Territorial Growth of the United States

CANADA

Lake Superior

MINNESOTA 1858

WISCONSIN 1848

MICHIGAN 1837

Lake Michigan

Lake Huron

Lake Ontario

Lake Erie

St. Lawrence R.

MAINE 1820

VT. 1791

N.H.

MASS.

CONN.

R.I.

NEW YORK

IOWA 1846

ILLINOIS 1818

INDIANA 1816

OHIO 1803

PENNSYLVANIA

NEW JERSEY 1790

MASON-DIXON LINE

DELAWARE

MARYLAND

COLONIES

THIRTEEN

MISSOURI 1821

KENTUCKY 1792

WEST VIRGINIA 1863

VIRGINIA

2010

THE ORIGINAL UNITED STATES
(By Treaty with Britain, 1783)

THE ORIGINAL

36°30'N MISSOURI COMPROMISE LINE

ARKANSAS 1836

TENNESSEE 1796

NORTH CAROLINA

SOUTH CAROLINA

Mississippi R.

MISSISSIPPI 1817

ALABAMA 1819

GEORGIA

LOUISIANA 1812

(Seized from Spain, 1810, 1813)

ATLANTIC OCEAN

Territorial Growth of the United States

1820 Date of states admission to the Union

● Geographic center of population by decade

0   150   300 Km.

0   150   300 Mi.

Gulf of Mexico

FLORIDA
(By Treaty with Spain, 1819)

FLORIDA 1845

BAHAMAS

N

PUERTO RICO
(Acquired from Spain, 1898)

VIRGIN IS.
(Acquired from Denmark, 1916–1917)

19°N

68°W

PUERTO RICO

VIRGIN ISLANDS

18°N

67°W

66°W

65°W

0   25   50 Km.

0   25   50 Mi.

CUBA

DOMINICAN REPUBLIC

HAITI

THE ENDURING
VISION
A HISTORY OF THE AMERICAN PEOPLE
NINTH EDITION
VOLUME 1: TO 1877

Paul S. Boyer
University of Wisconsin

Clifford E. Clark, Jr.
Carleton College

Karen Halttunen
University of Southern California

Joseph F. Kett
University of Virginia

Neal Salisbury
Smith College

Harvard Sitkoff
University of New Hampshire

Nancy Woloch
Barnard College

Andrew Rieser
State University of New York, Dutchess Community College

CENGAGE
Learning

Australia • Brazil • Mexico • Singapore • United Kingdom • United States

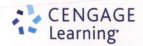

The Enduring Vision: A History of the American People, Ninth Edition
Volume 1: to 1877
Paul S. Boyer, Clifford E. Clark, Jr., Karen Halttunen, Joseph F. Kett, Neal Salisbury, Harvard Sitkoff, Nancy Woloch, Andrew Rieser

Product Director: Paul Banks

Product Manager: Joseph Potvin

Content Developer: Tonya Lobato

Product Assistant: Emma Guiton

Product Marketing Manager: Valerie Hartman

Senior Content Project Manager: Cathy Brooks

Senior Art Director: Cate Rickard Barr

Manufacturing Planner: Fola Orekoya

IP Analyst: Alexandra Ricciardi

IP Project Manager: Nick Barrows

Production Service and Compositor: SPi Global

Text and Cover Designer: Melissa Welch, Studio Montage

Cover Image: Yellowstone National Park (Corbis/Getty Images)

© 2018, 2014, 2011 Cengage Learning

For product information and technology assistance, contact us at
Cengage Learning Customer & Sales Support, 1-888-915-3276

For permission to use material from this text or product, submit all requests online at **www.cengage.com/permissions.** Further permissions questions can be emailed to **permissionrequest@cengage.com.**

Library of Congress Control Number: 2016951802

Student Edition:
ISBN: 978-1-337-11376-2

Loose-leaf Edition:
ISBN: 978-1-337-26986-5

Cengage Learning
20 Channel Center Street
Boston, MA 02210
USA

Cengage Learning is a leading provider of customized learning solutions with employees residing in nearly 40 different countries and sales in more than 125 countries around the world. Find your local representative at **www.cengage.com.**

Cengage Learning products are represented in Canada by Nelson Education, Ltd.

To learn more about Cengage Learning Solutions, **visit www.cengage.com** To find online supplements and other instructional support, please visit **www.cengagebrain.com.**

Printed in the United States of America
Print Number: 01 Print Year: 2016

In March 2012, shortly after completing his revisions to *The Enduring Vision*, our colleague Paul Boyer died, leaving both the text's authors and the editors at Cengage Learning deeply regretting our loss. Paul was a distinguished cultural and intellectual historian of the twentieth-century United States who served as a quiet leader on *The Enduring Vision* team ever since its inception more than 25 years ago. For every successive edition, he worked tirelessly to bring the textbook up to date, not only by adding recent events, but often overhauling the final chapters of the text from the new perspective generated by those recent events. He was a gentle and generous colleague, and we dedicate this Ninth Edition to him with gratitude and affection.

BRIEF Contents

Contents

Appendix A-1

SPECIAL Features

GOING TO THE SOURCE

Maps

Figures

Tables

Preface

The history of the United States has been shaped by an *enduring vision*, a shared commitment to a set of beliefs and values—including individual freedom, social equality, the rule of law, and openness to diversity—that run like threads through the lives of the American people. Those powerful beliefs and values express the people's collective determination to give meaning to America. Over the course of U.S. history, even when those values have been violated, that central vision of America has endured. *The Enduring Vision, Ninth Edition*, continues its authors' commitment, first undertaken nearly 30 years ago, to convey the strength of that enduring vision over centuries of often destabilizing change.

Over the past 50 years, the discipline of history itself has changed dramatically, moving from an earlier focus on national political narrative toward a rich and complex array of approaches—such as social, cultural, environmental, and global history. *The Enduring Vision* aims to integrate the best recent scholarship in all fields of American history without abandoning a clear political and chronological framework. In keeping with our central theme, our primary emphasis from the first edition to this new ninth edition has been social and cultural history, the fields that have shaped the authors' own teaching and scholarship. We are attentive to the lived historical experiences of women, African Americans, Hispanic Americans, Asian Americans, and Native Americans—that is, of men and women of all ethnic groups, regions, and social classes who make up the American mosaic. It was in their daily lives, their lived experience of American history, that the enduring vision of America was articulated—and it was their actions that put those visionary values to the test.

The Enduring Vision is designed for both college classrooms and Advanced Placement courses in U.S. history. Though it offers an appropriately complex treatment of the American past, it requires no prerequisite knowledge from students. Our approach is not only comprehensive, but readable, lively, and illuminating. *The Enduring Vision* is also attentive to the process of historical learning. Recent research on history education has emphasized the crucial importance of teaching students the fundamental skills of historical thinking, such as addressing both continuity and change over time, using evidence to construct and test their own hypotheses, understanding past events in their own contexts, and coming to terms with the contingency of history. *The Enduring Vision* is especially effective in helping students understand the connections between particular historical events and larger trends and developments.

Newer Approaches to the American Past

This new ninth edition of *The Enduring Vision* sustains the emphasis on social and cultural history that was established in the first edition. Religious history remains an important focus, from the spiritual values of pre-Columbian communities to the political activism of contemporary conservative Christian groups. Family history and the history of education receive serious attention. Visual culture—paintings, photographs, cartoons, and other illustrations—is investigated through all chapters in the volume. For the ninth edition, Andrew Rieser of the State University of New York, Dutchess Community College, is an important addition to the author team, bringing notable expertise in cultural history.

Environmental History

From the first edition on, *The Enduring Vision* has also paid close attention to the environmental history of America's past because it is clear that geography, land, and landscape have played an important role throughout human history. *The Enduring Vision*'s unique **Prologue** on the American Land solidly establishes those themes early on, and our extensive coverage of environmental history, the land, and the West is fully integrated into the narrative and treated analytically—not simply "tacked on" to a traditional account. We seek to encourage students' spatial thinking about historical developments by offering a **map program** rich in information, easy to read, and visually appealing. And our primary source feature, **Going to the Source** (described in more detail later), offers a number of primary sources involving the land, including excerpts from Meriwether Lewis's Journal, Thoreau's essay "Walking," and a Dust Bowl diary.

Global History

In response to newer developments in the history discipline, recent editions of *The Enduring Vision* have underscored the global context of American history. We continue to engage with new literature on global history throughout the narrative. In addition, our online MindTap resource includes a special feature titled **Beyond America—Global Interactions**, which was first introduced in the sixth edition. From the origins of agriculture ten millennia ago to the global impact of environmental changes today, we have emphasized how all facets of our historical experience emerge with fresh new clarity when viewed within a broader world framework.

Histories of Technology and Medicine

Students show a particular fascination with the histories of technology and medicine. In our popular **Technology & Culture** feature (available in MindTap), and throughout the print text, we continue to highlight the historical importance of new inventions and technological innovations. In addition to discussing the applications of science and technology, we note the often unanticipated cultural, social, and political consequences of such innovations—from new hunting implements developed by Paleo-Indians to contemporary breakthroughs in information processing and debates over net neutrality. Medicine and disease receive extensive coverage, and we look at the epidemics brought by European explorers and settlers as well as today's AIDS crisis, bioethics debates, and controversies over health care financing.

Organization and Special Features of *The Enduring Vision*

The general organization of the text is chronological, with individual chapters conforming to important historical periods. In keeping with our emphasis on social and cultural history, some chapters take a more thematic approach, overlapping chronologically with those that precede and follow them, thus introducing students to a more sophisticated understanding of the different levels—political, cultural, economic, social—of historical periodization.

Pedagogical Structure

Within each chapter, we offer a number of features designed to help students grasp its structure and purpose. A brief chapter introduction prepares students for the broader developments, themes, and historical problems that are addressed in that chapter. A **chapter outline** lists both the major headings and the subheads of the chapter, while also providing **focus questions** for each section—questions designed to help students read the chapter actively rather than passively. Those questions also appear under the major headings within the body of each chapter. **Chronologies** appear near the beginning of each chapter to provide an overview of key events. The chapter **conclusion**, The Whole Vision, addresses and answers the focus questions, providing students with an opportunity to review what they've read.

As a further pedagogical aid, each chapter includes **key terms and definitions** that appear in marginal boxes near where the boldfaced term first appears in the chapter. All terms are also grouped at the end of the chapter for quick and easy review. In addition, an annotated, up-to-date list of core readings, available on the website, offers guidance for those wishing to explore a particular topic in depth.

Special Features

In MindTap, every chapter of *The Enduring Vision* provides students with either a **Beyond America—Global Interactions** feature or a **Technology & Culture** feature. **Beyond America—Global Interactions** offers provocative, in-depth discussions of America's place in world history, focusing on such global developments as the origins and spread of agriculture, slave emancipation in the Atlantic World, and global climate change. **Technology & Culture** provides fascinating insight into such subjects as sugar production in the Americas, guns and gun culture, and the interstate highway system. Both features address important developments in U.S. history from the perspective of major new approaches to the past, with an intensity of detail geared to engaging students' curiosity and analytic engagement.

Among the many new exciting additions to *The Enduring Vision*'s MindTap is a thought-provoking unit reflection activity titled "Thinking Like an Historian" that challenges students' critical thinking skills by walking them through a brief historiography based on recent scholarship, asking them to analyze a related set of primary source images, and finally presenting them with an overarching essay question that aims at the heart of a core unit theme.

Every chapter in the print version of *The Enduring Vision* also includes a primary source feature, **Going to the Source**, first introduced in the seventh edition. Its pedagogical purpose is not only to bring history alive for our students, but to offer opportunities for their direct engagement in historical interpretation and analysis. **Going to the Source** offers a rich selection of primary sources, drawing on speeches, diaries, letters, and other materials created by Americans who lived through and helped shape the great events and historical changes of successive periods. In selecting documents, we focused especially, but not exclusively, on environmental themes. A brief introduction places each selection in context, and focus questions suggest assignment and discussion possibilities. The voices captured in **Going to the Source** include both prominent historical figures (from Christopher Columbus to Barack Obama) and lesser-known men and women (such as the Cherokee named Swimmer who explained the place of human beings in the natural world to an early anthropologist, and North Dakota farm girl Anna Marie Low who endured the terrible dust storms of the 1930s).

Chapter-by-Chapter Updates to the Ninth Edition

This edition of *The Enduring Vision* brings the work fully up to date, incorporating major developments and scholarship since the eighth edition went to press. In our chapter revisions, we have introduced new material and new visual images, tightened and clarified lines of argument, and responded to reviewers' suggestions for strengthening our work.

For the ninth edition of *The Enduring Vision*, we have carefully assessed the coverage, interpretations, and analytic framework of each chapter to incorporate the latest scholarship and emerging themes. This process is reflected both in our textual revisions and in the new works of scholarship cited in the end-of-chapter bibliographies. A chapter-by-chapter glimpse of some of the changes highlights new content and up-to-the-minute scholarship.

Chapter 1 significantly revises and expands coverage on Native American food ways, spirituality, marriage, and gender roles, while providing a more focused discussion of regional differences between native peoples. **Chapter 2** enhances the treatment of initial contact between Europeans and Native Americans, updates the material on West Africa and African slavery, and provides a stronger treatment of gender throughout. In **Chapter 3**, the topics of race and slavery in the Chesapeake and gender dynamics in colonial New England and New Netherland have been refined and extended. **Chapter 4** extends treatment of the Middle Passage and includes new material on women in the Great Awakening.

Chapter 5 includes expanded treatment of the role of women in colonial resistance against British policies. **Chapter 6** increases the coverage of slave experiences and women's roles during the revolutionary war and also contributes new material on the impact of the war on Native American culture and society. **Chapter 7** supplies a new chapter opener and greatly enhanced treatment of women and African Americans in the new republic. **Chapter 8** expands coverage of women's roles in the War of 1812 and broadens the discussion of the economic significance of the cotton gin. **Chapter 9** expands the treatment of the Trail of Tears and elaborates on women's factory work and the ideology of separate spheres. **Chapter 10** extends the treatment of abolitionism and the experience of free blacks. **Chapter 11** sharpens the discussion of the impact of mechanization on workers' lives and brings in new material on the impact of the rising market economy for women's household roles.

Chapter 12 includes new material on yeoman farmers' wives, southern paternalism, and secret slave churches. **Chapter 13** provides new details on gender roles for families on the trek west, Native American experiences, and Lincoln's reactions to the U.S. war with Mexico. **Chapter 14** consolidates sections on the Compromise of 1850 and the Fugitive Slave Act while providing new material on the southern response to *Uncle Tom's Cabin*. **Chapter 15** increases discussion of the role of women in the Civil War and the effect of the war on women's lives.

Chapter 16 adds new material on the Memphis Riot of 1866 and a new section analyzing the successes and failures of Reconstruction. **Chapter 17** includes new material on Plains Indians family structure and gender roles. **Chapters 18** and **19** include condensed opening vignettes and other revisions for improved clarity and readability. **Chapter 20** improves the treatment of the Populist support for women's suffrage and enhanced analysis of the political impact of Populism's defeat in 1896. **Chapter 21** condenses and consolidates two sections on the national phase of the Progressive Movement into one section.

Chapter 22 updates the treatment of the 1918 influenza epidemic, reflecting new scientific research. **Chapter 23** includes new material on the formation of the credit industry and its role in facilitating consumerism. **Chapter 24** improves the coverage of Hollywood's "Golden Age" while **Chapters 25** and **26** provide condensed opening vignettes and other improvements in clarity and readability.

Chapter 27 enhances the treatment of the interstate highway system and racial segregation in the North. **Chapter 28** offers expanded discussions of the Civil Rights Act of 1964 and new paragraphs on the post–civil rights struggle for black equality, with particular emphasis on mass incarceration. **Chapter 29** expands the treatment of 1960s student protest, including new material comparing U.S. protests in 1968 with those in Mexico and Europe. Taking advantage of new scholarship on the conservative movement, **Chapter 30** supplies a thoroughly reorganized section on that topic, including new material tracing the origins of modern conservatism to anti–New Deal activism in the 1930s. Supply-side economics is now clearly defined and its contribution to conservatism in the 1970s and 1980s explained.

Chapter 31 has been significantly reworked and updated with new narratives and analysis of the Obama presidency and foreign policy challenges. The chapter updates readers on recent climate change agreements and trade pacts; the status of the Afghan war; worsening U.S. relations with Russia; and events in the Middle East (including the Syrian Civil War and the ISIS threat). The chapter also provides improved treatment of the Tea Party and new sections on political polarization, congressional gridlock, and the 2014 midterm elections; developments in civil liberties, including NSA spying, marriage equality, and voting rights; current demographic and economic trends, stressing the uneven quality of the economic recovery and the ongoing racial inequities that prompted a wave of urban unrest in 2014 and 2015; and the 2016 presidential primaries and general election.

Supplements

- MindTap Instant Access Code (Full Volume): ISBN 9781337113724
- MindTap Instant Access Code (Volume 1): ISBN 9781337111287
- MindTap Instant Access Code (Volume 2): ISBN 9781337113809
- MindTap Printed Access Card (Full Volume): ISBN 9781337113731
- MindTap Printed Access Card (Volume 1): ISBN 9781337111294
- MindTap Printed Access Card (Volume 2): ISBN 9781337113816

MindTap for *The Enduring Vision, Ninth Edition*, is a personalized, online learning platform that provides students with an immersive learning experience to build and foster critical thinking skills. Through a carefully designed chapter-based learning path, MindTap allows students to easily identify learning objectives; draw connections and improve writing skills by completing unit-level essay assignments; read short, manageable sections from the e-book; and test their content knowledge with map- and timeline-based critical thinking questions.

MindTap allows instructors to customize their content, providing tools that seamlessly integrate YouTube clips, outside websites, and personal content directly into the learning path. Instructors can assign additional primary source content through the Instructor Resource Center and Questia primary and secondary source databases that house thousands of peer-reviewed journals, newspapers, magazines, and full-length books.

The additional content available in MindTap mirrors and complements the authors' narrative, but also includes primary source content and assessments not found in the printed text. To learn more, ask your Cengage Learning sales representative to demo it for you—or go to *www.Cengage.com/MindTap*.

Instructor's Companion Website The Instructor's Companion Website, accessed through the Instructor Resource Center (*login.cengage.com*), houses all of the supplemental materials you can use for your course. This includes a Test Bank, Instructor's Resource Manual, and PowerPoint Lecture Presentations. The Test Bank, offered in Microsoft Word and Cognero formats, contains multiple-choice, short-answer, map-based, and essay questions for each chapter. Cognero is a flexible, online system that allows you to author, edit, and manage test bank content for *The Enduring Vision*. Create multiple test versions instantly and deliver through your LMS from your classroom, or wherever you may be, with no special installs or downloads required. The Instructor's Resource Manual includes chapter outlines, a review of each chapter's core themes, suggested lecture topics, and additional teaching resources. Finally, the PowerPoint lectures are ADA-compliant slides that collate the key takeaways from each chapter in concise visual formats perfect for in-class presentations or for student review.

Cengagebrain.com Save your students time and money. Direct them to www.cengagebrain.com for a choice in formats and savings and a better chance to succeed in your class. *Cengagebrain.com*, Cengage Learning's online store, is a single destination for more than 10,000 new textbooks, eTextbooks, eChapters, study tools, and audio supplements. Students have the freedom to purchase à la carte exactly what they need when they need it. Students can save 50 percent on the electronic textbook and can purchase an individual eChapter for as little as $1.99.

Doing History: Research and Writing in the Digital Age, Second Edition (ISBN: 9781133587880), Prepared by Michael J. Galgano, J. Chris Arndt, and Raymond M. Hyser of James Madison University. Whether you're starting down the path as a history major or simply looking for a straightforward, systematic guide to writing a successful paper, this text's "soup-to-nuts" approach to researching and writing about history addresses every step of the process: locating your sources, gathering information, writing and citing according to various style guides, and avoiding plagiarism.

Writing for College History (ISBN: 9780618306039), Prepared by Robert M. Frakes of Clarion University. This brief handbook for survey courses in American, western, and world history guides students through the various types of writing assignments they may encounter in a history class. Providing examples of student writing and candid assessments of student work, this text focuses on the rules and conventions of writing for the college history course.

The Modern Researcher, Sixth Edition (ISBN: 9780495318705), Prepared by Jacques Barzun and Henry F. Graff of Columbia University. This classic introduction to the techniques of research and the art of expression thoroughly covers every aspect of research, from the selection of a topic through the gathering of materials, analysis, writing, revision, and publication of findings. They present the process not as a set of rules but through actual cases that put the subtleties of research in a useful context. Part One covers the principles and methods of research; Part Two covers writing, speaking, and getting one's work published.

Reader Program Cengage Learning publishes a number of readers. Some contain exclusively primary sources, others are devoted to essays and secondary sources, and still others provide a combination of primary and secondary sources. All of these readers are designed to guide students through the process of historical inquiry. Visit *www.cengage.com/history* for a complete list of readers.

Custom Options Nobody knows your students like you, so why not give them a text that tailor-fits their needs? Cengage Learning offers custom solutions for your course—whether it's making a small modification to *World Civilizations, Ninth Edition*, to match your syllabus or combining multiple sources to create something truly unique. Contact your Cengage Learning representative to explore custom solutions for your course.

Acknowledgments

In undertaking revisions of our textbook, we have drawn on our own scholarly work and teaching experience. We have also kept abreast of new work of historical interpretation, as reported by our U.S. history colleagues in their books, scholarly articles, and papers at historical meetings. We list much of this new work in the books cited in the bibliographies on *The Enduring Vision* website. We are much indebted to all these colleagues.

A special thanks goes to Debra Michals of Merrimack College whose expertise as a U.S. history author and women's history scholar helped round out Volume I of the ninth edition of *The Enduring Vision* with numerous important scholarly details and insights.

We have also benefited from the comments and suggestions of instructors who have adopted *The Enduring Vision*; from colleagues and students who have written us about specific details; and from the following scholars and teachers who offered systematic evaluations of specific chapters. Their perceptive comments have been most helpful in the revision process.

Charles deWitt, *Nashville State Community College*

Gabrielle Everett, *Jefferson College*

Kristen Foster, *Marquette University*

William Grose, *Wytheville Community College*

John Hayes, *Georgia Regents University*

Charles Hughes, *Oklahoma State University*

Johnny Moore, *Radford University*

Earl Mulderink, *Southern Utah University*

Melanie Storie, *East Tennessee State University*

Finally, we salute the skilled professionals at Cengage Learning and its partners whose expertise and enthusiastic commitment to this new ninth edition guided us through every stage and helped sustain our own determination to make this the best book we could possibly write. Senior Content Developer Tonya Lobato managed the day-to-day challenges of keeping us all on track. Cathy Brooks, Senior Content Production Manager at Cengage, and Patty Donovan, Senior Production Editor at partner SPi Global, ably shepherded the work through the crucial stages of production.

While Paul Boyer is no longer with us, his example of professionalism and attention to detail served as an ongoing inspiration for everyone involved in the project. Paul was a distinguished cultural and intellectual historian who served as the leader of *The Enduring Vision* team for 25 years until his death in 2012. For every successive edition, he worked tirelessly to bring the textbook up to date and incorporate new perspectives and authors. He was a gentle and generous colleague; he is missed and fondly remembered; and we dedicate this volume to him.

Paul S. Boyer (deceased)
Clifford E. Clark, Jr.
Karen Halttunen
Joseph F. Kett
Andrew Rieser
Neal Salisbury
Harvard Sitkoff
Nancy Woloch

ABOUT THE Authors

PAUL S. BOYER was the Merle Curti Professor of History at the University of Wisconsin, Madison. He earned his Ph.D. from Harvard University. He was also a visiting professor at the University of California, Los Angeles; Northwestern University; and the College of William and Mary. An editor of *Notable American Women, 1607–1950* (1971), Dr. Boyer also coauthored *Salem Possessed: The Social Origins of Witchcraft* (1974), for which, with Stephen Nissenbaum, he received the John H. Dunning Prize of the American Historical Association. His other works include *Urban Masses and Moral Order in America, 1820–1920* (1978), *By The Bomb's Early Light: American Thought and Culture at the Dawn of the Atomic Age* (1985), *When Time Shall Be No More: Prophecy Belief in Modern American Culture* (1992), and *Promises to Keep: The United States Since World War II* (third edition, 2005). Dr. Boyer was also editor-in-chief of the *Oxford Companion to United States History* (2001). His articles and essays appeared in the *American Quarterly, New Republic,* and other journals.

CLIFFORD E. CLARK, Jr., M.A. and A.D. Hulings Professor of American Studies and Professor of History at Carleton College, earned his Ph.D. from Harvard University. He has served as both the chair of the History Department and director of the American Studies program at Carleton. Dr. Clark is the author of *Henry Ward Beecher: Spokesman for a Middle-Class America* (1978), *The American Family Home, 1800–1960* (1986), *The Intellectual and Cultural History of Anglo-America Since 1789* in the General History of the Americas Series, and, with Carol Zellie, *Northfield: The History and Architecture of a Community* (1997). He also has edited and contributed to *Minnesota in a Century of Change: The State and Its People Since 1900* (1989). A past member of the Council of the American Studies Association, Dr. Clark is active in the fields of material culture studies and historic preservation, and he serves on the Northfield, Minnesota, Historical Preservation Commission.

KAREN HALTTUNEN, Professor of History at the University of Southern California, earned her Ph.D. from Yale University. Her works include *Confidence Men and Painted Women: A Study of Middle-Class Culture in America, 1830–1870* (1982) and *Murder Most Foul: The Killer and the American Gothic Imagination* (1998). She edited *The Blackwell Companion to American Cultural History* (2008) and coedited, with Lewis Perry, *Moral Problems in American Life: New Essays on Cultural History* (1998). As president of the American Studies Association and as vice-president of the Teaching Division of the American Historical Association, Dr. Halttunen has actively promoted K–16 collaboration in teaching history. She has held fellowships from the Guggenheim and Mellon Foundations, the National Endowment for the Humanities, the Huntington Library, and the National Humanities Center and has been principal investigator on several Teaching American History grants from the Department of Education.

JOSEPH F. KETT, James Madison Professor of History at the University of Virginia, received his Ph.D. from Harvard University. His works include *The Formation of the American Medical Profession: The Role of Institutions, 1780–1860* (1968), *Rites of Passage: Adolescence in America, 1790–Present* (1977), *The Pursuit of Knowledge under Difficulties: From Self-Improvement to Adult Education in America, 1750–1990* (1994), and *The New Dictionary of Cultural Literacy* (2002), of which he is coauthor. A forthcoming book, *Merit: The History of a Founding Ideal from the American Revolution to the Twenty-First Century*, will be released in early 2013. As the former History Department chair at Virginia, Dr. Kett also has participated on the Panel on Youth of the President's Science Advisory Committee, has served on the Board of Editors of the *History of Education Quarterly*, and is a past member of the Council of the American Studies Association.

ANDREW RIESER, Professor of History at State University of New York, Dutchess Community College, received his Ph.D. from the University of Wisconsin–Madison. He coedited the *Dictionary of American History* (third edition, 2002) and coauthored both the sixth and seventh editions of the concise volumes of *The Enduring Vision* (2010, 2013). Dr. Rieser is the author of *The Chautauqua Moment: Protestants, Progressives, and the Culture of Modern Liberalism* (2003) and other articles, chapters, and reviews in the field of U.S. cultural and intellectual history.

NEAL SALISBURY, Barbara Richmond 1940 Professor Emeritus in the Social Sciences (History), at Smith College, received his Ph.D. from the University of California, Los Angeles. He is the author of *Manitou and Providence: Indians, Europeans, and the Making of New England, 1500–1643* (1982), editor of *The Sovereignty and Goodness of God*, by Mary Rowlandson (1997), and coeditor, with Philip J. Deloria, of *The Companion to American Indian History* (2002). With R. David Edmunds and Frederick E. Hoxie, he has written *The People: A History of Native America* (2007). Dr. Salisbury has contributed numerous articles to journals and edited collections and coedits a book series, Cambridge Studies in North American Indian History. He is active in the fields of colonial and Native American history and has served as president of the American Society for Ethnohistory and on the Council of the Omohundro Institute of Early American History and Culture.

HARVARD SITKOFF, Emeritus Professor of History at the University of New Hampshire, earned his Ph.D. from Columbia University. He is the author of *A New Deal for Blacks* (Thirtieth Anniversary Edition, 2009), *The Struggle for Black Equality* (Twenty-Fifth Anniversary Edition, 2008), *King: Pilgrimage to the Mountaintop* (2008), *Toward Freedom Land, The Long Struggle for Racial Equality in America* (2010), and *Postwar America: A Student Companion* (2000); coauthor of the National Park Service's *Racial Desegregation in Public Education in the United States* (2000) and *The World War II Homefront* (2003); and editor of *Fifty Years Later: The New Deal Reevaluated* (1984), *A History* of *Our Time* (2012), and *Perspectives on Modern America: Making Sense of the Twentieth Century* (2001). Dr. Sitkoff's articles have appeared in *American Quarterly*, the *Journal of American History*, and the *Journal of Southern History*, among others. A frequent lecturer at universities abroad, he has been awarded the Fulbright Commission's John Adams Professorship of American Civilization in the Netherlands and the Mary Ball Washington Professorship of American History in Ireland.

NANCY WOLOCH received her Ph.D. from Indiana University. She is the author of *Women and the American Experience* (fifth edition, 2011), editor of *Early American Women: A Documentary History, 1600–1900* (third edition, 2013), and coauthor, with Walter LaFeber and Richard Polenberg, of *The American Century: A History of the United States Since the 1890s* (seventh edition, 2013). Dr. Woloch is also the author of *Muller v. Oregon: A Brief History with Documents* (1996). She teaches American history and American studies at Barnard College, Columbia University.

PROLOGUE
Enduring Vision, Enduring Land

IN THE VISION THAT Americans have shared, the American land has been central. For the Native Americans who spread over the land thousands of years ago, for the Europeans who began to arrive in the sixteenth century, and for the later immigrants who poured in by the tens of millions from all parts of the world, North America was a haven for new beginnings. If life was hard elsewhere, it would be better here. Once here, the immigrants continued to be lured by the land. If times were tough in the East, they would be better in the West. New Englanders migrated to Ohio; Ohioans migrated to Kansas; Kansans migrated to California. For Africans, the migration to America was forced and brutal. But after the Civil War, newly freed African Americans embraced the vision and dreamed of traveling to a Promised Land of new opportunities. Interviewed in 1938, a former Texas slave recalled a verse that he and other blacks had sung when emancipated:

> *I got my ticket,*
>
> *Leaving the thicket,*
>
> *And I'm a-heading for the Golden Shore!*

For most of America's history, its peoples have celebrated the land—its beauty, its diversity, and its ability to sustain and even enrich those who tapped its resources. But within this shared vision have been deep-seated tensions. Even Native Americans—who regarded the land and other natural phenomena as spiritual—sometimes depleted the resources on which they depended. Europeans, considering "nature" a force to be mastered, were even less restrained. The very abundance of America's natural resources led them to think of these resources as infinitely available and exploitable. In moving from one place to another, some sought to escape starvation or oppression, while others pursued wealth despite the environmental consequences. Regardless of their motives, migrants often left behind a land bereft of wild animals, its fertility depleted by intensive farming, its waters dammed and polluted or dried up altogether. If the land today remains part of Americans' vision, it is because they realize its vulnerability, rather than its immunity, to irreversible degradation at the hands of people and their technology.

To comprehend fully Americans' relationship with the land, we must know the land itself. The North American landscape, as encountered by its human inhabitants, formed over at least 3 billion years, culminating in the last Ice Age. From the earliest peopling to more recent waves of immigration, the continent's physical characteristics have shaped human affairs, including cycles of intensive agriculture and industrialization; the rise of cities; the course of politics; and even the basic themes of American literature, art, and music. Geology, geography, and environment are among the fundamental building blocks of human history.

The Continent and Its Regions

Differences in climate, physical features, soils and minerals, and organic life are the basis of America's geographic diversity (see Maps P.1, P.2, and P.3). As each region's human inhabitants utilized available resources, geographic diversity contributed to a diversity of regional cultures, first among Native Americans and then among the immigrant peoples who spread across America after 1492. Taken together, the variety of these resources would also contribute to the rise to wealth and global preeminence of the United States.

Arctic
Subarctic
Highland
Semiarid
Arid
Humid continental
Humid subtropical
Marine west coast
Mediterranean
Humid tropical

0 500 1000 Km.
0 500 1000 Mi.

MAP P.1 NORTH AMERICAN CLIMATIC REGIONS America's variety of mostly temperate climates is key to its environmental and economic diversity.

The West

With its extreme climate and profuse wildlife, Alaska recalls the land that North America's earliest peoples encountered (see Chapter 1). Alaska's far north is a treeless tundra of grasses, lichens, and stunted shrubs. This region, the Arctic, appears as a stark wilderness in winter and is reborn in fleeting summers of colorful flowers and returning birds. In contrast, the subarctic of central Alaska is a heavily forested country known as taiga. Here rises North America's highest peak, 20,310-foot Denali (formerly known as Mt. McKinley). Average temperatures in the subarctic range from the fifties above zero Fahrenheit in summer to well below zero in the long, dark winters, and the soil is permanently frozen except during summer surface thaws and where, ominously, global warming is having an effect.

The Pacific coastal region is in some ways a world apart. Vegetation and animal life, isolated from the rest of the continent by mountains and deserts, include many species unfamiliar farther east. Warm, wet westerly winds blowing off the Pacific create a climate more uniformly temperate than anywhere else in North America. From Anchorage to south of San Francisco Bay, winters are cool, humid, and foggy, and the coast's dense forest cover includes the largest living organisms on Earth—the giant redwood trees. Along the southern California coast, winds and currents generate a warmer, Mediterranean climate, and vegetation includes a heavy growth of shrubs and short trees, scattered stands of oak, and grasses able to endure prolonged seasonal drought.

To the east of the coastal region, the rugged Sierra Nevada, Cascade, and coastal ranges stretch the length of Washington, Oregon, and California. Their majestic peaks trap abundant Pacific Ocean moisture carried eastward by gigantic clockwise air currents. Between the ranges nestle flat, fertile valleys that have been major agricultural centers in recent times.

Still farther east lies the Great Basin, encompassing Nevada, western Utah, southern Idaho, and eastern Oregon. The few streams here have no outlet to the ocean. A remnant of an inland sea that once held glacial meltwater survives in Utah's Great Salt Lake. Today, however, the Great Basin is dry and severely eroded, a cold desert rich in minerals and imposing in its austere grandeur and lonely emptiness. North of the basin, the Columbia and Snake Rivers, which drain the plateau country of Idaho and eastern Washington and Oregon, provide plentiful water for farming.

Western North America's "backbone" is the Rocky Mountains. The Rockies form part of the immense

MAP P.2 LAND USE AND MAJOR MINERAL RESOURCES IN THE UNITED STATES The land has been central to America's industrial as well as agricultural productivity.

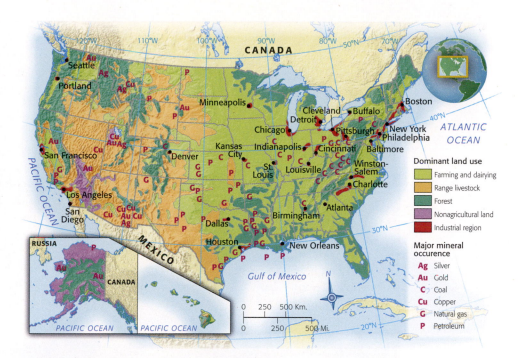

Dominant land use
- Farming and dairying
- Range livestock
- Forest
- Nonagricultural land
- Industrial region

Major mineral occurrence
- Ag   Silver
- Au   Gold
- C   Coal
- Cu   Copper
- G   Natural gas
- P   Petroleum

MAP P.3 NATURAL VEGETATION OF THE UNITED STATES The current distribution of plant life came about only after the last Ice Age ended, ca. 10,000 B.C.E., and Earth's climate warmed.

- Forest (broadleaf, coniferous, and mixed)
- Tall-grass prairie
- Short-grass prairie
- Desert and desert shrub
- Tundra/alpine
- Tropical rain forest
- Tropical grassland

mountain system that reaches from Alaska to the Andes of South America. Beyond the front range of the Rockies lies the Continental Divide, separating the rivers flowing eastward into the Atlantic from those draining westward into the Pacific. The climate and vegetation of the Rocky Mountain high country resemble those of the Arctic and subarctic regions.

Arizona, southern Utah, western New Mexico, and southeastern California form America's southwestern desert. The climate is arid, searingly hot on summer days and cold on winter nights. Adapted to these conditions, many plants and animals that thrive here could not survive elsewhere. Dust storms, cloudbursts, and flash floods have everywhere carved, abraded, and twisted the rocky landscape. The most monumental example is the Grand Canyon, where the Colorado River has been cutting down to Precambrian bedrock for 20 million years. In the face of such tremendous natural forces, human activity might well seem paltry and transitory. Yet it was in the Southwest that Native Americans cultivated the first crops in what is now the continental United States.

CARIBOU AND THE TRANS-ALASKA PIPELINE This scene from the open tundra of Alaska points to the uneasy co-existence between wildlife and the human pursuit of fossil fuels. *(Design Pics Inc / Alamy Stock Photo)*

The Heartland

North America's heartland comprises the area extending between the Rockies and the Appalachians. This vast region forms one of the world's largest drainage systems. From here, the Great Lakes empty into the North Atlantic through the St. Lawrence River, and the Mississippi–Missouri–Ohio river network flows southward into the Gulf of Mexico. By transporting peoples and goods, the heartland's network of waterways has supported commerce and communication for centuries, before—as well as since—the arrival of Europeans.

The mighty Mississippi—the "Great River" to the Ojibwe Indians and one of the world's longest rivers—has changed course many times. Southward from its junction with the Ohio River, the Mississippi meanders constantly, depositing rich sediments throughout its broad, ancient floodplain. It has carried so much silt over the millennia that its lower stretches flow above the surrounding valley, which it periodically floods when its high banks (levees) are breached. Only the Ozark Plateau and Ouachita Mountains remain exposed, forming the hill country of southern Missouri, north-central Arkansas, and eastern Oklahoma.

Below New Orleans, the Mississippi empties into the Gulf of Mexico through an enormous delta with an intricate network of grassy swamps known as bayous. The Mississippi Delta offers rich farm soil capable of supporting a large population. Swarming with waterfowl, insects, alligators, and marine plants and animals, this environment has nurtured a distinctive way of life for the Indian, white, and black peoples who have inhabited it.

North of the Ohio and Missouri Rivers, themselves products of glacial runoff, Ice Age glaciation distributed glacial debris. Spread even farther by wind and rivers, this fine-ground glacial dust slowly created the fertile farm soil of the Midwest. Glaciers also dug out the five Great Lakes (Superior, Michigan, Huron, Erie, and Ontario), collectively the world's largest body of fresh water. Water flowing from Lake Erie to the lower elevation of Lake Ontario created Niagara Falls, a testimony like the Grand Canyon to the way that water can shape a beautiful landscape.

Most of the heartland's eastern and northern sectors were once heavily forested while thick, tallgrass prairie covered Illinois, parts of adjoining states, and much of the Missouri and middle Arkansas river basins. Beyond the Missouri, the prairie gave way to short-grass steppe—the Great Plains, cold in winter, blazing hot in summer, and often dry. The great distances that separate the heartland's prairies and Great Plains from the moderating effects of the oceans continue to make this region's annual temperature range the most extreme in North America. As one moves westward, elevations rise gradually;

HARVESTING WHEAT A team of combines harvest wheat adjacent to the farm shop in the Palouse region of Washington. *(Rick Dalton - Ag / Alamy)*

trees grow only along streambeds; long droughts alternate with violent thunderstorms and tornadoes; and water and wood are ever scarcer.

During the nineteenth and twentieth centuries, much of this forested, grassy world became open farming country. Gone are the flocks of migratory birds that once darkened the daytime skies of the plains; gone are the free-roaming bison. Forests now only fringe the heartland: in the lake country of northern Minnesota and Wisconsin, on Michigan's upper peninsula, and across the hilly uplands of the Appalachians, southern Indiana, and the Ozarks. The settlers who largely displaced the region's Native Americans plowed up prairie grass and cut down trees. Destruction of the forest and grassy cover made the heartland both a "breadbasket" for the world market and, during intervals of drought, a bleak "dust bowl." With farming now in decline, the heartland's future is uncertain.

The Atlantic Seaboard

The eastern edge of the heartland is formed by the Appalachian Mountains, which over the course of 210 million years have been ground down to gentle ridges paralleling one another southwest to northeast. Between the ridges lie fertile valleys such as Virginia's Shenandoah. The Appalachian hill country's wealth is in thick timber and mineral beds—particularly coal deposits—whose heavy exploitation since the nineteenth century has accelerated destructive soil erosion in this softly beautiful, mountainous land.

Descending gently from the Appalachians' eastern slope is the Piedmont region. In this broad, rolling upland extending from Alabama to Maryland, the rich, red soil has been ravaged in modern times by excessive cotton and tobacco cultivation. The Piedmont's modern piney-woods cover constitutes "secondary growth," replacing the sturdy hardwood trees that Native Americans and pioneering whites and blacks once knew. The northward extension of the Piedmont from Pennsylvania to New England has more broadleaf vegetation and a harsher winter climate, and was shaped by glacial activity. The terrain in upstate New York and New England comprises hills contoured by advancing and retreating ice, and numerous lakes scoured out by glaciers. Belts of rocky debris remain, and in many places granite boulders shoulder their way up through the

ABANDONED "RUST BELT" FACTORY The American landscape is littered with reminders that large-scale factory production has ended or been diminished in many industries. *(Photo by Jeff Kowalsky/Bloomberg via Getty Images)*

mountains and valleys, oceangoing craft may find numerous small anchorages. South of Massachusetts Bay, the Atlantic shore and the Gulf of Mexico coastline form a shoreline of sandy beaches and long barrier islands paralleling the mainland. Tropical storms boiling up from the open seas regularly lash North America's Atlantic shores, and at all times brisk winds make coastal navigation treacherous.

For millions, the Atlantic coastal region of North America offered a welcome. Ancient Indian hunters and more recent European colonists alike found its climate and its abundance of food sources alluring. Offshore, well within their reach, lay such productive fishing grounds as the Grand Banks, off Newfoundland, and Cape Cod's coastal bays where cool-water upwellings on the continental shelf had lured swarms of fish and crustaceans. "The abundance of sea-fish are almost beyond believing," wrote a breathless English settler in 1630, "and sure I should scarce have believed it, except I had seen it with my own eyes."

soil. Though picturesque, the land is the despair of anyone who has tried to plow it.

The character of the Atlantic coastal plain varies strikingly from south to north. At the tip of the Florida peninsula in the extreme south, the climate and vegetation are subtropical. The southern coastal lands running north from Florida to Chesapeake Bay and the mouth of the Delaware River compose the tidewater region. This is a wide, rather flat lowland, heavily wooded with a mixture of broadleaf and coniferous forests, ribboned with numerous small rivers, occasionally swampy, and often miserably hot and humid in summer. North of Delaware Bay, the coastal lowlands narrow and flatten to form the New Jersey pine barrens, Long Island, and Cape Cod—all created by the deposit of glacial debris. Here the climate is noticeably milder than in the interior. North of Massachusetts Bay, the land beyond the immediate shoreline becomes increasingly mountainous.

North America's true eastern edge is not the coastline but the offshore continental shelf, whose relatively shallow waters extend as far as 250 miles into the Atlantic before plunging deeply. Along the rocky Canadian and Maine coasts, where at the end of the Ice Age the rising ocean half-covered glaciated

A Legacy and a Challenge

North America's fertile soil, extensive forests, and rich mineral resources long nourished visions of limitless natural abundance that would yield untold wealth to its human inhabitants. Such visions have contributed to the acceleration of population growth, intensive agriculture, industrialization, urbanization, and hunger for material goods—processes that are exhausting resources, polluting the environment, and raising temperatures to the point of endangering human health and well-being.

In searching for ways to avoid environmental catastrophe, Americans would do well to recall the Native American legacy. Although Indians often wasted, and occasionally exhausted, a region's resources to their detriment, their practices generally encouraged the renewal of plants, animals, and soil over time. Underlying these practices were Indians' beliefs that they were spiritually related to the land and all living beings that shared it. In recapturing the sense that they are intimately related to the land they inhabit, rather than alien to it, future American generations could revitalize the enduring vision of those who came before them.

THE ENDURING
VISION
A HISTORY OF THE AMERICAN PEOPLE

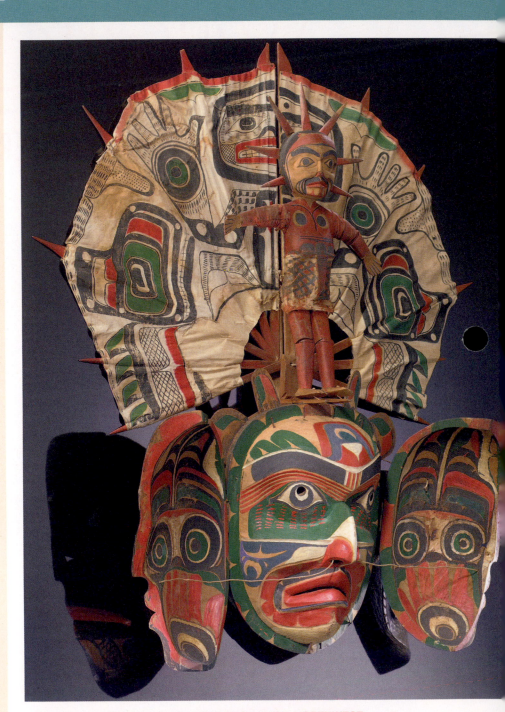

KWAKWAKA'WAKW SUN TRANSFORMATION MASK, NORTHWEST COAST Worn during Peace Dance ceremonies in the late nineteenth century, this mask drew on the deep-seated religious and artistic traditions of Northwest Coast Native Americans. *(Courtesy, National Museum of the American Indian, Smithsonian Institution #D115235)*

CHRONOLOGY 13,000 B.C.E.–C.E. 1500

ca. 13,000 B.C.E.	Human communities in the Americas.	**ca. C.E. 1**	Rise of chiefdoms on Northwest Coast and in California. Ancestral Pueblo culture begins in Southwest.
ca. 9000 B.C.E.	Paleo-Indians established throughout Western Hemisphere. Extinction of big-game mammals.	**ca. 300**	Hohokam culture begins in Southwest.
ca. 8000 B.C.E.	Earliest Archaic societies. Domesticated squash grown in Peru.	**ca. 700**	Mississippian culture begins.
ca. 7000 B.C.E.	Athapaskan-speaking peoples enter North America.	**ca. 900**	Urban center arises at Cahokia.
ca. 5000 B.C.E.	First maize grown in Mesoamerica.	**ca. 1000**	Norse attempt to colonize Vinland (Newfoundland).
ca. 3000–2000 B.C.E.	Inuit and Aleut peoples enter North America from Siberia.	**ca. 1200**	Ancestral Pueblo and Hohokam peoples disperse in Southwest.
ca. 2500 B.C.E.	Archaic societies begin giving way to a more diverse range of cultures. First maize grown in North America.	**ca. 1200–1400**	Cahokia declines and inhabitants disperse.
ca. 1200–900 B.C.E.	Poverty Point flourishes in Louisiana.	**ca. 1400**	Iroquois Confederacy formed.
ca. 400–100 B.C.E.	Adena culture flourishes in Ohio Valley.	**1428**	Aztec empire expands.
		1438	Inca empire expands.
ca. 100 B.C.E.–C.E. 600	Hopewell culture thrives in Midwest.	**1492**	Christopher Columbus reaches Western Hemisphere.

American history began with the people now referred to as Native Americans, thousands of years before the arrival of Europeans. Because Indians did not communicate through alphabetic writing before Europeans arrived, the principal sources of evidence about them are **archaeology**, **oral traditions**, graphic images and inscriptions, and cultural patterns (sometimes noted later by observant Europeans). As with all sources, historians have examined and interpreted this evidence critically to form a picture of the American past.

The earliest Native Americans lived in small, mobile bands of hunter-gatherers. They spread over the Americas and adapted to a variety of regional environments. As a result, their cultures diverged and diversified. By the time Europeans arrived, Indians lived in communities numbering from a few dozen to several thousand. All residents' contributions to these communities were vital, but each community had its own political, social, and gender organization. A group's regional location determined how they obtained food, which in turn helped shape their social structure. Some focused on farming, others hunting and gathering, and others fishing, but all drew on a variety of food sources. Although Indians' customs and spiritual beliefs varied widely, there were often similarities and shared cultural characteristics between peoples with different tribal, ethnic, and linguistic backgrounds.

archaeology
The scientific study of human history and prehistory using material remains such as artifacts, buildings, monuments, fossils, and inscriptions, often excavated.

oral traditions
A group's cultural practices and history passed from one generation to the next by word of mouth and often using the device of storytelling; verbal retelling of the past, not written down.

1-1 The First Americans, ca. 13,000–2500 B.C.E.

What tools have historians used to convey a sense of the American past and its peoples before the arrival of Europeans?

Exactly how and when the Western Hemisphere was first settled remains uncertain. Many Indians believe their ancestors originated in the Americas, but most scientific findings indicate that humans began arriving from northeastern Asia sometime during the last Ice Age (ca. 33,000–10,700 B.C.E.), when land linked Siberia and Alaska. There would have been no reason for these travelers to realize that they were passing from one of Earth's hemispheres to the other. Thereafter, as the Ice Age waned and global temperatures rose, they and their descendants dispersed throughout the Americas, adapting to environments ranging from tropical to frigid. Though divided into small, widely scattered groups, they interacted through trade and travel. Over several thousand years, indigenous Americans learned from one another and developed ways of life that had much in common despite their diverse backgrounds.

1-1.1 Peopling New Worlds

Most archaeologists agree that humans had spread to many parts of North America by 13,000 B.C.E. Often small foraging **bands** in search of food, most of the newcomers apparently traveled by watercraft, following the then-continuous coastline from Siberia to Alaska and progressing southward along the Pacific. As they went, groups stopped and either settled nearby or traveled inland to establish new homes. Coastal sites as far south as Monte Verde, Chile, reveal evidence from about 12,000 B.C.E. of peoples who fed on marine life, birds, small mammals, and wild plants, as well as an occasional mastodon. (Archaeologists estimate dates by measuring the radioactive carbon 14 [radiocarbon] in organic materials such as food remains.) Evidence of human encampments from the same period have been found at several North American sites. Some of the earliest Americans arrived by land. As the glaciers gradually melted, a corridor developed east of the Rocky Mountains through which these travelers passed before dispersing over much of the Western Hemisphere (see Map 1.1). A few archaeologists conjecture that some of the earliest Americans may have crossed the Atlantic from one or another western European site.

Although most Native Americans are descended from these early migrants, the ancestors of some native peoples came later from northeastern Asia, after the land connecting Siberia with Alaska had submerged. The Athapaskan (or Dene) people settled in Alaska and northwestern Canada in about 7000 B.C.E. Some of their descendants later migrated to the Southwest to form the Apaches and Navajos (as mentioned later). After 3000 B.C.E., Inuits (Eskimos) and Aleuts crossed the Bering Sea from Siberia to Alaska.

Native American oral traditions offer conflicting support for scientists' theories, depending on how the traditions are interpreted. Pueblos and Navajos in the Southwest tell how their forebears experienced perilous journeys through other worlds before emerging from underground in their present homelands, while the Iroquois in the region of modern-day New York and Ontario, Canada, trace their ancestry to a pregnant woman who fell from the "sky world." In accounts from the Iroquois and other peoples, the original humans could not settle on the water-covered planet until a diving bird or mammal brought soil from the ocean bottom, creating an island on which they could walk. Still other traditions recall large mammals, monsters, or "hairy people" with whom the first people shared Earth. Many Native Americans today insist that such accounts confirm that their ancestors originated in the Western Hemisphere. However, others note that the stories do not specify a place of origin and may well reflect the experiences of their ancestors as they journeyed from Asia—across water, ice, and unknown lands—and encountered large mammals before settling in their new homes. If not taken literally, they maintain, the traditions support rather than contradict scientists' theories.

Paleo-Indians, as archaeologists call the earliest Americans, established the foundations of Native American life. Paleo-Indians appear to have traveled within well-defined hunting territories in bands consisting of several families and totaling about fifteen to fifty people. Men hunted while women prepared food and cared for the children. Bands left their territories when traveling to quarries to obtain stone for making tools and other objects. There they encountered other bands, with whom they exchanged ideas and goods, intermarried, and participated in religious ceremonies. As in nonmarket economies and non-state societies throughout history, these exchanges followed the principle of **reciprocity**—the mutual bestowing of gifts and favors—rather than the notion that one party should accumulate profits or power at the expense of the other. These encounters enabled Paleo-Indians to develop a broad cultural life that transcended their small bands.

As at Monte Verde, Paleo-Indians everywhere exploited a variety of plant and animal foods available in their local environments. Initially, they focused on the large mammals—mammoths, mastodons, and giant species of horses, camels, bison, caribou, and moose—that proliferated then in the Americas. But suddenly in about 9000 B.C.E., the megafauna became extinct. Although some scholars believe that Paleo-Indian hunters killed off the large mammals, most maintain that the mammals were doomed not just by humans but by the warming climate, which disrupted the food chain on which they depended. Human beings, on the other hand, were major beneficiaries of environmental changes associated with the end of the Ice Age.

bands
Paleo-Indian traveling groups within hunting territories; these groups consisted of several families and totaled 15–50 people.

Paleo-Indians
Earliest peoples of the Americas, 13,000–8000 B.C.E.

reciprocity
Mutual bestowing of gifts and favors rather than competition for resources.

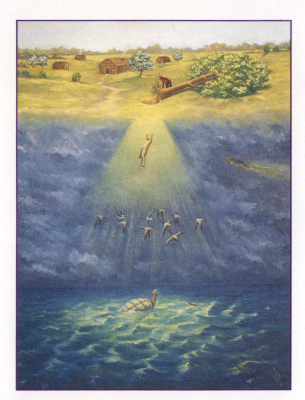

***SKY WOMAN*, ERNEST SMITH (1936)** A visual depiction of the Iroquois people's account of their origins, in which a woman fell from the sky to a watery world. *(Granger, NYC—All rights reserved)*.

1-1.2 Archaic Societies

After about 8000 B.C.E., Native Americans began modifying their Paleo-Indian ways. The warming of Earth's atmosphere continued until about 4000 B.C.E., with far-reaching global effects. Sea levels rose, flooding coastal areas, while glacial runoff filled interior waterways. The glaciers receded northward, along with the arctic and subarctic environments that had formerly extended into what are now the lower forty-eight states of the United States. Treeless plains and evergreen forests gave way to deciduous forests in the East, grassland prairies on the Plains, and desert in much of the West. The regional environments we know today emerged during this period.

Archaic peoples, as archaeologists term Native Americans who flourished in these new environments, lived off the wider varieties of flora and fauna that were now available. With more sources of food, communities required less land and supported larger populations. Some Indians in temperate regions resided in year-round villages. From about 3900 to 2800 B.C.E., for example, the 100 to 150 residents of a community near Kampsville, Illinois, obtained ample supplies of fish, mussels, mammals, birds, nuts, and seeds—without moving their homes.

Over time, Archaic Americans expanded women's and men's roles. Men took responsibility for fishing as well as hunting, while women procured wild plant products. Gender roles are apparent in burials at Indian Knoll, Kentucky, where tools relating to hunting, fishing, woodworking, and leatherworking were usually buried with men and those relating to cracking nuts and grinding seeds with women. Yet gender-specific distinctions did not apply to all activities, for objects used by religious healers were distributed equally between male and female graves.

Archaic Indians—usually women in North America—honed their skills at harvesting wild plants. Through generations of close observation, they determined how to weed, prune, irrigate, transplant, and otherwise manipulate their environments to favor plants that provided food and medicine. They also developed specialized tools for digging and grinding as well as more effective methods of drying and storing seeds. The most sophisticated early plant cultivators lived in **Mesoamerica** (central and southern Mexico and Central America), where maize agriculture was highly developed by 2500 B.C.E.

1-2 The Emergence of Tribal Societies, ca. 2500 B.C.E.–C.E. 1500

What was the relationship between the environment, available food supplies, and the development and success of various Native American societies from 2500 B.C.E. to 1500 C.E.?

After about 2500 B.C.E., most Native American societies moved beyond the ways of their Archaic forebears, particularly in their relations with the environment and with one another. The greatest change occurred among peoples whose environments enabled them to produce food surpluses by cultivating crops or other means. Surpluses enabled most of these societies to support larger populations in smaller territories than previously. Some of the most densely populated societies transformed trade networks into extensive religious and political systems linking several—sometimes dozens of—local communities. A few of these groupings became

> **Archaic peoples**
> Native Americans from 8000 until 2500 B.C.E.
>
> **Mesoamerica**
> Roughly, land extending from modern Mexico to Columbia; Central America plus Mexico.

MAP 1.1 **THE PEOPLING OF THE AMERICAS** Scientists postulate two probable routes by which the earliest peoples reached America. By 9500 B.C.E., their Paleo-Indian descendants had settled throughout the Western Hemisphere.

Iroquois Confederacy
The council of chiefs from the Onondaga, Mohawk, Oneida, Cayuga, and Seneca Iroquois nations.

formal confederacies and even states. The five Iroquois nations (Onondaga, Mohawk, Oneida, Cayuga, and Seneca) united around 1400 C.E. to become the powerful **Iroquois Confederacy**, for example. Two of the states—the Aztecs and Incas—went still further by becoming empires. But mobile hunting-fishing-gathering bands persisted in environments where food sources were few and widely scattered.

By 1500 C.E., the vast array of tribal societies encountered by the earliest Europeans had been established in the Americas.

1-2.1 Mesoamerica and South America

As Mesoamerican farmers refined their practices, their crops improved. When they planted beans alongside maize, the beans released an amino acid, lysine, into the maize, which heightened its nutritional value. Higher yields and improved nutrition led societies to structure their lives around farming. Over the next eight centuries, maize-based farming societies spread throughout Mesoamerica.

After 2000 B.C.E., some Mesoamerican societies produced crop surpluses that they traded to less populous, nonfarming neighbors. Expanding their trade contacts, a number of these societies established formal exchange networks that enabled them to enjoy more wealth and power than their partners. After 1200 B.C.E., a few communities, such as those of the Olmecs in Mesoamerica (see Map 1.2) and Chavín de Huántar in the Andes (see Map 1.3), developed into large urban centers, subordinating smaller neighbors. Unlike in earlier societies, the cities were highly unequal. A few wealthy elites dominated thousands of residents, and hereditary rulers claimed kinship with religious deities. Laborers built elaborate temples and palaces—including the first American pyramids—and artisans created statues of rulers and gods.

Although the earliest hereditary rulers exercised absolute power, their realms consisted of a few closely clustered communities. Anthropologists term such political societies **chiefdoms**, as opposed to **states** in which a ruler or government exercises direct authority over

MindTap

Beyond America
The Origins and Spread of Agriculture

chiefdoms
Political societies in Mesoamerica where the earliest hereditary rulers exercised absolute power over a few closely clustered communities.

states
Political societies in Mesoamerica where a ruler or government exercised direct authority over many communities.

MAP 1.2 MAJOR MESOAMERICAN CULTURES, CA. 1000 B.C.E.–C.E. 1519 Mesoamerica was a center of cultural and political ferment, culminating in the rise of the Aztecs. The Aztecs were still expanding when they were invaded by Spain in 1519.

many communities. Besides Mesoamerica and the Andes, chiefdoms eventually emerged in the Mississippi and Amazon valleys. A few states arose in Mesoamerica after 1 C.E. and in South America after 500 C.E. Although men ruled most chiefdoms and states, women served as chiefs in some Andean societies until the Spanish arrived.

The capital of the largest early state, Teotihuacán, was situated about fifty miles northeast of modern-day Mexico City. Numbering at least a hundred thousand people between the second and seventh centuries C.E., it was one of the largest cities in the world at the time. At its center was a complex of pyramids, the largest of which, the Pyramid of the Sun, was about 1 million cubic meters in volume. Teotihuacán dominated the peoples of the valley of Mexico, and its trade networks extended over much of present-day Mexico. Although Teotihuacán declined in the eighth century, it exercised enormous influence on the religion, government, and culture of its neighbors.

Teotihuacán's greatest impact was on the Maya, whose kingdom-states flourished from southern Mexico to Honduras between the seventh and fifteenth centuries. The Maya developed a calendar, a numerical system (which included the concept of zero), and a system of phonetic, hieroglyphic writing. Maya scribes produced thousands of books on bark paper glued into long, folded strips, which recorded religious ceremonies, historical traditions, and astronomical observations.

Other powerful states flourished in Mesoamerica and South America until the fifteenth century, when two mighty empires arose to challenge them. The first was the empire of the **Aztecs** (known then as the Mexica), who had migrated from the north during the thirteenth century and settled on the shore of Lake Texcoco as subjects of the local inhabitants. Overthrowing their rulers in 1428, the Aztecs conquered other cities and extended their domain to the Gulf Coast (see Map 1.2). In the 1450s, the Aztecs interpreted a four-year drought as a sign that the gods, like themselves, were hungry. Aztec priests maintained that the only way to satisfy the gods was to serve them human blood and hearts. From then on, conquering Aztec warriors sought captives for sacrifice to nourish the gods.

Aztecs
The empire that migrated from the north during the thirteenth century and settled on the shore of Lake Texcoco as subjects of the local inhabitants.

PYRAMID OF THE SUN, TEOTIHUACÁN Begun during the first century C.E., this pyramid remained the largest structure in the Americas until after the Spanish arrived. *(Richard A. Cooke/Corbis)*

A massive temple complex at the capital of Tenochtitlán formed the sacred center of the Aztec empire. The Great Temple consisted of two joined pyramids surrounded by smaller pyramids and buildings. Most of the more than two hundred deities the Aztecs honored originated with other societies, including those they had subjugated.

To support the nearly two hundred thousand people residing in and around Tenochtitlán, the Aztecs maximized food production. They drained swampy areas and created artificial islands with rich soil from the lake bottom. Aztec farmers grew food on the islands to supply the urban population. Aztec engineers devised an elaborate irrigation system to provide fresh water for both people and crops.

The Aztecs continued expanding into the early sixteenth century and collected taxes from subjects living within about a hundred miles of the capital. Conquered peoples farther away paid tribute, which replaced the free exchanges of goods formerly carried on with neighbors. Trade beyond the Aztec domain was conducted by *pochteca*, traders who traveled in armed caravans. The *pochteca* sought salt, cacao, jewelry, feathers, jaguar pelts, cotton, and precious stones and metals, including gold and turquoise, the latter from the American Southwest. Whether the Aztecs would have expanded still farther remains a mystery because they were violently crushed in the sixteenth century by the Spanish (see Chapter 2).

Meanwhile, a second empire, that of the **Incas**, arose in the Western Hemisphere. From their sumptuous capital at Cuzco, the Incas conquered and subordinated societies over much of the Andes and adjacent regions after 1438. One key to the Incas' expansion was their ability to produce and distribute a wide range of surplus crops, including maize, beans, potatoes, and meats. They constructed terraced irrigation systems for watering crops on mountainous terrain, perfected freeze-drying and other preservation techniques, built large storehouses, and constructed a vast network of roads and bridges. Like the Aztecs, the Incas were still expanding when Spanish invaders crushed them in the sixteenth century.

1-2.2 The Southwest

The Southwest is a uniformly arid region with a variety of landscapes. Waters from rugged mountains and forested plateaus follow ancient channels through vast expanses of desert on their way to the gulfs of Mexico and California. The amount of water has fluctuated over time, but securing water has always been a challenge for southwestern peoples. Nonetheless, some of them became farmers.

Maize first reached the Southwest via Mesoamerican trade links in about 2500 B.C.E. Yet full-time farming began only after 400 B.C.E. with the introduction of a more drought-resistant strain. Thereafter, southwestern populations rose and Indian cultures were transformed. The two most influential Southwestern cultures were Hohokam and Ancestral Pueblo.

Hohokam culture emerged about 300 C.E., several centuries after Native Americans had begun farming in the Gila and Salt River valleys of southern Arizona. Hohokam peoples—organized in large workforces—built irrigation canals that enabled them to harvest two crops a year. They also built permanent towns, usually consisting of several hundred inhabitants. While many towns remained independent, others joined confederations with several towns linked by canals. The central village in each

> **Incas**
> The empire that conquered and subordinated societies over much of the Andes and adjacent regions after 1438.
>
> **Hohokam**
> Early agricultural society of the Southwest.

MAP 1.3 **MAJOR ANDEAN CULTURES, 900 B.C.E.–1432 C.E.** Despite the challenges posed by the rugged Andes Mountains, native peoples there developed several complex societies and cultures, culminating in the Inca Empire.

confederation coordinated labor, trade, religion, and political life for member communities.

Although unique, Hohokam culture drew on Mesoamerican materials and ideas. From about the sixth century C.E., the large villages had ball courts and platform mounds similar to those in Mesoamerica. Archaeologists have uncovered rubber balls, macaw feathers, cottonseeds, and copper bells from Mesoamerica at Hohokam sites. Mesoamerican influence was also apparent in the creations of Hohokam artists, who worked in clay, stone, turquoise, and shell.

Ancestral Pueblo culture originated in about 1 C.E. in the Four Corners area where Arizona, New Mexico, Colorado, and Utah meet. By around 700 C.E., Ancestral Pueblos were harvesting crops, living in permanent villages, and making pottery. Thereafter, they expanded over a wide area and became the most powerful people in the Southwest.

Distinctive for their architecture, Ancestral Pueblo villages consisted of extensive complexes of attached apartments and storage rooms, along with *kivas*—partly underground structures in which male religious leaders conducted ceremonies. To this day, similar apartments and kivas remain central features of Southwestern Pueblo Indian architecture.

Ancestral Pueblo culture reached its height between about 900 and 1150, during an unusually wet period in the Southwest. In Chaco Canyon, a cluster of twelve large towns forged a powerful confederation numbering about fifteen thousand people. A system of roads radiated from the canyon to satellite towns as far as sixty-five miles away. Road builders carved out stairs or footholds on steep cliffs rather than go around them. By controlling rainwater runoff through small dams and terraces, the towns fed themselves and their satellites. The largest town, Pueblo Bonito, had about twelve hundred inhabitants. People traveled over the roads from the satellites to Chaco Canyon's two Great Kivas—about fifty feet in diameter—for religious ceremonies. The canyon was also a major trade center, with links to Mesoamerica, the Great Plains, the Mississippi Valley, and California.

Ancestral Pueblo culture—as manifested at Chaco Canyon, Mesa Verde in southwestern

> **Ancestral Pueblo**
> Southwest Native American culture known especially for its architecture, which consisted of apartments and kivas.

CLIFF PALACE, MESA VERDE Modern tourists help demonstrate the scale of this remarkable Ancestral Pueblo community site. *(Jose Fuste Raga/Corbis)*

Colorado, and other sites—declined in the twelfth and thirteenth centuries. The overriding cause was drought. As often has happened in human history, an era of abundant rainfall ended abruptly. Without enough water, inhabitants abandoned the great centers, dispersing to form smaller modern Pueblo communities, many of them on the Rio Grande. Hohokam communities also dispersed, forming the Akimel O'odham and Tohono O'odham tribes of southern Arizona. With farming peoples now living in the few areas with enough water, the drier lands of the Southwest attracted the nonfarming Apaches and Navajos, whose arrival at the end of the fourteenth century ended their long migration from the far north (mentioned earlier in this chapter).

1-2.3 The Eastern Woodlands

Unlike the Southwest, the Eastern Woodlands—stretching from the Mississippi Valley to the Atlantic Ocean—had abundant water. That and deciduous forests provided Woodlands Indians with a rich variety of food sources, while the region's extensive river systems facilitated long-distance travel. As a result, many eastern Indians established populous villages and complex confederations.

By 1200 B.C.E., about five thousand people lived at **Poverty Point** on the lower Mississippi River. The town featured earthworks consisting of two large mounds and six concentric embankments, the outermost of which spanned more than half a mile in diameter. During the spring and autumn equinoxes, a person standing on the larger mound could watch the sun rise directly over the village center. As elsewhere in the Americas, solar observations were the basis for religious beliefs and a calendar.

Poverty Point was the center of a larger political and economic unit. The settlement imported quartz, copper, obsidian, crystal, and other materials from long distances for redistribution to nearby communities. Poverty Point's general design and organization indicate Olmec influence from Mesoamerica. Poverty Point flourished for about three centuries and then declined, for unknown reasons. Nevertheless, it foreshadowed later developments in the Eastern Woodlands.

A different kind of mound-building culture, called **Adena**, emerged in the Ohio Valley around 400 B.C.E. Adena villages were smaller than Poverty Point, rarely exceeding four hundred inhabitants. But Adena people spread over a wide area and built hundreds of mounds, most of them containing graves. The treatment of Adena dead varied according to social or political status. Some corpses were

cremated; others were placed in round clay basins or given elaborate tombs.

After 100 B.C.E., Adena evolved into a more complex and widespread culture known as **Hopewell**, which spread from the Ohio Valley to the Illinois River Valley. Some Hopewell centers contained two or three dozen mounds within enclosures of several square miles. Hopewell elites were buried with thousands of freshwater pearls or copper ornaments or with sheets of mica, quartz, or other sacred substances, many of which originated in locales east of the Rockies. Through trade networks, Hopewell religious and technological influence spread to communities as far away as Wisconsin, Missouri, Florida, and New York. Although the great Hopewell centers were abandoned by about 600 B.C.E. (for reasons that are unclear), they had an enormous influence on subsequent developments in eastern North America.

The peoples of Poverty Point and the Adena and Hopewell cultures did little farming. Indian women in Kentucky and Missouri had cultivated small amounts of squash as early as 2500 B.C.E., and maize first appeared east of the Mississippi by 300 B.C.E. But agriculture did not become the primary food source for Woodlands people until between the seventh and twelfth centuries C.E.

The earliest societies in the East that were primarily agricultural were located on the floodplains of

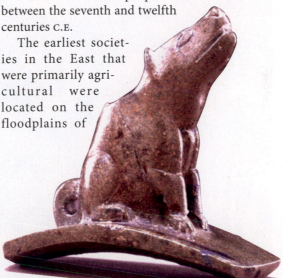

HOPEWELL EFFIGY PIPE This depiction of a coyote was carved between 200 B.C.E. and 1900 B.C.E. *(Ohio Historical Society)*

Poverty Point
The town on the lower Mississippi River that was the center of the Indian communities around 1200 B.C.

Adena
An early Native American culture centered in the Ohio River valley from about the tenth century B.C. to about the second century C.E., noted for its elaborate burial mounds and highly developed artistic style.

Hopewell
An early Native American culture centered in the Ohio River valley from about the second century B.C. to the fourth century A.D., noted for the construction of extensive earthworks and large conical burial mounds and for its highly developed arts and crafts.

the Mississippi River and its major tributaries. Beginning around 700 C.E., they developed a new culture, called **Mississippian**. Mississippian craft production and long-distance trade dwarfed that of Adena and Hopewell peoples. As in Meso-america, Mississippian centers, numbering hundreds or even thousands of people, arose around open plazas. Large platform mounds adjoined the plazas, topped by sumptuous religious temples and the residences of chiefs and other elites. Religious ceremonies focused on the worship of the sun as the source of agricultural fertility. The people considered chiefs to be related to the sun. When a chief died, his wives and servants were killed to accompany him in the afterlife. Largely in connection with their religious and funeral rituals, Mississippian artists produced highly sophisticated work in clay, stone, shell, copper, wood, and other materials.

After 900 C.E., Mississippian centers formed extensive networks based on river-borne trade and shared religious beliefs, each

dominated by a single metropolis. The largest, most powerful such system centered on **Cahokia**, located near modern St. Louis, Missouri, where about twenty thousand people inhabited a 125-square-mile metropolitan area.

For about two and a half centuries, Cahokia reigned supreme in the Mississippi Valley. After 1200 C.E., however, Cahokia and other valley centers experienced shortages of food and other resources. As in the Southwest, densely concentrated societies had taxed a fragile environment with a fluctuating climate. Competition for suddenly scarce resources led to warfare and undermined Cahokia and its allies. The survivors fled to the surrounding prairies and westward to the lower valleys of the Plains, where they regrouped in decentralized villages. Mississippian chiefdoms and temple mound centers persisted in the Southeast, where Spanish explorers would later encounter them as the forerunners of Cherokees, Creeks, and other southeastern Indian peoples (see Chapter 2).

Despite Cahokia's decline, Mississippian culture profoundly affected Native Americans in the Eastern Woodlands. Although Mississippian-style mounds and other earthworks did not spread elsewhere, life for the Iroquois and other peoples as far north as the Great Lakes and southern New England eventually

Mississippian

An early Native American culture formed in about A.D. 700 C.E in the floodplains of the Mississippi River and noted for the construction of extensive earthworks and large conical burial mounds, religious ceremonies, and its highly sophisticated arts and crafts.

Cahokia

Area located near modern St. Louis, Missouri, where about twenty thousand people inhabited a 125-square-mile metropolitan area.

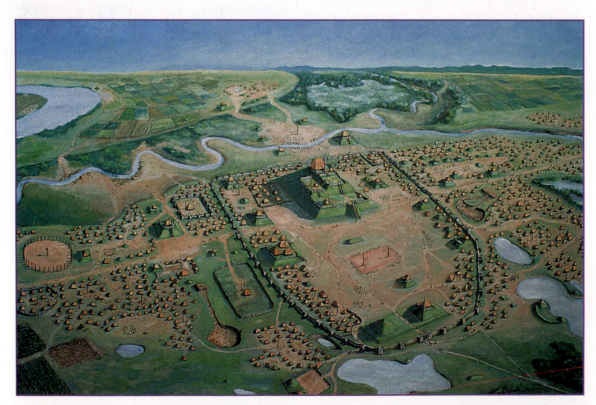

CAHOKIA MOUNDS This contemporary painting conveys Cahokia's grand scale. Not until the late eighteenth century did another North American city (Philadelphia) surpass the population of Cahokia, ca. 1200. *(Cahokia Mounds Historic Site, painting by William R. Iseminger)*

revolved around village-based farming. Women developed new strains of maize and beans, along with techniques and tools for cultivating crops. Only in more northerly Eastern Woodlands areas was the growing season too short for maize (which required one hundred or more frost-free days) to be a reliable source of food.

Eastern Indians' land management practices were environmentally sound and economically productive. Indian men systematically burned hardwood forests, eliminating, as an early New England colonist put it, "all the underwood and rubbish which would otherwise overgrow the country, making it unpassable and spoil their . . . hunting." Hunting was enhanced because burned-over tracts favored the growth of grass and berry bushes that attracted deer and other game. The men cleared fields so that women could plant corn, beans, and squash in soil enriched by ash. After several years of abundant harvests, yields declined, and the Indians moved to another site to repeat the process. Ground cover eventually reclaimed the abandoned clearing, restoring fertility naturally, and the Native Americans could return. Most early European colonists would settle on lands long cultivated by Eastern Woodlands peoples.

1-2.4 Nonfarming Societies

Outside the Southwest and the Eastern Woodlands, farming north of Mesoamerica was either impossible because of inhospitable environments or impractical because native peoples could obtain ample food from wild sources. On the Northwest coast, from the Alaskan panhandle to northern California, and in the Columbia Plateau, Native Americans devoted brief periods to catching salmon and other spawning fish, which they dried and stored in quantities sufficient to last the year. Their seasonal movements gave way to a settled lifestyle in permanent villages where they had access to fish in rivers and the ocean as well as to whales and other sea mammals, shellfish, land mammals, and wild plants.

By 1 C.E., most Northwest coast villages numbered several hundred people who lived in multifamily houses built of cedar planks. Trade and warfare with interior groups strengthened the wealth and power of chiefs and other elites. From the time of the earliest contacts, Europeans were amazed by the artistic and architectural achievements of the Northwest coast Indians. "What must astonish most," wrote a French explorer in 1791, "is to see painting everywhere, everywhere sculpture, among a nation of hunters."

At about the same time, Native Americans on the coast and in the valleys of what is now California were clustering in villages of about a hundred people to coordinate the processing of nutritious and easily stored acorns. After gathering millions of acorns from California's oak groves each fall, tribal peoples such as the Chumash and Ohlones ground the acorns into meal, leached them of their bitter tannic acid, and then roasted, boiled, or baked them prior to storage. Facing intense competition, California Indians combined their villages into chiefdoms and defended their territories. Chiefs conducted trade, diplomacy, war, and religious ceremonies. Along with other wild species, acorns enabled the Indians of California to prosper.

Between the Eastern Woodlands and the Pacific coast, the Plains and deserts were too dry to support large human settlements. Dividing the region are the Rocky Mountains, to the east of which lie the grasslands of the Great Plains, while to the west are several deserts of varying elevations that ecologists call the Great Basin. Except in the Southwest, Native Americans in this region remained in mobile hunting-gathering bands.

Plains Indian hunters pursued game animals, including antelope, deer, elk, and bear, but their favorite was buffalo, or bison. Buffalo provided Plains Indians with meat and hides, from which they made clothing, bedding, portable houses (tipis), kettles, shields, and other items. They made tools from buffalo bones and containers and arrowheads from buffalo horns. Limited to travel by foot, Plains hunters stampeded herds of bison into small box canyons or over cliffs, killing dozens, or occasionally hundreds. Because a single buffalo could provide two hundred to four hundred pounds of meat and a band had no means of preserving and storing most of it, the practice was especially wasteful. Yet humans were so few in number that they had no significant impact on the bison population before the arrival of Europeans.

During and after the Mississippian era, refugees from Cahokia and elsewhere in the Eastern Woodlands moved to the lower river valleys of the Plains, where the rainfall had increased enough to support cultivated plants. In contrast to Native Americans already living on the Plains, such as the Blackfeet and the Crow, farming newcomers such as the Mandans and Pawnees built year-round villages and permanent earth lodges. They also hunted buffalo and other animals.

As Indians elsewhere increased their food production, the Great Basin grew warmer and drier, further limiting already scarce food sources. Ducks and other waterfowl on which Native Americans formerly feasted disappeared as marshlands dried up after 1200 B.C.E., and the number of buffalo and other game animals also dwindled. Great Basin

WAHKPA CHU'GN BISON KILL SITE, MONTANA This artist's sketch shows one of the several ways that Plains Indians procured buffalo before the advent of horses and guns. *(Linda Rayner/Ethos Consultants)*

Indians such as the Shoshones and the Utes countered these trends by relying more heavily on *piñon* nuts, which they harvested, stored, and ate in winter camps. Hunting improved after about 500 c.e., when Indians adopted the bow and arrow.

In western Alaska, Inuits and Aleuts, carrying sophisticated tools and weapons from their Siberian homeland, arrived after 3000 b.c.e. Combining ivory, bone, and other materials, they fashioned harpoons and spears for the pursuit of sea mammals and—for the Inuits—caribou. Through continued contacts with Siberia, Inuits introduced the bow and arrow in North America. As they perfected their ways of living in the cold tundra environment, many Inuit groups spread westward across upper Canada and to Greenland.

The earliest contacts between Native Americans and Europeans occurred in about 980 c.e., five centuries before the arrival of Columbus, when Norse expansionists from Scandinavia colonized parts of Greenland. The Greenland Norse hunted furs, obtained timber, and traded with Inuit groups. They also made several attempts, beginning in about 1000, to colonize Vinland, as they called Newfoundland. The Vinland Norse initially exchanged metal goods for ivory with the local Beothuk Indians, but peaceful trade gave way to hostile encounters. Beothuk resistance soon led the Norse to withdraw from Vinland.

1-3 Native American Kinship, Gender, and Culture, ca. 1500 c.e.

What role did gender and kinship play in shaping the various Native American cultures that emerged by 1500?

By 1500 c.e., native peoples had transformed the Americas into a dazzling array of cultures and societies (see Map 1.4). The Western Hemisphere numbered about 75 million people, most of them in Mesoamerica and South America. Between 7 million and 10 million Indians were unevenly distributed across North America. As they had for thousands of years, small, mobile hunting bands peopled the Arctic, Subarctic, Great Basin, and much of the Plains. More sedentary societies based on fishing or gathering predominated along the Pacific coast, while village-based agriculture was typical in the Eastern Woodlands and the river valleys of the Southwest and Plains. Mississippian urban centers still prevailed in much of the Southeast. North American Indians grouped themselves in several hundred nations and tribes, and spoke hundreds of languages and dialects.

Despite differences among Native American societies, all were based on kinship, reciprocity, and communal ownership of resources. While some tasks were performed by both men and women, each gender also had its own distinctive roles and expectations, though these, too, varied from one Indian group to another. Trade facilitated the exchange of goods, technologies, and ideas. Thus over time, the bow and arrow, ceramic pottery, and certain religious values and practices had spread to Indians everywhere.

1-3.1 Kinship and Marriage

Like their Archaic forebears, native North Americans were bound together primarily by kinship. Ties among biological relatives created complex patterns of social obligation and interdependence. **Nuclear families** (a husband, a wife, and their biological children) never stood alone. Instead, they lived with one of the parents' relatives in multigenerational **extended families**.

In **patrilocal** societies, the extended families of men took precedence and couples went to live with the husband's family upon marriage. In **matrilocal** societies, the opposite was true, and couples would reside with the wife's relatives. Lineage varied, too. Hunter-gather cultures were typically **patrilineal**, with the line of descent and inheritance (power over the land) traced through the father. Farming-based cultures, such as the Pueblos, tended to be **matrilineal**, tracing the line of descent and inheritance through the mother. In matrilineal cultures, the primary male adult in a child's life was the mother's oldest brother, not the father. Some other cultures did not distinguish sharply between the status of female and male family lines.

Customs regulating marriage varied considerably. Some male leaders had more than one wife, and either husbands, wives, or both could terminate a marriage and begin a relationship with someone new. This flexibility to end and begin new relationships was especially true in matrilineal cultures such as the Pueblos, where a person's identity was based not on who they married, but rather on who their mother was. In most cultures, young people married in their teens, usually after engaging in sexual relationships. Native American cultures also included homosexuality and "two-spirit" people, more often men but also some women who cross-dressed and lived as the opposite gender. Believed to possess both male and female natures, in some societies, they were hailed for their unique spiritual power.

Kinship was also often the basis for armed conflict. Indian societies typically considered homicide a matter to be resolved by the extended families of the victim and the perpetrator. If the perpetrator's family offered a gift that the victim's family considered appropriate, the question was settled; if not, political leaders attempted to resolve the dispute. Otherwise, the victim's family members and their supporters might seek to avenge the killing by armed retaliation. Such feuds could escalate into wars between communities.

The potential for war rose when densely populated societies competed for scarce resources, as on the Northwest and California coasts. Yet Native American warfare generally remained minimal, with rivals seeking to humiliate one another and seize captives rather than inflict massive casualties or conquer land. The risk of being taken captive and incorporated into an enemy's culture was especially high for women and their children, though men might be taken to replace the death of a family member killed in battle.

1.3.2 Gender and Work

While Native American societies considered the contributions of both men and women vital to a group's survival, work was largely divided along gender lines. This varied, too, based on the nature and location of a particular group. Women did most of the cultivating in farming societies, except in the Southwest (where women and men shared the responsibility). In Pueblo cultures, men managed trade with other Indian groups and built homes, while women made clothing, pottery, and prepared food. In Iroquois society, men likewise managed trade, but they also hunted and got the soil ready for farming. Women cultivated the crops. In the hunting societies of the Plains, men killed the buffalo, bison, and other animals, while women skinned the animals and prepared hides and meat. In the sea-based cultures of the Northwest, women fished alongside men.

In cultures where women produced the greater share of the food supply, they could gain power, albeit indirectly. Among the Iroquois, for example, women collectively owned the fields and distributed food. They supplied men going off to battle, and by determining whether or not to provide food, they could also decide when to begin and end a

nuclear families
Families that consist of a husband, a wife, and their biological children.

extended families
Extension of the nuclear family that included additional relatives.

patrilocal
Social custom in which, upon marriage, a wife goes to live with her husband's family or community.

matrilocal
Social custom in which, upon marriage, a husband goes to live with his wife's family or community.

patrilineal
A kinship system in which the line of descent or inheritance/property is traced through the father/male line.

matrilineal
A kinship system in which the line of descent or inheritance/property is traced through the mother/female line.

GUALE INDIANS PLANTING CROPS, 1564 A French explorer sketched this scene on the Florida coast in which men are breaking up the soil while women sow corn, bean, and squash seeds. *(Library of Congress Prints and Photographs Division)*

war. Women might seek to prompt a war, for example, if they wanted to avenge the loss of a family member or wanted to bring new captives into the community.

The supreme authority of chief typically rested with men in Native American cultures, though there were some rare exceptions of women as sachems (chiefs) in New England, for example. In most societies, however, women's political power took the form of influence. Among the Iroquois, women played a decisive role in selecting chiefs, which gave them a kind of indirect power.

1-3.3 Spirituality, Rituals, and Beliefs

Native American religions revolved around the conviction that all nature was alive, pulsating with spiritual power. A mysterious force, such power united all nature, including human beings, in an unbroken web. Native Americans endeavored to conciliate the spiritual forces in their world—living things, rocks and water, sun and moon, even ghosts. For example, Indian hunters prayed to the animals they killed, begging their pardon and thanking them for the gift of food. (For one example, see Going to the Source.) Native people also looked to nature for stories of how they came into being, and women were often featured. The Iroquois origin story of Sky Woman (mentioned earlier), as well as the Penobscot Corn Mother and the Acoma tale of two sisters, all highlight women as primary creative forces in peopling the world.

Native Americans had several ways of gaining access to spiritual power. One was through dreams and visions, which most Native Americans interpreted as spiritual instructions. Sometimes a dreamer received a message for his or her people. Those who could interpret dreams were prized, and in some cultures, such as the Seneca, women could be both interpreters and spiritual healers.

Native people also sought power through physical ordeals and rituals. Power-seeking rituals, such as the Sun Dance performed by

Indians of the Plains and Great Basin, were often practiced by entire communities. Young men in many societies gained recognition as adults through a vision quest—a solitary venture that entailed fasting and envisioning a spirit who would endow them with special powers. Some tribes initiated girls at the onset of menstruation into the spiritual world from which female reproductive power flowed. In fact, women's sexuality was highly valued in most Indian cultures as the source of new life (reproduction) as well as a means to squelch hostile spirits. Female sexuality played a role in adopting new members into the community, too.

1-3.4 Native American Social Values

Native American societies demanded a strong degree of cooperation. Using physical punishment sparingly, if at all, Indians punished children psychologically by public shaming. Communities sought unity through consensus rather than tolerating lasting divisions. Political leaders articulated slowly emerging agreements in dramatic oratory. The English colonizer John Smith noted that the most effective Native American leaders spoke "with vehemency and so great passions that they sweat till they drop and are so out of breath they scarce can speak."

MAP 1.4 LOCATIONS OF SELECTED NATIVE AMERICAN PEOPLES, 1500 c.e. Indian nations were well established in homelands across the continent when Europeans first arrived. Many would combine with others or move in later centuries, either to avoid white invaders or because they were forced.

A Cherokee Oral Tradition

The following story is an example of a Native American oral tradition. Since before Europeans arrived, Indians have told and retold such stories as one means of conveying their beliefs and histories through the generations. This account was related by a Cherokee man named Swimmer to an anthropologist, James Mooney, in the 1880s. Mooney titled the story "Origin of Disease and Medicine," but it also sets out Cherokee beliefs on relations between humans, animals, and plants.

In the old days the beasts, birds, fishes, insects, and plants could all talk, and they and the people lived together in peace and friendship. But as time went on the people increased so rapidly that their settlements spread over the whole earth, and the poor animals found themselves beginning to be cramped for room. This was bad enough, but to make it worse Man invented bows, knives, blowguns, spears, and hooks, and began to slaughter the larger animals, birds, and fishes for their flesh or their skins, while the smaller creatures, such as the frogs and worms, were crushed and trodden upon without thought, out of pure carelessness or contempt. So the animals resolved to consult upon measures for their common safety.

The Bears were the first to meet in council in their townhouse under Kuwâ'hi mountain, the "Mulberry Place," and the old White Bear chief presided. . . . [But the bears could not devise a workable] plan, so the old chief dismissed the council and the Bears dispersed to the woods and thickets without having concerted any way to prevent the increase of the human race. Had the result of the council been otherwise, we should now be at war with the Bears, but as it is, the hunter does not even ask the Bear's pardon when he kills one.

The Deer next held a council under their chief, the Little Deer, and after some talk decided to send rheumatism to every hunter who should kill one of them unless he took care to ask their pardon for the offense. . . . No hunter who has regard for his health ever fails to ask pardon of the Deer for killing it.

Next came the Fishes and Reptiles, who had their own complaints against Man. They held their council together and determined to make their victims dream of snakes twining about them in slimy folds and blowing foul breath in their faces, or to make them dream of eating raw or decaying fish, so that they would lose appetite, sicken, and die. This is why people dream about snakes and fish.

Finally the Birds, Insects, and smaller animals came together for the same purpose, and the Grubworm was chief of the council. It was decided that each in turn should give an opinion, and then they would vote on the question as to whether or not Man was guilty. . . . They began then to devise and name so many new diseases, one after another, that had not their invention at last failed them, no one of the human race would have been able to survive.

When the Plants, who were friendly to Man, heard what had been done by the animals, they determined to defeat the latter's evil designs. Each Tree, Shrub, and Herb, down even to the Grasses and Mosses, agreed to furnish a cure for some one of the diseases named, and each said: "I shall appear to help Man when he calls upon me in his need." Thus came medicine; and the plants, every one of which has its use if we only knew it, furnish the remedy to counteract the evil wrought by the revengeful animals. Even weeds were made for some good purpose, which we must find out for ourselves. When the doctor does not know what medicine to use for a sick man the spirit of the plant tells him.

Source: James Mooney, Myths of the Cherokee, in 19th Annual Report of the Bureau of American Ethnology, 1897–98, Part I (Washington, D.C.: Smithsonian Institution, 1900), pp. 250–252.

QUESTIONS

1. How would you characterize relationships among humans, animals, and plants in the story?
2. What is the principal lesson for human beings in the story?

BIG HORN MEDICINE WHEEL, WYOMING The medicine wheel was constructed between three and eight centuries ago as a center for religious ceremonies, including those relating to the summer solstice. *(University of Saskatchewan, University Library, University Archives & Special Collections, Courtney Milne fonds, image 460-008)*

Native Americans reinforced cooperation with a strong sense of order. Custom, the demands of social conformity, and the rigors of nature strictly regulated life and people's everyday affairs. Exacting familial or community revenge was a ritualized way of restoring order that had broken down. On the other hand, the failure of measures to restore order could bring fearful consequences—blind hatred, unending violence, and the most dreaded of evils, witchcraft. In fearing witchcraft, Native Americans resembled the Europeans and Africans they would encounter after 1492.

The principle of reciprocity was central to Native Americans. Reciprocity involved mutual give-and-take. Its aim was to maintain equilibrium and interdependence even between individuals of unequal power and prestige. Most Indian leaders' authority depended on the obligations they bestowed rather than on coercion. By distributing gifts, they obligated members of the community to support them and to accept their authority, however limited. The same principle applied to relations between societies. Powerful communities distributed gifts to weaker neighbors who reciprocated with tribute in the form of material goods along with labor and other services. A French observer in seventeenth-century Canada clearly understood: "For the savages have that noble quality, that they give liberally, casting at the feet of him whom they will honor the present that they give him. But it is with hope to receive some reciprocal kindness, which is a kind of contract, which we call. . . . 'I give thee, to the end thou shouldst give me.'"

The Whole Vision

■ *What tools have historians used to convey a sense of the American past and its peoples before the arrival of Europeans?*

Historians rely on multiple sources to convey the past, but when few or no written records are available they must piece the story together using other evidence. In studying the history of Native American cultures before the arrival of Europeans, historians have had to rely heavily on archeological sources along with Native American oral accounts passed from generation to generation. These materials, along with other scientific data, have painted a picture of the geological changes that facilitated the peopling of North America by 13,000 B.C.E. Archeological sources indicate who these people may have been, how they probably arrived, how and where they dispersed throughout the region, what food sources they developed, how they established societies and cultures, and how they interacted with each other. Archeological findings also point to environmental changes that for better or worse altered Indians' ways of life. Finally, historians can compare scientific data with the oral traditions of native peoples, looking for ways these stories may verify or differ from archeological and scientific findings to provide a rich and complex portrait of the past.

■ *What was the relationship between the environment, available food supplies, and the development and success of various Native American societies from 2500 B.C.E. to 1500 C.E.?*

Whether a particular Native American society rose, endured, or failed had much to do with its relationship to the environment and, in turn, its access to food supplies. Regional variations in environment, weather, and terrain helped shape not only the types of food available but also the social, economic, and political organization of the people within native societies. Indians with surplus food could engage in trade, which brought different native societies into contact with each other and fueled cultural exchanges and adaptation. The greater the trade opportunities for a society, the wealthier and more powerful it became. It also helped shape whether communities organized independently, communally, or as chiefdoms extending over wide areas. Environmental changes over time influenced whether a society would continue to thrive or exist at all. In addition, scarcity of food supplies shaped the political organization of various societies, as they sometimes combined to safeguard their supplies from outsiders or waged war on intruders.

■ *What role did gender and kinship play in shaping the various Native American cultures that emerged by 1500?*

All native peoples looked to kinship systems to organize their communities and to reinforce accepted cultural and spiritual values. Ideas about gender roles—what was considered acceptable for men and women to do—structured daily life and the individual experiences of members within all Native American communities. The ways in which a group defined and prescribed gender, however, varied based on the community's location and economic foundation (farming, hunting, nonfarming). Gender and kinship systems determined everything from what constituted a family, when and who a person married, where married couples would live, to lines of descent and inheritance. In every society, the contributions of all members were vital to its survival, but gender determined the types of work done by men and women. The political aspects of native societies (who their leaders were and who elected those leaders) were also gendered. Finally, religious and spiritual practices and rituals were defined in gender terms, from the beliefs about creation to who could be spiritual healers and leaders to rites of passage.

2 The Rise of the Atlantic World, 1400–1625

BARTHOLOMEW GOSNOLD TRADING WITH WAMPANOAG INDIANS AT MARTHA'S VINEYARD (1602) BY THEODORE DE BRY, 1634 Exchanges between Native Americans and Europeans transformed the Atlantic Ocean from a barrier to a bridge linking Earth's two hemispheres. *(MPI/Getty Images)*

C. 1400–1600	European Renaissance. Coastal West African kingdoms rise and fall as slave trade expands.		**1558**	Elizabeth I becomes queen of England.
C. 1440	Portuguese slave trade in West Africa begins.		**1565**	St. Augustine founded by Spanish.
C. 1450	Songhay succeeds Mali as major power in West African grassland.		**1585–1590**	English colony of Roanoke established, then disappears.
1492	Christian "reconquest" of Spain. Columbus lands at Guanahaní.		**1588**	England defeats the Spanish Armada.
1498	Vasco da Gama rounds the Cape of Good Hope and reaches India.		**1598**	Oñate founds Spanish colony of New Mexico.
1517	Protestant Reformation begins in Germany.		**1603**	James I becomes king of England.
1519–1521	Cortés leads Spanish conquest of Aztec empire.		**1607**	English colonies founded at Jamestown and Sagadahoc.
1519–1522	Magellan's expedition circumnavigates the globe.		**1608**	Champlain founds New France.
1532–1536	Pizarro leads Spanish conquest of Inca empire.		**1609**	Henry Hudson explores the Hudson River.
1534	Church of England breaks from Roman Catholic Church.		**1610–1614**	First Anglo-Powhatan War.
			1614	New Netherland founded.
1539–1543	De Soto attempts conquests of southeastern Native Americans.		**1619**	Virginia begins exporting tobacco. First Africans arrive in Virginia.
1540–1542	Coronado attempts conquests of southwestern Native Americans.		**1620**	English colony of Plymouth founded.
			1622–1632	Second Anglo-Powhatan War.
1541–1542	Cartier attempts to colonize eastern Canada.		**1624**	James I revokes Virginia Company's charter.

At ten o'clock on a moonlit evening, the tense crew spotted a glimmering light. At two the next morning—October 12, 1492—came the shout, "Land! Land!" The captain, **Christopher Columbus**, went ashore with the royal flag, knelt to give thanks, and claimed for Spain the island in the Bahamas that he named San Salvador.

Yet Columbus and his crew were not alone. Witnessing their landing were the local Taino Indians, who called the island Guanahaní and had never heard of Spain. Far from a one-sided act of discovery, Columbus's landing facilitated the mutual discovery by two peoples of one another.

The meeting of Spaniards with Tainos was a critical step in the formation of what historians call the **Atlantic world**. After 1492, an emergent Atlantic world linked peoples from Europe, Africa, and North and South America, in colonial societies, coercive labor systems, trade networks, religious missions, and wars. Whether traveling to new lands—voluntarily or under duress—or experiencing the transformation of familiar homelands, Atlantic peoples experienced repeated challenges to their customary ways of thinking and acting. Their exchanges also included new animals, plants, and germs with far-reaching environmental and demographic consequences. In this sense, the Atlantic world was a "new world" for indigenous Americans, Europeans, and Africans. In much of what is now Latin America, the coming of Europeans was quickly transformed into conquest. In the future United States and Canada, European mastery would come more slowly. More than a hundred years would pass before self-sustaining colonies

Christopher Columbus
Italian explorer who claimed the island of San Salvador in the Bahamas for the king and queen of Spain.

Atlantic world
The emerging stage upon which peoples from Europe, Africa, and North and South America would increasingly interact after Columbus's voyage to the Bahamas in 1492.

CHRISTOPHER COLUMBUS *(Snark/Art Resource, NY)*

appeared in North America. Nevertheless, from the moment of Columbus's landing, the Americas became the stage for a variety of encounters of Native American, European, and African peoples in the new Atlantic world.

2-1 The Context for European Exploration

How does an awareness of the social and political context in Europe enrich our understanding of early American exploration and history?

When the Atlantic world emerged in the fifteenth and sixteenth centuries, all four of the continents facing the Atlantic Ocean were undergoing internal change. In North and South America, some societies rose, others fell, and still others adapted to new circumstances (see Chapter 1). A new market society emerged in western Europe and West Africa, which coexisted alongside older systems of barter and local exchange. Wealthy merchants financed dynastic rulers seeking to extend their domains, and religion played a critical role in supporting some merchants and rulers.

Western Europe's transformation was especially thoroughgoing. Its population nearly doubled in size, the distribution of wealth and power shifted radically, and new modes of thought and spirituality undermined established beliefs and knowledge. The result was social, political, and religious upheaval alongside remarkable expressions of creativity and innovation. Together, these factors provided the push that would lead some western European countries to seek new opportunities to expand their borders, increase their wealth, and deal with the complex socioeconomic problems they increasingly faced. Exploration would prove all too enticing within this context.

2-1.1 European Culture and Society

When Columbus reached Guanahaní in 1492, western Europe was undergoing a cultural **Renaissance** (literally, rebirth). Intellectuals and poets rediscovered Europe's descent from a classical tradition originating in ancient Greece and Rome but obscured for a thousand years. Western European scholars found scores of forgotten ancient texts in philosophy, science, medicine, geography, and other subjects, and a rich tradition of commentary on them by Muslim, Eastern Orthodox, and Jewish scholars. Armed with the new learning, Renaissance authors strove to reconcile ancient philosophy with Christian faith, to explore the mysteries of nature, to map the world, and to explain the motions of the heavens.

> **Renaissance**
> An era of intense artistic creativity in Europe after the Middle Ages.

The Renaissance was also an era of intense artistic creativity. Wealthy Italian merchants and rulers—especially in the city-states of Florence and Venice, and in Rome (controlled by the papacy)—commissioned magnificent architecture, painting, and sculpture. Artists such as Leonardo da Vinci and Michelangelo created works rooted in classical tradition and based on close observations of nature (including the human body) and attention to perspective. Europeans celebrated these artistic achievements, along with those of writers, philosophers, scientists, and explorers, as the height of "civilization" to which other cultures should aspire.

But European society was also quivering with tension. Renaissance creativity was partly inspired by intense social and spiritual stress. Europeans groped for stability by glorifying order and hierarchy in the universe and in society. Writing near the end of the Renaissance, William Shakespeare (1564–1616) expressed these values with eloquence:

The heavens themselves, the planets and this center [earth]
Observe degree, priority, and place . . .
Take but degree away, untune that string,
And hark, what discord follows!

Gender, age, and social class defined every European's status, and few lived outside the reach of some political authority's taxes and laws. But this order was shaky. Conflicts between states, between religions, and between social classes constantly threatened the balance.

Beneath these conflicts lay deep-seated forces of change. By the end of the fifteenth century, strong national monarchs in Spain, France, and England had consolidated royal authority at the expense of the Catholic Church and the nobility. The "new monarchs" cultivated powerful merchants by promoting their enterprises in exchange for financial support. King Ferdinand of Aragon had married Queen Isabella of Castile in 1479 to create the Spanish monarchy. France's boundaries expanded as a series of kings absorbed neighboring lands through inter-dynastic marriage and military conquest. England's Tudor dynasty gradually suppressed the aristocracy's ability to plunge the nation into deadly civil war.

Most Europeans—about 75 percent—were peasants, frequently driven to starvation by taxes, rents,

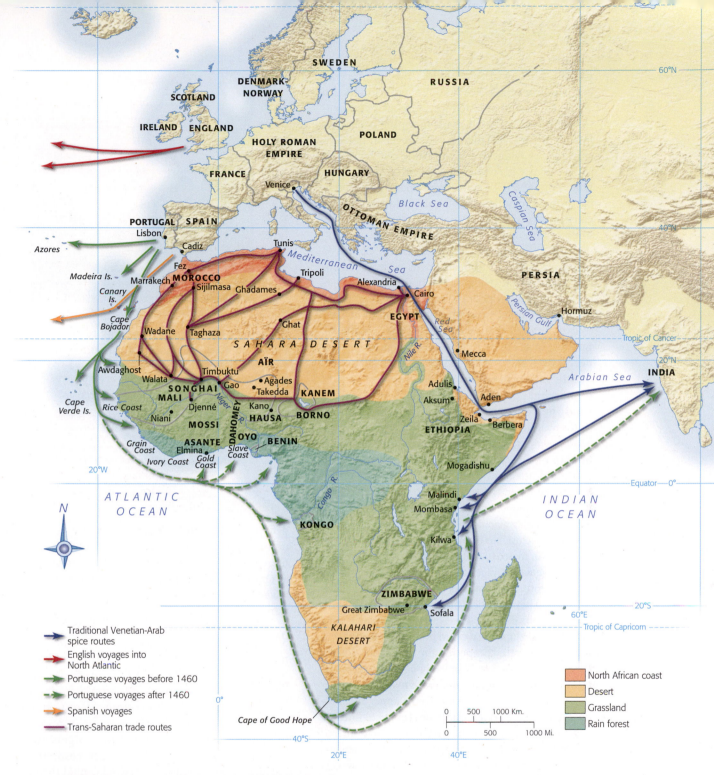

MAP 2.1 **EUROPE, AFRICA, AND SOUTHWESTERN ASIA IN 1500** During the fifteenth century, Portuguese voyages established maritime trade links between Africa and Europe, circumventing older trans-Saharan routes. Several voyages near the end of the century extended Europe's reach to India and the Americas.

Legend:
- Traditional Venetian-Arab spice routes
- English voyages into North Atlantic
- Portuguese voyages before 1460
- Portuguese voyages after 1460
- Spanish voyages
- Trans-Saharan trade routes

- North African coast
- Desert
- Grassland
- Rain forest

and other dues owed to landlords and Catholic Church officials. Not surprisingly, peasant revolts were frequent, often mercilessly suppressed by the authorities.

Conditions among European peasants were made worse by a sharp rise in population, from about 55 million in 1450 to almost 100 million by 1600.

Neighboring families often cooperated in plowing, sowing, and harvesting as well as in grazing their livestock on jointly owned "commons." But with new land at a premium, landlords, especially in England, wanted to "enclose" the commons—that is, convert the land to private property. Peasants who had no written title to their land were especially vulnerable to these pressures.

Environmental factors further exacerbated peasants' circumstances. Beginning in the fourteenth century, lower-than-average temperatures marked a "Little Ice Age" that lasted for more than four centuries. During this time, many European crops were less abundant or failed to grow. Hunger and malnutrition were widespread, with full-scale famine in some areas. With population growth came deforestation, prompted by increased demand for wood to use as fuel and building materials. Deforestation also caused the disappearance of wild foods and game, important food sources for many peasants.

Such pressures accelerated peasants' exodus to towns and cities. European towns were numerous but small, typically with several thousand inhabitants each. A great metropolis such as London, whose population ballooned from fifty-five thousand in 1550 to two hundred thousand in 1600, was exceptional. But towns were dirty and disease-ridden, and townspeople lived closely packed with their neighbors.

Still, many men and women preferred towns to the rural poverty they left behind. Immigration from the countryside—rather than an excess of births over deaths—accounted for towns' expansion. Most people who flocked into towns remained at the bottom of the social order as servants or laborers and could not accumulate enough money to marry and live independently.

The consequences of rapid population growth were particularly acute in England, where the number of people doubled from about 2.5 million in 1500 to 5 million in 1620. As throughout western Europe, prices rose while wages fell during the sixteenth and early seventeenth centuries (see Figure 2.1), widening the gap between rich and poor. Although English entrepreneurs expanded textile production by assembling spinners and weavers in household workshops, the workers were competing for fewer jobs. Enclosures of common lands severely aggravated unemployment, forcing large numbers of people to wander the country in search of work. To the upper and middle classes, these poor vagabonds seemed to threaten law and order. Parliament passed laws that ordered vagrants whipped and sent home, but most offenders only moved on to other towns. Some English writers viewed overseas colonies as places where the unemployed, landless poor could find work, thereby enriching their countries rather than draining resources.

2-1.2 Traditional Values in Flux

As in America and Africa, traditional society in Europe rested on maintaining long-term, reciprocal relationships. European reciprocity required the upper classes to act with self-restraint and dignity and the lower classes to

joint-stock company
A business corporation that amassed capital through sales of stock to investors.

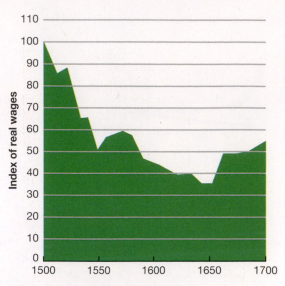

FIGURE 2.1 **DECLINE IN REAL WAGES IN ENGLAND, 1500–1700** The income of English workers declined by about two-thirds from 1500 to 1630. Widespread poverty led to social unrest, prompting some in England to advocate sending the poor to overseas colonies.

Source: (E. H. Phelps Brown and S. V. Hopkins, "Builders' Wage-Rates, Prices and Population: Some Further Evidence," Economica, XXVI (1959): 18–38; adapted from D. C. North and R. P. Thomas, The Rise of the Western World: A New Economic History (Cambridge, UK: Cambridge University Press, 1973), 111.)

defer to their "betters." It also demanded strict economic regulation to ensure that no purchaser paid more than a "just price"—one that permitted a seller a "reasonable" profit but that barred him from taking advantage of buyers' misfortunes to make "excessive" profits.

Yet for several centuries many Europeans had been compromising the ideals of traditional economic behavior. "In the Name of God and of Profit," thirteenth-century Italian merchants had written on their ledgers. By the sixteenth century, nothing could stop lenders' profiting from interest on borrowed money or sellers' raising prices in response to demand. New forms of business organization emerged—especially the **joint-stock company**, a business corporation that amassed capital through sales of stock to investors. Demand rose for capital investment, and so did the supply of accumulated wealth. Gradually, a new economic outlook justified the unimpeded acquisition of wealth and insisted that individuals owed one another nothing but the money necessary to settle their transactions. This new outlook, the central value system of capitalism or the "market economy," rejected traditional demands that economic activity be regulated to ensure social reciprocity and maintain "just prices."

Sixteenth- and seventeenth-century Europeans therefore held conflicting attitudes toward economic enterprise and social change. A restless desire for fresh opportunity kept European life simmering with competitive tension. But those who prospered still sought the entitlements and deference from inferiors afforded by their high social status, whereas the poor longed for the age-old values that would restrain irresponsible greed.

Perhaps the most sensitive barometer of social change was the family. The household was not only a family but also the principal economic unit in European society. Peasants on their tiny farms, artisans and merchants in their shops, and even nobles in their castles all lived and worked in households. Throughout Europe, the typical household consisted of a small nuclear family—two parents and several children—in which the husband and father functioned as a head whose authority was not to be questioned. The role of the wife and mother was to bear and rear children as well as assist her husband in providing for the family's subsistence. Children were regarded as potential laborers who would aid in these tasks until they left home to start their own families. People who did not live with their own families resided as dependents in the households of others as servants, apprentices, or relatives. Europeans regarded those who lived outside family-based households with extreme suspicion, often accusing them of crimes or even witchcraft.

Europeans frequently characterized the nuclear family as a "little commonwealth." A father's authority over his family supposedly mirrored God's rule over Creation and a king's power over his subjects. Even grown children knelt for their father's blessing. "Wives," according to a German writer, "should obey their husbands and not seek to dominate them; they must manage the home efficiently. Husbands . . . should treat their wives with consideration and occasionally close an eye to their faults." Repeated male complaints, such as that of an English author in 1622 about wives "who think themselves every way as good as their husbands, and no way inferior to them," suggest that some women found ways to undermine male domination.

2-1.3 Religious Fractures

Although Europe was predominantly Christian in 1400, it was also home to significant numbers of Muslims and Jews. Adherents to these three religious traditions worshiped a single supreme being, based on the God of the Hebrew Bible. While they often coexisted peacefully in lands bordering the Mediterranean, hatred and violence also marked their shared history. For more than three centuries, European Christians conducted numerous Crusades against Muslims in Europe and the Middle East, and Muslims retaliated with "holy war." Eventually, ambitious rulers transformed the religious conflicts into wars of conquest.

While the Islamic Ottoman Empire seized Christian strongholds in southeastern Europe, the Catholic monarchies of Portugal and Spain undertook a "reconquest" of the Iberian Peninsula. The "reconquest" was completed in 1492 when Spain drove the last Muslim rulers from Iberia and expelled all Jews who refused to convert to Catholicism.

The Spanish reconquest completed the Roman Catholic Church's domination of western and central Europe. The Catholic Church taught that Christ's sacrifice was repeated every time a priest said Mass and that divine grace flowed to sinners through the sacraments that priests alone could administer—above all, baptism, confession, and communion. The Church set its personnel, male and female, apart from laypeople by forbidding them to marry. At the top was the pope, the "vicar (representative) of Christ" on Earth.

Besides conducting services, priests heard the confessions of sinners and assigned them penance, usually devotional exercises and good works to demonstrate repentance. Recently the Church had assumed the authority to grant extra blessings, or "indulgences," to repentant sinners. Indulgences promised cancellation both of penance and of time in purgatory, where the dead atoned for sins they had already confessed and been forgiven. (Hell, from which there was no escape, awaited those who died unforgiven.) By the early sixteenth century, many religious authorities granted indulgences in exchange for such "good works" as donating money to the Church. The jingle of one enterprising German friar promised that

As soon as the coin in the cash box rings,
The soul from purgatory's fire springs.

The sale of indulgences provoked charges that the materialism and corruption infecting economic life had spread to the Church. In 1517, German monk Martin Luther (1483–1546) openly attacked the practice. When the pope censured him, Luther broadened his criticism to encompass the Mass, purgatory, priests, and the papacy. After Luther refused to recant, the Roman Church excommunicated him. Luther charged that through the sale of indulgences, the Church gave people false confidence that they could be forgiven for their sins and earn salvation simply by doing good works. His own agonizing search for salvation had convinced Luther that God saved sinners not because of their worldly deeds, but solely because of their faith. Luther's revolt initiated what became known as the **Protestant Reformation**, which changed Christianity forever. (The word *Protestant* comes from the *protest* of Luther's princely supporters against the anti-Lutheran policies of Holy Roman Emperor Charles V.)

> **Protestant Reformation**
> A movement led by Martin Luther in the sixteenth century in which people split from the Catholic Church.

MARTIN LUTHER AT THE DIET OF WORMS BY ANTON VON WERNER (1843–1915) Long critical of the Catholic Church, Luther was summoned to answer charges of heresy in April 1521 in Worms, Germany. After he refused to recant, some saw him as a hero, others a heretic. The case resulted in the Edict of Worms, which made Luther's anti-Church writings illegal. *(Ivy Close Images/Alamy)*

Other Protestant reformers followed Luther in breaking from Catholicism, most notably John Calvin (1509–1564), who fled his native France for Geneva, Switzerland. Contrary to Luther, Calvin insisted on the doctrine of predestination. By this he meant that an omnipotent God predestined most sinful humans to hell, saving a few to demonstrate his power and grace. Only these few—called the "elect," "godly," or "saints"—would have a true conversion experience and feel God's transcending power.

Despite their differences, Protestants shared much common ground. For one thing, they denied that God had endowed priests with special powers. A proper church, Luther claimed, was a "priesthood of all believers." Protestant reformers insisted that laypeople take responsibility for their own spiritual and moral conditions. Accordingly, they placed a high value on reading and demanded that the Bible be translated from Latin into spoken languages so that believers could read it for themselves. The new faith was spread by the recently invented printing press. Wherever Protestantism became established, basic education and religious study followed. Finally, Protestantism (initially) condemned the replacement of traditional reciprocity by marketplace values. Protestantism's greatest appeal was to those—ordinary individuals, merchants, and aristocrats alike—who brooded over their chances for salvation and valued the traditional performance of duty.

In the face of the Protestant challenge, the **Catholic or Counter-Reformation** was born. Reformers such as Teresa of Ávila (1515–1582), a Spanish nun from a *converso* (converted Jewish) family, urged members of Catholic holy orders to repudiate corruption and to lead the Church's renewal by living piously and austerely. Another Spanish reformer, Ignatius Loyola (1491–1556), founded a militant religious order, the Society of Jesus, whose members (Jesuits) would distinguish themselves in coming centuries as royal advisers and missionaries to non-Christians throughout the world. The high point of Catholic reform came during the Council of Trent (1545–1563), convened by the pope. While denouncing Protestants, the council reformed Church administration to combat corruption and broaden public participation in religious observances. This revival brought the modern Roman Catholic Church into existence.

The Protestant Reformation changed the religious map of Europe (see Map 2.2). Lutheranism became the state religion in the Scandinavian countries, while Calvinism made significant inroads in France, the Netherlands (which a royal marriage had brought under Spanish rule), England, and Scotland. The tiny states comprising the modern nations of Germany and Switzerland were divided among Catholics, Lutherans, and Calvinists.

2-1.4 The Impact of the Reformation in England, 1533–1625

England's Reformation began at the top, started not by a theologian with popular support but by a king and a compliant Parliament. King Henry VIII (ruled 1509–1547) had married Catherine of Aragon,

Catholic or Counter-Reformation
The movement in the sixteenth century within the Catholic Church to reform itself as a result of the Protestant Reformation.

SAINT TERESA OF ÁVILA One of the leading Catholic reformers, Saint Teresa was a nun whose exemplary life and forceful views helped reshape the Roman church during the Catholic or Counter-Reformation. *(Institut Amatller d'Art Hispanic)*

daughter of the Spanish monarchs, Ferdinand and Isabella, in a match that was intended to strengthen both countries and the ties between them. Although Catherine had borne a daughter and a son who died at birth, she did not bear a living male heir in more than twenty years of marriage. Henry asked the pope to annul his marriage, but the pope refused. Frustrated and determined, Henry abandoned Catherine and secretly married the already pregnant Anne Boleyn. He then persuaded Parliament to pass a series of acts in 1533–1534 dissolving his marriage to Catherine and proclaiming him supreme head of the **Church of England** (or Anglican Church). The move justified Henry's seizure of income-producing Catholic Church properties, further consolidating royal power and financial independence.

Religious differences divided England for more than a century after Henry's break with Rome. Under Edward VI (ruled 1547–1553), Henry's son by the third of his six wives, the church veered sharply toward Calvinism, giving rise to a militant movement. But Edward's successor was the daughter of Catherine, Mary I (ruled 1553–1558), who tried to restore Catholicism by burning several hundred Protestants at the stake and by marrying the King of Spain, Phillip II.

After the short, divisive reigns of Edward and Mary, the ascension of Elizabeth I (ruled 1558–1603), the daughter of Anne Boleyn, marked a crucial turning point. After the reign of "Bloody Mary," support for Catholicism declined in England and most people were

> **Church of England**
> Also known as the Anglican Church.

MAP 2.2 MAJOR RELIGIONS IN EUROPE, CA. 1560 By 1560, some European lands were solidly Catholic, Lutheran, or Calvinist. Others remained bitterly divided for another century or more.

Predominant religion in 1560

- Lutheran
- Calvinist (Reformed)
- Church of England
- Roman Catholic
- Eastern Orthodox Christian
- Significant Muslim population
- Calvinist stronghold
- ▲ Calvinist center
- ✶ Significant Jewish presence
- Ottoman Empire, 1566

ready to become Protestant; but just *how* Protestant remained a divisive question. Elizabeth took a middle road by affirming the monarch's role as head of the Anglican hierarchy of archbishops, bishops, and parish priests while allowing individuals and parish churches wide latitude in deciding whether to follow conservative or more radical customs.

Militant Calvinists, whose opponents derisively called them **Puritans**, wanted a more thorough purification of the Church of England from "popish [Catholic] abuses." Puritans insisted that membership in a congregation be limited to those who had had a conversion experience and that each congregation be independent from each other and from the Anglican hierarchy. Some "nonseparating" Puritans remained nominally within the Church of England, hoping to reform it. Others, called Separatists, withdrew, insisting that a "pure" church had to be entirely free of Anglican "pollution."

The severe self-discipline and moral uprightness of Puritanism appealed primarily to the small but growing number of people in the "middling" ranks of English society—landowning gentry, yeomen (small independent farmers), merchants, shopkeepers, artisans, and university-educated clergy and intellectuals. From their ranks, and particularly from among farmers, artisans, and clergy, would later come the settlers of New England (discussed in Chapter 3).

Elizabeth distrusted Puritan militancy; but, after 1570 when the pope declared her a heretic and, backed by Spain, urged Catholics to overthrow her, she regarded England's small number of Catholics as even more dangerous. Thereafter, she courted influential Puritans and embraced militant anti-Catholicism.

2-2 Exploration, Interaction, and Early Contact in the Atlantic World, 1400–1600

What shaped the early exchanges between Europeans, Native Americans, and Africans during their initial contact in the late fifteenth and sixteenth centuries?

Puritans
Militant Calvinists who insisted that membership in a congregation be limited to those who had had a conversion experience and that each congregation be independent of other congregations and of the Anglican hierarchy.

The forces transforming Europe quickly reverberated beyond that continent and inspired Europe to look beyond its borders for solutions and opportunities. During the fifteenth and sixteenth centuries, dynastic monarchs and allied merchants in several western European countries organized commercial and imperial ventures to Africa, Asia, and the Americas, bringing these cultures into contact with each other. Besides seeking wealth and power, expanding Europeans proclaimed it their mission to introduce Christianity and "civilization" to the "savages" and "pagans" of alien lands. Two prominent outcomes of the new imperialism were a transatlantic slave trade and the colonization of the Americas. These quests for the riches, land, and labor of non-Europeans significantly shaped the emerging Atlantic world.

2-2.1 Portugal and the Atlantic, 1400–1500

During the fifteenth century, some European merchants sought to enhance their profits by circumventing costly Mediterranean-overland trade routes to and from Asia and Africa. Instead, they hoped to establish direct contacts with sources of prized imports via the seas. Africa would prove a good source of gold, which had become the standard for all European currencies. The growing demand for both gold and slaves would bring thousands of newcomers from Europe to trade in Africa in the fifteenth century.

Important changes in maritime technology in the early fifteenth century facilitated this quest. Shipbuilders and mariners along Europe's stormy Atlantic coast added the triangular Arab sail to their heavy cargo ships. They created a more maneuverable vessel, the caravel, which sailed more easily against the wind. Sailors also mastered the compass and astrolabe, by which they got their bearings on the open sea. Without this maritime revolution, European exploration would have been impossible.

Led by Prince Henry "the Navigator" (1394–1460), Portugal was the first nation to capitalize on these developments. Henry gained the support of merchants seeking to circumvent Moroccan control of the African–European gold trade. He encouraged Portuguese seamen to pilot the new caravels southward along the African coast, mastering the Atlantic's currents while searching for opportunities to trade or raid profitably.

By the time of Henry's death, Portugal had begun acquiring gold and slaves from as far south as the African Gold Coast. After he died, the Portuguese further expanded their vision of a trading empire. In 1488, Bartolomeu Días reached the Cape of Good Hope at Africa's southern tip. A decade later, Vasco da Gama led a Portuguese fleet around the Cape of Good Hope and on to India (see Map 2.1).

Although the Portuguese did not destroy older European commercial links, they showed western Europeans, first, a way around the Sahara to West Africa and, then, how to go around Africa to Asia. In the process, they brought Europeans face-to-face with West Africans and an already flourishing slave trade.

2-2.2 African Trade, the "New Slavery," and Racism

Slavery was well established in fifteenth-century Africa, and while trade was important, most people relied on agriculture—just as Europeans did—for their survival. The institution of slavery took two basic forms prior to European contact. Many Africans were enslaved as captives in war or because of indebtedness. Their debts were purchased by kings and emperors who made them servants or by families seeking additional laborers on their farms. They or their children were either absorbed into their new families over time or released from bondage when they worked off their debts. As an example of the flexibility of slave status, Queen Nzinga, who came to power in 1623, was the daughter of a former slave. As did Native Americans, West Africans lived within networks of mutual obligation to kinfolk (see Chapter 1). Not just parents but also aunts, uncles, distant cousins, and persons sharing clan ties formed an African's extended family and claimed his or her first loyalty. In centuries to come, the tradition of strong extended families would help enslaved Africans in the Americas endure the forced breakup of nuclear families by sale.

A long-distance commercial trade in slaves was expanding rapidly in Africa. Middle East and North African traders furnished fellow Muslim rulers south of the Sahara with a range of fine, imported products in exchange for black laborers, mostly non-Muslims. By the middle of the fifteenth century, Europeans—initially the Portuguese—entered the slave trade, mostly in West Africa. Male slaves comprised the majority of those sold to the external trade with Europeans because within Africa, women were in greater demand for their reproductive potential and roles as agricultural workers. African women might also purchase female slaves as household workers.

Portuguese traders quickly realized how lucrative the trade in slaves could be. One fifteenth-century Italian who witnessed North African and Portuguese slave trading noted, "Slaves are brought to the market town of Hoden; there they are divided . . . [Some] are taken . . . and sold to the Portuguese leaseholders. As a result every year the Portuguese carry away . . . a thousand slaves."

In 1482, the Portuguese built a major outpost, Elmina, on West Africa's Gold Coast; however, they primarily traded through African-controlled commercial networks. Although women in the matrilineal society of Africa engaged in trade of all kinds, most slave traders interacting with the Europeans were African men. The local African kingdoms were too strong for the Portuguese to attack, and African rulers traded—or chose not to trade—according to their own self-interest.

Despite preventing the Portuguese from directly colonizing them, West African societies were profoundly affected by the new Atlantic slave trade. Portuguese traders enriched favored African rulers not only with luxury products but also with guns. As a result, heavily armed slave raiders would capture yet more people for sale to the Portuguese as slaves. In Guinea and Senegambia, where most sixteenth-century slaves came from, small kingdoms expanded to "service" the trade. Some of their rulers became comparatively rich. Farther south, the kings of **Kongo** (the point of origin for many American slaves) used the slave trade to expand their regional power and voluntarily adopted Catholicism, just as rulers farther north had converted to Islam. Queen Nzinga, for example, forged an alliance with Portugal—solidified by her conversion to Catholicism—to thwart threats to her kingdom from other parts of Africa. Later, amid Portugal's heightened demand for slaves and fears that Portugal might attempt to seize control of her country, she began a war against Portugal.

Although slavery had long been practiced in many parts of the Eastern Hemisphere, including in Europe, there were ominous differences between these older practices and the **"new slavery"** initiated by Portugal and later adopted by other western Europeans. First, the unprecedented magnitude of the trade resulted

AFRICAN VIEW OF PORTUGUESE, CA. 1650–1700
A carver in the kingdom of Benin, on Africa's west coast, created this salt holder depicting Portuguese officials and their ship. (© Werner Forman/Universal Images Group/ Getty Images)

ELMINA, PORTUGUESE SLAVE-TRADING FORTRESS Thousands of enslaved Africans passed through Elmina while it was controlled by Portugal and, after 1637, by the Netherlands. *(akg-images / Mark De Fraeye)*

in a demographic catastrophe for West Africa and its peoples. Before the Atlantic slave trade finally ended in the nineteenth century, nearly 12 million Africans would be shipped in terrible conditions across the sea. Slavery on this scale had been unknown to Europeans since the collapse of the Roman Empire. Second, African slaves were subjected to new extremes of dehumanization. In medieval Europe, in much of North Africa, and in West Africa itself, most slaves lived in their masters' households and primarily performed domestic service. But by 1450, the Portuguese and Spanish had created large slave-labor plantations on their Atlantic and Mediterranean islands. These plantations produced sugar for European markets, using capital supplied by Italian investors to buy African slaves, who toiled until death. In short, Africans enslaved by Europeans were regarded as property rather than as persons of low status; as such, they were consigned to labor that was unending, exhausting, and mindless. By 1600, the "new slavery" had become a central, brutal component of the Atlantic world.

Finally, race became the ideological basis of the new slavery. Africans' blackness, along with their alien religions and customs and nakedness, increasingly dehumanized them in European eyes. In 1555, English traveler William Towerson compared the Africans—especially the women—he encountered to animals, writing, "men and women go so alike that one cannot know a man from a woman but by their breasts which in the most part be very foule and long, hanging down low like the udder of a goat." Significantly for the future treatment of slaves, Towerson saw little difference between the sexes, claiming women's "masculine physique" made them men's equals in labor. From the fifteenth century onward, as their prejudice hardened, European Christianity made few attempts to soften slavery's rigors, and race defined a slave. Slavery would become a lifelong, hereditary, and despised status.

2-2.3 To the Americas and Beyond, 1492–1522

Europeans' varying motivations for expanding their horizons converged in the contradictory figure of Christopher Columbus (1451–1506), the son of a weaver from the Italian port of Genoa. Columbus's maritime experience and keen imagination led him to conclude that Europeans could reach Asia more directly by sailing westward across the Atlantic rather than around Africa and across the Indian Ocean. Like most literate Europeans of his time, he knew that Earth was round but he underestimated its size. Religious fervor led Columbus to dream of carrying Christianity around the globe and liberating Jerusalem from Muslim rule, but he also burned with ambition to win wealth and glory.

Columbus was unique in the persistence with which he hawked his "enterprise of the Indies" in the royal courts of western Europe. John II of Portugal showed interest until Bartolomeu Días's discovery of the Cape of Good Hope confirmed a sure way to the Indies. Finally, in 1492, he turned to Queen Isabella and King Ferdinand of Spain. Hoping to continue the Christian crusading of the just completed "reconquest" (discussed earlier) and to break Portugal's threatened monopoly on direct trade with Asia, the Spanish monarchs accepted Columbus's offer. Queen Isabella saw in exploration both a mission to spread Christianity globally and an opportunity to expand Spain's empire. She financed Columbus's journey with property taken from Jews and Muslims forced from Spain during the reconquest.

Picking up the westward-blowing trade winds at the Canary Islands, Columbus's three small ships reached Guanahaní within a month. After his meeting with the Tainos there, he sailed on in search of gold, making additional contacts with Tainos in Cuba (which he thought was Japan) and Hispaniola, the Caribbean island today

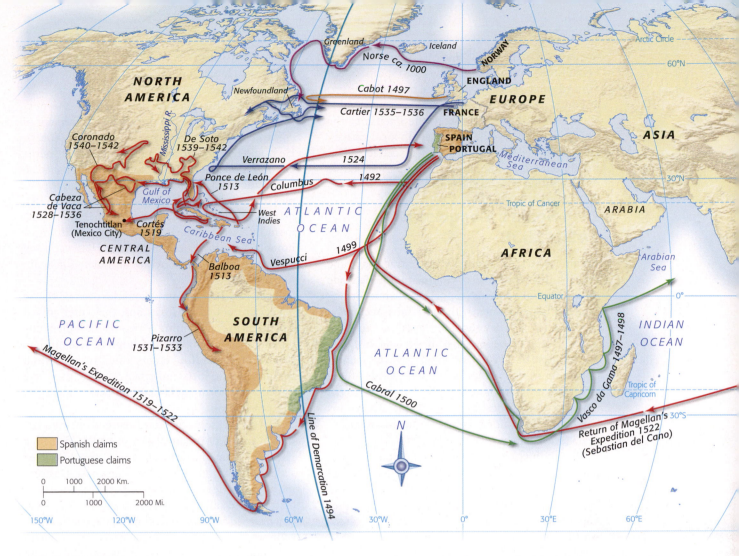

MAP 2.3 MAJOR TRANSATLANTIC EXPLORATIONS, 1000–1542 Following Columbus's 1492 voyage, Spain's rivals began laying claim to parts of the New World based on the voyages of Cabot for England, Cabral for Portugal, and Verrazano for France.

occupied by Haiti and the Dominican Republic (see Map 2.3). Finding gold on Hispaniola, he traveled back to Spain to tell Isabella and Ferdinand about his discovery.

Meanwhile, word of Columbus's discovery caught Europeans' imaginations. To forestall competition between them and to deter potential rivals, Isabella and Portugal's King John II in 1494 signed the **Treaty of Tordesillas** (see Map 2.4). The treaty drew a line in the mid-Atlantic, dividing all future discoveries between Spain and Portugal.

Ignoring the Treaty of Tordesillas, England attempted to join the race for Asia in 1497 when Henry VII (ruled 1485–1509) sent an Italian navigator, John Cabot, to explore the North Atlantic. Sailing past Nova Scotia and Newfoundland, Cabot claimed everything he saw and the lands beyond them for England. But England failed to follow up on Cabot's voyage for another sixty years.

The more Europeans explored, the more apparent it became that a vast landmass blocked the route to Asia. In 1500, a Portuguese voyage headed for India unexpectedly stumbled on Brazil (much of which lay east of the Tordesillas line). Other voyages soon revealed a continuous coastline from the Caribbean to Brazil. In 1507, this landmass got its name when a publisher brought out a collection of voyagers' tales. One of the chroniclers was an Italian named Amerigo Vespucci. With a shrewd marketing touch, the publisher devised a catchy name for the new land: *America*.

Getting past America and reaching Asia remained the early explorers' primary aim. In 1513, the Spaniard Vasco Núñez de Balboa came upon the Pacific Ocean when he crossed

Treaty of Tordesillas
Treaty between Spain and Portugal, and decreed by the pope, to resolve disputes over control of the newly discovered lands in the late fifteenth century by creating a line of demarcation, with Spain getting control of everything west of that line and Portugal getting everything east.

the narrow isthmus of Panama. Then in 1519, Ferdinand Magellan, sailing for Spain, went around the stormy straits (later named for him) at South America's southern tip. In an incredible feat of endurance, he crossed the Pacific to the Philippines, only to die fighting with local natives. One of his five ships and fifteen emaciated sailors finally returned to Spain in 1522, the first people to have sailed around the world.

2-2.4 Spain's Conquistadors, 1492–1536

Columbus was America's first slave trader and the first Spanish conqueror, or **conquistador**. He made his assumptions and his plans clear when recording his very first encounter with the Tainos (see Going to the Source). "They should be good servants," he wrote, ". . . and I believe that they would easily be made Christians." When the Tainos gave the Spanish gifts in return for "trifles," Columbus derided them as simplistic, failing to realize they were engaging in the kind of reciprocal exchange Native Americans had conducted among themselves for thousands of years (see Chapter 1).

Placed in charge of Spain's first colony on Hispaniola, Columbus and the settlers there started the first American gold rush. While fighting among themselves, they enslaved native peoples and forced them to mine gold and supply the Spanish with food and other needs, including access to women. Queen Isabella, however, wanted to see the native people converted to Christianity, not enslaved. When she died in 1504, the sanctions against enslaving native people died, too, and the practice continued in full force. Columbus, meanwhile, proved a poor administrator. Although he made two more voyages (1498–1502), he was shunted aside and died an embittered man, still convinced he had reached Asia only to be cheated of his rightful rewards. After the crown took direct control of Hispaniola, Spain extended the search for gold to nearby islands, establishing colonies at Puerto Rico (1508), Jamaica (1510), and Cuba (1511).

The enslaved Tainos and other Native Americans in the Caribbean colonies died off in shockingly large numbers from imported diseases such as smallpox and measles. To replace the perishing Indians, the colonists began importing enslaved Africans. Spanish missionaries who came to Hispaniola to convert Native Americans had sent back grim reports of Spanish exploitation of Indians, most notably Bartolomé

conquistador
A conquerer, usually referring to the Spanish explorers who set out to conquer the territories of the so-called new world.

encomiendas
Grants awarding Indian labor to wealthy colonists.

de las Casas. Initially arriving in Hispaniola in 1502 with a land grant, de las Casas later became a friar, renounced his land grant, released his slaves, and made it his personal mission for the next several decades to battle the abusive treatment of enslaved Native Americans by Spanish explorers. He would become the most outspoken critic of the **encomienda** system that explorers established to exact labor and tribute from enslaved native peoples in the early Spanish territories. In 1552–1553, he published several accounts of the harsh treatment of Native Americans by the Spanish, most notably *Very Brief Account of the Destruction of the Indies*, seeking to convince authorities in Spain to intervene.

But while most other missionaries deemed Native Americans potential Christians, they often joined colonizers in condemning Africans as less than fully human and thereby beyond hope of redemption. Blacks could therefore be exploited without limit. In Cuba, Puerto Rico, and other colonies, they were forced to perform backbreaking work on Spanish sugar plantations.

Meanwhile, some Spaniards fanned out even farther in search of Indian slaves and gold. In 1519, a restless nobleman, Hernán Cortés (1485–1547), led six hundred troops to the Mexican coast. Destroying his boats, he enlisted the support of enemies and discontented subjects of the Aztecs (see Chapter 1) in a quest to conquer that empire. Besides military support, Cortés gained the services of Malintzin (or Malinche), later known as Doña Marina, an Aztec woman brought up among the Maya who was one of the female captives gifted to the Spanish. Malintzin served as Cortés's interpreter, diplomatic broker, and mistress. She was also the mother of his son, though Spain's attitude toward native people was evident when Cortés handed her off to his lieutenant and instead married a prominent Spanish woman.

Upon reaching the Aztec capital of Tenochtitlán, the Spanish were stunned by its size and wealth. "We were amazed and said that it was like the enchantments they tell of [in stories], and some of our soldiers even asked whether the things that we saw were not a dream," recalled one soldier. Certainly, the golden gifts that Aztec emperor Moctezuma II (ruled 1502–1520) initially offered the invaders were no dream. "They picked up the gold and fingered it like monkeys," one Aztec recalled. "Their bodies swelled with greed, and their hunger was ravenous. They hungered like pigs for that gold."

The Spanish ignored Moctezuma's offer, raiding his palace and treasury and melting down all the gold they could find. Despite their emperor's imprisonment, the Aztecs regrouped and drove the invaders from the city, killing three hundred Spanish and four thousand of their Indian allies. Yet just as the Aztecs took back Tenochtitlán, a smallpox epidemic struck. Lacking any previous contact with the disease, the Aztecs' immune systems were ill-equipped to resist it. When the Spanish finally recaptured the city, wrote one Spanish chronicler, "the streets were so filled with dead and sick people that our men walked over nothing but bodies." The epidemic enabled the Spanish to consolidate their control over much of central Mexico. By 1521, Cortés had overthrown the Aztecs and began to build a Spanish capital, Mexico City, on the ruins of Tenochtitlán.

Over the remainder of the sixteenth century, other conquistadors and officials established a great Spanish empire stretching from New Spain (Mexico) southward to Chile (see Map 2.4). The most important of these later conquests was that of the Inca empire (see Chapter 1) between 1532 and 1536 by a second reckless conquistador, Francisco Pizarro

(c. 1478–1541). As with the Aztecs, smallpox and native unfamiliarity with European ways and weapons enabled a small army to overpower a mighty emperor and his realm.

The human cost of the Spanish conquest was enormous. An Aztec survivor later recalled his people's despair:

Broken spears lie in the roads;
We have torn our hair in our grief
The houses are roofless now . . .
And the walls are splattered with gore . . .
We have pounded our hands in despair
Against the adobe walls.

When Cortés landed in 1519, central Mexico's population was between 13 and 25 million. By 1600, it had shrunk to about seven hundred thousand. Peru and other regions experienced similar devastation. The Americas had witnessed the greatest demographic disaster in world history.

MindTap

Technology & Culture
Sugar Production in the Americas

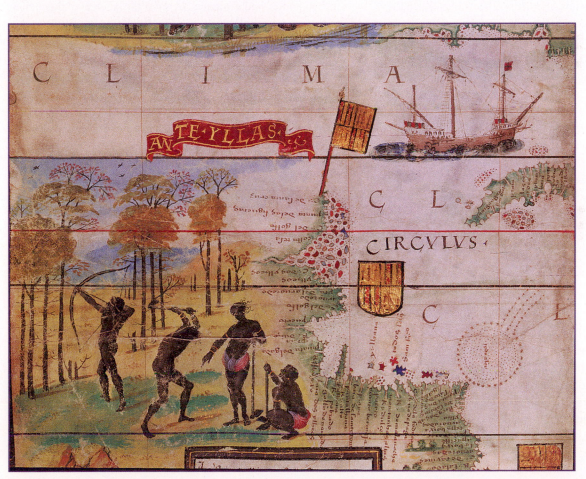

SPANISH MAP OF THE ANTILLES, 1519 This map offers a rare glimpse of Spain's early colonies in the West Indies. It depicts African laborers, forcibly imported to replace Native Americans lost to disease and harsh treatment. *(Bibliotheque Nationale de France)*

SOURCE

First Encounter

As he encountered the Taino Indians for the first time on October 12, 1492, Christopher Columbus recorded the meeting in words that he would later include in his report to King Ferdinand and Queen Isabella. They are the first words written by Europeans about Native Americans since those of the Norse several centuries earlier (see Chapter 1).

As I saw that they were very friendly to us, and perceived that they could be much more easily converted to our holy faith by gentle means than by force, I presented them with some red caps, and strings of beads to wear upon the neck, and many other trifles of small value, wherewith they were much delighted, and became wonderfully attached to us. Afterwards they came swimming to the boats, bringing parrots, balls of cotton thread, javelins, and many other things which they exchanged for articles we gave them, such as glass beads, and hawk's bells; which trade was carried on with the utmost good will. But they seemed on the whole to me, to be a very poor people. They all go completely naked, even the women, though I saw but one girl. All whom I saw were young, not above thirty years of age, well made, with fine shapes and faces; their hair short, and coarse like that of a horse's tail, combed toward the forehead, except a small portion which they suffer to hang down behind, and never cut. Some paint themselves with black, which makes them appear like those of the Canaries [Canary Islands, where Columbus had sold enslaved Africans to Spanish planters], neither black nor white; others with white, others with red, and others with such colors as they can find. Some paint the face, and some the whole body; others only the eyes, and others the nose. Weapons they have none, nor are acquainted with them, for I showed them swords which they grasped by the blades, and cut themselves through ignorance. They have no iron, their javelins being without it, and nothing more than sticks, though some have fish-bones or other things at the ends. They are all of a good size and stature, and handsomely formed. I saw some with scars of wounds upon their bodies, and demanded by signs the [source] of them; they answered me in the same way, that there came people from the other islands in the neighborhood who endeavored to make prisoners of them, and they defended themselves. I thought then, and still believe, that these were from the continent [Asia]. It appears to me, that the people are ingenious, and would be good servants and I am of opinion that they would very readily become Christians, as they appear to have no religion. They very quickly learn such words as are spoken to them. If it please our Lord, I intend at my return to carry home six of them to your Highnesses, that they may learn our language. I saw no beasts in the island, nor any sort of animals except parrots.

Source: Internet Medieval Source Book. www.fordham.edu/halsall/source/columbus1.html

---

QUESTIONS

1. What assumptions and biases shape Columbus's depictions of the Taino people?
2. Despite Columbus's biases, does he convey any information at all about the Tainos, their culture, and their motives during their first encounter with him?
3. How do you think that the Tainos would have described the Spanish?

2-2.5 The Columbian Exchange

The emerging Atlantic world linked not only peoples but also animals, plants, and germs from Europe, Africa, and the Americas in what has come to be called the **Columbian exchange**. The biological encounter of the Eastern and Western Hemispheres affected the everyday lives of peoples throughout the Atlantic world. After 1492, vast numbers of Native Americans died because they lacked antibodies that could resist infectious diseases brought by Europeans and Africans—especially deadly, highly communicable smallpox. From the first years of contact, epidemics scourged defenseless Indian communities. A Spanish observer estimated that the indigenous population of the West Indies declined from about 1 million in 1492 to just five hundred a half century later. Such devastation directly facilitated European colonization everywhere in the Americas, whether accompanied by a military effort or not.

Besides diseases, Europeans, Africans, and Native Americans exchanged agricultural products and techniques, animals, and other goods. Sixteenth-century Europeans introduced horses, cattle, sheep, swine, chickens, wheat and other grains, coffee, sugar, numerous fruits and garden vegetables, and many species of weeds, insects, and rodents to America. In the next century, enslaved Africans carried rice and yams with them across the Atlantic. The list of American gifts to Europe and Africa was equally impressive: corn, many varieties of beans, white and sweet potatoes, tomatoes, squash, pumpkins, peanuts, vanilla, cacao (for making chocolate and cocoa), avocados, pineapples, chilis, tobacco, and turkeys. Often, several centuries passed before new plants became widely accepted. For example, many Europeans initially suspected that potatoes were aphrodisiacs and that tomatoes were poisonous.

European weeds and domestic animals drastically altered many American environments and, in turn, Native American ways of life. Especially in temperate zones, livestock devoured indigenous plants, enabling hardier European weeds to take over. As a result, wild animals that had fed on the plants stayed away, depriving Indians of a critical source of food. Free-roaming livestock, especially hogs, also invaded Native Americans' cornfields. Settlers' crops, intensively cultivated on lands never replenished by lying fallow, often exhausted American soil. But the worldwide exchange of food products also enriched human diets and later made enormous population growth possible.

Another dimension of the Atlantic world was the mixing of peoples. During the sixteenth century, about three hundred thousand Spaniards immigrated, 90 percent of them male. Particularly in towns, a racially blended people emerged as these men had marriage-like relationships with Indian women (living as if wed although not legally married), giving rise to the large mestizo (mixed Spanish-Indian) population of Mexico and other Latin American countries. Lesser numbers of *métis*, as the French termed people of both Indian and European descent, would appear in the French and English colonies of North America. Throughout the Americas, particularly in plantation colonies, European men fathered mulatto children after forcing themselves upon their female African slaves, and African-Indian unions occurred in most regions. Colonial societies differed significantly in their official attitudes toward the different

> **Columbian Exchange**
> The widespread exchange of animals, plants, germs, and peoples from Europe, Africa, and the Americas.

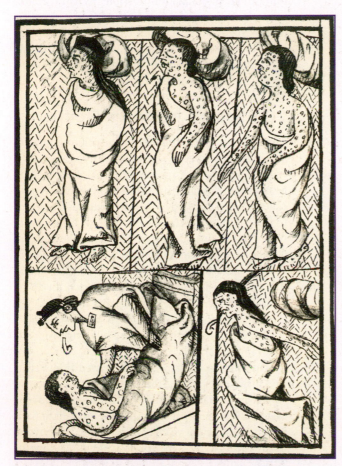

SMALLPOX IN THE CONQUEST OF MEXICO Illustrations from a Spanish account depict the impact of smallpox on the Aztecs, making clear how it prevented them from continuing their resistance to Spanish invaders. (*Biblioteca Medicea Laurenziana, Florence, Italy*)

kinds of interracial unions and in their classifications of the children who resulted. The English outright banned unions with Native Americans; the Spanish tolerated marriage-like relationships that incorporated native women into their camps but that could end when a Spanish man decided to enter a legal marriage with a Spanish woman; and the French participated in what they called "country marriages" with native women, meaning they were wed but without the sanction of the church.

The Americas supplied seemingly limitless wealth for Spain. More important sources of wealth than gold and sugar were the immense quantities of silver that crossed the Atlantic after rich mines in Mexico and Peru began producing in the 1540s. But Spanish kings squandered this wealth. Bent on dominating Europe, they needed ever more American silver to finance their wars there. Several times they went bankrupt, and in the 1560s their efforts to squeeze more taxes from their subjects helped provoke the revolt of Spain's rich Netherlands provinces (discussed later in this chapter). In the end, American wealth proved to be a mixed blessing for Spain.

MAP 2.4 THE SPANISH AND PORTUGUESE EMPIRES, 1610 By 1610, Spain dominated Latin America, including Portugal's possessions. Having devoted its energies to exploiting Mexico and the Caribbean, Spain had not yet expanded into what is now the United States, beyond outposts in Florida and New Mexico.

2-3 Footholds in North America, 1512–1625

What is the best way to understand the differences between the early settlements that various European countries established in North America?

Most European immigrants in the sixteenth century flocked to Mexico, the Caribbean, and points farther south. But a minority extended the Atlantic world to North America. Except for a tiny Spanish base at St. Augustine, Florida, the earliest attempts to plant colonies failed, generally because they were predicated on unrealistic expectations of fabulous wealth and natives who would be easily conquered.

After 1600, the ravaging of Indian populations by disease and the rise of English, French, and Dutch power made colonization possible. By 1614, Spain, England, France, and the Netherlands had established North American footholds (see Maps 2.5 and 2.6). Within another decade, each colony developed a distinct economic orientation and its own approach to Native Americans.

2-3.1 Spain's Northern Frontier

The Spanish had built their American empire by subduing the spectacularly wealthy Aztecs and Incas. The dream of more such finds drew would-be conquistadors northward to what would later be called Florida and New Mexico. "As it was his object to find another treasure like that . . . of Peru," a witness wrote of one such man, Hernando de Soto, he "would not be content with good lands nor pearls."

The earliest of these invaders was Juan Ponce de León, who had founded Puerto Rico. In 1513, he explored the coast of a peninsula he named "La Florida." Returning to Florida in 1521 to found a colony, Ponce de León was killed in a skirmish with Calusa Indians.

The most astonishing early expedition began in Florida in 1527. After provoking attacks by Apalachee Indians, the three hundred explorers separated into several parties. All were thought to have perished until eight years later, when four survivors, led by Alvar Nuñez Cabeza de Vaca and including an African slave, Esteban, arrived in northern Mexico. They had been shipwrecked on the Texas coast and made the rest of the journey on foot, living in dozens of Native American communities along the way.

Cabeza de Vaca provided direct inspiration for two more formidable attempts at Spanish conquest. Hernando de Soto and his party in 1539–1543 blundered from Tampa Bay to the Appalachians to the southern Plains, scouring the land for gold and alienating native people wherever they went. "Think, then," one Indian chief appealed to de Soto in vain,

what must be the effect on me and mine, of the sight of you and your people, whom we have at no time seen, astride the fierce brutes, your horses, entering with such speed and fury into my country, that we had no tidings of your coming—things so absolutely new, as to strike awe and terror into our hearts.

In 1540, a coalition of Native Americans gathered at the Mississippian city of Mábila to confront de Soto. Although the Spanish were victorious militarily, their own losses doomed them. Most of their horses died from arrow wounds while their livestock (their principal source of food aside from the corn they seized) scattered. Thereafter, the expedition floundered.

Although de Soto died without finding gold or extending Spanish rule, his and other expeditions spread epidemics that destroyed most of the remaining Mississippian societies (see Chapter 1). By the time Europeans returned to the southeastern interior late in the seventeenth century, only the Natchez on the lower Mississippi River still inhabited their sumptuous temple-mound center and remained under the rule of a Great Sun monarch. Depopulated groups like the Cherokees and Creeks had adopted the less centralized village life of other eastern Indians.

Meanwhile, Cabeza de Vaca had reported hearing of golden cities in the Southwest. In 1540–1542, Francisco Vásquez de Coronado led a massive expedition northward from Mexico to find and conquer these cities. Coronado plundered several pueblos

MAP 2.5 NATIVE AMERICAN-EUROPEAN CONTACTS, 1497–1600 Native peoples and European expeditions encountered one another in much of North America before Europeans established extensive colonies in the seventeenth century.

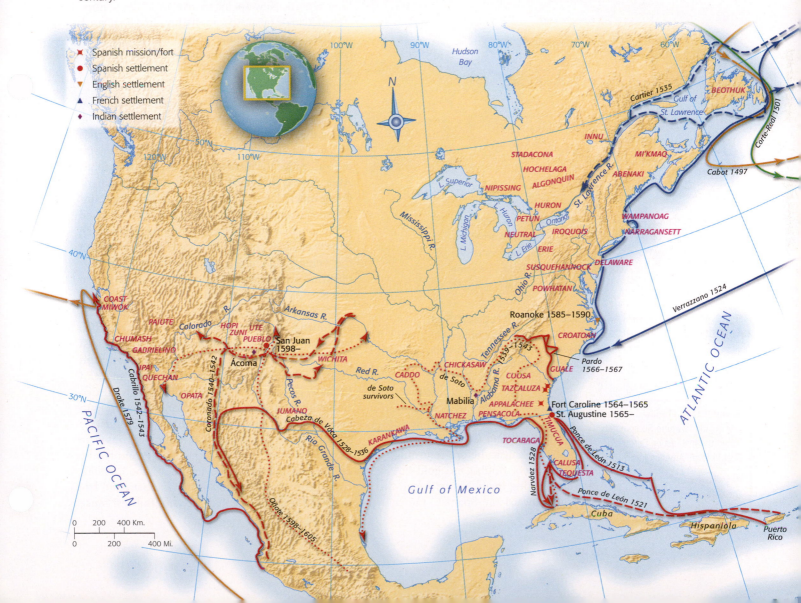

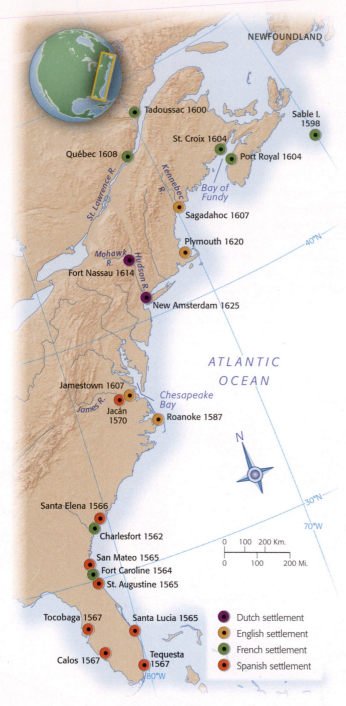

MAP 2.6 EUROPEAN IMPERIAL CLAIMS AND SETTLEMENTS IN EASTERN NORTH AMERICA, 1565–1625 By 1625, four European nations contended for territory on North America's Atlantic coast. Except for St. Augustine, Florida, all settlements established before 1607 had been abandoned by 1625.

St. Augustine, Florida
City in Florida where Spain established the first lasting European post in North America in 1565.

New Mexico
The Spanish colony in the upper Rio Grande Valley.

expeditions along the California coast and up the Colorado River likewise proved fruitless.

For several decades after these failed ventures, Spain's principal interest in North America lay in establishing strategic bases to keep French and English intruders away from Mexico and the Caribbean. In 1565, Spain established the first lasting European post in North America, a fortress at **St. Augustine, Florida**. While remaining a lone military stronghold, St. Augustine also served as a base for a chain of Catholic missions on the Florida peninsula and Atlantic coast as far northward as Chesapeake Bay. Rejecting missionary efforts to reorder their lives, the Guale, Powhatan, and other Indians rebelled and forced the closing of all the missions before 1600. Franciscan missionaries renewed their efforts in Florida in the early seventeenth century and secured the nominal allegiance of about sixteen thousand Guale and Timucua Indians. But epidemics in the 1610s killed about half the converts.

Beginning in the 1580s, Spanish missionaries also looked to the Southwest, preaching Christianity and scouting the area's potential wealth. Encouraged by their reports, New Spain's viceroy in 1598 commissioned Juan de Oñate to lead five hundred Spaniards, mestizos, Mexican Indians, and enslaved Africans into the upper Rio Grande Valley. Oñate seized a pueblo of the Tewa Indians, renamed it San Juan, and proclaimed the royal colony of **New Mexico**.

The Spanish encountered swift resistance at the mesa-top pueblo of Ácoma in December 1598. When the Ácoma Indians refused Spanish demands for corn and other provisions, fifteen Spanish soldiers ascended the mesa to obtain the goods by force. After Ácoma defenders killed most of the soldiers, Oñate ordered massive retaliation. In January, Spanish troops captured the pueblo, killing eight hundred inhabitants. Oñate sentenced surviving Ácoma men to have one foot cut off and forced them, along with the women and children, to be servants of the soldiers and missionaries. Two prominent leaders also had their right hands amputated.

Despite having crushed Ácoma and imposed encomiendas on other Pueblo Indians, New Mexico barely survived. The Spanish government replaced Oñate in 1606 because of mismanagement and excessive brutality toward Native Americans, and seriously considered withdrawing from New Mexico altogether. But Franciscan missionaries, aiming to save Pueblo Indian souls, persuaded the authorities to keep New Mexico alive. By 1630, Franciscans were present in more than fifty pueblos. Prompted by deadly epidemics and believing that Catholic rituals could be reconciled with traditional practices, a few thousand Indians accepted baptism. But resistance

on the Rio Grande and wandered from the Grand Canyon to present-day Kansas before returning to Mexico, finding no gold but embittering many Native Americans toward the Spanish. Other

was common because, as the leading Franciscan summarized it, "the main and general answer given [by the Pueblos] for not becoming Christians is that when they do . . . they are at once compelled to pay tribute and render personal service." New Mexico began, then, amid uneasy tensions between colonists and natives.

2-3.2 France: Colonizing Canada

France entered the imperial competition in 1524 when King Francis I (ruled 1515–1547) dispatched Giovanni da Verrazano to find a "northwest passage" to the Pacific. Verrazano explored the North American coast from the Carolinas to Newfoundland. In 1534 and 1535–1536, French explorer Jacques Cartier probed the coasts of Newfoundland, Quebec, and Nova Scotia and sailed up the St. Lawrence River as far as present-day Montreal but found neither gold nor a northwest passage.

France made its first colonizing attempt in 1541 when Cartier returned to the St. Lawrence Valley with ten ships carrying four hundred soldiers, three hundred sailors, and a few women. They abandoned the colony after two years due to ongoing battles with local Indians and harsh winters.

Success came as the French began trading with local Beothuck Indians off the coast of Newfoundland for beaver skins. By the late sixteenth century, European demand for beaver hats was skyrocketing, and a French-dominated fur trade blossomed. Before the end of the century, French traders were returning annually to sites from Newfoundland to New England and along the lower St. Lawrence.

Most fur traders recognized the importance of reciprocity in dealing with Native Americans. In exchange for pelts, they traded axes, knives, copper kettles, cloth, and glass beads. Usually dismissed by Europeans as "trinkets," glass beads were valued by northeastern Indians for possessing spiritual power comparable to that of quartz, mica, and other sacred

NAVAJO VIEW OF SPANISH COLONIZERS This pictograph (a painting or drawing on rock) was sketched in the early colonial period in Cañón del Muerto, Arizona. (© George H. H. Huey)

THE BEAVER AS WORKER AND AS PREY This French engraving illustrates beavers' environmental impact and Indian methods of hunting them for commercial purposes. *(National Archives of Canada)*

substances they had long obtained via trade networks (see Chapter 1). By the next century, specialized factories in Europe would be producing both cloth and glass for the "Indian trade."

Seeing the lucrative Canadian trade as a source of revenue, the French government dispatched Samuel de Champlain to establish the colony of **New France** at Quebec in 1608. The French concluded that a colony was the surest means of deterring English, Dutch, and independent French traders. Champlain shrewdly allied with the Innu and Algonquins of the St. Lawrence and the Hurons (or Wendat) of the lower Great Lakes. He agreed to help these allies defeat the Mohawks of the Iroquois Confederacy, who sought to control Indian-European trade on the St. Lawrence. In July 1609, Champlain and two other French soldiers accompanied sixty Innu and Huron warriors to Lake Champlain (which the explorer named for himself), where they fought and defeated two hundred Mohawks at Point Ticonderoga near the lake's southern tip. The battle at Lake Champlain marked a turning point in Indian-European relations in the Northeast. Except in a few isolated places, casual encounters between small parties gave way to trade, diplomacy, and warfare coordinated by Indian and European governments. Through their alliance with the powerful Hurons, the French

gained access to the thick beaver pelts of the Canadian interior while providing their Indian allies with European goods and armed protection from Iroquois attacks. These economic and diplomatic arrangements, and Iroquois reactions (noted later in this chapter), defined the course of New France's history for the rest of the seventeenth century.

2-3.3 England and the Atlantic World, 1558–1603

When Elizabeth I became queen in 1558, Spain and France were grappling for supremacy in Europe, and England was a minor power. But largely Protestant England resented Spain's suppression of Calvinists in the Netherlands and the pope's call for Elizabeth's overthrow. Elizabeth adopted a militantly anti-Spanish foreign policy, with Anglicans and Puritans alike hailing England as an "elect nation" whose mission was to elevate "true" Christianity and to overthrow Catholicism, represented by Spain. Secretly, she stepped up her aid to Dutch Calvinists and encouraged English privateers (armed private ships), commanded by "sea dogs" like John Hawkins and Francis Drake, to attack Spanish ships.

The Anglo-Spanish rivalry extended to Ireland after 1565, when Spain and the pope began directly

New France
Areas in North America under French colonial rule.

aiding Irish Catholics' longtime resistance to English rule. In a war that ground on to the seventeenth century, the English drove the Irish clans off their lands, especially in northern Ireland, or Ulster, and established their own settlements ("plantations") of English and Scottish Protestants. The English practiced "scorched earth" warfare to break the rebellious population's spirit, inflicting starvation and mass slaughter by destroying villages in the winter.

Elizabeth's generals justified these atrocities by claiming that the Irish were "savages" and that Irish customs, religion, and methods of fighting absolved the English from guilt in waging exceptionally cruel warfare. Ireland thus furnished precedents for later English tactics and rationales for crushing Native Americans.

England had two objectives in the Western Hemisphere in the 1570s. The first was to find the northwest passage to Asia and discover gold on the way; the second, in Drake's words, was to "singe the king of Spain's beard" by sacking Spanish fleets and ports. The search for the northwest passage led only to such embarrassments as explorer Martin Frobisher's voyages to the Canadian Arctic. Frobisher returned with several thousand tons of an ore that looked like gold but proved worthless. However, privateering raids proved spectacularly successful and profitable for their financial backers, including merchants, gentry, government leaders, and Elizabeth herself. The most breathtaking enterprise was Drake's voyage around the world (1577–1580) in a quest of sites for colonies, including on the northern California coast, where he traded with Miwok Indians.

Now deadly rivals, Spain and England sought to outmaneuver one another in North America. In 1572, the Spanish tried to fortify a Jesuit mission on the Chesapeake Bay. They failed, largely because Powhatan Indians resisted. Although she was dubbed the "virgin queen," the unmarried Elizabeth had a fondness for some of the men in her court, including Sir Walter Raleigh. To him, she granted a royal patent (charter) to start an English colony farther south, closer to the Spanish. After an exploratory expedition returned singing the praises of Roanoke Island, its peaceable natives, and its ideal location as a base for anti-Spanish privateers, Raleigh persuaded Elizabeth to dispatch an expedition in 1585 to found Roanoke colony. He named the colony **Virginia** in tribute to the virgin queen.

At first all went well, but by winter, the English had alienated the Roanoke Indians with their incessant demands for food. Fearing that the natives were about to attack, English soldiers killed Wingina, the Roanoke leader, in June 1586. When Drake visited soon after on his way back to England, the starving colonists joined him.

The determined Raleigh dispatched a second group of colonists, including seventeen women and nine children in 1587. The civilian leader, John White, soon went back to England for supplies, but war between England and Spain prevented him from returning to Roanoke until 1590. Upon finally arriving, White found only rusty armor, moldy books, and the word CROATOAN cut into a post. Although the stranded colonists were presumably living among the Croatoan Indians of Cape Hatteras, the exact fate of the "lost colony" remains a mystery.

In 1588, while Roanoke struggled, England won a spectacular naval victory over the Armada, a huge invasion fleet sent into the English Channel by Spain's Philip II. This famous victory preserved England's independence and confirmed its status as a major power in the Atlantic and a dominant force in the American colonies.

2-3.4 Failure and Success in Virginia, 1603–1625

Anglo–Spanish relations took a new turn after 1603, when the unmarried Elizabeth died and was succeeded by James I (ruled 1603–1625), a distant cousin who was king of Scotland. The cautious, peace-loving James signed a truce with Spain in 1604. Alarmed by Dutch naval victories, the Spanish now considered England the lesser danger. Consequently, Spain's new king, Philip III (ruled 1598–1621), renounced Spanish claims to Virginia.

In 1606, James I granted a charter authorizing overlapping grants of land to two separate joint-stock companies. The Virginia Company of Plymouth received a grant extending south from modern Maine to the Potomac River, while the Virginia Company of London's lands ran north from Cape Fear, North Carolina, to the Hudson River. Both companies dispatched colonists in 1607.

The Virginia Company of Plymouth sent 120 men to Sagadahoc, on the Maine coast. After bickering among themselves, alienating nearby Abenaki Indians, and enduring a hard New England winter, the colonists returned to England and the company disbanded.

The Virginia Company of London barely avoided a similar failure. Its expedition included many gentlemen who, considering themselves above manual work, expected Native Americans to feed them and riches to fall into their laps. Choosing a site on the James River, they called it Jamestown. Discipline quickly fell apart and, as at Roanoke, the colonists neglected to plant crops. The local Powhatan Indians sold them some corn but, with their own supplies running low, declined to offer more. By December, the English were running out of food. As with Roanoke

> **Virginia**
> North American colony established by the British.

and numerous Spanish ventures, Virginia's military leader, Captain John Smith, led some soldiers in an attempt to seize corn from the Powhatans. After capturing and releasing Smith, the Powhatan *weroance* (chief), also named Powhatan, did share some of his people's remaining supplies with the English. (Many years later, Smith would claim that Powhatan's ten-year-old daughter, Pocahontas, saved him at the last minute from execution. Because Smith claimed to have been similarly rescued by females on two other occasions during his military adventures, the story's accuracy is doubtful. More than likely, Pocahontas was helping to incorporate Smith into her tribe, a common role for Native American women.)

When relief ships arrived in January 1608 with reinforcements, only thirty-eight survivors remained out of 105 immigrants. By September 1608, three councilors had died, and three others had returned to England, leaving Smith in complete charge of the colony. Smith shrewdly noted that the healthy Powhatans moved away from the James River each spring after planting their crops, not returning until the fall at harvest time. Without understanding why moving left the Powhatans healthier, Smith ordered the colonists to do the same. (Scientists have determined that tidal patterns at Jamestown at the time were such that the colonists were drinking salty, contaminated water, and that even more died from dysentery, typhoid fever, and salt poisoning than from starvation.) During the next winter (1608–1609), Virginia lost just a dozen men out of two hundred. Smith prevented Virginia from disintegrating as Sagadahoc had. But when he returned to England in 1609 after being wounded in a gunpowder explosion, discipline again crumbled and the deadly diseases returned. Of the five hundred residents at Jamestown in September 1609, about four hundred died by May 1610.

An influx of new recruits, coupled with renewed military rule, enabled Virginia to recover enough to challenge the Powhatans again. When Powhatan refused to submit to the new governor's authority, the colony waged the First Anglo-Powhatan War (1610–1614). After the English captured Powhatan's daughter, Pocahontas, and she converted to Christianity, the war ended when the aging weroance agreed that she could marry a colonist named John Rolfe. Nevertheless, the English population remained small—just 380 in 1616—and had yet to produce anything of value for Virginia Company stockholders.

Tobacco emerged as Virginia's salvation, and Pocahontas likely aided Rolfe in the cultivation of the plant that would become Virginia's staple and a valuable trade item,

since Powhatan women were responsible for growing tobacco within their culture. Rolfe spent several years adapting a salable variety of Caribbean tobacco to conditions in Virginia. By 1619, tobacco commanded high prices, and Virginia exported large amounts to a newly emergent European market. Pocahontas would become the token celebrated Native American in British culture. She and Rolfe had one son, and she journeyed with them to England in 1616, where she was presented to the court and hailed as proof of the value in developing the American colonies. She died in England at age twenty-one, likely from an illness though the exact cause remains unknown.

To attract labor and capital to its suddenly profitable venture, the Virginia Company awarded a fifty-acre "headright" for each person ("head") entering the colony, to whomever paid that person's passage. By paying the passage of prospective laborers, some enterprising planters accumulated sizable tracts of land. Thousands of young men and a few hundred women calculated that uncertainty in Virginia was preferable to continued unemployment and poverty in England. In return for their passage and such basic needs as food, shelter, and clothing, they agreed to work as **indentured servants** for fixed terms, usually four to seven years.

The Virginia Company abandoned military rule in 1619 and provided for an assembly to be elected by the "inhabitants" (apparently meaning only the planters and not the laborers). Although the assembly's actions were subject to the company's veto, it was the first representative legislature in North America.

By 1622, Virginia faced three serious problems. First, local officials systematically defrauded the shareholders by embezzling treasury funds, overcharging for supplies, and using company laborers to work their own tobacco fields. They profited, but the company sank deep into debt. Second,

POCAHONTAS A Dutch artist engraved this portrait of the Powhatan woman when she traveled to England in 1616. *(Library of Congress Prints and Photographs Division)*

---

indentured servants
Young men and women, usually unemployed and poor, who were given free passage to America, plus basic needs such as food, shelter, and clothing, in exchange for labor, usually for four to seven years.

despite massive immigration, the colony's population continued to experience an appallingly high death rate. Most of the 3,500 immigrants entering Virginia from 1618 to 1622 died within three years, primarily from malnutrition or from the diseases that had plagued earlier colonists. Finally, relations with Native Americans steadily worsened after both Powhatan and Pocahontas died. Leadership passed to Powhatan's younger brother, Opechancanough, who at first sought to accommodate the English. But relentless English expansion provoked Indian discontent and the rise of a powerful religious leader, Nemattenew, who urged the Powhatans to expel the English. After some settlers killed Nemattenew, the Indians launched a surprise attack in 1622 that killed 347 of the 1,240 colonists. With much of their livestock destroyed, spring planting prevented, and disease spreading through cramped fortresses, hundreds more colonists died in the ensuing months. Writing to his parents in England, indentured servant Richard Frethorne lamented that, besides more Indian attacks, he and other servants could expect nothing "but sickness and death. . . . I have . . . not a shirt to my back but two rags, nor clothes but one poor suit, . . . one pair of shoes, . . . one pair of stockings, but one cap. . . . My cloak is stolen by one of my fellows, and to his dying hour [he] would not tell me what he did with it."

After the Virginia Company sent more men, Governor Francis Wyatt reorganized the settlers and took the offensive during the Second Anglo-Powhatan War (1622–1632). Using tactics developed during the Irish war, Wyatt inflicted widespread starvation by destroying food supplies and driving Indians from their homes during winter. By 1625, the English had effectively won the war, and the Powhatans had lost their best chance of driving out the intruders.

The clash left the Virginia Company bankrupt. After receiving a report critical of the company's management, James I revoked its charter in 1624 and placed Virginia directly under his rule as a royal colony. Only about five hundred non-Indians now lived there, including a handful of Africans who had been brought in since 1619. With its combination of fabulous profits, unfree labor, and massive mortality, Virginia was truly a land of contradictions.

2-3.5 New England Begins, 1614–1625

The next English colony, after Virginia, that proved permanent arose in New England. John Smith, exploring its coast in 1614, gave New England its name. "Who," he asked, "can but approve this most excellent place, both for health and fertility?" Smith hoped to establish a colony there, but in 1616–1618 a terrible epidemic spread by fishermen or traders devastated New England's coastal Native American communities by about 90 percent. Later visitors found the ground littered with the "bones and skulls" of the unburied dead and acres of overgrown cornfields.

Against this tragic backdrop, the Virginia Company of London gave a patent to some merchants headed by Thomas Weston for a settlement. In 1620, Weston sent over twenty-four families (a total of 102 people) in a small, leaky ship called the *Mayflower*. The colonists promised to send lumber, furs, and fish back to Weston in England for seven years, after which they would own the tract.

The expedition's leaders, but only half its members, were Separatist Puritans who had withdrawn from the Church of England and fled to the Netherlands to practice their religion freely. Fearing that their children were assimilating into Dutch culture, they decided to emigrate to America.

In November 1620, the *Mayflower* landed at Plymouth Bay in present-day Massachusetts, north of the Virginia Company's grant. Knowing they had no legal right to be there, the expedition's leaders insisted that all adult males in the group (including non-Puritans) sign the Mayflower Compact before they landed. By this document, they constituted themselves a "civil body politic," or government, and claimed the land for King James, establishing **Plymouth** colony.

Weakened by their journey and unprepared for winter, half the Pilgrims, as the colonists later came to be known, died within four months of landing. Those still alive in the spring of 1621 owed much to the aid of two English-speaking Native Americans. One was Squanto, a Wampanoag Indian who had been taken to Spain as a slave in 1614 but was freed and lived in England for several years. Returning home with a colonizing expedition, he learned that most of the two thousand people of his village had perished in the recent epidemic. The other Native American, an Abenaki from Maine named Samoset, had experience trading with the English. To prevent the colonists from stealing the natives' food, Squanto showed them how to grow corn, using fish as fertilizer. Plymouth's first harvest was marked by a festival, "at which time . . . we exercised our arms, many of the Indians coming amongst us, . . . some 90 men, whom for three days we entertained and feasted." Although often thought of as the "first Thanksgiving," the national holiday of that name only began during the Civil War.

Plymouth's relations with the Native Americans soon worsened. The alliance that Squanto and Samoset had arranged between Plymouth and the Wampanoags,

Plymouth
Colony established by English emigrants, half of which were Puritans. They sailed across the Atlantic on the *Mayflower* and signed the Mayflower Compact.

headed by Massasoit, had united two weak parties. But news of the Powhatan attack in 1622 hastened the colony's militarization. Miles Standish, its military commander, threatened Plymouth's "allies" with the colony's monopoly of firepower. For although Massasoit remained loyal, other Indians were offended by the colonists' conduct.

Plymouth soon became economically self-sufficient. After the colony turned from communal farming to individually owned plots, its more prosperous farmers produced corn surpluses, which they traded to nonfarming Abenaki Indians in Maine for furs. Within a decade, Plymouth's elite had bought out the colony's London backers and several hundred colonists had arrived.

Although a tiny colony, Plymouth was significant as an outpost for Puritans dissenting from the Church of England and for proving that a self-governing society consisting mostly of farm families could flourish in New England. In these respects, it proved to be the vanguard of a massive migration of Puritans to New England in the 1630s (covered in Chapter 3).

2-3.6 A "New Netherland" on the Hudson, 1609–1625

Among the most fervently Calvinist regions of Europe were the Dutch-speaking United Provinces of the Netherlands. The provinces had come under Spanish rule during the sixteenth century, but Spain's religious intolerance and high taxes drove the Dutch to revolt, beginning in 1566. Exhausting its resources trying to quell the revolt,

New Netherland
Dutch colony in America.

Spain finally recognized Dutch independence in 1609. By then, the Netherlands (also known as the Dutch Republic) was a wealthy commercial power. The Dutch built an empire stretching from Brazil to South Africa to Indonesia, and played a key role in colonizing North America

Just as the French were routing the Mohawk Iroquois at Lake Champlain in 1609, Henry Hudson sailed up the river later named for him, traded with Native Americans, and claimed the land for the Netherlands. When Dutch traders returned the following year, some of their most eager customers were—not surprisingly—Mohawks. Having established lucrative ties with Native Americans on the lower Hudson River, Dutch traders in 1614 built Fort Nassau near what would become Albany, and established the colony of **New Netherland**. In 1626, local Munsee Indians allowed the Dutch to settle on an island at the mouth of the Hudson. The Dutch named the island Manhattan and the settlement, New Amsterdam.

The earliest New Netherlanders lived by the fur trade. Through the Mohawks, they relied on the Five Nations Iroquois, much as the French depended on the Hurons, as commercial clients and military allies. To stimulate a flow of furs to New Netherland, Dutch traders obtained from coastal Indians large quantities of wampum—sacred shells like those used by Deganawidah and Hiawatha to convey solemn "words" of condolence in rituals (see Chapter 3)—for trade with the Iroquois. The Dutch–Iroquois and French–Huron alliances became embroiled in an ever-deepening contest to control the movement of goods between Europeans and Indians (discussed in Chapter 3).

The Whole Vision

■ *How does an awareness of the social and political context in Europe enrich our understanding of early American exploration and history?*

Historians recognize that when a people looks beyond its own borders—either as leaders or as individuals—there are several factors within that society that are pushing them to do so. People typically do not want to leave their homelands if social conditions are good; but when society is influx, as it was in Europe in the late fifteenth and early sixteenth centuries, then they begin to consider faraway alternatives that may offer better prospects for social mobility. That is true for those in leadership positions, seeking to fortify a nation's power base or economy, but it is also true for individual citizens. Europe's economic, religious, and political upheavals provided the push factors for its exploration of previously unknown regions. Countries such as Portugal, Spain, and England faced population pressures, land shortages, and religious crises, along with ongoing battles for power and status between them. This context not only provides insight into the benefits that exploration (even with its associated financial and other costs) might afford, but it also sheds light on when a country might begin to look elsewhere, why, and how its exploration and colonization would take shape. In effect, without those push factors, exploration and colonization of the Americas may not have taken place, or certainly not at this particular moment in history or in the way that it transpired.

■ *What shaped the early exchanges between Europeans, Native Americans, and Africans during their initial contact in the late fifteenth and sixteenth centuries?*

One of the most important factors that shaped the encounters between peoples in the Atlantic world was the advent of new sailing technologies, without which exploration and subsequent contact would have been slowed or far less likely to occur in this time period. The other factors influencing the relationships between these disparate people include the drive for gold and other sources of wealth, rivalries between European nations, religious imperatives, and notions of race. Religious goals and ideas about race were particularly important in shaping how European people understood their mission in the so-called "new world," and it played a role in how some responded to efforts to enslave native peoples. The intersection of racial ideologies and European goals for exploration would determine not only their relationships to native peoples, but also their regard for African slaves and the slave trade. As people from these three different continents—Europe, Africa, and the Americas—interacted, they exchanged everything from new types of food to everyday objects to germs and diseases. Sometimes, the results were positive, as in the case of new foods; other times, disastrous, as exposure to new and devastating diseases.

KEY TERMS

Christopher Columbus (p. 23)

Atlantic world (p. 23)

Renaissance (p. 24)

joint-stock company (p. 26)

Protestant Reformation (p. 27)

Catholic or Counter-Reformation (p. 28)

Church of England (p. 29)

Puritans (p. 30)

Kongo (p. 31)

"new slavery" (p. 31)

Treaty of Tordesillas (p. 33)

conquistador (p. 34)

encomiendas (p. 34)

Columbian exchange (p. 37)

St. Augustine, Florida (p. 40)

New Mexico (p. 40)

New France (p. 42)

Virginia (p. 43)

indentured servants (p. 44)

Plymouth (p. 45)

New Netherland (p. 46)

■ *What is the best way to understand the differences between the early settlements that various European countries established in North America?*

While the Spanish dominated initial exploration and colonization of the Americas, they were soon joined in the early seventeenth century by the rising powers of England, France, and the Netherlands. All early settlers faced questions of survival and how to interact with the native people they encountered, and their relationship to native people varied depending on their goals in the new world and their beliefs about nonwhite people. Either way, however, all early settlers would require assistance—voluntarily or coercively—from Native Americans to survive. If a country's primary goal from colonization was wealth, its settlers would treat Native Americans as resources to aid in that goal, sometimes violently so. If a country's goal was religious conversion of native peoples, its explorers would be either sensitive to its converts or harsh in its judgment and treatment of those who might resist conversion. If a country's goal was to establish trade with native peoples, its approach would be potentially more balanced. Even when European explorers benefited from food supplies and other assistance the Native Americans provided by choice or force, their notions of racial superiority often guided their interactions.

3 The Emergence of Colonial Societies, 1625–1700

LORD BALTIMORE, BY GERARD SOEST (1670) The English proprietor of Maryland holds a map of his colony along with his grandson, who would eventually inherit the proprietorship. Their enslaved African servant stands in attendance. *[Portrait of Cecilius Calvert with his grandson and houseboy (oil on canvas), Soest, Gerard (c.1600–81) / Private Collection / Peter Newark American Pictures / The Bridgeman Art Library]*

1625	Charles I crowned King of England.	**1661**	Maryland defines slavery as a lifelong, inheritable racial status.
1629	Massachusetts Bay colony founded.	**1664**	English conquer New Netherland; establish New York and New Jersey.
1630–1642	"Great Migration" to New England.		
1634	Lord Baltimore establishes Maryland.	**1670**	Charles Town, Carolina, founded. Virginia defines slavery as a lifelong, inheritable racial status.
1636	Roger Williams founds Providence.		
1636–1637	Antinomian crisis in Massachusetts Bay.		
1637	Pequot War in Connecticut.	**1675–1676**	King Philip's War in New England.
1638	New Sweden established.	**1676**	Bacon's Rebellion in Virginia.
1642–1649	English Civil War.	**1680**	Pueblo Revolt begins in New Mexico.
1643–1645	Kieft's War in New Netherland.	**1681**	William Penn founds Pennsylvania.
1644–1646	Third Anglo-Powhatan War in Virginia.	**1682**	La Salle claims Louisiana for France.
1648–1657	Iroquois "beaver wars."	**1691**	Spain establishes Texas.
1649	Maryland's Act for Religious Toleration. King Charles I executed in England.	**1692–1700**	Spain "reconquers" New Mexico.
		1692–1693	Salem witchcraft trials.
1655	New Netherland annexes New Sweden.	**1698**	End of Royal African Company's monopoly on English slave trade. First French settlements in Louisiana.
1660	Restoration in England; Charles II crowned king.		

The seventeenth century witnessed a flood of English migration across the Atlantic. In 1600 no English person lived along the North American seacoast. By 1700, however, almost 250,000 people of European birth or ancestry lived within the modern-day United States and Canada. In addition, nearly 30,000 enslaved Africans also resided in North America in 1700, most of them in the Chesapeake colonies and Carolina. Whereas European immigrants could at least hope to realize economic opportunity or religious freedom, nearly all Africans and their children remained the property of others.

The migration of Europeans and Africans to North America was possible only because of yet another demographic upheaval, the depopulation and uprooting of Native Americans. Having begun in the sixteenth century (see Chapter 2), the process expanded in the seventeenth, primarily as a result of epidemic diseases, but also because of Europeans' often violent encroachments on Indian lands. Although some Native populations partly recovered, about 1 million North American Indians died as a result of contact with Europeans before 1700. European colonists built their farms, plantations, towns, and cities not in wildernesses but on lands long inhabited and worked by Native Americans.

Indian depopulation and European and African immigration transformed North America during the seventeenth century. By 1625, Europeans had established just a few scattered outposts north of Mexico and the Caribbean. Thereafter, they expanded their territorial domains at Native American expense and by 1700 had begun a number of self-sustaining colonies.

The vast majority of European immigrants were from England, ensuring that nation's domination of North America's eastern coast as well as the Caribbean (see Map 3.1). Before 1700, the English would force the Dutch out of mainland North America and leave France and Spain with lands less attractive to colonists. The rise of England in the Americas was central to its emergence as a major power in the Atlantic world. Among England's mainland colonies, four distinct regions emerged: the Chesapeake, New England, Carolina, and the middle colonies. These regions varied in numerous ways, including their physical environments, patterns of population growth, economies, social structures, religious practices, modes of government, and ethnic and racial compositions. There were no "typical" colonists in the seventeenth century.

3-1 Chesapeake Society

What set the Chesapeake apart in its social and economic development from other regions in British colonial America?

Building on the tobacco boom of the 1620s, two English colonies on Chesapeake Bay—Virginia and Maryland—were the first to prosper in North America. Despite differences between their political and religious institutions, Virginia and Maryland had similar economies, populations, and patterns of growth that gave them a distinct regional identity.

Chesapeake society was highly unequal and unstable before 1700. Life for most colonists was short, good health was rare, and the familiar comforts of family and community were missing. After a civil conflict, Bacon's Rebellion, the English seized yet more Native American land for growing tobacco. Planters also increasingly shifted from white indentured servitude to black slavery as the principal source of labor. On this racial foundation, white Chesapeake colonists finally achieved economic stability and built their society.

3-1.1 State and Church in Virginia

King James I had reorganized Virginia as a **royal colony**, in which a crown-appointed governor would name leading planters to an advisory council. James did not reconvene Virginia's elected assembly. With civil war threatening in England, James's successor Charles I (ruled 1625–1649) in 1639 restored the assembly as a means of securing tobacco revenues and the support of Virginia's planters. The elected representatives initially met as a single body with the council to pass laws. During the 1650s, the legislature split into two chambers—the elected House of Burgesses and the Governor's Council—whose members held lifetime appointments.

Virginia adopted England's county-court system for local government. Justices of the peace served as judges and, along with sheriffs, as executives who administered local affairs. These officials were chosen by the governor. Everywhere south of New England, unelected county courts became the basic unit of local government.

As in England, Virginia's established church was the Church of England to which taxpayers were legally obliged to pay fixed rates. In each parish, six vestrymen managed church finances, distributed poor relief, and prosecuted moral offenses such as fornication or drunkenness. Vestries were elected until 1662, when the assembly made them self-perpetuating and independent of the voters.

Because Anglican priests could only be trained in England and usually found pulpits there, few were attracted to Virginia. Consequently, Virginia experienced a chronic shortage of clergymen, and most priests rotated among two or three parishes. But when a minister was conducting services in a parish, church attendance was required (as in Puritan New England); violators were subject to fines payable in cash or labor on public works projects.

3-1.2 State and Church in Maryland

After 1632, the crown created new colonies by awarding portions of the Virginia Company's forfeited territory to wealthy, trusted English elites. One or more proprietors, as they were called, were responsible for peopling, governing, and defending each **proprietary colony**.

In 1632, Charles I awarded the first such grant to a Catholic nobleman, **Lord Baltimore**, for a large tract of land north of the Potomac River and east of Chesapeake Bay. The grant guaranteed Lord Baltimore freedom from royal taxation, the power to appoint sheriffs and judges, and the privilege of creating a local nobility. The only checks on the proprietor's power were the crown's control of war and trade and the requirement that an elected assembly approve all laws.

Naming his colony Maryland, Lord Baltimore intended it as a refuge for English Catholics, who constituted about 2 percent of England's population and

---

royal colony
A type of colony that is administered by a crown-appointed governor, who would appoint and dismiss leading gentlemen in the colony to an advisory council.

proprietary colony
A type of colony that is administered by proprietors, usually one or two English elites.

Lord Baltimore
Catholic nobleman who received a proprietary grant from Charles I for a large tract of land north of the Potomac River and east of Chesapeake Bay.

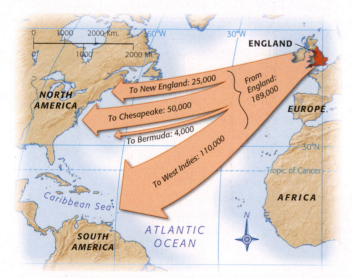

MAP 3.1 ENGLISH MIGRATION, 1610–1660 During the first phase of English transatlantic migration, more than half of the colonists settled in the West Indies.

suffered from religious discrimination. Many English Catholics were wealthy and a few held political office, but (like the Puritans and other dissenters) they were not allowed to worship in public and were required to pay taxes to support the Anglican Church.

To avoid antagonizing Protestants, Baltimore introduced the English institution of the manor—an estate on which a lord could maintain private law courts and employ a Catholic priest as his chaplain. Local Catholics could go to the manor to hear Mass and receive the sacraments privately. Baltimore adapted Virginia's headright system (see Chapter 2) by offering a two-thousand-acre manor to anyone transporting five adults (a requirement raised to twenty by 1640).

Maryland's beginnings were promising. In 1634, the first two hundred immigrants landed. Maryland was the first colony spared a starving time, thanks to Baltimore's attention to Virginia's early history. Thereafter, however, colonization did not proceed as the proprietor envisioned. Baltimore stayed in England, governing as an absentee proprietor, and few Catholics went to Maryland. From the outset, Protestants formed the majority of the population. With land prices low, those of modest means purchased property and avoided becoming tenants on the manors, which doomed Baltimore's dream of a manorial system. By 1675, all of Maryland's sixty nonproprietary manors had evolved into plantations.

Religious tensions soon emerged. In 1642, Catholics and Protestants in the capital at St. Mary's argued over use of the city's chapel, which the two groups had shared. As antagonisms intensified, Baltimore drafted the **Act for Religious Toleration**, or Toleration Act, which the Protestant-dominated assembly passed in 1649. The act affirmed toleration of Catholics and Protestants but did not protect non-Christians.

The Toleration Act failed to maintain peace between Catholics and Protestants. In 1654, the Protestant majority repealed the Toleration Act, barred Catholics from voting, and ousted Governor William Stone (a pro-tolerance Protestant). In 1655, Stone raised an army of both faiths to regain the government but was defeated. The victors imprisoned Stone and hanged three Catholic leaders.

Lord Baltimore resumed control of Maryland in 1658, but he and his descendants would encounter continued Protestant resistance to Catholic rule (as discussed in Chapter 4).

3-1.3 Gender, Kinship, and Demographics in the Chesapeake

Tobacco sustained a sharp demand for labor that lured about 110,000 English to the Chesapeake from 1630 to 1700. Ninety percent of these

VIEW OF JAMESTOWN, 1625 As Virginia's tobacco production boomed, the capital expanded beyond the fort that had originally confined it. *("Jamestown, 1614" by Sidney King. Colonial National Historical Park.)*

immigrants were indentured servants, people who agreed to work for four to seven years for whoever paid their passage over. Because men were more valued as field hands than women, 80 percent of arriving servants were male. The servants' lot was harsh. Most were poorly fed, clothed, and housed, and masters often extended servants' terms as penalties for even minor infractions. Women were also sexually vulnerable. If a female servant became pregnant before her term of service was up—and roughly one-fifth did—she would be whipped and fined, and if she could not pay the fine, additional years would be added to her service.

So few women initially moved to the Chesapeake that only a third of male colonists found brides before 1650. Servants married late—in their mid-twenties—because their indentures forbade them to wed before completing their contractual service. Their scarcity gave women an advantage in negotiating favorable marriages. Some female servants found prosperous planters who would buy their remaining time of service and marry them. Others married men closer to their own social status or formed unions with African slaves.

Gender and family life was also influenced by life expectancy. The high death rates that characterized the early Chesapeake persisted after tobacco production became routine. The greatest killers were typhoid fever and, after 1650, malaria. Malaria became endemic as sailors and slaves arriving from Africa brought a particularly virulent form and carried it into marshy lowlands, where mosquitoes spread it rapidly. Life expectancy in the 1600s was about forty-eight for men and forty-four for women—slightly lower than in England and nearly

Act for Religious Toleration Passed in 1649, it affirmed religious toleration in Maryland. It was also known as the Toleration Act.

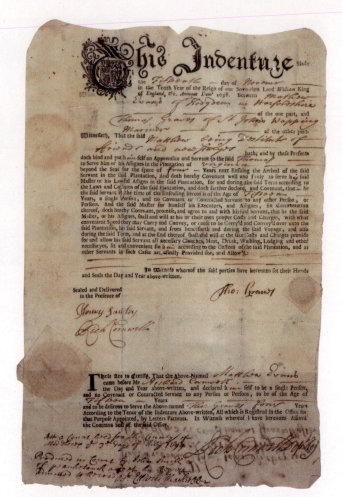

INDENTURE CONTRACT In 1698 Matthew Evans, age fifteen, agreed to work for four years for Thomas Graves or for anyone in Virginia to whom Graves sold his contract. *(The Library of Virginia)*

twenty years lower than in New England. Servants died at horrifying rates, with perhaps 40 percent going to their graves within six years of arrival and 70 percent by age forty-nine. Such high death rates crippled family life. Half of all people married in Charles County, Maryland, during the late 1600s became widows or widowers within seven years. The typical Maryland family saw half of its four children die in childhood.

Chesapeake colonies—like all English colonies—followed English common law of **coverture** regarding marriage. Under coverture, when a woman married, she was considered a *feme covert*, which meant that she was considered legally "covered by," or subsumed under, her husband. The man became the public representative of his wife in the world. All of her possessions and any wages she might earn would belong to him, just as their children would. She could not make any contracts, sue or be sued, vote, or run for political office. If a wife committed a crime, her

> **coverture**
> English common law referring to a woman's legal status upon marriage as being subsumed under—or covered by—her husband. He served as her protection but also her authority. Her property, body, children, and wages were all considered his.

husband could be held responsible. If a husband died, his wife would receive dower rights, one-third of his property to use for the rest of her life. Single women and widows, or *femes soles* (literally, "women without a husband"), had a few more rights under the law, such as the ability to transact business and own property. New England adhered more closely to the rules of coverture, but with high death and infant mortality rates, Chesapeake widows tended to enjoy greater economic power than widowed women elsewhere. Chesapeake husbands often gave their wives complete control of their estates in widowhood and not simply the one-third dower right. A widow in such circumstances gained economic independence yet typically still needed to marry a man who could produce income by farming her fields. But because there were so many more men than women, she had a wider choice of husbands than widows in most societies.

The combination of predominantly male immigration and devastating death rates sharply limited population growth. Although the Chesapeake had received about 110,000 English immigrants by 1700, its white population stood at about seventy thousand that year. By contrast, a benign disease environment and a more balanced gender ratio among the 28,000 immigrants to New England during the 1600s allowed that region's white population to grow to ninety-one thousand by 1700.

The Chesapeake's dismal demographic history began improving in the late seventeenth century. By then, resistance acquired from childhood immunities allowed native-born colonists to survive into their fifties, ten years longer than immigrants. As a result, more laborers lived beyond their terms of indenture instead of dying before tasting freedom.

3-1.4 Social Life in Tobacco Country, 1630–1675

Compared to colonists in New England's compact towns, Chesapeake residents had few neighbors. A typical community contained about two dozen families in an area of twenty-five square miles, or about six persons per square mile. Friendship networks typically extended for a two- to three-mile walk from one's farm and included about fifteen other families.

The isolated folk in Virginia and Maryland shared a way of life based on the production of tobacco. The plant grew best on level ground with good internal drainage, so called light soil, which was usually found beside rivers. Locating a farm along Chesapeake Bay or one of its tributary rivers also minimized transportation costs by permitting tobacco to be loaded on ships near home. Approximately 80 percent of early Chesapeake homes lay within a half-mile of a riverbank, and most were within just six hundred feet of the shoreline (see Map 3.2).

From such waterfront bases, the wealthiest planters built wharves that served both as depots for tobacco exports and as distribution centers for imported goods. Planters' control of commerce stunted the growth of towns and the emergence of a merchant class. Urbanization proceeded slowly in the Chesapeake; even Maryland's capital, St. Mary's, had just thirty scattered houses as late as 1678.

Tobacco had dominated Chesapeake agriculture since 1618, when demand for the crop exploded and prices spiraled to dizzying levels. The boom ended in 1629 when prices sank a stunning 97 percent (see Figure 3.1). After stabilizing, tobacco remained profitable for most growers as long as it sold for more than two pence per pound. But after 1660, it fell to a penny a pound. Large planters offset their tobacco losses through income from rents, trade, interest on loans to small planters, and fees earned as government officials. Small planters had no such options.

Taking advantage of the headright system, a few planters built up large landholdings and grew wealthy from their indentured servants' labor. The exploitation of labor in the Chesapeake was unequaled anywhere in the English-speaking world outside the West Indies, and the gap between rich and poor whites far exceeded that of New England.

Although after 1660 servants increasingly lived long enough to complete their terms, their futures remained bleak. Having received no pay, they entered into freedom impoverished. Virginia obliged masters to provide a new suit of clothes and a year's supply of corn to a freed servant. Maryland required these items plus a hoe, an ax, and the right to claim fifty acres—if the freedman paid to have the land surveyed and deeded. Thus, Maryland's policy enabled many freedmen to become landowners. Two-thirds of all Chesapeake servants lived in Virginia, however, where no such opportunity existed. Moreover, large planters and absentee English speculators monopolized the best planting land in Virginia. Lacking capital, and with tobacco selling for less than ever, many freedmen toiled as tenants or wage laborers on large plantations.

Even freedmen who managed to obtain their own land usually remained poor. A typical family inhabited a shack barely twenty feet by sixteen feet and had no more possessions than did Adam Head of Maryland when he died in 1698: three mattresses without bedsteads, a chest and barrel that served as table and chair, two pots, a kettle, "a parcell of old pewter," a gun, and some books. Most tobacco farmers lacked furniture, lived on mush or stew because they had just one pot, and slept on the ground—often on a pile of rags. Having fled poverty in England for the promise of a better life, they remained impoverished in the Chesapeake.

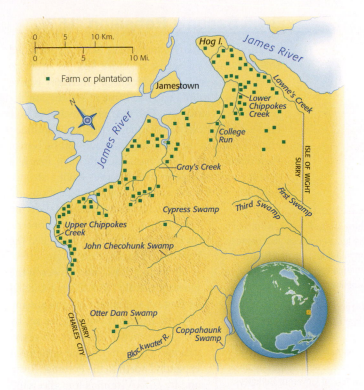

MAP 3.2 **PATTERN OF SETTLEMENT IN SURRY COUNTY, VIRGINIA, 1620–1660** In contrast to New Englanders (see Map 3.4), Chesapeake colonists spread out along the banks of rivers and creeks to facilitate the cultivation and exporting of tobacco.

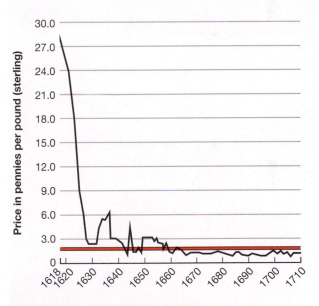

Break-even price for producers

FIGURE 3.1 **CHESAPEAKE TOBACCO PRICES, 1618–1710** Even after the tobacco boom ended in 1629, tobacco remained profitable until about 1660, when its price fell below the break-even point—the income needed to support a family or pay off a farm mortgage.

Source: (Russell R. Menard, "The Chesapeake Economy, 1618–1720: An Interpretation" (unpublished paper presented at the Johns Hopkins University Seminar on the Atlantic Community, November 20, 1973) and "Farm Prices of Maryland Tobacco, 1659–1710," Maryland Historical Magazine, LVIII (Spring 1973): 85.)

3-1.5 Bacon's Rebellion, 1676

By the 1670s, many Chesapeake whites concluded that they needed access to more land in order to prosper. Accordingly, they focused on nearby Native Americans. Virginia had been free of serious conflict with Indians since the **Third Anglo-Powhatan War** (1644–1646). Resentful of tobacco planters' continued encroachments on their land, a coalition of Native Americans led by Opechancanough, then nearly a century old but able to direct battles from a stronghold, killed five hundred of the colony's eight thousand whites before being defeated. Defying Governor William Berkeley's orders, an English soldier shot and killed the captured Opechancanough, effectively ending Powhatan power in the Chesapeake. By 1653, tribes encircled by English settlement began agreeing to remain within boundaries set by the government—in effect, on reservations. Thereafter, white settlement expanded north to the Potomac River, and by 1675 Virginia's four thousand Indians were greatly outnumbered by forty thousand whites.

> **Third Anglo-Powhatan War**
> The last serious conflict between Virginia colonists and Native Americans before Bacon's Rebellion.
>
> **Bacon's Rebellion**
> A war of Indian extermination waged by farmers in Virginia, led by Nathaniel Bacon, in 1676. The rebels burned the capital and forced Governor Berkeley to flee, but the rebellion fizzled when Bacon died later that year.

POOR FARMER'S HOUSE Many poor white farm families in the Chesapeake lived in a single room with a dirt floor, an unglazed window, and minimal furnishings. (*Historic St. Mary's City/Picture Research Consultants & Archives*)

Tensions flared in both Chesapeake colonies between Native Americans struggling to retain land and independence and expanding settlers, especially white freedmen who often squatted illegally on tribal lands. The conflict also divided colonists because both Governor Berkeley and Lord Baltimore, along with a few wealthy cronies, held fur-trade monopolies that profited from friendly relations with local Indians. The monopolies alienated poor freedmen and some wealthier planters who wished to expand their landholdings. As a result, colonists' resentments against the governor and proprietor became fused with those against Native Americans. In June 1675, a dispute between some Doeg Indians and a Virginia farmer escalated until some Virginia and Maryland militiamen pursuing the Doegs instead murdered fourteen friendly Susquehannocks and then assassinated the Susquehannocks' leaders during a peace conference. The Susquehannocks retaliated by killing an equal number of settlers and then offered to make peace. But with most colonists refusing to trust any Indians, the violence was now unstoppable.

Tensions were especially acute in Virginia, reflecting the greater disparities among whites there. Governor Berkeley proposed defending the panic-stricken frontier with a chain of forts linked by patrols. Stung by low tobacco prices and taxes that took almost a quarter of their yearly incomes, small farmers preferred the less costly solution of waging a war of extermination. Nathaniel Bacon, a newly arrived, wealthy planter and Berkeley's distant relative, inspired them. Defying the governor's orders, three hundred colonists elected Bacon to lead them against nearby Native Americans in April 1676, thereby initiating **Bacon's Rebellion**. Bacon's expedition found only peaceful Indians but massacred them anyway.

Returning in June 1676, Bacon and his armed followers demanded authority to wage war "against all Indians in generall," which an intimidated Berkeley granted. The assembly defined as enemies any Indians who left their villages without English permission (even if they did so out of fear of attack by Bacon), and declared their lands forfeited. Bacon's troops were free to seize enemy Indians' food and possessions and to keep Native American prisoners as slaves.

Berkeley soon had second thoughts and called Bacon's men back. The thirteen hundred rebels returned with their guns pointed toward Jamestown. Forcing Berkeley to flee, the rebels burned the capital, offered freedom to any Berkeley supporters' servants or slaves who joined the uprising, and looted their enemies' plantations. But at the very moment of triumph in late 1676, Bacon died of dysentery and his followers dispersed.

A royal commission dispatched from England in 1677 found that Berkeley had mismanaged the crisis and that some lands seized by Bacon's followers were lands that had been guaranteed peaceful tribes in the 1650s. In a series of treaties, the tribes and the colony renewed their peace, English-held captives were freed, and tribal lands were guaranteed in perpetuity. The leading tribe, the Pamunkeys, agreed to present the governor of Virginia with three arrowheads and twenty beaver pelts annually, a provision they honor to this day.

Most Indian-held land seized during Bacon's Rebellion was not protected by formal treaties. The colony retained most of this land and opened it to settlers (see Map 3.3). Captives from nontreaty tribes fed a growing trade in Indian slaves.

Bacon's Rebellion revealed a society under stress. It was an outburst of long pent-up frustrations by marginal taxpayers and former servants seeking land, but also by wealthier planters. Although land-hunger was one motive for the uprising, the willingness of whites to murder, enslave, or expel all Native Americans demonstrated that racial hostility was also a motive.

3-1.6 From Servitude to Slavery: Racializing the Chesapeake

Even before Bacon's uprising, planters had begun shifting from white indentured servants to black slaves as laborers. Between 1650 and 1700, wages rose in England by 50 percent, removing many poor people's incentive to move to the Chesapeake and raising the cost of indentures for those who did. Slavery, as it would turn out, proved far more cost-effective for planters. As slavery expanded, it not only replaced indentured servitude as the principal labor system in the Chesapeake, it became increasingly racialized, formalized, and codified in laws.

Racial slavery developed in three stages in the Chesapeake since the first Africans arrived in 1619. Until about 1640, colonists distinguished between blacks and whites in official documents but did not assume that every African sold was a slave for life. The same was true for Native Americans captured in the colony's early wars. Some Africans gained their freedom during this period, and a few owned their own tobacco farms.

During the second phase, from 1640 to 1660, growing numbers of blacks and some Indians were treated as slaves for life, in contrast to white indentured servants who had fixed terms of service. Slaves' children inherited their parents' status. At the same time, white and black laborers on their own often cooperated as equals. They frequently ran away or rebelled against a master together, and, once their term of service was up, several white female indentured servants married black slave men.

Possibly in reaction to such incidents, the colonies began legally distinguishing whites from blacks and consigning the latter to slavery. Maryland first defined slavery as a lifelong, inheritable racial status in 1661. Virginia followed suit in 1662 with its law, making slave status inherited from the mother. If a mother was a slave, her children automatically were, even if the father was white. Significantly, the law also banned "fornication" (sex) between "any Christian" (read: whites) and any "negro man or woman." In doing so, it effectively ended the long-term practice of marriage and nonmarital sex between white, indentured female servants and black male slaves. While it also made sex between white men and black women illegal, this was rarely enforced. Masters could and did have sex with slave women—often in the form of rape—without any legal consequences, and any offspring produced simply increased the number of slaves the master owned.

MAP 3.3 CHESAPEAKE EXPANSION, 1607–1700 The Chesapeake colonies expanded slowly before midcentury. By 1700, settlers, servants, and slaves had spread throughout the low-lying tidewater region.

By 1705, strict legal codes defined the place of slaves in society and set standards of racial etiquette. By then, free blacks had all but disappeared from the Chesapeake. In formally codifying slavery and deeming nonwhites unfit for freedom, planter elites created a common, exclusive identity for whites as free or potentially free persons. This process began before slavery became economically significant. As late as 1660, fewer than a thousand slaves lived in Virginia and Maryland. The number in bondage first became truly significant in the 1680s when the Chesapeake's slave population almost tripled, rising from forty-five hundred to about twelve thousand. By 1700, slaves made up 22 percent of the inhabitants and more than 80 percent of all unfree laborers.

Even as demand for slaves rose among Chesapeake planters, until the 1690s, the Royal African Company, which held a monopoly on selling slaves to the English colonies, shipped most of its cargoes to the West Indies. Some of these slaves were then transported to the Chesapeake and other mainland regions of English America, but at prices only rich planters could afford. In 1698, the English Parliament lifted this monopoly, and rival companies began shipping massive numbers of Africans directly to the Chesapeake.

The rise of a direct trade in slaves between the Chesapeake and West Africa exacerbated the growing gap between whites and blacks in another way. Before 1698, most blacks in the Chesapeake had either been born, or spent many years, in West African ports or in other American colonies. As a consequence, they were familiar not only with Africans from other cultures but with Europeans and European languages, often including English. Some had also gained their freedom in New Netherland or other colonies where enslavement was not invariably permanent. Such experiences had enabled some blacks to become free landowners and had facilitated marriages and acts of resistance across racial lines among laborers. But after 1698, far larger numbers of slaves poured into Virginia and Maryland, arriving directly from the West African interior without having interacted with Europeans. Language and culture now became barriers rather than bridges to mutual understanding among blacks as well as between blacks and whites, reinforcing the overt racism arising among whites.

The changing composition of the white population also contributed to the emergence of race as the foundation of Chesapeake society. As increasing numbers of colonists lived long enough to marry and form their own families, the number of such families slowly rose, and the ratio of men to women became more equal because half of all children were girls. By 1690, an almost even division existed between males and females. Thereafter, the white population grew primarily through an excess of births over deaths rather than through immigration, so that by 1720 most Chesapeake colonists were native-born and lived longer lives. Whites' shared attachments

to the colony heightened their sense of a common racial identity vis-à-vis an increasingly fragmented and seemingly alien black population.

3-2 New England: Puritanism and Its Decline

How unshakable were New England's religious foundations over time?

After the Chesapeake, New England was the next colonial region to prosper in North America. Separatist Puritans had established Plymouth in 1620 (see Chapter 2), but Plymouth was dwarfed after 1630 when a massive Puritan-led "Great Migration" to New England began. By the time England's civil war halted the migration in 1642, about twenty-one thousand newcomers had established the colonies of Massachusetts Bay, Connecticut, New Haven (absorbed by Connecticut in 1662), and Rhode Island. A clear majority were committed Puritans, and most of the rest were prepared to live under Puritan rule. But serious internal divisions quickly emerged among the Puritans, and over time, the ideals of New England's founders would give way to a more worldly outlook among the colonists. Nevertheless, Puritanism provided the foundation for New England's distinctive regional identity.

New England offered a sharp contrast to the Chesapeake colonies. The religions, economies, social structures, local communities, families, and living standards in the two regions differed completely. While the Chesapeake became a society dominated by plantation slavery, New England was made up of mostly family farms with a small but dynamic commercial sector. Chesapeake and New England colonists did, however, share English nationality and a determination to expand at Native Americans' expense.

3-2.1 A City upon a Hill

While insisting that Puritans in England conform outwardly to Anglican practices, King James I had tolerated those who did not publicly proclaim their dissent. But upon succeeding his father in 1625, Charles I reversed James's policy and began a systematic campaign to eliminate Puritan influence within the Church of England. Anglican authorities insisted that services be conducted according to the Book of Common Prayer, which prescribed rituals similar to Catholic practices. Church courts fined or excommunicated Puritans who protested.

In the face of such harassment, a group of wealthy Puritans successfully petitioned the crown for a charter to colonize at Massachusetts Bay, north of Plymouth. Organizing as the Massachusetts Bay Company, they sent four hundred colonists to Salem, Massachusetts, in 1629. Like Plymouth, Massachusetts Bay would be a Puritan-dominated, self-governing colony rather than one controlled from England by stockholders, proprietors, or the crown. In 1630, eleven ships and seven hundred passengers under Governor **John Winthrop** arrived at the new capital of Boston, where Winthrop distributed an essay titled **"A Model of Christian Charity."** In it, he declared that Massachusetts "shall be as a city upon a hill, the eyes of all people are upon us." The settlers would build a harmonious, godly community in which individuals would subordinate their personal interests to a higher purpose. The result would be an example to the world.

Winthrop denounced the economic jealousy that bred class resentments. God intended that "in all times some must be rich and some poor," he asserted. The rich had an obligation to show charity and mercy toward the poor, who should humbly accept rule by their social superiors as God's will. God expected the state to keep the rich from exploiting the needy and to prevent the poor from burdening their fellow citizens. In outlining a divine plan in which all people, rich and poor, served one another, Winthrop voiced Puritans' dismay at the forces of individualism and class that were battering—and changing—English society.

By fall 1630, six towns had sprung up around Boston. During the unusually severe first winter, 30 percent of Winthrop's party died, and another 10 percent went home in the spring. By mid-1631, however, thirteen hundred new settlers had landed, and more were on the way. The worst was over. The colony would never suffer another starving time. Like Plymouth, Massachusetts Bay primarily attracted landowning farm families of modest means, most of them receptive if not actively committed to Calvinism. There were few indentured servants and almost no slaves. New Englanders quickly established a physically healthier, more stable colonial region than their Chesapeake contemporaries.

Political participation was broader in New England than elsewhere in Europe and its colonies. Instead of requiring voters or officeholders to own property, Massachusetts permitted voting by every adult male "saint," as Puritans termed church members. By 1641, about 55 percent of the colony's twenty-three hundred men were eligible to vote. Because the other New England colonies based voting on property ownership, an even higher proportion of their male residents voted. By contrast, property requirements in England allowed fewer than 30 percent of adult males to vote.

In 1634, after protests that the governor (Winthrop) and council held too much power, the General Court (legislature) allowed each town to send two delegates. Initially resisting this effort, Winthrop was defeated for reelection and did not return

JOHN WINTHROP The future Massachusetts Bay leader most likely commissioned this portrait in 1629, a year before inaugurating the Great Migration to New England. It depicts a gentleman who projects wisdom and patriarchal authority. *(Courtesy, American Antiquarian Society)*

to the governorship for three years. In 1644, the General Court became a bicameral (two-chamber) lawmaking body when the towns' elected deputies separated from the appointed Governor's Council.

3-2.2 New England Ways

Although most New Englanders nominally belonged to the Church of England, their self-governing congregations, like those in Separatist Plymouth, ignored Anglican bishops' authority. Control of each congregation lay squarely in the hands of its male "saints." By majority vote, these men chose a minister, elected a board of elders to handle finances, and admitted new members.

Although congregations were supposedly independent and controlled by their male members, the clergy quickly asserted its power in New England's religious life. Upon arriving in New England, many ministers feared that complete congregational independence would undermine Puritan unity and lead to religious and social disorder. Accordingly, the ministers in Massachusetts, Connecticut, New Haven, and

John Winthrop
Governor of Massachusetts Bay colony who wrote "A Model of Christian Charity."

"A Model of Christian Charity."
This spelled out the Massachusetts Bay colony's social and political ideals. It declared that Massachusetts "shall be as a city upon a hill, the eyes of all people are upon us." The settlers would build a harmonious, godly community in which individuals would subordinate their personal interests to a higher purpose. The result would be an example for all the world and would particularly inspire England to live up to its role as God's "elect nation."

(eventually) Plymouth developed a set of official practices—often referred to as the **"New England Way"**—that strengthened their authority at the expense of church members.

In its church membership requirements, the New England Way diverged from other Puritans' practices. English Puritans accepted as saints any adult who correctly professed the Calvinist faith, repented his or her sins, and lived free of scandal. New England Puritans, however, insisted that candidates for membership stand before their congregation and provide a convincing, soul-baring "relation," or account, of their conversion experience (see Chapter 2). The conversion relation would prove to be the New England Way's most controversial feature.

Education also helped ensure orthodoxy. Like most European Protestants, Puritans insisted that conversion required familiarity with the Bible and, therefore, literacy. In 1647, Massachusetts Bay ordered every town of fifty or more households to appoint a teacher to instruct its children, and every town of at least one hundred households to maintain a grammar school—New England's first steps toward public education. None of these laws required school attendance, however, and boys were more likely to be taught reading and especially writing than were girls.

To ensure a supply of ministers trained in the New England Way, Massachusetts founded Harvard College in 1636. From 1642 to 1671, its 201 graduates included 111 ministers, making New England the only part of English America to produce its own clergy and college-educated elite before 1700.

Puritans agreed that the church must be free of state control, and they opposed theocracy (government by clergy). But Winthrop and other New England leaders insisted that a holy commonwealth required cooperation between church and state. Except for Rhode Island, the colonies obliged all adults to attend services and levied taxes to support local churches. Thus these colonies, like England and Virginia, had an established church. The established clergy did not welcome Puritans whose views threatened to divide churchgoers.

Roger Williams, a Separatist minister who arrived in Massachusetts in 1631, aroused elite anxieties by advocating religious toleration and the complete separation of church and state. He opposed any civil government connection to religious matters, even swearing oaths on the Bible in court, as well as compulsory church service. His objection was not that all religions deserved equal respect, but that the state (a creation of sinful human beings) would corrupt the church.

As Williams's popularity grew, Winthrop and other authorities declared his opinions subversive and banished him in 1635. Williams moved south to a place he called Providence, which he purchased from the Narragansett Indians. At Williams's invitation, a steady stream of dissenters drifted to settlements near Providence, which in 1647 joined to form Rhode Island colony. Rhode Island was the only New England colony to practice religious toleration. The colony's four towns had eight hundred settlers by 1650.

A second major challenge to the New England Way began when **Anne Hutchinson**, a deeply religious member of the Boston congregation, publicly criticized the clergy for judging prospective church members on the basis of "good works"—the Catholic standard for salvation that Protestants had repudiated during the Reformation (see Chapter 2). Supposedly, Puritans followed John Calvin in maintaining that God had "predestined" all persons for either salvation or damnation (see Chapter 2). But Hutchinson argued that ministers who scrutinized a person's outward behavior for "signs" of salvation were substituting their own judgment for God's. Critics charged that her beliefs would lead people to think

ANNE HUTCHINSON Artist rendering of Anne Hutchinson testifying at her 1637 trial. She is shown speaking before a group of Massachusetts judges (which actually included Governor John Winthrop), all of whom were male. *(North Wind Picture Archives/Alamy)*

they were accountable to no one but themselves. Winthrop branded her followers Antinomians, meaning those opposed to the rule of law.

By 1637, Massachusetts Bay had split into two camps. Hutchinson's supporters, primarily Bostonians, included merchants (like her husband) who disliked the government's economic restrictions on their businesses, young men chafing against the rigid control of church elders, and women impatient with their second-class status in church affairs. Even the colony's governor, Henry Vane, was an Antinomian. But most colonists outside Boston were alarmed by what they regarded as religious extremism. In the election of 1637, voters rejected Vane and returned Winthrop to the governorship.

Winthrop brought Hutchinson to trial for heresy before a panel of magistrates and ministers, whose members peppered her with questions (see Going to the Source). Hutchinson's knowledge of Scripture so exceeded that of her interrogators, however, that she might have been acquitted had she not claimed, in a moment of fatigue, to be converted through a direct revelation from God. Like most Christians, Puritans believed that God had ceased to make himself known by personal revelation after New Testament times.

But Hutchinson's real crime was that she defied gender norms. Hutchinson had led other women and some men in discussions of ministers' sermons, asserting her own opinions, including her criticisms of the clergy. Brought to court and tried, her accusers stated that she went beyond women's prescribed roles. As one put it, "You have stepped out of your place; you [would] have rather been a husband than a wife, a preacher than a hearer; and a magistrate than a subject."

The General Court banished the leading Antinomians from the colony, and others followed them into exile. The largest group, led by Hutchinson, settled in Rhode Island. Some Rhode Island Antinomians later converted to Quakerism (discussed later in this chapter), returning to Massachusetts and again defying political and religious authorities. Antinomianism's defeat was followed by new restrictions on women's religious independence that increasingly prohibited the kind of public religious roles claimed by Hutchinson.

3-2.3 Towns, Families, and Farm Life

To ensure that colonists would settle in communities with congregations, all New England colonies provided for the establishment of towns, which would distribute land. Legislatures authorized a town by awarding a grant of land to several dozen landowners. These men then laid out the settlement, organized its church, distributed land among themselves, and established a town meeting—a distinctly New England institution that persists in much of the region to this day. At the center of each town lay the meetinghouse, which served as both church and town hall.

Whereas appointed justices of the peace in England and Virginia administered local government through county courts, New England's county courts served strictly as courts of law; the town meeting conducted local administration. Town meetings decentralized authority over political and economic decisions far more than in England and its other colonies. Each town determined its own qualifications for voting and holding office in the town meeting, although most allowed all male taxpayers (including non-saints) to participate. The meeting could exclude anyone from settling in town and granted newcomers the right to share in future land distributions.

Few aspects of early New England life are more revealing than the first generation's attempt in many towns to promote unity by keeping residents tightly clustered. They did so by assigning house lots near the town center and by granting families just enough cropland to support their families (see Map 3.4). Dedham's forty-six founders, for example, received 128,000 acres from Massachusetts Bay in 1636, yet gave themselves just 3,000 acres by 1656, or about 65 acres per family. The rest remained in trust for future generations.

With families clustered within a mile of one another, the physical settings of New England towns were conducive to traditional reciprocity. They also fostered an atmosphere of mutual watchfulness that Puritans hoped would promote godly order and behavior. Although women's religious roles had been sharply curtailed following the Antinomian crisis, women—especially female saints—remained a social force in their communities. With their husbands and older sons attending the family's fields and business, women remained at home in the tightly knit neighborhoods at the center of each town. Neighboring women exchanged not only goods—say, a pound of butter for a section of spun wool—but advice and news of other neighbors as well. They also gathered at the bedside when one of them gave birth, an occasion supervised by a midwife (one of the few professions open to women) and entirely closed to men. They trained daughters in the skills of housewifery and prepared them for marriage. In these settings, women confided in one another, creating a "community of women" within each town that helped enforce morals and protect the poor and vulnerable. In 1663, Mary Rolfe of Newbury, Massachusetts, was sexually harassed by a high-ranking gentleman while her fisherman husband was at sea. Rolfe confided in her mother, who in turn consulted with a neighboring woman of influence before filing formal charges. Clearly influenced by the town's women, a male jury convicted the gentleman of attempted adultery.

Chesapeake Society Anne Hutchinson versus John Winthrop

The following excerpt from the transcript of the trial of Anne Hutchinson, held in Boston in 1637, consists of an exchange between her and Governor John Winthrop regarding meetings of women that she held in her home. It reveals the differences between her views and those of the colony's male political and religious leaders on the proper role and place of women in church affairs.

Winthrop: Why do you keep such a meeting at your house as you do every week upon a set day?

Hutchinson: It is lawful for me to do so, as it is all your practices, and can you find a warrant for yourself and condemn me for the same thing? The ground of my taking it up was, when I first came to this land, because I did not go to such meetings, . . . it was . . . reported that I did not allow of such meetings but held them unlawful and therefore . . . they said I was proud and did despise all ordinances. Upon that a friend came unto me and told me of it and I to prevent such aspersions took it up, but it was in practice before I came. Therefore I was not the first.

Winthrop: By what warrant do you continue such a course?

Hutchinson: I conceive there lies a clear rule in Titus that the elder women should instruct the younger and then I must have a time wherein I must do it . . .

Winthrop: You know that there is no rule that crosses another, but this rule crosses that in the Corinthians. But you must take it in this sense that elder women must instruct the younger about their business and to love their husbands and not to make them to clash.

Hutchinson: Will it please you to answer me this and to give me a rule for then I will willingly submit to any truth. If any come to my house to be instructed in the ways of God what rule have I to put them away? . . . Do you think it not lawful for me to teach women and why do you call me to teach the court?

Winthrop: We do not call you to teach the court but to lay open yourself . . .

Winthrop: Your course is not to be suffered for. Besides that we find such a course as this to be greatly prejudicial to the state. Besides the occasion that it is to seduce many honest persons that are called to those meetings and your opinions being known to be different from the word of God, may seduce many simple souls that resort unto you. Besides that the occasion which hath come of late hath come from none but such as have frequented your meetings, so that now they are flown off from magistrates and ministers and since they have come to you. And besides that it will not well stand with the commonwealth that families should be neglected for so many neighbors and dames and so much time spent. We see no rule of God for this. We see not that any should have authority to set up any other exercises besides what authority hath already set up and so what hurt comes of this you will be guilty of and we for suffering you.

Hutchinson: Sir, I do not believe that to be so.

Winthrop: Well, we see how it is. We must therefore put it away from you or restrain you from maintaining this course.

Hutchinson: If you have a rule for it from God's word you may.

Winthrop: We are your judges, and not you ours and we must compel you to it.

QUESTIONS

1. On what grounds do Hutchinson and Winthrop base their respective arguments?
2. In what ways does the transcript reflect the emotions behind these legal and theological arguments?

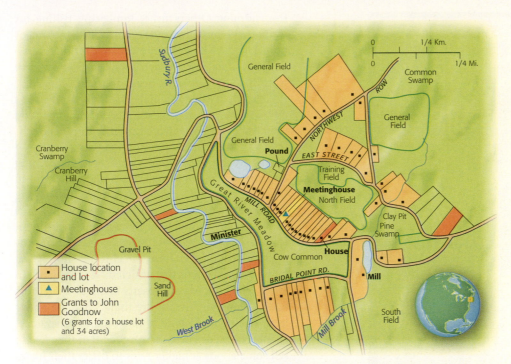

MAP 3.4 LAND DIVISIONS IN CENTRAL SUDBURY, MASSACHUSETTS, 1639–1656 Most early New England towns clustered homes around a meetinghouse and a town commons, used for grazing. Sudbury, like many towns, followed an English practice of distributing croplands in scattered strips. For example, one original settler, John Goodnow, eventually owned a house lot and eleven additional plots (some beyond the bounds of this map) totaling ninety-one acres.

Puritans defined matrimony as a contract rather than a religious sacrament, and justices of the peace rather than ministers married New England couples. As a civil institution, a marriage could be dissolved in cases of desertion, bigamy, adultery, or physical cruelty. By permitting divorce, the colonies diverged from practices in England, where Anglican authorities rarely annulled marriages and civil divorces required a special act of Parliament. Still, New Englanders saw divorce as an exceptional remedy for extremely wronged spouses, such as the Plymouth woman who discovered that her husband was also married to women in Boston, Barbados, and England. Massachusetts courts allowed just twenty-seven divorces before 1692. Despite their greater legal protections, New England wives suffered the same legal disabilities as all Englishwomen, including those in other colonies. An English wife had no property rights independent of her husband unless he consented to a prenuptial agreement leaving her in control of property she already owned. Only if a husband had no other heirs or so stipulated in a will could a widow claim more than the third of the estate reserved by law for her lifetime use.

In contrast to the Chesapeake, New England benefited from a remarkably benign disease environment. Most families owned farms and produced the foods needed for an adequate diet, thereby improving resistance to disease and lowering death rates associated with childbirth. Malaria and other tropical diseases did not thrive in New England's frozen winters. Before 1700, New Englanders seldom traveled far beyond their own towns, so communicable diseases rarely spread inland from Boston and other ports.

Consequently, New Englanders lived longer and raised larger families than their contemporaries in England and in other colonial regions. Life expectancy for men reached sixty-five, and women lived nearly that long. More than 80 percent of all infants survived long enough to get married. Because most settlers came as members of family groups, the population was evenly divided between males and females from the beginning. This permitted rapid population growth without heavy immigration.

Most colonists relied on the labor of their large, healthy families to sustain them and secure their futures. Married men managed the family's crops and livestock, conducted most of its business transactions, and represented it in town government. Their wives bore, nursed, and reared their children and were in charge of work in the house, preparing food, and making clothing. They also tended gardens, using some of their surplus to trade with neighbors.

More than in England and the other colonies, the sons of New England's founding generation depended on their parents to provide them with

MARY HOLLINGSWORTH EMBROIDERED SAMPLER Many New England women found in embroidery a creative outlet that was compatible with their domestic duties. *[(c) 2006 Peabody Essex Museum, Salem, MA. Photography by Jeffrey R. Dykes]*

farmland. With eventual landownership guaranteed and few other opportunities available, sons delayed marriage and worked in their fathers' fields until receiving their own land, usually after age twenty-five. Because the average family raised three or four boys to adulthood, parents could depend on thirty to forty years of sons' labor.

While daughters performed equally vital labor, their future lay with another family—the one into which they would marry. Being young, with many childbearing years ahead of them, enhanced their value to that family. Thus first-generation women, on average, were only twenty-one when they married.

3-2.4 Economic and Religious Tensions

Despite a short growing season and rocky soil, most New Englanders managed to feed large families and keep ahead of their debts, but few became wealthy from farming. Others turned lumbering, fishing, fur trading, shipbuilding, and rum distilling into major industries. As its economy became more diversified, New England prospered, colonists grew more worldly, and their values began to shift.

The most fundamental threat to Winthrop's city upon a hill was that colonists would abandon the ideal of a close-knit community to pursue self-interest. Other colonies—most pointedly, Virginia—displayed the acquisitive impulses transforming England, but in New England, as one writer put it, "religion and profit jump together." While hoping for prosperity, Puritans believed there were limits to legitimate commercial behavior. Government leaders tried to regulate prices so that consumers would not suffer from the chronic shortage of manufactured goods that afflicted New England. In 1635, when the Massachusetts General Court forbade pricing any item more than 5 percent above its cost, Robert Keayne of Boston and other merchants objected. These men argued that they had to sell some goods at higher rates to offset their losses from other sales, shipwrecked cargoes, and inflation. In 1639, after selling nails at 25 to 33 percent above cost, Keayne was fined heavily in court and was forced to make a humiliating apology before his congregation.

Controversies between the Puritan clergy and rural elites on one hand and urban merchants on the other were part of a struggle for New England's soul. Some merchants favored less rigid variants of Calvinism. Merchants, especially those with trans-Atlantic connections, figured prominently among the followers of both Roger Williams and Anne Hutchinson. As such, political and religious leaders sought to minimize merchants' influence on public opinion.

Other social and economic changes further undermined Winthrop's vision. After about 1660, farmers eager to expand their agricultural output and provide land for their sons voted themselves larger amounts of land and insisted that their scattered parcels be consolidated. For example, Dedham, Massachusetts, which distributed only three thousand acres from 1636 to 1656, allocated five times as much in the next dozen years. Rather than continue living closely together, many farmers built homes on their outlying tracts. The dispersal of settlers away from town centers generated friction between townspeople settled near the meetinghouse and "outlivers," whose distance from the town center limited their influence over town affairs. Although groups of outlivers often formed new towns (see Map 3.5), John Winthrop's vision of a closely knit society was slowly giving way to the more individualistic society that the original immigrants had fled in England.

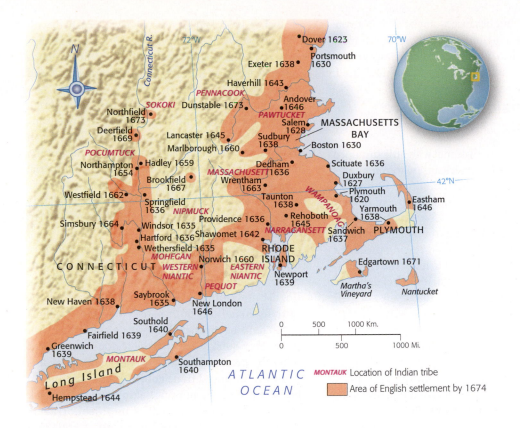

MAP 3.5 NEW ENGLAND EXPANSION, 1620–1674 Population growth and land-hunger drove whites' expansion. The resulting pressures on Native Americans and their land was a major cause of King Philip's War (1675–1676).

As New England slowly prospered, England fell into chaos. The efforts of Charles I to impose taxes without Parliament's consent sparked a civil war in 1642. Alienated by years of religious harassment, Puritans gained control of the successful revolt and beheaded Charles in 1649. Puritan Oliver Cromwell's consolidation of power raised orthodox New Englanders' hopes that England would establish a truly reformed church. But Cromwell supported religious toleration and favored Rhode Island's Roger Williams over other New Englanders. After Cromwell died, chaos returned to England until a provisional government proclaimed the **Restoration** of the monarchy and crowned King Charles II (ruled 1660–1685). Charles sought to undermine Puritan rule, especially in Massachusetts (covered in Chapter 4), putting its leaders increasingly on the defensive. Contrary to Winthrop's vision, "the eyes of all people" were no longer (if ever they had been) fixed on New England.

The erosion of Winthrop's social vision was accompanied by the decline of the religious vision embodied in the New England Way. A crisis over church membership arose as many first-generation Puritans' children stopped joining congregations. By 1650, for example, fewer than half of Boston's adults belonged to its church. Because Puritan ministers baptized only babies born to saints, the second generation's disinterest in becoming church members meant that most third-generation children would remain unbaptized. Unless a solution was found, saints' numbers would dwindle and Puritan rule would end. In 1662, a meeting of clergy proposed a compromise that would permit the children of baptized adults to receive baptism. Derisively termed the "halfway" covenant by its opponents, the proposal would allow the founders' descendants to transmit potential church membership to their grandchildren, leaving their adult children "halfway" members who could not take communion or vote in church affairs. Congregations divided bitterly over limiting membership to pure saints or compromising purity to maintain Puritan power in New England. In the end, most opted for worldly power over spiritual purity.

The crisis in church membership signaled a weakening of the New England Way. Most second-generation adults remained in "halfway" status for life, and the saints became a shrinking minority as the third and fourth generations matured. Sainthood tended to flow in certain families, and soon there were more women than men among the elect. But because women could not vote in church affairs, religious authority stayed in male hands. Nevertheless, ministers publicly recognized women's role in upholding piety and the church itself.

3-2.5 Expansion and Native Americans

New England's first colonists met with little sustained resistance from Native Americans, whose numbers were drastically reduced by the ravages of disease. After one epidemic killed about 90 percent of New England's coastal Indians (see Chapter 2), smallpox inflicted comparable casualties on Indians throughout the Northeast in 1633–1634. Having dwindled from twenty thousand in 1600 to a few dozen survivors by the mid-1630s, the coastal Massachusett and Pawtucket Indians were pressed to sell most of their land to the English. During the 1640s, Massachusetts Bay passed laws that prohibited them from practicing their own religion and authorized missionaries to convert them to Christianity. Thereafter, they ceded more land to the colonists and moved into "praying towns" like Natick, a reservation established by the colony. In the praying towns, Puritan missionary John Eliot hoped to teach the Native Americans Christianity and English "civilization."

By that time, English expansion inland had aroused Native American resistance. Beginning in 1633, Massachusetts settlers moved into the Connecticut River Valley and in 1635 organized the new colony of Connecticut. Friction quickly developed with the Pequot Indians, who controlled the trade in furs and wampum between local Native Americans and New Netherland (see Chapter 2). After tensions escalated into violence, Massachusetts and Connecticut took military action in 1637, thereby beginning the **Pequot War**. Having gained the support of the Mohegan and Narragansett Indians, they waged a ruthless campaign. In a predawn attack, English troops surrounded and set fire to a Pequot village at Mystic, Connecticut, and cut down all who tried to escape. Several hundred Pequots, mostly women and children, were killed. The English found a cause for celebration in the grisly massacre. Wrote Plymouth's Governor William Bradford,

It was a fearful sight to see them [the Pequots] thus frying in the fire and the streams of blood quenching the same, and horrible was the stink and scent thereof; but the victory seemed a sweet sacrifice, and they [the English] gave the praise to God, who had wrought so wonderfully for them, thus to enclose their enemies in their hands and give them so speedy a victory over so proud and insulting an enemy.

Pequot War
War in 1637 between the colonists of Connecticut and the Pequot Indians. The colonists won, and they took over the Pequots' land.

By late 1637, Pequot resistance was crushed, with the survivors taken by pro-English Indians as captives or by the English as slaves. The Pequots' lands were awarded to the colonists of Connecticut and New Haven.

As settlements grew and colonists prospered, the numbers and conditions of Native Americans in New England declined. Although Indians began to recover from the initial epidemics by midcentury, the settlers brought new diseases such as diphtheria, measles, and tuberculosis as well as new outbreaks of smallpox, which took heavy tolls. New England's Indian population fell from 125,000 in 1600 to 10,000 in 1675.

Native Americans felt the English presence in other ways. Intercultural trade, by which Natives exchanged the furs of beavers and other furs to the English for cloth and other manufactured goods, initially benefited both sides. But once Indians began hunting for trade instead of just for their own needs, they quickly depleted the region's beavers and other fur-bearing animals. Because English traders shrewdly advanced trade goods on credit to Indian hunters before the hunting season began, the lack of pelts pushed many Natives into debt. Traders thereupon began taking Indian land as collateral and selling it to settlers. The expansion of English settlement often separated Native villages from one another and from hunting, gathering, and fishing areas.

English expansion put new pressures on native peoples and the land. As early as 1642, Miantonomi, a Narragansett sachem (chief), warned neighboring Indians, "These English having gotten our land, they with scythes cut down the grass, and with axes fell the trees; their cows and horses eat the grass, and their hogs spoil our clam banks, and we shall all be starved."

Within a generation, Miantonomi's fears were borne out. By clearing away trees for fields and for use as fuel and building material, colonial farmers altered an entire ecosystem. Deer were no longer attracted, and the wild plants upon which Native Americans depended for food and medicine ceased to grow. The soil became drier and flooding more frequent in the face of this deforestation. The settlers' domestic livestock, according to English custom, ranged freely. Pigs damaged Indian cornfields (until the natives adopted the alien practice of fencing their fields) along with shellfish-gathering sites. Settlers replaced the native grasses, which English cattle and horses quickly devoured, with English varieties.

With their leaders powerless to halt the alarming decline of their population, land, and food sources, many Indians became demoralized. In their despair, some turned to alcohol, increasingly available during the 1660s despite colonial efforts to suppress its sale to Native Americans. Domestic violence also escalated within Native American families and communities. Interpreting the crisis as one of belief, other natives responded to an expanded initiative by Puritan missionaries to convert them to Christianity. By 1675, about 2,300 Indians inhabited thirty praying towns in eastern Massachusetts, Plymouth, and offshore islands. Regularly visited by supervising missionaries, each praying town had its own Native American magistrate, usually a sachem, and some congregations had Indian preachers. Although the missionaries struggled to convert the Indians to "civilization" (meaning English culture and lifestyles) as well as Christianity, most praying Indians integrated the new faith with their native cultural identities.

Anglo–Indian conflict became acute during the 1670s because of pressures imposed on unwilling Indians to sell more land and to accept missionaries and the legal authority of colonial courts. Tension ran especially high in Plymouth colony where Metacom, or "King Philip," the son of the colony's one-time ally Massasoit (see Chapter 2), was now the leading Wampanoag sachem. The English had engulfed the Wampanoags, persuaded many of them to renounce their loyalty to Metacom, and forced several humiliating concessions on the sachem.

In 1675, Plymouth hanged three Wampanoags for killing a Christian Indian and threatened to arrest Metacom. The resulting tensions ignited the conflict known as **King Philip's War**. Eventually, two-thirds of southern New England's Native Americans rallied around Metacom. Unlike Indians in the Pequot War, they were familiar with guns and were as well armed as the colonists. Indian raiders attacked fifty-two of the region's ninety towns (entirely destroying twelve), burned twelve hundred houses, slaughtered eight thousand head of cattle, and killed twenty-five hundred colonists (5 percent).

The tide turned against Metacom's forces in 1676 after the Mohawk Iroquois of New York and many local Indians joined the English against him. The colonists and their Native American allies scattered their enemies and destroyed their food supplies. About five thousand Indians starved or fell in battle, including Metacom himself, and others fled to New York and Canada. After crushing the uprising, the English sold hundreds of captives into West Indian slavery, including Metacom's wife and child.

King Philip's War further reduced southern New England's Indian population by about 40 percent and eliminated organized resistance to English expansion. It also deepened English hostility toward all Native Americans, even Christians and others who had supported the colonies. In Massachusetts, ten praying towns were disbanded, and native peoples restricted to the remaining four; all Indian courts were dismantled; and English "guardians" were appointed to supervise the reservations. In the face of poverty and discrimination, remaining Indians struggled to survive and maintain their communities.

3-2.6 Salem Witchcraft, 1691–1693

The devastation of the ongoing Indian wars combined with other forces of social change in New England to further destabilize Puritan society and help pave the way for the Salem, Massachusetts, witch hysteria in 1692. In that event, over 200 people were accused and nineteen hanged—more than 80 percent of them women. Of the men accused, nearly half were relatives or spouses of the women initially accused.

Historians have struggled to make sense of this complicated event in colonial New England's history. While Salem's hysteria would prove unique for the size and scope of the tragedy, witchcraft accusations were not unusual in seventeenth-century Europe and its colonies. In New England, however, most earlier witchcraft accusations had one defendant and cases that either never went to trial or proceeded with little fanfare.

In part, witchcraft accusations and beliefs can be explained in terms of Puritans' understanding of their relationship to the supernatural world. Puritans looked for signs all around them—in a bountiful or failed harvest, in the illness or loss of a child—that they had curried God's favor. Witches were believed to be people (usually women) whose pride, envy, discontent, or greed supposedly led them to sign a pact with the devil. Thereafter, they allegedly used *maleficium* (the devil's supernatural power of evil) to torment neighbors and others by causing illness, destroying property, or—as with the girls in Salem Village—inhabiting or "possessing" their victims' bodies and minds. Because they lived in close proximity to each other, New Englanders sometimes blamed neighbors for the ills that befell them. For example, if a woman had a miscarriage, she might accuse a troublesome neighbor of having used witchcraft to cause it.

Salem, Massachusetts, like much of Puritan New England in 1692, was in flux. Trade made Salem prosperous but also destroyed the relatively equal society of first-generation fishermen and farmers. Salem's divisions were especially sharp in

King Philip's War
War in 1675 between the Wampanoags and the Plymouth colonists, which was ignited by the hanging of three Wampanoags for killing a Christian Indian.

IMAGES OF WITCHCRAFT Most seventeenth-century Europeans and colonists feared that, at any time, Satan and those in his grip (witches) could attack and harm them with the power of evil. *(The Huntington Library & Art Collections, San Marino, California)*

destructive conflict with Indians a decade later. As such, anyone who had been to the frontier was also suspect, given fears about another possible Indian attack. Many of Salem's residents had indeed fled to the town from Indian wars.

These factors combined with others to make Salem in some ways ripe for the crisis that ensued. The town experienced an influx of immigrants and population growth that heightened demand for the increasingly scarce supplies of land. Younger people resisted the control of parents and similarly pressed for land of their own. That, combined with declining church membership and the growth of what some regarded as more worldly values emphasizing personal gain, had Puritan Salem on edge.

In the 1692 witchcraft crisis, the most consistent and undeniable pattern was that both accusers and accused were predominantly female. Two-thirds of all "possessed" accusers were females aged eleven to twenty, and more than half had lost one or both parents in Anglo–Indian conflicts in Maine. Having fled to Massachusetts, most were now servants in other families' households. These young women likely gained momentary power and prominence by voicing the anxieties and hostilities of others in their community and by virtually dictating the course of events in and around Salem for several months.

The witch crisis began in January 1692 when several Salem Village girls began displaying odd behavior and fits. Their parents went looking for the cause, and the girls—two of whom resided with the minister Samuel Parris—were pressured to name who was doing this to them. They pointed to an enslaved woman, Tituba, of African and/or Native American descent who had been brought from Barbados, and two local white women, who were promptly arrested.

By April 1692, as the accusations increased, fears of witchcraft soon overrode doubts about the girls' credibility and led local judges to sweep aside normal procedural safeguards. In particular, the judges ignored the law's ban on "spectral evidence"—testimony that a spirit resembling the accused had been seen tormenting a victim. Thereafter, accusations multiplied until the jails overflowed with 342 accused witches.

Another factor seemed to undergird the nature of the accusations: fear of "disorderly women." While many of the accused were poor women, they also included those who were known for publically speaking their mind, not a sanctioned behavior for women in Puritan New England. Some may have been known for debating with others, particularly male neighbors. It is likely that the accusing girls had heard their parents or other authority figures describe the women they accused of witchcraft as evil or problematic.

the precinct of Salem Village (now Danvers), an economically stagnant district located northwest of Salem Town. Residents of the village's eastern section farmed richer soils and benefited from nearby Salem Town's commercial expansion, whereas those in the less fertile western half did not share in this prosperity and had lost the political influence they once held in Salem.

The pattern of hysteria in Salem Village reflected that community's internal divisions and fears about social change. Most accusations originated in the village's poorer western division and were directed largely at wealthier families in the eastern village or in Salem Town (see Map 3.6). Residents remained shaken by King Phillip's War as well as a second

Accusers and witnesses most frequently named as witches middle-aged wives and widows—those past childbearing age, which was a key source of women's social value. A disproportionate number of accused women had inherited, or stood to inherit, property beyond the one-third of a husband's estate normally bequeathed to widows. In some cases, the inherited land may have been coveted by other family members or the source of a boundary dispute. In other words, some of the accused tended to be women who had or soon might have more economic power and independence than many men—a problematic situation in traditional, patriarchal New England. To New Englanders who felt the need to limit female independence and economic individualism, witchcraft accusations represented the dangers awaiting those who disregarded such limits.

The number of persons facing trial multiplied quickly. Those found guilty desperately tried to stave off death by implicating others. As the pandemonium spread beyond Salem, fear dissolved ties of friendship and family. A minister heard himself condemned by his own granddaughter. A seven-year-old girl helped send her mother to the gallows. Fifty persons saved themselves by confessing. Twenty others who refused to confess falsely or to betray other innocents went to their graves. Shortly before she was hanged, a victim named Mary Easty begged the court to come to its senses: "I petition your honors not for my own life, for I know I must die . . . [but] if it be possible, that no more innocent blood be shed."

By late 1692, most Massachusetts ministers came to doubt that justice was being done. They objected that spectral evidence, crucial in most convictions, was suspect because the devil could manipulate it. Backed by the clergy (and alarmed by an accusation against his wife), Governor William Phips forbade further imprisonments for witchcraft in October—by which time over a hundred individuals were in jail and twice that many stood accused. Shortly thereafter, he suspended all trials, and in early 1693 he pardoned all those convicted or suspected of witchcraft.

Along with the revocation of Massachusetts' charter (discussed in Chapter 4), the witchcraft hysteria ended what was left of "Puritan" New England. Already the "New England Way" had disappeared and most colonists were turning toward the pursuit of self-interest. Those reaching maturity thereafter would reinforce this trend, becoming "Yankees" who shrewdly pursued material gain. True to their Puritan roots, they would retain their forceful convictions and self-discipline, giving New England a distinctive regional identity that would endure.

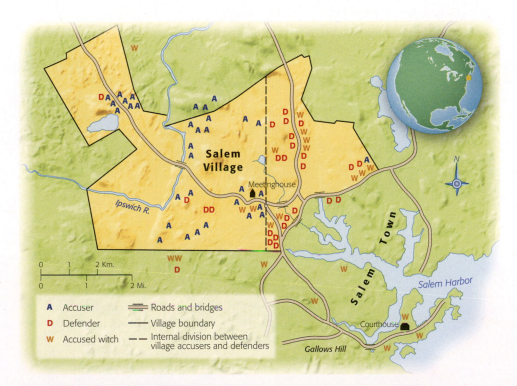

MAP 3.6 THE GEOGRAPHY OF WITCHCRAFT: SALEM VILLAGE, 1692 Most of those who leveled accusations of witchcraft lived in western Salem Village while those they targeted, along with those who defended the accused, lived in the eastern village and in Salem Town.

3-3 The Spread of Slavery: The Caribbean and Carolina

What connections exist between colonial development in the Caribbean and Carolinas and that of the other British colonies?

As the Chesapeake and New England flourished, an even larger wave of settlement swept the West Indies (see Maps 3.1 and 3.7). Between 1630 and 1642, more than half of the eighty thousand English who emigrated to the Americas went to the Caribbean. Beginning in the 1640s, English planters began using slave labor to produce sugar on large plantations. As a result, England's Caribbean colonies became its wealthiest and most productive during the seventeenth century. After 1670, many English islanders moved to the new mainland colony of Carolina, thereby facilitating the spread of large-scale plantation slavery to North America.

3-3.1 Sugar and Slaves: The West Indies

As on the North American mainland, the Netherlands, France, and England entered the colonial race in the West Indies during the early seventeenth century and expanded thereafter. Challenging Spain's monopoly, each nation seized islands in the region, but it was the English who became the most powerful and prosperous during the 1600s.

The tobacco boom that powered Virginia's economy until 1630 led early English settlers on the island of Barbados to cultivate that plant. But with most colonists farming small plots, few realized spectacular profits.

During the 1640s, an even greater boom—in sugar—revolutionized the islands' economy and society. Dutch planters in Brazil (where the Netherlands had captured some territory) showed English West

MAP 3.7 THE CARIBBEAN COLONIES, 1670 By 1660, nearly every West Indian island had been colonized by Europeans and was producing sugar with slave labor. Ten years later, English colonists from Barbados began settling the new mainland colony of Carolina.

Indian planters how to raise and process sugar cane, which the Dutch then marketed. Turning spectacular profits, sugar production quickly moved beyond Barbados to other English islands.

Because sugar production required three times as many workers per acre as tobacco, West Indian planters increasingly purchased enslaved Africans from Dutch traders to do fieldwork and used English indentured servants as overseers and skilled artisans.

Sugar planters preferred black slaves to white servants because slaves could be driven harder and cost less to maintain. Whereas most servants ended their indentures after four years, slaves toiled until death. Although slaves initially cost two to four times more than servants, they were a more lucrative long-term investment. In this way, the profit motive and the racism that emerged with the "new slavery" (see Chapter 2) reinforced one another.

By 1670, the sugar revolution had transformed the English West Indies into a predominantly slave society. Thereafter, the number of enslaved Africans rose from approximately 40,000 to 130,000 in 1713 while the white population remained stable at about 33,000.

Three victorious wars with the Dutch and enactment of the Navigation Acts (covered in Chapter 4) enabled English merchants and shippers to monopolize the West Indian trade in sugar and slaves from the 1660s onward. The profits from this trade, far more than from all mainland trade, enabled England to become the wealthiest nation in the Atlantic world by 1700.

Declining demand for white labor in the West Indies diverted the flow of English immigration from the islands to mainland North America and so contributed to population growth there. Furthermore, because land was priced beyond the reach of most whites, about thirty thousand people left the islands from 1655 to 1700. Most whites who left the West Indies migrated to the mainland colonies, especially Carolina.

3-3.2 Rice and Slaves: Carolina

In 1663, King Charles II bestowed the swampy coast between Virginia and Spanish Florida on several English supporters, making it the first of several Restoration colonies. The grateful proprietors named their colony Carolina in honor of Charles (*Carolus* in Latin).

One of the proprietors, Anthony Ashley Cooper, and his young secretary, future philosopher John Locke (further discussed in Chapter 4), drew up a plan for Carolina's settlement and government. Their Fundamental Constitutions provided for a nobility that would hold two-fifths of all land while

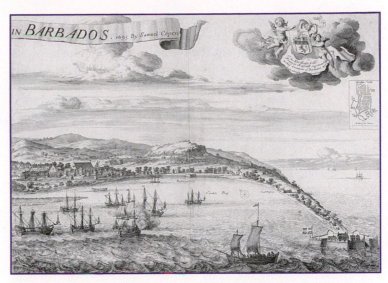

"A PROSPECT OF BRIDGETOWN IN BARBADOS" (1696) Slaves and sugar were the primary cargoes on ships anchored in Bridgetown, the wealthiest and busiest port in Britain's American colonies at the end of the seventeenth century. *(Courtesy of the John Carter Brown Library at Brown University)*

controlling the upper house of the legislature and the judiciary. Ordinary Carolinians with smaller landholdings were expected to defer to this nobility, although they would enjoy religious toleration and English common law and could elect an assembly. To induce settlement, the proprietors offered a headright of one hundred fifty acres to planters for each arriving family member or slave as well as one hundred acres to each servant who completed a term of indenture.

Uninterested in moving themselves, the proprietors arranged for settlers from Barbados to get their colony started. Accordingly, in 1670, two hundred white Barbadians and their slaves landed near modern-day Charleston, "in the very chops of the Spanish." The settlement called Charles Town formed the colony's nucleus.

Until the 1680s, most settlers were from Barbados, with smaller numbers from other colonies and some French Huguenots (Calvinists). Obtaining all the land they needed, the colonists saw little reason to obey absentee lords' plans drawn up for them across the Atlantic. Southern Carolinians raised livestock and exported Indian slaves (as discussed shortly), while colonists in northern Carolina produced tobacco, lumber, and pitch, giving local people the name "tarheels." At first, these activities did not produce enough profit to warrant maintaining many slaves, so self-sufficient white families predominated in the area.

But some southern Carolinians, particularly those from Barbados, sought a staple crop that could make them rich. By the 1690s, they found it in rice.

Because rice, like sugar, enormously enriched a few men with capital to invest in costly dams, dikes, and slaves, it remade southern Carolina into a society resembling the one from which Barbadians came. By earning annual profits of 25 percent, rice planters within a generation became the one mainland colonial elite whose wealth rivaled that of the Caribbean sugar planters.

Even when treated humanely, indentured English servants simply did not survive in humid rice paddies swarming with malaria-bearing mosquitoes. The planters' solution was to import an ever-growing force of enslaved Africans. West Africans had developed immunities to malaria and yellow fever—infectious, mosquito-borne diseases that were endemic to their homelands. Enslaved Africans, along with slave ship crews, carried both diseases to North America. (Tragically, the antibody that helps ward off malaria also tends to produce the sickle-cell trait, a genetic condition often fatal to the children who inherit it.) Because a typical Carolina rice planter farming 130 acres needed sixty-five slaves, a great demand for black slave labor resulted. As agriculturalists who had farmed rice in their homeland, African women would prove especially vital. They shared techniques for planting, harvesting, and processing rice that aided its development as a staple crop. The proportion of enslaved Africans in southern Carolina's population rose from just 17 percent in 1680 to about half by 1700. Thereafter, Carolina would have a black majority.

Rice thrived only within a forty-mile-wide coastal strip extending from Cape Fear to present-day Georgia. Carolinians grimly joked that the malaria-infested rice belt was a paradise in spring, an inferno in summer, and a hospital in the wet, chilly fall. In the worst months, planters' families usually escaped to the relatively cool and more healthful climate of Charles Town and let overseers supervise their slaves during harvests.

Enslavement in Carolina was not confined to Africans. In the 1670s, traders in southern Carolina armed nearby Native Americans and encouraged them to raid rival tribes for slaves. After local supplies of Indian slaves were exhausted, the English-allied Indians captured unarmed Guale, Apalachee, and Timucua Indians at Spanish missions in Florida and traded them to the Carolinians for guns and other European goods. The English in turn sold the enslaved Native Americans, mostly to planters in the West Indies—where most died quickly because they lacked immunities to European and tropical diseases—but also on the mainland as far north as New England. By the mid-1680s, the Carolinians had extended the trade through alliances with the Yamasees and the Creeks, a powerful confederacy centered in what is now western Georgia and

northern Alabama. For three decades, these Indian allies of the English terrorized Indians in Florida with their slave raids. Between thirty thousand and fifty thousand Native Americans were enslaved in Carolina between 1670 and 1715.

3-4 The Middle Colonies: Ethnic and Religious Diversity

What made the Middle Colonies distinctive?

Between the Chesapeake and New England, two non-English nations established colonies (see Map 3.8). New Netherland and New Sweden began as small commercial outposts, but the Dutch colony eventually flourished and took over New Sweden. Then England seized New Netherland from the Dutch in 1664 and carved New York, New Jersey, Pennsylvania, and Delaware out of the former Dutch territory. These actions together created a fourth English colonial region, the middle colonies.

The middle colonies differed from the three other English mainland regions in several crucial respects: the ethnic and religious diversity of their populations, the fertility of their lands, and the dynamism of their urban commercial centers. These characteristics gave the middle colonies a distinct regional identity.

3-4.1 Precursors: New Netherland and New Sweden

New Netherland was North America's first multiethnic colony. Barely half of its colonists were Dutch; most of the rest were Germans, French, English, Scandinavians, and Africans, free as well as enslaved; and eighteen European and African languages were spoken. In 1643, the population included Protestants, Catholics, Jews, and Muslims. But religion counted for little (in 1642, the colony had seventeen taverns but not one place of worship), as did loyalty to Dutch authority. Although the Dutch West India Company—a consortium of merchants—nominally controlled trade in New Netherland, private individuals persisted in illegally trading with Native Americans. In 1639, the company bowed to mounting pressure and legalized private trading.

Privatization led to a rapid rise in Dutch exports of beaver pelts, obtained primarily from the Five Nations Iroquois, who demanded increasing numbers of guns in return. As overhunting depleted local supplies of beaver skins and as smallpox epidemics ravaged their communities, armed Iroquois attacked convoys of pro-French Indians carrying pelts to Montreal. The Iroquois seized not only the pelts but also captives whom they adopted into their families to replace the dead. Between 1648 and 1657, the Iroquois, in a series of bloody **"beaver wars,"** dispersed the Hurons and other French allies, incorporating many members of these nations into their own ranks. They also attacked French settlements along the St. Lawrence. "They come like foxes, they attack like lions, they disappear like birds," wrote a French Jesuit of the Iroquois.

Although the Dutch allied successfully with the inland Iroquois, their relations with nearby coastal Indians paralleled native–settler relations in England's seaboard colonies. In 1643, all-out war erupted when Governor Willem Kieft ordered the massacre of previously friendly Indians who were protesting settler encroachments on Long Island. By 1645, the Dutch prevailed over these Indians and their allies, only with English help and by inflicting additional atrocities. But "Kieft's War" helped reduce New Netherland's Indian population from sixteen hundred to seven hundred.

Another European challenger distracted the Dutch as they sought to suppress neighboring Native Americans. In 1638, Sweden had planted a small colony in the lower Delaware Valley that, like New Netherland, was ethnically diverse. Also like New Netherland, New Sweden included traders who obtained furs from Native Americans, in this case from the Delaware and Susquehannock Indians. Viewing the Swedes as interlopers, the Dutch colony's governor, Peter Stuyvesant, led seven warships and three hundred troops into New Sweden in 1655. Overwhelmed, the three hundred residents of the tiny colony peacefully accepted Dutch annexation.

Although they were short-lived, the Dutch and Swedish colonies were historically significant. New Netherland had attained a population of nine thousand and featured a wealthy, thriving port city—New Amsterdam—by 1664. Some of the nation's first Jewish emigrants landed in New Amsterdam. Women in New Netherland had far more rights than their English counterparts—they retained their legal independence within marriage and all marital property was considered jointly held. When husbands died, their wives were their sole inheritors, with children waiting until both parents passed to receive anything. Dutch wives could even own property and businesses, something only single English women could do. Even New Sweden left a mark—the log cabin, that durable symbol of the American frontier, which Finnish settlers in the Swedish colony first introduced to the continent. Above all, the two colonies bequeathed a social environment characterized by ethnic and religious diversity that would continue in England's middle colonies.

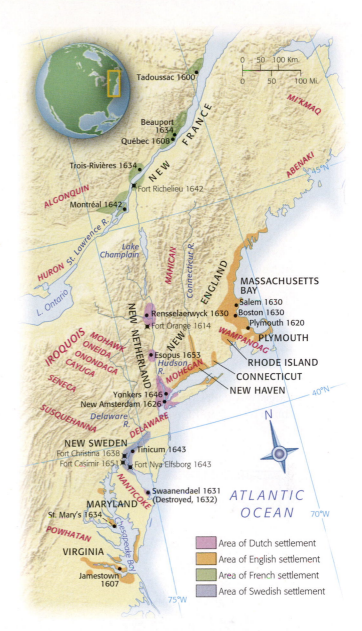

MAP 3.8 EUROPEAN COLONIZATION IN THE MIDDLE AND NORTH ATLANTIC, CA. 1650 North of Spanish Florida, Swedish, Dutch, English, and French colonizers competed for territory and trade with Native Americans. By 1664, England had assumed control of the former Swedish and Dutch territories.

3-4.2 English Conquests: New York and New Jersey

Like Carolina, New York and New Jersey originated as proprietary colonies, awarded by King Charles II to favored upper-class supporters. Here, too, proprietors hoped to create hierarchical societies in which they would profit from settlers' rents. These plans failed in New Jersey, as in Carolina. Only in rural New York did they achieve some success.

> **"beaver wars"**
> Series of conflicts among the members of the Iroquois nation in a quest for pelts and captives who could be adopted into Iroquois families to replace the dead.

In 1664, as part of a broader war against the Dutch Republic, Charles II dispatched a naval force to conquer New Netherland. With Dutch forces tied down elsewhere and with Puritan settlers on Long Island supporting England, Stuyvesant and four hundred poorly armed civilians could not defend New Amsterdam. After a peaceful surrender, most of the Dutch remained in the colony on generous terms. For women, promises to retain Dutch inheritance practices faded over time, and Dutch women were increasingly governed by English notions of coverture.

Charles II appointed his brother James, Duke of York, proprietor of the new province and renamed it New York. When the duke became King James II in 1685, he proclaimed New York a royal colony. Immigration from New England, Britain, and France boosted the population from nine thousand in 1664 to twenty thousand in 1700, of whom just 44 percent were of Dutch descent.

New York's governors rewarded their wealthiest political supporters, both Dutch and English, with large land grants. By 1703, five families held approximately 1.75 million acres in the Hudson River Valley (see Map 3.9), on which they created manors with rent-paying tenants. Earning an enormous income from their rents over the next half-century, the New York **patroons** (the Dutch name for manor lords) formed a landed elite second in wealth only to the Carolina rice planters.

Ambitious plans collided with American realities in New Jersey, which also was carved out of New Netherland. Immediately after the conquest of 1664, the Duke of York awarded New Jersey to a group of proprietors. About four thousand Delaware Indians and a few hundred Dutch and Swedes inhabited the area at the time. From the beginning, New Jersey's proprietors had difficulty controlling their province. By 1672, several thousand New Englanders had settled along the Atlantic shore. After the Puritans rejected their authority, the proprietors sold the region to a group of Quakers who split the territory into the two colonies of West Jersey (1676) and East Jersey (1682).

The Jerseys' Quakers, Anglicans, Puritans, Scottish Presbyterians, Dutch Calvinists, and Swedish Lutherans got along poorly with one another and even worse with the proprietors. Both governments collapsed between 1698 and 1701 as mobs disrupted

DUTCH COUPLE AT NEW AMSTERDAM Dutch wealth and enslaved African labor contributed to New Amsterdam's early prosperity. *(Archive Photos/Getty Images)*

the courts. In 1702, the disillusioned proprietors surrendered their political powers to the crown, which combined the colonies into a single royal province, New Jersey.

3-4.3 Quaker Pennsylvania

In 1681, Charles II paid off a huge debt by making a supporter's son, **William Penn**, the proprietor of the last unallocated tract of his American domain. Perhaps the most distinctive of all English colonial founders, Penn (1644–1718) had two aims in developing Pennsylvania (Penn's Woods). While he wanted to launch a "holy experiment" based on Quaker teachings and religious freedom, he was quick to add, "yet I want some recompense for my trouble."

Quakers in late-seventeenth-century England stood well beyond the fringe of respectability. Quakerism appealed strongly to men and women at the bottom of the economic ladder who challenged the social order. George Fox, the new religion's originator, had received his inspiration while wandering civil war–torn England and searching for spiritual meaning among distressed common people. Tried on one occasion for blasphemy, he warned the judge to "tremble at the word of the Lord" and was ridiculed as a "quaker." Fox's followers called themselves Friends, but the name Quaker stuck.

At the core of Quakerism was the belief that the Holy Spirit or "Inner Light" could inspire every soul. Mainstream Christians, by contrast, believed that humans were basically sinful unless saved and found any claim of direct, personal communication between God and individuals highly dangerous, as Massachusetts' persecution of Antinomians demonstrated. Friends trusted direct inspiration and disavowed the need for a clergy. In their simple religious services ("meetings"), they sat silently until the Inner Light began prompting participants to speak.

Friends' emphasis on religious individualism and equality extended to the social and political arenas. For example, insisting that individuals deserved recognition for their spiritual state rather than their worldly wealth or status, Quakers refused to tip their hats to their social betters. Finally, Quakers accorded women unprecedented equality. The Inner Light, Fox insisted, could "speak in the female as well as the male." Acting on these beliefs, Quakers suffered persecution and occasionally death in England, Massachusetts, and Virginia.

Not all Quakers came from the bottom of society. The movement's emphasis on quiet introspection and its refusal to adopt a formal creed also attracted some well-educated and prosperous individuals disillusioned by the quarreling of rival faiths. Besides William Penn, who possessed a great fortune, there were significant numbers of merchants among the estimated sixty thousand Friends in the British Isles in the early 1680s. Moreover, their religious self-discipline carried over into worldly pursuits, ensuring that many humble Quakers accumulated money and property.

Careful planning gave Pennsylvania the most successful

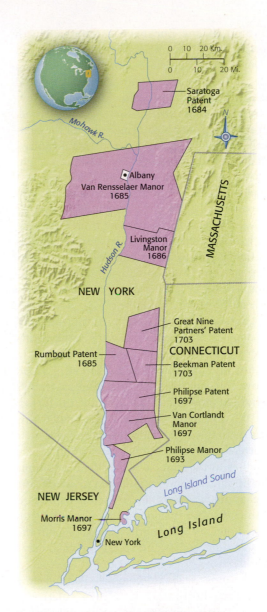

MAP 3.9 NEW YORK MANORS AND LAND GRANTS Between 1684 and 1703, English governors awarded vast tracts of land along the Hudson River as manors to prominent supporters.

William Penn
The proprietor of the last unallocated tract of American territory at the king's disposal.

Quakers
A religious sect that appealed strongly to men and women at the bottom of the economic ladder. They believed that the Holy Spirit or the "Inner Light" could inspire every soul. Mainstream Christians, by contrast, found any such claim of direct, personal communication to God highly dangerous.

beginning of any European colony in North America. In 1681, Penn sent an advance party to the Delaware Valley, where about five thousand Delaware Indians and one thousand Swedes and Dutch already lived. Then, after an agonizing voyage in which one-third of the passengers died, Penn arrived in 1682. Choosing a site for the capital and principal port, he named it Philadelphia—the "City of Brotherly Love." By 1687, some eight thousand settlers had arrived in Pennsylvania—primarily Quakers from the British Isles, but also Presbyterians, Baptists, and Anglicans, as well as Lutherans and radical sectarians from Germany. Most were attracted by Pennsylvania's religious toleration as well as its agricultural and commercial prospects. As in New England, most immigrants arrived in families rather than as single males, so the population grew rapidly.

After wavering between authoritarian and more democratic plans, Penn gave Pennsylvania a government with a strong executive branch (a governor and governor's council) and granted the lower legislative chamber (the assembly) only limited powers. Friends, forming the majority of the colony's population, dominated this elected assembly. Penn named Quakers and their supporters as governor, judges, and sheriffs. Like most elites of the time, he feared "the ambitions of the populace," and he intended to check "the rabble" as much as possible. To prevent haphazard growth and social turmoil in Philadelphia, Penn designed the city with a grid plan, laying out the streets at right angles and reserving small areas for parks.

Unlike most seaboard colonies, Pennsylvania avoided early hostilities with Native Americans. This was partly because the native population had been reduced by epidemics. But it was also a testament to Penn's Quaker tolerance. To the Delaware Indians, Penn expressed a wish "to live together as Neighbours and Friends," and he made it the colony's policy to purchase land it wanted for settlement from them.

Land was a key to Pennsylvania's early prosperity. Rich, level lands and a lengthy growing season enabled immigrants to produce bumper crops, including staples of wheat and flaxseed. With little regulation, no taxation, a culture of individualism, and vast opportunities for settlers, the region came to be regarded by its white male settlers as the "best poor man's country in the world." West Indian demand for the colony's grain rose sharply and by 1700 made Philadelphia a lively port city with more than two thousand residents. Thereafter, Philadelphia grew rapidly and became a major urban center (discussed in Chapter 4).

Like other attempts to base new colonies on preconceived plans or lofty ideals, Penn's "peaceable kingdom" soon met with resistance. After Penn returned to England in 1684, an opposition party attacked his efforts to monopolize foreign trade and to require each landowner pay him a small annual fee. Bitter struggles between Penn's supporters in the governor's council and opponents in the assembly deadlocked the government. From 1686 to 1688, the legislature passed no laws, and the council once ordered the lower house's speaker arrested. During a brief return (1699–1701), Penn made the legislature a unicameral (one-chamber) assembly and allowed it to initiate legislation.

William Penn met his strongest opposition in the counties on the lower Delaware River, where Swedes and Dutch had taken up the best lands. In 1704, these counties became the separate colony of Delaware, but Penn continued to name their governors.

The middle colonies demonstrated the benefits of encouraging religious toleration and ethnic pluralism. New Jersey and, for the most part, New York successfully integrated New Netherland's Swedish and Dutch population, and neither Pennsylvania, New Jersey, nor Delaware required taxpayers to support an established church. These features attracted a wide range of farmers, merchants, and laborers who enabled the middle colonies very quickly to rival the other three English colonial regions in their wealth and importance. They also provided some of the ideals that would inspire the founding of the United States a century later.

3-5 Rivals for North America: France and Spain

How did the experiences of Spain and France in the Americas differ from that of Britain?

In marked contrast to England's compact, densely populated settlements on the Atlantic, France and Spain established far-flung networks of fortified trading posts and missions in North America. Unable to attract large numbers of colonists, they enlisted Native Americans as trading partners and military allies, and the two Catholic nations had far more success than English Protestants in converting Indians to Christianity. Nevertheless, both also struggled fiercely against hostile Native Americans before securing their colonies.

By 1700, French and Spanish missionaries, traders, and soldiers—and relatively few settlers—were spreading European influence well beyond the range of England's colonies, to much of Canada and what is now the American Midwest, Southeast, and Southwest. Along with the English colonies, much of this French and Spanish territory would later become part of the United States. As such, it contributed to the shaping of American society.

3-5.1 France Claims a Continent

After briefly losing Canada to England (1629–1632), France resumed and extended its colonization there. Paralleling the early English and Dutch colonies, a privately held company initially assumed responsibility for settling New France. The Company of New France granted extensive tracts to large landlords, who either imported indentured servants or rented out small tracts to prospective farmers. Although some farmers spread along the St. Lawrence River as far inland as Montreal (see Map 3.8), Canada's harsh winters and short growing season sharply limited their numbers.

More successful in New France were commercial traders who obtained furs from Native Americans. Indeed, the more lucrative opportunities offered by trade diverted many French men who had initially arrived to take up farming. By 1670, one-fifth of male colonists were *voyageurs*, or *coureurs de bois*—independent traders unconstrained by government authority. Living in Indian villages and often marrying native women, the *voyageurs* built an empire for France. From Canadian and Great Lakes Indians, they obtained furs in exchange for European goods, including guns to use against the Iroquois and other rivals. In their commercial interactions, the French and Indians observed Native American norms of reciprocity (see Chapter 1). Their exchanges of goods sealed bonds of friendship and alliance, which served their mutual interests in trade and in war against common enemies.

Catholic religious workers, especially Jesuit missionaries and Ursuline nuns, also helped to shape New France's relations with Native Americans. Given a virtual monopoly on missions to Native Americans in 1633, the Jesuits followed the fur trade into the North American interior. Although the missionaries often feuded with the traders, whose morality they condemned, the two groups together spread French influence westward to the Great Lakes, securing commercial and diplomatic ties with the region's

LAMERE MARIE DE L'INCARNATION
Première Supérieure des Ursulines de la nouvelle
france decedée a Quebec en odeur de Sainteté le
dernier jour d'avril 1672. ageé de 72 ans 6 mois 13 j.s

SISTER MARIE DE L'INCARNATION As Mother Superior of the Ursuline order in New France, Sister Marie oversaw missionary work among female Native Americans and became one of the colony's most powerful women. *(Thomas Fisher Rare Book Library, University of Toronto)*

Indians. The Ursulines ministered particularly to Native American women and girls nearer Quebec, ensuring that Catholic piety and morality reached all members of Indian families. Many Indians resisted Christianity altogether, but even those who embraced the new faith combined it with their own beliefs and practices.

The chief minister of France's King Louis XIV (reigned 1661–1715), Jean-Baptiste Colbert, was a forceful proponent of the doctrine of mercantilism (covered more fully in Chapter 4), which held that colonies should provide their home country with raw materials for manufacturing and markets for manufactured goods. Accordingly, Colbert hoped that New France could increase its output of furs, ship agricultural surpluses to France's new sugar-producing colonies in the West Indies, and export timber to those colonies and for the French navy. To begin realizing these goals, Louis XIV made New France a royal colony in 1663.

With the colony under its direct control, the French government sought to stifle the Iroquois threat to New France's economy. In 1666, France dispatched fifteen hundred soldiers to Canada to take the offensive against the Iroquois. French troops sacked and burned four Mohawk villages that were well stocked with winter food. After the alarmed Iroquois made a peace that lasted until 1680, New France enormously expanded its fur exports.

Meanwhile, Colbert encouraged French immigration to Canada. Within a decade of the royal takeover, the French population rose from twenty-five hundred to eighty-five hundred. Most of the new arrivals were indentured servants who earned wages and received land after three years' work. Others were former soldiers and officers who were given land grants and other incentives to remain in New France and farm while strengthening the colony's defenses. The officers were encouraged to marry among the "king's girls," wealthy female orphans shipped from France with dowries.

The upsurge in French immigration petered out after 1673 as two-thirds of French immigrants returned to their native land. They told tales of disease and other hazards of the transatlantic voyage, of Canada's hard winters, and of wars with the "savage" Iroquois. New France would grow slowly, relying on the natural increase of its small population rather than on newcomers from Europe.

Alarmed by the rapid expansion of England's colonies and fearing that Spain would link Florida with New Mexico, France boldly sought to dominate the North American heartland. In 1672, fur trader Louis Jolliet and Jesuit missionary Jacques Marquette became the first Europeans known to have reached the upper Mississippi River; they later paddled twelve hundred miles downstream to the Mississippi's junction with the Arkansas River. Ten years later, **Robert Cavelier de La Salle**, an upper-class adventurer, descended the entire Mississippi to the Gulf of Mexico. When he reached the delta, La Salle formally claimed the entire Mississippi basin—half of the present-day continental United States—for Louis XIV, for whom he named it Louisiana.

Having asserted title to this vast empire, the French began settling its southern gateway. In 1698, the first colonizers arrived on the Gulf of Mexico coast. A year later,

Robert Cavelier de La Salle
An ambitious upper-class adventurer who descended the entire Mississippi to the Gulf of Mexico. When he reached the delta, he formally claimed the entire Mississippi basin for Louis XIV, in whose honor he named the territory of Louisiana.

the French erected a fort near present-day Biloxi, Mississippi. In 1702, they occupied the former Mississippian city of Mábila, where De Soto's expedition had faltered a century and a half earlier (see Chapter 2), founding a trading post and calling it Mobile. But Louisiana's growth would stall for another decade.

3-5.2 New Mexico: The Pueblo Revolt

Lying at the northerly margin of Spain's vast empire, New Mexico and Florida remained small and weak through the seventeenth century. With few settlers, they needed ties with friendly Native Americans to obtain land, labor, and security. But Spanish policies made friendly relations hard to come by in both places.

From the beginning, the Spanish sought to rule New Mexico by subordinating the Pueblo Indians to their authority in several ways. First, Franciscan missionaries supervised the Indians' spiritual lives by establishing churches in most of the Indian communities (pueblos) and attempting to force the natives to practice Catholicism. Second, Spanish landowners were awarded *encomiendas* (discussed in Chapter 2), which allowed them to exploit Indian labor and productivity for personal profits. Finally, the Spanish drove a wedge between the Pueblo Indians and their nonfarming neighbors, the Apaches and Navajos. Because the Spanish collected corn as tribute, the Pueblo Indians could no longer trade their surplus crops to their neighbors. Having incorporated corn into their diets, the Apaches and Navajos raided the pueblos for the grain. They also raided the colonists because Spanish slave traders were capturing and selling some of their people to work in Mexican silver mines. Several outlying pueblos made common cause with the Apaches, but most Pueblo Indians relied on the Spanish for protection from the raids.

Although local rebellions erupted sporadically, most Pueblo Indians initially accepted Spanish rule and tried to reconcile Catholicism with their own religious traditions. Beginning in the 1660s, however, their crops withered under several consecutive years of sustained drought. Starvation plus deadly epidemic diseases sent the Pueblo population plummeting from about eighty thousand in 1598 to just seventeen thousand in the 1670s. In response, many Christian Indians openly resumed traditional Pueblo ceremonies, hoping to restore the spiritual balance that had brought ample rainfall, good health, and peace before the Spanish arrived. Seeking to suppress this religious revival, Franciscan missionaries entered sacred kivas (underground ceremonial centers), destroyed religious objects, and publicly whipped native religious leaders and their followers.

Matters came to a head in 1675 when Governor Juan Francisco Treviño ordered soldiers to sack the kivas and arrest Pueblo religious leaders. Three leaders were sentenced to the gallows; a fourth hanged himself; and forty-three others were jailed, whipped, and sold as slaves. In response, armed warriors from several pueblos converged on Santa Fe and demanded the prisoners' release. With most of his soldiers off fighting the Apaches, Treviño complied.

Despite Treviño's concession, there was no cooling of Pueblo resentment against the Spanish. Pueblo leaders, both Christian and traditionalist, began gathering secretly to plan the overthrow of Spanish rule. At the head of this effort was Popé, a traditionalist and one of those arrested in 1675.

In August 1680, Popé and his cohorts were ready to act. On the morning of August 10, some Indians from the pueblo of Taos and their Apache allies attacked the homes of the seventy Spanish colonists residing near Taos and killed all but two. Then, with Indians from neighboring pueblos, they proceeded south and joined a massive siege of New Mexico's capital, Santa Fe. Thus began the **Pueblo Revolt** of 1680, the most successful Indian uprising in American history.

At each pueblo, rebels destroyed the churches and religious paraphernalia and killed those missionaries who did not escape. All told, about four hundred colonists were slain. Then the Pueblos "plunge[d] into the rivers and wash[ed] themselves with amole," a native root, to undo their baptisms. As a follower later testified, Popé also called on the Indians "to break and enlarge their cultivated fields,

TAOS PUEBLO, NEW MEXICO Although this photo was taken in 1880, Taos's appearance had changed little during the two centuries since the Pueblo Revolt. *(Palace of the Governors, New Mexico History Museum.)*

saying now they were as they had been in ancient times, free from the labor they had performed for the religious and the Spaniards."

After the siege of Santa Fe, the colonists fled southward to El Paso and beyond as far as Mexico City. Only in 1692 did a new governor, Diego de Vargas, arrive to "reconquer" New Mexico. Exploiting divisions that had emerged among the Pueblos since Popé's recent death, Vargas used violence and threats of violence to reestablish Spanish rule. Even then, Spain did not effectively quash Pueblo resistance until 1700, and thereafter its control of the province was more limited than before. The Spanish needed Pueblo military support against the Apaches, who now attacked them on horses the colonists had left behind when abandoning the colony. To appease the Pueblos, Spanish authorities abolished the hated *encomienda* and ordered the Franciscans to permit the Pueblos to practice their traditional religion.

Pueblos' suspicions of the Spanish lingered after 1700, but they did not again attempt to overthrow them. With the missions and *encomienda* less intrusive, they sustained their cultural identities within, rather than outside, the bounds of colonial rule.

3-5.3 Florida and Texas

The Spanish fared no better in Florida. For most of the seventeenth century, Florida's colonial population numbered only in the hundreds, primarily Spanish soldiers and Franciscan missionaries. Before 1680, the colony faced periodic rebellions from Guale, Timucua, and Apalachee Indians protesting forced labor and Franciscan attempts to impose religious conformity. Thereafter, Creeks and other outside Native Americans added to the Florida Indians' miseries. As the Spanish, with their small numbers of soldiers and arms, looked on helplessly, the invading Indians killed and captured thousands of Florida's natives and sold them to English slave traders in Carolina (as discussed earlier). Even before a new round of warfare erupted in Europe at the turn of the century, Spain was ill-prepared to defend its beleaguered North American colonies.

English expansion threatened Florida, while the French establishment of Louisiana defied Spain's hope of one day linking that colony with New Mexico. To counter the French, Spanish authorities in Mexico proclaimed the province of Texas (Tejas) in 1691. But no permanent Spanish settlements appeared there until 1716 (covered in Chapter 4).

The Whole Vision

■ *What set the Chesapeake apart in its social and economic development from other regions in British colonial America?*

The best way to think about what made any of the early colonies or regions distinct is to start first with the physical environment the settlers encountered and, second, with the types of people who came to settle the region and their motivations for doing so. Other important factors include the role of religion in settlement, whether the economy would be based on subsistence farming or the commercial development of a staple crop, the amount and type of labor needed for its economic development, and finally, the relationship between settlers and native peoples. The physical environment determined the resources available for economic survival and the life expectancy of its settlers, and that in turn would shape the colony's focus and economic and social development. It would also influence ideas about inheritance and gender. The way in which the Chesapeake addressed its labor needs shaped not only the region's racial but also class composition in lasting ways. Next, it is important to consider what type of people arrived first—was it mostly men or family groups, Protestants or Catholics, poor white servants hoping to one day become landowners? The tensions around the availability and means of acquiring land in the Chesapeake would also have lasting consequences.

■ *How unshakable were New England's religious foundations over time?*

Each colonial region of the Americas was settled with its own distinct mission and vision; New England's was in part driven by a spiritual desire to serve as an example of religious purity for the rest of the world, a beacon that its founders called a "city upon a hill." Even if such a utopian model were possible, social change over time within the colony and beyond it (within England) would add pressures that put the Puritan way to the test. Wars abroad and with nearby Indians complicated the picture of simplicity that New Englanders hoped for in important ways, ranging from outright physical destruction to loss of authority to the mother country. Challenges about belief from fellow colonists—male and female—showed the difficulties of orthodoxy and also raised new questions about gender. As the colony grew and people moved further away from the core community, the ability of the Puritan leadership to assert its authority was also challenged. Economic development, too, had an impact on the composition of church membership, and fears about the impact of social change sparked a massive witch hysteria that forever altered the New England Way.

■ *What connections exist between colonial development in the Caribbean and Carolinas and that of the other British colonies?*

Even with their differences, all British colonies had some parallels and overlaps, and at times they interacted commercially. The development of the Caribbean and Carolinas had much to do with the goals of settlement and the timing of the British arrival and investment there. The nature of economic development in the Caribbean and Carolinas and the labor systems they employed would reverberate throughout British colonies with similar staple-based agriculture. Both the Caribbean and Carolinas were plantation societies; they, too, quickly came to see benefits in slave labor over indentured servitude, and notions of race would play an important role in how workers were treated. Their use and misuse of slaves—and the economic benefits they saw in such a system—would not only shape their development but that of slavery in the mainland colonies. As England pushed competitors out of the sugar market, it also gained a foothold in the slave market, which would provide an entrée to trade with mainland colonies for slaves.

KEY TERMS

royal colony (p. 52)

proprietary colony (p. 52)

Lord Baltimore (p. 52)

Act for Religious Toleration (p. 53)

coverture (p. 54)

Third Anglo-Powhatan War (p. 56)

Bacon's Rebellion (p. 56)

John Winthrop (p. 59)

"A Model of Christian Charity" (p. 59)

"New England Way" (p. 60)

Roger Williams (p. 60)

Anne Hutchinson (p. 60)

Restoration (p. 65)

Pequot War (p. 66)

King Philip's War (p. 67)

"beaver wars" (p. 73)

patroons (p. 74)

William Penn (p. 75)

Quakers (p. 75)

Robert Cavelier de la Salle (p. 78)

Pueblo Revolt (p. 79)

■ *What made the Middle Colonies distinctive?*

The Middle Colonies were not founded in quite the same way as New England or the Chesapeake. The region referred to as the Middle Colonies included New York, New Jersey, Pennsylvania, and Delaware. Parts of this region were settled by the Dutch and Swedish initially, part as British royal charters, and Pennsylvania as its own unique British colony under the helm of William Penn. Later, England seized the Dutch and Swedish territories and consolidated the region within the English colonies. But again, the issue of initial settlement and the motivations of settlers such as William Penn would indeed make this region unlike the Chesapeake, New England, or the South. For starters, the role of religion was different, and none of these colonies relied on staple-based agriculture. For another, the settlers were not solely British, and included a vast array of people who engaged in trade with Indians. That trade influenced the kinds of relationships settlers had with native peoples—far different from those of all other regions. Women's roles, too, were much different within Dutch culture than English, a fact that would be reconciled as England assumed complete control of the region.

■ *How did the experiences of Spain and France in the Americas differ from that of Britain?*

The experiences of France and Spain in the Americas varied greatly from that of Britain. While Britain's settlements grew rapidly, the French and Spanish colonies did not attract comparably large numbers of settlers. Their relationships with natives quickly became the hallmark of their colonial experiences, and in this, they competed also with each other. The French focused its colonies to the north, largely Canada, building trade networks with the native people. The Spanish settled further south and southwest—modern-day Florida, Texas, and New Mexico. Both groups attempted to Christianize the Indians. But the success of their efforts at trade or religious conversion would depend greatly on how well they were able to integrate with the Indians they encountered, whether relationships were built on respect and mutuality, or whether violence became the primary instrument of European encounters with native people. Both countries, too, not only competed with each other, but feared England's further encroachment into their territories. This, too, would influence their relationships with native people, seeing them as possible enemies or allies. When treatment was harsh, native people rebelled, often—though not always—with dire consequences.

4 The Bonds of Empire, 1660–1750

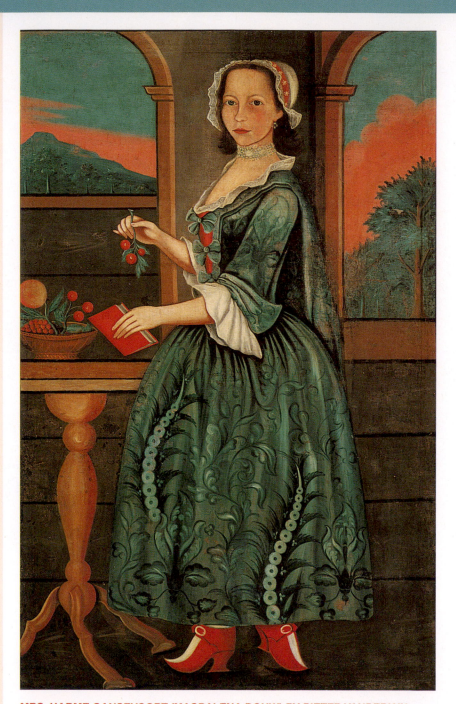

MRS. HARME GANSEVOORT (MAGDALENA BOUW) BY PIETER VANDERLYN, C. 1740 This New York "lady" personified the ideal of gentility that developed in the eighteenth century, as affluent colonists consciously emulated the lifestyles of English elites and indulged in such luxuries as having portraits painted. *(Courtesy, Winterthur Museum, Painting Magdalena Douw by John Heaton, 1737–1740, Hudson Valley, NY, Gift of Henry Francis du Pont, 1963.852 DETAIL)*

1651–1663	England enacts first three Navigation Acts.	1715–1716	Yamasee War in Carolina.
1660	Restoration of the English monarchy.	1716	San Antonio de Béxar founded.
1686–1689	Dominion of New England.	1718	New Orleans founded.
1688–1689	Glorious Revolution in England.	1733	Georgia founded.
1689	English Bill of Rights.	1733	Molasses Act.
1689–1691	Uprisings in Massachusetts, New York, and Maryland.	1735	John Peter Zenger acquitted of seditious libel in New York. Jonathan Edwards leads revival in Northampton, Massachusetts.
1689–1697	King William's War (in Europe, War of the League of Augsburg).	1737	Walking Purchase of Delaware Indian lands in Pennsylvania.
1690	John Locke, *Essay Concerning Human Understanding*.	1739	Great Awakening begins with George Whitefield's arrival in British colonies. Stono Rebellion in South Carolina.
1693	Spain offers freedom to English-owned slaves escaping to Florida.	1740–1748	King George's War (in Europe, War of the Austrian Succession).
1701	Iroquois Grand Settlement with England and France.	1743	Benjamin Franklin founds American Philosophical Society.
1702–1713	Queen Anne's War (in Europe, War of the Spanish Succession).	1750	Slavery legalized in Georgia.
1711–1713	Tuscarora War in Carolina.		

Two men, George Whitefield and Benjamin Franklin, exemplified the major cultural currents that swept across the Atlantic from Europe to the colonies in the mid-eighteenth century. The embodiment of the powerful revival of piety that reinvigorated Protestantism on both sides of the Atlantic, Whitefield also demonstrated and reinforced the close ties that bound England and the colonies. Franklin, considered the leading American scientist of his time, personified the faith in reason known as the **Enlightenment**.

Whitefield, an Englishman in America, and Franklin, a colonist who traveled frequently to England, also signaled the close ties that increasingly bound Britain and America. Beginning in the late seventeenth century, England tightened the political and economic bonds linking the colonies' fortunes with its own. Coupled with the astonishing growth of its population, enslaved as well as free, the new imperial relationship enabled the British colonies by 1750 to achieve a level of growth and collective prosperity unknown elsewhere in the Americas.

GEORGE WHITEFIELD *(Granger, NYC)*

> **Enlightenment**
> A European ideological movement beginning in the seventeenth and eighteenth century that stressed reason and scientific inquiry, as well as individualism.

4-1 England's Wars and Colonial Reverberations, 1660–1713

How did periods of upheaval and conflict in England affect its relationship with its American colonies?

The Restoration (1660) of the monarchy did not resolve England's deep-seated political antagonisms. Charles II and James II (ruled 1685–1688) attempted to strengthen the crown at Parliament's expense and to centralize royal authority in the colonies. After

England overthrew James and replaced him with his daughter, Mary, and her husband, William, in 1689, Massachusetts, New York, and Maryland carried out their own revolts. Thereafter, both royal authority and representative legislatures became stronger in the colonies.

The overthrow of James, a pro-French Catholic, led directly to a period of warfare between England and France. By the time peace was restored in 1713, the colonists had become closely tied to a new, powerful British empire.

4-1.1 Royal Centralization, 1660–1688

The Restoration monarchs had little use for representative government. Charles II rarely called Parliament into session. James II, Charles's younger brother, hoped to reign as an "absolute" monarch like France's Louis XIV, who never faced an elected legislature. Not surprisingly, the two English kings had little sympathy for American colonial assemblies. Royal intentions of extending direct political control to North America first became evident in New York. The proprietor, the future James II, considered elected legislatures "of dangerous consequence" and forbade New York's assembly (lower legislative chamber) to meet, except briefly between 1682 and 1686.

Puritan-led Massachusetts proved most persistent in defending self-government and resisting English authority. Puritans refused to grant any religious freedom to non-Puritans, and they implemented other laws that defied English practices. The crown insisted that Massachusetts base voting rights on property ownership rather than church membership, that it tolerate Anglicans and Quakers (which Puritans had resisted), and that it observe the Navigation Acts (discussed later in this chapter). As early as 1661, the General Court (legislature) defiantly declared Massachusetts exempt from all parliamentary laws and royal decrees except declarations of war. Charles II moved to break the Puritan establishment's power. There was also concern that massive smuggling occurred in New England. In 1679, he carved a new royal colony, New Hampshire, out of its territory. Then, in 1684, he declared Massachusetts a royal colony and revoked its charter, the very foundation of the Puritan city upon a hill.

Royal centralization accelerated after James II succeeded Charles. In 1686, the new king consolidated Massachusetts, New Hampshire, Connecticut, Rhode Island, and Plymouth into a single administrative unit, the **Dominion of New England**, with its capital at Boston. He added New York and the Jerseys to the dominion in 1688, and the charters of all these colonies were revoked. With these bold strokes, the legislatures in these colonies were eliminated, and a single governor, Sir Edmund Andros, headed the new supercolony with substantial power. Andros needed only the approval of an appointed council to impose taxes or implement new laws.

Massachusetts burned with hatred for the dominion and its governor. Many historians point to the colonists' response to the Dominion of New England as the first real colonial rebellion in British North America (see further discussion of rebellions below). By "Exercise of an arbitrary Government," preached Salem's minister, "ye wicked walked on Every Side & ye Vilest of men ware [sic] exalted." Andros was indeed arbitrary. He limited towns to a single annual meeting and strictly enforced religious toleration. Tensions also ran high in New York, where Catholics held prominent political and military posts under James. By 1688, colonists feared these Catholic officials would betray New York to France, England's chief imperial rival. When Andros's local deputy allowed the harbor's forts to deteriorate and downplayed rumors that Native Americans would attack, New Yorkers suspected the worst.

4-1.2 The Glorious Revolution, 1688–1689

Not only colonists but also most people in England were alarmed by the direction in which the monarchy was taking the nation. Charles II and James II ignored Parliament, issued decrees allowing Catholics to hold high office and worship openly, and expressed their friendship with France's King Louis XIV, just as Louis was persecuting Protestant Huguenots.

The English initially tolerated James's Catholicism because his daughters, Mary and Anne, remained Anglican. But in 1688, James's wife bore a son who would be raised a Catholic and, as a male, precede his sisters to the throne. Aghast at the thought of another Catholic monarch, England's leading political and religious figures invited Mary and her husband, Prince William of Orange (head of state in the Protestant Netherlands), to intervene. When William led a small Dutch army to England in

> **Dominion of New England**
> Made up of Massachusetts, New Hampshire, Connecticut, Rhode Island, and Plymouth.

November 1688, most royal troops defected to them, and James II fled to France.

This revolution of 1688, called the **Glorious Revolution**, created a "limited monarchy" as defined by the **English Bill of Rights** (1689). The crown was required to summon Parliament annually, sign all its bills, and respect traditional civil liberties. This circumscribing of monarchial power and vindication of representative government burned deeply into the English political consciousness, and Anglo-Americans never forgot it. Many decades later, authors of the American Declaration of Independence in 1776 would be influenced by this parliamentary document.

News that James II had fled England electrified New Englanders. Protestantism had prevailed. On April 18, 1689, well before confirmation of the revolt's success, Boston's militia arrested Andros and his councilors. (The governor tried to flee in women's clothing but was caught after an alert guard spotted a "lady" in army boots.) Massachusetts political leaders acted in the name of William and Mary, risking their necks should James return to power in England.

Although William, now King William III, dismantled the Dominion of New England and permitted Connecticut and Rhode Island to resume electing their own governors, he and Mary shared James's belief in the need to more tightly control the colonies. William reined in Massachusetts' independent leanings. He issued a new charter for the colony in 1691, stipulating that the crown would continue to choose the governor. In addition, property ownership, not church membership, became the criterion for voting. Finally, the new charter required Massachusetts to tolerate all Protestants. While Plymouth and Maine remained within Massachusetts, New Hampshire became a separate royal colony. For Puritans already demoralized by the demise of the "New England Way," this was indeed bitter medicine.

The Glorious Revolution sparked revolts across the colonies, such as **Leisler's Rebellion** in New York. Emboldened by news of Boston's coup, the city's militia—consisting mainly of Dutch and other non-English artisans and shopkeepers—seized the harbor's main fort on May 31, 1689. Militia Captain Jacob Leisler took command of the colony, repaired its rundown defenses, and called elections for an assembly. When English troops arrived at New York in 1691, Leisler, fearing (wrongly) that their commander was loyal to James II, denied them entry to key forts. A skirmish resulted, and Leisler was arrested.

"Hott brain'd" Leisler had jailed many elite New Yorkers for questioning his authority, but now his enemies persuaded the new governor to charge Leisler with treason for firing on royal troops. In the face of popular outrage, a packed jury found Leisler and his son-in-law, Jacob Milborne, guilty. Both men went to the gallows insisting that they were dying "for the king and queen and the Protestant religion."

News of England's Glorious Revolution heartened Maryland's Protestant majority, which continued to resent Catholic rule. Hoping to prevent a religious uprising, Lord Baltimore sent a messenger from England in early 1689, ordering colonists to obey William and Mary. But the courier died en route, leaving Maryland's Protestants fearful that their Catholic proprietor still supported James II.

Acting on this fear, John Coode and three others organized the **Protestant Association** to secure Maryland for William and Mary. Coode's group seized the capital in July 1689, removed all Catholics from office, and requested a royal governor. They got their wish in 1691, and the Church of England became the established religion in 1692. Catholics, who composed less than one-fourth of the population, lost the right to vote and thereafter could worship only in private. Maryland stayed in royal hands until 1715, when the fourth Lord Baltimore regained his proprietorship after joining the Church of England.

The revolutionary events of 1688–1689 changed the colonies' political climate by reestablishing representative government while strengthening English authority. The success of the Glorious Revolution also ensured religious freedom for Protestants. Dismantling the Dominion of New England and directing governors to call annual assemblies, William encouraged colonial elites to return to politics. By encouraging the assemblies to work with royal and proprietary governors, he expected elites to identify their interests with those of England. A foundation was thus laid for an empire based on voluntary allegiance rather than submission to raw power imposed from faraway London. The crowning of William and Mary opened a new era in which Americans drew rising confidence from their relationship to the English throne. "As long as they reign," wrote

Glorious Revolution
Revolution of 1688 that resulted in the overthrow of James II by William of Orange.

English Bill of Rights
Under its terms, the crown was required to summon Parliament annually, sign all its bills, and respect traditional civil liberties.

Leisler's Rebellion
Led by Captain Jacob Leisler, it was an uprising in New York in 1689 against the British.

Protestant Association
Association formed by John Coode and three others to secure Maryland for William and Mary.

a Bostonian who helped topple Andros, "New England is secure."

4-1.3 A Generation of War, 1689–1713

The Glorious Revolution ushered in a quarter-century of warfare, convulsing both Europe and North America. In 1689, the War of the League of Augsburg between England and France, which Anglo-Americans called **King William's War**, would be the first of several European wars that would be fought partly on North American soil.

When King William's War began in Europe, New Yorkers and New Englanders launched an invasion of New France in 1690, targeting Montreal and Quebec. Failing, the war devolved into cruel border raids against civilians carried out by both English and French troops and their Indian allies.

Having fought pro-French Indians since 1680, the Five Nations Iroquois Confederacy bore the bloodiest fighting. While their English allies failed to offer adequate support, the Iroquois faced the French as well as virtually all Indians from Maine to the Great Lakes. Although King William's War ended in 1697, the Five Nations staggered until 1700 under additional invasions by pro-French Indians. The total Iroquois population declined 20 percent over twelve years, from eighty-six hundred to fewer than seven thousand. (By comparison, the

war cost about thirteen hundred English, Dutch, and French lives.)

By 1700, the Confederacy was divided into pro-English, pro-French, and neutralist factions. The neutralists set the tone, however, for Iroquois diplomacy. In two separate treaties, together called the **Grand Settlement of 1701**, the Five Nations made peace with France and its Indian allies in exchange for access to western furs, and redefined their alliance with Britain to exclude military cooperation. Skillful negotiations allowed the Iroquois to keep control of their lands, expand trade, rebuild their decimated population, and avoid more losses in Europe's destructive wars.

In 1702, European war again erupted when England fought France and Spain in the War of the Spanish Succession, called **Queen Anne's War** by England's American colonists. With the Iroquois Confederacy remaining neutral, French and Indian forces from Canada raided Massachusetts and Maine, destroying settlements and seizing captives. Spanish forces invaded Carolina and nearly took Charles Town in 1706, while Anglo-American sieges of Quebec and St. Augustine ended as expensive failures. England's forces seized Hudson Bay and Acadia (renamed Nova Scotia) from France.

The most important consequence of the imperial wars for Anglo-Americans was that they reinforced colonists' allegiance to post-1689 England as a bastion of Protestantism and political liberty. Recognizing their own military weakness and the extent to which the Royal Navy had protected their shipping, colonists acknowledged their dependence on the newly formed United Kingdom of Great Britain (created by the formal union of England and Scotland in 1707). As a new generation of English colonists matured, war buttressed their loyalty to Great Britain and the crown.

4-2 Colonial Economies and Societies, 1660–1750

What marked the economic growth of the American colonies from 1660 to 1750?

For a generation after achieving peace in 1713, Britain, France, and Spain competed economically rather than militarily. During the late seventeenth century, England and France had developed maritime empires that successfully seized control of Atlantic commerce from the Dutch. Thereafter,

THE GRAND SETTLEMENT OF 1701 Artist's rendition of the treaty conference that ended Iroquois hostilities with New France and forty groups of pro-French Native Americans. *(Francis Back)*

all three powers hoped to expand their American colonies and integrate them into single, imperial economies. Spain and France gained territory but realized few benefits from their mainland colonies north of Mexico. Meanwhile, Britain and its American colonies thrived. By 1739, tensions in Europe brought a return to war that spread to North America.

4-2.1 England's Mercantilist Empires in America

The imperial practices of Britain, France, and Spain were rooted in a set of political-economic assumptions known as **mercantilism**, and it would make England one of the wealthiest nations in the world. Mercantilist theory held that each nation's power was measured by its wealth, especially in gold. To secure wealth, a country needed to maximize its sale of goods abroad while minimizing foreign purchases and use of foreign shippers. In pursuit of this goal, mercantilist nations—especially France and England—sought to produce everything they needed without relying on other nations, while obliging other nations to buy from them. Although the home country would do most manufacturing, colonies would supply vital raw materials. If needed, a country would go to war to gain raw materials or markets, or to prevent a rival from doing the same.

Britain's mercantilist policies were articulated in a series of **Navigation Acts** governing imperial commerce. Parliament enacted the first Navigation Act in 1651, requiring that trade be carried on in English, including colonial-owned, vessels to replace Dutch shippers with English. After the Restoration, Parliament enacted the Navigation Act of 1660, requiring that certain "enumerated" commodities (discussed shortly) be exported via England or Scotland and barring imports from arriving in non-English ships. The Navigation Act of 1663 stipulated that imports to the colonies arrive via England rather than directly from another country. Later, the Molasses Act (1733) taxed, at sixpence per gallon, all foreign molasses (produced from sugar cane and imported primarily for distilling rum) entering the mainland colonies. This act was intended less to raise revenue than to serve as a tariff that would protect British West Indian sugar producers at the expense of French rivals.

The Navigation Acts affected the English colonial economy in four major ways. First, they limited all imperial trade to English-owned ships whose crews were at least three-quarters English. This restriction benefited the colonies as well as England because it classified all colonists, including slaves, as English. As a result, the acts not only contributed to Britain's

rise as Europe's foremost shipping nation but also laid the foundations of an American shipbuilding industry and merchant marine. By the 1750s, one-third of all "English" or "British" vessels were owned by Anglo-American merchants. The swift growth of this merchant marine diversified the northern colonial economy and made it more commercial. The expansion of colonial shipping also hastened urbanization by creating a need for centralized docks, warehouses, and repair shops in the colonies. By midcentury Philadelphia, New York City, Boston, and Charles Town had emerged as important transatlantic ports.

The second effect of the Navigation Acts on the colonies lay in their stipulating that "enumerated" exports pass through England or Scotland. The colonies' major "enumerated" exports were sugar (by far the most profitable commodity), tobacco, rice, furs, indigo (a Carolina plant that produced a blue dye for cloth), and naval stores (masts, hemp, tar, and turpentine). Parliament never restricted grain, livestock, fish, lumber, or rum, which together made up 60 percent of mainland colonial exports. Parliament further reduced the burdens on exporters of tobacco and rice—the chief mainland commodities affected—with two significant concessions. First, it gave tobacco growers a monopoly over the British market by excluding foreign tobacco, even though this hurt British consumers. (Rice planters enjoyed a natural monopoly because they had no foreign competitors.) Second, it minimized the added cost of landing tobacco and rice in Britain by refunding customs duties when those products were later shipped to other countries. With about 85 percent of all American tobacco and rice eventually sold outside the British Empire, the acts reduced planters' profits by less than 3 percent.

The navigation system's third effect on the colonies was to encourage economic diversification. Parliament used British tax revenues to pay modest bounties to Anglo-Americans producing such items as silk, iron, dyes, hemp, and lumber, and it imposed protective tariffs on imports of these products from other countries. The laws did prohibit Anglo-Americans from competing with British manufacturing of certain products, most notably clothing. However, colonial tailors, hatters, and housewives could continue to make any item of dress in their households or small shops. Manufactured by low-paid labor, British clothing imports generally undersold whatever the colonists could have

mercantilism
The theory that holds that each nation's power was measured by its wealth, especially in gold. To secure wealth, a country needed to maximize its sale of goods abroad in exchange for gold while minimizing foreign purchases paid for gold.

Navigation Acts
A series of laws that governed commerce between England and its colonies.

exported. The colonists were also free to produce iron, and by 1770 they had built two hundred and fifty ironworks employing thirty thousand men, a workforce larger than the entire population of Georgia or of any provincial city.

Finally, the Navigation Acts made the colonies a protected market for low-priced exports from Britain. Steady demand for colonial products in the British Isles and the European continent spawned a prosperity that enabled white colonists to purchase ever larger amounts not only of clothing but also of dishware, furniture, tea, and a range of other imports from British and other overseas sources. Retail shops sprang up in cities and rural crossroads throughout the colonies, while itinerant peddlers took imported wares into more remote areas of the countryside. One such peddler arrived in Berwick, Maine, in 1721 and sold several kinds of cloth, a "pair of garters," and various "small trifles" before local authorities confiscated his goods because he lacked a license. Other traders traveled to Native American communities to exchange cloth and other commodities for furs. As a result of colonial consumption, the share of British exports bound for North America spurted from just 5 percent in 1700 to almost 40 percent by 1760. Mercantilism had given rise to a "consumer revolution" in British America while helping to make Britain itself the wealthiest nation in Europe and the Atlantic world.

4-2.2 Mercantilism in the Hands of France and Spain

The economic development of the French and Spanish colonies in North America paled beside that of the British. Although the French government had difficulty implementing mercantilist policies, New France did become agriculturally self-sufficient and exported some wheat to the French West Indies. It also exported small amounts of fish and timber to the Caribbean and to France. Although European demand for Canada's chief export—furs—had flattened, the French government expanded the fur trade, even losing money, to retain Native Americans as military allies against Britain. Moreover, France maintained a sizable army in Canada that also drained the royal treasury. French Canadians enjoyed a comfortable if modest standard of living but lacked the private investment, extensive commercial infrastructure, vast consumer market, and manufacturing capacity of their British neighbors.

France's wealthiest colonies were in the West Indies, where French planters, following the example

BALTIMORE IRONWORKS Whereas free laborers and indentured servants did most manufacturing work in the colonies, about half the workers at this furnace (established in 1733) were enslaved Africans. *(Catoctin Furnace DTA_0006 © C. Kurt Holter)*

of their English neighbors, imported large numbers of enslaved Africans to produce sugar under appalling conditions. French sugar planters' success was partly a result of their defying mercantilist policies. In St. Domingue, Martinique, and Guadeloupe, many planters built their own sugar refineries and made molasses instead of shipping their raw sugar to refineries in France, as French regulations prescribed. They sold much of their molasses to merchants in Britain's mainland colonies, especially Massachusetts, which similarly ignored British mercantilist laws.

Although Spain had squandered the wealth from gold and silver extracted by the conquistadors and early colonists (see Chapter 2), its economy and that of Latin America revived during the eighteenth century. However, that revival did not extend to the northern borderlands of New Mexico, Texas, and Florida, where colonists conducted little overseas commerce.

Britain's colonies differed fundamentally from those of France and Spain in their respective economies and societies. While mercantilist principles governed all three nations, the monarchy, the nobility, and the Catholic Church controlled most wealth in France and Spain. Most private wealth was inherited and took the form of land. England, on the other hand, had become a mercantile-commercial economy, and a significant portion of its wealth was in the form of capital held by merchants who reinvested it in commercial and shipping enterprises. Moreover, the British government used much of its considerable income from duties, tariffs, and other taxes to enhance commerce. For example, the government strengthened Britain's powerful navy to protect the empire's trade and created the Bank of England in 1694 to ensure a stable money supply and lay the foundation for a network of lending institutions. These benefits extended not only to Britain but also to colonists. Indeed the colonies' per capita income rose 0.6 percent annually from 1650 to 1770, a pace twice that of Britain.

4-2.3 Population Growth and Diversity

Britain's economic advantage over its rivals in North America was reinforced by its sharp demographic edge. In 1700, approximately 250,000 Europeans and Africans resided in England's colonies, compared to only 15,000 in French territory and 4,500 in Spain's possessions. During the first half of the eighteenth century, all three colonial populations at least quadrupled in size—the British to 1,170,000, the French to 60,000, and the Spanish to 19,000—but these increases only magnified Britain's advantage.

Spanish emigrants could choose from among that nation's many Latin American colonies, most of which offered more opportunities than remote, poorly developed Florida, Texas, and New Mexico. Reports of Canada's harsh winters and Louisiana's poor economy deterred most potential French colonists. France and Spain attracted few immigrants to North America from outside their own empires. And both limited immigration to Roman Catholics, a restriction that diverted French Huguenots to the English colonies. Meanwhile, England's colonies boasted good farmlands, healthy economies, and a willingness to absorb Europeans of most Protestant denominations. While anti-Catholicism remained strong, small Jewish communities formed in several Anglo-American cities.

Spain regarded its northernmost colonies less as centers of population than as buffers to shield their more valued colonies to the south from Indian raids and from French and English encroachments. While hoping to lure civilian settlers, the Spanish relied heavily on soldiers stationed in *presidios* (forts) for defense plus missionaries who attempted to attract Native Americans to strategically placed missions. Most colonists in Spanish North America did not come directly from Spain but from Mexico and other Spanish colonies.

Although boasting more people than the Spanish colonies, New France and Louisiana were also limited. The military played a strong role in Canada, while missionaries and traders enhanced the colony's relations with Native Americans. New France's population growth in the eighteenth century resulted largely from natural increase rather than immigration. Some rural Canadians established new settlements along the Mississippi River in what are now Illinois and Missouri. To boost Louisiana's population, the government sent paupers and criminals, recruited some German Catholic refugees, and encouraged large-scale slave imports. By 1732, two-thirds of Louisiana's 5,800 people were black and enslaved.

The British colonies outpaced the population growth of not only their French and Spanish rivals but of Britain itself. White women in the colonies had an average of eight children and forty-two grandchildren, compared to five children and fifteen grandchildren for British women. The ratio of England's population to that of the mainland colonies plummeted from 20 to 1 in 1700 to 3 to 1 in 1775.

4-2.4 New Immigrants—Free and Unfree—to the British Colonies

Although contributing less to eighteenth-century population growth than natural increase, immigration remained important. In the forty years after

Queen Anne's War, the British colonies absorbed 350,000 newcomers, approximately 210,000 of whom were non-English Europeans (see Figure 4.1). Rising employment and higher wages in England made voluntary immigration to America less attractive than before. But economic hardship elsewhere in the British Isles and northern Europe supplied a steady stream of immigrants, who contributed to greater ethnic diversity among white North Americans.

One of the largest contingents was made up of 100,000 newcomers from Ireland, two-thirds of them "Scots-Irish" descendants of Scottish Presbyterians who had first sought economic opportunity in northern Ireland. After 1718, Scots-Irish fled to America to escape rack renting (frequent sharp increases in farm rents), usually moving as complete families.

Meanwhile, from German-speaking regions in central Europe came 125,000 settlers, most of them fleeing wartime devastation and severe land shortages in the Rhine Valley. One-third of German immigrants financed their voyage by indenturing themselves or their children as servants. Most Germans were either Lutherans or Calvinists, but some belonged to small, pacifist religious sects that desired above all to be left alone.

Overwhelmingly, eighteenth-century white immigrants were poor. Those who were indentured servants worked from one to four years for an urban or rural master. Servants could be sold or rented out, beaten, granted minimal legal protection, kept from marrying, and sexually harassed. Attempted escape usually meant an extension of their service. But at the end of their terms, most managed to collect "freedom dues," which could help them marry and acquire land.

Few white immigrants settled in crowded New England or in the southern tidewater, where land was most scarce and expensive. Philadelphia became immigrants' primary port of entry. Building on the ethnic diversity that characterized its founding (see Chapter 3), Pennsylvania absorbed so many non-English that by 1755 the English accounted for only one-third of that colony's population. Most of the newcomers arrived from northern Ireland and Germany; they settled in central and western Pennsylvania or moved on to the Piedmont region, stretching along the eastern slope of the Appalachians from New York to Carolina. A significant German community developed in upper New York, and thousands of other Germans as well as Scots-Irish fanned southward from Pennsylvania. Others from Germany and Ireland arrived in the second-most popular American gateway, Charles Town. They too moved on to the Carolina Piedmont and raised grain, livestock, and tobacco, generally without slaves. After 1750, both streams of immigration merged with an outpouring of Anglo-Americans from the Chesapeake in the rolling, fertile hills of western Virginia and North Carolina. In 1713, few colonists lived more than fifty miles from the sea, but by 1750 one-third of all colonists resided in the Piedmont (see Map 4.1).

The least-free white immigrants were English convict laborers. Between 1718 and 1775, about fifty thousand condemned prisoners arrived, mostly in the Chesapeake colonies. A few of the convicts were murderers; most were guilty of more trivial offenses, like a young Londoner who "got intoxicated with liquor, and in that condition attempted to snatch a handkerchief from the body of a person in the street to him unknown." (English law authorized the death penalty for 160 offenses, including what today would be considered petty theft.) Convicts were sold

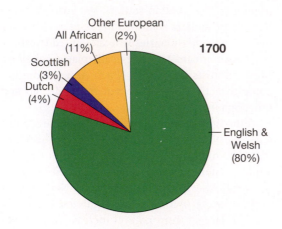

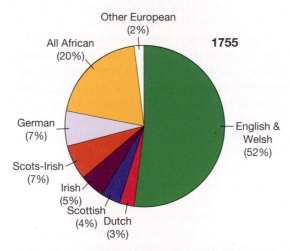

FIGURE 4.1 DISTRIBUTION OF EUROPEANS AND AFRICANS WITHIN THE BRITISH MAINLAND COLONIES, 1700–1755 Immigration from Germany and Ireland, plus the transatlantic slave trade, transformed the ethnic makeup of the colonial population.

Source: Thomas L. Purvis, "The European Ancestry of the United States Population," William & Mary Quarterly, LXI (1984): 85–101.

as servants on arrival. Relatively few committed crimes in America, and most returned to England upon completing their terms.

Many English-descended colonists resented the influx of so many people different from themselves. "These confounded Irish will eat us all up," snorted one Bostonian. Benjamin Franklin spoke for many when he asked, "Why should Pennsylvania, founded by the English, become a colony of aliens, who will shortly be so numerous as to Germanize us instead of us Anglicizing them, and will never adopt our language or customs any more than they can acquire our complexion?"

In the same ungenerous spirit, Franklin (himself a slaveholder) objected to the slave trade not because it was inhumane but because it would increase America's black population at the expense of industrious whites, and suggested that the colonists send rattlesnakes to Britain in return for its convict laborers.

About 40 percent (140,000) of newcomers to the British mainland colonies were African-born slaves who arrived as cargo. All but a few slave ships departed from West African ports with captives from dozens of West and Central African ethnic groups (see Map 4.2). Most planters deliberately mixed slaves who came from various regions and spoke different languages to minimize the potential for collective rebellion.

Conditions aboard slave ships during the **Middle Passage**, from Africa to America, were appalling by any standard. Africans were crammed into tight quarters with inadequate sanitary facilities. Men were chained together two by two and kept below, except for brief bits of exercise on the decks above. Perceived as far less threatening, slave women and children were allowed to move about and work cleaning or cooking meals. Women were also at risk for sexual exploitation by crew members. Up to 20 percent of slaves in the Middle Passage died of diseases before ever reaching the Americas, and many others perished in the weeks after arrival. Crew members also died from illnesses caught during the journey. A Guinea-born slave, later named Venture Smith, was one of 260 who were on a voyage in 1735. But "smallpox . . . broke out on board," Smith recalled, and "when we reached [Barbados], there were found . . . not more than two hundred alive."

Slaves sometimes resisted by refusing to eat, staging or joining rebellions, or hurling themselves into the sea in a last desperate act of defiance against those who would profit from their misery. Those who defied shipboard authority were flogged and, in extreme cases, thrown overboard. So many sick, dead, and condemned Africans were tossed overboard that sharks routinely followed slave ships,

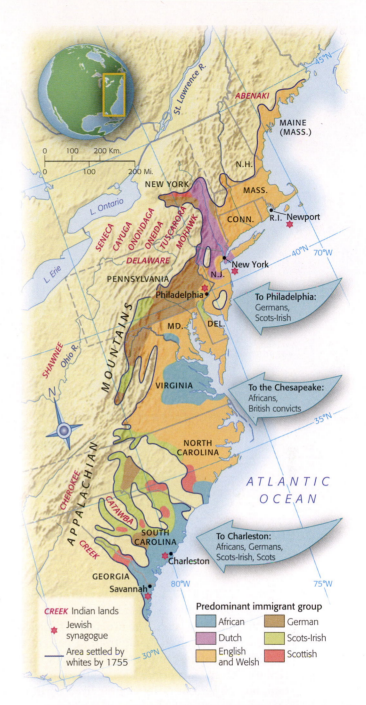

MAP 4.1 **IMMIGRATION AND BRITISH COLONIAL EXPANSION TO 1755** Black majorities emerged in much of the Chesapeake tidewater and the Carolina-Georgia low country. Immigrants from Germany, Ireland, and Scotland predominated among settlers in the Piedmont. A significant Jewish population emerged in the seaports.

awaiting their next meals. Slave rebellions, large and small, erupted on about one in ten slave voyages. The rebellions forced shippers to hire full-time guards and install barricades to confine slaves. Shippers then passed the cost on to American buyers.

Middle Passage
The journey in which millions of slaves were transported from Africa to the Americas, packed into cramped, unsanitary quarters in the dungeons of ships for weeks at a time. Estimates are that up to 20 percent of the human cargo died on board.

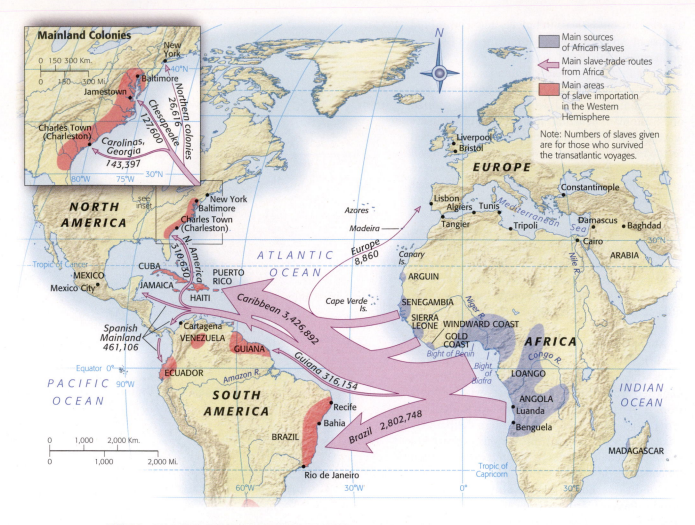

Mainland Colonies

0 150 300 Km.
0 150 300 Mi.

New York
40°N
Baltimore
Jamestown

Northern colonies
26,616

Chesapeake
127,600

Charles Town
(Charleston)

Carolinas,
Georgia
143,397

80°W   75°W   30°N

Main sources
of African slaves

Main slave-trade routes
from Africa

Main areas
of slave importation
in the Western
Hemisphere

Note: Numbers of slaves given
are for those who survived
the transatlantic voyages.

NORTH
AMERICA

New York
Baltimore
Charles Town
(Charleston)

see
inset

CUBA
JAMAICA
HAITI
PUERTO
RICO

MEXICO
Mexico City

N. America
310,630

Spanish
Mainland
461,106

Cartagena
VENEZUELA

GUIANA

ECUADOR

Equator 0°
90°W

PACIFIC
OCEAN

Tropic of Cancer

SOUTH
AMERICA

Amazon R.

Recife
Bahia
BRAZIL

Rio de Janeiro

Caribbean 3,426,892

Guiana 316,154

Brazil 2,802,748

ATLANTIC
OCEAN

Europe
8,860

Azores
Madeira
Canary
Is.
Cape Verde
Is.

EUROPE

Liverpool
Bristol

Lisbon
Algiers Tunis
Tangier
Tripoli

Mediterranean
Sea

Constantinople

Damascus
Cairo
Baghdad

ARABIA

30°N

ARGUIN
SENEGAMBIA
SIERRA
LEONE
WINDWARD COAST
GOLD
COAST
Bight of Benin

AFRICA

Niger R.

Bight
of
Biafra

LOANGO

Congo R.

ANGOLA
Luanda
Benguela

INDIAN
OCEAN

MADAGASCAR

Tropic of
Capricorn

60°W   30°W   0°   30°E

N

0 1,000 2,000 Km.
0 1,000 2,000 Mi.

MAP 4.2   **MAIN SOURCES OF AFRICAN SLAVES,** CA. 1500–1800 The vast majority of enslaved Africans were taken to plantation colonies between Chesapeake Bay and the Brazilian coast.

From 1713 to 1754, five times as many enslaved Africans poured onto mainland North America as in all the preceding years. The proportion of blacks in the colonies doubled, rising from 11 percent at the beginning of the century to 20 percent by mid-century. Slavery was primarily a southern institution, but 15 percent of its victims lived north of Maryland, mostly in New York and New Jersey.

Because slaves were far cheaper in Brazil and the West Indies than farther north, only 5 percent of enslaved Africans arrived in the present-day United States. To economize, rice and tobacco planters purchased African women and protected their investments by minimally maintaining slaves' health, which increased life expectancy far beyond the Caribbean's low levels (see Chapter 3). Masters also encouraged female slaves to mate by pairing them with male slaves, often coercively and forcibly, with the express goal of producing more slaves. This did in some ways lead to family formation and population growth. By 1750, the rate of natural increase for mainland blacks almost equaled that for whites.

4-2.5 Rural White Men and Women

Although most whites benefited from rising living standards in the British colonies, they enjoyed these advantages unevenly. Except for Benjamin Franklin and a few others, most wealthy colonists inherited their fortunes. For the vast majority of whites, most of them rural, personal success was limited and came through hard work, if at all.

Because most farm families owned just enough acreage for a working farm, they could not provide all their children with land of their own when they married. A young male typically worked from about age sixteen to twenty-three as a field hand for his father or neighbors. After marrying, he often supported his growing family by renting a farm until his early or mid-thirties. In some areas, especially the oldest colonized areas of New England, the continued high birthrates of rural families combined with a shortage of productive land to close off farming opportunities altogether. As a result, growing numbers of young men turned elsewhere to make their livings—the frontier, the port cities, or the high seas.

Families who did acquire land worked off mortgages slowly because the long-term cash income from a farm (6 percent) about equaled the interest on borrowed money (5 to 8 percent). Only by their late fifties, just as their youngest offspring got ready to leave home, did most colonial parents free themselves of debt.

Remote or poor rural families depended heavily on wives' and daughters' making items that more affluent families could purchase. Besides cooking, cleaning, and washing, wives preserved food, boiled soap, made clothing, and tended the garden, dairy, orchard, poultry house, and pigsty. They also sold dairy products to neighbors or merchants, spun yarn into cloth for tailors, knitted garments for sale, and even sold their own hair for wigs.

Legally, however, white women in the British colonies were constrained (see Chapter 3). A woman's single most autonomous decision was her choice of a husband. Once married, she lost control of her dowry, unless she was a New Yorker subject to Dutch custom, which allowed her somewhat more authority, but only until Dutch laws were replaced by English ones. Women in the French and Spanish colonies retained ownership of, and often augmented, the property they brought to a marriage. Widows did

control between 8 and 10 percent of all property in eighteenth-century Anglo-America, and a few—such as Eliza Pinckney of South Carolina—owned and managed large and profitable estates (her father's and later her deceased husband's) and introduced the cultivation of indigo to the British colonies.

4-2.6 Colonial Farmers and the Environment

The rapid expansion of Britain's colonies hastened environmental change east of the Appalachians. Despite the labor involved in removing trees, eighteenth-century settlers, especially those using slave labor, preferred to establish farms on heavily forested areas where the soil was most fertile. New England farmers also had to clear innumerable heavy rocks, with which they built walls around their fields. Colonists everywhere used timber for buildings and as fuel for heating and cooking. Farmers and planters also sold firewood to the inhabitants of cities and towns.

Removing the trees drove away forest animals while attracting grass- and seed-eating rabbits, mice, and possums. Fewer trees meant less protection from winds and the sun as well as warmer summers and colder winters, further increasing colonists' demand for firewood. In turn, less stable temperatures and water levels, along with impediments created by mills

PREPARING A SLAVE VOYAGE Africans weep as relatives or friends are taken to a slave vessel. *(The Granger Collection, NYC)*

A NEW ENGLAND WOMAN'S CUPBOARD Modest prosperity enabled some married women to exercise power as consumers and even to express their individuality. Hannah Barnard, a Hadley, Massachusetts, farm woman, commissioned this cupboard for storing linens and other fine textiles, in about 1720. *(From the Collections of The Henry Ford)*

and by floating timber downstream, rapidly reduced the fish in colonial waters. Writing in 1766, naturalist John Bartram noted that fish "abounded formerly when the Indians lived much on them & was very numerous," but that "now there is not the 100th or perhaps the 1000th [portion of] fish to be found."

Native Americans, recognizing the soil-depleting effects of intensive cultivation, rotated their crops, letting fields lie fallow (unplanted) for several years while vital nutrients replenished the soil. But most colonial farmers did not have enough land to leave some unplanted.

As early as 1637, one New England farmer discovered that his soil "after five or six years [of planting corn] grows barren beyond belief and puts on the face of winter in the time of summer." Chesapeake planters' tobacco yields declined after only three or four years in the same plot. Like farmers elsewhere, they used animal manure to fertilize their food crops but not their tobacco, fearing that manure would spoil the taste for consumers.

Confronting a shortage of land and resources, Europe's well-to-do farmers were already turning their attention to conservation and "scientific" farming. But most colonists ignored such techniques, either because they could not afford to implement them or because they believed that American land, including that still held by Native Americans, would sustain them indefinitely.

4-2.7 The Urban Paradox

The cities were British North America's economic paradox. As major ports of entry and exit, they were keys to the colonies' rising prosperity; yet they held only 4 percent of the colonies' population, and a growing percentage of city-dwellers were caught in a downward spiral of declining opportunity.

As colonial prosperity reached new heights after 1740, poverty spread among residents of the major seaports—Philadelphia, New York, Boston, and Charles Town. The cities' poor rolls bulged as poor white men, women (often widowed), and children arrived from Europe and the colonial countryside. High population density and poor sanitation allowed contagious diseases to run rampant, so that half of all city children died before age twenty-one and urban adults lived ten years less on average than country folk.

Changing labor practices also contributed to poverty. Urban artisans traditionally trained apprentices and employed them as journeymen for many years until they could open their own shops. By midcentury, however, employers increasingly kept laborers only as long as business was brisk, releasing them when sales slowed. In 1751, a shrewd Benjamin Franklin recommended this practice to employers as a way to reduce labor costs. Except in Boston, poor whites in cities competed for work with slaves whose masters rented out their labor. Recessions hit more frequently after 1720 and created longer spells of unemployment that made it difficult for many to afford rent, food, and firewood.

Insignificant before 1700, urban poverty became a major problem. By 1730, Boston ceased providing shelter for its growing number of homeless residents. The proportion of residents considered too poor to pay taxes climbed even as the total population leveled (see Figure 4.2). For example, the number of Philadelphia families listed as poor on tax rolls jumped from 3 percent in 1720 to 11 percent by 1760.

Wealth, however, remained highly concentrated. New York's wealthiest 10 percent (mostly merchants) owned about 45 percent of the city's property throughout the eighteenth century. Similar patterns existed in Boston and Philadelphia. Charles Town offered gracious living to wealthy planters who flocked from their plantations to townhouses during the worst months of heat and insect infestation, while shanties on the city's outskirts sheltered a growing crowd of destitute whites. Such trends underscored the polarization of status and wealth in urban America.

Although urban middle-class women performed less manual drudgery than farm women, they managed complex households that often included servants, slaves, and apprentices. While raising poultry

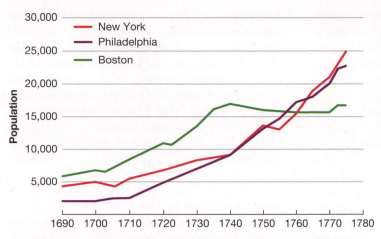

FIGURE 4.2 **POPULATIONS OF BOSTON, NEW YORK, AND PHILADELPHIA, 1690–1776** Transatlantic commerce contributed to the rapid growth of the three northern seaports. But Boston's growth halted in 1740, while New York and Philadelphia continued to flourish.

Source: Gary B. Nash, The Urban Crucible: Social Change, Political Consciousness, and the Origins of the American Revolution. *Copyright © 1978 by the President and Fellows of Harvard College.*

and vegetables as well as sewing and knitting, city wives purchased cloth and most of their food in daily trips to public markets. Servants, usually young single women or widows, helped with cooking, cleaning, and laundering. Urban standards of cleanliness and appearance were higher than in the country. Wives also worked in family businesses or their own shops, which were located in owners' homes.

Less affluent wives and widows had the fewest opportunities of all. They housed boarders rather than servants, and many spun and wove cloth in their homes for local merchants. Poor widows with children looked to the community for relief. Whereas John Winthrop and other Puritans had deemed it a Christian's duty to care for poor dependents (see Chapter 3), affluent Bostonians now scorned the needy. Preaching in 1752, the city's leading minister, Charles Chauncy, lamented "the swarms of children, of both sexes, that are continually strolling and playing about the streets of our metropolis, clothed in rags, and brought up in idleness and ignorance." Another clergyman warned that charity for widows and their children was money "worse than lost."

4-2.8 Slavery

For slaves, the economic progress achieved in colonial America meant only that most masters could afford to keep them healthy. Rarely did masters choose to make their human property comfortable. A visitor to a Virginia plantation from Poland (where peasants lived in dire poverty) recorded this impression of slaves' quality of life:

We entered some Negroes huts—for their habitations cannot be called houses. They are far more miserable than the poorest of the cottages of our peasants. The husband and wife sleep on a miserable bed, the children on the floor . . . a little kitchen furniture amid this misery . . . a tea-kettle and cups . . . five or six hens, each with ten or fifteen chickens, walked there. That is the only pleasure allowed to the negroes.

Slaves were far cheaper than indentured servants; to maintain slaves, masters spent just 40 percent of what they paid for the upkeep of indentured servants. White servants ate two hundred pounds of meat yearly; black slaves consumed fifty pounds. The value of the beer and hard cider given to a typical servant equaled

Just imported in Capt. *Partilge* from LONDON and to be Sold by

Suſanna Renken,

At her Ship in Fore-Street near the Draw-Bridge, BOSTON, Viz.

EARLY Charlton, Hotſpur, Marrowfat, Golden Hotſpur, and blue Marrowfat Peas; Large Windſor, early Hotſpur, early yellow Kidney, early Spaniſh Beans:——Early *Yorkſhire*, Dutch, Batterſea, Red, and large Winter Cabbage: yellow and green Savoy; Purple and Colliflower Brocoli; white Goſs-Cabbage, Marble, white Sileſia, green Sileſia, and ſcarlet Lettice, green and yellow Hyſſop; Turkey Melons; and Winter Savory; with all ſorts of other Garden Seeds, among which are a great Variety of Flower-Seeds:——Red and white Clover, Herd Graſs and Trefoile.

Juſt Imported from LONDON, and to be Sold

By Sarah DeCoſter,

At the Sign of the Walnut-Tree in Milk-Street in Boſton, a little below the Rev. Dr. Sewall's Meeting-Houſe,

WINDSOR Beans; Early Peas of ſeveral Sorts; Early Cabbage-Seeds, and other Sorts of Garden-Seeds; too many to enumerate: All at reaſonable Rates.

WOMEN ENTREPRENEURS Women shopkeepers were common in the cities, especially in trades that required only a small investment. These Boston women advertised imported garden seeds in a city newspaper. *(Chicago History Museum)*

the entire expense of feeding and clothing the average slave. Masters usually provided adult slaves corn and meat but expected them to grow their own vegetables, forage for wild fruits, and perhaps raise poultry.

Blacks worked for a far longer portion of their lives than whites. Slave children entered the fields as part-time helpers after reaching age seven and began working full time between ages eleven and fourteen. Whereas most white women worked in their homes, barns, and gardens, black females routinely tended tobacco or rice crops, even when pregnant, and often worked outdoors in the winter. Most slaves toiled until they died, although those over age sixty were usually spared hard labor.

As the numbers of American-born or "**creole**" slaves grew, sharp differences emerged between them and African-born blacks in the southern colonies. Unlike African-born slaves, creoles spoke a single language, English, and were familiar from birth with their environment and with the ways of slaveowners. As wealthier, longer-established planters diversified economically and developed more elaborate lifestyles (as discussed shortly), they diverted favored creoles toward such services as shoeing horses, repairing and driving carriages, preparing and serving meals, sewing and mending clothing, and caring for planters' children.

Africans and creoles alike proved resourceful at maximizing opportunities within this harsh, confining system. House slaves aggressively demanded that guests tip them for shining shoes and stabling horses. They also sought presents on holidays, as a startled New Jersey visitor to a Virginia plantation discovered early one Christmas morning when slaves demanding gifts of cash roused him from bed.

In the Carolina-Georgia rice country, slaves working under the task system gained some control of about half their waking hours. Under tasking, each slave spent some hours tending rice and food crops, after which his or her plantation duties ended for the day. Thereafter, slaves managed their own crops and sold any surplus, but enjoyed little truly "free time" (see Going to the Source). Women were crucial to rice production and toiled alongside men.

The gang system used on tobacco plantations afforded Chesapeake slaves even less relief than those in Carolina. As one white observer noted, Chesapeake blacks labored "from daylight until the dusk of evening and some part of the night, by moon or candlelight, during the winter."

Despite the task system's relative benefits, racial tensions ran high in Carolina. After 1700, as a black majority emerged, whites increasingly used force and fear to control "their" blacks.

For example, a 1735 law, noting that many Africans wore "clothes much above the condition of slaves," imposed a dress code limiting slaves' apparel to fabrics worth less than ten shillings per yard and even prohibited them from wearing their owners' cast-off clothes. Of even greater concern were large gatherings of slaves uncontrolled by whites. In 1721, Charles Town enacted a 9:00 P.M. curfew for blacks, while Carolina's assembly placed all local slave patrols under the colonial militia. Slaves responded to such measures with increased instances of arson, theft, flight, and violence.

Violence by slaves peaked in 1739, when the **Stono Rebellion** rocked South Carolina (separated from North Carolina in 1729). It began when twenty Africans seized guns and ammunition from a store at the Stono River Bridge, outside Charles Town. Marching under a makeshift flag and crying "Liberty!" eighty men headed south toward Florida, a well-known refuge for escapees (as discussed later). Along the way, they burned seven plantations and killed twenty whites, but they spared a Scottish innkeeper known for being "a good Man and kind to his slaves." Within a day, mounted militia surrounded the slaves near a riverbank, cut them down mercilessly, and spiked a rebel head on every milepost between that spot and Charles Town. Uprisings elsewhere in the colony required more than a month to suppress, with insurgents generally "put to the most cruel Death." Thereafter, whites enacted a new slave code, essentially in force until the Civil War, that kept South Carolina slaves under constant surveillance. Furthermore, it threatened masters with fines for not disciplining slaves and required legislative approval for manumission (freeing of individual slaves). The Stono Rebellion and its cruel aftermath thus reinforced South Carolina's emergence as a rigid, racist, and fear-ridden society.

Slavery and racial tensions were by no means confined to plantations. By midcentury, enslaved blacks made up 20 percent of

ASANTE DRUM Enslaved Africans carried their cultures with them to the Americas. This drum, made from African wood, was found in Virginia. (© Trustees of the British Museum)

SOURCE

A Planter Describes the Task System

In 1750 Johann Bolzius, a German-born Georgia planter, described how slaves' labor sustained rice plantations on the swampy coastal plain of South Carolina and Georgia under the task system.

The order of planting is the following. 1) The Negroes plant potatoes at the end of March unless the weather is too cold. This keeps all Negroes busy, and they have to loosen the earth as much as they can. The potatoes are cut into several pieces and put into long dug furrows, or mounds. . . . 2) As soon as one is through with the potatoes, one plants Indian corn. A good Negro man or woman must plant half an acre a day. Holes are merely made in the earth 6 feet from one another, and five or six kernels put into each hole. 3) After the corn the Negroes make furrows for rice planting. A Negro man or woman must account for a quarter acre daily. On the following day the Negroes sow and cover the rice in the furrows, and half an acre is the daily task of a Negro. 4) Now the Negroes start to clean the corn of the grass, and a day's work is half an acre, be he man or woman. . . . 5) When they are through with that, they plant beans together among the corn. At this time the children must weed out the grass in the potato patches. 6) Thereupon they start for the first time to cultivate the rice and to clean it of grass. A Negro must complete 1/4 acre daily. 7) Now the corn must be cleaned of the grass for the second time, and a little earth put around the stalks like little hills. . . . Their day's task in this work is half an acre for each. 8) As soon as they are through with the corn, they cultivate the rice a second time. The quality of the land determines their

day's work in this. 9) Corn and rice are cultivated for the third and last time. A Negro can take care of an acre and more in this work, and 1/2 an acre of rice. . . . Afterwards the Negroes are used for all kinds of housework, until the rice is white and ripe for cutting, and the beans are gathered, which grow much more strongly when the corn has been bent down. The rice is cut at the end of August or in September, . . . Towards the middle of August all Negro men of 16 to 60 years must work on the public roads, to start new ones or to improve them, namely for 4 or 5 days, or according to what the government requires, and one has to send along a white man with a rifle or go oneself. At the time when the rice is cut and harvested, the beans are collected too, which task is divided among the Negroes. They gather the rice, thresh it, grind it in wooden mills, and stamp it mornings and evenings. The corn is harvested last. During the 12 days after Christmas they plant peas, garden beans, transplant or prune trees, and plant cabbage. Afterwards the fences are repaired, and new land is prepared for cultivating.

They ["Negroes"] are given as much land as they can handle. On it they plant for themselves corn, potatoes, tobacco, peanuts, water and sugar melons, pumpkins, bottle pumpkins . . . They plant for themselves also on Sundays. For if they do not work they make mischief and do damage. . . . They sell their own crops and buy some necessary things.

QUESTIONS

1. What was the role of enslaved Africans in producing wealth and sustenance from the land on rice plantations?
2. In what ways does Bolzius indicate his own racial attitudes?

New York City's population and formed a majority in Charles Town and Savannah. Southern urban slave owners augmented their incomes by renting out the labor of their slaves, who were cheaper to employ than white workers. Slave artisans worked as coopers, shipwrights, rope makers, and, in a few cases, goldsmiths and cabinetmakers. Some artisans supplemented their work as slaves by earning income of their own. Slaves in northern cities were more often unskilled. Urban slaves in both the North and South typically lived apart from their masters in rented quarters alongside free blacks.

Although city life afforded slaves greater freedom of association than did plantations, urban blacks remained the property of others and chafed at racist restrictions. In 1712, rebellious slaves in New York City killed nine whites in a calculated attack. As a result, eighteen blacks were hanged or tortured to death, and six others committed suicide to avoid similar treatment. In 1741, a wave of thefts and fires was attributed on dubious testimony to conspiring New York slaves. Of one hundred fifty-two blacks arrested, thirteen were burned at the stake, seventeen were hanged (along with four whites), and seventy were sent to the West Indies.

4-2.9 The Rise of Colonial Elites

A few colonists benefited disproportionately from the growing wealth of Britain and its empire. Most elite colonists inherited their advantages at birth and augmented them by marrying a spouse from a similarly wealthy family. Most elite males were large planters or farmers, merchants, or attorneys, clergymen, and other professionals who catered to fellow elites. They constituted British America's upper class, or gentry.

Before 1700, the colonies' class structure was less apparent because elites spent their limited resources buying land, servants, and slaves rather than luxuries. As late as 1715, a traveler noticed that one of Virginia's richest planters, Robert Beverley, owned "nothing in or about his house but just what is necessary, . . . [such as] good beds but no curtains and instead of cane chairs he hath stools made of wood."

As British mercantilist trade flourished, higher incomes enabled elite colonists to display their wealth more openly, particularly in their housing. The greater gentry—the richest 2 percent, owning about 15 percent of all property—constructed elaborate showcase mansions that broadcast their elite status. The lesser gentry, or second wealthiest 2 to 10 percent holding about 25 percent of all property, lived in more modest two-story dwellings. In contrast, middle-class farmers commonly inhabited one-story wooden buildings with four small rooms and a loft.

Colonial gentlemen and ladies also exhibited their status by imitating the "refinement" of upper-class Europeans. A gentleman was expected to behave with an appropriate degree of responsibility, to display dignity and generosity, and to be a community leader. His wife, a "lady," was to be a skillful household manager and, in the presence of men, a refined yet deferring hostess. Elites wore costly English fashions, drove carriages instead of wagons, and bought expensive chinaware, books, furniture, and musical instruments. They pursued

JOHN POTTER AND HIS FAMILY The Potters of Matunuck, Rhode Island, relax at tea. In commissioning a portrait depicting themselves at leisure and attended by a black slave, the Potters proclaimed their elite status. *(Newport Historical Society)*

a gracious life by studying foreign languages, learning formal dances, and cultivating polite manners. A few young gentlemen even traveled abroad to get an English education. Thus, elites led colonists' growing taste for British fashions and consumer goods.

4-3 Competing for a Continent, 1713–1750

How did competition in the first half of the seventeenth century between the three leading European powers for control of the North American colonies affect both Native Americans and the fate of the colonies?

After a generation of war, Europe's return to peace in 1713 only heightened British, French, and Spanish imperial ambitions in North America. Europeans expanded their territorial claims, intensifying both trade and warfare with Native Americans and carving out new settlements. Native Americans welcomed some of these developments and resisted others, depending on how they expected their sovereignty and livelihoods to be affected. But peace too lasted for only a generation before a new round of imperial warfare began in 1739.

4-3.1 France and the American Heartland

To limit British and Spanish expansion in North America, France sought to strengthen its hold on the Mississippi Valley. In 1718, Louisiana officials established New Orleans as the colony's capital and port. Louisiana's staunchest Indian allies were the Choctaws, through whom the French hoped to counter both the expanding influence of Carolina's traders and the Spanish presence in Florida. But during the 1730s, inroads by traders from South Carolina divided the Choctaws into pro-English and pro-French factions that fought a civil war.

Life was dismal in Louisiana for whites as well as blacks. A thoroughly corrupt government ran the colony. With tobacco and indigo exports failing to sustain them, Louisiana's settlers and slaves found other means of survival. Like the Native Americans, they hunted, fished, gathered wild plants, and cultivated gardens. In 1727, a priest

described how some whites eventually prospered: "A man with his wife or partner clears a little ground, builds himself a house on four piles, covers it with sheets of bark, and plants corn and rice for his provisions; the next year he raises a little more for food, and has also a field of tobacco; if at last he succeeds in having three or four Negroes, then he is out of difficulties."

Many Native American, white, and black Louisianans depended on exchanges with one another to stay "out of difficulties." Nearby Native Americans provided corn, bear oil, tallow (for candles), and above all deerskins to French merchants in return for blankets, kettles, axes, chickens, hogs, guns, and alcohol. Indian and Spanish traders from west of the Mississippi brought horses and cattle. Familiar with cattle from their homelands, enslaved Africans managed many of Louisiana's herds, and some became rustlers and illicit traders of beef.

French settlers in Upper Louisiana, or Illinois, were somewhat better off, but by 1752 more than a third of its twenty-six hundred inhabitants were enslaved Africans. Illinois' principal export was wheat, potentially a more profitable crop than the plantation commodities grown farther south. But Illinois' remote location limited exports and attracted few whites, obliging it to depend on Native American allies to defend it from Indian enemies.

With Canada and the Mississippi Valley secure from European rivals, France sought to counter growing British influence in the Ohio Valley. Since the Iroquois declared their neutrality in the Grand Settlement of 1701, many Indian refugees had been settling in the "Ohio country." Some, such as the Shawnees, returned from elsewhere to reoccupy homelands. Others were

HURON (WENDAT) WOMAN Along with her traditional attire, this mother and farmer in the Great Lakes region wears glass beads and cloth while carrying an iron hoe, all acquired from French traders. *(Granger, NYC—All rights reserved).*

MAP 4.3 **EUROPEAN OCCUPATION OF NORTH AMERICA TO 1750** Spanish and French occupation depended on frequently uncertain ties with Native Americans. By contrast, British colonists, often aided by the Iroquois, had dispossessed coastal native peoples and densely settled the eastern seaboard.

newcomers, such as Delawares escaping settler encroachments in Pennsylvania. Hoping to secure commercial and diplomatic ties with these natives, the French expanded their trade subsidies. Several French posts, most notably Detroit, became sizable towns housing Indians, French, and mixed-ancestry *métis*. But wherever English traders introduced better goods at lower prices, Indians steered a more independent course.

Although generally more effective in Indian diplomacy than the English, the French were not always successful and could be equally violent. They and their native allies brutally suppressed the Natchez in Louisiana, and for nearly forty years waged war against the Mesquakie (or Fox) Indians in the upper Midwest. The French sold Native Americans captured in these wars as slaves in Louisiana, Illinois, Canada, and the West Indies.

By 1744, French traders were traveling as far west as the Rocky Mountains and were buying buffalo hides and Indian slaves at Indian trade centers on the Great Plains. These traders and their British competitors spread European-made goods, including guns, to Native Americans throughout central Canada and the Plains. Meanwhile, Indians in the Great Basin and southern Plains were acquiring horses, thousands of which had been left behind by the Spanish when they fled New Mexico during the Pueblo Revolt of 1680. Native peoples such as the Lakota Sioux, from the upper Mississippi Valley, and Comanches, from the Rocky Mountains, moved to the Plains and built a new, highly mobile way of life based on horses, firearms, the pursuit of buffalo, and trade with Europeans, particularly the French. By 1750, France had an immense domain, but one that depended on often-precarious relations with Native Americans.

4-3.2 Native Americans and British Expansion

As in the seventeenth century, British colonial expansion was made possible by the depopulation and dislocation of Native Americans. Epidemic diseases, environmental changes, war, and political pressures on Indians to sell and move off their land all combined to make new territory available to European immigrants.

Conflict came early to Carolina, where a trade in Indian slaves (see Chapter 3) and imperial war had already produced violence. The **Tuscarora War** (1711–1713) began when Iroquoian-speaking Tuscaroras, provoked by encroaching settlers, destroyed New Bern, a nearby town of seven hundred Swiss immigrants. Troops from Carolina and Virginia, along with Indian allies, retaliated. By 1713, after about a thousand Tuscaroras (one-fifth of the total population) had been killed or enslaved, the nation surrendered. Most Tuscarora survivors migrated northward to what is now upstate New York and in 1722 became the sixth nation of the Iroquois Confederacy. (The Five Nations would be known thereafter as the Six Nations.)

After helping defeat the Tuscaroras, Carolina's Indian allies experienced abuses, including cheating, violence, and enslavement by English traders and encroachments on their land. The Yamasees were the most seriously affected. In the **Yamasee War** (1715–1716), they were joined by Catawbas, Creeks, and other disaffected Carolina allies in attacking English trading houses and settlements. Only by enlisting the Cherokee Indians, and allowing four hundred enslaved Africans to bear arms, did Carolina crush the uprising. Yamasees not killed or captured fled to Florida or to Creek towns in the interior.

The defeat of the Yamasees left their Catawba supporters vulnerable to pressures from English on one side and Iroquois on the other. As settlers moved uncomfortably close to some villages, the Catawbas moved inland. Having escaped the settlers, however, the Catawbas faced rising conflict with the Iroquois, who raided them for captives whom they could adopt. To counter the well-armed Iroquois, the Catawbas turned back to Carolina. By ceding land and helping defend Carolina against outside Indians, the Catawbas received guns, food, and clothing. Their relationship with the English allowed the Catawbas to survive and maintain their communities. However, the growing gap in numbers between Catawbas and colonists greatly favored the English in the two peoples' competition for resources.

To the north, the Iroquois Confederacy accommodated English expansion while consolidating its own power among Native Americans. Late in the seventeenth century, the Iroquois and several colonies forged a series of treaties known as the **Covenant Chain**. Under these treaties, the Confederacy helped the colonies subjugate Indians whose lands the English wanted. Under one such agreement, the Iroquois assisted Massachusetts in subjugating that colony's natives following King Philip's War. Under another, the Susquehannock Indians, after being crushed in Bacon's Rebellion, moved northward from Maryland to a new homeland adjacent to the Iroquois' own. By relocating non-Iroquois on their periphery as well as by inviting the Tuscaroras into their Confederacy, the Iroquois controlled a center of Native American power that was independent of, but cooperative with, the British. In this way, the Iroquois hoped to deflect English expansion to lands other than their own.

Although not formally belonging to the Covenant Chain, Pennsylvania maintained a similar relationship with the Iroquois. With immigration and commercial success, William Penn's early idealism waned in Pennsylvania, along with his warm ties with the Delaware Indians. Between 1729 and 1734, Penn's sons, now the colony's proprietors, and his former secretary coerced the Delawares into selling more than fifty thousand acres. Then the Penn brothers produced a patently fraudulent "deed," which alleged that the Delawares had agreed in 1686 to sell their land as far westward as a man could walk in a day and a half. After selling much of the land to settlers and speculators in a lottery, the Penns in 1737 hired two men to make the walk. After practicing, the men covered sixty-four miles, meaning that the Delawares, in what became known as the **Walking Purchase**, had to hand over an additional twelve hundred square miles of land and move inland under Iroquois supervision. Settlers began pouring in and, within a generation, the Delawares' former lands were among the most productive in the British Empire.

Tuscarora War
War in the Carolinas in 1711–1713 between the Tuscarora Indians and the colonists.

Yamasee War
A series of attacks in 1715–1716 led by Catawbas, Creeks, and other Indian allies on English trading houses and settlements. Only by enlisting the aid of the Cherokee Indians, and allowing four hundred slaves to bear arms, did the colony crush the uprising.

Covenant Chain
A series of treaties between the Iroquois and the colonists. Under these treaties, the Iroquois helped the colonies subjugate Indians whose lands the English wanted.

Walking Purchase
William Penn's sons produced a patently fraudulent "deed," which alleged that the Delawares had agreed in 1686 to sell their land as far westward as a man could walk in a day and a half. After selling much of the land to settlers and speculators in a lottery and hiring two men to rehearse the walk, the Penns in 1737 sent the two men to conduct an "official" walk. The men covered sixty-four miles, meaning that the Delawares had to hand over an additional twelve hundred square miles of land.

4-3.3 British Expansion in the South: Georgia

Britain moved to expand southward toward Florida in 1732 when Parliament authorized the new colony of Georgia. Although expecting Georgia to export such expensive commodities as wine and silk, the colony's sponsors intended it as a refuge for honest debtors who would otherwise have to serve time in an English prison. A board of trustees was formed to oversee the colony for twenty-one years, when it would become a royal colony. During that time, the trustees decreed, Georgia would do without slavery, alcohol, landholdings over five hundred acres, and representative government.

One of the trustees, **James Oglethorpe**, moved to Georgia and dominated it for a decade. Ignoring Spain's claims, Oglethorpe purchased the colony's land from the Creek Indians, with whom he cultivated close ties. Oglethorpe founded the port of Savannah in 1733, and by 1740 twenty-eight hundred colonists had arrived. Almost half the immigrants came from Germany, Switzerland, and Scotland, and most had their overseas passage paid by the government. A small number of Jews were among the early colonists. Along with Pennsylvania, early Georgia was the most inclusive of the British colonies.

Oglethorpe was determined to keep slavery out of Georgia. "They live like cattle," he wrote to the trustees after viewing Charles Town's slave market. "If we allow slaves, we act against the very principles by which we associated together, which was to relieve the distressed." Slavery, he thought, degraded blacks, made whites lazy, and presented the terrible risk of slave revolts, which the Spanish could then exploit. But most of all, he recognized that slavery undermined the economic position of poor whites like those he sought to settle in Georgia.

Oglethorpe's plans failed completely. Few English debtors arrived because Parliament set impossibly stringent conditions for their release from prison. Limitations on settlers' rights to sell or enlarge their holdings, as well as the ban on slavery, also discouraged immigration. Raising exotic export crops proved impractical. Looking to neighboring South Carolina, some Georgians recognized that rice, which required large estates, substantial capital, and many cheap laborers, could flourish in Georgia's lowlands. Under pressure from planters, the trustees lifted limits on the size of landholdings in 1744 and the ban on slavery in 1750. The trustees also authorized a representative assembly in 1750, just two years before turning the colony over to the crown. By 1760, sixty-five hundred whites and thirty-five hundred enslaved blacks were making Georgia profitable.

James Oglethorpe
One of the trustees of the Georgia colony. He purchased land for the colony from the Creek Indians, with whom he cultivated close ties. He founded the port of Savannah in 1733, and by 1740 twenty-eight hundred colonists had arrived. He was determined to keep slavery out of Georgia because slaves, he thought, degraded blacks, made whites lazy, and presented a terrible risk of slave revolts.

JAMES OGLETHORPE Portrait of James Oglethorpe, who established the colony of Georgia and originally hoped to keep slavery out of it. *(Stock Montage/Archive Photos/Getty Images)*

4-3.4 Spain's Borderlands

Spain sought with limited success to maintain its North American presence in the face of Native American, French, and British adversaries. Seeking to strengthen New Mexico after the Pueblo Revolt, Spain awarded grants of approximately twenty-six square miles wherever ten or more families founded a town. As in early New England, settlers built homes on small lots around a church plaza, farmed separate fields nearby, grazed livestock farther away, and shared a community wood lot and pasture.

The livestock-raising ranchos, radiating out for many miles from little clusters of houses, monopolized vast tracts along the Rio Grande and blocked further town settlement. On the ranchos, mounted cattle herders created the way of life later associated with the American cowboy, featuring roping skills, cattle drives, roundups (rodeos), and livestock branding.

By 1750, New Mexico residents numbered about 14,000, but more than half of them were

SLAVE-RAIDING EXPEDITION IN NEW MEXICO This surviving portion of a painting on buffalo hide, dating to the 1720s, depicts Spanish soldiers and allied Indians as they attack an encampment, probably of Apaches. Women and children look on from behind a palisade surrounding the encampment. *(Courtesy Museum of New Mexico, Neg. No.149796)*

Pueblo Indians. Most Pueblos now cooperated with the Spanish, and although many had converted to Catholicism, they also practiced their traditional religion. Like the colonists, the Pueblos were village-dwellers who grew crops and raised livestock, making them equally vulnerable to horse-mounted raiders. Apache raids were now augmented by those of armed and mounted Comanches from the north and east. The raiders sought livestock and European goods as well as captives, often to replace those of their own people who had been seized by Spanish raiders and sent to mine silver in Mexico.

Spain had established Texas to counter growing French influence among the Comanches and other Native Americans on the southern Plains. Colonization began after 1716. Among several outposts, the most prominent center was at San Antonio de Béxar, where two towns, a presidio, and a mission (later known as the Alamo) were clustered. But lack of security against attacking Indians deterred immigrants, so that by 1760 only twelve hundred Spaniards inhabited Texas.

Although Spain claimed Texas, the dominant power there was actually the Comanche Indians. Acquiring firearms from French traders on the Missouri River, horse-mounted Comanches expanded their power and influence across the southern Plains and into New Mexico. They attacked Spaniards, Pueblos, and Apaches for captives, driving most Apaches farther south and west from Texas and eastern New Mexico. The Comanches periodically made truces with New Mexico, enabling them to trade with colonists and Pueblo Indians there. In a reversal of typical Indian-European trade patterns, the better-armed Comanches frequently sold guns to the Spanish. Some historians maintain that the Comanches were an empire, one that was stronger in the region than Spain's.

The Spanish position in Florida was only slightly less precarious than in Texas. As early as 1700, thirty-eight hundred English were already in recently founded Carolina, compared to just fifteen hundred Spanish in Florida. This disparity widened thereafter, especially with the founding of Georgia.

Florida found ways to offset its small number of colonists. After the Yamasee War, the Creeks declared their neutrality in conflicts among Europeans. As a result, some Spaniards traded with the Creeks for deerskins, but profits remained

FORT MOSE This artist's reconstruction of the free black community at St. Augustine is based on archaeological and documentary evidence. *(Florida Museum of Natural History, Fort Mose Exhibition)*

King George's War
Also known as the War of Austrian Succession. It started out as a conflict between Britain and Spain, but then escalated when France sided with Spain.

limited because Floridians lacked cheap, desirable trade goods.

Florida gained more at English expense through its recruitment of escaped slaves from Carolina. From the time of Carolina's founding, some enslaved Africans had found their way to the Spanish colony. In 1693, Spain's King Charles II ruled that any English-owned slaves arriving in Florida would be freed upon converting to Catholicism. Word of the ruling spread to Carolina, prompting more slaves to flee to Florida. In 1726, Spanish authorities created an all-black militia unit under the command of Francisco Menéndez, a former South Carolina slave, to help defend Florida. In 1738, the colony built a fortified village, Mose, for Menéndez's men and their families adjacent to the capital at St. Augustine.

By 1750, Spain maintained a presence in a few parts of the Southeast and Southwest, while France exercised influence among Native Americans in the Mississippi, Ohio, and Missouri River valleys, as well as around the Great Lakes and in Canada (see Map 4.3). Both empires were thinly populated by colonists and depended on subsidies from their home governments. In contrast, British North America was compact, wealthy, deeply involved in

transatlantic trade, densely populated by colonists and slaves, and aggressively expansionist.

4-3.5 The Return of War, 1739–1748

After decades of war ended in 1713, the American colonies enjoyed a generation of peace and rising prosperity. But Britain feared that it was losing wealth because French sugar production in the West Indies now exceeded that of its own planters there. The British first sought to regain their advantage by undermining France's ally, Spain. In 1739, Spanish authorities in the Caribbean captured a British smuggler, Robert Jenkins, and cut off his ear. Britain used the incident to declare the "War of Jenkins' Ear" against Spain. In 1740, James Oglethorpe led a massive British assault on Florida. The English captured Mose but withdrew after Francisco Menéndez's militiamen and other troops recaptured the town. In 1741, 3,500 Anglo-Americans joined a British assault on the Spanish port of Cartagena in what is now Colombia. As Spain repulsed the attack, more than half the colonial troops died from yellow fever. Britain's only satisfaction came two years later when Oglethorpe and 650 Georgians repelled 3,000 Spanish troops invading the colony from Florida.

By then, the War of Jenkins' Ear had merged with a larger one in Europe, the War of the Austrian Succession, called **King George's War** in British America (1740–1748). King George's War followed the pattern of earlier imperial conflicts. Few battles involved more than six hundred men, and most were attacks and counterattacks on civilians in the Northeast. Many noncombatants, mostly New Englanders in isolated towns, were killed and others captured. Although prisoners were exchanged at the end of the war, some English women and children elected to remain with their French or Indian captors.

King George's War produced just one major engagement in North America. In 1745, almost four thousand New Englanders besieged and captured the French bastion of Louisbourg, guarding the entrance to the St. Lawrence River. After three years of inconclusive warfare, Britain signed the Treaty of Aix-la-Chapelle (1748), exchanging Louisbourg for a British outpost in India that the French had seized.

The return of hard-won Louisbourg to France fanned Anglo-Americans' suspicions that Britain had neglected them. Opposition members of Parliament joined the criticism, noting how vital the colonists now were to Britain's wealth and power.

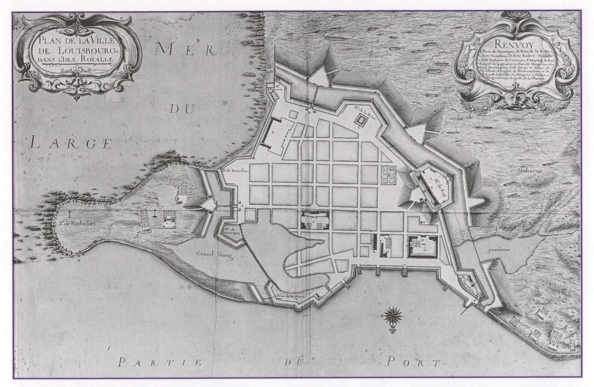

PLAN OF LOUISBOURG, 1744 Built to defend New France, Louisbourg fell to New Englanders in 1745 but was returned to France by the Treaty of Aix-la-Chapelle (1748). France would lose the fortress for good when British troops seized it in 1758 (covered in Chapter 5). *(Library and Archives Canada/Maps, Plans and Charts/MIKAN 4153172)*

British officials vowed to be more attentive to colonists' concerns in future wars.

4-4 Public Life in British America, 1689–1750

How did new ideologies and trends that reached America in the late seventeenth and early eighteenth century contribute to political consciousness in the British colonies?

The growing ties between Britain and its colonies included movements of ideas and beliefs as well as of goods and peoples. England's new Bill of Rights was the foundation of government and politics in the colonies. English thinkers initially inspired the intellectual movement known as the Enlightenment, while English preacher George Whitefield (discussed at the beginning of this chapter) helped transform the practice of Protestantism in British America. While reinforcing the colonies' links with Britain, these developments also led many more colonists than before to participate actively in politics, intellectual life, and religious movements. Taken as a whole, this wider participation signaled the emergence of a broad Anglo-American "public."

4-4.1 Colonial Politics

The most significant political result in the colonies of the Glorious Revolution was the rise of representative assemblies as a major political force. Except in Connecticut and Rhode Island, the crown or a proprietor in England chose each colony's governor. In most colonies, the governor named a council, or upper house of the legislature. The assembly, the legislative lower house, was therefore the only political body whose members were chosen by colonists rather than by English officials. Before 1689, governors and councils took the initiative in drafting laws, and the assemblies followed their lead; thereafter, however, the assemblies governed more actively.

Anglo-Americans saw their assemblies as comparable to England's House of Commons, which represented the people and defended their liberty against centralized authority, particularly through its exclusive power to originate revenue-raising measures. After Parliament won supremacy over the monarchy through the Bill of Rights, assemblymen

SEAT OF GOVERNMENT, BOSTON, MASSACHUSETTS Built in 1713, this building (now called "The Old State House") housed the royal governor, his council, and the General Court (assembly). A public gallery (the first in British America) in the General Court chamber enabled citizens to observe their elected legislators in action. *(Archive Photos/Getty Images)*

insisted that their governors' powers were similarly limited.

The lower houses asserted their prestige and authority by refusing to permit outside meddling in their proceedings, by taking firm control over taxes and budgets, and especially by keeping a tight rein on executive salaries. Although governors had considerable powers (including the right to veto acts, call and dismiss assembly sessions, and schedule elections), they were vulnerable to legislatures' pressure because their income came solely from the assemblies. Using this "power of the purse," assemblies could sometimes force governors to sign laws opposed by the crown.

British policy reinforced the assemblies' growing importance. The Board of Trade, established in 1696 to monitor American developments, could have persuaded the crown to disallow objectionable laws signed by governors. But it rarely exercised this power before midcentury. The resulting political vacuum enabled the colonies to become self-governing in most respects except for trade regulation, restrictions on printing money, and declaring war. Representative government in the colonies originated and was nurtured within the protective environment of the British Empire.

The elite landowners, merchants, and attorneys who monopolized colonial wealth also dominated politics. Most assemblymen ranked among the wealthiest 2 percent of colonists. To placate them, governors invariably appointed other members of the gentry to their councils and to judgeships. Only men could participate in formal politics. Outside New England (where any voter was eligible for office), legal requirements barred 80 percent of white men from running for the assembly, most often by specifying that a candidate own a minimum of a thousand acres. (Farms then averaged 180 acres in the South and 120 acres in the middle colonies.) Even without property qualifications, few ordinary colonists could have afforded to hold elective office. Assemblymen received only living expenses, which might not fully cover the cost of staying at their province's capital, much less compensate a farmer for his absence from home for six to ten weeks a year. As a result, a few wealthy families in each colony dominated the highest political offices. Nine families, for example, provided one-third of Virginia's councilors after 1680. John Adams, a rising young Massachusetts politician, estimated that most towns in his colony chose their representatives from among just three or four families.

By eighteenth-century standards, Anglo-American voting qualifications were liberal, but all provinces barred women and nonwhites from voting. In seven colonies, male voters had to own a minimal amount of land. About 40 percent of free white men—mostly indentured servants and young men—could not meet these requirements. Still, most white males in British North America could vote by age forty, whereas two-thirds of all men in England and nine-tenths in Ireland were never eligible.

In rural areas, voter participation averaged about 45 percent. Most governors called elections when they saw fit, so that elections might lapse for years and then suddenly take place on short notice. Thus, voters in isolated areas often had no knowledge of upcoming contests. That polling took place at the county seat discouraged many electors from traveling long distances over poor roads to vote. In several colonies, voters stated their choices orally and publicly, often with the candidates present. This procedure inhibited humbler men from participating or choosing freely if their views differed from those of elites, especially elites they depended on for credit, shipping privileges, or other favors. Finally, most rural elections before 1750 were uncontested. Local elites decided in advance who would "stand" for office. They regarded officeholding as a gentleman's public duty and considered it demeaning to show interest in being chosen, much less to compete or "run" for a position.

Given all these factors, many rural voters were indifferent about politics at the colony level. For example, to avoid paying legislators' expenses at the capital, many smaller Massachusetts towns refused to elect assemblymen. Thirty percent of men elected to South Carolina's assembly neglected to take their seats from 1731 to 1760, twice including a majority of those chosen.

Despite these limitations, rural elections slowly emerged as community events in which many nonelite white men participated. In time, rural voters would follow urban colonists and express themselves more forcefully.

Competitive politics first developed in the major northern cities. Depending on their economic interests and family ties, wealthy colonists aligned themselves with or against royal and proprietary governors. To gain advantage over rivals, some factions courted artisans and shopkeepers whose fortunes had stagnated or declined as the distribution of urban wealth increasingly favored the rich. In courting nonelite voters, they scandalized rival elites who feared that unleashing popular passions could disturb the social order.

New York was the site of the bitterest factional conflicts. In one episode, Governor William Cosby's supporters in 1734 engineered the arrest of newspaper printer John Peter Zenger. The charge was that in printing accusations of corruption against the governor, he had seditiously libeled Cosby. Following a celebrated trial in August 1735, Zenger was acquitted.

Although it neither led to a change in New York's libel law nor greatly enhanced freedom of the press at the time, the Zenger verdict was significant for several reasons. Zenger's brilliant lawyer, Andrew Hamilton, effectively employed the growing practice among colonial attorneys of speaking directly to a jury on behalf of a defendant. He persuaded the jury that it alone, without the judge's advice, could reject a charge of libel "if you should be of the opinion that there is no falsehood in [Zenger's] papers." Until then, a statement's truth was not, by itself, a sufficient defense against a charge of libel in British and colonial courts of law. Beyond its legal implications, the Zenger trial empowered nonelites as voters, readers, and jurors, and in New York and elsewhere it encouraged broader political discussion and participation beyond a small circle of elites.

4-4.2 The Enlightenment

If property and wealth were keys to political participation and officeholding, literacy and education permitted Anglo-Americans to participate in the transatlantic world of ideas and beliefs. Perhaps 90 percent of New England's adult white men and 40 percent of white women could write well enough to sign documents, thanks to the region's system of primary education. Among white male colonists elsewhere, the literacy rate varied from about 35 percent to more than 50 percent. (In England, by contrast, no more than one-third of all men could read and write.)

The best-educated colonists—members of the gentry, well-to-do merchants, educated ministers, and growing numbers of artisans and farmers—embraced a wider world of ideas and information. Though costly, books, newspapers, and writing paper brought the excitement of eighteenth-century European civilization to reading men and women. Scientific advances seemed to explain the laws of nature; human intelligence appeared poised to triumph over ignorance, prejudice, superstition, and irrational tradition. For those who had the time to read and to ponder ideas, an age of optimism and boundless progress was dawning, an age known as the Enlightenment.

Enlightenment ideals combined confidence in human reason with skepticism toward beliefs not

BENJAMIN FRANKLIN This earliest known portrait of Franklin dates to about 1740, when he was a rising leader in bustling Philadelphia. *(Harvard University Art Museums, Fogg Art Museum, Bequest of Dr. John Collins Warren, 1856, H47 Photo: Imaging Department © President and Fellows of Harvard College)*

founded on science or strict logic. A major source of Enlightenment thought was English physicist Sir Isaac Newton (1642–1727), who in 1687 explained how gravitation ruled the universe. Newton's work appealed to educated Europeans by demonstrating the harmony of natural laws and stimulated others to search for rational principles in medicine, law, psychology, and government.

Before 1750, no American more fully embodied the Enlightenment spirit than **Benjamin Franklin**. Born in Boston in 1706, Franklin migrated to Philadelphia at age seventeen. He brought skill as a printer, considerable ambition, and insatiable intellectual curiosity. In moving to Philadelphia, Franklin put himself in the right place at the right time, for the city was growing much more rapidly than Boston and was attracting merchants and artisans who shared Franklin's zest for learning and new ideas. Franklin organized some of these men into a reading-discussion group called the Junto, and they helped him secure printing

Benjamin Franklin
A skilled printer who had a zest for learning and new ideas. He later on devoted his life to science and public service.

contracts. In 1732, he first published *Poor Richard's Almanack*, a collection of maxims and proverbs that made him famous. By age forty-two, Franklin had earned enough money to retire and devote himself to science and public service.

These dual goals—science and public benefit—were intimately related in Franklin's mind, for he believed that all true science would be useful in making everyone's life more comfortable. For example, experimenting with a kite, Franklin demonstrated in 1752 that lightning was electricity, a discovery that led to the lightning rod.

Although some southern planters, such as Thomas Jefferson, later championed progress through science, the Enlightenment's earliest and primary American centers were cities, where the latest European books and ideas circulated and where gentlemen and self-improving artisans met to discuss ideas and conduct experiments. Franklin organized one such group, the American Philosophical Society, in 1743 to encourage "all philosophical experiments that let light into the nature of things, tend to increase the power of man over matter, and multiply the conveniences and pleasures of life." By 1769, this society had blossomed into an intercolonial network of amateur scientists. The societies emulated, and corresponded with, the Royal Society in London, the foremost learned society in the English-speaking world. In this respect, the Enlightenment strengthened the ties between colonial and British elites.

Just as Newton inspired the scientific bent of Enlightenment intellectuals, English philosopher John Locke, in his *Essay Concerning Human Understanding* (1690), led many to embrace "reasonable" or "rational" religion. Locke contended that ideas, including religion, are not inborn but are acquired by toilsome investigation of and reflection upon experience. To most Enlightenment intellectuals, the best argument for the existence of God was the harmony and order of nature, which pointed to a rational Creator. Some individuals, including Franklin and, later, Jefferson and Thomas Paine, carried this argument a step farther by insisting that where the Bible conflicted with reason, one should follow the dictates of reason. Called Deists, they concluded that God, having created a perfect universe, did not thereafter intervene in its workings but rather left it alone to operate according to natural laws.

Most colonists influenced by the Enlightenment described themselves as Christians and attended church. But they feared those Christians who persecuted others in religion's name or who emphasized emotion rather than reason in the practice of piety. Above all, they distrusted zealots and sectarians. Typically, Franklin contributed money to most of the churches in Philadelphia because they encouraged virtue and morality, but he deplored theological hair-splitting.

In 1750, the Enlightenment's greatest contributions to American life still lay in the future. A quarter-century later, Anglo-Americans drew on the Enlightenment's revolutionary ideas as they declared their independence from Britain and created the foundations of a new nation (discussed in Chapters 5 and 6). Meanwhile, a series of religious revivals known as the **Great Awakening** challenged the Enlightenment's most basic assumptions.

4-4.3 The Great Awakening

Viewing the world as orderly and predictable, rationalists often expressed smug self-satisfaction. Writing his will in 1750, Franklin thanked God for giving him "such a mind, with moderate passions" and "such a competency of this world's goods as might make a reasonable mind easy." But many Americans lacked such a comfortable competency of goods and lived neither orderly nor predictable lives. Earlier generations of young people coming of age had relied on established authority figures— parents, local leaders, clergy—for wisdom and guidance as they faced the future. But the world had changed by the middle decades of the eighteenth century. Older authorities were of little help when one's economic future was uncertain, when established elites seemed to act out of self-interest, or when one encountered more strangers than familiar faces on a daily basis. The result was a widespread spiritual hunger among ordinary people that neither traditional religion nor Enlightenment philosophy could satisfy.

In addition, as more men went into the world of business, they found the restrictive and finite authority of the church less compelling. For women, the submission the church required was comparable to that of their gender role in daily life. As such, in New England churches especially, there were more women than men. In 1739, an outpouring of European Protestant revivalism spread to British North America that would, at least for a time, prompt a return of men to the church.

Marked by evangelicalism, this burst of religiosity and revivals—which historians later termed the "Great Awakening"—cut across lines of class, gender, and even race. Women and blacks were not only present, they were encouraged to participate, sharing stories of how they experienced Jesus coming into their lives. Above all, the revivals represented an unleashing of anxiety and longing among ordinary people—anxiety about sin, and longing for

assurances of salvation. The answers they received were conveyed through the powerful preaching of ministers who appealed to their audiences' emotions rather than to their intellects.

In contrast to rationalists, who stressed the potential for human improvement, revivalist ministers aroused their audiences by depicting the sinfulness of human beings and the need for immediate repentance. Although well read in Enlightenment philosophy and science, Congregationalist Jonathan Edwards, who led a revival at Northampton, Massachusetts, in 1735, drove home this message with breathtaking clarity. "The God that holds you over the pit of Hell, much as one holds a spider or other loathsome insect over the fire, abhors you," Edwards intoned in a famous sermon, "Sinners in the Hands of an Angry God." "His wrath toward you burns like fire; He looks upon you as worthy of nothing else but to be cast into the fire." Audiences, in turn, wept, cried out, and flailed about.

The work of Edwards and other local revivalists was brought together with the arrival from Britain in 1739 of **George Whitefield**. So overpowering was Whitefield that some joked he could make crowds swoon simply by uttering "Mesopotamia." In an age without microphones, crowds exceeding twenty thousand could hear his booming voice clearly, and many wept at his eloquence.

Whitefield's American tour inspired thousands to seek salvation. Most converts were young adults in their late twenties. In Connecticut alone, church membership jumped from 630 in 1740 to 3,217 after Whitefield toured in 1741. Whitefield's allure was so powerful that he even awed potential critics. Hearing him preach in Philadelphia, Benjamin Franklin first vowed to contribute nothing to the collection. But so admirably did Whitefield conclude his sermon, Franklin recalled, "that I empty'd my Pocket wholly into the Collector's Dish, Gold and all."

Divisions over the revivals quickly developed and were often exacerbated by social and economic tensions. For example, after leaving Boston in October 1740, Whitefield invited another preacher, Gilbert Tennent, to follow "in order to blow up the divine flame lately kindled there." Denouncing Boston's established clergymen as "dead Drones" and lashing out at aristocratic fashion, Tennent built a following among the city's poor and downtrodden. Another preacher, James Davenport, spoke daily on the Boston Commons and then led processions of "idle or ignorant persons, and those of the lowest

Great Awakening
An evangelical Protestant religious revival movement that swept through Europe and the American colonies in the 1730s and 1740s.

George Whitefield
A significant preacher during the Great Awakening.

REVEREND SAMSON OCCOM, MOHEGAN INDIAN PREACHER Born in a wigwam in Connecticut, Occom converted to Christianity under the influence of the Great Awakening and preached to other Native Americans. He helped to develop a distinctly Native American variant of Protestant Christianity. *(Courtesy of the Trustees of the Boston Public Library/ Prints)*

Rank" through the streets. Brought before a grand jury, Davenport was expelled for asserting that "Boston's ministers were leading the people blind-folded to hell."

As Whitefield's exchange with Alexander Garden showed, the lines hardened between the revivalists, known as New Lights, and the rationalist clergy, or Old Lights, who dominated the Anglican, Presbyterian, and Congregational churches. Writing in 1740, Tennent hinted that most Presbyterian ministers lacked saving grace and urged parishioners to abandon them for the New Lights. By sowing seeds of doubt about individual ministers, Tennent undermined one of the foundations of social order. For if the people could not trust their own ministers, whom would they trust?

Old Light rationalists fired back. Charles Chauncy, Boston's leading Congregationalist minister, condemned the revival as an epidemic of the "enthusiasm" that enlightened intellectuals loathed. He even provided a kind of checklist for spotting enthusiasts: "a certain wildness" in their eyes, the "quakings and tremblings" of their limbs, and foaming at the mouth. Put simply, the revival had unleashed "a sort of madness" that overheated imaginations mistook for the experience of divine grace.

The Great Awakening opened unprecedented splits in American Protestantism. In 1741, New and Old Light Presbyterians formed rival branches that did not reunite until 1758, when the revivalists emerged victorious. The Anglicans lost many members to New Light congregations. The Congregationalists splintered so badly that by 1760, New Lights had seceded from one-third of New England's churches and formed New Light congregations or joined new denominations such as the Baptists.

The secession of New Lights was especially bitter in Massachusetts and Connecticut, where the Congregational church was established by law. Old Lights denied new churches legal status, meaning that New Lights' taxes would go to their former churches. Connecticut passed repressive laws forbidding revivalists to preach or perform marriages, and the colony expelled New Lights from the legislature.

Although New Lights made steady gains until the 1770s, the Great Awakening peaked in New England in 1742. The revival then crested everywhere but in Virginia, where its high point came after 1755 with an upsurge of conversions by Baptists, who also suffered legal harassment. For all the commotion it raised at the time, the Great Awakening's long-term effects exceeded its immediate impact. First, the revivals undermined Anglicans and Congregationalists, the colonies' two officially established denominations. As these churches' importance waned after 1740, the number of Presbyterians and Baptists increased.

The Great Awakening also stimulated the founding of new colleges as both Old and New Lights sought institutions free of one another's influence. In 1746, New Light Presbyterians established the College of New Jersey (Princeton). Then followed King's College (Columbia) for Anglicans in 1754, the College of Rhode Island (Brown) for Baptists in 1764, and Queen's College (Rutgers) for Dutch Reformed in 1766.

The revivals were also significant because they spread beyond the ranks of white society. The emphasis on piety over intellectual learning as the key to God's grace led some preachers to reach out to Africans and Native Americans. The Great Awakening marked the beginnings of black Protestantism when some slaves and free blacks joined white churches and even preached at revival meetings. New Light Christianity also attracted Native Americans residing within the colonies. A few

Christian Indians trained in a special school to become missionaries to other Native Americans, and one, Samson Occom, a Mohegan born in Connecticut, became widely known among whites. Despite these breakthroughs, blacks and Indians still faced considerable religious discrimination, even among New Lights. Occom and other Christian Indians in New England became bitterly disillusioned with such treatment, criticizing whites for their un-Christian practices. Some even formed their own all-native congregations.

The Great Awakening also added to white women's religious prominence. Some New Light churches, mostly Baptist and Congregationalist, granted women the right to speak and vote in church meetings. Mother Ann Lee, who founded the "Shaking Quakers," or Shakers, joined Jemima Wilkinson in becoming charismatic preachers of new sects. Like Anne Hutchinson in Puritan New England, some women led prayer and discussion groups that became overtly political. One such woman, Sarah Osborn of Newport, Rhode Island, conducted "private praying Societies Male and female" that included black slaves in her home. In 1770, Osborn and her followers won a bitter fight over their congregation's choice of a new minister. While most assertive women were prevented from exercising as much power as Osborn, none was persecuted as Hutchinson had been.

Finally, the revivals blurred denominational differences among Protestants. Although George Whitefield was an Anglican who defied his superior, Garden, and later helped found Methodism, he preached with Presbyterians such as Tennent and Congregationalists like Edwards. By emphasizing the need for salvation over details of doctrine and church governance, revivalism emphasized Protestants' common experiences and promoted mutual toleration among religious denominations.

Historians have disagreed over whether the Great Awakening had political as well as religious effects. Although Tennent and Davenport called the poor "God's people" and condemned the material wealth and display of elites, they never advocated revolution per se, and the Awakening did not produce a distinct political ideology. Yet the revivals did empower many ordinary people to express and act publicly on beliefs that countered those in authority. But in challenging the traditional social structure, elite power, and the system of deference, the Great Awakening articulated a more egalitarian sensibility consistent with that which would later imbue revolutionary ideology. By questioning the status quo and asserting the right of a people to dissent, New Light ministers modeled an ideology that would become central to colonial beliefs and political practices for decades to come. Along with competitive politics, the Great Awakening helped to create a pro-active public, thereby laying some of the groundwork for political revolutionaries a generation later.

The Whole Vision

■ *How did periods of upheaval and conflict in England affect its relationship with its American colonies?*

Without question, political turmoil and a transition from one monarchy to another in England had a direct impact on the British colonies. Kings who were Protestant took positions that Protestant colonists liked; Kings who were Catholic did likewise. As power changed hands, so, too, did ideas in England about the amount of political control and centralization that might be required for its colonies. Decisions were made that reshaped colonial boundary lines as well as notions of local rule in ways that prompted resistance in some colonies. This ongoing tug-of-war about political autonomy and British rule also showed early cracks in the foundation between the mother country and her colonies. England's own Glorious Revolution produced new ideas about rights that would have lasting implications at home and abroad. That event, too, sparked revolts in the colonies.

■ *What marked the economic growth of the American colonies from 1660 to 1750?*

By the mid-1600s, Britain, France, and Spain would seek to not only fortify their colonial holdings in America, but they would also look to them as increased sources of economic and political power globally. Long competitors in Europe, each country saw in their colonies a way to push past the other two and solidify their status as a leading power. All three countries embraced mercantilism in varying degrees and with varying success as the lynchpin to their strategies for economic growth. For Britain, the centerpiece was the Navigation Acts, which established rules about raw materials, production of goods, and trade within and outside the colonies. France focused on its fur trade and alliances with Indians, where Spain's emphasis was largely on its Latin American colonies. Whether any wealth gained via mercantilism was controlled privately or by the Church, monarchy, or nobility would affect the impact of a country's economic growth. The population size of each country's American colonies would also provide an advantage, including the influx of immigrants and slaves. The quest to beat each other upped the ante on the slave trade. Whether colonists benefitted from this growth would depend on the region in which they lived, whether they were enslaved or free, and whether they had access to land, as well as the class to which they belonged.

■ *How did competition in the first half of the seventeenth century between the three leading European powers for control of the North American colonies affect both Native Americans and the fate of the colonies?*

After extensive wars in Europe and a brief period of peace in the colonies, by 1713, Britain, France, and Spain ramped up their efforts to secure and expand their colonial holdings. Native Americans were often caught in the middle, at times allying with one country or the other, as deemed most advantageous. All three nations looked to Indians as a way to help them thwart the advances of their European territorial rivals. Indians also warred and formed alliances with other native peoples in facing Indian and European enemies. These unions met with varying degrees of success. As Britain, France, and Spain began to battle with each other on colonial soil once again, Native Americans were forced to choose sides; the decisions made along these lines by various Indian groups would seal their fate in the postwar era. The outcome of these wars would also help seal the fate of which European country would control the largest colonial empire in North America.

■ *How did new ideologies and trends that reached America in the late seventeenth and early eighteenth century contribute to political consciousness in the British colonies?*

Whenever new ideas became popular in England, it was not long before they reached the British colonies. Within the American context, however, these ideas would take on a significance of their own, often with lasting implications. Three trends specifically took root in the Americas: the impact of the English Bill of Rights, the Enlightenment, and the Great Awakening. While vastly different, all three would affect not only the notion of an American public, but also colonial political and social consciousness and ideas about responsibilities and rights. As colonists continued to establish governments and contemplate their identity as both English citizens and Americans, these ideas would prove influential. These ideological currents also made their way to America as the colonies were grappling with changes in religiosity, voting rights, increased factionalism, and whether to accept or question authority and the status quo. The Enlightenment and the Great Awakening in particular inspired men and women (even slaves) to contemplate new realities for themselves and society and, more importantly, to participate in bringing them to fruition.

5 Roads to Revolution, 1750–1776

THE BOSTON MASSACRE, 1770, ENGRAVING BY PAUL REVERE After this incident, a Bostonian remarked, "unless there is some great alteration in the state of things, the era of the independence of the colonies is much nearer than I once thought it, or now wish it." *(Library of Congress Prints & Photographs Division)*

CHRONOLOGY 1750–1776

Year	Event
1754	Albany Congress.
1754–1761	Seven Years' War (in Europe, 1756–1763).
1755	Britain expels Acadians from Nova Scotia.
1760	George III becomes king of England. Writs of assistance.
1762	Treaty of San Ildefonso.
1763	Treaty of Paris. Pontiac's War. Proclamation of 1763.
1763–1764	Paxton Boys uprising in Pennsylvania.
1764	Sugar Act.
1765	Stamp Act. African Americans demand liberty in Charles Town. First Quartering Act.
1766	Stamp Act repealed. Declaratory Act.
1767	Townshend Acts. American Board of Customs Commissioners created.
1768	Massachusetts "circular letters." John Hancock's ship *Liberty* seized by Boston customs commissioner.
1768	First Treaty of Fort Stanwix. St. George's Fields Massacre in London.
1770	Townshend Acts, except tea tax, repealed. Boston Massacre.
1771	Battle of Alamance Creek in North Carolina.
1772–1774	Committees of correspondence formed.
1772	Somerset decision in England.
1773	Tea Act and Boston Tea Party.
1774	Lord Dunmore's War. Coercive Acts and Quebec Act. First Continental Congress.
1775	Battles of Lexington and Concord. Lord Dunmore's Proclamation. Olive Branch Petition. Battles at Breed's Hill and Bunker Hill. George III and Parliament declare colonies to be in rebellion.
1776	Thomas Paine, *Common Sense*. Declaration of Independence.

With the end of the **Seven Years' War** in 1763, Britain had defeated France, its chief competitor for preeminence in North America, and stood at the height of eighteenth-century imperial power. British rule ran undisputed from the Atlantic seacoast to the Mississippi River and from northernmost Canada to the Florida straits. Yet this greatest of British triumphs would turn into one of Britain's greatest defeats.

The imperial reorganization that occurred after 1763 as a result of war and conquest radically altered Britain's relationship with its American colonies. Conflict arose between Britain and the colonies when Parliament, as it searched for ways to pay off the enormous debt accumulated during the war, attempted to tighten control over colonial affairs. The colonists, accustomed to legislating for themselves, resisted this effort to centralize decision making in London. American leaders interpreted Britain's clampdown as calculated antagonism, intended to deprive them of both prosperity and relative independence.

Conflict spilled out beyond constitutional issues. In port cities, crowds of poor and working people engaged in direct, often violent demonstrations against British authority. Settlers in the backcountry invoked the ideas of urban radicals when resisting large landowners and distant colonial governments dominated by elites. These movements reflected political and economic tensions within the colonies, as well as growing defiance of elites by ordinary colonists. Women participated, too, a reflection of their growing impatience with the restraints imposed by traditional gender norms. Nonwhites, both African American and Native American, often perceived the colonists as greater threats to their liberty than the British. Within Britain, many opposed the government's colonial policies.

Colonial resistance to British policies also reflected democratic stirrings in America and throughout the North Atlantic world. Among the products of this democratic surge were both the American Revolution, which erupted in 1776, and the French Revolution, which began in 1789 and sparked unrest over much of Europe and the Americas.

Despite their apprehension, most colonial politicians expressed their opposition peacefully from 1763 to 1775 through legislative resolutions and commercial boycotts.

Seven Years' War
Known to the colonists as the French and Indian War, a clash between Britain and France that eventually extended to Europe and other parts of the world. Fighting in North America occurred from 1754 to 1761, and resulted in Britain gaining most of France's former territories in North America.

Even after fighting erupted, the colonists agonized for more than a year about whether to sever their political relationship with Britain—which even native-born Americans sometimes referred to affectionately as "home." Of all the world's colonial peoples, none became rebels more reluctantly than Anglo-Americans in 1776.

5-1 Triumph and Tensions: The British Empire, 1750–1763

What was the impact of the Seven Years' War on the relationship between England and its colonies?

King George's War ended in 1748 with Britain and France still intent on defeating one another. Even before war returned to Europe, British and French forces clashed in North America in the Seven Years' War, known to Anglo-Americans as the French and Indian War. After Austria shifted its allegiance from Britain to France, and Britain aligned with Prussia, the Seven Years' War expanded to Europe and elsewhere. British and French forces fought one another in every continent except Australia.

CHIEF HENDRICK (THEYANOGUIN) OF THE MOHAWK IROQUOIS (1692–1755) A longtime (but often critical) ally of the British, Hendrick led the Mohawk delegation to the Albany Congress. *(Courtesy of the John Carter Brown Library at Brown University)*

After Britain and the colonies together defeated France, the French were expelled from mainland North America, leaving all of its territory east of the Mississippi to a triumphant Britain. Yet even as war wound down, tensions erupted within the victorious coalition of Britons, colonists, and Native Americans.

5-1.1 A Fragile Peace, 1750–1754

The tinderbox for Anglo-French conflict in North America was the Ohio Valley, claimed by Virginia, Pennsylvania, France, and the Six Nations Iroquois, as well as by the Native Americans who actually lived there.

Traders from Virginia and Pennsylvania were strengthening British influence among Indians in the Ohio Valley. Seeking to drive out the traders, the French began building a chain of forts there in 1753. Virginia retaliated by sending troops under a twenty-one-year-old surveyor, planter, and speculator, George Washington, to persuade or force the French to leave. Fearing that Virginia had designs on their land, Native Americans refused to support Washington, and in 1754 French troops drove the Virginians back to their homes.

While Washington was in Ohio, British officials called a meeting in mid-1754 of delegates from Virginia and colonies to the north to negotiate a treaty with the Six Nations Iroquois. Support from the Six Nations would be vital in any effort to drive the French from the Ohio Valley. Seven colonies (but neither Virginia nor New Jersey) sent delegates to the Albany Congress in Albany, New York. Long allied with Britain in the Covenant Chain, the Iroquois were also bound by the Grand Settlement of 1701 to remain neutral in any Anglo-French war. Moreover, the easternmost Mohawk Iroquois were angry because New York settlers were encroaching on their land. Although the delegates obtained expressions of friendship from the Six Nations, Iroquois suspicions of Britain persisted.

The delegates also endorsed a proposal for a colonial confederation, the Albany Plan of Union, largely based on the ideas of Pennsylvania's Benjamin Franklin and Massachusetts' Thomas Hutchinson. The plan called for a Grand Council representing, and funded by, all the colonial assemblies. A crown-appointed executive officer would head the council, which would coordinate military defense and Indian

affairs. Although later regarded as a precedent for American unity, the Albany Plan in fact came to nothing because no colonial legislature approved it.

5-1.2 The Seven Years' War in America, 1754–1760

Although France and Britain remained at peace in Europe until 1756, Washington's 1754 clash with French troops began the war in North America. In response, the British dispatched General Edward Braddock and a thousand regular troops to North America to seize Fort Duquesne at the headwaters of the Ohio River.

Scornful of colonial soldiers and friendly Indians, Braddock expected his disciplined redcoats to make short work of the enemy. On July 9, 1755, about 600 Native Americans and 250 French and Canadians ambushed Braddock's force of 2,200 Britons and Virginians (including George Washington) nine miles east of Fort Duquesne. Riddled by steady fire,

Braddock's troops retreated. Nine hundred British and provincial soldiers, including Braddock, died, compared to just twenty-three French and Indians.

Braddock's disastrous loss was the first of a string of setbacks for Britain and its colonists. French-armed Shawnees, Delawares, and Ohio Senecas (or Mingos, who had recently migrated from their Iroquois homeland) struck hard at encroaching settlers in western Pennsylvania, Maryland, and Virginia. For three years, these attacks halted English expansion and prevented the three colonies from joining the British war against France.

Although numerically superior, the Anglo-Americans were badly disorganized. As a result, the French and their Native American allies—now including the Six Nations Iroquois—captured Fort Oswego on Lake Ontario in 1756 and Fort William Henry on Lake George in 1757, and threatened central New York and western New England (see Map 5.1). In Europe, too, the war began badly for Britain, which by 1757 seemed to be facing defeat on all fronts.

MAP 5.1 **THE SEVEN YEARS' WAR IN NORTH AMERICA, 1754–1760** After experiencing major defeats early in the war, British and Anglo-American forces turned the tide against the French in 1758 by taking Fort Duquesne and Louisbourg. After Canada fell in 1760, the fighting shifted to Spain's Caribbean colonies.

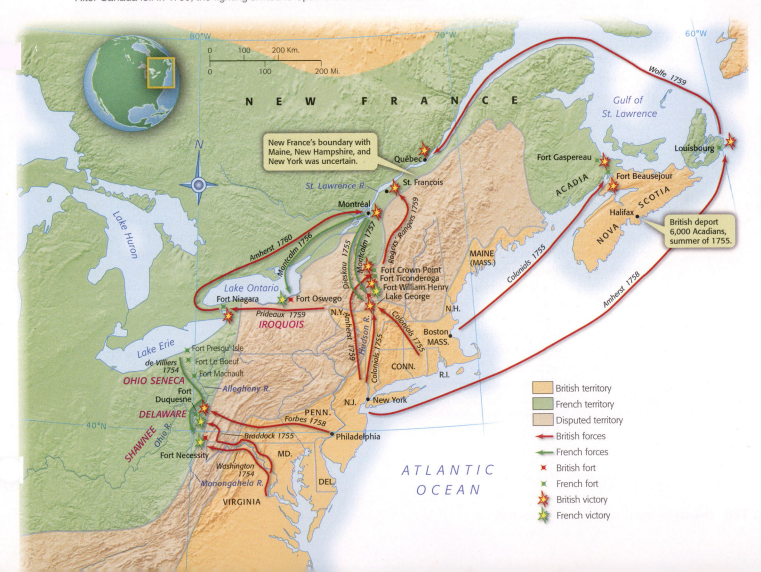

DESTRUCTION OF QUEBEC, 1759 After their relentless attack secured Quebec for British forces, France's defeat in North America was virtually certain. *(National Archives of Canada)*

In this dark hour, two developments turned the tide for Britain. One occurred when the Six Nations Iroquois and most Ohio Native Americans agreed at a treaty conference at Easton, Pennsylvania, in 1758 to abandon their alliances with the French. Resenting French officers' high-handed treatment of them, the Native Americans determined that a complete French victory would threaten their land and sovereignty as seriously as would a British triumph. The Indians' subsequent withdrawal from Fort Duquesne enabled the British to capture it and other French forts. Many Native Americans withdrew from the fighting altogether, while others actively joined Britain's cause.

Another decisive development occurred when William Pitt took control of military affairs in the British cabinet and reversed the downward course. Pitt saw himself as the man of the hour. "I know," he declared, "that I can save this country and that no one else can." True to his word, Pitt reinvigorated British patriotism throughout the empire. By war's end, he was the symbol of what Americans and the English could accomplish when united.

Needing British troops in Europe to face France and its allies (which included Spain after 1761), Pitt sought instead to use colonial soldiers on the North American front. He promised the colonies that if they raised the necessary men, Parliament would bear most of the cost of fighting the war. Pitt's offer generated unprecedented Anglo-American support. The colonies provided more than forty thousand troops in 1758–1759, far more soldiers than the crown sent to North America during the entire war.

The impact of Pitt's decision was immediate. Anglo-American troops under General Jeffery Amherst captured Fort Duquesne and Louisbourg in 1758 and drove the French from northern New York the next year. In September 1759, Quebec fell after General James Wolfe defeated the French commander-in-chief, Louis Joseph Montcalm, on the Plains of Abraham, where both commanders died in battle. French resistance ended in 1760 when Montreal surrendered.

5-1.3 The End of French North America, 1760–1763

Although the fall of Montreal dashed French hopes of victory in North America, the war continued in Europe and elsewhere. Finally, with defeat inevitable, France in 1762 began negotiating with its enemies. The Seven Years' War officially ended with the signing of the Treaty of Paris in 1763.

Under terms of the treaty, France gave up all its lands and claims east of the Mississippi (except New Orleans) to Britain. In return for Cuba, seized by the British in 1762, Spain ceded Florida to Britain. Neither France nor Britain wanted the other to control Louisiana, so in the Treaty of San Ildefonso (1762), France ceded the vast territory to Spain. Thus, France's once mighty North American empire was reduced to a few tiny fishing islands off New-foundland and several prosperous sugar islands in the West Indies. Britain reigned supreme in eastern North America while Spain now claimed the west below Canada (see Map 5.2).

Several thousand French colonists suddenly found themselves subjects of Spain or Britain, not always happily. While Anglo-Americans were resisting Britain's Townshend Acts (discussed later) in 1768, armed French residents of New Orleans drove the Spanish governor of Louisiana out of the colony. A new governor arrived the following year along with three thousand Spanish troops. The Spanish arrested the leaders of the uprising and, after a brief trial, executed five of them.

The most adversely affected Franco-Americans were the Acadians, who had been nominal British subjects since England took over Acadia in 1713 and renamed it Nova Scotia. Britain left the Acadians alone until 1755 when, with Anglo-French war looming, Nova Scotia's government ordered them to swear loyalty to the King of England. After most Acadians refused to take the oath, British soldiers drove them from their homes. About 7,000 of the 18,000 Acadians were forcibly dispersed among Britain's other colonies, while others were sent to France or French colonies. Facing poverty and intense anti-French, anti-Catholic prejudice in the British colonies and seeking to remain together, a majority of the exiles and refugees eventually moved to rural Louisiana, where their descendants became known as Cajuns.

King George's War and the Seven Years' War produced ironically mixed effects. On one hand, they fused the bonds between the British and the Anglo-Americans. Fighting side by side against the French Catholic enemy, Britons and colonists had further strengthened their common identity. On the other hand, each war also planted seeds of mutual misunderstanding and suspicion.

5-1.4 Anglo-American Friction

During the Seven Years' War, British officers regularly complained about colonial troops, not only their inability to fight but also their tendency to return home—even in the midst of campaigns—when their terms were up or when they were not paid on time. For their part, colonial soldiers

MAP 5.2 EUROPEAN TERRITORIAL CLAIMS, 1763 The treaties of San Ildefonso (1762) and Paris (1763) divided France's North American empire between Britain and Spain. Britain in 1763 established direct imperial authority west of the Proclamation Line.

complained of British officers who, as one put it, treated their troops "but little better than slaves."

Tensions between British officers and colonial civilians also flared. Officers complained about colonists being unwilling to provide food and shelter while Anglo-Americans resented the officers' arrogant manners. One general groused that South Carolinians were "extremely pleased to have Soldiers to protect their Plantations but will feel no inconveniences for them." Quakers in the Pennsylvania assembly, acting from pacifist convictions, refused to vote funds to support the war effort, while assemblies in New York and Massachusetts opposed the quartering of British troops on their soil as an encroachment on English liberties. English authorities regarded such actions as affronts to the crown and as undermining Britain's efforts to defend its territories.

Pitt's promise to reimburse the colonial assemblies for their military expenses angered many in Britain, who concluded that the colonists were escaping scot-free from the war's financial burden. Colonists had profited enormously from the war, as military contracts and spending by British troops brought an influx of British currency into the hands of farmers, artisans, and merchants. Some merchants had even traded with the French enemy during wartime. Meanwhile, Britain's national debt nearly doubled during the war, from £72 million to more than £132 million. Whereas in 1763 the total debt of all thirteen colonies amounted to £2 million, the interest charges alone on the British debt came to more than £4 million a year. This debt was assumed by British landowners through a land tax and, increasingly, by ordinary consumers through excise duties on such everyday items as beer, tea, salt, and bread.

Colonists felt equally burdened. Those who profited during the war spent their additional income on

British imports, the annual value of which doubled during the war. Thus, the war accelerated the Anglo-American "consumer revolution" in which colonists' purchases of British goods greatly stimulated Britain's economy, particularly its manufacturing sector. But when peace returned in 1760, the wartime boom in the colonies ended as abruptly as it had begun. To maintain their lifestyles, many colonists went into debt. British creditors obliged their American merchant customers by extending the usual period for remitting payments from six months to a year. Nevertheless, many recently prosperous colonists found themselves overloaded with debts and, in some cases, bankrupt. As colonial indebtedness to Britain grew, some Americans began to accuse the British of deliberately plotting to "enslave" the colonies.

The ascension to the British throne of King **George III** (ruled 1760–1820) at age twenty-two reinforced Anglo-American tensions. The new king was determined to have a strong influence on government policy, but neither his experience, his temperament, nor his philosophy suited him to the formidable task of building political coalitions and pursuing consistent policies. Until 1774, George III made frequent abrupt changes in government leadership that destabilized politics in Britain and exacerbated relations with the colonies.

5-1.5 Frontier Tensions

Victory over the French spurred new Anglo-Indian conflicts that drove the British debt even higher. With the French gone, Ohio and Great Lakes Native Americans recognized that they could no longer play the two imperial rivals off against each other. Their fears that the British would treat them as subjects rather than as allies were confirmed when General Jeffery Amherst, Britain's commander in North America, ordered troops occupying former French posts not to distribute food, ammunition (needed for hunting), and other gifts as the French had done. Moreover, squatters from the colonies were moving onto Indian lands and harassing the occupants, and Native Americans feared that the British occupation was intended to support these incursions.

As tensions mounted, a Delaware Indian religious prophet named Neolin reported a vision in which the "Master of Life," or Great Spirit, instructed him to urge Native Americans of all tribes to unify and to take back their land and live as they had before Europeans—particularly the British—arrived (see Going to the Source). Drawing on Neolin's message and inspired by Pontiac, an Ottawa, Indians throughout the Ohio-Great Lakes region, unleashed **Pontiac's War**. During the spring and summer of 1763, they sacked eight British forts and besieged four others. But over the next six months, shortages

GEORGE III, STUDIO OF A. RAMSAY, 1767
Although emotionally unpredictable and prone to making rash decisions, George III possessed a deep moral sense and a fierce determination to rule as well as to reign. *(World History Archive/Alamy)*

Pontiac Recounts a Prophet's Vision

Pontiac was an *ogema* (civil leader) of the Ottawa people. Like many eastern Indians, he distrusted British intentions after the Seven Years' War. Speaking to an intertribal audience in spring 1763, Pontiac recounted the vision of the Delaware religious prophet, Neolin. In the following excerpt from that speech (recorded by a French colonist), Pontiac repeats the words spoken to Neolin by the Master of Life. Note how the Master of Life accounts for the absence of wild animals, which others might attribute to commercial overhunting and the environmental effects of European settlement.

I am the Master of Life, whom you desire to know and to whom you would speak. Listen well to what I am going to say to you and all the red brethren. I am He who made heaven and earth, the trees, lakes, rivers, all men, and all that you see, and all that you have seen on earth. Because of this and because I love you, you must do what I say and leave what I hate. I do not like it that you drink until you lose your reason, as you do; or that you fight with each other; or that you take two wives, or run after the wives of others; . . . I hate that. You must have but one wife, and keep her until death. When you are going to war, you [must] . . . join the medicine dance, and believe that I am speaking. . . . It is . . . Manitou to whom you [should] speak. It is a bad spirit who whispers to you nothing but evil, and to whom you listen because you do not know me well. This land, where you live, I have made for you and not for others. How comes it that you suffer the whites on your lands? Can't you do without them? I know that those whom you call the children of your Great Father supply your wants, but if you were not bad, as you are, you would well do without them. You might live wholly as you did before you knew them. Before those whom you call your brothers came on your lands, did you not live by bow and arrow? You had no need of gun nor powder, nor the rest of their things, and nevertheless you caught animals to live and clothe yourselves with their skins, but when I saw that you went to the bad, I called back the animals into the depths of the woods, so that you had need of your brothers to have your wants supplied and cover you. You have only to become good and do what I want, and I shall send back to you the animals to live on. I do not forbid you, for all that, to suffer among you the children of your father [whites who live peaceably among the Indians]. I love them, they know me and pray to me, and I give them their necessities and all that they bring to you, but as regards those [whites] who have come to trouble your country, drive them out, make war on them! I love them not, they know me not, they are my enemies and the enemies of your brothers! Send them back to the country which I made for them! There let them remain.

Source: *Michigan Pioneer and Historical Collections (1886) 8:270–271.*

QUESTIONS

1. Why, according to the Master of Life, are Native Americans suffering?
2. What does the Master of Life say Indians must do so that the animals will return?

of food and ammunition, a smallpox epidemic at Fort Pitt (triggered when British officers deliberately distributed infected blankets at a peace parley), and a recognition that the French would not return led the Indians to make peace with Britain.

Although not a military victory, Pontiac's War gained some political concessions for Native Americans. Hoping to conciliate the Indians and end the fighting, George III issued the **Proclamation of 1763**, asserting direct British control of land transactions, settlement, trade, and other activities of non-Indians west of a Proclamation line along the Appalachian crest (see Map 5.2). The government sought to control Anglo-American expansion by asserting its authority over the various (and often competing) colonies claiming western lands. The proclamation recognized existing Indian land titles everywhere west of the "proclamation line" until such time as tribal governments agreed to cede their land to Britain through treaties. Although addressing Native Americans' concerns, the proclamation

Proclamation of 1763
This was issued by George III to assert direct British control of land transaction, settlement, trade, and other activities of non-Indians west of the Proclamation line along the Appalachian crest.

angered the colonies by subordinating their western claims to imperial authority and, they feared, by blocking expansion. (Actually, roads built to the forts—and land grants to settlers who would provision the forts—encouraged expansion.)

Pontiac's War was also a factor in the British government's decision to leave ten thousand soldiers in France's former forts on the Great Lakes and in the Ohio Valley to enforce the Proclamation of 1763. The cost of maintaining this military presence would reach almost a half million pounds a year, fully 6 percent of Britain's peacetime budget. Britons considered it perfectly reasonable for the colonists to help underwrite this expense. Although the troops would help offset the colonies' unfavorable balance of payments with Britain, many Anglo-Americans regarded them as a peacetime "standing army" that threatened their liberty and blocked their expansion onto Indian lands.

5-2 Imperial Authority, Colonial Opposition, 1760–1766

What was at the core of the tensions between the colonists and the British in the years following the Seven Years' War?

After the Seven Years' War, Anglo-American tensions centered on Britain's efforts to finance its suddenly enlarged empire through a series of revenue measures and to enforce these and other measures directly rather than relying on local authorities. Following passage of the Stamp Act, opposition movements arose in the mainland colonies to protest not only the new measures' costs but also what many people considered a dangerous extension of Parliament's power. Opponents came from all segments of colonial society, including poor and working people. The crisis revealed a widening gulf between British and colonial perceptions of the proper relationship between Great Britain and its colonies.

5-2.1 Writs of Assistance, 1760–1761

Even before the Seven Years' War ended, British authorities attempted to halt American merchants' trade with the French enemy in the West Indies. In 1760, the royal governor of Massachusetts authorized revenue officers to employ a search warrant called a writ of assistance to seize illegally imported goods. The writ permitted customs officials to

INDIAN-BRITISH DIPLOMACY IN THE OHIO COUNTRY, 1764 A brief truce during Pontiac's War brought Indian and British leaders together to talk peace. Here, a Native American speaker presents a wampum belt to his counterparts. *(Library of Congress Prints and Photographs Division Washington, D.C[LC-USZ62-104])*

enter any ship or building (including a merchant's residence) where smuggled goods might be hidden. Because the document required no evidence of probable cause for suspicion, opponents considered it unconstitutional.

Writs of assistance proved effective against smuggling. In quick reaction, some Boston merchants hired lawyer James Otis to challenge the constitutionality of the writs. Before the Massachusetts Supreme Court in 1761, Otis argued that "an act against the Constitution is void"—even one passed by Parliament. But the court, influenced by Chief Justice Thomas Hutchinson, who noted the use of identical writs in England, ruled against the merchants.

Despite losing the case, Otis expressed the fundamental conception of many, both in Britain and in the colonies, of Parliament's role under the British constitution. The British constitution was not a written document but instead a collection of customs and accepted principles that guaranteed certain rights to all citizens. Most British politicians assumed that Parliament's laws were themselves part of the constitution and hence that Parliament could alter the constitution at will. But Otis contended that Parliament possessed no authority to violate the "rights of Englishmen," and he asserted that there were limits "beyond which if Parliaments go, their Acts bind not." Such challenges to parliamentary authority would be renewed once peace was restored.

5-2.2 The Sugar Act, 1764

Following the British victory over France and the Proclamation of 1763, Parliament in 1764 passed the **Sugar Act**. The measure's goal was to raise revenues to help pay for "defending, protecting, and securing" North America, and thus ended the exemption of colonial trade from revenue-raising measures. Under the Navigation Acts, English importers, not American producers, paid taxes on colonial products entering Britain, and then passed the cost on to consumers. So little revenue did the Navigation Acts bring in (just £1,800 in 1763) that they did not even pay the cost of their own enforcement.

The Sugar Act amended the Molasses Act of 1733, the last of the Navigation Acts, which taxed foreign (primarily French West Indian) molasses and rum entering the mainland colonies at sixpence per gallon. But colonial merchants had simply continued to import the cheaper French molasses after 1733, bribing customs officials 1½ pence per gallon when it was unloaded. Hoping to end the bribery, Parliament lowered the duty to three pence per gallon.

The Sugar Act also vastly complicated the requirements for shipping goods. Merchants and captains now had to fill out a confusing series of documents to certify that their commerce was legal, and merchants were required to post expensive bonds to ensure their compliance.

Finally, the Sugar Act disregarded many traditional English protections for a fair trial. Although customs officials needed to show "probable cause" for prosecuting a case, the defendant was presumed to be guilty until proven innocent. The law stipulated that smuggling cases be heard in vice-admiralty courts, where a British-appointed judge gave the verdict, rather than in colonial courts, in which juries decided the outcome. The government established a vice-admiralty court in Halifax, Nova Scotia, to hear American cases, a location far from any merchant's home port. Because the Sugar Act (until 1768) awarded vice-admiralty judges 5 percent of any confiscated cargo, judges had a financial incentive to find defendants guilty.

The British navy vigorously enforced the Sugar Act. A Boston resident complained in 1764 that "no vessel hardly comes in or goes out but they find some pretense to seize and detain her." That same year, Pennsylvania's chief justice reported that customs officers were extorting fees from small boats carrying lumber across the Delaware River to Philadelphia from New Jersey and seemed likely "to destroy this little River-trade."

Rather than pay the three-pence tax, Americans continued smuggling molasses until 1766. Then, to discourage smuggling, Britain lowered the duty to a penny—less than the customary bribe American shippers paid to get their cargoes past inspectors. The law thereafter raised about £30,000 annually in revenue.

Because the burden of the Sugar Act fell overwhelmingly on Massachusetts, New York, and Pennsylvania, other provinces had little interest in resisting it. The Sugar Act's immediate effect was minor, but it irritated urban merchants and heightened colonists' sensitivities to the new direction of imperial policies.

5-2.3 The Stamp Act Crisis, 1765–1766

The revenue raised by the Sugar Act did little to ease Britain's financial crisis. The national debt escalated, and Britons bemoaned the second-highest tax rates in Europe. Particularly irritating: By 1765 their rates averaged 26 shillings per person, whereas the colonial tax burden varied from ½ to 1½ shillings per inhabitant. British prime minister George Grenville thought colonists should make a larger contribution to the empire's American expenses.

> **Sugar Act**
> This amended the Molasses Act of 1733. It reduced tax on molasses to three pence per gallon.

As such, Parliament passed the **Stamp Act** in March 1765. The law obliged colonists to purchase and use special stamped (watermarked) paper for newspapers, customs documents, various licenses, college diplomas, playing cards, and legal forms used for recovering debts, transferring property, and making wills. As with the Sugar Act, violators would face prosecution in vice-admiralty courts, without juries. The prime minister projected yearly revenues of £60,000 to £100,000, which would offset 12 to 20 percent of North American military expenses.

Unlike the Sugar Act, which was an external tax levied on imports, the Stamp Act was an internal tax, or a duty levied directly on property, goods, and government services within the colonies. Whereas external taxes were intended to regulate trade and fell mainly on merchants and ship captains, internal taxes were designed to raise revenue for the crown and affected most people at least occasionally.

To Grenville and his supporters, the new tax seemed a small price for the benefits of empire. Nevertheless, some in England, notably William Pitt, objected, emphasizing that the colonists had never been subject to British revenue bills and that they already taxed themselves through their own elected assemblies.

Grenville and his followers believed that while Americans did not directly elect members of Parliament, they were "virtually" represented there. The principle of virtual representation held that Parliament considered the welfare of all subjects when deciding issues. By definition, then, British subjects, including colonists, were not represented by particular individuals but by all members of Parliament. Grenville and his supporters also alleged that American assemblies were comparable to British local governments, whose powers did not nullify Parliament's authority over them. But colonists had long maintained that their assemblies exercised legislative powers equivalent to those of the House of Commons in Britain (see Chapter 4).

Many colonists felt that the Stamp Act forced them either to confront the issue of parliamentary taxation or to surrender any claim to self-government. Most colonists accepted the validity of virtual representation for England and Scotland but denied that it extended to the colonies. Instead, they argued, their self-governance was similar to that of Ireland, whose Parliament alone could tax its people but could not interfere with laws, like the Navigation Acts, passed by the British Parliament. In essence, the colonists assumed that the empire was a loose federation in which their legislatures possessed considerable autonomy, rather than an extended nation governed directly from London.

To many colonists, passage of the Stamp Act demonstrated both Parliament's indifference to their interests and the shallowness of the theory of virtual representation. Provincial assemblies as well as colonial lobbyists in London had urged the act's defeat, but Parliament had dismissed these appeals without a hearing. In late May 1765, Patrick Henry, a twenty-nine-year-old Virginia lawyer and planter with a talent for fiery oratory, dramatically conveyed the rising spirit of resistance. Henry urged the Virginia House of Burgesses to adopt seven strongly worded resolutions denying Parliament's power to tax the colonies. Viewing some of the language as treasonous, the legislators passed only the mildest four of Henry's resolutions. By year's end, seven other assemblies had passed resolutions against the act.

It was no accident that Boston set the pace in opposing Parliament. There, in late summer, a group of middle-class artisans and small business owners formed the Loyal Nine to fight the Stamp Act. They recognized that the stamp distributors, who alone could accept money for watermarked paper, were the law's weak link. If the public could pressure them into resigning before taxes became due on November 1, the Stamp Act would become inoperable.

No other port suffered as much as Boston from the Sugar Act's trade restrictions. Worse, for several decades, its shipbuilding industry had lost significant ground to New York and Philadelphia, and the output of its rum and sugar producers had fallen by half in a decade. British impressment (forced recruitment) of Massachusetts fishermen for naval service had undermined the fishing industry. The resulting unemployment led to increased local taxes for poor relief. The taxes, along with fewer customers, drove many marginal artisans out of business and into the ranks of the poor.

Widespread economic distress produced an explosive situation in Boston. Already resentful of an elite whose fortunes had risen spectacularly while they suffered, many poor and working-class Bostonians blamed British officials and policies for the town's hard times. The morning of August 14 found a likeness of Boston's stamp distributor, Andrew Oliver, swinging from a tree guarded by a menacing crowd organized by the Loyal Nine. By dusk, Oliver had not resigned, so several hundred Bostonians demolished a building of Oliver's. Thereafter, the Loyal Nine withdrew, and the crowd continued on its own. The men surged toward Oliver's house, where they beheaded his effigy and "stamped" it to pieces. They then shattered the windows of his home and smashed his furniture. The next morning, Oliver announced his resignation.

Stamp Act

This obliged colonists to purchase and use special stamped (watermarked) paper for newspapers, customs documents, various licenses, college diplomas, and legal forms used for recovering debts, buying land, and making wills.

Bitterness against the Stamp Act unleashed spontaneous violence. Twelve days after Oliver resigned, a crowd demolished the home of Lieutenant Governor and Chief Justice Thomas Hutchinson. Boston's smugglers begrudged Hutchinson for some of his decisions as chief justice while many more citizens saw him as a symbol of the royal policies crippling Boston's economy. Ironically, Hutchinson privately opposed the Stamp Act.

Thereafter, groups similar to the Loyal Nine calling themselves **Sons of Liberty** formed throughout the colonies. The leaders of the Sons of Liberty sought to prevent more violent outbreaks. They recognized that the crowds were casting aside their customary deference toward their social "superiors," a development that could broaden to include all elites if not contained. Fearful of alienating wealthy opponents of the Stamp Act, the Sons of Liberty focused their demonstrations strictly against property and forbade their followers to carry weapons.

In October 1765, representatives of nine colonial assemblies met in New York City in a **Stamp Act Congress**. The session was remarkable for the colonies' agreement on and bold articulation of the principle that Parliament lacked authority to levy taxes outside Great Britain and to deny any person a jury trial. "The Ministry never imagined we could or would so generally unite in opposition to their measures," wrote a Connecticut delegate, "nor I confess till I saw the Experiment made did I."

By late 1765, most stamp distributors had resigned or fled, and without the watermarked paper required by law, most royal customs officials and court officers were refusing to perform their duties. In response, legislators threatened to withhold their pay. At the same time, merchants obtained sailing clearances by insisting they would sue if cargoes spoiled while delayed in port. By late December, the courts and harbors of almost every colony were again functioning.

Thus, colonial elites moved to keep an explosive situation from escalating by supporting the moderate Sons of Liberty over radical groups, by expressing opposition through the Stamp Act Congress, and by having colonial legislatures restore normal business. Elite leaders feared that chaos could break out, particularly if British troops landed to enforce the Stamp Act. Pennsylvania's John Dickinson feared that revolutionary turmoil would lead to "a multitude of Commonwealths, Crimes, and Calamities."

To force the Stamp Act's repeal, New York's merchants agreed on October 31, 1765, to boycott all British goods, and businessmen and elite women in other cities soon followed their example. Because American colonists purchased about 40 percent of England's manufactures, this nonimportation strategy put the English economy in danger of recession.

THOMAS HUTCHINSON As lieutenant governor and, later, governor of Massachusetts, Hutchinson believed that social and political order under British authority must be maintained at all costs. *(Thomas Hutchinson (1711–80) 1741 (oil on canvas), Truman, Edward (18th century) / © Massachusetts Historical Society, Boston, MA, USA / Bridgeman Images)*

Panicked English businessmen descended on Parliament to warn that continuation of the Stamp Act would stimulate a wave of bankruptcies, massive unemployment, and political unrest.

By early 1766, support was growing in Parliament for repeal of the Stamp Act. In March 1766, Parliament revoked the Stamp Act, but only in conjunction with passage of the **Declaratory Act**, which affirmed parliamentary power to legislate for the colonies "in all cases whatsoever."

Because the Declaratory Act was written in general language, Anglo-Americans interpreted it to their own advantage. To them, the measure seemed no more than a parliamentary exercise in saving face to compensate for the Stamp Act's repeal. The House of Commons, however, intended that the colonists take the Declaratory Act literally to mean that they could not claim exemption from any parliamentary statute, including a tax law. The Stamp Act crisis thus

Sons of Liberty
Groups of colonists who opposed the Stamp Act and extension of British rule. At times, they rebelled by destroying the property of the elites.

Stamp Act Congress
October 1765 meeting of colonial representatives to protest the Stamp Act, notable for the unity shown by colonists in defying Parliament.

Declaratory Act
This affirmed parliamentary power to legislate for the colonies "in all cases whatsoever."

ANTI–STAMP ACT TEAPOT Some colonists signaled their opposition to the Stamp Act on the pots from which they drank tea (ironically, purchased from British merchants). Less than a decade later, they would protest a British tax on tea itself. *(The Colonial Williamsburg Foundation)*

ended in a fundamental disagreement between Britain and America over Parliament's authority in the colonies.

5-2.4 Ideology, Religion, and Resistance

The Stamp Act and the conflicts around it revealed a chasm between Britain and its colonies that startled Anglo-Americans. For the first time, some of them critically reconsidered the imperial relationship. To put their concerns into perspective, educated colonists turned to the works of philosophers, historians, and political writers. Many more, both educated and uneducated, looked to religion.

By the 1760s, many colonists were familiar with the political writings of European Enlightenment thinkers, particularly John Locke (see Chapter 4). Locke argued that humans originated in a "state of nature" in which each man enjoyed the "natural rights" of life, liberty, and property. Thereafter, groups of men entered into a "social contract," under which they formed governments for the sole purpose of protecting those individual rights. A government that encroached on natural rights, then, broke its contract with the people. In such cases, people could resist their government, although Locke cautioned against outright rebellion except in the most extreme cases. To many colonial readers, Locke's concept of natural rights appeared to justify opposition to arbitrary legislation by Parliament.

Colonists also read European writers who emphasized excessive concentrations of executive power as tyrannical threats. Some of them developed a set of ideas termed "republican," in which they balanced Locke's emphasis on individual rights with an emphasis on the good of the people as a whole. "Republicans" especially admired the

sense of civic duty that motivated citizens of the Roman republic. Like the early Romans, they maintained that a free people had to avoid moral and political corruption, and practice a disinterested "public virtue." An elected leader of a republic, one author noted, would command obedience "more by the virtue of the people, than by the terror of his power."

Among those influenced by republican ideas were a widely read group of English political writers known as oppositionists. According to the oppositionists, Parliament—consisting of the elected representatives of the people—formed the foundation of England's unique political liberties and protected those liberties against the inherent corruption and tyranny of executive power. But recent prime ministers, the oppositionists argued, had exploited the treasury's resources to bribe politicians and voters. Most members of Parliament, in their view, no longer represented the true interests of the people; rather, they had created self-interested "factions" and joined in a "conspiracy against liberty." Often referring to themselves as the "country party," the oppositionists feared that a power-hungry "court party" of unelected officials close to the king was using a corrupted Parliament to gain absolute power for themselves.

Over the next decade, a proliferation of pamphlets denounced British efforts to "enslave" the colonies through excessive taxation and the imposition of officials, judges, and a standing army directed from London. In such assaults on liberty and natural rights, some Americans found principled reasons for opposing British policies and actions.

Beginning with the Stamp Act protest, many Protestant clergymen, both Old Lights and New Lights (see Chapter 4), wove resistance to British authority into their sermons, summoning their congregations to protect their God-given liberty. "A just regard to our liberties . . . is so far from being displeasing to God that it would be ingratitude to him who has given them to us to . . . tamely give them up," exhorted one New England minister. Most Anglican ministers, whose church was headed by the king, tried to stay neutral or opposed the protest, but to large numbers of Congregationalist, Presbyterian, and Baptist preachers, battling for the Lord and defending liberty were one and the same.

Voicing such a message, ministers exerted an enormous influence on public opinion. Far more Americans heard sermons than had access to newspapers or pamphlets. Provincial proclamations of days of "fasting and public humiliation"—a traditional means of focusing public attention on an issue and invoking divine aid—inspired sermons on the theme of God's sending the people woes only to strengthen and sustain them until victory. Moreover, protest leaders' calls for boycotting British luxuries fit neatly with traditional pulpit warnings against self-indulgence and wastefulness. Few ordinary Americans escaped the unceasing public reminders that community solidarity against British tyranny and "corruption" meant rejecting sin and obeying God.

5-3 Resistance Resumes, 1766–1770

Why did colonial resistance continue even after the Stamp Act was withdrawn?

Although Parliament's repeal of the Stamp Act momentarily quieted colonial protests, its search for new sources of revenue soon revived them. While British leaders condemned the colonists for evading their financial responsibilities and for insubordination, growing numbers of Anglo-Americans became convinced that the Stamp Act had not been an isolated mistake but rather part of a deliberate design to undermine colonial self-governance. In this, they were joined by many in Britain who opposed policies that seemed to threaten Britons and colonists alike.

5-3.1 Opposing the Quartering Act, 1766–1767

Hoping to end disarray in Parliament, George III in August 1766 summoned William Pitt to form a cabinet. Previously sympathetic to the colonies, Pitt might have repaired the Stamp Act's damage, for no Englishman was more respected in America. But after Pitt's health collapsed in March 1767, effective leadership passed to his Chancellor of the Exchequer (treasurer) Charles Townshend.

Just as Townshend took office, a conflict arose with the New York assembly over the Quartering Act, enacted in 1765. This law ordered colonial legislatures to pay for housing and provisioning British soldiers stationed within their respective borders. Despite its minimal cost, the Quartering Act aroused resentment, for it constituted an indirect tax; that is, although it did not (like the Stamp Act) empower royal officials to collect money directly from the colonists, it obligated assemblies to raise a stated amount of revenue. Such obligations clashed with the assemblies' claimed power to initiate all revenue-raising measures. The law fell lightly or not at all on most colonies, but New York, where many soldiers had recently been transferred from western forts, refused to comply.

New York's resistance to the Quartering Act produced a torrent of anti-American feeling in Parliament, whose members remained bitter at having had to withdraw the Stamp Act. In response, they passed the New York Suspending Act (1767), which would delay the assembly until it appropriated the funds. The assembly quickly complied before the measure became law.

Although New York's retreat averted further confrontation, the Quartering Act demonstrated that British leaders would not hesitate to defend Parliament's authority through the most drastic of all steps: by interfering with American claims to self-governance.

5-3.2 Crisis over the Townshend Acts, 1767–1770

As Parliament passed the New York Suspending Act, Townshend expanded his efforts to subordinate the colonies to Parliament's authority and raise revenues in America. He sought to tax the colonists by exploiting an oversight in their arguments against the Stamp Act. In confronting the Stamp Act, Americans had emphasized their opposition to internal taxes but had said little about Parliament's right to tax imports as they entered the colonies. Townshend chose to interpret this silence as evidence that the colonists accepted Britain's power to tax their trade—to impose external taxes. Yet not all British politicians were so mistaken. "They will laugh at you," predicted a now wiser George Grenville, "for your distinctions about regulations of trade." Brushing aside Grenville's warnings, Parliament passed the **Townshend Acts** in 1767. The new law taxed glass, paint, lead, paper, and tea imported to the colonies from England.

The Townshend Acts differed significantly from what Americans had long seen as a legitimate way of regulating trade through taxation. To the colonists, charging a duty was a lawful way for British authorities to control trade—but only if that duty was levied against foreign goods, thereby making them prohibitively expensive to consumers. The Townshend Acts, however, set moderate rates that did not price goods out of the colonial market; clearly, its purpose was to collect money for the treasury. Thus, from the colonial standpoint, Townshend's duties were taxes just like the Stamp Act duties.

In reality, the new duties would never yield anything like the income that Townshend anticipated. Of the various items taxed, only tea produced any significant revenue—£20,000 of the £37,000 that the law was expected to yield. And because the measure would

> **Townshend Acts**
> Passed in June and July 1767, these taxed glass, paint, lead, paper, and tea imported to the colonies from England.

serve its purpose only if British tea were afford-able to colonial consumers, Townshend eliminated £60,000 worth of import fees paid on tea entering Britain from India before transshipment to America. On balance, the Townshend Acts worsened the British treasury's deficit by £23,000. But by 1767, Parliament was less concerned with raising revenues than with asserting its authority over the colonies.

Colonial opposition to the Townshend Acts began in December 1767, when John Dickinson published twelve essays titled *Letters from a Farmer in Pennsylvania*. The essays argued that although Parliament could regulate trade by imposing duties, no tax designed to produce revenue could be considered constitutional unless a people's elected representatives voted for it. Dickinson said nothing that others had not stated or implied during the Stamp Act crisis. Rather, his contribution lay in persuading recent opponents of the Stamp Act that their arguments also applied to the Townshend Acts.

Other Anglo-Americans quickly embraced Dickinson's arguments. In early 1768, the Massachusetts assembly condemned the Townshend duties and commissioned Samuel Adams to draft a "circular letter" calling on other colonial legislatures to join it. Adams's letter condemned taxation without representation. But it acknowledged Parliament as the "supreme legislative Power over the whole Empire," and it advocated no illegal activities. Three other colonies approved Adams's message and Virginia sent out a more strongly worded circular letter of its own. But most colonial legislatures reacted indifferently. In fact, resistance to the Townshend Acts might have disintegrated had the British government not overreacted to the circular letters.

Parliamentary leaders regarded even the mild Massachusetts letter as "little better than an incentive to Rebellion." Following Townshend's sudden death in 1767, Lord Hillsborough, first appointee to the new post of secretary of state for the colonies, took charge of British policy. Hillsborough flatly told the Massachusetts assembly to disown its letter, forbade all colonial assemblies to endorse it, and commanded royal governors to dissolve any legislature that violated his instructions. George III later commented that he never met "a man of less judgment than Lord Hillsborough."

To protest Hillsborough's bullying, many legislatures previously indifferent to the Massachusetts circular letter now adopted it enthusiastically. In obedience to Hillsborough, royal governors responded by dismissing legislatures in Massachusetts and elsewhere. These moves played directly into the hands of Samuel Adams, James Otis, and others who sought to ignite widespread public opposition to the Townshend duties.

Although outraged over the Townshend Acts, colonial activists needed some effective means of pressuring Parliament for their repeal. One approach, nonimportation, seemed especially promising because it offered an alternative to violence and would distress Britain's economy. In August 1768, Boston's merchants therefore adopted a nonimportation agreement, and the tactic slowly spread southward. "Save your money, and you save your country!" became the watchword of the Sons of Liberty, who began reorganizing after two years of inactivity. The success of nonimportation depended on the compliance of merchants whose livelihood relied on buying and selling imports. In several major communities, including Philadelphia, Baltimore, and Charles Town, merchants continued buying British goods until 1769. Nevertheless, the boycott did significantly limit British imports and mobilized colonists into resuming resistance to British policies.

By 1770, a new British prime minister, Lord North, favored eliminating most of the Townshend duties to prevent the American boycott from widening. But to underscore British authority, he insisted on retaining the highly profitable tax on tea. Parliament agreed, and in April 1770, giving in for the second time in four years to colonial pressure, it repealed most of the Townshend duties.

Parliament's partial repeal produced a dilemma for American politicians. They considered it intolerable that taxes remained on tea. Colonial leaders were unsure whether they should press on with the nonimportation agreement until they achieved total victory, or whether it would suffice to maintain a selective boycott of tea. When the nonimportation movement collapsed in July 1770, colonists resisted external taxation by voluntary agreements not to drink British tea. Through nonconsumption, they succeeded in limiting revenue from tea to about one-sixth the level originally expected. Yet colonial resistance leaders took little satisfaction in having forced Parliament to compromise. The tea duty remained a galling reminder that Parliament refused to retreat from the broadest possible interpretation of the Declaratory Act.

5-3.3 Women and Colonial Resistance

Colonial boycotts of British goods provided a unique opportunity for white women to join the resistance to British policies. White women purchased most of their families' household items, including food and clothing, and therefore, it was not a big leap for them to participate politically by boycotting British imports. As early as 1765, a contingent of upper-class female patriots had played a part in defeating the Stamp Act. Some had attended political rallies during the crisis, and many more had influenced family and friends through discussions and correspondence. As colonial protests against British measures widened, groups of white female activists—often calling themselves the **Daughters of Liberty**—played increasingly prominent roles, utilizing their black female slaves to assist in their endeavors.

Women assumed an even more prominent political role during the crisis over the Townshend Acts by boycotting British imports. To protest Parliament's continuation of the tax on tea in 1770, more than three hundred "mistresses of families" in Boston denounced consumption of the beverage. Instead, they created their own teas from local herbs or drank coffee. In some ways, the threat of nonconsumption was even more effective than that of nonimportation because women served and drank most of the tea consumed by colonists. The protests extended far beyond Boston: In Edenton, North Carolina, fifty-one women signed a proclamation attesting to their support of the nonimportation resolutions. Women's efforts were mocked and their femininity called into question in British political cartoons.

Nonconsumption agreements were extended to include other English manufactures, especially cloth and clothing. Responding to leaders' pleas that they expand domestic cloth production, women of all social ranks—even those who customarily did not weave their own fabric or sew their own clothing—organized spinning bees to make homespun cloth. As part of the protest, large groups of women would later wear their homespun apparel in public as a demonstration of their support for the colonial cause. These events attracted intense publicity as evidence of American determination to forgo luxury and idleness for the common defense of liberty. Women were praised in newspapers for their efforts. One historian calculates that more than sixteen hundred women participated in spinning bees in New England alone from 1768 to 1770. The colonial cause, noted a New York woman, had enlisted "a fighting army of amazons . . . armed with spinning wheels."

Spinning bees not only helped undermine the notion that women had no place in public life but also endowed spinning and weaving, previously considered routine household tasks, with special political virtue. "Women might recover to this country the full and free enjoyment of all our rights, properties and privileges," exclaimed the Reverend John Cleaveland of Ipswich, Massachusetts, in 1769, adding that this "is more than the men have been able to do." Other male observers favorably compared the sober discipline of spinning women with the mob violence of rioting men. For many colonists, such logic enlarged the arena of supposed feminine

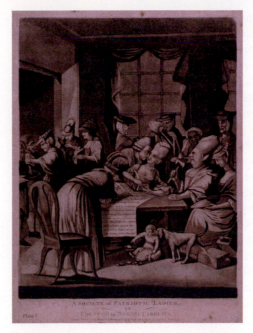

A SOCIETY OF PATRIOTIC LADIES, 1774 British political cartoonists mocked colonial women's efforts to support the patriots' rebellion. This one takes a swipe at the Edenten, North Carolina, women who signed a pledge to boycott British goods. *(Library of Congress Prints and Photographs Division [Robert Sayer and John Bennett/LC-DIG-ppmsca-19468])*

virtues from strictly religious and domestic matters to include political issues.

Combined with female support for boycotting tea, spinning bees dramatically demonstrated that American resistance ran far deeper than the protests of a few male merchants and the largely male crowds in American seaports. Women's participation showed that colonial protests extended into the heart of American households and congregations, and were leading to broader popular participation in politics. Women's political participation would, in the years ahead, lead some women to envision expanded possibilities for their gender. Abigail Adams famously wrote to her husband John Adams in early 1776, urging that he and other members of the Continental Congress "remember the ladies" in the laws that they might make.

5-3.4 Customs "Racketeering," 1767–1770

Besides taxing colonial imports, Townshend had sought additional means of financing British rule in America. Traditionally, royal governors had depended on colonial legislatures to vote their salaries, and assemblies used this power to

> **Daughters of Liberty**
> Name for groups of colonial female activists who participated in boycotts, attended political rallies, and influenced others through correspondence to resist British policies.

influence governors' actions. At Townshend's urging, Parliament authorized paying the salaries of governors and other royal officials in America from revenues raised there, thus freeing officials from the assemblies' control and influence. In effect, by stripping the assemblies of their most potent weapon, the power of the purse, Parliament's action threatened to tip the balance of power away from elected colonial representatives and toward unelected royal officials.

Townshend hoped to increase revenue through stricter enforcement of existing customs laws. Accordingly, he persuaded Parliament in 1767 to establish the American Board of Customs Commissioners. The law raised the number of port officials, funded a colonial coast guard, and provided money for secret informers. It awarded an informer one-third of the value of all goods and ships appropriated through a conviction for smuggling. Smuggling cases were heard in vice-admiralty courts where the probability of conviction was extremely high. But the law quickly drew protests because of the way it was enforced and because it assumed those accused to be guilty unless they could prove otherwise.

Customs commissioners even invaded the traditional rights of sailors, who had long supplemented their incomes by making small sales between ports. Anything stored in a sailor's chest had been considered his private property. Under the new policy, crewmen saw their trunks broken open by inspectors who confiscated trading stock worth several months' wages because it was not listed on the captain's loading papers.

To merchants and seamen alike, the commissioners had embarked on a program of "customs racketeering" that was little more than a system of legalized piracy. Customs agents and informers were especially detested in Boston, where in June 1768 citizens retaliated against them. The occasion was the seizure, on a technicality, of Boston merchant John Hancock's sloop *Liberty*. Hancock, reportedly North America's richest merchant and a leading opponent of British taxation, had become a target of customs commissioners. Now they fined him £9,000, an amount almost thirteen times greater than the taxes he supposedly evaded on a shipment of Madeira wine. A crowd, "chiefly sturdy boys and Negroes," in Thomas Hutchinson's words, tried to prevent the towing of Hancock's ship and then began assaulting customs agents. Growing to several hundred, the mob drove all revenue inspectors from Boston.

Under Lord North, the British government, aware of customs officers' excesses, took steps to dampen colonial protests. Prosecutors dropped the charges against Hancock, but British officials conceded nothing to the colonists. At the same time, they dispatched four thousand troops to Boston, making clear that they would not tolerate further violent defiance of their authority.

5-3.5 "Wilkes and Liberty," 1768–1770

Although wealthy Britons blamed the colonists for their high taxes, others in England found common cause with the Americans. They formed a popular movement that arose during the 1760s to oppose the domestic and foreign policies of George III and a Parliament dominated by wealthy landowners. Their leader was John Wilkes, a fiery London editor and member of Parliament who acquired notoriety in 1763 when his newspaper regularly denounced George III's policies. The government finally arrested Wilkes for seditious libel, but to popular acclaim, he won his case in court. The government, however, succeeded in shutting down his newspaper and in persuading a majority in the House of Commons to deny Wilkes his seat. After subsequently offending the government with a publication, Wilkes fled to Paris.

Defying a warrant for his arrest, Wilkes returned to England in 1768 and again ran for Parliament. By this time, British policies were sparking widespread protests. Merchants and artisans in London, Bristol, and other cities demanded the dismissal of the "obnoxious" ministers who were "ruining our manufactories by invidiously imposing and establishing the most impolitic and unconstitutional taxations

ABIGAIL ADAMS Portrait of Abigail Adams, who gave voice to the political visions of activist, patriot women during the American Revolution in letters to her husband John Adams. *(Harris & Ewing/Library of Congress)*

and regulations on your Majesty's colonies." They were joined by (nonvoting) weavers, coal heavers, seamen, and other workers who protested low wages and high prices that stemmed in part from government policies. All of these people rallied around the cry "Wilkes and liberty!"

After being elected again to Parliament, Wilkes was arrested. The next day, twenty to forty thousand angry "Wilkesites" gathered on St. George's Fields, outside the prison where he was held. When members of the crowd began throwing stones, soldiers and police responded with gunfire, killing eleven protesters. The "massacre of St. George's Fields" had given the movement some martyrs. Wilkes and an associate were elected twice more and were both times denied their seats. Wilkes was besieged by outpourings of popular support from the colonies as well as from Britain. Some Virginians sent him tobacco, and the South Carolina assembly voted to contribute £1,500 to help defray his debts. He maintained a regular correspondence with the Boston Sons of Liberty and, upon his release in

April 1770, was hailed in a massive Boston celebration as "the illustrious martyr to Liberty."

Wilkes's cause sharpened the political thinking of government opponents in Britain and the colonies alike. Thousands of English voters signed petitions to Parliament protesting its refusal to seat Wilkes as an affront to the electorate's will. Some of them formed a Society of the Supporters of the Bill of Rights "to defend and maintain the legal, constitutional liberty of the subject," including the colonists. Wilkes's movement also provided powerful reinforcement for colonists' challenges to the authority of Parliament and the British government.

5-4 The Deepening Crisis, 1770–1774

What fed colonists' growing rebelliousness and fears of British authority from 1770 to 1774?

After 1770, the imperial crisis grew more ominous. Colonists and British troops clashed on the streets of Boston. Resistance leaders in the colonies developed means of systematically coordinating their actions and policies. After Bostonians defied a new act of Parliament, the Tea Act, Britain was determined to subordinate the colonies once and for all. Adding to the tensions of the period were several violent conflicts that erupted in the colonial West.

5-4.1 The Boston Massacre, 1770

As noted, in response to the violence provoked by Hancock's case, British authorities had dispatched four thousand troops to Boston in the summer and fall of 1768. Resentful Bostonians regarded the redcoats as a standing army that threatened their liberty, as well as a financial burden.

With so many soldiers, Boston took on the atmosphere of an occupied city and crackled with tension. Armed sentries and resentful civilians traded insults. The overwhelmingly Protestant townspeople were especially angered that many soldiers were Irish Catholics. The poorly paid enlisted men, moreover, were free to seek employment when off-duty. Often agreeing to work for less than local laborers, they generated hostility from a community plagued by persistently high unemployment.

Poor Bostonians' deep-seated resentment against British authority erupted on February

JOHN WILKES, BY WILLIAM HOGARTH, 1763 Detesting Wilkes and all he stood for, Hogarth depicted the radical leader as menacing and untrustworthy. (*William L. Clements Library. University of Michigan*)

MERCY OTIS WARREN, BY JOHN SINGLETON COPLEY, 1763 An essayist and playwright, Warren was the most prominent woman intellectual of the Revolutionary era. *(Museum of Fine Arts, Boston, Bequest of Winslow Warren. Photograph @ 2009 Museum of Fine Arts, Boston)*

guarding the customs office. When an officer tried to disperse the civilians, his men endured a steady barrage of flying objects and dares to shoot. A private finally did fire, after having been knocked down by a block of ice, and then shouted, "Fire! Fire!" to his fellow soldiers. The soldiers' volley hit eleven persons, five of whom, including Attucks, died.

The shock that followed the March 5 bloodshed marked the emotional high point of the Townshend crisis. Royal authorities in Massachusetts tried to defuse the situation by isolating all British soldiers on a fortified island in the harbor, and Governor Thomas Hutchinson promised that the soldiers who had fired would be tried. John Adams, an elite patriot who opposed crowd actions, served as their attorney. Adams appealed to the Boston jury by claiming that the soldiers had been provoked by a "motley rabble of saucy boys, negroes and mulattoes, Irish teagues, and outlandish jack tarres"—in other words, people not considered "respectable" by the city's elites and middle class. All but two of the soldiers were acquitted, and those found guilty suffered only a branding on their thumbs.

Burning hatreds produced by an intolerable situation underlay the **Boston Massacre**, as it came to be called in conscious recollection of the St. George's Fields Massacre in London. The shooting of unarmed American civilians by British soldiers and the light punishment given the soldiers forced the colonists to confront the stark possibility that the British government was bent on coercing and suppressing them through force. In a play written by Mercy Otis Warren (wife of politically active attorney James Otis), a character predicted that soon "Murders, blood and carnage/Shall crimson all these streets" as patriots rose to defend their republican liberty against tyrannical authority.

5-4.2 The Committees of Correspondence, 1772–1773

In the fall of 1772, Lord North was preparing to implement Townshend's goal of paying the royal governors' salaries using customs revenue. The colonists viewed efforts to free the governors from financial dependence on the legislatures as a threat to representative government. In response, Samuel Adams persuaded Boston's town meeting to request that every Massachusetts community appoint a committee whose members would be responsible for exchanging information and coordinating measures to defend colonial rights. Of approximately 260 towns, about half immediately established **"committees of correspondence,"** and most others did so within a year. The idea soon spread throughout New England.

22, 1770, when a customs informer shot into a crowd picketing the home of a customs-paying merchant, killing an eleven-year-old boy. While elite Bostonians had disdained the unruly exchanges between soldiers and crowds, the horror at a child's death momentarily united the community. "My Eyes never beheld such a funeral," wrote John Adams. "A vast Number of Boys walked before the Coffin, a vast Number of Women and Men after it. . . . This Shews there are many more Lives to spend if wanted in the Service of their country."

Although the army had played no part in the shooting, it became a target for popular frustration and rage. A week after the boy's funeral, a crowd led by Crispus Attucks, a seaman of African and Native American descent, and including George Robert Twelves Hewes, confronted redcoats who were

Boston Massacre
A conflict that took place on March 5, 1770, when an angry crowd of poor and working-class Bostonians protested a British soldier's abusive treatment a few hours earlier of a Boston apprentice who was trying to collect a debt from the officer. Shots rang out, and as a result, four Bostonians lay dead and seven more were wounded, one mortally.

"committees of correspondence"
Groups that linked almost every interior community to Boston through a network of dedicated activists. Members were responsible for exchanging information and coordinating measures to defend colonial rights.

The committees of correspondence were resistance leaders' first attempt to maintain close and continuing political cooperation over a wide area. By linking almost every interior community to Boston through a network of dedicated activists, the system enabled Adams to send out messages for each local committee to read at its own town meeting, which would then debate the issues and adopt a formal resolution. Involving tens of thousands of colonists to consider evidence that their rights were in danger, the system enabled them to take a personal stand by voting.

Adams's most successful effort to mobilize popular sentiment came in June 1773, when he publicized letters written by Massachusetts Governor Thomas Hutchinson that Benjamin Franklin had obtained. Massachusetts town meetings discovered through the letters that Hutchinson had advocated "an abridgement of what are called English liberties" and "a great restraint of natural liberty." The publication of Hutchinson's correspondence confirmed many colonists' suspicions of a plot to destroy basic freedoms.

In March 1773, Patrick Henry, Thomas Jefferson, and Richard Henry Lee proposed that Virginia establish committees of correspondence. Within a year, every province but Pennsylvania had followed its example. By early 1774, a communications web linked colonial leaders for the first time since the Stamp Act crisis of 1766.

5-4.3 Conflicts in the Colonial West

Although most of the turbulence between 1763 and 1775 swirled in the eastern seaports, numerous clashes, involving Native Americans, colonists, and colonial governments, erupted in the colonial West. These conflicts were rooted in the rapid population growth that had spurred the migration of whites toward the Appalachians and beyond.

In Paxton, Pennsylvania, on the western frontier, recently arrived Scots-Irish Presbyterians resented the Quaker-dominated assembly for failing to provide them with adequate military protection against "savage" Indians and for denying them equal representation in the legislature. They also concluded that all Native Americans, regardless of wartime conduct, were their racial enemies. In December 1763, armed settlers attacked two villages of peaceful Conestoga Indians, killing and scalping men, women, and children. In February 1764, about 200 "Paxton Boys," as they were called, set out for Philadelphia, with plans to kill Christian Indian refugees there. A government delegation headed by Benjamin Franklin met the armed, mounted mob on the outskirts of the city. After Franklin promised that the assembly

would consider their grievances, the Paxton Boys returned home. Nevertheless, popular sympathy for the settlers' plight weakened the Quakers politically.

Speculators such as George Washington sought western land, and settlers, traders, hunters, and thieves regularly trespassed on Indian territory, often responding violently when Indians resisted. Land pressures and the lack of adequate revenue from the colonies left the British government helpless in enforcing the Proclamation of 1763 and other Indian laws and treaties. Britain also struggled to maintain garrisons at many of its forts. Under such pressure, Britain and its Six Nations Iroquois allies agreed in the Treaty of Fort Stanwix (1768) to grant lands along the Ohio River that were occupied and claimed by Shawnees, Delawares, and Cherokees to the governments of Pennsylvania and Virginia.

The treaty only heightened western tensions, especially in the Ohio country, where settlers agitated to establish a new colony, Kentucky. Growing violence culminated in 1774 in the unprovoked slaughter by colonists of thirteen Shawnees and Ohio Senecas, including eight members of the family of Logan, until then a moderate Ohio Seneca leader. Logan and a force of Shawnees and Ohio Senecas retaliated by killing an equal number of white Virginians and then offered to make peace. Virginia declined and mobilized for what became known as Lord Dunmore's War (1774), for the colony's governor. The English defeated Logan's people, and in the peace conference that followed, Virginia gained uncontested rights to lands south of the Ohio in exchange for its claims on the northern side. But Anglo–Indian resentments persisted, and fighting would resume once Britain and its colonies went to war.

Other western disputes led to conflict among the colonists. In 1769, settlers moving west from New Hampshire came into conflict with New York. After four years of guerrilla warfare, the New Hampshire settlers, calling themselves the Green Mountain Boys, established an independent government that much later became the state of Vermont. Expansion also provoked conflicts between western settlers and their colonial governments. In North Carolina, a group known as the Regulators aimed to redress the grievances of westerners who, underrepresented in the colonial assembly, found themselves exploited by eastern officeholders. The Regulator movement climaxed on May 16, 1771, at the battle of Alamance Creek. Leading an army of perhaps thirteen hundred eastern militiamen, North Carolina's royal governor defeated about twenty-five hundred Regulators in a clash that produced almost three hundred casualties. Although the Regulator uprising disintegrated, it crippled the colony's subsequent ability to resist British authority.

PREPARING FOR THE PAXTON BOYS Militia units organize in Philadelphia, ready to defend the city against the Paxton Boys if necessary. *(Granger, NYC)*

An armed Regulator movement also arose in western South Carolina, in this case to counter the government's unwillingness to prosecute bandits who were terrorizing settlers. But the South Carolina government did not dispatch its militia westward for fear that the colony's restive slave population might use the occasion to revolt. Instead, it conceded to the principal demands of the Regulators by establishing four new judicial circuits and allowing jury trials in the newly settled areas.

All of these episodes reflected the tensions generated by an increasingly land-hungry white population and its willingness to resort to violence against Native Americans, other colonists, and British officials. As Anglo-American tensions mounted in older settled areas, the western settlers' anxious mood spread.

5-4.4 The Tea Act, 1773

Colonial smuggling and nonconsumption had taken a heavy toll on the British East India Company, which enjoyed a legal monopoly on the sale of tea within Britain's empire. By 1773, with tons of tea rotting in its warehouses, the company was teetering on the brink of bankruptcy. Lord North could not afford to let the company fail. Not only did it pay substantial duties on the tea it shipped to Britain, but it also subsidized British rule in India (as discussed in Chapter 6).

In May 1773, to save the beleaguered East India Company from financial ruin, Parliament passed the **Tea Act**, which eliminated all remaining import duties on tea entering England and thus lowered the selling price to consumers. To lower the price still further, the Tea Act also permitted the company to sell its tea directly to consumers rather than through wholesalers. These two concessions reduced the cost of company tea in the colonies well below the price of all smuggled competition. Parliament expected simple economic self-interest to overcome Anglo-American scruples about buying taxed tea.

But the Tea Act alarmed many Americans, above all because it would raise revenue with which the British government would pay royal governors. The law thus threatened to corrupt Americans into accepting the principle of parliamentary taxation by taking advantage of their weakness for a frivolous luxury. Quickly, therefore, the committees of correspondence decided to prevent East India Company cargoes from being landed, either by pressuring the company's agents to refuse acceptance or by intercepting the ships at sea and ordering them home. In Philadelphia, an anonymous "Committee for Tarring and Feathering" warned harbor pilots not to guide any ships carrying tea into port.

In Boston, however, this strategy failed. On November 28, 1773, the first ship came under the jurisdiction of the customs house, where duties would have to be paid on its cargo within twenty days. Otherwise, the cargo would be seized from the captain and the tea claimed by the company's agents and placed on sale. When Samuel Adams, John Hancock, and other popular leaders requested

Tea Act
Eliminated all remaining import duties on tea entering England and thus lowered the selling price to customers.

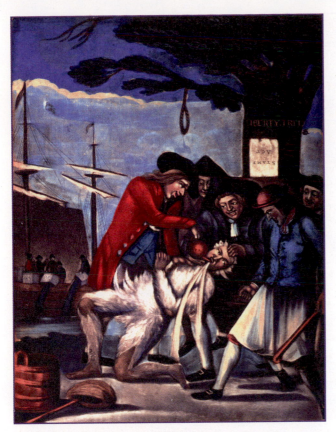

BOSTONIANS PAYING THE EXCISE (TAX) MAN In this engraving, a crowd protests the Tea Act by forcing a British tax collector to drink tea. *(Courtesy of the John Carter Brown Library at Brown University)*

a special clearance for the ship's departure, Thomas Hutchinson refused.

On the evening of December 16, five thousand Bostonians gathered at Old South Church. Samuel Adams informed them of Hutchinson's insistence upon landing the tea and proclaimed that "this meeting can do no more to save the country." About fifty young men, including George Robert Twelves Hewes, stepped forward and disguised themselves as Mohawk Indians—symbolizing a virtuous, proud, and assertive American identity distinct from that of corrupt Britain. Armed with "toma-hawks," they headed for the wharf, followed by most of the crowd.

The disciplined band assaulted no one and damaged nothing but the hated cargo. For almost an hour, thousands of onlookers stood silently trans-fixed, as if at a religious service, peering through the crisp, cold air of a moonlit night. The only sounds were the steady chop of hatchets breaking open wooden chests and the soft splash of tea—forty-five tons in all—on the water. When Boston's "Tea Party," as it was later called, was finished, the participants left quietly, and the town lapsed into a profound hush.

5-5 Toward Independence, 1774–1776

Why was reconciliation between Britain and its American colonies ultimately impossible?

The calm that followed the Boston Tea Party would preceed a storm. The incident inflamed the British government and Parliament, which now determined once and for all to quash colonial insubordination. Colonial political leaders responded with equal determination to defend self-government and liberty. The empire and its American colonies were on a collision course, leading by spring 1775 to armed clashes. Yet even after blood was shed, colonists hesitated before declaring their inde-pendence from Britain. In the meantime, free and enslaved African Americans pondered how best to realize their own freedom.

5-5.1 Liberty for African Americans

Throughout the imperial crisis, African Americans, as a deeply alienated group within society, quickly responded to calls for liberty and equality. In January 1766, a group of blacks, inspired by anti–Stamp Act protests, had marched through Charles Town, South Carolina, shouting "Liberty!" Instead of being hailed as patriotic heroes, they were arrested for inciting a rebellion. Thereaf-ter, unrest among slaves—usually in the form of vio-lence or escape—kept pace with that among white rebels. Then in 1772, a court decision in England electrified much of the black population. A Mas-sachusetts slave, James Somerset, had accompanied his master to England, where he ran away but was recaptured. Aided by Quaker abolitionists, Somerset sued for his freedom. Writing for the King's Court, Lord Chief Justice William Mansfield ruled that because Parliament had never explicitly established slavery in England, Somerset must be freed.

Although the decision applied only to Somerset and had no force in the colonies, it inspired African Americans to pursue their freedom. In January 1773, several Massachusetts blacks filed the first of three petitions to the legislature, arguing that the Somerset decision should be extended to the colony. In Virginia and Maryland, dozens of enslaved persons ran away from their masters and sought passage aboard ships bound for England. As Anglo-American tensions mounted in 1774, many slaves, especially in the

A List of Negroes that went off to Dunmore) April 14 1776

Women	Ages	Girls	Boys	Negro Men	Ages
Pleasant	55	1		Sawer a Sawer	60
Nancy	46	4		Tobey Do	54
Mary	50	2	2	Ned	44
Judey	28	3	2	Peter a house Carpenter	37
Lucy	25	1	5	James a Shoemaker	35
Hezziah	23		3	Robin a Sawer	25
Cate	30	2	1	Bob	30
Rachel	25		4	Charles	24
Easter	27		6	Glascow	21
Betise	23	1		Will	21
Jenny	42			Anthony	19
Lindah	27	2	2	George	18
Manda	25		5	Jacob	20
Dynah	26	2		Isack	16
Lidia	26	2	1		
Abey	29		3		
Biss	23	1		Total. 87	
Jenny	30				
Josie	16			Entailed.	
Nell	25	2		Brister a Sawer	25
Pegg	18			Moses a house Sevt	23

Fee Simple

Women	Girls	Boys	Men
21	23	27	16

"LIST OF NEGROES THAT WENT OFF TO DUNMORE" In this petition, Virginia colonist John Willoughby, Jr. is seeking compensation from the General Assembly for eighty-seven of his slaves who escaped from his father's property at Willoughby Point to join Lord Dunmore. Although Lord Dunmore invited only able-bodied men to flee their masters and aid the British, this list shows that enslaved African Americans of all ages and both genders sought freedom by responding to his proclamation. *(The Library of Virginia)*

Lord Dunmore's Proclamation
In November 1775, Virginia's governor, Lord Dunmore, promised freedom to any able-bodied male slave who enlisted in the cause of restoring royal authority.

Chesapeake colonies, looked for war and the arrival of British troops as a means to their liberation. The young Virginia planter James Madison remarked that "if America and Britain come to a hostile rupture, I am afraid an insurrection among the slaves may and will be promoted" by England.

Madison's fears were borne out in November 1775 when Virginia's governor, Lord Dunmore, promised freedom to any able-bodied enslaved man who enlisted in the cause of restoring royal authority. Like Florida's offer of refuge to escaping South Carolina slaves (see Chapter 4), **Lord Dunmore's Proclamation** intended to undermine a planter-dominated society by appealing to slaves' longings for freedom. About one thousand Virginia blacks flocked to Dunmore. Those who fought donned uniforms proclaiming "Liberty to Slaves." Dunmore's proclamation associated British forces with slave liberation in the minds of both blacks and whites in the southern colonies, an association that continued during the war that followed (as discussed in Chapter 6).

5-5.2 The "Intolerable Acts"

Following the Boston Tea Party, Lord North fumed that only "New England fanatics" could imagine themselves oppressed by inexpensive tea. A member of Parliament drew wild applause by declaring that "the town of Boston ought to be knocked about by the ears, and destroy'd." In vain the Americans' supporter, Edmund Burke, pleaded for the one action that could end the crisis: "Leave America . . . to tax herself. . . . Leave the Americans as they anciently stood." The British government, however, swiftly asserted its authority by enacting four "Coercive Acts" that, together with the unrelated Quebec Act, became known to colonists as the **"Intolerable Acts."**

The first of the Coercive Acts, the Boston Port Bill, became law on April 1, 1774. It ordered the navy to close Boston harbor unless the town arranged to pay for the ruined tea by June 1. Lord North's cabinet deliberately imposed this impossibly short deadline to ensure the harbor's closing, which would lead to serious economic distress.

The second Coercive Act, the Massachusetts Government Act, revoked the Massachusetts charter and restructured the government. The colony's upper house would no longer be elected annually by the assembly but instead be appointed for life by the crown. The governor would independently appoint all judges and sheriffs, while sheriffs would appoint jurymen, who previously had been elected. Finally, towns could hold no more than one meeting a year without the governor's permission. These changes brought Massachusetts into line with other royal colonies.

The third of the new acts, the Administration of Justice Act, which some colonists cynically called the Murder Act, permitted any person charged with murder while enforcing royal authority in Massachusetts (such as the British soldiers indicted for the Boston Massacre) to be tried in England or in other colonies. Finally, a new Quartering Act went beyond the earlier act of 1765 by allowing the governor to requisition empty private buildings for housing troops.

Americans learned of the Quebec Act along with the previous four statutes and associated it with them. Intended to cement loyalty to Britain among conquered French-Canadian Catholics, the law retained Roman Catholicism as Quebec's established religion. This provision alarmed Protestant Anglo-Americans who widely believed that Catholicism went hand in hand with despotism. Furthermore, the Quebec Act gave Canada's governors sweeping powers but established no legislature. It also permitted property disputes (but not criminal cases) to be decided by French law, which did not use juries. Finally, the law extended Quebec's territorial claims south to the Ohio River and west to the Mississippi, a vast area populated by Native Americans and some French. Although it had been designated off-limits by the Proclamation of 1763, several colonies continued to claim portions of the region.

Along with the appointment of General Thomas Gage, Britain's military commander in North America, as governor of Massachusetts, the "Intolerable Acts" convinced Anglo-Americans that Britain was plotting to abolish traditional English liberties throughout North America. Rebel pamphlets fed fears that Gage would starve Boston into submission and appoint corrupt sheriffs and judges to crush political dissent through rigged trials. By this reasoning, the new Quartering Act would repress any resistance by forcing troops on an unwilling population, and the "Murder Act" would encourage massacres by preventing local juries from convicting soldiers who killed civilians. Once resistance in Massachusetts had been smashed, the Quebec Act would serve as a blueprint for extinguishing representative government throughout the colonies. Parliament would revoke every colony's charter and introduce a government like Quebec's. Elected assemblies, freedom of religion for Protestants, and jury trials would all disappear.

Intended by Parliament simply to punish Massachusetts—and particularly that rotten apple in the barrel, Boston—the acts instead pushed most colonies to the brink of rebellion. Repeal of these laws became, in effect, the colonists' non-negotiable demand. Of the twenty-seven reasons justifying the break with Britain that Americans later cited in the Declaration of Independence, six concerned these statutes.

5-5.3 The Continental Congress

In response to the "Intolerable Acts," the extralegal committees of correspondence of every colony but Georgia sent delegates to a **Continental Congress** in Philadelphia. The fifty-six delegates assembled on September 5, 1774, to

> **"Intolerable Acts"**
> A series of laws that was made up of the Boston Port Bill, the Massachusetts Government Act, the Administration of Justice Act, the Quartering Act, plus the unrelated Quebec Act. Intended by the British Parliament to simply punish Massachusetts, the acts instead pushed most colonies to the brink of rebellion.
>
> **Continental Congress**
> Group of representatives appointed by the legislatures of a dozen North American colonies of Great Britain.

find a way to defend the colonies' rights in common. Those in attendance included Samuel and John Adams of Massachusetts; John Jay of New York; Joseph Galloway and John Dickinson of Pennsylvania; and Patrick Henry, Richard Henry Lee, and George Washington of Virginia.

The Continental Congress opened by endorsing a set of statements called the Suffolk Resolves. Recently adopted at a convention of Massachusetts towns, the resolves declared that the colonies owed no obedience to any of the Coercive Acts, that a provisional government should collect all taxes until the former Massachusetts charter was restored, and that defensive measures should be taken in the event of an attack by royal troops. The Continental Congress also voted to boycott all British imports after December 1 and to halt almost all exports to Britain and its West Indian possessions after September 1775 unless a reconciliation had been accomplished. This agreement, the Continental Association, would be enforced by locally elected committees of "observation" or "safety," whose members in effect would be seizing control of American trade from the royal customs service.

Such bold defiance displeased some delegates. Jay, Dickinson, Galloway, and other moderates who dominated the middle-colony contingent feared the internal turmoil that would surely accompany a head-on confrontation with Britain. These "trimmers" (John Adams's scornful phrase) unsuccessfully opposed nonimportation and tried in vain to win endorsement of Galloway's plan for an American legislature that would share the authority to tax and govern the colonies with Parliament.

Finally, however, the delegates summarized their principles and demands in a petition to the king. This document affirmed Parliament's power to regulate imperial commerce, but it argued that all previous parliamentary efforts to impose taxes, enforce laws through admiralty courts, suspend assemblies, and unilaterally revoke charters were unconstitutional. By addressing the king rather than Parliament, Congress was imploring George III to end the crisis by dismissing those ministers responsible for passing the Coercive Acts. At the same time, the extralegal Congress was claiming to act as the legitimate representatives of the king's American subjects. Should independence come to pass, it would necessarily constitute the foundation of a new government.

5-5.4 From Resistance to Rebellion

The divisions within the Continental Congress mirrored those within Anglo-American society at large.

Tensions between moderates and radicals ran high, and bonds between Americans formerly united in outlook sometimes snapped. John Adams's one-time friend Jonathan Sewall, for example, charged that the Congress had made the "breach with the parent state a thousand times more irreparable than it was before." Fearing that Congress was enthroning "their High Mightinesses, the MOB," he and like-minded Americans refused to defy the king.

To solidify their defiance, resistance leaders coerced colonists who refused to support them. Thus, the elected committees that Congress had created to enforce the Continental Association often became vigilantes, compelling merchants who still traded with Britain to burn their imports and make public apologies, browbeating clergymen who preached pro-British sermons, and pressuring Americans to adopt simpler diets and dress in order to relieve their dependence on British imports. Additionally, the committees established provincial "congresses" that paralleled and rivaled the existing assemblies headed by royal governors.

Activists in several colonies prepared for the worst by collecting arms for volunteer militia units (known in Massachusetts as minutemen) whose members could respond instantly to an emergency. On April 19, 1775, Massachusetts's Governor Gage sent seven hundred British soldiers to seize military supplies that colonists had stored at Concord. Two couriers, William Dawes and Paul Revere, rode out to warn nearby towns of the troop movements. At Lexington, about seventy minutemen confronted the soldiers. After a confused skirmish in which eight minutemen died and a single redcoat was wounded, the British pushed on to Concord. There they found few munitions but encountered a growing swarm of armed Yankees. When some minutemen mistakenly thought the town was being burned, they exchanged fire with the British regulars and touched off a battle that continued for most of the sixteen miles back to Boston. By day's end, the redcoats had suffered 273 casualties, the minutemen, 92. These engagements awakened the countryside, and by the evening of April 20, some twenty thousand New Englanders were besieging the British garrison in Boston.

Three weeks later, a Second Continental Congress convened in Philadelphia. Most delegates still opposed independence and at Dickinson's urging agreed to send a "loyal message" to George III. Dickinson composed the **Olive Branch Petition** listing three demands: a ceasefire at Boston, repeal of the Coercive Acts, and negotiations to establish guarantees of American rights. Yet while pleading for peace, the delegates also passed measures that Britain could only construe as rebellious. In particular, they voted in May 1775 to establish an "American

Olive Branch Petition
A "loyal message" to King George III from the Second Continental Congress that presented three demands: a ceasefire at Boston, repeal of the Coercive Acts, and negotiations to establish guarantees of American rights.

A VIEW OF THE TOWN OF CONCORD, 1775 British troops enter Concord to search for armaments. A few hours later, hostilities with the townspeople would erupt. *(Attributed to Timothy Martin Minot, ca. 1825. Concord Museum)*

continental army" and appointed George Washington its commander.

The Olive Branch Petition reached London along with news of the Continental Army's formation and of a battle fought just outside Boston on June 17. In this engagement, British troops attacked colonists entrenched on Breed's Hill and Bunker Hill. Although they succeeded in dislodging the Americans, the British suffered 1,154 casualties out of twenty-two hundred men, compared to a loss of 311 patriots.

After Bunker Hill, many Britons wanted retaliation, not reconciliation. On August 23, George III proclaimed New England in a state of rebellion, and in October he extended that pronouncement to include all the colonies. In December, Parliament likewise declared all the colonies rebellious, outlawing all British trade with them and subjecting their ships to seizure.

5-5.5 *Common Sense*

Despite the turn of events, many Americans clung to hopes of reconciliation with Britain. Even John Adams, who believed in the inevitability of separation, described himself as "fond of reconciliation, if we could reasonably entertain Hopes of it on a constitutional basis."

Through 1775, such colonists comforted themselves with the notion that Parliament and evil ministers rather than the king were forcing unconstitutional measures on them. But with George III having declared the colonies to be in "open and avowed rebellion . . . for the purpose of establishing an independent empire," Anglo-Americans had no choice but either to submit or to acknowledge their goal of national independence.

Most colonists' sentimental attachment to the king, the last emotional barrier to their accepting independence, finally crumbled after January 1776, when Thomas Paine published *Common Sense*. A failed corset maker and schoolmaster, Paine had immigrated to the colonies from England late in 1774 with a letter of introduction from Benjamin Franklin, a penchant for radical politics, and a gift for writing plain and pungent prose that anyone could understand.

Paine told Americans what they had been unable to bring themselves

> **Common Sense**
> A pamphlet written by Thomas Paine that advocated freedom from British rule.

to say: monarchy was an institution rooted in super-stition, dangerous to liberty, and inappropriate to Americans. The king was "the royal brute" and a "hardened, sullen-tempered Pharaoh." Whereas previous writers had maintained that certain corrupt politicians were directing an English conspiracy against American liberty, Paine argued that such a conspiracy was rooted in the very institutions of monarchy and empire. Moreover, he argued, America had no economic need for the British connection. As he put it, "The commerce by which she [America] hath enriched herself are the necessaries of life, and will always have a market while eating is the custom in Europe." In addition, he pointed out that the events of the preceding six months had made independence a reality. Finally, Paine linked America's awakening nationalism with the sense of religious mission felt by many when he proclaimed, "We have it in our power to begin the world over again. A situation, similar to the present, hath not happened since the days of Noah until now." America, in Paine's view, would be not only a new nation but a new kind of nation, a model society founded on republican principles and unburdened by the oppressive beliefs and corrupt institutions of the European past.

Printed in both English and German, *Common Sense* sold more than one hundred thousand copies within three months, equal to one for every fourth or fifth adult male, making it a best-seller. Readers passed copies from hand to hand and read passages aloud in public gatherings. The *Connecticut Gazette* described Paine's pamphlet as "a landflood that sweeps all before it." *Common Sense* had dissolved lingering allegiance to George III and Great Britain, removing the last psychological barrier to American independence.

5-5.6 Declaring Independence

As Americans absorbed Paine's views, the military conflict between Britain and the colonies escalated, making the possibility of reconciliation even less likely. In May 1775, irregular troops from Vermont and Massachusetts had captured Fort Ticonderoga and Crown Point on the key route connecting New York and Canada. Six months later, Washington ordered Colonel Henry Knox, the army's senior artillerist, to bring the British artillery seized at Ticonderoga to reinforce the siege of Boston. Knox and his men built crude sleds to haul their fifty-nine cannons through dense forest and rugged, snow-covered mountains. Forty days and three hundred miles after leaving Ticonderoga, Knox and his exhausted troops reported to

Declaration of Independence
Proposed by the Second Continental Congress, this document proclaimed independence of the Thirteen Colonies from British rule.

Washington in January 1776. They had accomplished one of the Revolution's great feats of endurance. The guns from Ticonderoga placed the outnumbered British in a hopeless position and forced them to evacuate Boston on March 17, 1776.

Regrouping and augmenting its forces at Halifax, Nova Scotia, Britain planned an assault on New York to drive a wedge between rebellious New England and the other colonies. Recognizing New York's strategic importance, Washington led most of his troops there in April 1776.

Other military moves reinforced the drift toward all-out war. In June, Congress ordered a two-pronged assault on Canada in which forces under General Philip Schuyler would move northward via Fort Ticonderoga to Montreal while Benedict Arnold would lead a march through the Maine forest to Quebec. Schuyler succeeded but Arnold failed. As British troops poured into Canada, the Americans withdrew. At the same time, a British offensive in the southern colonies failed after an unsuccessful attempt to seize Charles Town.

By spring 1776, Paine's pamphlet, reinforced by the growing reality of war, had stimulated dozens of local gatherings—artisan guilds, town meetings, county conventions, and militia musters—to pass resolutions favoring American independence. The groundswell quickly spread to the colonies' extralegal legislatures. New England was already in rebellion, and Rhode Island declared itself independent in May 1776. The middle colonies hesitated to support independence because they feared, correctly, that any war would largely be fought over control of Philadelphia and New York. Following the news in April that North Carolina's congressional delegates were authorized to vote for independence, several southern colonies pressed for separation. Virginia's legislature instructed its delegates to propose independence, which Richard Henry Lee did on June 7. Formally adopting Lee's resolution on July 2, Congress created the United States of America.

The task of drafting a statement to justify the colonies' separation from England fell to a committee of five, including John Adams, Benjamin Franklin, and Thomas Jefferson, with Jefferson as the principal author. Among Congress's revisions to Jefferson's first draft: insertion of the phrase "pursuit of happiness" in place of "property" in the Declaration's most famous sentence, and its deletion of a statement blaming George III for foisting the slave trade on unwilling colonists. The **Declaration of Independence** (reprinted in the Appendix at the back of this volume) never mentioned Parliament by name because Congress had moved beyond arguments over legislative representation and now wanted to separate America altogether from Britain and its head of state, the king. Jefferson listed twenty-seven "injuries and usurpations" committed by George III against the colonies. And he drew on a familiar line of radical thinking when he added that the king's actions had as their "direct object the establishment of an absolute tyranny over these states."

Like Paine, Jefferson elevated the colonists' grievances from a dispute over English freedoms to a struggle of universal dimensions. In the tradition of Locke and other Enlightenment figures, Jefferson argued that the English government had violated its contract with the colonists, thereby giving them the right to replace it with a government of their own design. And his eloquent emphasis on the equality of all individuals and their natural entitlement to justice, liberty, and self-fulfillment expressed republicans' deepest longing for a government that would rest on neither legal privilege nor exploitation of the majority by the few.

Jefferson addressed the Declaration of Independence as much to Americans uncertain about the wisdom of independence as to world opinion, for even at this late date a significant minority opposed independence or were uncertain whether to endorse it. Above all, he wanted to convince his fellow citizens that social and political progress could no longer be accomplished within the British Empire. But he left unanswered just which Americans were and were not equal to one another and entitled to liberty. All the colonies endorsing the Declaration countenanced, on grounds of racial inequality, the enslavement of blacks and severe restrictions on the rights of free blacks. Moreover, all had property qualifications that prevented many white men from voting. The proclamation that "all men" were created equal accorded with the Anglo-American assumption that women could not and should not function politically or legally as autonomous individuals. And Jefferson's accusation, echoing the Paxton Boys and other Indian-haters, that George III had unleashed "the merciless Indian savages" on innocent colonists placed Native Americans outside the bounds of humanity.

Was the Declaration of Independence a statement that expressed the sentiments of all but a minority of colonists? In a very narrow sense it was, but by framing the Declaration in universal terms, Jefferson and the Continental Congress made it something much greater. The ideas motivating

"DRAFTING OF THE DECLARATION OF INDEPENDENCE" (1900) BY JEAN LOUIS GERMORE FERRIS Franklin, John Adams, and Jefferson work on the Declaration. The artist makes clear that they went through several drafts before producing the renowned final version. (© Bettmann/Corbis)

Jefferson and his fellow delegates had moved thousands of ordinary colonists to political action over the preceding eleven years, both on their own behalf and on behalf of the colonies in their quarrel with Britain. For better or worse, the struggle for national independence had hastened, and become intertwined with, a quest for equality and personal independence that, for many Americans, transcended boundaries of class, race, or gender. In their reading, the Declaration never claimed that perfect justice and equal opportunity existed in the United States; rather, it challenged the Revolutionary generation and all who later inherited the nation to bring this ideal closer to reality.

The Whole Vision

■ *What was the impact of the Seven Years' War on the relationship between England and its colonies?*

Wars have a way of bringing people together under the notion of a shared enemy or desired outcome. That was initially the case with England and its American colonies during the Seven Years' or French and Indian War. England emerged victorious with the aid of its colonies and a brief sense of unity resulted. But the war had other consequences. Each side had a different view of the other's involvement during the war and obligations thereafter, as well as how to handle Indians and their land claims. That dispute would pose new challenges and strain relations in enduring ways. As victors, England also gained new territory and subjects who did not share its heritage or feel any sense of loyalty. England's efforts to cope with its postwar circumstances, particularly its economic difficulties and ongoing tensions over Indian lands, would lead to colonial policies that would erode whatever unity the war itself had forged between England and America.

■ *What was at the core of the tensions between the colonists and the British in the years following the Seven Years' War?*

In a nutshell, the conflict between England and her colonies after the Seven Years' War was one of rights and governance, and its origins actually predate the war. England had long sought to enforce its power over the colonies in various trade, revenue, and political policies, and colonists at times resisted. But the Seven Years' War created new difficulties for England that, in turn, inspired it to take a closer look at the colonies. The policies that England devised for its colonies—both as its subjects and as beneficiaries in the war—triggered a dispute about local rule and representation. That, in turn, inspired a deeper question about the nature of the relationship between the colonies and the mother country and the powers they each possessed. The differences over British colonial policies would lead to a continuous cycle of rebellions (sometimes violent) within the colonies, followed by new assertions of British power. Along the way, colonists would forge new alliances and look for answers in Enlightenment and religious ideas to their questions about the relationship between government and the people.

■ *Why did colonial resistance continue even after the Stamp Act was withdrawn?*

The Stamp Act was one of many new pieces of legislation passed by Parliament in the mid to late 1760s and imposed on the colonies. All of this legislation raised colonists' ire because it often clashed directly with colonists' beliefs about which powers belonged to them and which powers were held by England. Some of the legislation had little financial or other impact on the colonies; others were experienced as great impositions. Either way, the issue for colonists seemed to be one of trust and of control. After the Stamp Act, colonists were dubious about England's motives for each new piece of legislation. The more they experienced British legislation as an assertion of authority and assault on colonial self-rule, the more they rebelled. Ongoing resistance led, in turn, to the formation of a political consciousness among men and women in the colonies, and a small, but supportive movement on their behalf in England.

■ *What fed colonists' growing rebelliousness and fears of British authority from 1770 to 1774?*

Increased assertions of British authority—along with evidence that proved colonists' worst fears about Britain's motivations to suppress and control the colonists and their legislatures—inspired ongoing rebellions. Britain's response to each act of defiance also played an important role in escalating the tensions. At the same time, colonial leaders and organizations emerged, giving voice to dissent and organizing the rebellion and the response of colonial governments. Earlier protests were more disparate and random; as resistance escalated, organization and links between urban and rural areas and between the colonies became increasingly important. As population surged and land was at a premium, tensions heightened within the colonies and with the British. As clashes intensified, suspicions escalated and with it resistance (sometimes accompanied by violence) among the colonists, even to the point of at times going against their self-interest.

■ *Why was reconciliation between Britain and its American colonies ultimately impossible?*

When colonists began their rebellion, they did not articulate notions of independence or breaking from Britain to form their own nation. Nor did any of the colonists even conceive of waging a war against the mother country. But after years of animosity and distrust on both sides, positions hardened and provocations worsened, even extending to issues of slavery in the colonies. The more colonists asserted their rights or resisted, the more Britain asserted its authority and right to control the colonies. Even as they formed their own Congress, colonists were divided about the steps they were willing to take to preserve their rights. Negotiations, petitions, and rebellions were all aimed at reconciliation. But experience is transformative, and as Britain offered what colonists regarded as an ultimatum, it pushed them closer to a break and toward embracing newly articulated—and increasingly popular—views about the potential of an independent America.

6 Securing Independence, Defining Nationhood, **1776–1788**

THE DEATH OF GENERAL MERCER AT THE BATTLE OF PRINCETON (DETAIL) BY JOHN TRUMBULL The American victory at Princeton secured control of New Jersey. The martyred Mercer was one of George Washington's most trusted officers. *(Francis G. Mayer/Corbis)*

CHRONOLOGY 1776–1788

1776	British force American troops from New York City.
1777	Congress approves Articles of Confederation. American victory at Saratoga.
1777–1778	British troops occupy Philadelphia. Continental Army winters at Valley Forge.
1778	France formally recognizes the United States; declares war on Britain.
1779	Spain declares war on Britain. John Sullivan leads American raids in Iroquois country.
1780	British seize Charles Town.
1781	Articles of Confederation ratified. Battle of Yorktown; British General Cornwallis surrenders.
1783	Treaty of Paris.

1784	Spain closes New Orleans to American trade. Economic depression begins in New England. Second Treaty of Fort Stanwix.
1785	Ordinance of 1785. Treaty of Fort McIntosh.
1786	Congress rejects Jay-Gardoqui Treaty. Treaty of Fort Finney. Joseph Brant organizes Indian resistance to U.S. expansion.
1786–1787	Shays's Rebellion in Massachusetts.
1787	Northwest Ordinance. Philadelphia convention frames federal Constitution.
1787–1788	Alexander Hamilton, James Madison, and John Jay, *The Federalist*.
1788	Constitution ratified.

ON MAY 1, 1777, eighteen-year-old Agrippa Hull, a free African American man from Stockbridge, Massachusetts, enlisted in the Continental Army. Like most black recruits and some whites, Hull enlisted for the duration of the Revolutionary War. He spent four years as an orderly for General Thaddeus Kósciuszko, a Polish republican and abolitionist who had volunteered for the American cause.

Upon discharge, Hull returned to Stockbridge, where he was welcomed as a hero and became a New England celebrity until his death at age eighty-nine. A gifted storyteller, Hull regaled locals and visitors with accounts of his wartime experiences—of horrors such as assisting surgeons performing amputations, of glorious American victories at Saratoga and Monmouth (discussed in this chapter), and of lighter moments such as Kósciuszko finding him entertaining his black friends in the general's uniform. When Kósciuszko made a return visit to the United States in 1797, he reunited with Hull in New York to public acclaim.

For the new nation as well as for patriots like Hull, a distinctive identity as American emerged gradually over the course of the war. In July 1776, the thirteen colonies had jointly declared their independence from Britain and formed a loosely knit confederation of states. Shaped by the collective hardships experienced during eight years of terrible fighting, the former colonists shifted from seeing themselves primarily as military allies to accepting one another as fellow citizens.

But even with their newfound unity, Americans remained divided over the distribution of power and

AGRIPPA HULL (*Universal Images Group/Getty Images*)

authority within the new nation. During the war, the United States of America was formalized with the adoption of the Articles of Confederation. But states struggled to adopt constitutions of their own, and tensions between the states flared in the national contest over replacing the Articles. The ratification of the Constitution in 1787 marked a triumph for those favoring more centralization of power at the national level. It also left most of Agrippa Hull's fellow African Americans in slavery.

6-1 The Prospects of War

How did British colonists choose sides as the American Revolution approached?

The Revolution was both a collective struggle that pitted the independent states against Britain and a civil war among American peoples. American opponents of independence constituted one of several factors working in Britain's favor as war began. Others included Britain's larger population and its superior military resources and preparation. America, on the other hand, was located far from Britain and enjoyed the intense commitment to independence of patriots and the Continental Army, led by the formidable George Washington.

6-1.1 Loyalists and Other British Sympathizers

Even after the Declaration of Independence, some Americans remained opposed to secession from Britain, including about 20 percent of all whites. Although these internal enemies of the Revolution called themselves **loyalists**, they were "Tories" to their patriot, or Whig, opponents. The question of which side to support during the Revolution divided friends, neighbors, and families. While Benjamin Franklin had been a firm patriot since well before war erupted, his son, William, was an equally firm loyalist.

Loyalists shared many political beliefs with patriots. In particular, most opposed Parliament's claim of authority to tax the colonies. Finding themselves fighting for a cause with which they did not entirely agree, some loyalists would change sides during the war. Loyalists disagreed, however, with the patriots' insistence that independence was the only way to preserve the colonists' constitutional rights. The loyalists denounced separation as an illegal act certain to ignite an unnecessary war. Above all, they retained a profound reverence for the crown and believed that, without firm monarchial rule, America would flounder in violence and anarchy.

The mutual hatred between Whigs and Tories exceeded that of patriots and the British. Each side saw its cause as so sacred that opposition by a fellow American was an unforgivable act of betrayal. Americans inflicted the worst atrocities committed during the war upon each other. Loyalists were often harassed, had property damaged or confiscated, and in some cases were tarred and feathered. When loyalist husbands fled during the war, wives who remained behind were presumed by patriots to share their husbands' allegiances. Many—though not all—wives did, and some women acted as spies or messengers for the British side.

The most important factor in determining loyalist strength in any area was the political power of local Whigs and their success in convincing their neighbors that Britain threatened their liberty. For several years, colonial resistance leaders in New England towns, tidewater Virginia, and coastal South Carolina had vigorously pursued a program of political education and popular mobilization. As a result, only about 5 percent of whites in these areas were committed loyalists in 1776. Where elites and other leaders were divided or indecisive, however, loyalist sentiment flourished. Loyalist strength was greatest in New York and New Jersey, where elites were especially reluctant to declare their allegiance to either side. Those two states eventually furnished about half of the twenty-one thousand white Americans who fought as loyalists.

The next most significant factor influencing loyalist military strength was the geographic distribution of recent British immigrants, who remained closely identified with their homeland. Newcomers included thousands of British soldiers who had served in the Seven Years' War and remained in the colonies, usually in New York, where they could obtain land grants of two hundred acres. An additional 125,000 English, Scots, and Scots-Irish landed from 1763 to 1775. In New York, Georgia, and the backcountry of North and South Carolina, where the recent immigrants were heavily concentrated, the proportion of white loyalists ranged from 25 to 40 percent in 1776. During the war, these newcomers would form Tory units. After the Revolution, foreign-born loyalists were a majority of those whom the British compensated for wartime

loyalists
Colonists who retained a profound reverence for, and loyalty to, the British crown and believed that if they failed to defend their king, they would sacrifice their personal honor.

property losses—including three-quarters of all such claimants from the Carolinas and Georgia.

Quebec's religious and secular elites comprised another significant white minority with pro-British sympathies. After the British had conquered New France in the Seven Years' War, the Quebec Act of 1774 (Chapter 5) retained Catholicism as the established religion in Quebec and continued partial use of French civil law, measures that reconciled Quebec's provincial leaders to British rule. Quebec's elites worked closely with Britain's military, enabling it to retain control of Canada throughout the war.

The rebels never attempted to win over three other mainland colonies—Nova Scotia and East and West Florida—whose small British populations consisted of recent immigrants and British troops. Nor was independence seriously considered in Britain's thirteen West Indian colonies, which were dominated by British absentee plantation owners

6-1.2 Slaves and Native Americans During the War

The British cause would draw significant wartime support from nonwhites. Before the war began, African Americans made clear that they considered their own liberation from slavery a higher priority than the colonies' independence from Britain. After Virginia slaves flocked to Lord Dunmore's ranks (see Chapter 5), hundreds of South Carolina slaves had escaped and had taken refuge on British ships in Charles Town's harbor. During the war, about twenty thousand enslaved African Americans, mostly from the southern and middle colonies, escaped their owners. About a third of the slaves who fled to the British were women, often with children.

Most slaves were recaptured or died, especially from epidemics, but a small minority achieved freedom, often after serving as laborers or soldiers in the Royal Army. In one tragic example, a group of several hundred slaves who had contracted smallpox were not treated but instead sent by the British military into patriot territory with the intention of inflicting the rebels with the dreaded disease. Meanwhile, about five thousand enslaved and free African Americans, mostly from New England, calculated that supporting the rebels would hasten their own emancipation and equality.

Slaves who remained behind faced greater hardships during the war years. Masters who struggled with shortages of food and other supplies often doled out less to slaves. Still, the climate of crisis that accompanied the war also made room for some slaves to assert themselves and make more demands, which led masters to worry about possible slave rebellions.

Although Native Americans were deeply divided, most supported the British, either from the beginning or after being pressured by one side or the other to abandon neutrality. Most did so because they had had ongoing problems keeping settlers off their land, and these Native Americans thought they would fare better with a British victory. In the Ohio country, most Shawnees, Delawares, Ohio Senecas, and other Indians continued to resent settlers' incursions, but some sought to remain neutral and a few communities initially supported the Americans. After Pontiac's War, Native Americans in the Great Lakes region had developed improved relations with British agents and now supported Britain's cause.

The most powerful Native American confederacies—the Six Nations Iroquois, the Creeks, and the Cherokees—were badly divided when the war broke out. Among the Six Nations, the central council fire at Onondaga, a symbol of unity since Hiawatha's time (see Chapter 1), died out. Most Iroquois followed the lead of the Mohawk chief **Joseph Brant** (Thayendagea) in supporting Britain.

Joseph Brant
Mohawk chief who supported the British.

BENEDICT ARNOLD, PATRIOT TURNED LOYALIST Arnold was an American general who defected to the British. A patriot street parade in Philadelphia in 1780 portrayed him as a two-faced tool of the devil. *(Library of Congress Prints and Photographs Division)*

But the Oneidas and Tuscaroras, influenced by a New England missionary, actively sided with the rebels against other Iroquois. Creeks' allegiances depended on each village's earlier trade ties. Those who traded with the British supported Britain's cause, while those with ties to Spain advocated neutrality. Cherokee ranks were split between anti-American militants who saw an opportunity to drive back settlers and those who thought that Cherokees' best hope was to steer clear of the Anglo-American conflict.

The patriots also had other sources of Indian support. Native Americans in upper New England, easternmost Canada, and the Illinois and Wabash valleys were initially anti-British because of earlier ties with the French, though some of them became alienated from the colonists during the war. In coastal areas, where surviving Indians had long been subjugated to colonial governments, most native men fought on the patriot side.

6-1.3 Military Preparedness on Both Sides

Britain entered the war with two major advantages. First, in 1776 the 11 million inhabitants of the British Isles greatly outnumbered the 2.5 million colonists, one-third of whom were either slaves or loyalists. Second, Britain possessed the world's largest navy and one of its best professional armies. Even so, the royal military establishment grew during the war years to a degree that strained Britain's resources. The number of soldiers stationed in North America, the British Isles, and the West Indies more than doubled from 48,000 to 111,000 men, especially after the war became a global conflict. To meet its manpower needs, the British government obtained the services of 30,000 German troops known as Hessians and enlisted 21,000 loyalists.

Britain's ability to crush the rebellion was further weakened by the decline in its sea power, a result of budget cuts after 1763. Midway through the war, half of the Royal Navy's ships sat in dry dock awaiting major repairs. Although the navy expanded rapidly from 18,000 to 111,000 sailors, it lost 42,000 men to desertion and 20,000 to disease or injuries. In addition, Britain's merchant marine suffered from raids by American privateers. During the war, rebel privateers and the fledgling U.S. navy would capture more than 2,000 British merchant vessels and 16,000 crewmen.

Britain could ill afford these losses, for it faced a colossal task in trying to supply its troops in America. In fact, it had to import from Britain most of the food consumed by its army, a third of a ton per soldier per year. Seriously overextended, the navy barely kept the army supplied and never effectively blockaded American ports.

Because of the enormous strain that the war imposed, British leaders faced problems maintaining their people's support for the conflict. The war more than doubled the national debt, thereby adding to the burdens of a people already paying record taxes. Voters could not be expected to vote against their pocketbooks forever.

The United States faced different but no less severe wartime problems. Besides the fact that many colonists, slaves, and Native Americans favored the British, the patriots faced a formidable military challenge. American men were accustomed to serving as citizen-soldiers in colonial (now state) militias. Although militias often performed well in hit-and-run guerrilla skirmishes, they were not trained to fight pitched battles against professional armies like Britain's. Congress recognized that independence would never be secured if the new nation relied on guerrilla tactics, avoided major battles, and allowed the British to occupy its major population centers. Moreover, these scenarios would undermine the confidence of potential European allies in the colonial army's ability to drive the British out.

For the United States to succeed, the Continental Army would have to supersede the state militias and would need to fight in the standard European fashion. Professional eighteenth-century armies relied on the precisely executed movements of mass formations. Victory often depended on rapid maneuvers to crush an enemy's undefended flank or rear. Attackers needed exceptional skill in close-order drill to fall on an enemy before the enemy could re-form and return fire. Because muskets had a range of less than one hundred yards, armies in battle were never far apart. The troops advanced within musket range of each other, stood upright without cover, and fired at one another until one line weakened from its casualties. Discipline, training, and nerve were essential if soldiers were to stay in ranks while comrades fell beside them. The stronger side then attacked at a quick walk with bayonets drawn and drove off its opponents.

In 1775, Britain possessed a well-trained and disciplined army known for its bravery under fire. In contrast, the Continental Army lacked a deep pool of experienced officers and sergeants who could turn raw recruits into crack units. European officers such as Kósciuszko helped make up for the shortage of leaders. Although the United States mobilized about 220,000 troops, compared to the 162,000 who served the British, most served short terms. Even with bounties (signing bonuses), promises of land after service, and other incentives, the army had difficulty attracting men for the long term. Most whites and blacks who did sign up for multiyear or indefinite lengths of time were poor and landless. Such men joined not out of patriotism but because, as one of them, a jailed debtor named Ezekiel Brown, put it, they had "little or nothing to lose."

The Americans experienced a succession of heartbreaking defeats in the war's early years, and the new nation would have been hard-pressed had it not been for the military contributions of France and Spain in the war's later stages. Yet, to win the war, the Continentals did not have to destroy the British army but only prolong the rebellion until Britain's taxpayers lost patience with the struggle. Until then, American victory would depend on the ability of one man to keep his army fighting: the brilliant, ambitious Virginian, **George Washington**.

The young Washington's mistakes and defeats in the Ohio Valley (see Chapter 5) taught him about the dangers of overconfidence and the need to demonstrate determination even in the face of defeat. He also learned much about American soldiers, notably that they performed best when led by example and treated with respect.

After resigning his commission in 1758, Washington had served in the Virginia House of Burgesses, where his influence grew as he shrewdly positioned himself as a wise counselor whose opinions others sought. Having emerged as an early, though not outspoken, opponent of parliamentary taxation, he later sat in the Continental Congress. Given his military and political reputation, Washington was Congress's logical choice to head the Continental Army.

6-2 War and Peace, 1776–1783

What turned the tide of war in the colonists' favor and ensured their victory in the American Revolution?

Until mid-1778, the Revolutionary War remained centered in the North, where each side won some important victories. Meanwhile, American forces prevailed over British troops and their Native American allies to gain control of the trans-Appalachian West. The war was ultimately decided in the South when American and French forces won a stunning victory at Yorktown, Virginia, in 1781. In the peace treaty that followed, Britain finally acknowledged American independence.

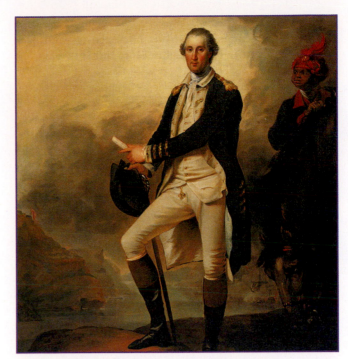

GEORGE WASHINGTON, BY JOHN TRUMBULL, 1780
Washington posed for this portrait at the height of the Revolutionary War, accompanied by his enslaved servant, William Lee. *(Image copyright © The Metropolitan Museum of Art/Art Resource, NY)*

6-2.1 Shifting Fortunes in the North, 1776–1778

During the second half of 1776, the two sides focused on New York. Under two brothers—General William Howe and Admiral Richard, Lord Howe—130 British warships carrying 32,000 royal troops landed at New York in the summer of 1776 (see Map 6.1). Defending the city were 18,000 poorly trained soldiers of the Continental Army (knicknamed "Continentals") under George Washington.

By the end of the year, William Howe's men had killed or captured one-quarter of Washington's troops and had forced the survivors to retreat from New York across New Jersey and the Delaware River into Pennsylvania. Thomas Paine aptly described these demoralizing days as "the times that try men's souls."

With the British nearing Philadelphia, Washington decided to seize the offensive before the morale of his army and country collapsed completely. On Christmas night 1776, his troops returned to New Jersey and attacked a Hessian garrison at Trenton, where they captured 918 Germans and lost only

George Washington
American military leader and the first president of the United States (1789-1797). Commander of the American forces in the Revolutionary War (1775-1783), he presided over the Second Constitutional Convention (1787) and was elected president of the fledgling country (1789). He shunned partisan politics and in his farewell address (1796) warned against foreign involvement.

four Continentals. Washington's men then attacked twelve hundred British at Princeton on January 3, 1777, and killed or captured one-third of them while sustaining only forty casualties.

The American victories at Trenton and Princeton had several important consequences. At a moment when defeat seemed inevitable, they boosted civilian and military morale. In addition, they drove a wedge between New Jersey's five thousand loyalists and the British army. Washington's victories forced the British to remove virtually all their New Jersey garrisons to New York early in 1777. Once the British were gone, New Jersey's militia disarmed known loyalists, jailed their leaders, and kept a constant watch on suspected Tories. Bowing to the inevitable, most remaining loyalists swore allegiance to the Continental Congress. Some even joined the patriots.

After the Battle of Princeton, the Marquis de Lafayette, a young French aristocrat, joined Washington's staff. The twenty-year-old Lafayette was brave, idealistic, and optimistic. Given Lafayette's close connections with the French court, his presence indicated France's growing interest in the American cause. (France had already secretly provided the Americans with funds.) Before providing French military support to the new nation, however, King Louis XVI wanted proof that the Americans could win a major battle, a feat they had not yet accomplished.

Louis did not have to wait long. In the summer of 1777, the British planned a two-pronged assault

MAP 6.1 THE WAR IN THE NORTH, 1775–1778 During the early years of the war, most of the fighting took place from Philadelphia northward.

intended to crush American resistance in New York State and thereby isolate New England. From Montreal, a force of regulars and their Iroquois allies under Lieutenant Colonel Barry St. Leger would march south along Lake Ontario and invade central New York from Fort Oswego in the west. At the same time, General John Burgoyne would lead the main British force south from Quebec through eastern New York and link up with St. Leger near Albany.

Nothing went according to British plans. St. Leger's force of nineteen hundred British and Iroquois advanced one hundred miles and halted to besiege 750 Continentals at Fort Stanwix. Unable to take the post after three weeks, St. Leger retreated in late August 1777.

Burgoyne's campaign appeared more promising after his force of eighty-three hundred British and Hessians recaptured Fort Ticonderoga. But as Burgoyne continued southward, nearly seven thousand American troops under General Horatio Gates prepared to challenge him near Saratoga. In two battles in the fall, the British suffered twelve hundred casualties while failing to dislodge the Americans. Surrounded and hopelessly outnumbered, Burgoyne surrendered on October 17, 1777.

The **Battle of Saratoga** would prove to be the war's turning point. The victory convinced France that the Americans could win the war. Negotiated by Benjamin Franklin, in February 1778, France formally recognized the United States by signing treaties of friendship and commerce and of military alliance with the new nation. The second of these agreements, the Treaty of Alliance, solidified the bonds between the two countries, as they pledged that neither would agree to a peace treaty with the British without the other's involvement. Four months later, France joined the patriots and went to war with Britain, sending troops, supplies, and war materiel to aid the Continentals. Spain declared war on Britain in 1779, but as an ally only of France, not the United States, and the Dutch Republic joined the war against Britain late in 1780. Britain faced a formidable coalition of enemies, without allies of its own.

Meanwhile, as Gates and Burgoyne maneuvered in upstate New York, Britain's General Howe landed eighteen thousand troops near Philadelphia. With Washington at their head and Lafayette at his side, sixteen thousand Continentals occupied the imperiled city in late August 1777.

The two armies collided on September 11, 1777, at Brandywine Creek, Pennsylvania. In the face of superior British discipline, most Continental units crumbled, and Congress fled Philadelphia in panic, enabling Howe to occupy the city. Howe again defeated Washington at Germantown on October 4.

In one month's bloody fighting, 20 percent of the Continentals were killed, wounded, or captured.

While the British army wintered comfortably in Philadelphia, the Continentals huddled eighteen miles away in the bleak hills of Valley Forge. Joseph Plumb Martin, a seventeen-year-old Massachusetts recruit, recorded the troops' condition in his diary: "The greatest part were not only shirtless and barefoot but destitute of all other clothing, especially blankets." However, he concluded, "we had engaged in the defense of our injured country and were willing nay, we were determined, to persevere as long as such hardships were not altogether intolerable." Shortages of provisions, especially food, would continue to undermine morale and, on some occasions, discipline among American forces.

The army also lacked training. At Saratoga, the Americans' overwhelming numbers more than their skill had forced Burgoyne to surrender. Indeed, when Washington's men had met Howe's forces on equal terms, they lost badly.

Battle of Saratoga
A turning point in the American Revolution. The American victory in this battle convinced France that Americans could win the war, and it allied itself with the Americans.

BARON FRIEDRICH WILHELM VON STEUBEN Portrayed here by Charles Willson Peale, the German general was instrumental in transforming the Continental Army into a formidable fighting force. *(Courtesy of Independence National Historical Park)*

The Continental Army received a desperately needed boost in February 1778, when a German soldier of fortune, Friedrich von Steuben, arrived at Valley Forge. The short, squat Steuben did not look like a soldier, but he had a talent for motivating men (sometimes by staging humorous tantrums featuring German, English, and French swearing). In a mere four months, General Steuben almost single-handedly turned the army into a formidable fighting force.

British officials evacuated Philadelphia in June 1778 to free up several thousand troops for action against France in the West Indies. General Henry Clinton, the new commander-in-chief in North America, led the troops northward for New York. The Continental Army got its first opportunity to demonstrate Steuben's training when it caught up with Clinton's rear guard at Monmouth, New Jersey, on June 28, 1778. The battle raged for six hours in one-hundred-degree heat until Clinton broke off contact. Expecting to renew the fight at daybreak, the Americans slept on their arms, but Clinton's army slipped away before then. The British would never again win easily, except when they faced more militiamen than Continentals.

The Battle of Monmouth ended the contest for the North. Clinton occupied New York, which the Royal Navy made safe from attack while Washington's army remained nearby to keep an eye on Clinton.

6-2.2 The War in the West, 1776–1782

A different kind of war developed from the Appalachians westward, consisting of small-scale skirmishes rather than major battles involving thousands of troops. Long-standing tensions between native peoples and land-hungry settlers continued to simmer. In one sense, the warfare between them only continued an older frontier struggle. Despite its smaller scale, the war in the West was fierce and the stakes—for the new nation, for the British Empire, and for French settlers and Native Americans in the region—were enormous.

The war in the West erupted in 1776 when Cherokees began attacking settlers from North Carolina and nearby states who had encroached on their homelands (see Map 6.2). After suffering heavy losses, the states recovered and organized retaliatory expeditions. Within a

year, these expeditions had burned most Cherokee towns, forcing the Cherokees to sign treaties that ceded most of their land in South Carolina and substantial tracts in North Carolina and Tennessee.

The intense fighting lasted longer in the Northwest. Largely independent of American and British coordination, Ohio Indians and white settlers fought for two years in Kentucky, with neither side gaining a clear advantage. But after British troops occupied French settlements in what is now Illinois and Indiana, Colonel George Rogers Clark led 175 Kentucky militiamen north of the Ohio River. After capturing and losing Vincennes, Clark retook the French town for good in February 1779. With the British unable to offer assistance, their Native American allies were vulnerable. In May, John Bowman led a second Kentucky unit in a campaign that destroyed most Shawnee villages, and in August a move northward from Pittsburgh by Daniel Brodhead inflicted similar damage on the Delawares and Ohio Senecas. Although these raids depleted their populations and food supplies, most

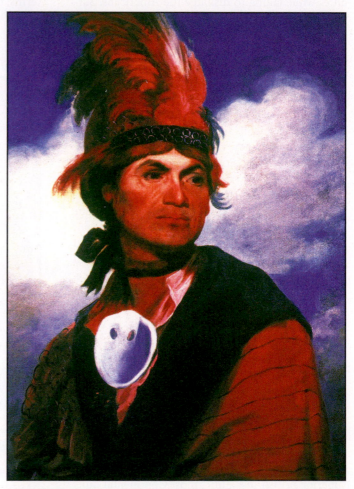

JOSEPH BRANT, BY GILBERT STUART, 1786 The youthful Mohawk leader was a staunch ally of the British during the Revolutionary War, and thereafter resisted U.S. expansion in the Northwest. *(Granger, NYC — All rights reserved.)*

MAP 6.2 **THE WAR IN THE WEST, 1776–1782** The war's western front was closely tied to Native Americans' defense of their homelands against expansionist settlers.

Ohio Indians resisted the Americans until the war's end.

Meanwhile, pro-British Iroquois, led by the gifted Mohawk leader Joseph Brant, devastated the Pennsylvania and New York frontiers in 1778, killing about seven hundred settlers. In 1779, American General John Sullivan retaliated by invading Iroquois country with thirty-seven hundred Continental troops, along with several hundred Tuscaroras and Oneidas who had broken with the other Iroquois nations. Sullivan fought just one battle, near present-day Elmira, New York, in which his artillery routed Brant's warriors. Then he burned two dozen Iroquois villages and destroyed a million bushels of corn, causing most Iroquois to flee without food into Canada. Untold hundreds starved during the next winter, when more than sixty inches of snow fell.

In 1780, Brant's thousand warriors took revenge on the Tuscaroras and Oneidas, and then laid waste to Pennsylvania and New York for two years. But this final whirlwind masked reality: Sullivan's campaign had devastated the pro-British Iroquois.

Fighting continued in the West until 1782. Despite their intensity, the western campaigns did not determine the outcome of the war itself. Nevertheless, they would have a significant impact on the future shape of the United States and on Native American populations as well.

6-2.3 Victory in the South, 1778–1781

In 1778, the war's focus shifted to the South. By securing southern ports, the British expected to acquire the flexibility needed to move their forces back and forth between the West Indies—where they faced French and Spanish opposition—and the mainland, as necessity dictated. General Clinton expected to seize key southern ports and, with the aid of loyalist militiamen, move back toward the North, pacifying one region after another.

The plan unfolded smoothly at first. In the spring of 1778, British troops from East Florida took control of Georgia. After a two-year delay caused by political bickering at home, Clinton sailed from New York

MindTap

Beyond America
The American Revolution as an International War

with nine thousand troops and forced the surrender of Charles Town, South Carolina, and its thirty-four-hundred-man garrison on May 12, 1780 (see Map 6.3). However, the British quickly found that there were fewer loyalists than they had expected.

Southern loyalism had declined considerably since the war began. When the Cherokees had attacked the Carolina frontier in 1776, they killed whites indiscriminately. Numerous Tories had switched sides, joining the rebel militia to defend their homes. The arrival of British troops sparked a renewed exodus of enslaved Africans from their plantations. About one-third of Georgia's blacks and one-fourth of South Carolina's fled to British lines or to British-held Florida in quest of freedom. Although British officials attempted to return runaway slaves to loyalist masters, they met with limited success. Planters feared that loss of control over their human property

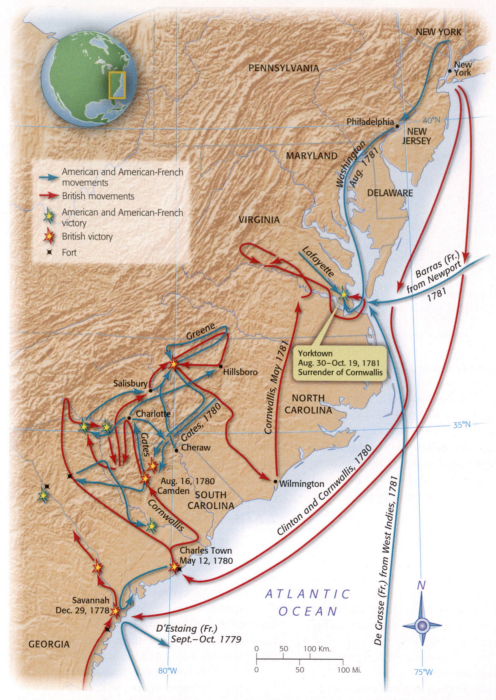

MAP 6.3 THE WAR IN THE SOUTH, 1778–1781 The South was the setting for the final and decisive phase of the war. After the British overran Georgia and captured Charles Town, they fought repeatedly with the Continentals in the interior before Cornwallis surrendered at Yorktown.

SURRENDER OF THE BRITISH AT YORKTOWN, 1781 French naval power combined with American military savvy to produce the decisive defeat of the British. *(Library of Congress Prints and Photographs Division)*

would lead to a black uprising. Despite British efforts to placate them, many white loyalists abandoned the British and welcomed the rebels' return to power in 1782. Those who remained loyalists, embittered by countless instances of harsh treatment under patriot rule, took revenge. Patriots struck back whenever possible, perpetuating an ongoing cycle of revenge, retribution, and retaliation among whites.

Meanwhile, Horatio Gates took command of American forces in the South. With only a small force of Continentals at his disposal, Gates had to rely on poorly trained militiamen. In August 1780, Lord Charles Cornwallis inflicted a crushing defeat on Gates at Camden, South Carolina. Fleeing after firing a single volley, Gates's militia left his badly outnumbered Continentals to be overrun. Camden was the worst rebel defeat of the war.

Washington and Congress responded by relieving Gates of his command and sending General Nathanael Greene to confront Cornwallis. Greene subsequently fought and lost three major battles between March and September 1781. Still, Greene won the campaign, for he gave the Whig militia the protection they needed to hunt down loyalists, stretched British supply lines until they snapped, and weakened Cornwallis by inflicting much heavier casualties than the British general could afford. Greene's dogged resistance forced Cornwallis to leave the Carolina backcountry in American hands and to lead his battered troops into Virginia.

Cornwallis established a base at Yorktown, Virginia, where he allied with American traitor Benedict Arnold and his pro-British army. There, Cornwallis and his soldiers waited for supplies and additional troops. Britain's undoing began on August 30, 1781, when a French fleet dropped anchor off the Virginia coast and landed troops near Yorktown. Lafayette and a small force of Continentals from nearby joined the French while Washington arrived with his army from New York. Meanwhile, French admiral Francois Jean Paul De Grasse intercepted and defeated British Royal Navy ships stocked with supplies and troops for Cornwallis, leaving him trapped and isolated. In the **Battle of Yorktown**, six thousand British troops stood off eighty-eight hundred Americans and seventy-eight hundred French for three weeks before surrendering with military honors on October 19, 1781.

6-2.4 Peace at Last, 1782–1783

Cornwallis's surrender drained the will of England's overtaxed people to continue fighting and forced Britain to negotiate for peace. John Adams, Benjamin Franklin, and John Jay were America's principal delegates to the peace talks in Paris, which began in June 1782.

Military realities largely influenced the terms of the **Treaty of Paris**

> **Battle of Yorktown**
> The battle in Virginia where Lord Cornwallis surrendered to George Washington.
>
> **Treaty of Paris**
> A treaty signed in 1783 when the British recognized American independence and agreed to withdraw all royal troops from the colonies.

(1783). Britain recognized American independence and agreed to withdraw all royal troops from the new nation's soil. The British had little choice but to award the United States all lands east of the Mississippi. Although the vast majority of Americans were clustered near the eastern seaboard, twenty thousand Anglo-Americans now lived west of the Appalachians. Moreover, Clark's victories had given Americans control of the Northwest, while Spain had kept Britain out of the Southwest.

On the whole, the settlement was highly favorable to the United States, but it left some disputes unresolved. Under a separate treaty, Britain returned East and West Florida to Spain, but the boundaries designated by this treaty were ambiguous. Spain interpreted the treaty to mean that it regained the same Florida territory that it had ceded to Britain in 1763 (see Chapter 5). But the Treaty of Paris (not signed by Spain) named the thirty-first parallel as Florida's northern border, well south of the area claimed by Spain. Spain and the United States would dispute the northern boundary of Florida until 1795 (as discussed later in this chapter and in Chapter 7).

The Treaty of Paris failed to prevent several future disputes between Britain and America. Not bound by the treaty, which extended only to national governments, state governments refused to compensate loyalists for their property losses and erected barriers against British creditors' attempts to collect prewar debts. In retaliation, the British refused to honor treaty pledges to abandon forts in the Northwest and to return American-owned slaves under their control.

Notably missing in the Treaty of Paris was any reference to Native Americans, most of whom had supported the British to avert the alternative—an independent American nation whose citizens would covet their lands. In effect, the treaty left native peoples to deal with the United States on their own, without any provision for their status or treatment. Joseph Brant and other Native American leaders were outraged. Not surprisingly, most Indians did not acknowledge the new nation's claims to sovereignty over their territory.

The Treaty of Paris ratified American independence, but winning independence had exacted a heavy price. At least 5 percent of Americans between the ages of sixteen and forty-five—white, black, and Native American—died fighting the British. Only the Civil War produced a higher ratio of casualties to the nation's population.

The American victory drove about sixty thousand white loyalists, African Americans, and Native Americans into exile. More than half the refugees moved to Canada, with the rest dispersing to Great Britain and to British colonies in the West Indies, Africa, and India. About six thousand white southerners carried at least twice that many still-enslaved African Americans to new plantations in the British colonies of Jamaica and the Bahamas. After finding that both the land and inhabitants in Nova Scotia were inhospitable, about twelve hundred freed blacks moved from there to the British colony of Sierra Leone in West Africa, which had been recently founded by abolitionists as a haven for emancipated slaves.

Finally, although the war secured American independence, it did not address two important issues: what kind of society America would become and what sort of government the new nation would possess.

6-3 The Revolution and Social Change

How did the American Revolution change people's lives during and after the conflict ended?

As Chapter 5 explained, during the decade preceding the Revolution, nonelite colonists had become more politically active than previously. After 1776, the principles articulated in the Declaration of Independence and dislocations caused by the war forced questions of class, gender, and race into public discussion. As a result, popular attitudes regarding the rights of nonelite white men and of white women, and the future of slavery, shifted somewhat. Although the resulting changes were not substantive, the discussions ensured that these issues would continue to be debated in the United States. For Native Americans, however, the Revolution was a definite step backward.

6-3.1 Egalitarianism Among White Men

For much of the eighteenth century, members of the colonial gentry emphasized their social position by conspicuously consuming expensive English imports. By the late 1760s, however, many elite politicians began wearing homespun clothes made by wives and other colonial women rather than imported English clothes to win popular political approval during the colonial boycott of British goods. When Virginia planters organized militia companies in 1775, they put aside their expensive officers' uniforms and dressed in buckskin or homespun hunting shirts of a sort that even the poorest farmer could afford. By 1776, the anti-British movement had persuaded many elites to maintain the appearance, if not the substance, of equality with common people.

Then came war, which accelerated the trend toward equality by pressuring the gentry, who held officers' rank, to show respect to the ordinary men serving under them. Indeed, the soldiers demanded to be treated with consideration, especially in light of the ringing words of the Declaration of Independence, "All men are created equal." The soldiers would follow commands, but not if they were addressed as inferiors.

A few officers, among them General Israel Putnam of Connecticut, went out of their way to show that they felt no superiority to their troops. While inspecting a regiment digging fortifications around Boston in 1776, Putnam saw a large stone nearby and told a soldier to throw it onto the outer wall. The individual protested, "Sir, I am a corporal." "Oh," replied Putnam, "I ask your pardon, sir." The general then dismounted his horse and hurled the rock himself, to the immense delight of the troops working there.

Still, many officers insisted that soldiers remain disciplined and subordinate under all circumstances. In May 1780—more than two years after the terrible winter at Valley Forge—Continental Army troops in New Jersey were again, in Joseph Plumb Martin's words, "starved and naked. . . . They could not stand it any longer." After a day of exercising with their arms, Martin's regiment defied orders to disarm and return to its quarters, instead urging two nearby regiments to join in protesting the lack of provisions. A colonel, who "considered himself the soldier's friend," was wounded when trying to prevent his men from getting their weapons. After several officers seized one defiant soldier, his comrades pointed their rifles at the officers until they released the soldier. The soldiers' willingness to defy their superiors paid off. Within a few days, more provisions arrived.

After returning to civilian life, the soldiers carried this egalitarian spirit into their postwar life, insisting on respectful treatment by elites. As these feelings of personal pride gradually translated into political behavior and beliefs, candidates often took care not to scorn the common people. The war thus subtly democratized Americans' political assumptions.

Still, many elites did not welcome the apparent trend toward democracy. These men insisted that each social class had its particular virtues and that a chief virtue of the lower classes was deference to those possessing the wealth and education necessary to govern. Writing to a friend in 1776, John Adams expressed alarm that "a jealousy or an Envy taking Place among the Multitude" would exclude "Men of Learning . . . from the public Councils and from Military Command." "A popular government is the worse Curse," he concluded, "despotism is better." Such concerns about deference would divide leaders as they considered the allocation of power in the American republic.

Nevertheless, most Revolutionary-generation Americans came to insist that virtue and sacrifice defined a citizen's worth independently of his wealth. Voters still elected the wealthy to office, but not if they flaunted their money or were condescending toward common people. The new emphasis on equality did not extend to propertyless males, women, and non-whites, but it undermined the tendency to believe that wealth or distinguished family background conferred a special claim to public office.

Egalitarian attitudes aside, the Revolution left the actual distribution of wealth in the nation unchanged. The exodus of loyalists did not affect the class structure because the 3 percent who fled the United States represented a cross-section of society and equally well-to-do Whig gentlemen usually bought up their confiscated estates. Overall, the American upper class seems to have owned about as much of the national wealth in 1783 as it did in 1776.

6-3.2 White Women in Wartime

White women's support of colonial resistance before the Revolution (see Chapter 5) broadened into an even wider range of activities during the war. Female "camp followers," most of them poor though some of them soldiers' wives, served military units on both sides by cooking, laundering, and nursing the wounded. Although the services they were provided were vital, George Washington found their presence bothersome, especially the poorer women who he thought degraded the image of his upstanding Continentals. He also worried that feeding camp followers might take from supplies needed for soldiers.

Other women served as spies or couriers for the Continental army. A few female patriots, such as Massachusetts's Deborah Sampson, disguised themselves as men and joined in the fighting. Sampson, the most famous example, dubbed herself Robert Shurtleff and served for a year and a half in 1782. She was wounded a few times before officials discovered Shurtleff was actually a woman. She later married and had a family, but also gave talks about her military service. In 1790, she began petitioning Congress for a military pension. In 1804, after Paul Revere argued that she was "more deserving than hundreds to whom Congress have been generous," she was finally awarded a pension.

Even traditional female roles took on new meaning with the wartime absence of male household heads. After her civilian husband was seized by loyalists and turned over to the British on Long Island, Mary Silliman of Fairfield, Connecticut, tended to her four children (and bore a fifth), oversaw several servants and slaves, ran a commercial farm that had to be evacuated when the British attacked Fairfield, and launched repeated appeals to male authorities for her husband's release.

Left to manage households as well as spouses' businesses on their own, women gained newfound confidence to think and act on matters typically reserved for men. During the prewar era, wives did as they were told regarding business when filling in for traveling husbands. During the Revolution, however, they no longer strictly followed a spouse's instructions and often acted as they saw best—at times boldly referring to the business as "ours" in the letters they exchanged, much to the men's chagrin. "I have the vanity," wrote Mary Fish of Connecticut to a female friend, "to think I have in some measure acted the *heroine* as well as my dear Husband the Hero."

DEBORAH SAMPSON, REVOLUTIONARY WAR HERO. Portrait of Deborah Sampson, Revolutionary war hero, which appeared in *The Female Review,* Herman Mann's 1797 account of Sampson's life, and one of the leading primary sources about Sampson.*(Portrait of Deborah Sampson, 1787 (litho), American School, (18th century) / American Antiquarian Society, Worcester, Massachusetts, USA / Bridgeman Images)*

As in all wars, women's public roles were heightened during the Revolution. In 1779, Esther de Berdte Reed and Sally Franklin Bache (Benjamin Franklin's daughter) organized a campaign among Philadelphia women to raise money for the troops. Not content to see their movement's role as secondary, they compared it to those of Joan of Arc and other female heroes and proclaimed that American women were "born for liberty" and would never "bear the irons of a tyrannic Government." They raised $300,000—a sizable sum for the day—which they hoped to distribute to needy soldiers. But General Washington suggested they use the money instead to make shirts, an action more in keeping with, and perhaps a reminder of, women's appropriate gender roles.

The most direct wartime challenge to established gender relations came from **Abigail Adams**. "In the new Code of Laws which I suppose it will be necessary for you to make," Adams wrote to her husband John in 1776, "I desire that you would Remember the Ladies." Otherwise, she continued, "we are determined to foment a Rebellion and will not hold ourselves bound by any Laws in which we have no voice, or Representation." Abigail made clear that, besides participating in boycotts and spinning bees, women recognized that colonists' arguments against arbitrary British rule also applied to gender relations. Despite his high regard for his wife's intellect, John dismissed her plea as yet another effort to extend rights and power to those who were unworthy. The assumption that women were naturally dependent—either as children subordinate to their parents or as wives to their husbands—continued to dominate discussions of the female role. For that reason, married women's property remained, in Abigail's bitter words, "subject to the control and disposal of our partners, to whom the law have given a sovereign authority."

6-3.3 A Revolution for African Americans

The wartime situation of African Americans contradicted the ideals of equality and justice for which Americans were fighting. About a half million blacks—20 percent of the total population—inhabited the United States in 1776, all but about twenty-five thousand of whom were enslaved. Even those who were free could not vote, lived under curfews and other galling restrictions, and lacked the guarantees of equal justice held by the poorest white criminal. Free blacks could expect no more than grudging toleration, and few slaves had ever gained their freedom.

The early fighting in New England drew several hundred blacks into militia and Continental units. Some slaves, among them Jehu Grant of Rhode Island, ran off and posed as free persons. Grant later recalled that "when I saw liberty poles and the people all engaged for the support of freedom, . . . I could not but like and be pleased with such a thing." But pressure from white southern politicians led Washington to ban blacks from serving on November 12, 1775, ironically just five days after Lord Dunmore's proclamation invited enslaved Virginians to join the British.

Most wartime opportunities for African American men grew out of the army's need for personnel rather than a white commitment to equal justice. Just six weeks after barring all black enlistments, Washington decided to admit free blacks to the army. Two years later, he agreed to Rhode Island's plea that it be allowed to raise a nonwhite regiment. Slaves could enlist and would be freed, in return for which the state paid their masters about $2,400 in today's currency. The regiment of African Americans and Native Americans distinguished itself in several battles, including at Yorktown.

The arming of enslaved African Americans was more controversial among white patriots. In 1779, as British troops poured from Georgia into South Carolina, a South Carolina officer, with the support of Congress, urged the two states to organize a battalion of three thousand enslaved Africans. As in Rhode Island, the slaves would be freed and their masters compensated. But the two states vetoed the plan.

Until the mid-eighteenth century, few Europeans and white Americans had criticized slavery at all. But in the decade before the Revolution, American opposition to slavery had swelled, especially as resistance leaders increasingly compared the colonies' relationship with Britain to that between slaves and a master.

Given Quakers' beliefs in human equality, it is not surprising that the earliest organized white initiatives against slavery originated among Quakers. The yearly meeting of the New England Friends abolished slavery among its members in 1770, and yearly meetings in New York and Philadelphia followed suit in 1776. By 1779, Quaker slave owners had freed 80 percent of their slaves.

Although the Quakers aimed mainly to abolish slave-holding within their own ranks, some activists, most notably Anthony Benezet and John Woolman, broadened their condemnations to include slavery everywhere. Discussions of liberty, equality, and natural rights, particularly in the Declaration of Independence, also spurred antislavery legislation. Between 1777 and 1784, Vermont, Pennsylvania, Massachusetts, Rhode Island, and Connecticut began phasing out slavery. New York did not do so until 1799, and New Jersey until 1804. New Hampshire, unmoved by petitions like that written in 1779 by twenty Portsmouth slaves demanding liberty "to dispose of our lives, freedom, and property," never officially freed its slaves, but by 1810 none remained in the state.

Rather than immediately abolishing slavery, the northern states took steps that weakened the institution, paving the way for its eventual demise. Most state abolition laws provided for gradual emancipation, typically declaring all children born of a slave woman after a certain date—often July 4—free. (They still had to work, without pay, for their mother's master up to age twenty-eight.) Furthermore, northern politicians did not press for decisive action against slavery in the South. They argued that the Confederation, already deeply in debt as a result of the war, could not finance abolition in the South and feared that any attempt to do so without compensation would drive that region into secession.

Yet even in the South, where it was most firmly entrenched, slavery troubled some whites. When one of his slaves ran off to join the British and later was recaptured, James Madison of Virginia concluded that it would be hypocritical to punish the runaway "merely for coveting that liberty for which we have paid the price of so much blood." Still, Madison did not free the slave, and no state south of Pennsylvania abolished slavery. Nevertheless, all states except South Carolina and Georgia ended slave imports and all but North Carolina passed laws making it easy for masters to manumit (set free) slaves. The number of free African Americans in Virginia and Maryland rose from about four thousand in 1775 to nearly twenty-one thousand, or about 5 percent of the black population there, by 1790.

These "free persons of color" faced the future as often destitute and definitely second-class citizens. Most had purchased their freedom by spending small cash savings earned in off-hours and were past their physical prime. Once free, they found whites reluctant to hire them or to pay equal wages. Black ship carpenters in Charleston (formerly Charles Town), South Carolina, for example, earned one-third less than their white coworkers in 1783. Under such circumstances, most free blacks remained poor laborers, domestic servants, and tenant farmers.

One of the most prominent free blacks to emerge during the Revolutionary period was Boston's **Prince Hall**. Born a slave, Hall received his freedom in 1770 and took a leading role among Boston blacks protesting slavery. During the war, he formed a separate African American Masonic lodge, beginning a movement that spread to other northern cities and becoming an important source of community support for black Americans. In 1786, Hall petitioned the Massachusetts legislature for support of a plan that would enable interested blacks "to return to Africa, our native country . . . where we shall live among our equals and be more comfortable and happy than

Prince Hall
One of the most prominent free blacks to emerge during the Revolutionary period. Born a slave, he received his freedom in 1770 and immediately took a leading role among Boston blacks protesting slavery.

we can be in our present situation." Hall's request was unsuccessful, but later activists would revive his call for blacks to "return to Africa."

Among whites, the most widely recognized African American was an enslaved Boston poet, Phillis Wheatley. Wheatley drew on Revolutionary ideals in considering her people's status. Several of her poems explicitly linked the liberty sought by white Americans with a plea for the liberty of slaves, including one that was autobiographical:

I, young in life, by seeming cruel fate
Was snatch'd from Afric's fancy'ed happy seat:
Such, such my case. And can I then but pray
Others may never feel tyrannic sway?

Most states granted some civil rights to free blacks during and after the Revolution. Free blacks had not participated in colonial elections, but those who were male and met the property qualification gained this privilege in a few states during the 1780s. Most northern states repealed or stopped enforcing curfews and other colonial laws restricting free African Americans' freedom of movement. These same states generally changed their laws to guarantee free blacks equal treatment in court hearings.

PHILLIS WHEATLEY, AFRICAN AMERICAN POET Wheatley was America's best-known poet at the time of the Revolution. Despite her fame, she remained a slave and died in poverty in 1784. *(Library of Congress Prints and Photographs Division)*

The Revolution neither ended slavery nor brought equality to free blacks, but it did begin a process by which slavery eventually might have been extinguished. Slavery had begun to crack, and free blacks had made some gains. But events in the 1790s would reverse the tentative move toward egalitarianism (as discussed in Chapter 7).

6-3.4 Native Americans and the Revolution

Whereas Revolutionary ideology held out at least an abstract hope for white women, blacks, and others seeking liberty and equal rights within American society, it made no provision for Native Americans wishing to remain independent of the United States. Regardless of which side they had fought on—or whether they had fought at all—Native Americans suffered worse than any group during the war. During the three decades encompassed by the Seven Years' War and the Revolution (1754–1783), the Native population east of the Mississippi declined by about half, and many Indian communities were completely uprooted. Moreover, in the overwhelmingly agrarian society of the United States, the Revolution's implicit promise of equal economic opportunity for all white male citizens set the stage for massive encroachments onto Native American landholdings. Even where Indians initially retained some land, newly arrived white neighbors posed dangers in the form of deadly diseases, violence, fraudulent purchases, farming practices inimical to Indian subsistence (see Chapter 3), and alcohol.

After the war, Native Americans experienced pressure to adopt white practices and assimilate to white cultural norms in ways that would have long-term repercussions for women and for gender roles. Men were urged to give up hunting—often their primary role—and take up farming, much as European men did. Women were pressed to turn over the farming they typically did and take on domestic roles more in keeping with white women's practices. These changes, as well as the ongoing land losses, strained Native American men's sense of social value and masculinity. That fueled increased alcohol consumption, which in turn sparked increased domestic violence against women, who already saw much of their traditional tribal influence and prominence stripped away.

For several centuries since initial contact, native peoples in eastern North America had selectively adopted European-made products, domestic animals, and even aspects of Christianity into their lives. Many Indians, especially those no longer resisting American expansion, participated in the American economy by working for wages or by selling food, crafts, or other products. But Native Americans never gave up their older ways altogether; rather, they worked hard to combine elements of the old and the new.

Native Americans did insist on retaining control of their homelands and their communities, both of which were fundamental to their identities. But many Indians on already crowded lands near the eastern seaboard were forced to choose between these alternatives. While some of their tribespeople stayed behind, Samson Occom (see Chapter 4) and several hundred other disillusioned Christian Indians left New England in 1784. They founded the communities of Brothertown and New Stockbridge on land granted them by the Oneida Iroquois in upstate New York. Farther west, the Chickasaws of the Mississippi Valley sought to avoid the same predicament. While asking Congress in 1783 "from whare and whome we are to be supplyed with necessaries," they also requested that the Confederation "put a stop to any encroachments on our lands, without our consent, and silence those [white] People who . . . inflame and exasperate our Young Men." Other, more westerly native peoples allied, or threatened to ally, with Britain or Spain in order to protect themselves from American expansion (discussed later).

6-4 Forging New Governments, 1776–1787

How did the new United States of America implement a system of government?

In establishing new political institutions, revolutionary Americans endeavored to guarantee liberty at the state level by minimizing executive power and by subjecting all officeholders to frequent scrutiny by voters. In turn, the new national government was subordinate, under the Articles of Confederation, to the thirteen states. Only after several years did elites, fearing that excessive decentralization and democracy were weakening the states, push through more hierarchical frames of government. Meanwhile, challenges facing the Confederation made clear to many elites the need for more centralized authority at the national level as well.

6-4.1 From Colonies to States

Before 1776, colonists had regarded their popularly elected assemblies as the bulwark of their liberties against encroachments by governors wielding executive power. Thereafter, the legislatures retained that role even when voters, rather than the British crown, chose governors.

In keeping with colonial practice, eleven states established bicameral (two-chamber) legislatures. Colonial legislatures had consisted of an elected lower house (or assembly) and an upper house (or council), usually appointed by the governor (see Chapter 4). These two-part legislatures mirrored Parliament's division into the House of Commons and House of Lords, symbolizing the assumption that a government should have separate representation by the upper class and the common people.

Despite participation by people from all classes in the struggle against Britain, few questioned the long-standing practice of setting property requirements for voters and elected officials. In the prevailing view, the ownership of property, especially land, gave voters a direct stake in the outcome of elections. Whereas propertyless men might vote to please landlords, creditors, or employers, sell their votes, or be fooled by a demagogue, property owners supposedly had the financial means and the education to vote freely and responsibly. Nine of the thirteen states reduced property requirements slightly for voting, but none abolished such qualifications entirely.

Another colonial practice that persisted beyond independence was the equal (or nearly equal) division of legislative seats among all counties or towns, regardless of differences in population. As a result, a minority of voters usually elected a majority of assemblymen. Only the most radical constitution, Pennsylvania's, sought to avoid such outcomes by attempting to ensure that election districts would be roughly equal in population.

Despite the holdover of certain colonial-era practices, the state constitutions in other respects departed radically from the past. Above all, they were written documents that usually required popular ratification and could be amended only by the voters. In short, Americans jettisoned the British conception of a constitution as a body of customary arrangements and practices, insisting instead that constitutions were written compacts that defined and limited the powers of rulers. Moreover, as a final check on government power, the Revolutionary constitutions spelled out citizens' fundamental rights. By 1784, all state constitutions included explicit bills of rights that outlined certain freedoms that lay beyond the control of any government.

The earliest state constitutions strengthened legislatures at governors' expense. In most states, the governor became an elected official, and elections themselves occurred far more frequently. Whereas most colonial elections had been called at the governor's pleasure, after 1776 all states scheduled annual elections except South Carolina, which held them every two years. In most states, the power of appointments was transferred from the governor to the legislature. Legislatures usually appointed judges and could reduce their salaries, and legislatures could impeach both judges and governors (try them for wrongdoing). By depriving governors of most appointive powers, denying them the right to veto laws, and making them subject to impeachment, the constitutions gave governors little to do except chair councils that made militia appointments and supervised financial matters. Pennsylvania went further, simply eliminating the office of governor.

As the new state constitutions weakened the executive branch and vested more power in the legislatures, they also made the legislatures more responsive to the will of the voters. Nowhere could the governor appoint the upper chamber. Eight constitutions written before 1780 allowed voters to select both houses of the legislature; one (Maryland) used a popularly chosen "electoral college" for its upper house; and the remaining "senates" were filled by vote of their assemblies. Pennsylvania and Georgia abolished the upper house altogether. States' weakening of the executive branch and enhancement of legislative and popular authority reflected Americans' fears of centralized authority, rooted in bitter memories of royal governors and other imperial officials who had acted arbitrarily.

Despite their high regard for popularly elected legislatures, Revolutionary leaders described themselves as republicans rather than democrats. These words had different connotations in the eighteenth century than they do today. To many elites, democracy suggested mob rule or, at least, the concentration of power in the hands of an uneducated multitude. In contrast, **republicanism** presumed that government would be entrusted to virtuous leaders who would put the public good above their self-interests and ambitions. For most republicans, the ideal government would delicately balance the interests of different classes to prevent any one group from gaining absolute power. Many colonial leaders, including Thomas Paine, embraced republicanism over monarchy, which they increasingly saw as corrupt and in which power is absolute rather than derived from consent of the governed, as in republics. But they differed in how they interpreted republicanism and over what constituted a virtuous citizenry. Some thought that only those in the upper rungs of society could afford to set aside personal gain for the public good, and were, by virtue of talent and education, best prepared to lead. Others disagreed, arguing for egalitarianism, and saw virtue as embodied in the common man. A few, including John Adams, thought that a republic could include a hereditary aristocracy or even a monarchy if needed to counterbalance democratic tendencies. Having rid themselves of one king, even most elites, however, did not wish to enthrone another. Either way, leaders recognized that their republican experiment would struggle with the delicate balance between power and liberty. As such, ensuring that citizens were virtuous would prove a vital and ongoing task of the American republican experiment and would provide an opening for women—as mothers raising sons who might one day become leaders—to gain access to education (see Chapter 7).

In the first flush of revolutionary enthusiasm, elites had to content themselves with state governments dominated by popularly elected legislatures. Gradually, however, wealthier landowners, bankers, merchants, and lawyers reasserted their desires for centralized authority and the political prerogatives of wealth. In Massachusetts, where voters had thus far resisted having a constitution at all, an elite-dominated convention in 1780 pushed through a constitution largely authored by John Adams. The document stipulated stiff property qualifications for voting and holding office, state senate districts that were apportioned according to property values, and a governor with considerable powers in making appointments and vetoing legislative measures. The Massachusetts constitution signaled a general trend. Georgia and Pennsylvania substituted bicameral for unicameral legislatures by 1790. Other states raised property qualifications for members of the upper chamber in a bid to strengthen the "senatorial element" and to make room for men of "Wisdom, remarkable integrity, or that Weight which arises from property."

6-4.2 Formalizing a Confederation, 1776–1781

In keeping with their revolt against Britain and their early state constitutions, Americans' first national government reflected widespread fears of centralized authority and its potential for corruption and tyranny. It also reflected their strong attachments to their states (the former colonies) and the states' elected legislatures, as opposed to the newly declared nation. And while Americans embraced the notion of their nation as a republican experiment, some feared that republics were only possible in small states—not in a nation as large as the United States was and would further become. Such concerns began as early as the meeting of the first Continental Congress and would continue well after the war as efforts to establish a national government ramped up. In 1776, John Dickinson, who had stayed in the Continental Congress despite his refusal to sign the

republicanism
A system of government in which power derives from the people, and in which virtuous citizens are counted on to sacrifice self-interest for the greater good.

Declaration of Independence, drafted a proposal for a national constitution. Congress adopted a weakened version of Dickinson's proposal, called the **Articles of Confederation**, and sent it to the states for ratification in 1777. But only in February 1781—six months before the American victory at Yorktown—did the last state, Maryland, agree to ratification.

The Articles of Confederation explicitly reserved to each state—and not to the national government—"its sovereignty, freedom and independence." The "United States of America" was "a firm league of friendship" among sovereign states, more like today's European Union than like a unified nation-state. As John Adams later explained, Congress never thought of "consolidating this vast Continent under one national Government" but instead erected "a Confederacy of States, each of which must have a separate government."

Under the Articles, the national government consisted of a single-chamber Congress, elected by the state legislatures, in which each state had one vote. Congress could request funds from the states but could not enact any tax without every state's approval and could not regulate interstate or overseas commerce. The approval of seven states was required to pass minor legislation; nine states had to approve declarations of war, treaties, and the coining and borrowing of money. Unanimous approval was required to impose any new taxes and to ratify and amend the Articles. The Articles did not provide for an independent executive branch. Rather, congressional committees oversaw financial, diplomatic, military, and Indian affairs, and resolved interstate disputes. Nor was there a judicial system by which the national government could compel allegiance to its laws. The Articles did eliminate all barriers to interstate travel and trade, and guaranteed that all states would recognize one another's judicial decisions.

6-4.3 Finance, Trade, and the Economy, 1781–1786

Aside from finishing the war on the battlefield, the greatest challenge facing the Confederation was putting the nation on a sound financial footing. The war cost a staggering $160 million, a sum that exceeded by 2,400 percent the taxes raised to pay for the Seven Years' War. Yet even this was not enough; to finance the war fully, the government had borrowed funds from abroad and printed its own paper money, called Continentals. Lack of public faith in the new currency destroyed 98 percent of its value from 1776 to 1781, an inflationary disaster that gave rise to the expression "not worth a Continental."

Seeking to overcome the national government's financial weakness, Congress in 1781 appointed a wealthy Philadelphia merchant, Robert Morris, as Superintendent of Finance. Morris proposed that the states authorize the collection of a national import duty of 5 percent, which would finance the congressional budget and guarantee interest payments on the war debt. Because the Articles required that every state approve any national tax, the import duty failed because Rhode Island alone rejected it.

Meanwhile, seeing themselves as sovereign, most states had assumed some responsibility for the war debt and begun compensating veterans and creditors within their borders. But Morris and other nationally minded elites insisted that the United States needed sources of revenue independent of the states to attract capital and to establish a strong national government. Hoping to panic the country into seeing things their way, Morris and New York Congressman Alexander Hamilton engineered a dangerous gamble known later as the Newburgh Conspiracy. In 1783, the two men secretly persuaded some army officers, then encamped at Newburgh, New York, to threaten a coup d'état unless the treasury obtained the taxation authority needed to raise their pay, which was months in arrears. But George Washington, learning of the conspiracy before it was carried out, ended the plot by delivering a speech that appealed to his officers' honor and left them unwilling to proceed. Although Morris may not have intended for a coup to actually occur, his willingness to take such a risk demonstrated the new nation's perilous financial straits and the vulnerability of its political institutions.

When peace came in 1783, Congress sent another tax measure to the states, but once again a single legislature, this time New York's, blocked it. From then on, the states steadily decreased their contributions to Congress. By the late 1780s, the states had fallen behind nearly 80 percent in providing the funds that Congress requested to operate the government and honor the national debt.

Nor did the Confederation succeed in prying trade concessions from Britain. The continuation after the war of British trade prohibitions contributed to an economic depression that gripped New England beginning in 1784. A short growing season and poor soil kept yields so low, even in the best of times, that farmers barely produced enough grain for local consumption. New Englanders also faced both high taxes to repay the money borrowed to finance the Revolution and a tightening of credit that spawned countless legal actions against debtors. Rural overpopulation and high unemployment only aggravated the region's miseries.

The mid-Atlantic states, on the other hand, were less dependent on British-controlled markets for their

> **Articles of Confederation**
> Government that focused more on states' rights. It reserved to each state "its sovereignty, freedom and independence."

Ordinance of 1785

Established uniform procedures for surveying land north of the Ohio River. The law established a township six miles square as the basic unit of settlement. Every township would be subdivided into 36 sections of 640 acres each, one of which would be reserved as a source of income for schools. It imposed an arbitrary grid of straight lines and right angles across the landscape that conformed to European–American notions of private property while utterly ignoring the land's natural features and Native American inhabitants.

exports. As famine stalked Europe, farmers in Pennsylvania and New York prospered from climbing export prices. By 1788, the region had largely recovered from the Revolution's ravages.

Southern planters faced frustration at the failure of their principal crops, tobacco and rice, to return to prewar export levels. Whereas nearly two-thirds of American exports originated in the South in 1770, less than half were produced by southern states in 1790. In an effort to stay afloat, many Chesapeake tobacco planters shifted to wheat, while others began growing hemp. But these changes had little effect on the region's exports and, because wheat and hemp required fewer laborers than tobacco, left slave owners with a large amount of underemployed, restless "human property."

6-4.4 The Confederation and the West

Another formidable challenge confronting the Confederation was the postwar settlement and administration of American territory outside the states. White American squatters and speculators were already encroaching on these lands, and Native Americans were determined to keep them out. To strengthen their own positions between the Appalachians and the Mississippi, Britain and Spain supported the Indian nations and encouraged settlers to consider seceding from the United States. Congress hoped to strengthen its authority in the region by persuading eastern states to relinquish their western claims, establishing orderly procedures for settling and governing these lands and gaining revenue through sales of individual tracts.

After the states surrendered claims to more than 160 million acres north of the Ohio River (see Map 6.4), Congress passed the **Ordinance of 1785**, which outlined procedures for surveying the land. Reflecting Enlightenment rationality, the

MAP 6.4 **STATE CLAIMS TO WESTERN LANDS, AND STATE CESSIONS TO THE FEDERAL GOVERNMENT, 1782–1802** Eastern states' surrender of land claims paved the way for new state governments in the West.

Ordinance imposed an arbitrary grid of straight lines and right angles (the boundaries of townships and private landholdings) across the natural landscape (see Map 6.5). Then, in the **Northwest Ordinance** (1787), Congress defined a series of steps for establishing the Northwest Territory and subsequently organizing new states and admitting them to the Union (see Going to the Source).

The most significant achievements of the Confederation, the Ordinance of 1785 and the Northwest Ordinance had lasting effects. Besides laying out procedures for settling and establishing governments in the Northwest, they later served as models for organizing territories farther west. The Northwest Ordinance also established a significant precedent by banning slavery from the new territory, although voters could legalize the institution after statehood.

To most whites, the Northwest Territory seemed to offer enough land to guarantee property to American citizens for centuries. This assumption satisfied republicans such as Thomas Jefferson who feared that the rapidly growing white population would quickly exhaust available land east of the Appalachians. The result would be a large class of landless poor who would be deprived of the virtues of agrarian life (as discussed in Chapter 7) and who could not vote. Such a development would undermine the equality of opportunity among whites that expansionist republicans thought essential for a healthy nation.

The realization of these expansionist dreams was by no means inevitable. Most "available" territory from the Appalachians to the Mississippi River belonged to those peoples whom the Declaration of Independence had condemned as "merciless Indian savages." Divided into more than eighty tribes and numbering perhaps 150,000 people in 1789, Native Americans were struggling to preserve their own independence. At postwar treaty negotiations, they repeatedly heard Confederation commissioners scornfully declare, "You are a subdued people . . . we claim the country by conquest."

Under threats of continued warfare with the United States, some northwestern Indian leaders yielded to American pressure. The Iroquois, who had

Northwest Ordinance Defined the steps for the creation and admission of new states. It designated the area north of the Ohio River as the Northwest Territory and provided for its later division into states. It forbade slavery while the region remained a territory, although citizens could legalize the institution after statehood.

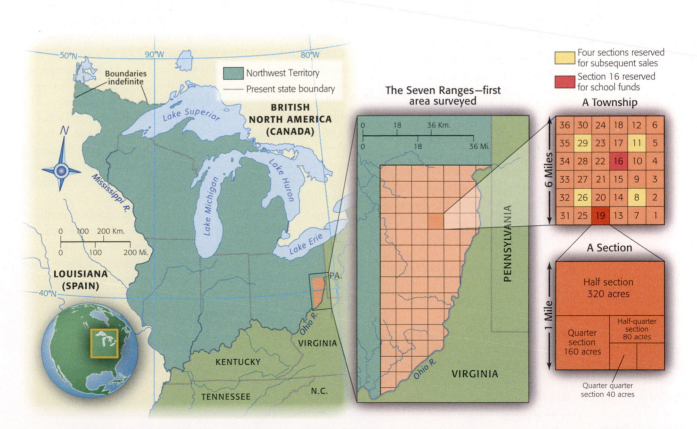

MAP 6.5 THE NORTHWEST TERRITORY, 1785–1787 The Ordinance of 1785 mandated the surveying of land into townships of thirty-six sections, each supporting four families on 160-acre plots. In 1787, the Northwest Ordinance provided for the establishment of a territory and, subsequently, states in the region.

The Northwest Ordinance

Perhaps the single most important measure passed by Congress under the Articles of Confederation, the Northwest Ordinance established the first United States territory and provided for its later division into states.

An Ordinance for the Government of the Territory of the United States Northwest of the River Ohio

Section 1. Be it ordained by the United States in Congress assembled, That the said territory, for the purposes of temporary government, be one district.

. . .

Sec. 3. Be it ordained by the authority aforesaid, That there shall be appointed from time to time by Congress, a governor, whose commission shall continue in force for the term of three years, . . .

. . .

Sec. 9. So soon as there shall be five thousand free male inhabitants of full age in the district, upon giving proof thereof to the governor, they shall receive authority, with time and place, to elect a representative from their counties or townships to represent them in the general assembly: . . .

. . .

Sec. 12. . . . As soon as a legislature shall be formed in the district, the [legislative] council and house assembled in one room, shall have authority, by joint ballot, to elect a delegate to Congress, who shall have a seat in Congress, with a right of debating but not voting during this temporary government.

Sec. 13. And, for extending the fundamental principles of civil and religious liberty, which form the basis whereon these republics, their laws and constitutions are erected; to fix and establish those principles as the basis of all laws, constitutions, and governments, which forever hereafter shall be formed in the said territory: to provide also for the establishment of States, and permanent government therein, and for their admission to a share in the federal councils on an equal footing with the original States, at as early periods as may be consistent with the general interest:

Sec. 14. . . .[T]he following articles shall be considered as articles of compact between the original States and the people and States in the said territory and forever remain unalterable, unless by common consent, to wit:

Art. 1. No person, demeaning himself in a peaceable and orderly manner, shall ever be molested on account of his mode of worship or religious sentiments, in the said territory.

Art. 2. The inhabitants of the said territory shall always be entitled to the benefits of the writ of habeas corpus, and of the trial by jury; of a proportionate representation of the people in the legislature; and of judicial proceedings according to the course of the common law. . . .

Art. 3. Religion, morality, and knowledge, being necessary to good government and the happiness of mankind, schools and the means of education shall forever be encouraged. The utmost good faith shall always be observed towards the Indians; their lands and property shall never be taken from them without their consent; and, in their property, rights, and liberty, they shall never be invaded or disturbed, unless in just and lawful wars authorized by Congress; . . .

Art. 4. The said territory, and the States which may be formed therein, shall forever remain a part of this Confederacy of the United States of America, subject to the Articles of Confederation, and to such alterations therein as shall be constitutionally made; and to all the acts and ordinances of the United States in Congress assembled, conformable thereto.

Art. 5. There shall be formed in the said territory, not less than three nor more than five States; . . . And, whenever any of the said States shall have sixty thousand free inhabitants therein, such State shall be admitted, by its delegates, into the Congress of the United States, on an equal footing with the original States in all respects whatever, and shall be at liberty to form a permanent constitution and State government: . . . and, so far as it can be consistent with the general interest of the confederacy, such admission shall be allowed at an earlier period, and when there may be a less number of free inhabitants in the State than sixty thousand.

Art. 6. There shall be neither slavery nor involuntary servitude in the said territory, otherwise than in the punishment of crimes whereof the party shall have been duly convicted: Provided, always, That any person escaping into the same, from whom labor or service is lawfully claimed in any one of the original States, such fugitive may be lawfully reclaimed and conveyed to the person claiming his or her labor or service as aforesaid.

Source: The Avalon Project: Documents in Law, History, and Diplomacy, Yale Law School, Lillian Goldman Law Library; http:// avalon.law.yale.edu/18th_century/nworder.asp; Documents Illustrative of the Formation of the Union of the American States. Government Printing Office, 1927. House Document No. 398. Selected, Arranged and Indexed by Charles C. Tansill.

QUESTIONS

1. What were the most important steps in the Ordinance's procedures for establishing state governments?

2. How did the Ordinance provide for the treatment of nonwhites?

suffered heavily during the war, lost about half their land in New York and Pennsylvania in the second Treaty of Fort Stanwix (1784). In the treaties of Fort McIntosh (1785) and Fort Finney (1786), Delaware and Shawnee leaders, respectively, were obliged to recognize American sovereignty over their lands. But upon hearing of the treaties, most tribal members angrily repudiated them on the grounds that they had never authorized their negotiators to give up territory.

Native Americans' resistance to Confederation encroachments also stemmed from their confidence that the British would provide the arms and ammunition they needed to defy the United States. In discussing the Treaty of Paris, the British had refused to abandon seven northwestern forts within U.S. boundaries. With Indian support, Britain hoped eventually to reclaim lands that lay within the Northwest Territory.

Mohawk Joseph Brant emerged as the initial leader of Native American resistance in the Northwest. Courageous in battle, skillful in diplomacy, and highly educated in English ways (he had translated an Anglican prayer book and the Gospel of Mark into Mohawk), Brant became a celebrity when he visited King George III in London in 1785. At British-held Fort Detroit in 1786, he helped organize some northwestern Indians into a coalition that would negotiate to defend Indian lands north of the Ohio River. But Brant and his followers, who had relocated beyond American reach in Canada, could not win support from Iroquois still in New York, who feared that alienating their white neighbors would cost them more land. Nor could he count on the support of the Shawnees and other Ohio Indians, whom the Iroquois had betrayed in the past (as discussed in Chapters 4 and 5).

Seizing on disunity within Indian ranks, western settlers organized militia raids into the Northwest Territory. These raids gradually forced the Miamis, Shawnees, and Delawares to evacuate southern Indiana and Ohio. The Indians' withdrawal northward, toward the Great Lakes, tempted whites to make their first settlements north of the Ohio River. In spring 1788, about fifty New Englanders sailed down the river in a bulletproof barge named the *Mayflower* and founded the town of Marietta. Later that year, other newcomers established a second community on the site of modern-day Cincinnati. By then, another phase in the long-running contest for the Ohio Valley was nearing a decisive stage (as discussed in Chapter 7).

The Confederation confronted similar challenges in the Southeast, where Spain and its Indian allies took steps to keep American settlers off their lands. The Spanish found a brilliant ally in the Creek leader Alexander McGillivray. In some fraudulent treaties, two Creeks had surrendered extensive territory to Georgia that McGillivray intended to regain. McGillivray negotiated a secret treaty in which Spain promised weapons so that the Creeks could protect themselves "from the Bears and other fierce Animals." Attacking in 1786, the Creeks shrewdly expelled only those whites occupying the disputed lands and then offered Georgia a ceasefire. Eager to avoid approving taxes for a costly war, Georgia politicians let the Creeks keep the land.

Spain also sought to prevent American infiltration by denying western settlers permission to ship their crops down the Mississippi River to New Orleans. As noted earlier, Spain had negotiated a separate treaty with Britain and had not signed the Treaty of Paris, by which Britain promised the United States export rights down the Mississippi. In 1784, the Spanish closed New Orleans to American commerce. Spain and the United States negotiated the Jay-Gardoqui Treaty (1786), which opened Spanish markets to American merchants and renounced Spanish claims to disputed lands—at the cost, however, of postponing American exporters' access to New Orleans for another twenty years. Westerners and southerners charged that the treaty sacrificed their interests to benefit northern commerce, and Congress rejected it.

Unable to prevent American settlers from occupying territory it claimed in the Southeast (see Map 7.3), Spain sought to win the newcomers' allegiance by bribes and offers of citizenship. Noting that Congress seemed ready to accept the permanent closing of New Orleans in return for Spanish concessions elsewhere, many settlers began talking openly of secession. As young Andrew Jackson (the future U.S. general and president) concluded in 1789, making some arrangements with the Spanish seemed "the only immediate way to obtain peace with the Savage [Indians]." Although only a few settlers actually conspired with Spain against the United States, the incident revealed the new nation's weak authority in newly settled areas.

6-5 Toward a New Constitution, 1786–1788

What were the key concerns about replacing the Articles of Confederation with the Constitution?

The Jay-Gardoqui Treaty revealed deep-seated tensions beneath the surface appearance of American national unity. Despite the nation's general prosperity outside New England, a growing minority was dissatisfied with the Confederation. Bondholders, merchants, and shippers wanted a central government powerful enough to secure trading privileges for them abroad and to strengthen America's standing in the Atlantic economy. Land speculators and western settlers sought a government that would pursue a more activist policy against Spain, Britain, and Native Americans in the West, and prevent citizens there from defecting. Urban artisans hoped for a national government that could impose uniformly high tariffs that would protect them from foreign competition. Meanwhile, wealthy elites decried state governments that refused to clamp down on debtors and delinquent taxpayers, many of whom were organizing resistance movements.

Impatience turned to anxiety in 1786 after some Massachusetts farmers threatened to seize a federal arsenal and march on Boston. A national convention called to consider amendments to the Articles instead proposed a radical new frame of government, the Constitution. In 1788, the states ratified the Constitution, setting a bold new course for the United States.

6-5.1 Shays's Rebellion, 1786–1787

The depression that had begun in 1784 persisted in New England, which had never recovered from the loss of its prime export market in the British West Indies. With farmers already squeezed financially, the Massachusetts legislature, dominated by commercially minded elites, voted early in 1786 to pay off its Revolutionary debt in three years. This ill-considered policy necessitated a huge tax hike. Meanwhile, the state's unfavorable balance of payments with Britain had produced a shortage of specie (gold and silver coin) because British creditors refused any other currency. Fearing a flood of worthless paper notes, Massachusetts bankers and merchants insisted that they, too, be paid in specie, while the state mandated the same for payment of taxes. Lowest in this cycle of debt were thousands of small family farmers, who rarely if ever possessed specie.

The plight of small farmers was especially severe in western Massachusetts, where agriculture was least profitable. Facing demands that they pay their debts and taxes in hard currency, farmers held public meetings. As in similar meetings more than a decade earlier, the farmers—most of whom were Revolutionary War veterans—discussed "the Suppressing of tyrannical government," referring this time to the Massachusetts government rather than the British. Reminiscent of pre-Revolutionary backcountry

Shays's Rebellion
An event in which a group of small farmers protested taxes and the use of specie. The group, led by Daniel Shays, managed to shut down the courts in five counties in Massachusetts but were turned back by troops at the federal arsenal of Springfield in 1786–1787.

"regulators" (see Chapter 5), farmers led by Daniel Shays in 1786 shut down the courts in five counties, initiating what became known as **Shays's Rebellion**. Then in January 1787, they marched on a federal arsenal at Springfield, Massachusetts. But troops, funded by Boston elites to quell the uprising, reached the arsenal first and beat back the rebels. Thereafter, the troops scattered or routed bands of insurgents. Although the movement was defeated militarily, sympathizers of Shays won control of the Massachusetts legislature in elections later that year and then cut taxes and secured a pardon for their leader.

The Shaysites had limited objectives, were dispersed with relatively little bloodshed, and never seriously threatened anarchy. But their uprising, and similar but smaller movements in other states, became the rallying cry for advocates of a stronger central government. By threatening to seize weapons from a federal arsenal, the Shaysites unintentionally enabled nationalists to argue that the United States had become vulnerable to "mobocracy," as Adams and others feared for the American republican experiment. Writing to a fellow wartime general, Henry Knox, for news from Massachusetts, an anxious George Washington worried that "there are combustibles in every state, which a spark might set fire to," destroying the Republic.

Instead of igniting an uprising from below, Shays's Rebellion sparked elite nationalists into action from above. Shortly before the outbreak of the rebellion, delegates from five states had assembled at Annapolis, Maryland. They had intended to discuss means of promoting interstate commerce but instead called for a general convention to propose amendments to the Articles of Confederation. Accepting their suggestion, Congress asked the states to appoint delegations to meet in Philadelphia.

6-5.2 The Philadelphia Convention, 1787

In May 1787, fifty-five delegates from every state but Rhode Island gathered at the Pennsylvania State House in Philadelphia, later known as Independence Hall. Among them were established figures such as George Washington and Benjamin Franklin, as well as talented newcomers such as Alexander Hamilton and James Madison. Most were wealthy and in their thirties or forties, and nineteen owned slaves. More than half had legal training.

The convention closed its sessions to the press and the public, kept no official journal, and even monitored the aged and talkative Franklin at dinner parties lest he disclose details of its discussions. Although these measures opened the convention to charges of being undemocratic and conspiratorial, the delegates insisted on secrecy to minimize public pressure on their debates.

The delegates shared a "continental" or "nationalist" perspective, drawn from their extended involvement with the national government. Thirty-nine had sat in Congress, where they had seen the Confederation's limitations firsthand. In the post-war years, they had become convinced that unless the national government was freed from the control of state legislatures, the country would disintegrate. Although their mission was to consider amendments to the Articles, most were prepared to frame a new constitution that gave more power to the national government.

The first debate among the framers concerned the conflicting interests of large and small states. **James Madison** of Virginia boldly called for the establishment of a strong central government rather than a federation of states. Madison's **Virginia Plan** gave Congress virtually unrestricted powers to legislate, levy taxes, veto state laws, and authorize military force against the states. As one delegate immediately saw, the Virginia Plan was designed "to abolish the State Govern[men]ts altogether." The Virginia Plan specified a bicameral legislature and fixed representation in both houses of Congress proportionally to each state's population. In keeping with republican notions of the sovereignty of the people, voters would elect the lower house, which would then choose delegates to the upper chamber from nominations submitted by the legislatures. Both houses would jointly name the country's president and judges.

Madison's scheme aroused immediate opposition, however, especially his call for state representation according to population—a provision highly favorable to his own Virginia. On June 15, William Paterson of New Jersey offered a counterproposal, the so-called **New Jersey Plan**, which recommended a single-chamber congress in which each state had an equal vote, as under the Articles.

The two plans exposed one of the convention's greatest stumbling

James Madison
One of the delegates of the Articles of Federation, he introduced the Virginia Plan and played a central role in the Constitution's adoption.

Virginia Plan
Called for the establishment of a strong central government rather than a federation of states. It gave Congress virtually unrestricted rights of legislation and taxation and power to veto any state law, and authority to use military force against the states. It specified a bicameral legislature and fixed representation in both houses of Congress proportionally to each state's population.

New Jersey Plan
A counterproposal to the Virginia Plan, it recommended a single-chamber congress in which each state had an equal vote, just as the Articles.

INDEPENDENCE HALL, PHILADELPHIA, 1776 While the Continental Congress deliberated inside on the grave issues of the day, city residents outside carried on with their everyday lives. *(Picture Research Consultants & Archives)*

blocks: the question of representation. The Virginia Plan would have given the four largest states a majority in both houses. Under the New Jersey Plan, the seven smallest states, which included just 25 percent of all Americans, could have controlled Congress. By July 2, the convention had arrived "at a full stop," as one delegate put it. Finally, a "grand committee," consisting of one delegate from each state, proposed the Great (or Connecticut) Compromise, whereby each state would have an equal vote in the upper house while representation in the lower house would be based on population. Although Madison and the Virginians doggedly opposed this compromise, it passed on July 17.

Despite their differences over representation, Paterson's and Madison's proposals would both have strengthened the national government at the states' expense. No less than Madison, Paterson wished to empower Congress to raise taxes, regulate interstate commerce, and use military force against the states. The New Jersey Plan, in fact, defined congressional laws and treaties as the "supreme law of the land" and would also have established courts to force reluctant states to accept these measures. But other delegates were wary of undermining the sovereignty of the states altogether. Only after a good deal of bargaining did they reconcile their differences.

As finally approved on September 17, 1787, the **Constitution of the United States** (reprinted in the Appendix) was an extraordinary document, and not merely because it reconciled the conflicting interests of large and small states. In contrast to the Articles of Confederation, the Constitution provided for a vigorous national authority that superseded that of the states in several significant ways. Although it did not incorporate Madison's proposal to give Congress a veto over state laws, it followed the New Jersey Plan by asserting in "the supremacy clause" that all acts and treaties of the United States were "the supreme law of the land." The Constitution vested in Congress the authority to lay and collect taxes, to regulate interstate commerce, and to conduct diplomacy. States could no longer coin money, interfere with contracts and debts, or tax interstate commerce. All state officials had to swear to uphold the Constitution, even against acts of their own states. The national government could use military force against any state. Beyond these powers, the Constitution empowered Congress to enact "all laws which shall

be necessary and proper" for the national government to fulfill its constitutional responsibilities. These provisions added up to a complete abandonment of the principle on which the Articles had rested: that the United States was a federation of sovereign states, with ultimate authority concentrated in their legislatures.

To allay the concerns of more moderate delegates, the Constitution's framers devised two means of restraining the power of the new central government. First, in keeping with republican political theory and the state constitutions, they established a **separation of powers** among the national government's three distinct branches—executive, legislative, and judicial; second, they designed a system of **checks and balances** to prevent any one branch from dominating the other two. In the bicameral Congress, states' equal representation in the Senate was offset by proportional representation, by population, in the House; and each chamber could block measures approved by the other. Furthermore, where the state constitutions had deliberately weakened the executive, the Constitution gave the president the power to veto acts of Congress; to prevent abuse of the veto, Congress could override the president by a two-thirds majority in each house. The president could conduct diplomacy, but the Senate had to ratify treaties. The president appointed a cabinet, but only with Senate approval. The president and any presidential appointee could be removed from office by a joint vote of Congress, but only for "high crimes," not for political disagreements.

To further ensure the independence of each branch, the Constitution provided that the members of one branch would not choose those of another, except for justices of the Supreme Court, whose independence would be protected because they were appointed for life by the president with the "advice and consent" of the Senate. For example, the president was to be selected by electors, whom the states would select as their legislatures saw fit. The number of electors in each state would equal the number of its senators and representatives. In the event of a deadlock among the electors, the House of Representatives, with one vote per state, would choose the president. The state legislatures would elect the members of the Senate, whereas members of the House of Representatives would be chosen by direct popular vote.

In addition to checks and balances, the founders devised a system of shared power and dual lawmaking by the national and state governments—**"federalism"**—in order to place limits on central authority. Not only did the state legislatures have a key role in electing the president and senators, but the Constitution could be amended by the votes of three-fourths of the states. Thus, the convention

Constitution of the United States
Reconciled the conflicting interests of large and small states, and stated the laws of the United States.

separation of powers
Each branch of government has separate powers from one another.

checks and balances
Designed to prevent one branch of government from dominating the other two.

"federalism"
Shared power and dual lawmaking by the national and state governments.

departed sharply from Madison's plan to establish a "consolidated" national government entirely independent of, and superior to, the states.

A key assumption behind federalism was that the national government would limit its activities to foreign affairs, national defense, regulating interstate commerce, and coining money. Most other political matters would be left to the states. Regarding slavery in particular, each state retained full authority.

The delegates to the Philadelphia convention debated not whether slavery would be allowed but only the narrower question of whether slaves should be counted as persons when it came to determining a state's representation at the national level. For most legal purposes, slaves were regarded as the chattel property of their owners, meaning that they were on a par with other living property such as horses and cattle. But southern states saw their large numbers of slaves as a means of augmenting their numbers in the House of Representatives and in the electoral meetings ("colleges") that would elect the nation's presidents. So strengthened, they hoped to prevent northerners from ever abolishing slavery.

Representing states that had begun ending slavery, northern delegates opposed giving southern states a political advantage by allowing them to count people who had no civil or political rights. As Madison—himself a slave owner—observed, "it seemed now to be pretty well understood that the real difference of interests lay, not between the large & small [states] but between the N. & South." But after Georgia and South Carolina threatened to secede if their demands were not met, northerners agreed to the **"three-fifths clause,"** allowing three-fifths of all slaves to be counted for congressional representation and, thereby, in the electoral college.

The Constitution also reinforced slavery in other ways. Most notably, it forbade citizens of any state to prevent the return of escaped slaves to another state. The Constitution limited slavery only to the extent of prohibiting Congress from banning the importation of slaves before 1808, and by maintaining Congress's earlier ban on slavery in the Northwest Territory. Neither of these limitations weakened the assumption that enslaved persons were property rather than human beings.

Although leaving much authority to the states, the Constitution established a national government whose sovereignty, unlike under the Articles of Confederation, clearly superseded that of the states. Having thus strengthened national authority, the convention had to face the issue of ratification. For two reasons, it seemed unwise to submit the Constitution to state legislatures for ratification. First, the delegates realized that the state legislatures

would reject the Constitution, which shrank their power relative to the national government. Second, most of the framers rejected the idea—implicit in ratification by state legislatures—that the states were the foundation of the new government. The opening words of the Constitution, "We the People of the United States," underlined the delegates' conviction that the government had to be based on the consent of the American people themselves, "the fountain of all power" in Madison's words, and not of the states.

In the end, the Philadelphia convention provided for the Constitution's ratification by special state conventions composed of delegates elected by the voters. Approval by nine such conventions would put the new government in operation. Because any state refusing to ratify the Constitution would legally remain under the Articles, the possibility existed that the country would divide into two nations.

Under the Constitution, the framers expected the nation's elites to continue exercising political leadership. Seeking to rein in the democratic currents set in motion by the Revolution, they curtailed what they considered the excessive power of popularly elected state legislatures. And while they located sovereignty in the people rather than in the states, they stipulated that an electoral college, whose members were selected by the states, would actually elect the president. The framers did provide for one crucial democratic element in the new government, the House of Representatives. Moreover, by making the Constitution flexible and amendable (though not easily amendable), and by dividing political power among competing branches of government, the framers made it possible for the national government to be slowly democratized, in ways unforeseen in 1787.

6-5.3 The Struggle over Ratification, 1787–1788

The Constitution's supporters began the campaign for ratification without significant popular support. Expecting the Philadelphia convention to offer some amendments to the Articles of Confederation, most Americans hesitated to replace the entire system of government. Undaunted, the Constitution's friends moved decisively to marshal political support. In a shrewd public relations stroke, they called themselves "Federalists," a term implying that the Constitution would more nearly balance the relationship between the national and state governments, and thereby undermined the arguments of those hostile to a centralized national government.

> **"three-fifths clause,"**
> Allowed three-fifths of all slaves to be counted for congressional representation and, thereby, in the Electoral College that selected the president.

The Constitution's opponents became known as **"Antifederalists."** This negative-sounding title probably hurt them, for it did not convey the crux of their argument against the Constitution—that it was not "federalist" at all since it failed to balance the power of the national and state governments. By augmenting national authority, Antifederalists maintained, the Constitution would weaken the states and undermine the people's liberty. Both sides would claim to be the true torchbearers of the Revolution and protectors of the subsequent American experiment in republicanism.

The Antifederalist arguments reflected Anglo-Americans' long-standing suspicion of centralized executive power, reiterated by Americans from the time of the Stamp Act crisis, through the Revolution, to the framing of the first state constitutions and the Articles of Confederation. Patrick Henry feared that a president "of ambition and abilities" could, as commander in chief, use the army to "render himself absolute," while another Antifederalist feared that the national government would "fall into the hands of the few and the great." Compared to a distant national government, Antifederalists argued, state governments were far more responsive to the popular will. They acknowledged that the framers had guarded against tyranny by preserving limited state powers and devising a system of checks and balances, but doubted that these devices would succeed. The proposed constitution, concluded one Antifederalist, "nullified and declared void" the constitutions and laws of the states except where they did not contradict federal mandates. Moreover, for all its checks and balances, opponents noted, the Constitution provided no guarantees that the new government would protect the liberties of individuals.

Although the Antifederalists advanced some formidable arguments, they confronted a number of disadvantages in publicizing their cause. While Antifederalist ranks included some prominent figures, none had the stature of George Washington or Benjamin Franklin. As state and local leaders, the Antifederalists lacked their opponents' contacts and experience at the national level, acquired through service as Continental Army officers, diplomats, or members of Congress. Moreover, most American newspapers were pro-Constitution and did not hesitate to bias their reporting in favor of ratification.

The Federalists' advantages in funds and political organizing proved decisive. The Antifederalists failed to create a sense of urgency among their supporters, assuming incorrectly that a large majority would rally to them. Only one-quarter of the voters turned out to elect delegates to the state ratifying conventions, and most had been mobilized by Federalists.

The Constitution became the law of the land when the ninth state, New Hampshire, ratified it on June 21, 1788. Federalist delegates prevailed in seven of the first nine state conventions by margins of at least two-thirds. Such lopsided votes reflected the Federalists' organizational skills and aggressiveness rather than the degree of popular support for the Constitution. The Constitution's advocates rammed through approval in some states "before it can be digested or deliberately considered," in the words of a Pennsylvania Antifederalist.

But unless Virginia and New York—two of the largest states—ratified, the new government would be fatally weakened. In both states (and elsewhere), Antifederalist sentiment ran high among small farmers, who saw the Constitution as a scheme favoring city dwellers and moneyed interests (see Map 6.6). Prominent Antifederalists in these two states included New York governor George Clinton and Virginia's Patrick Henry, Richard Henry Lee, George Mason, and future president James Monroe.

At Virginia's convention, Federalists won crucial support from the representatives of the Allegheny counties—modern West Virginia—who wanted a strong national government capable of ending Indian raids from north of the Ohio River. Western Virginians' votes, combined with James Madison's leadership among tidewater planters, proved too much for Henry's spell-binding oratory. On June 25, the Virginia delegates ratified by a narrow 53 percent majority.

The struggle was even closer and more hotly contested in New York. Antifederalists had solid control of the state convention and would probably have voted down the Constitution, but then news arrived that New Hampshire (the ninth state) and powerful Virginia had approved. Federalist leaders Alexander Hamilton and John Jay threatened that if the convention failed to ratify, pro-Federalist New York City and adjacent counties would secede from the state and join the Union alone, leaving upstate New York landlocked. When several Antifederalist delegates took alarm at this threat and switched sides, on July 26 New York ratified by a 30 to 27 vote.

So the Antifederalists went down in defeat, and they did not survive as a political movement. Yet their influence was lasting. At their insistence, the Virginia, New York, and Massachusetts conventions approved the Constitution with the accompanying request that it be amended to include a bill of rights protecting Americans' basic freedoms. Moreover, Antifederalists' concerns for the sovereignty of states under the Constitution's federal framework would be echoed in the bitter political debates that roiled

Antifederalists
The derogatory nickname given to those who opposed ratification of the Constitution.

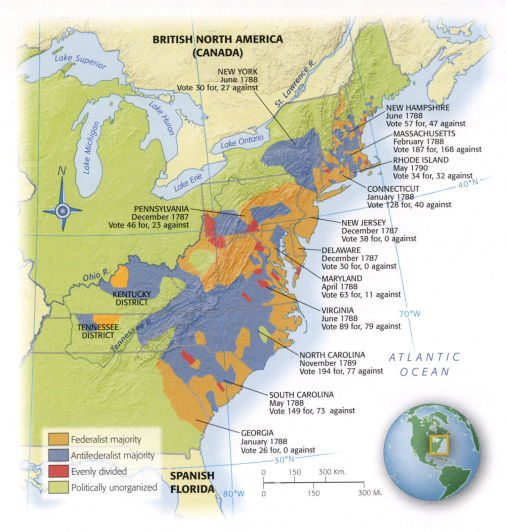

MAP 6.6 **FEDERALIST AND ANTIFEDERALIST STRONGHOLDS, 1787–1790** Federalists drew their primary backing from densely populated areas, while Antifederalist support was strongest among small farmers in interior regions.

On the map:

BRITISH NORTH AMERICA (CANADA)

NEW YORK
June 1788
Vote 30 for, 27 against

NEW HAMPSHIRE
June 1788
Vote 57 for, 47 against

MASSACHUSETTS
February 1788
Vote 187 for, 168 against

RHODE ISLAND
May 1790
Vote 34 for, 32 against

CONNECTICUT
January 1788
Vote 128 for, 40 against

PENNSYLVANIA
December 1787
Vote 46 for, 23 against

NEW JERSEY
December 1787
Vote 38 for, 0 against

DELAWARE
December 1787
Vote 30 for, 0 against

MARYLAND
April 1788
Vote 63 for, 11 against

KENTUCKY DISTRICT

TENNESSEE DISTRICT

VIRGINIA
June 1788
Vote 89 for, 79 against

NORTH CAROLINA
November 1789
Vote 194 for, 77 against

SOUTH CAROLINA
May 1788
Vote 149 for, 73 against

GEORGIA
January 1788
Vote 26 for, 0 against

SPANISH FLORIDA

ATLANTIC OCEAN

Legend:
Federalist majority
Antifederalist majority
Evenly divided
Politically unorganized

the new government during its first decade and long thereafter.

Antifederalists' objections in New York also stimulated a response in the form of one of the great classics of political thought, *The Federalist*, a series of eighty-five newspaper essays penned by Alexander Hamilton, James Madison, and John Jay. *The Federalist Papers*, as they are commonly termed, had little influence on voting in the New York convention. Rather, their importance lay in articulating arguments defending the Constitution and addressing Americans' wide-ranging concerns about the powers and limits of the new federal government, thereby shaping a new political philosophy. The Constitution, insisted *The Federalist's* authors, had a twofold purpose: First, to defend the rights of political minorities against majority tyranny and, second, to prevent a stubborn minority from blocking well-considered measures that the majority believed necessary for the national interest. Critics, argued *The Federalist*, had no reason to fear that the Constitution would allow a single economic or regional interest to dominate. "Extend the sphere," Madison argued in *Federalist* No. 10, "and . . . you make it less probable [than in a small republic] that a majority of the whole will have a common motive to invade the rights of other citizens, . . . [or will be able to] act in unison with each other." The country's very size and diversity would neutralize the attempts of factions to push unwise laws through Congress.

Madison's analysis was far too optimistic, however. As the Antifederalists predicted, the Constitution afforded enormous scope for special interests to influence the government. The great challenge for Madison's generation would be to maintain a government that commanded Americans' respect and allegiance.

The Federalist
A series of 85 newspaper essays penned by Alexander Hamilton, James Madison, and John Jay. It defended the rights of political minorities against majority tyranny, and it prevented a stubborn minority from blocking well-considered measures that the majority believed necessary for the national interest.

The Whole Vision

■ *How did British colonists choose sides as the American Revolution approached?*

As war became inevitable, people in the colonies were faced with a difficult question: Ally with those who wanted to permanently break with England, cast their lot with the British, or remain neutral (the latter would become increasingly difficult as the war waged on). People's allegiances ultimately depended on which side they perceived would be most beneficial to their long-term vision of the nation, region, and their personal aims. For white Americans, key factors were whether they considered the break with England to be legal and how much they revered the crown, whether they were recent immigrants, and how well established the patriot cause was in a given area. The economic and political development of the region in which they resided would also influence whether they would be pro-British or pro-colonist. Native Americans would join forces with the side they believed would be less inclined to encroach on their lands and more inclined to support their territorial claims. Enslaved African Americans, who comprised the vast majority of American blacks, would assist or flee to those they believed might offer freedom from slavery after the war.

■ *What turned the tide of war in the colonists' favor and ensured their victory in the American Revolution?*

The British had many advantages heading into the American Revolution—among them a more experienced military and strong navy—that led to early victories. But colonists would take decisive measures during the course of the war that would enable them to become increasingly and ultimately victorious. Their knowledge of the vast American frontier and their passionate sense of purpose proved advantageous. The Continental Army, which benefited from the leadership of General George Washington, would forge alliances with British rivals France and Spain that facilitated the colonial victory on multiple levels, from aid in training Continental troops to supplying additional forces, naval assistance, weapons, ammunition, and other war materiel. Homefront and political issues in Britain, along with wartime strategy—including errors in the final battles—also ensured the Continentals' victory.

■ *How did the American Revolution change people's lives during and after the conflict ended?*

The political climate of the American Revolution, as well as the personal contributions and sacrifices people made for the cause, had a transformative effect on their lives during and after the war. White men and women were influenced by the egalitarian spirit that undergirded the war effort; and their experiences during those years also changed what they believed their social status should be after the battle ended. Most importantly, it altered ordinary people's expectations of their relationship to political leaders and the state, as they embraced notions of democracy and chipped away at older systems of class and deference. Women who aided the war effort, too, had newfound confidence in their capabilities that led some to wonder about expanded roles in a postwar world. African Americans also embraced the war's language of liberty, seeing in it and in some postwar antislavery measures hope for freedom and the ultimate abolition of slavery. Native Americans fared the worst after the war, as their hopes of preserving their land were increasingly dashed and they faced pressures to assimilate to white cultural norms.

How did the new United States of America implement a system of government?

During the war and its immediate aftermath, leaders of the former colonies faced the task of establishing both a national and state government. States adopted their own constitutions and sought to preserve their power and independence. In fact, the biggest challenge facing the founding fathers was how to balance the power of the states against that of a central or national government. During the war, the need for a central governing authority that could raise and fund a military proved crucial, but it would be even more vital as the new United States sought to establish itself as an independent nation among other nations. The ideology that imbued the process was that of republicanism, but leaders differed over the form it would take and how to address the interests of the various social classes, as well as fears among elites about the downside of democracy. The experience under the British monarchy also led many leaders to worry about granting too much authority to a central power. The governing document that resulted—the Articles of Confederation—provided an early, though flawed, constitutional document for the new nation.

What were the key concerns about replacing the Articles of Confederation with the Constitution?

Efforts to fix the problems evident in the Articles of Confederation ultimately led to the process for a new constitution. But once again, political leaders debated the form that document should take and how to divide powers between the national and state governments. Events such as Shays's Rebellion only furthered calls for efforts to safeguard the republic with a more cohesive national government. Concerns about the document that came to be known as the Constitution included how to balance the interests of large versus small states, as well as how much to empower the national government. James Madison would emerge as the chief negotiator, offering his Virginia Plan, and the final version of the Constitution would prove a compromise between his vision and that embodied in an alternative, the New Jersey Plan. Even then, debates about ratifying the document divided people into camps known as Federalist and Antifederalist, depending on their visions about the type of government they hoped to see established, with both sides claiming to preserve the true legacy of the Revolution and the postwar republican ideals. Debates about protecting individual liberty ultimately led to inclusion of a bill of rights, a compromise that helped facilitate ratification.

7 Launching the New Republic, 1788–1800

JUDITH SARGENT STEVENS (MURRAY) BY JOHN SINGLETON COPLEY, CA. 1770
Judith Sargent Murray was the foremost American advocate of women's rights at the end of the eighteenth century. *(Terra Foundation for American Art, Chicago/Art Resources, NY)*

CHRONOLOGY 1788–1800

1788	First election under the Constitution.
1789	First Congress convenes in New York.
	George Washington inaugurated as first president.
	Judiciary Act.
	French Revolution begins.
1790	Alexander Hamilton submits Reports on Public Credit and National Bank to Congress.
	Treaty of New York.
	Judith Sargent Murray, "On the Equality of the Sexes."
	First Indian Trade and Intercourse Act.
1791	Bank of the United States established with twenty-year charter.
	Bill of Rights ratified.
	Uprising begins in Saint Domingue.
	Society for the Encouragement of Useful Manufactures founded.
1792	Washington reelected president.
1793	Planters and slaves arrive from St. Domingue.
	Fugitive Slave Law.
	Citizen Genet active in United States.
	Jefferson resigns from Washington's cabinet.
	First Democratic societies established.

1794	Whiskey Rebellion.
	Battle of Fallen Timbers.
1795	Treaty of Greenville.
	Jay's Treaty.
1796	Treaty of San Lorenzo.
	Washington's Farewell Address.
	John Adams elected president.
1798	XYZ Affair.
	Alien and Sedition Acts.
1798–1799	Virginia and Kentucky Resolutions.
1798–1800	Quasi-War between United States and France.
1799	Russia establishes colony in Alaska.
	Fries Rebellion in Pennsylvania.
	Handsome Lake begins reform movement among Senecas.
1800	Gabriel's Rebellion in Virginia.
	Thomas Jefferson elected president.

When George Washington took office as the new United States' first president, it was by several measures cause for celebration. Not only did this mark the establishment of a firm and visible leader, but it also proved to be a brief moment of complete unity between the various states. While they all agreed on Washington, from the start leaders debated the nature, shape, and form the new republic should take, just as they continued to debate the very meaning of republicanism itself. Many of those disputes would focus on the power of the central government relative to that of the states, but they would also center on the role of individuals and groups. Leaders differed, too, about how to stimulate economic growth and on foreign policy matters as the United States took its position in the international world.

For most Americans, the 1790s was a decade marked by social, political, and economic transformation. Since 1750, the former colonies had grown from just under 2 million people to more than 5 million, 90 percent of whom lived and worked on the land. White planters and farmers equated the ownership of land with liberty and political rights, and they considered Native Americans an obstacle to those goals. Whether accommodating the expansionist republic would actually improve prospects for the 125,000 Indians east of the Mississippi was questionable at best.

Meanwhile, the liberty so fundamental to white American men came at enormous cost not only to Native Americans but to African Americans and all women as well—groups that had hoped for more rights and opportunities in the new republic. While women and free blacks saw some small gains, progress halted overall and in some cases reversed itself. If anything, prospects for improving the political and economic standings of nonwhite males worsened during the 1790s, just as the United States launched its new frame of government under the Constitution.

Although the new federal government began on a harmonious note under President George Washington, white male interest groups grew increasingly divided over the political and diplomatic course the United States should take. Splitting into factions during Washington's first term, they hardened by 1798 into political parties, each of which accused the other of threatening republican liberty. Only when the election of 1800 had been settled—by the narrowest of margins—did it seem certain that the United States would endure.

7-1 Economic and Social Change

Which groups experienced the greatest gains and losses in the early years of the new republic?

During the nation's first twelve years under the Constitution, the spread of economic production for markets, even by family farms, dramatically altered the lives of many Americans. These transformations marked the United States' first small steps toward industrial capitalism and prompted early debates about the effects of factory production on workers and American society at large.

Meanwhile, other disagreements during the 1790s centered on questions of gender and race in American society. Contrary to the hopes for greater liberty and equality that many found in the Declaration of Independence, legal and political barriers to gender and racial equality actually became more entrenched during the first decade of the constitutional era.

7-1.1 Producing for Markets

For centuries most economic production in European societies and their colonial offshoots took place in household settings. At the core of each household was a patriarchal nuclear family—the male head, his wife, and their unmarried children. Many American households included additional people—relatives; boarders; apprentices and journeymen in artisan shops; servants and slaves in well-off urban households; and slaves, "hired hands," and tenant farmers in rural settings. Unlike in our modern world, before the nineteenth century most people except mariners worked at what was temporarily or permanently "home." The notion of "going to work" would have struck them as odd. Even most slaves living in separate "quarters" on large plantations labored in enterprises centered on planters' households.

Although households varied greatly in the late eighteenth century, most were on small farms and consisted of only an owner and his family. By 1800, such farm families typically included approximately seven children whose labor contributed to production. While husbands and older sons worked in fields away from the house, wives, daughters, and young sons maintained the barns and gardens near the house. Wives, of course, reared the children as well. As in the colonial period, most farm families produced food and other products largely for their own consumption and created small surpluses for bartering with neighbors or local merchants. Some women also found work as midwives, treating members of the community during illness and especially helping with the birth of children.

After the American Revolution, households in the most densely populated regions of the Northeast began to change. Relatively prosperous farm families increasingly directed their surplus production to meet the growing demands of urban customers for produce, meat, and dairy products. These families often turned to agricultural experts, whose advice their parents and grandparents had usually spurned. Accordingly, men introduced clover into their pastures, expanded acreage devoted to hay, and built barns to shelter their cows in cold weather and to store the hay. A federal census in 1798 revealed that about half the farms in eastern Pennsylvania had barns, usually of logs or framed but occasionally of stone. Consequently, by 1800 dairy production rose as mid-Atlantic farmwomen, or "dairymaids," milked an average of six animals twice a day, with each "milch cow" producing about two gallons per day during the summer. Farmwomen turned much of the milk into butter for sale to urban consumers.

Poorer farm families, especially in New England, found less lucrative ways to produce for commercial markets. Small plots of land on New England's thin, rocky soil no longer supported large families, leading young people to look elsewhere for a living. While many young men and young couples moved west and other young men went to sea, unmarried daughters more frequently remained at home, where they helped satisfy a growing demand for ready-made clothing. After the Revolution, enterprising merchants began catering to urban consumers as well as southern slave owners seeking to clothe their slaves as cheaply as possible. Making regular circuits through rural areas, the merchants supplied cotton for spinning and weaving to mothers and daughters in farm households. A few weeks later, they would return and pay the women in cash for their handiwork. They or other merchants also purchased wool and flax (made from linen) that were produced by the women's families.

A comparable transition began in some artisans' households. The shoemakers of Lynn, Massachusetts, had expanded their production during the Revolution when filling orders from the Continental Army. After the war, some more successful artisans transformed their shops to small factories that employed young men from the countryside, while others contracted with rural families to assemble one or another part of a shoe. The artisan-entrepreneurs then sold the finished products throughout the country, filling an annual demand that rose from 175,000 pairs in 1789 to 400,000 in 1800.

Numerous other enterprises likewise emerged, employing men as well as women to satisfy demands that self-contained households could never have met on their own. For example, a traveler passing through Middleborough, Massachusetts, observed,

In the winter season, the inhabitants . . . are principally employed in making nails, of which they send large quantities to market. This business is a profitable addition to their husbandry; and fills up a part of the year, in which, otherwise, many of them would find little employment.

Behind the new industries was an ambitious, aggressive class of businessmen, most of whom had begun as merchants and now invested their profits in factories, ships, government bonds, and banks. Such entrepreneurs stimulated a flurry of innovative business ventures that pointed toward the future. The country's first private banks were founded in the 1780s in Philadelphia, Boston, and New York. Philadelphia merchants created the Pennsylvania Society for the Encouragement of Manufactures and the Useful Arts in 1787. This organization promoted the immigration of English artisans familiar with the latest industrial technology, including Samuel Slater, a pioneer of American industrialization who helped establish a cotton-spinning mill at Pawtucket, Rhode Island, in 1790 (see Chapter 9). In 1791, investors from New York and Philadelphia, with Secretary of the Treasury Alexander Hamilton's enthusiastic endorsement, formed the Society for the Encouragement of Useful Manufactures, which attempted to demonstrate the potential of large-scale industrial enterprises by building a factory town at Paterson, New Jersey. That same year, New York merchants and insurance underwriters organized America's first formal association for trading government bonds, out of which the New York Stock Exchange evolved.

For many Americans, the choice between manufacturing and farming was moral as well as economic. Hamilton's aggressive support of entrepreneurship and industrialization was consistent with his larger vision for America and contradicted that of Secretary of State Thomas Jefferson. As outlined in his Report on the Subject of Manufactures (1791), Hamilton admired efficiently run factories in which a few managers supervised large numbers of workers. Manufacturing would provide employment opportunities, promote emigration, and expand the applications of technology. It would also offer "greater scope for the talents and dispositions [of] men," afford "a more ample and various field for enterprise," and create "a more certain and steady demand for the surplus produce of the soil." Hamilton endorsed that factories hire unmarried farm girls, as they were increasingly becoming surplus labor on family farms and he believed they could aid families by providing much-needed cash. He also saw them as a temporary labor pool, working only until they wed.

For Hamilton, capital, technology, and managerial discipline were the surest roads to national order and wealth, and he saw no incompatibility of either with notions of republicanism—government in which the people are sovereign (Chapter 6). Jefferson, putting more trust in white male citizens, envisioned land as the key to prosperity and liberty for all. He idealized white, landowning family farmers as bulwarks of republican liberty and virtue. "Those who labour in the earth are the chosen people," he wrote in 1784, whereas the dependency of European factory workers "begets subservience and venality, suffocates the germ of virtue, and prepares fit tools for the designs of ambition." The argument over these two ideals would remain a constant in American politics and culture in future centuries.

7-1.2 White Women in the Republic

Alongside the growing importance of women's economic roles, whites' discussions about republicanism and virtue prompted women to raise questions about their broader roles and rights in the new republic, socially and politically. Debates begun during the Revolution would intensify in subsequent years, especially after 1792, when U.S. publications printed British women's rights activist Mary Wollstonecraft's *A Vindication of the Rights of Woman*. Socially, American women did see some gains; politically, however, change would prove more challenging and elusive.

There was no talk during or immediately after the Revolution about voting rights for women, for example. Women were able to vote in one place—New Jersey in 1776—but that proved short-lived. New Jersey's new state constitution did not specify gender and race in its voting requirements, leaving a loophole that enabled female and black property owners to vote, which many began to do. In a hotly contested legislative race in 1797, seventy-five women voters nearly gave the victory to a Federalist candidate. His victorious Republican opponent, John Condict, would get his revenge in 1807 by successfully advocating a bill to disenfranchise women—who, it was argued, are too easily influenced (along with free blacks). The law, however, widened the pool of white male voters by permitting even those without land (the usual requirement) to vote.

But socially, there were some signs of progress. American republicans increasingly recognized the right of a woman to choose her husband—a striking departure from the continued practice among some elites whereby fathers approved or even arranged marriages. Thus in 1790, on the occasion of his daughter Martha's marriage, Jefferson wrote to a friend that, following "the usage of my country, I scrupulously suppressed my wishes, [so] that my daughter might indulge her sentiments freely."

Republican ideals also influenced notions of male-female relations. "I object to the word 'obey' in the marriage-service," wrote a female author calling herself Matrimonial Republican, ". . . The obedience between man and wife is, or ought to be mutual." As new laws sanctioned the right to divorce (previously prohibited except in cases of desertion), lack of mutuality was one reason for a rising number of divorce petitions from women. In Connecticut, for example, the number rose from fewer than fourteen divorce petitions annually before the Revolution to forty-five in 1795. A few women also challenged the sexual double standard that allowed men to indulge in extramarital affairs while their female partners, single or married, were condemned. Writing in 1784, an author calling herself "Daphne" pointed out how a woman whose illicit affair was exposed was "forever deprive[d] . . . of all that renders life valuable," while "the base [male] betrayer is suffered to triumph in the success of his unmanly arts, and to pass unpunished even by a frown." Daphne called on her "sister Americans" to "stand by and support the dignity of our own sex" by publicly condemning seducers rather than their victims.

Within even the happiest marriages, white women had fewer children overall than had their mothers and grandmothers. In Sturbridge, Massachusetts, women in the mid-eighteenth century had averaged nearly nine children per marriage, compared with six in the first decade of the nineteenth century. Whereas 40 percent of Quaker women had nine or more children before 1770, only 14 percent bore that many thereafter. Such statistics testify to declining farm sizes and urbanization, both of which were incentives for having fewer children. But they also indicate that some women were finding relief from the near-constant state of pregnancy and nursing that had consumed their grandmothers.

Motherhood, in fact, would provide some rationale for expanding women's roles within and later beyond the home. Advocates of republicanism and its need for virtuous citizens—those who would put the common good above their own self-interest—had from the start wondered about how virtuous citizens come to be. The answer, it seemed, was in how they were raised from childhood. It was, many quickly argued, the republican duty of mothers to inculcate these values in their sons—the nation's future leaders—as well as their daughters. As such, advocates of what historians have dubbed "**republican motherhood**" emphasized the importance of educating white women in the values of liberty and independence to strengthen virtue in the new nation. John Adams reminded his daughter that she was part of "a young generation, coming up in America . . . [and] will be responsible for a great share of the duty and opportunity of educating a rising family, from whom much will be expected."

Two of the leading proponents of women's education—Judith Sargent Murray and Benjamin Rush—embraced these notions of republican motherhood and used them to expand women's access to education. They challenged prevailing fears that educating women would prove problematic—that it would "unsex" them (make them more masculine) and make them unhappy with their gender roles. Before the 1780s, only a few women had acquired an advanced education through private tutors. Rush, a physician who was among the signers of the Declaration of Independence, advocated for expanding women's traditional learning about female crafts such as sewing to include geography and reading—but he stopped short of including topics that were standard in male education, such as philosophy or mathematics.

Murray, the daughter of a prominent Gloucester, Massachusetts, merchant, took a more radical position, seeking complete education for women. In "On the Equality of the Sexes" (1790), Murray contended that the genders had equal intellectual ability and deserved equal education. She hoped that "sensible and informed" women would improve their minds rather than rush into marriage (as she had at eighteen). Murray, who experienced financial hardship as a widow and even after she remarried, saw in education the potential for women to not only raise virtuous sons, but also find a means to economically provide for themselves. Either way, by the late eighteenth century educational opportunities for women increased. Urban elites founded numerous private schools, or

"republican motherhood"
Emphasized the importance of educating white women in the values of liberty and independence in order to strengthen virtue in the new nation. It was the republican duty of mothers to inculcate these values in their sons—the nation's future leaders—as well as in their daughters.

academies, for girls, and Massachusetts also established an important precedent in 1789 when it forbade any town to exclude girls from its elementary schools.

Although the great struggle for female political equality would not begin until the next century, assertions that women were intellectually and morally men's peers, and that republican mothers played a vital public role, provoked additional calls for equality beyond those voiced by Abigail Adams and a few other women during the Revolution (see Chapter 6). In 1793, Priscilla Mason, a student at a female academy, blamed "*Man*, despotic man" for shutting women out of the church, the courts, and government. In her graduation speech, she urged that a women's senate be established by Congress to evoke "all that is human—all that is *divine* in the soul of woman." Mason pointed out that while women could be virtuous wives and mothers, the world outside their homes still offered them few opportunities to apply their education. And neither she nor anyone else at the time challenged prohibitions against married women's ownership of property.

7-1.3 Land and Culture: Native Americans

Native Americans occupied the most tenuous position in American society. By 1800, Indians east of the Mississippi had suffered severe losses of population, territory (see Map 7.3), and political and cultural self-determination. Thousands of deaths had resulted from battle, famine, and disease during successive wars since the 1750s and from poverty, losses of land, and discrimination during peacetime. From 1775 to 1800, the Cherokee population declined from sixteen thousand to ten thousand, and Iroquois numbers fell from about nine thousand to four thousand. During the same period, Native Americans lost more land than the area inhabited by whites in 1775. Squatters, liquor dealers, and criminals trespassed on Indian lands, often defrauding, stealing, or inflicting

ADVOCATING WOMEN'S RIGHTS, 1792 In this illustration from an American magazine for women, the "Genius of the Ladies Magazine" and the "Genius of Emulation" present Liberty with a petition based on English feminist Mary Wollstonecraft's *Vindication of the Rights of Woman*. *(Granger, NYC—All rights reserved.)*

NANCY WARD Statue of Nancy Ward, created by James Abraham Walker (circa 1876) for Ward's Tennessee gravesight. It was stolen in the early 1980s and was seen again in 2006 as part of the American Antiques Show in New York. *(Photo by D. Ray Smith.)*

violence on Native Americans and provoking them to retaliate. Indians who sold land or worked for whites were often paid in the unfamiliar medium of cash and then found little to spend it on in their isolated communities except alcohol.

During the war, peaceful Cherokees, including Nancy (Nanye'hi) Ward, sought an agreement with the United States. Known as "War Woman" (or Beloved Woman), in 1755 Ward had picked up her husband's gun after he was killed in a battle against the Creeks and defeated them. She was among those, too, who had urged that the Cherokee remain neutral during the Revolution, splitting with more militant Cherokees who supported Britain in the hope of preventing further land losses. At a treaty conference with the United States in 1781, Ward and other speakers persuaded the Americans not to take additional Cherokee land. But after the war ended, U.S. treaty commissioners pressured the Cherokees in 1783 and 1785 to cede another eight thousand square miles. Thereafter, Ward urged those Cherokees still resisting the Americans to make peace. Only in 1794, after their Shawnee allies were crushed at the Battle of Fallen Timbers (discussed in this chapter), did the last Cherokees submit to U.S. rule. Ward advocated peace with the United States, not because she embraced the new republic and its values, but because she recognized that resistance to its military power was futile.

While employing military force against Native Americans who resisted U.S. authority, George Washington and Secretary of War Knox recognized that American citizens' actions often contributed to Indians' resentment. Accordingly, they pursued a policy similar to Britain's under the Proclamation of 1763 (see Chapter 5) in which the federal government sought to regulate relations between Indians and non-Indians. Congress enacted the new policy gradually in a series of **Indian Trade and Intercourse Acts** (1790–1796). (Thereafter, Congress periodically renewed and amended the legislation until making it permanent in 1834.) To halt fraudulent land cessions, the acts prohibited transfers of tribal lands to outsiders except as authorized in formal treaties or by Congress. Other provisions regulated the conduct of non-Indians on lands still under tribal control. To regulate intercultural trade and reduce abuses, the acts required that traders be licensed by the federal government. (But until 1802, the law did not prohibit the sale of liquor on Indian lands.) The law also defined murder and other abuses committed by non-Indians against Indians on tribal lands as federal offenses. Finally, the legislation authorized the federal government to establish programs that would "promote civilization" among Native Americans as a replacement for traditional culture. By "civilization," Knox and his supporters meant Anglo-American culture, particularly private property and a strictly agricultural way of life, with men replacing women in the fields. By abandoning communal landownership and seasonal migrations for hunting, gathering, and fishing, they argued, Indians would no longer need most of the land they were trying to protect, thereby making it

available for whites. But before 1800, the "civilization" program was offered to relatively few Native Americans, and the Indian Trade and Intercourse Acts went largely unenforced (see Map 7.1).

Among the most devastated Native Americans in the 1790s were the Seneca Iroquois of western New York and Pennsylvania. Most surviving Iroquois had moved to Canada after the Revolution, and those like the Seneca who stayed behind were pressured to sell, or were simply defrauded of, most of their land, leaving them isolated from one another on tiny reservations. Unable to hunt, trade, or find work, Seneca men frequently resorted to heavy drinking, often becoming violent. All too typical were the tragedies that beset Mary Jemison, born a half-century earlier to white settlers but a Seneca since her wartime capture and adoption at age ten. Jemison saw one of her sons murder his two brothers in alcohol-related episodes before meeting a similar fate himself.

RED JACKET, SENECA IROQUOIS CHIEF (CA. 1750–1830) Red Jacket was an eloquent defender of Seneca traditions against the efforts of both Christian missionaries and Handsome Lake to change Seneca religion and culture. *(Red Jacket (c.1756-1830) (w/c on paper)/Catlin, George (1796-1872)/PETER NEWARK'S PICTURES/ Private Collection/Bridgeman Images)*

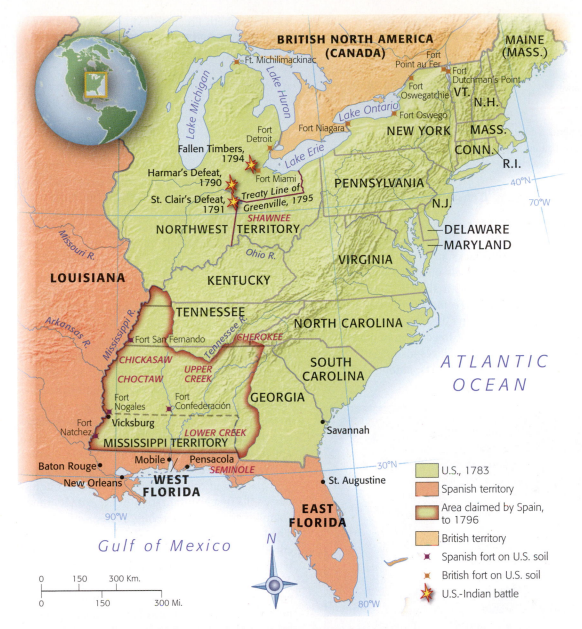

MAP 7.1 AMERICAN EXPANSION AND INDIAN LAND CESSIONS, 1768–1800 As the U.S. population grew, Native Americans were forced repeatedly to give up extensive homelands.

In 1799, a Seneca prophet, **Handsome Lake**, emerged and led his people in a remarkable spiritual revival. Severely ill, alcoholic, and near death, he experienced a series of visions, which Iroquois and many other Native American societies interpreted as prophetic messages. As in the visions of the Iroquois prophet Hiawatha in the fourteenth century (see Chapter 1), spiritual guides appeared to Handsome Lake and instructed him in his own recovery and in that of his people. Invoking Iroquois religious traditions, Handsome Lake preached against alcoholism and sought to revive unity and self-confidence among the Seneca. But whereas many Indian visionary prophets, such as Neolin (see Going to the Source in Chapter 5), rejected all white ways, Handsome Lake welcomed civilization, as introduced by

Quaker missionaries (who did not attempt to convert Native Americans) supported by federal aid. In particular, he urged a radical shift in gender roles, with Seneca men displacing women not only in farming but also as heads of their families. At the same time, he insisted that men treat their wives respectfully and without violence.

The most traditional Senecas rejected Handsome Lake's message that native men should work like white farmers. While many Seneca men welcomed the change, women often resisted because they stood to lose their control of farming and their considerable political influence. Some of Handsome Lake's

> **Handsome Lake**
> Seneca prophet who led his people to a spiritual revival that rejected alcoholism and promoted peaceful relationships with whites, including adopting some of their gender roles, while maintaining Iroquois religious traditions.

Fugitive Slave Law of 1793
Required judges to award possession of an escaped slave upon any formal request by a master or his representative.

supporters accused women who rejected his teachings of witchcraft, and even killed a few of them. The violence soon ceased and Handsome Lake's followers formed their own church, complete with traditional Iroquois religious ceremonies. But the Seneca case was unique because most missionaries continued to expect Native Americans to become Christians as well as adopt "civilization."

7-1.4 African American Struggles

The Republic's first years marked the high tide of African Americans' Revolutionary-era success in bettering their lot. Blacks and even many whites recognized that the ideals of liberty and equality were inconsistent with slavery. Some states passed laws gradually freeing slaves within their borders (as discussed in Chapter 6), while some others, giddy with liberty, freed them immediately or in slaveowners' wills. Slaves also legally sued for their freedom in the courts, among them, in

PORTRAIT OF ELIZABETH FREEMAN (ALSO KNOWN AS MUM BETT) (C. 1742-1829.) A slave, in 1781 she successfully sued in Massachusetts courts for her freedom. *(Portrait of Elizabeth 'Mumbet' Freeman (c.1742-1829) 1811 (w/c on ivory), Sedgwick, Susan Anne Livingston Ridley (fl 1811) / © Massachusetts Historical Society, Boston, MA, USA / Bridgeman Images)*

1781, Elizabeth Freeman (Mum Bett) as well as a male slave named Quock Walker, both in Massachusetts and both winning their cases (see Going to the Source). By 1790, 8 percent of all African Americans had been freed from slavery. Ten years later, 11 percent were free (see Figure 7.1). Various state measures meanwhile attempted to improve the conditions of those who remained enslaved. In 1791, for example, the North Carolina legislature declared that the former "distinction of criminality between the murder of a white person and one who is equally an human creature, but merely of a different complexion, is disgraceful to humanity" and authorized the execution of whites who murdered slaves. Although more for economic than humanitarian reasons, by 1794 most states had outlawed the Atlantic slave trade.

Hesitant measures to ensure free blacks' legal equality also appeared in the 1780s and early 1790s. Most states dropped restrictions on African Americans' freedom of movement and protected their property. By 1796, all but three of the sixteen states either permitted free blacks to vote or did not specifically exclude them. But by then a countertrend was reversing many of the Revolutionary-era advances. Before the 1790s ended, free blacks faced new obstacles to equality, while abolitionist sentiment ebbed among whites and slavery became more entrenched.

Federal law led the way in restricting the rights of free blacks and other nonwhites. When Congress passed the first Naturalization Act (1790), it limited eligibility for U.S. citizenship to "free white aliens." The federal militia law of 1792 required whites to enroll in local units but allowed states to exclude free blacks, which state governments increasingly did. The navy and the marine corps forbade nonwhite enlistments in 1798. State legislation followed the new trend. Delaware stripped free, property-owning black males of the vote in 1792, and by 1807 Maryland, Kentucky, and New Jersey had taken similar steps. Free black men continued to vote and to serve in some militia units after 1800 (including in the slave states of North Carolina and Tennessee), but the number of settings in which they were treated as the equals of whites dropped sharply.

Federal legislation also reinforced slavery and racism with the **Fugitive Slave Law of 1793**. This law required judges to award possession of an escaped slave upon any formal request by a master or his representative. Accused runaways not only were denied a jury trial but were also sometimes refused permission to present evidence of their freedom. Slaves' legal status as property disqualified them from claiming these constitutional privileges, but the Fugitive Slave Law denied free blacks the legal protections that the Bill of Rights guaranteed them as citizens. Congress nevertheless passed this

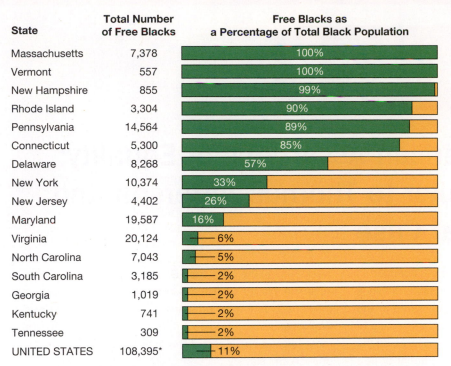

State	Total Number of Free Blacks	Free Blacks as a Percentage of Total Black Population
Massachusetts	7,378	100%
Vermont	557	100%
New Hampshire	855	99%
Rhode Island	3,304	90%
Pennsylvania	14,564	89%
Connecticut	5,300	85%
Delaware	8,268	57%
New York	10,374	33%
New Jersey	4,402	26%
Maryland	19,587	16%
Virginia	20,124	6%
North Carolina	7,043	5%
South Carolina	3,185	2%
Georgia	1,019	2%
Kentucky	741	2%
Tennessee	309	2%
UNITED STATES	108,395*	11%

FIGURE 7.1 NUMBER AND PERCENTAGE OF FREE BLACKS, BY STATE, 1800 Within a generation of the Declaration of Independence, a large free black population emerged that included every ninth African American. In the North, only in New Jersey and New York did most blacks remain slaves. Every sixth black in Maryland was free by 1800.

Source: U.S. Bureau of the Census.

* Total includes figures from the District of Columbia, Mississippi Territory, and Northwest Territory. These areas are not shown on the chart.

measure without serious opposition. All in all, the new laws of the 1790s marked a striking departure from the atmosphere of the preceding decade, when state governments had moved toward granting free blacks legal equality with whites.

Despite these growing restrictions, some free blacks became landowners or skilled artisans, and a few gained recognition among whites. Yet even free blacks who were acknowledged in some way by whites did not hesitate to insist on full liberty and equality for their people. Among the best-known free African Americans was Benjamin Banneker of Maryland, a self-taught mathematician and astronomer. In 1789, Banneker was one of three surveyors who laid out the new national capital in Washington, D.C., and after 1791 he published a series of widely read almanacs. Sending a copy of one to Thomas Jefferson, Banneker chided the future president for holding views of black inferiority that contradicted his words in the Declaration of Independence (see Going to the Source). In a brief reply, Jefferson expressed hope that blacks' physical and mental condition would be raised "as far as the imbecility of their present existence . . . will admit." (At the time, "imbecility" referred to nonmental as well as mental limitations.) The two men's exchange was published a year later.

In resisting limitations on their freedom and opportunities, free African Americans in the North turned to one another for support. Self-help among African Americans flowed especially through religious channels. During the 1780s, two free black Christians, Richard Allen and Absalom Jones, formed the Free African Society of Philadelphia, a community organization whose members pooled their scarce resources to assist one another and other blacks in need. After the white-dominated Methodist church they attended restricted black worshipers to the gallery, Allen, Jones, and most other black members withdrew and formed a separate congregation. Comparable developments in other northern communities eventually resulted in the formation of a new denomination, the African Methodist Episcopal Church (discussed in Chapter 9).

In 1793, Philadelphia experienced a yellow fever epidemic in which about four thousand residents died. (Carried by mosquitoes, yellow fever is a highly contagious and deadly virus in which infected persons' skin turns yellow.) As most affluent whites fled, Allen and Jones organized a relief effort in which African Americans, at great personal risk, tended to the sick and buried the dead of both races. But their only reward was a vicious publicity campaign wrongly accusing blacks of profiting at whites' expense. Allen and Jones vigorously defended the black community against these charges while condemning slavery and racism. Jones also delivered a petition to Congress on behalf of four escaped slaves who had been seized in free territory under provisions of the Fugitive Slave Law.

Two African American Assertions of Equality: Benjamin Banneker to Thomas Jefferson and the Quock Walker Case

African Americans tested the tenets of liberty embedded in the American Revolution and the ideological underpinnings of the new United States. These challenges came in the form of legal petitions claiming freedom—as in the case of the slave Quock Walker (below), as well as in attacks on the racism that undergirded slavery and the treatment of free blacks—as in the letter from Benjamin Banneker to Thomas Jefferson. Walker, whose case involved three trials, successfully sued his former master for damages from a beating Walker endured after fleeing slavery. Banneker issued the most forceful challenge of the time to Jefferson's positions on race and slavery.

Jury Instructions from Chief Justice William Cushing in the Quock Walker Case, 1783

As to the doctrine of slavery and the right of Christians to hold Africans in perpetual servitude, and selling and treating them as we do our horses and cattle, that (it is true) has been heretofore countenanced by the province Laws formerly, but no where is it expressly enacted or established. It has been a usage—a usage which took its origin from the practice of some of the European nations, and the regulations of British government respecting the then Colonies, for the benefit of trade and wealth. But whatever Sentiments have formerly prevailed in this particular or slid in upon us by the example of others, a different idea has taken place with the people of America, more favorable to the natural rights of mankind, and to that natural, innate desire of Liberty, with which Heaven (without regard to color, complexion, or shape of noses—features) has inspired all the human race. And upon this ground our Constitution of Government, by which the people of this Commonwealth have solemnly bound themselves, sets out with declaring that all men are born free and equal—and that every subject is entitled to Liberty, and to have it guarded by the laws, as well as life and property—and in short is totally repugnant to the idea of being born slaves. This being the case, I think the Idea of Slavery is inconsistent with our own conduct and Constitution; and there can be no such thing as perpetual servitude of a rational creature, unless his liberty is forfeited by some criminal conduct or given up by personal consent or contract.

Source: Massachusetts Historical Society, Online Collections. Legal notes by William Cushing about the Quock Walker case. From the William Cushing judicial note-book Sequence of 13 pages presented—pages 87 [second page 87]–99.

Letter, Benjamin Banneker to Thomas Jefferson August 19, 1791

Sir, I freely and cheerfully acknowledge, that I am of the African race, and in that color which is natural to them of the deepest dye; and it is under a sense of the most profound gratitude to the Supreme Ruler of the Universe, that I now confess to you, that I am not under that state of tyrannical thralldom, and inhuman captivity, to which too many of my brethren are doomed, but that I have abundantly tasted of the fruition of those blessings, which proceed from that free and unequalled liberty with which you are favored. . . .

Sir, suffer me to recall to your mind that time, in which the arms and tyranny of the British crown were exerted, with every powerful effort, in order to reduce you to a state of servitude: look back, I entreat you, on the variety of dangers to which you were exposed . . .

This, Sir, was a time when you clearly saw into the injustice of a state of slavery, and in which you had just apprehensions of the horrors of its condition. It was now that your abhorrence thereof was so excited, that you publicly held forth this true and invaluable doctrine, which is worthy to be recorded and remembered in all succeeding ages: "We hold these truths to be self-evident, that all men are created equal; that they are endowed by their Creator with certain unalienable rights, and that among these are, life, liberty, and the pursuit of happiness." . . . Sir, how pitiable is it to reflect, that although you were so fully convinced of the benevolence of the Father of Mankind, and of his equal and impartial distribution of these rights and privileges, which he hath conferred upon them, that you should at the same time counteract his mercies, in detaining by fraud and violence so numerous a part of my brethren, under groaning captivity and cruel oppression, that you should at the same time be found guilty of that most criminal act, which you professedly detested in others, with respect to yourselves.

I suppose that your knowledge of the situation of my brethren, is too extensive to need a recital here; neither shall I presume to prescribe methods by which they may be relieved, otherwise than by recommending to you and all others, to wean yourselves from those narrow prejudices which you have imbibed with respect to them, and as Job [a figure in the Bible] proposed to his friends, "put your soul in their souls' stead"; thus shall your hearts be enlarged with kindness and benevolence towards them; and thus shall you need neither the direction of myself or others, in what manner to proceed herein.

Source: American Multiculturalism Series. Unit One. *Documenting the African American Experience,* Special Collections, University of Virginia Library.

QUESTIONS

1. How do both the Quock Walker case and the Banneker letter tap into the language of liberty in the Declaration of Independence and post-Revolutionary discourse?
2. How does Banneker characterize Jefferson's ownership of slaves?

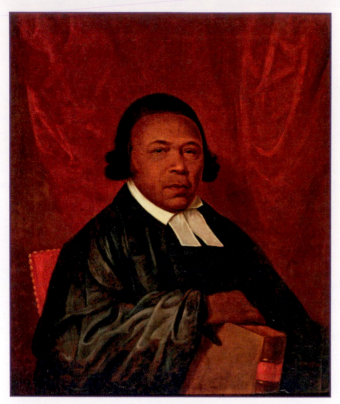

ABSALOM JONES, BY RAPHAEL PEALE, 1810 Born a slave, Jones was allowed to study and work for pay; eventually he bought his freedom. He became a businessman, a cofounder of the African Methodist Episcopal Church, and a stalwart in Philadelphia's free black community. *(Absalom Jones, 1810 (oil on paper), Peale, Raphaelle (1774–1825) / Delaware Art Museum, Wilmington, USA / Gift of Absalom Jones School / Bridgeman Images)*

Enslaved African Americans also banded together in the quest of freedom—especially in Virginia, where both blacks and whites closely followed news of developments in Saint Domingue. The slave revolution there, led by Touissant L'Ouverture, was on the verge of declaring an independent black republic (which in 1802 would be named Haiti, believed to be the indigenous Taino name of the land). Several thousand former French planters and their slaves now lived in Virginia, and the state's newspapers covered the black takeover extensively.

While slave owners feared violent retaliation by enslaved African Americans, the latter drew inspiration from the uprising. In August 1800, both sides' expectations seem to have been realized when a slave insurrection, known as **Gabriel's Rebellion**, broke out near Richmond, Virginia's capital. Amid the election campaign that year, in which Federalists and Republicans accused one another of endangering liberty and hinted at violence, a slave named Gabriel and his followers calculated that the split among whites afforded blacks an opportunity to gain their freedom. Having secretly assembled weapons, Gabriel led a march on Richmond by more than a thousand slaves. But the plot had been leaked on the eve of the march. Obtaining confessions from some participants, the authorities rounded up the rest and executed thirty-five of them, including Gabriel. "I have nothing more to offer than what General Washington would have had to offer, had he been taken by the British officers and put to trial by them," said one rebel before his execution. "I have ventured my life in endeavoring to obtain the liberty of my countrymen, and I am a willing sacrifice to their cause." In the end, Gabriel's Rebellion only confirmed whites' anxieties that Haiti's revolution could be replayed on American soil.

While concluding that slaves required brutal repression, many planters questioned slavery's economic necessity, especially with the decline of tobacco production in the Chesapeake. A technological development, however, reinvigorated the institution of slavery. During the 1790s, demand in the British textile industry stimulated the cultivation of cotton in coastal South Carolina and Georgia. The soil and climate were ideal for growing long-staple cotton, a variety whose fibers could be separated easily from its seed by squeezing it through rollers. In the South's upland and interior regions, however, the only cotton that would thrive was the short-staple variety, whose seed stuck so tenaciously to the fibers that rollers crushed the seeds and ruined the fibers. It was as if growers had discovered gold only to find that they could not mine it. But in 1793, a New Englander, Eli Whitney, invented a **cotton gin** that successfully separated the fibers of short-staple cotton from the seed. Quickly copied and improved upon by others, Whitney's invention removed a major obstacle to the westward spread of cotton cultivation. It thereby gave a new lease on life to plantation slavery and undermined the doubts of those who considered slavery economically outmoded.

By 1800, free blacks had suffered noticeable erosion of their post-Revolutionary gains, and southern slaves were farther from freedom than a decade earlier. Two vignettes poignantly communicate the plight of African Americans. By arrangement with her late husband, Martha Washington freed the family's slaves a year after George died. But many of the freed blacks remained impoverished and dependent on the Washington estate because Virginia law prohibited the education of blacks and otherwise denied them opportunities to realize their freedom. Meanwhile, across the Potomac at the site surveyed by Benjamin Banneker, enslaved blacks were performing most of the labor on the new national capital that would bear the first president's name. African Americans were manifestly losing ground.

Gabriel's Rebellion
A planned slave rebellion in Richmond led by Gabriel, a slave. The plan leaked out just before the march, and authorities rounded up the participants and executed thirty-five of them, including Gabriel.

cotton gin
Device created by Eli Whitney to make it easier to separate cotton seeds from the cotton itself; credited with reviving slavery at a time when it was in decline.

7-2 Constitutional Government and New Domestic Policies, 1788–1794

What were the points of unity and fissure in the new American government?

Although in 1788 the Constitution replaced the Articles of Confederation as the law of the land, its effectiveness had yet to be tested. Given the social and political divisions among Americans and their varying views on what a republic should be, the successful establishment of a national government was anything but guaranteed. Would Americans accept the results of a national election? Would the legislative, executive, and judicial branches of the new government function effectively? And would agreement on domestic policies be possible? Once the government was in place, Secretary of the Treasury Alexander Hamilton would be charged with promoting national economic development, but his program would spark new controversies with its emphasis on strengthening the national government and with his use of a distinctive brand of republicanism that disavowed widespread ideals of self-sacrifice and virtue.

7-2.1 Implementing Government

The first step in implementing the new government was the election of a president and Congress. The first elections under the Constitution, in fall 1788, pitted Federalist proponents of the new frame of government against its Antifederalist opponents. Solidifying their victory in the vote for ratification, the Federalists won an overwhelming mandate. Antifederalists won just two of twenty seats in the Senate and five of fifty-nine in the House of Representatives. An electoral college met in each state on February 9, 1789, with each elector voting for two presidential candidates. Although unaware of deliberations in other states, every elector designated George Washington as one of their choices. Having gotten the second-most votes, John Adams became the vice president. (The Twelfth Amendment would later change this procedure for choosing the president and vice president, as discussed in Chapter 8.)

There was nothing surprising about the unanimity of Washington's victory. His leadership during the Revolutionary War and the constitutional convention earned him a reputation as a national hero whose abilities and integrity far surpassed those of his peers. Because of his exalted stature, Washington

was able to calm Americans' fears of unlimited executive power.

Traveling slowly over the nation's miserable roads, the men entrusted with launching the federal experiment began assembling in New York, the new national capital, in March 1789. Because so few members were on hand, Congress opened its session a month late. President-elect Washington did not arrive until April 23 and took his oath of office a week later.

The Constitution required the president to obtain the Senate's "advice and consent" to his nominees to head executive departments. Otherwise, Congress was free to determine the organization and accountability of what became known as the cabinet. The first cabinet, established by Congress, consisted of five departments, headed by the secretaries of state, treasury, and war and by the attorney general and postmaster general. Vice President John Adams's tie-breaking vote defeated a proposal that would have forbidden the president from dismissing cabinet officers without Senate approval. This outcome strengthened the president's authority to make and carry out policy independently of congressional oversight, beyond what the Constitution required.

7-2.2 The Federal Judiciary and the Bill of Rights

The Constitution authorized Congress to establish federal courts below the level of the Supreme Court, but provided no plan for their structure. Many citizens feared that federal courts would ride roughshod over each state's distinctive blend of judicial procedures.

With the **Judiciary Act** of 1789, Congress quieted popular apprehensions by establishing in each state a federal district court that operated according to local procedures. As the Constitution stipulated, the Supreme Court exercised final jurisdiction. Congress had struck a compromise between nationalists and states' rights advocates, one that respected state traditions while offering wide access to federal justice.

The Constitution offered some protection of citizens' individual rights. It barred Congress from passing ex post facto laws (criminalizing previously legal actions and then punishing those who had engaged in them) and bills of attainder (proclaiming a person's guilt and stipulating punishment without a trial). Nevertheless, the absence of a comprehensive bill of rights had prompted several delegates at Philadelphia to refuse to sign the Constitution and had been a condition of ratification in several states. James Madison, who had been elected to the House of Representatives, led the drafting

> **Judiciary Act**
> This act established in each state a federal district court that operated according to local procedures.

GEORGE WASHINGTON'S INAUGURAL JOURNEY THROUGH TRENTON, 1789 Washington received a warm welcome in Trenton, site of his first victory during the Revolutionary War. *(Library of Congress Prints and Photographs Division)*

of the ten amendments that became known as the **Bill of Rights**.

The First Amendment guaranteed the most fundamental freedoms of expression—religion, speech, press, and political activity—against federal interference. The Second Amendment ensured that "a well-regulated militia" would preserve the nation's security by guaranteeing "the right of the people to bear arms." Along with the Third Amendment, it sought to protect citizens from what eighteenth-century Britons and Americans alike considered the most sinister embodiment of tyrannical power: standing armies. The Fourth through Eighth Amendments limited the police powers of the state by guaranteeing individuals' fair treatment in legal and judicial proceedings. The Ninth and Tenth Amendments reserved to the people or to the states powers not allocated to the federal government under the Constitution, but Madison headed off proposals to limit federal power more explicitly. In general, the Bill of Rights imposed no serious check on the framers' nationalist objectives. The ten amendments were submitted to the states and ratified by December 1791.

7-2.3 Establishing the Nation's Credit

With the new government in place, Secretary of the Treasury **Alexander Hamilton** turned his attention to fortifying the nation's economy and economic growth. In Hamilton's mind, the most immediate danger facing the United States was the possibility of war with Britain, Spain, or both. The republic could finance a major war only by borrowing heavily, but because Congress under the Confederation had not assumed responsibility for the Revolutionary War debt, the nation's credit was weakened abroad and at home.

Responding to a request from Congress, Hamilton in January 1790 issued the first of two **Reports on the Public Credit**. It outlined a plan to strengthen the country's credit, enable it to defer paying its debt, and entice wealthy investors to place their capital at its service. The report listed $54 million in U.S. debt, $42 million of which was owed to Americans, and the rest to Europeans. Hamilton estimated that on top of the national debt, the states had debts of $25 million, some of which the United States had promised to reimburse.

Hamilton recommended first that the federal government "fund" the $54 million national debt by selling an equal sum in new government bonds. Purchasers of these securities would choose from

Bill of Rights
The first ten amendments of the Constitution; designed to preserve individual liberty and rights.

Alexander Hamilton
Secretary of the Treasury under President George Washington.

Reports on the Public Credit
Hamilton's report that contained recommendations that would at once strengthen the country's credit, enable it to defer paying its debt, and entice wealthy investors to place their capital at its service.

several combinations of federal "stock" and western lands. Those who wished could retain their original bonds and earn 4 percent interest. All these options would reduce interest payments on the debt from the full 6 percent set by the Confederation Congress. Hamilton knew that creditors would not object to this reduction because their investments would now be more valuable and more secure. His report also proposed that the federal government pay off the $25 million in state debts remaining from the Revolution in the same manner.

Hamilton exhorted the government to use the money earned by selling federal lands in the West to pay off the $12 million owed to Europeans as quickly as possible. In his Second Report on the Public Credit, submitted to Congress in December 1790, he argued that the Treasury could accumulate the interest owed on the remaining $42 million by collecting customs duties on imports and an excise tax (a tax on products made, sold, or transported within a nation's borders) on whiskey. In addition, Hamilton proposed that money owed to American citizens should be made a permanent debt. That is, he urged that the government not attempt to repay the $42 million principal but instead keep paying interest to bondholders. Under Hamilton's plan, the only burden on taxpayers would be the small annual cost of interest. The government could uphold the national credit at minimal expense, without ever paying off the debt itself.

Hamilton advocated a perpetual debt as a lasting means of uniting the economic fortunes of the nation's creditors to the United States. In an age when financial investments were notoriously risky, the federal government would protect the savings of wealthy bondholders through conservative policies while offering an interest rate competitive with the Bank of England's. The guarantee of future interest payments would unite the interests of the moneyed class with those of the government. Few other investments would entail so little risk.

Hamilton's recommendations provoked immediate controversy. Although no one in Congress doubted that they would enhance the country's fiscal reputation, many objected that those least deserving of reward would gain the most. The original owners of more than three-fifths of the debt certificates issued by the Continental Congress were Revolutionary patriots of modest means who had long before sold their certificates for a fraction of their promised value, usually out of dire financial need. Foreseeing that the government would fund the debt, wealthy speculators had bought the certificates and now stood to reap huge gains at the expense of the original owners, even collecting interest that had accrued before they purchased the certificates. "That the case of those who parted with their securities from necessity is a hard one, cannot be denied," Hamilton admitted. But making exceptions, he argued, would be even worse.

To Hamilton's surprise, Madison—his longtime ally—emerged as a leading opponent of funding. Facing opposition to the plan in his home state of Virginia, Madison tried but failed to obtain compensation for original owners who had sold their certificates. Congress rejected his proposal primarily on the grounds that it would weaken the nation's credit.

Opposition to Hamilton's proposal that the federal government assume states' war debts also ran high. Only Massachusetts, Connecticut, and South Carolina had failed to make effective provisions for satisfying their creditors. The issue stirred the fiercest indignation in the South, which except for South Carolina had paid off 83 percent of its debt. Madison and others maintained that to allow residents of the laggard states to escape heavy taxes while others had liquidated theirs at great expense was to reward irresponsibility.

Southern hostility almost defeated assumption. In the end, however, Hamilton saved his proposal by enlisting Secretary of State Thomas Jefferson's help. Jefferson and other Virginians favored moving the capital to the Potomac River, hoping to make Virginia a national crossroads and thus preserve its position as the largest, most influential state. In return for the northern votes necessary to transfer the capital, Hamilton secured enough Virginians' support to win the battle for assumption. The capital would move in the following year to Philadelphia and remain there until a new capital city was built. Despite this concession, the debate over state debts confirmed many white southerners' suspicions that northern financial and commercial interests would benefit from Hamilton's policies at southerners' expense.

Congressional enactment in 1790 of Hamilton's recommendations dramatically reversed the nation's fiscal standing. European investors grew so enthusiastic about U.S. bonds that by 1792 some securities were selling at 10 percent above face value.

7-2.4 Creating a National Bank

Having significantly expanded the stock of capital available for investment, Hamilton intended to direct that money toward projects that would diversify the national economy through a federally chartered bank. Accordingly, in December 1790 he presented Congress with the **Report on a National Bank**.

The proposed Bank of the United States would raise $10 million through a public stock offering. Private investors could purchase shares by paying for three-quarters of their value in government bonds. In this way, the bank would capture a significant portion of the recently funded debt and

Report on a National Bank
Hamilton's report that proposed a Bank of the United States.

make it available for loans; it would also receive a steady flow of interest payments from the Treasury. Under these circumstances, shareholders were positioned to profit handsomely.

Hamilton argued that the bank would cost the taxpayers nothing and greatly benefit the nation. It would provide a safe place for the federal government to deposit tax revenues, make inexpensive loans to the government when taxes fell short, and help relieve the scarcity of hard cash by issuing paper notes that would circulate as money. Furthermore, it would possess authority to regulate the business practices of state banks and would provide much needed credit to expand the economy.

Hamilton's critics denounced his proposal for a national bank, interpreting it as a dangerous scheme that would give a small, elite group special power to influence the government. These critics argued that the Bank of England had undermined the integrity of government in Britain. Shareholders of the new bank could just as easily become the tools of unscrupulous politicians. Jefferson openly opposed Hamilton, claiming that the bank would be "a machine for the corruption of the legislature [Congress]." Another Virginian, John Taylor, predicted that the bank would take over the country, which would thereafter, he quipped, be known as the United States of the Bank.

Madison led the opposition to the bank in Congress, arguing that it was unconstitutional. Unless Congress closely followed the Constitution, he argued, the central government could oppress the states and trample on individual liberties, just as Parliament had done to the colonies. Strictly limiting federal power seemed the surest way of preventing the United States from degenerating into a corrupt despotism.

Congress approved the bank by only a thin margin. Uncertain of the bank's constitutionality, Washington turned to both Jefferson and Hamilton for advice before signing the measure into law. Like many southern planters whose investments in slaves left them short of capital and often in debt, Jefferson distrusted banking. Moreover, his fear of concentrated economic and political power led him, like Madison, to favor a "strict interpretation" of the Constitution. "To take a single step beyond the boundaries thus specifically drawn around the powers of Congress is to take possession of a boundless field of power no longer susceptible of any definition," warned Jefferson.

Hamilton fought back, urging Washington to sign the bill. Because the Constitution authorized Congress to enact all measures "necessary and proper" (Article I, Section 8), Hamilton contended, it could execute such measures. The only unconstitutional activities of the national government, he concluded, were those expressly prohibited. In the end, the president accepted Hamilton's argument for a "loose interpretation" of the Constitution. In February 1791, the Bank of the United States obtained a charter guaranteeing its existence for twenty years. Washington's acceptance of the principle of loose interpretation was an important victory for those advocating an active, assertive national government. But the split between Jefferson and Hamilton, and Washington's siding with the latter, signaled a deepening political divide within the administration.

7-2.5 Emerging Partisanship

Hamilton's attempt to build political support for Federalist policies by appealing to certain citizens' economic self-interest was successful but also divisive. His arrangements for rescuing the nation's credit provided enormous gains for speculators, merchants, and other investors in the port cities who by 1790 held most of the Revolutionary debt. As holders of bank stock, these groups had yet another reason to favor centralized national authority. Assumption of the state debts liberated New England, New Jersey, and South Carolina taxpayers from a crushing burden, enabling Federalists to dominate politics in these places. Hamilton's efforts to promote industry, commerce, and shipping also struck a responsive chord among northeastern entrepreneurs.

Opposition to Hamilton's program was strongest in sections of the country where it offered few benefits. Outside of Charleston, South Carolina, few southerners or westerners retained Revolutionary certificates in 1790, invested in the Bank of the United States, or borrowed from it. Resentment against a national economic program whose main beneficiaries seemed to be eastern "monied men" and New Englanders who refused to pay their debts gradually united westerners, southerners, and some mid-Atlantic citizens into a political coalition that challenged the Federalists and called for a return to the "true principles" of republicanism.

With Hamilton having presented his measures as "Federalist," Jefferson, Madison, and their supporters began referring to themselves as "republicans." In this way, they implied that Hamilton's schemes to centralize the national government threatened liberty. Having separated from the Federalists, Jefferson and Madison drew support from former Antifederalists whose ranks had been fatally weakened after the election of 1788. In 1791, they supported the establishment in Philadelphia of an opposition newspaper, *The National Gazette*, whose editor, Philip Freneau, had been an ardent Antifederalist. For the year preceding the election of 1792, Freneau attacked Hamilton relentlessly, accusing him of trying to create an aristocracy and monarchy in America. Hamilton responded vigorously to the attacks through his own column in Philadelphia's Federalist newspaper, *The Gazette of the United States*. Using pseudonyms, he also wrote columns in which he attacked Jefferson as an enemy of President Washington.

Although political partisanship intensified as the election approached, there was no organized political campaigning. For one thing, most voters believed that organized factions or parties were inherently corrupt and threatened liberty. The Constitution's framers had neither wanted nor planned for political parties. Indeed, in *Federalist* No. 10, James Madison had argued that the Constitution would prevent the rise of national political factions. For another thing, George Washington, by appearing to be above the partisan disputes, remained supremely popular.

Meeting in 1792, the electoral college was again unanimous in choosing Washington to be president. John Adams was reelected vice president but by a closer vote than in 1788, receiving 77 votes compared to 50 for George Clinton, the Antifederalist governor of New York.

7-2.6 The Whiskey Rebellion

Hamilton's program not only sparked an angry congressional debate but also helped ignite a civil insurrection in 1794 called the **Whiskey Rebellion**. Reflecting serious regional and class tensions, this popular uprising was the young republic's first serious crisis. It was also about competing visions of the republican ideals, as well as the legacy of the American Revolution.

As part of his financial program, Hamilton had recommended an excise tax on domestically produced whiskey. He insisted that such a tax would not only help in financing the national debt but would improve morals by inducing Americans to drink less liquor. Though Congress enacted the tax, some members doubted that Americans (who on average annually consumed six gallons of hard liquor per adult) would submit tamely to limitations on their drinking. James Jackson of Georgia, for example, warned the administration that his constituents "have long been in the habit of getting drunk and that they will get drunk in defiance of . . . all the excise duties which Congress might be weak or wicked enough to pass."

The validity of such doubts became apparent in September 1791 when a crowd tarred and feathered an excise agent near Pittsburgh. Western Pennsylvanians found the new tax especially burdensome. Unable to export crops through New Orleans, most farmers distilled their rye or corn into alcohol, which could be carried across the Appalachians at a fraction of the price charged for bulkier grain. Hamilton's excise equaled 25 percent of whiskey's retail value, enough to wipe out a farmer's profit.

The law also stipulated that trials for evading the tax be conducted in federal courts. Any western Pennsylvanian indicted for noncompliance would have to travel three hundred miles to Philadelphia. Besides facing a jury of unsympathetic easterners, the accused would have to bear the cost of the long journey and lost earnings while at court, in addition to fines and other penalties if found guilty. Moreover, Treasury officials rarely enforced the law rigorously outside western Pennsylvania. For all these reasons, western Pennsylvanians complained that the whiskey excise was excessively burdensome.

In a scene reminiscent of Revolutionary-era popular protests, large-scale resistance erupted in July 1794. One hundred western Pennsylvanians attacked a U.S. marshal serving sixty delinquent taxpayers with summonses to appear in court at Philadelphia. A crowd of five hundred burned the chief revenue officer's house after a shootout with federal soldiers. Roving bands torched buildings, assaulted tax collectors, harassed government supporters, and flew a flag symbolizing an independent country they hoped to create from six western counties.

Whiskey Rebellion
A civil insurrection in 1794 where one hundred men attacked a U.S. marshal serving sixty delinquent taxpayers with summonses to appear in court at Philadelphia. A crowd of five hundred burned the chief revenue officer's house after a shoot-out with federal soldiers assigned to protect him.

WHISKEY REBELLION, 1794 Rebels in Washington County, Pennsylvania, tar and feather a federal tax collector.
(Granger, NYC — All rights reserved.)

Echoing elites' denunciations of earlier protests, Hamilton condemned the rebellion as lawlessness. He noted that Congress had reduced the tax rate per gallon in 1792 and had recently voted to allow state judges in western Pennsylvania to hear trials. As during Shays's Rebellion (see Chapter 6), Washington concluded that failure to respond strongly to the uprising would encourage outbreaks in other western areas.

Washington accordingly mustered nearly thirteen thousand militiamen from Pennsylvania and neighboring states to march west under his command. Opposition evaporated once the troops reached the Appalachians, and the president left Hamilton in charge of making arrests. Of about 150 suspects seized, Hamilton sent twenty in irons to Philadelphia. Two men received death sentences, but Washington eventually pardoned them both, noting that one was a "simpleton" and the other "insane."

The Whiskey Rebellion resulted in severe limits on public opposition to federal policies. In the early 1790s, many Americans still believed it was legitimate to protest unpopular laws using the same tactics with which they had blocked parliamentary measures like the Stamp Act. Indeed, western Pennsylvanians had justified their resistance with exactly such reasoning. By firmly suppressing the first major challenge to national authority, Washington served notice that citizens who resorted to violent or other extralegal means of political action would feel the full force of federal authority. In this way, he gave voice and substance to elites' fears of "mobocracy," now resurfacing in reaction to the French Revolution (discussed shortly).

7-3 The United States in a Wider World, 1789–1796

How did foreign policy concerns inspire increased partisanship?

By 1793, debates about foreign affairs had emerged as the primary source of friction in American public life. The political divisions created by Hamilton's financial program hardened into ideologically oriented factions that argued vehemently over whether the country's foreign policy should favor industrial and overseas mercantile interests or those of farmers, planters, small businesses, and artisans. Moreover, having begun the Constitutional era in the year the French Revolution began (1789), the United States entered the international arena as

Alta California
Present-day American state of California.

European tensions were once again exploding. The rapid spread of pro-French revolutionary ideas and organizations alarmed Europe's monarchs and aristocrats. Perceiving a threat to their social orders as well as their territorial interests, most European nations declared war on France by early 1793. For most of the next twenty-two years—until Napoleon's final defeat in 1815—Europe and the Atlantic world remained in a state of war.

While most Americans hoped that their nation could avoid this European conflict, the interests or values of many citizens led them to be partial toward either Britain, France, or Spain. Thus, differences over foreign policy fused with differences over domestic affairs, further intensifying partisanship in American politics.

7-3.1 Spanish Power in Western North America

Stimulated by having won Louisiana from France in 1762 (see Chapter 5), Spain enjoyed a brief revival of its North American fortunes in the late eighteenth century. Strengthened by new presidios and additional troops north of the Rio Grande, Spain sought to force the powerful Comanches to end their damaging raids on Spanish colonists and allied Indians and to submit to Spanish authority. This effort succeeded, but only up to a point. By 1800, the Comanches and other nomadic Indians had agreed to cease their raids in New Mexico and Texas, but whether the truce would become a permanent peace depended on whether Spain could strengthen and broaden its imperial position in North America.

Spain's efforts in New Mexico and Texas were part of its larger effort to counter rivals for North American territory and influence. The first challenge arose in the Pacific Ocean, where Spain had enjoyed an unchallenged monopoly for more than two centuries until Russian traders entered Alaska.

Perceiving Russia's move into Alaska as a threat, Spain expanded northward on the Pacific coast from Mexico. In 1769, it established the province of **Alta California** (the present American state of California) (see Map 7.2). Efforts to encourage large-scale Mexican immigration to Alta California failed, leaving the colony to be sustained by a chain of religious missions among Native Americans, several military presidios, and a few large ranchos (ranches). Seeking support against inland adversaries, coastal California Indians welcomed the Spanish at first. But the Franciscan missionaries sought to convert them to Catholicism while imposing harsh disciplinary measures and putting them to work in vineyards and in other enterprises. Meanwhile, Spanish colonists' spreading of epidemic and venereal diseases precipitated a decline in the Native American population from about seventy-two thousand in 1770 to about eighteen thousand by 1830.

Between New Mexico and California, Spain attempted to make alliances with Indians in the area later known as Arizona. In this way, Spain hoped to dominate North America between the Pacific and the Mississippi River. But resistance from the Hopi, Quechan (Yuma), and other Native Americans thwarted these hopes. Fortunately for Spain, Arizona had not yet attracted the interest of other imperial powers.

7-3.2 Challenging American Expansion, 1789–1792

Although the Treaty of Paris (1783) (discussed in Chapter 6) granted sovereignty over all territory between the Appalachians and the Mississippi River to the United States, Spain, Britain, and numerous Indian nations resisted the new nation's efforts to assert its authority in the region (see Map 7.3).

Realizing that the United States was in no position to dictate developments immediately in the West, President Washington pursued a course of patient diplomacy that was intended "to preserve the country in peace if I can, and to be prepared for war if I cannot." The prospect of peace improved in 1789 when Spain unexpectedly opened New Orleans to American commerce, although exports remained subject to a 15 percent duty.

Thereafter, Spanish officials continued to bribe well-known political figures in Tennessee and Kentucky, among them a former general on Washington's staff, James Wilkinson. Thomas Scott, a congressman from western Pennsylvania, meanwhile schemed with the British. Between 1791 and 1796, the federal government anxiously admitted Vermont, Kentucky, and Tennessee to the Union, partly in the hope of strengthening their residents' flickering loyalty to the United States.

Washington also tried to weaken Spanish influence by neutralizing Spain's most important ally, the Creek Indians. The Creeks numbered more than twenty thousand, including perhaps five thousand warriors, and they bore a fierce hostility toward Georgian settlers, whom they called Ecunnaunuxulgee, or "the greedy people who want our lands." In 1790, Creek leader Alexander McGillivray signed the Treaty of New York with the United States. The treaty permitted American settlers to remain on lands in the Georgia piedmont fought over since 1786 (see Chapter 6), but in other respects preserved Creek territory against U.S. expansion. Washington also insisted that Georgia restore to the Creeks' allies, the Chickasaws and Choctaws, the vast area along the Mississippi River

MAP 7.2 SPANISH SETTLEMENTS IN ALTA CALIFORNIA, 1800 While the United States was struggling to win its independence, Spain was establishing a new colony on the Pacific coast.

known as the Yazoo Tract, which Georgia had begun selling off to white land speculators (as discussed in Chapter 8).

Washington and his secretary of war, Henry Knox, adopted a harsher policy toward Native Americans who resisted efforts by American citizens to occupy the Ohio Valley. In 1790, the first U.S. military effort collapsed when a coalition of tribes chased General Josiah Harmar and 1,500 troops from the Maumee River. A second campaign failed in November 1791, when a thousand Shawnee warriors surrounded an encampment of fourteen hundred soldiers led by General Arthur St. Clair. More than six hundred soldiers were killed and several hundred wounded before the survivors could flee for safety.

MindTap

Beyond America
Trade and Empire in the Pacific, to 1800

MISSION SAN ANTONIO DE PADUA The early colonization of Alta California depended on missions at which Native Americans were subjected to harsh treatment and Roman Catholic religion. *(Copyright © Tony Freeman / Photo Edit)*

With Native Americans having twice humiliated U.S. forces in the Northwest Territory, Washington's western policy was in shambles. Matters worsened in 1792 when Spain persuaded the Creeks to renounce the Treaty of New York and resume hostilities. The damage done to U.S. prestige by these setbacks convinced many Americans that the combined strength of Britain, Spain, and the Native Americans could be counterbalanced only by an alliance with France.

Saint Domingue
Site of a black uprising against slavery and French colonial rule in the Caribbean in 1791–1793, which increased southern slaveowners' distrust of Britain and support for the French Revolution.

7-3.3 France and Factional Politics, 1793

One of the most momentous events in world history, the French Revolution began in 1789. The French were inspired by America's revolution, and Americans were initially sympathetic as France overthrew the monarchy, abolished nobles' privileges, proclaimed itself a constitutional republic, and bravely repelled foreign invaders. But the Revolution took a radical turn in 1793 when France declared an international revolutionary war of all peoples against all kings and began a "Reign of Terror," executing not only the king but dissenting revolutionaries.

Americans grew bitterly divided in their attitudes toward the French Revolution and over how the United States should respond to it. While republicans such as Jefferson supported it as an assault on monarchy and tyranny, Federalists like Hamilton denounced France as a "mobocracy" and supported Britain in resisting French efforts to export revolution.

White southern slave owners were among France's fiercest supporters. The French Revolution had taken an earlier shocking turn in 1791 when it spread to the wealthy Caribbean colony of **Saint Domingue**. There it not only divided whites but inspired free and enslaved blacks to demand they, too, be granted liberty and equality. Following a bloody battle in Saint Domingue's leading port in 1793, thousands of terrified French planters fled to the United States, recounting how British (and Spanish) invaders were supporting the black revolutionaries. Recalling how Britain had encouraged their own slaves to escape and fight for the king during the Revolution, southern planters concluded that the British intentionally sparked a slave uprising in Saint Domingue and would do the same in their states.

Many northerners, on the other hand, were more repelled by the political, social, and religious upheaval in revolutionary France. The revolution was "an open hell," thundered Massachusetts's Fisher Ames, "still ringing with agonies and blasphemies, still smoking with sufferings and crimes." New England Protestants detested the French for worshiping Reason instead of God. Less religious Federalists condemned French leaders as evil radicals who incited the poor against the rich.

Northern and southern reactions to the French Revolution also diverged for economic reasons. Merchants, shippers, and ordinary sailors in New England, Philadelphia, and New York (which conducted most of the country's foreign trade) feared that an alliance with France would provoke British retaliation against American commerce. They argued that the United States could win valuable concessions by demonstrating friendly intentions toward Britain and noted that some influential

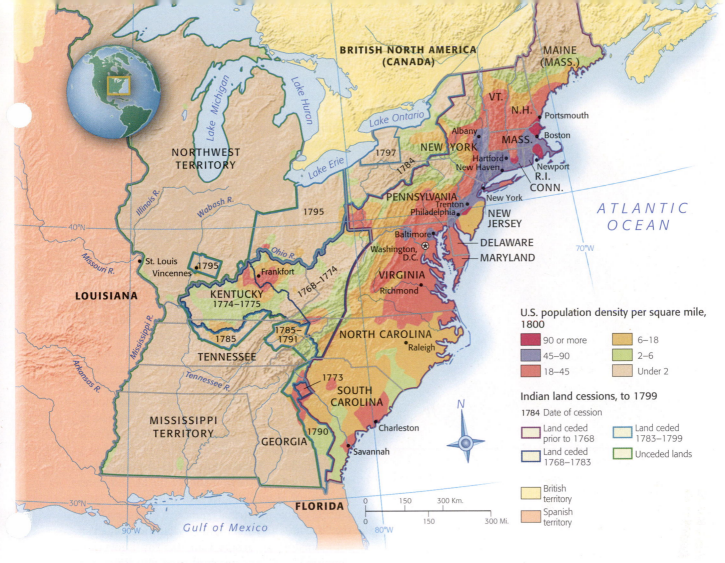

BRITISH NORTH AMERICA (CANADA)

NORTHWEST TERRITORY

Lake Michigan
Lake Huron
Lake Ontario
Lake Erie

MAINE (MASS.)

VT.
N.H.
Portsmouth
Albany
MASS.
Boston
Hartford
New Haven
Newport
R.I.
CONN.

NEW YORK

1797
1784

40°N

Illinois R.
Wabash R.

1795

PENNSYLVANIA
Trenton
Philadelphia
New York
NEW JERSEY

Baltimore
DELAWARE
Washington, D.C.
MARYLAND

70°W

A T L A N T I C
O C E A N

St. Louis
Vincennes
1795
Frankfort

Missouri R.

LOUISIANA

KENTUCKY
1774–1775

Ohio R.
1768–1774

VIRGINIA
Richmond

Mississippi R.

1785
1785–1791

TENNESSEE

Tennessee R.

NORTH CAROLINA
Raleigh

Arkansas R.

MISSISSIPPI TERRITORY

1773
SOUTH CAROLINA

GEORGIA
1790
Charleston
Savannah

30°N

FLORIDA

90°W
Gulf of Mexico
80°W

U.S. population density per square mile, 1800

90 or more	6–18
45–90	2–6
18–45	Under 2

Indian land cessions, to 1799

1784 Date of cession

Land ceded prior to 1768
Land ceded 1768–1783
Land ceded 1783–1799
Unceded lands

British territory
Spanish territory

N

0   150   300 Km.
0   150   300 Mi.

MAP 7.3 DISPUTED TERRITORIAL CLAIMS IN THE WEST, 1783–1796 Until 1796, Britain, Spain, and Native Americans controlled much of the western territory claimed by the United States.

members of Parliament leaned toward liberalizing trade with the United States.

Southern elites instead viewed Americans' reliance on British commerce as a menace to national self-determination and wished to divert most U.S. trade to France. Jefferson and Madison advocated reducing British imports through the imposition of steep duties. Federalist opponents countered that Britain, which sold more manufactured goods to the United States than to any other country, would not stand idly by under such circumstances. If Congress adopted a discriminatory tariff, Hamilton predicted in 1792, "there would be, in less than six months, an open war between the United States and Great Britain."

Enthusiasm for a pro-French foreign policy intensified in the southern and western states after France went to war against Spain and Great Britain in 1793. Increasingly, western settlers and speculators hoped for a French victory that, they reasoned, would induce Britain and Spain to cease blocking U.S. expansion. The United States could then insist on free navigation of the Mississippi, force the evacuation of British garrisons, and end both nations' support of Native American resistance.

After declaring war on Britain and Spain, France actively tried to embroil the United States in the conflict. The French dispatched Edmond Genet as minister to the United States with orders to mobilize republican sentiment in support of France, enlist American mercenaries to conquer Spanish territories and attack British shipping, and strengthen the French–American alliance. Responding to France's aggressive diplomacy, President Washington issued a proclamation of American neutrality on April 22, 1793.

Defying Washington's proclamation, Citizen Genet (as he was known in French Revolutionary

FRANÇOIS DOMINIQUE TOUISSANT L'OUVERTURE As leader of the movement to free Saint Dominigue from slavery and French colonial rule, L'Ouverture inspired enslaved African Americans and profoundly shaped political debates among whites in the United States. *(© Bettmann/Corbis)*

style) recruited volunteers for his American Foreign Legion. Making generals of George Rogers Clark of Kentucky and Elisha Clarke of Georgia, Genet directed them to seize Spanish garrisons at New Orleans and St. Augustine. Genet also contracted with American privateers. By the summer of 1793, almost a thousand Americans were at sea in a dozen ships flying the French flag. These privateers seized more than eighty British vessels and towed them to U.S. ports, where French consuls sold the ships and cargoes at auction. Refusing Secretary of State Jefferson's patient requests that he desist, Genet threatened to urge Americans to defy their own government.

7-3.4 Diplomacy and War, 1793–1796

Although the Washington administration swiftly closed U.S. harbors to Genet's buccaneers and demanded that France recall him, Genet's exploits provoked an Anglo-American crisis. George III's ministers decided that only a massive show of force would deter American support for France. Accordingly, on November 6, 1793, Britain's Privy Council ordered the Royal Navy to confiscate foreign ships trading with the French in the West Indies. The council purposely delayed publishing these instructions until after most American ships sailing to the Caribbean had left port, so that their captains would not know that they were entering a war zone. The British then seized more than 250 American vessels.

The Royal Navy added a second galling indignity—the impressment (forced enlistment) of crewmen from U.S. ships. Thousands of British sailors had previously fled to the U.S. merchant marine, where they hoped to find an easier life than under the tough, poorly paying British system. In late 1793, British naval officers began routinely inspecting American crews for British subjects, whom they then impressed as the king's sailors. Overzealous commanders sometimes broke royal orders by taking U.S. citizens, and in any case the British did not recognize former subjects' right to adopt American citizenship. Impressment scratched a raw nerve in most Americans, who argued that their government's willingness to defend its citizens from such abuse was a critical test of national character.

Meanwhile, Britain, Spain, and many Native Americans continued to challenge the United States for control of territory west of the Appalachians. During a large intertribal council in February 1794, the Shawnees and other Ohio Indians welcomed an inflammatory speech by Canada's royal governor denying U.S. claims north of the Ohio River and urging destruction of every American settlement in the Northwest. Soon British troops were building an eighth garrison on U.S. soil, Fort Miami, near present-day Toledo. Spanish troops also encroached on territory claimed by the United States by building Fort San Fernando in 1794 at what is now Memphis, Tennessee.

Hoping to halt the drift toward war, Washington launched three desperate initiatives in 1794. He authorized General Anthony Wayne to negotiate a treaty with the Shawnees and their Ohio Valley allies, sent Chief Justice John Jay to Great Britain, and dispatched Thomas Pinckney to Spain.

Having twice defeated federal armies, the Shawnees and their allies scoffed at Washington's peace offer. "Mad Anthony" Wayne then led thirty-five hundred U.S. troops deep into Shawnee homelands, building forts and ruthlessly burning every village within his reach. On August 20, 1794, his troops routed four hundred Shawnees at the Battle of Fallen Timbers just two miles from Britain's Fort Miami. As Shawnees fled toward the fort, the British closed its gates, denying entry to their allies. Wayne's army then built an imposing stronghold to challenge

British authority in the Northwest, appropriately named Fort Defiance. Native American morale plummeted, not only because of the American victory and their own losses but also because of Britain's betrayal.

In August 1795, Wayne compelled the Shawnees and eleven other tribes to sign the **Treaty of Greenville**, which opened most of modern-day Ohio and a portion of Indiana to American settlement. But aside from the older leaders who were pressured to sign the treaty, most Shawnees knew that U.S. designs on Indian land in the Northwest had not been satisfied and would soon resurface (as discussed in Chapter 8).

Wayne's victory at Fallen Timbers helped John Jay, in **Jay's Treaty**, win a British promise to withdraw troops from American soil by June 1796. Jay also managed to gain access to British West Indian markets for small American ships, but only by bargaining away U.S. rights to load cargoes of sugar, molasses, and coffee from French colonies during wartime.

Aside from fellow Federalists, few Americans interpreted Jay's Treaty as preserving peace with honor. The treaty left Britain free to violate American neutrality and to restrict U.S. trade with France. Opponents condemned the treaty's failure to end impressment and predicted that Great Britain would thereafter force even more Americans into the Royal Navy. Slave owners were resentful that Jay had not obtained compensation for slaves taken away by the British army during the Revolution. After the Senate barely ratified the treaty in 1795, Jay nervously joked that he could find his way across the country at night by the fires of rallies burning him in effigy.

Despite its unpopularity, Jay's Treaty prevented war with Britain and finally ended British occupation of U.S. territory. The treaty also helped stimulate an enormous expansion of American trade. Upon its ratification, Britain permitted Americans to trade with its West Indian colonies and with India. Within a few years, American exports to the British Empire shot up 300 percent.

On the heels of Jay's controversial treaty came an unqualified diplomatic triumph engineered by Thomas Pinckney. Ratified in 1796, the **Treaty of San Lorenzo** with Spain (also called Pinckney's Treaty) won westerners the right of unrestricted, duty-free access to world markets via the Mississippi River. Spain also agreed to recognize the thirty-first parallel as the United States' southern boundary, to dismantle its fortifications on American soil, and to discourage Native American attacks against western settlers.

By 1796, the Washington administration could claim to have successfully extended American authority throughout the trans-Appalachian West, opened the Mississippi for western exports, enabled northeastern shippers to regain British markets, and kept the nation out of a dangerous European war. As the popular outcry over Jay's Treaty demonstrated, however, the nation's foreign policy left Americans much more deeply divided in 1796 than they had been in 1789.

7-4 Parties and Politics, 1793–1800

How did political disputes in the early republic develop into the nation's first political parties?

By the time Washington was reelected, the deep divisions among voters over domestic and foreign policy were fostering distinct political factions. During the president's second term, these factions hardened into formal political parties, Federalists and Republicans, which advanced their members' interests, ambitions, and ideals. Thereafter, the two parties waged a bitter battle, culminating in the election of 1800.

7-4.1 Ideological Confrontation, 1793–1794

Conflicting attitudes about events in France, federal power, and democracy accelerated the polarization of American politics. Linking the French Revolution and the Whiskey Rebellion, Federalists trembled at the thought of guillotines and "mob rule." They were also horrified by the sight of artisans in Philadelphia and New York bandying the French revolutionary slogan "Liberty, Equality, Fraternity" and rallying around pro-French politicians such as Jefferson. Citizen Genet had openly encouraged opposition to the Washington administration, and had found hundreds of Americans willing to fight for France. Federalists worried that all of this was just the tip of a revolutionary iceberg.

By the mid-1790s, Federalists' worst fears of democracy seemed to have been confirmed. The people, they believed, were undependable and vulnerable to rabble rousers such as Genet. For Federalists, democracy meant "government

Treaty of Greenville
Opened most of modern-day Ohio and a portion of Indiana to white settlement and ended U.S.-Indian hostilities in the region for sixteen years.

Jay's Treaty
This treaty gave the Americans access to West Indian markets for small American ships, but only by bargaining away other American complaints as well as U.S. rights to load cargoes of sugar, molasses, and coffee from French colonies during wartime.

Treaty of San Lorenzo
Also called Pinckney's Treaty, it won westerners the right of unrestricted, duty-free access to world markets via the Mississippi River.

by the passions of the multitude." They argued that, as in colonial times, ordinary voters should not be presented with choices over policy, but should vote simply on the basis of the personal merits of elite candidates. Elected officials, they maintained, should rule in the people's name but be independent of direct popular influence.

Republicans offered a very different perspective on government and politics. Like the Federalists, they sought to preserve their interpretation of what a republic truly was and deemed themselves the keepers of the legacy of the American Revolution. They stressed the corruption inherent in a powerful government dominated by a highly visible few, and insisted that liberty would be safe only if power were widely diffused among white male property owners.

It might at first glance seem contradictory for southern slave owners to support a radical ideology like republicanism, with its emphasis on liberty and equality. While a few southern republicans advocated abolishing slavery gradually, most were far more concerned that the slave violence in Saint Domingue would spread to American shores. Many of the French planters who had escaped to the United States had brought their slaves with them, and whites feared that these blacks would foment rebellion among African Americans. Although expressed in universal terms, the liberty and equality advocated by southern republicans were intended for white men only.

Political ambition drove men like Jefferson and Madison to rouse ordinary voters' concerns about civic affairs. The widespread awe in which Washington was held inhibited open criticism of him and his policies. If, however, his fellow Federalists could be held accountable to the public, they would think twice before enacting measures opposed by the majority; if they persisted in advocating misguided policies, they would ultimately be removed from office. Such reasoning led Jefferson, a wealthy landowner and large slaveholder, to say, "I am not among those who fear the people; they and not the rich, are our dependence for continued freedom."

Jefferson's frustration at being overruled at every turn by Hamilton and Washington finally prompted his resignation from the cabinet in 1793, and thereafter not even the president could halt the widening political split. Each side portrayed itself as the guardian of republican virtue and attacked the other as an illegitimate "cabal" or "faction."

In 1793–1794, opponents of Federalist policies began organizing Democratic societies. The societies formed primarily in seaboard cities but also in the rural South and West. Their members included planters, small farmers and merchants,

artisans, distillers, and sailors; conspicuously absent were big businessmen, the clergy, the poor, nonwhites, and women.

7-4.2 The Republican Party, 1794–1796

In 1794, party development reached a decisive stage after Washington openly identified himself with Federalist policies. Republicans attacked the Federalists' pro-British leanings in many local elections and won a slight majority in the House of Representatives. The election signaled the Republicans' transformation from a coalition of officeholders and local societies to a broad-based party capable of coordinating local political campaigns throughout the nation.

Federalists and Republicans alike used the press to mold public opinion. In the 1790s, American journalism came of age as the number of newspapers rose from 92 to 242, mostly in New England and the mid-Atlantic states. By 1800, newspapers had about 140,000 paid subscribers (roughly one-fifth of eligible voters), and their secondhand readership probably exceeded 300,000. Newspapers of both camps did not hesitate to engage in fear-mongering and character assassination. Federalists accused Republicans of plotting a reign of terror and of conspiring to turn the nation over to France. Republicans charged Federalists with favoring a hereditary aristocracy and even a royal dynasty that would form when John Adams's daughter married George III. Despite the extreme rhetoric, newspaper warfare stimulated many citizens to become politically active.

Washington grew impatient with the nation's growing polarization into openly hostile parties, and he deeply resented Republican charges that he secretly supported alleged Federalist plots to establish a monarchy. "By God," Jefferson reported him swearing, "he [Washington] would rather be in his grave than in his present situation . . . he had rather be on his farm than to be made emperor of the world." Unhappy and surrounded by mediocre advisers after Hamilton returned to private life, Washington decided in the spring of 1796 to retire after two terms. Washington recalled Hamilton to write his Farewell Address.

The heart of Washington's message was a vigorous condemnation of political parties. Partisan alignments, he insisted, endangered the republic's survival, especially if they became entangled in disputes over foreign policy. Washington warned that the country's safety depended on citizens' avoiding "excessive partiality for one nation and excessive dislike of another." Otherwise, "real patriots" would be overwhelmed by demagogues championing foreign causes and paid by foreign governments. Aside from scrupulously fulfilling its existing treaty obligations and maintaining its foreign commerce, the United States should strive to avoid "political connection" with Europe and its wars. If the United States gathered its strength under "an efficient government," it could defy any foreign challenge; but if it became sucked into Europe's quarrels, violence, and corruption, the republican experiment was doomed. Washington and Hamilton had skillfully turned republicanism's fear of corruption against their Republican critics. They had also evoked a vision of an America virtuously isolated from foreign intrigue and power politics, which would remain a potent inspiration for long afterward.

Washington left the presidency in 1797 and died in 1799. Like many later presidents, he went out amid a barrage of partisan criticism.

7-4.3 The Election of 1796

With the **election of 1796** approaching, the Republicans cultivated a large, loyal body of voters. Their efforts to marshal popular support marked the first time since the Constitution was ratified that political elites had effectively mobilized nonelites to participate in politics. The Republicans' constituency included the Democratic societies, workingmen's clubs, and immigrant-aid associations.

Immigrants became prime targets for Republican recruiters. During the 1790s, the United States absorbed about twenty thousand French refugees from Saint Domingue and more than sixty thousand Irish, many of whom had been exiled for opposing British rule. Although potential immigrant voters made up less than 2 percent of the electorate, the Irish could make a difference in closely divided Pennsylvania and New York.

In 1796, the presidential candidates were the Federalist vice president John Adams and the Republicans' Jefferson. Republicans expected to win as many southern electoral votes and congressional seats as the Federalists counted on in New England, New Jersey, and South Carolina. The crucial "swing" states were Pennsylvania and New York, where the Republicans fought hard to win the large immigrant vote with their pro-French and anti-British rhetoric. In the end, the Republicans took Pennsylvania but not New York, so that Jefferson lost the presidency by just three electoral votes. As the second-highest vote-getter in the electoral college, he became vice president. The Federalists narrowly regained control of the House and maintained their firm grip on the Senate.

Adams's intellect and devotion to principle have rarely been equaled among American presidents.

SEAL OF THE GENERAL SOCIETY OF MECHANICS AND TRADESMEN OF NEW YORK Founded in 1785, the Society included artisans in a wide variety of crafts. During the 1790s, it was a major force in the emerging Republican Party. *(Picture Research Consultants & Archives)*

But the new president was more comfortable with ideas than with people. He inspired trust and often admiration but could not command personal loyalty or galvanize the public. Adams's stubborn personality and disdain for both ordinary people and most politicians left him ill-suited to govern; ultimately, he proved unable to unify either the country or his own party.

7-4.4 The French Crisis, 1798–1799

Even before the election, the French had recognized that Jay's Treaty was a Federalist-sponsored attempt to assist Britain in its war against France. On learning of Jefferson's defeat, France began seizing American ships carrying goods to British ports and within a year had plundered more than three hundred vessels. The French also directed that every American captured on a British naval ship (even those involuntarily impressed) should be hanged.

Hoping to avoid war, Adams sent a peace commission to Paris. But the French foreign minister, Charles de Talleyrand, refused to meet the delegation, instead promising through three unnamed agents ("X, Y, and Z") that talks could begin after he received

> **election of 1796**
> Federalist John Adams won by three votes, and as the second-highest vote-getter in the electoral college, Thomas Jefferson became vice president.

"PREPARATION FOR WAR TO DEFEND COMMERCE" (1800) BY WILLIAM BIRCH Birch's engraving depicts the building of the frigate *Philadelphia* during the Quasi-War. *(Library of Congress Prints and Photographs Division [LC-USZC4-569])*

$250,000 and France obtained a loan of $12 million. Americans were outraged at this barefaced demand for a bribe, which became known as the XYZ Affair. "Millions for defense, not one cent for tribute" became a popular slogan as the 1798 congressional elections began.

The XYZ Affair discredited the Republicans' foreign policy views, but the party's leaders compounded the damage by refusing to condemn French aggression and opposing Adams's call for military preparations. The Republicans tried to excuse French behavior, whereas the Federalists rode a wave of militant patriotism. In the 1798 elections, Republican candidates were routed almost everywhere, even in the South.

Adams responded to the XYZ Affair by joining Britain in a trade agreement with François Dominique Touissant L'Overture, a charismatic former slave who led what was now an independence movement that controlled most of Saint Domingue.

The administration and Congress also armed fifty-four ships to protect American commerce in the Caribbean. During an undeclared Franco-American naval conflict known as the Quasi-War (1798–1800), U.S. forces seized ninety-three French privateers while losing just one vessel. The British navy meanwhile extended the protection of its convoys to America's merchant marine. By 1799, the French were no longer a serious naval threat, and American commerce flourished.

Meanwhile, the Federalist-dominated Congress quadrupled the size of the regular army to twelve thousand men in 1798, with ten thousand more troops in reserve. Yet the risk of a land war with France was minimal. In reality, the Federalists wanted a military force ready in the event of a civil war, for the crisis had produced near-hysteria among them about conspiracies being hatched by French and Irish revolutionaries flooding into the United States.

7-4.5 The Alien and Sedition Acts, 1798

The most heated controversies of the late 1790s arose from the Federalists' insistence that the threat of war with France required strict laws to protect national security. In 1798, the Federalist-dominated Congress accordingly passed four measures known collectively as the **Alien and Sedition Acts**. Adams neither requested nor particularly wanted these laws, but he deferred to Federalist congressional leaders and signed them.

The least controversial of the laws, the Alien Enemies Act, authorized jailing or deporting those who were deemed spies or saboteurs. Because it was to operate only if Congress declared war, it was not used until the War of 1812 (discussed in Chapter 8).

Second, the Alien Friends Act, a temporary statute, authorized the president to expel any foreign residents whose activities he considered dangerous. The law did not require proof of guilt, on the assumption that spies would hide or destroy evidence of their crime. Republicans maintained that the law's real purpose was to deport immigrants critical of Federalist policies.

Republicans also denounced the third law, the Naturalization Act. This measure increased the residency requirement for U.S. citizenship from five to fourteen years (the last five continuously in one state), with the purpose of reducing Irish voting.

Finally came the Sedition Act, the only one of these measures enforceable against U.S. citizens. Although its alleged purpose was to punish attempts to encourage the violation of federal laws or to overthrow the government, the act defined criminal activity so broadly that it blurred any distinction between sedition and legitimate political discussion. For example, it prohibited an individual or group from opposing "any measure or measures of the United States"—wording that could be interpreted to ban any criticism of the party in power. Another clause made it illegal to speak, write, or print any statement about the president that would bring him "into contempt or disrepute." Under such restrictions, a newspaper editor could face imprisonment for criticizing an action by Adams. The Federalist *Gazette of the United States* expressed the twisted logic of the Sedition Act perfectly:

> **Alien and Sedition Acts**
> A series of laws passed in 1798 designed to protect national security.

He in a trice struck Lyon thrice Upon his head, enrag'd sir,

Who seiz'd the tongs to ease his wrongs, And Griswold thus engag'd, sir.

Congress Hall, in Philad.ª Feb. 15.1798. S.E. Cor 6ᵗʰ & Chesnut S.

VIOLENCE IN THE HOUSE OF REPRESENTATIVES, 1798 Partisan enmity turned violent when Republican Matthew Lyon (with tongs) and Federalist Roger Griswold fought on the House floor. *(Library of Congress Prints and Photographs Division)*

"It is patriotism to write in favor of our government—it is sedition to write against it." However one regarded it, the Sedition Act interfered with free speech. Ingeniously, the Federalists wrote the law to expire in 1801, so that it could not be turned against them if they lost the next election, while leaving them free to heap abuse on Vice President Jefferson (who did not participate in the making of government policy).

A principal target of Federalist repression was the opposition press. Four of the five largest Republican newspapers were charged with sedition just as the election campaign of 1800 was getting under way. The attorney general used the Alien Friends Act to threaten Irish journalist John Daly Burk with expulsion (Burk went underground instead), and Scottish editor Thomas Callender went to prison for criticizing the president.

Federalist leaders never intended to fill the jails with Republican martyrs. Rather, they hoped to use a few highly visible prosecutions to silence Republican journalists and candidates during the election of 1800. The attorney general charged seventeen persons with sedition and won ten convictions. Among the victims was Republican congressman Matthew Lyon of Vermont ("Ragged Matt, the democrat," to the Federalists), who spent four months in prison for publishing a blast against Adams.

In 1788, opponents of the Constitution had warned that giving the national government extensive powers would eventually endanger freedom. Ten years later, their prediction seemed to have come true. Shocked Republicans concluded that because the Federalists controlled all three branches of the government, neither the Bill of Rights nor the system of checks and balances reliably protected individual liberties. In this context, they advanced the doctrine of states' rights as a means of restraining the federal government.

Recognizing that opponents of federal power would never prevail in the Supreme Court, which was still dominated by Federalists, Madison and Jefferson anonymously wrote manifestos on states' rights known as the **Virginia and Kentucky Resolutions**, adopted respectively by the legislatures of those states in 1798. Repudiating his position at the constitutional convention (see Chapter 6), Madison in the Virginia Resolutions declared that state legislatures had never surrendered their right to judge the constitutionality of federal actions and that they retained an authority called *interposition*, which enabled them to protect the liberties of their citizens. Jefferson's resolution for Kentucky went further by declaring that ultimate sovereignty rested with the states, which empowered them to "nullify" federal laws to which they objected. Although Kentucky's legislature deleted the term "nullify" before approving the resolution in 1799, the intention of both resolutions was to invalidate any federal law in a state that had deemed the law unconstitutional. Although the resolutions were intended as nonviolent protests, they challenged the jurisdiction of federal courts and could have enabled state militias to march into a federal courtroom to halt proceedings at bayonet point.

No other state endorsed these resolutions (ten expressed disapproval), but their passage demonstrated the great potential for disunion in the late 1790s. So did several near-violent confrontations between Federalist and Republican crowds in Philadelphia and New York City. A minor insurrection, the Fries Rebellion, broke out in 1799 when crowds of German Pennsylvanian farmers released prisoners jailed for refusing to pay taxes needed to fund the national army's expansion. But the uprising collapsed when federal troops intervened.

The nation's leaders increasingly acted as if a crisis were imminent. Vice President Jefferson hinted that events might push the southern states into secession from the Union, while President Adams hid guns in his home. After passing through Richmond and learning that state officials were purchasing thousands of muskets for the militia, an alarmed Supreme Court justice wrote in January 1799 that "the General Assembly of Virginia are pursuing steps which will lead directly to civil war." A tense atmosphere hung over the Republic as the election of 1800 neared.

7-4.6 The Election of 1800

In the election campaign, the two parties again rallied around the Federalist Adams and the Republican Jefferson. The leadership of moderates in both parties helped to ensure that the nation survived the **election of 1800** without a civil war. Jefferson and

---

Virginia and Kentucky Resolutions
Written by Madison, the first declared that state legislatures had never surrendered their right to judge the constitutionality of federal actions and that they retained an authority called interposition, which enabled them to protect the liberties of their citizens. Written by Jefferson, the second declared that ultimate sovereignty rested with the states, which empowered them to "nullify" federal laws to which they objected.

election of 1800
Presidential election in which Thomas Jefferson defeated John Adams.

Madison discouraged radical activity that might provoke intervention by the national army, while Adams rejected demands by extreme "High Federalists" that he ensure victory by deliberately sparking an insurrection or asking Congress to declare war on France.

"Nothing but an open war can save us," argued one High Federalist cabinet officer. But when Adams suddenly learned in 1799 that France wanted peace, he proposed a special diplomatic mission. "Surprise, indignation, grief & disgust followed each other in quick succession," said a Federalist senator on hearing the news. Adams obtained Senate approval for his envoys only by threatening to resign and so make Jefferson president. Outraged High Federalists tried to dump Adams, but their ill-considered maneuver rallied most New Englanders around the stubborn, upright president.

Adams's envoys did not achieve a settlement with France until 1800, but his pursuit of peace with France prevented the Federalists from exploiting charges of Republican sympathy for the enemy. Without the immediate threat of war, moreover, voters grew resentful that in only two years, taxes had soared 33 percent to support an army that had done nothing except chase Pennsylvania farmers. As the danger of war receded, voters gave the Federalists less credit for standing up to France and more blame for adding $10 million to the national debt.

While High Federalists spitefully withheld the backing that Adams needed to win, Republicans redoubled their efforts to elect Jefferson. As a result of Republicans' mobilization of voters, popular interest in politics rose sharply. Voter turnout rose from about 15 percent in 1788 to almost 40 percent in 1800; in hotly contested Pennsylvania and New York, more than half the eligible voters participated.

Adams lost the presidency by just eight electoral votes out of 138. But Adams's loss did not ensure Jefferson's election. Because all 73 Republican electors voted for both Jefferson and their own choice for vice president, New York's Aaron Burr, the electoral college deadlocked in a tie between the two Republicans. Even more seriously than in 1796, the Constitution's failure to anticipate organized, rival parties affected the outcome of the electoral college's vote. The choice of president devolved upon the House of Representatives, where thirty-five ballots over six days produced no result. Aware that Republican voters and electors wanted Jefferson to be president, the wily Burr cast about for Federalist support. But after Hamilton—Burr's bitter rival in New York politics—declared his preference for Jefferson as "by far not so dangerous a man," a Federalist representative abandoned Burr and gave Jefferson the presidency by history's narrowest margin.

The Whole Vision

■ *Which groups experienced the greatest gains and losses in the early years of the new republic?*

The new United States underwent dramatic social, economic, and political changes during its first decades under the Constitution. Economically, the nation shifted from agricultural production for one's own use to production for market, and as it did, class and regional location would play a crucial role in who would fare best. Simply put, those best able to adapt to the changing landscape would do well, but that often had to do with status before the economy shifted. Farmers with larger landholdings in the Northeast who could serve the growing demand would fare better than smaller farmers and artisans, who were incorporated into the move toward factory-like production of manufactured goods. Women would benefit in some ways from the new awareness brought by the language of republicanism and virtue, but would find traditionalism remained a powerful and limiting force. Despite some efforts to aid Native Americans in safeguarding their lands, native peoples would see far more losses and increased pressure to assimilate to white ways, with dire consequences. Free blacks initially saw some progress in political rights, but would later experience new efforts to limit their social mobility and rights. Slavery, the institution that might have faded over time, was resuscitated by technological innovations and market demand for raw materials produced by slave labor.

■ *What were the points of unity and fissure in the new American government?*

Fears about the power of the central government that marked the debates about the Constitution continued as the new nation formed its first government. Some of those concerns were quelled by the unanimity that surrounded the choice of George Washington as the first president. As the federal government took shape, some powers were strengthened and others clarified, as the roles of president, Congress, and cabinet officials were outlined. Concerns about federal authority versus states' and individual rights were also eased by new legislative initiatives—compromises that sought to balance the visions of federalists and states' rights advocates, notably the Judiciary Act and the Bill of Rights. But tensions would again flare as Secretary of the Treasury Alexander Hamilton unveiled his program for promoting the nation's economic growth. His detailed report embraced the notion of debt—something most Americans were wary of—as a way of forging civic and political obligations. There were also concerns about his call to establish a national bank. Many also saw his programs as classist, benefiting one region over another, and giving some groups greater power to influence the central government. While his programs prevailed, they sparked factional dissent, early partisanship, and class tensions that manifested in the Whiskey Rebellion.

■ *How did foreign policy concerns inspire increased partisanship?*

The political divisiveness that began in the debates over Hamilton's program solidified as the nation sought to establish its footing in an international context, particularly one that became increasingly marked by conflict. Americans—both citizens and leaders—were divided in their opinions and loyalties concerning Spain (particularly as it sought to retain an American foothold) and Britain. There were serious divisions, too, over whether to support the French Revolution, especially as it became increasingly violent. Debates raged at the political level, as some leaders denounced the revolution as a "mobocracy" and others focused on the emphasis on liberty that it shared with the American Revolution. Opinions on France divided regionally, due largely to economic relationships both with that country and its rival, Britain. And after France went to war against Spain and Great Britain, the nation was torn about which side to support and opted instead for the equally unpopular neutrality. The U.S. was also plagued by divisions over how to resolve controversies over westward expansion, with Native Americans as well as Europeans still claiming parts of the region. Even treaties that ended disputes with native peoples and European nations provoked growing partisanship within the United States.

■ *How did political disputes in the early republic develop into the nation's first political parties?*

Political disagreements were a part of the new republic from the very beginning, but it was not until America faced early policy challenges that those differences began to harden into political parties. The first challenge came from Hamilton's programs and domestic policies; the second from foreign policy matters, most notably whether to ally with the French during its revolution. In fact, the French Revolution brought to the surface American leaders' differing views about democracy and split the former Federalists into Federalists and Republicans. These groups would debate the true meaning and legacy of the American Revolution and, in turn, the power of the people. The split had a direct impact on Washington's administration and would increasingly polarize the nation politically in ways the president—in his farewell address—deemed dangerous. The growing partisanship would shape the presidential election of 1796, the foreign policy views during the conflicts with France and Britain in 1798 and 1799, legislative initiatives such as the Alien and Sedition Acts, and the presidential election of 1800.

8 America at War and Peace, 1801–1824

WAR OF 1812 SCENE Captain Thomas Macdonough and his crew celebrate their victory over the British in the Battle of Lake Champlain, August 24, 1812. *(Granger, NYC—All rights reserved)*

CHRONOLOGY 1801–1824

1801	Thomas Jefferson's inauguration.
1801–1805	Tripolitan War.
1802	Repeal of the Judiciary Act of 1801.
	Yazoo land compromise.
1803	*Marbury* v. *Madison.*
	Conclusion of the Louisiana Purchase.
1804	Impeachment of Justice Samuel Chase.
	Aaron Burr kills Alexander Hamilton in a duel.
	Jefferson elected to a second term.
1804–1806	Lewis and Clark expedition.
1805	British court declares the broken voyage illegal.
1807	*Chesapeake* Affair.
	Embargo Act passed.
1808	James Madison elected president.
1809	Non-Intercourse Act passed.
	Embargo Act repealed.
1810	Macon's Bill No. 2.
1811	Battle of Tippecanoe.
1812	United States declares war on Britain.
	Madison reelected to a second term.

	General William Hull surrenders at Detroit.
	Battle of Queenston.
1813	Battle of the Thames.
1814	British burn Washington, D.C.
	Hartford Convention.
	Treaty of Ghent signed.
1815	Battle of New Orleans.
	Algerine War.
1816	James Monroe elected president.
	Second Bank of the United States chartered.
1817	Rush-Bagot Treaty.
1818	British-American Convention of 1818 sets U.S.–Canada border in West.
	Andrew Jackson invades East Florida.
1819	Adams-Onís (Transcontinental) Treaty.
	Dartmouth College v. *Woodward.*
	McCulloch v. *Maryland.*
1820	Monroe elected to a second term.
1820–1821	Missouri Compromise.
1823	Monroe Doctrine.

JEFFERSON'S TRIUMPH in the election of 1800, which Federalists interpreted as a victory for the "worthless, the dishonest, the rapacious, the vile and ungodly," left the bitter aftertaste of partisanship. Nevertheless, in his inaugural address, Jefferson struck a conciliatory note. He traced the political convulsions of the 1790s to different responses to the French Revolution, an external event whose fury had passed. What Americans needed to recognize, Jefferson stated, was that they agreed on essentials, that "we are all republicans, we are all federalists."

However, foreign affairs continued to agitate American politics. A month before Jefferson's inauguration, Tripoli, an Islamic state in North Africa, declared war on the United States. Since 1785, these "Barbary pirates" had been seizing American vessels and enslaving their crews. With its tiny navy, the United States had no choice but to pay exorbitant ransoms and bribes. The Muslim states sometimes justified their enslavement of Christian "infidels" on religious grounds, but Tripoli warred on the United States because its ruler wanted a bigger bribe.

Although he had opposed strengthening the navy during the 1798 Quasi-War with France in 1798—a view consistent with his loathing of expansive government—Jefferson now authorized hostilities. He believed that pirate states, once bribed, would demand greater "tributes and humiliations." The ensuing Tripolitan War (1801–1805) ended favorably for the United States. American naval success also depended on European events over which it had no control. Starting in 1805, Britain—alarmed by the French emperor Napoleon's military successes on the European continent—renewed its seizure of American merchant ships bound for ports controlled by Napoleon. Jefferson's answer to the renewed seizure of American ships was the Embargo Act of 1807, a self-blockade in which the United States sought to influence Britain and France by denying American trade to each. This policy of "peaceable coercion" failed, and in 1812 the United States

MAN OF THE PEOPLE, THOMAS JEFFERSON (*Library of Congress Prints and Photographs Division*)

211

went to war with Britain to secure respect for its trading rights as a neutral.

The treaty ending the War of 1812 did not guarantee neutral rights. But fortunately for the United States, the treaty coincided with Napoleon's decline. With peace in Europe, American trading ships enjoyed freedom of the seas for the next century. The American navy returned to the Mediterranean in 1815, trounced Algiers (the most aggressive of the pirate states), and then forced all the Barbary states to abandon forever their claims for tribute from the United States.

These developments fed American pride. However, the harmony for which Jefferson longed proved elusive. Between 1801 and 1824, the Federalist Party collapsed as a force in national politics. Yet the Federalists' decline opened the way to intensified factionalism within the Democratic-Republican Party, especially during Jefferson's second term (1805–1809) and during the mistakenly named Era of Good Feelings (1817–1824). Most ominously, between 1819 and 1821, northern and southern Democratic-Republicans split over the extension of slavery into Missouri.

8-1 The Age of Jefferson

Was Jefferson's election truly the "revolution" he claimed it to be?

Narrowly elected in 1800, Jefferson saw his popularity rise during his first term when he moved quickly to scale down government expenditures. Increasingly confident of popular support, he worked to loosen the Federalists' grip on appointive federal offices, especially in the judiciary. His purchase of Louisiana against Federalist opposition added to his popularity. In all of these moves, Jefferson was guided not merely by political calculation, but also by his philosophy of government—eventually known as Jeffersonianism.

8-1.1 Jefferson and Jeffersonianism

A man of extraordinary attainments, Jefferson was fluent in French, read Latin and Greek, and studied several Native American languages. He served for more than twenty years as president of America's foremost scientific association, the American Philosophical Society. A student of architecture, he designed his own mansion in Virginia, Monticello. Gadgets fascinated him. He invented a device for duplicating his letters, of which he wrote more than twenty thousand, and he improved the design for a revolving book stand, which enabled him to consult up to five books at once. His public career was luminous: principal author of the Declaration of Independence, governor of Virginia, ambassador to France, secretary of state under Washington, and vice president under John Adams.

Yet he was, and remains, a controversial figure. His critics, pointing to his doubts about some Christian doctrines and his early support for the French Revolution, portrayed him as an infidel and radical. Federalists alleged that he kept a slave

mistress, and in 1802 James Callender, a former supporter furious about not receiving a government job he wanted, wrote a newspaper account naming her as Sally Hemings, a house slave at Monticello. Drawing on the DNA of Sally's male descendents and linking the timing of Jefferson's visits to Monticello with the start of Sally's pregnancies, most scholars now view it as very likely that Jefferson, a widower, was the father of several of her children.

Callender's story did Jefferson little damage in Virginia because Jefferson had acted according to the rules of white Virginia gentlemen by never acknowledging any of Sally's children as his own. Although he freed two of her children (the other two ran away), he never freed Sally, the daughter of Jefferson's own father-in-law and so light-skinned that she could pass for white, nor did he ever mention her in his vast correspondence. Yet the story of Sally fed the charge that Jefferson was a hypocrite, for throughout his career he condemned the very "race-mixing" to which he appears to have contributed.

Jefferson did not believe that blacks and whites could live permanently side-by-side in American society. As the black population grew, he feared a race war so vicious that it could be suppressed only by a dictator. This view was consistent with his conviction that the real threat to republics rose less from hostile neighbors than from within. He believed that the French had turned to a dictator, Napoleon Bonaparte, to save them from the chaos of their own revolution. Only by colonizing blacks in Africa, an idea embodied in the American Colonization Society (1816), could America avert a similar fate, he believed.

Jefferson worried that high taxes, standing armies, and corruption could destroy American liberty by turning government into the master rather than servant of the people. He feared the monarchical tendencies he saw in the Federalists, which to Jefferson ran counter to the principles of the Revolution and the American republic. To prevent tyranny, he advocated that state governments retain considerable authority. In a vast republic, he reasoned, state governments would be more responsive to the popular will than would the central government in Washington.

He also believed that popular liberty required popular virtue. For republican theorists like Jefferson, virtue consisted of a decision to place the public good ahead of one's private interests and to exercise vigilance to keep governments from growing out of control. To Jefferson, the most vigilant and virtuous people were educated farmers who were accustomed to act and think with sturdy independence and as self-sufficient land-owners were beholden to no one. Jefferson regarded cities as breeding grounds for mobs and as menaces to liberty. Men who relied on merchants or factory owners for their jobs could have their votes influenced, unlike farmers who worked their own land. When the people "get piled upon one another in large cities, as in Europe," he wrote, "they will become corrupt as in Europe."

In fact, Jefferson's emphasis on "the people" likely fed the democratizing impulses of the early nineteenth century. By the 1790s, his party had added "Democratic" to its name, calling themselves Democratic-Republicans. The number of white male voters increased in the early decades of the nineteenth century, as states, such as New Jersey in 1807, removed property requirements from qualifications for voting. By 1830, ten states had adopted universal white manhood suffrage with no restrictions at all, and others had widened the pool of voters though with some qualifications. The tough economic times of the Panic of 1819 further fueled the trend (see Chapter 9) toward removing restrictions on voting and running for office. Though a democratizing trend, it occurred at the same time that access to voting was increasingly denied to free black men.

8-1.2 Jefferson's "Revolution"

Jefferson described his election as a revolution. But the revolution he sought was to restore the liberty and tranquility that (he thought) the United States had enjoyed in its early years and to reverse what he saw as a drift into despotism. The $10 million growth in the national debt under the Federalists alarmed Jefferson and his secretary of the treasury, Albert Gallatin. They rejected Hamilton's idea that a national debt would strengthen the government by giving creditors a stake in its health. Just paying the interest on the debt would require taxes, which would suck money from industrious farmers—the backbone of the Republic. The money would then fall into the hands of creditors, parasites who leeched off interest payments. Increased tax revenues might also tempt the government to establish a standing army, always a threat to liberty.

Jefferson and Gallatin secured the repeal of many taxes, and they slashed expenditures by closing some embassies overseas and reducing the army, which declined from an authorized strength of over 14,000 in 1798 to 3,287 in 1802. A lull in the war between Britain and France that had threatened American shipping in the 1790s persuaded Jefferson that minimal military preparedness was a sound policy: "We can now proceed without risks in demolishing useless structures of expense, lightening the burdens of our constituents, and fortifying the principles of free government." This may have been wishful thinking, but it rested on a sound economic calculation, for the vast territory of the United States could not be secured from attack without astronomical expense.

8-1.3 Jefferson and the Judiciary

Jefferson hoped to conciliate the moderate Federalists, but conflicts over the judiciary derailed this objective. Washington and Adams had appointed only Federalists to the bench, including the new chief justice, **John Marshall**. Still bitter about the zeal of federal courts in enforcing the Alien and Sedition Acts, Jefferson saw the Federalist-sponsored Judiciary Act of 1801 as the last straw. By reducing the number of Supreme Court justices from six to five, the act threatened to strip him of an early opportunity to appoint a justice. At the same time, the act created sixteen new federal judgeships, which outgoing president John Adams had filled by last-minute ("midnight") appointments of Federalists. To Jefferson, this was proof that the Federalists intended to use the judiciary as a stronghold from which "all the works of Republicanism are to be beaten down and erased." In 1802, he won congressional repeal of the Judiciary Act of 1801.

Jefferson's troubles with the judiciary were not over. On his last day in office, Adams had appointed a Federalist, William Marbury, as justice of the peace in the District of Columbia but failed to deliver Marbury's commission before midnight. When Jefferson's secretary of state, James Madison, refused to send him notice of the appointment, Marbury petitioned the Supreme Court to issue a writ compelling delivery. In *Marbury* v. *Madison* (1803), Chief Justice John Marshall

BURNING OF THE *PHILADELPHIA* The American frigate Philadelphia ran aground in the shallow waters guarding Tripoli harbor. Both the ship and its crew of more than 300 were captured. This incident prompted what a British admiral called "the most bold and daring act of the age" when, on the evening of February 16, 1804, a small American force led by Lt. Stephen Decatur slipped into Tripoli harbor and boarded and burned the *Philadelphia*. *(The Mariners' Museum, Newport News, VA)*

wrote the unanimous opinion. Marshall ruled that, although Madison should have delivered Marbury's commission, he was under no legal obligation to do so because part of the Judiciary Act of 1789 that had granted the Court the authority to issue such a writ as unconstitutional.

For the first time, the Supreme Court had asserted its authority to void an act of Congress on the grounds that it was "repugnant" to the Constitution. Jefferson did not reject this principle, known as the doctrine of judicial review and destined to become highly influential, but he was enraged that Marshall had used part of his decision to lecture Madison on his moral duty (as opposed to his legal obligation) to deliver Marbury's commission. This gratuitous lecture, which was really directed at Jefferson as Madison's superior, struck Jefferson as another example of Federalist partisanship.

While the *Marbury* decision was brewing, the Democratic-Republicans took the offensive against the judiciary by moving to impeach (charge with wrongdoing) two Federalist judges, John Pickering and Samuel Chase. Pickering, an insane alcoholic, was quickly removed from office, but Chase presented difficulties. He was a partisan Federalist notorious for jailing several Democratic-Republican editors under the Sedition Act of 1798. Nonetheless, the Constitution specified that judges could be impeached only for treason, bribery, and "high Crimes and Misdemeanors." Was impeachment appropriate because a judge was excessively partisan? Moderate Democratic-Republicans came to doubt it, and partly for that reason, the Senate narrowly failed to convict Chase.

Chase's acquittal ended Jefferson's skirmishes with the judiciary. Unlike his radical followers, Jefferson objected neither to judicial review nor to an appointed judiciary; he merely challenged Federalist use of judicial power for political goals. Yet there was always a gray area between law and politics. To Federalists, there was no conflict between protecting the Constitution and advancing their party's cause. Nor did the Federalists attempt to use their control of the federal judiciary to undo Jefferson's "revolution" of 1800. The Marshall court, for example, upheld the constitutionality of the repeal of the Judiciary Act of 1801. For his part, Jefferson never proposed to impeach Marshall.

8-1.4 Extending the Land: The Louisiana Purchase, 1803

Jefferson's goal of avoiding foreign entanglements would remain beyond reach as long as European powers had large landholdings in North America. Spain owned East Florida and the vast Louisiana Territory, including New Orleans, and it claimed West Florida (now the southern portions of Alabama and Mississippi). In 1800, a weakened Spain returned Louisiana to France, which, under Napoleon Bonaparte, was fast emerging as Europe's strongest military power. Jefferson was appalled.

The president had long imagined the inevitable expansion of the free and virtuous American people would create an "empire of liberty." Spain was no obstacle, but Jefferson knew that Bonaparte's capacity for mischief was boundless. Bonaparte was sure of his destiny as a conqueror, and he dreamed of re-creating a French New World empire bordering the Caribbean and the Gulf of Mexico. The island of Saint Domingue (modern Haiti and the Dominican Republic) would be the fulcrum of the empire, and Louisiana would be its breadbasket. Before this dream could become a reality, however, the French would have to subdue Saint Domingue, where by 1800 a bloody slave revolution had resulted in a takeover of the government by the former slave Toussaint L'Ouverture (see Chapter 7). Bonaparte dispatched an army to reassert French control and reestablish slavery, but yellow fever and fierce resistance by former slaves doomed the French force.

In the short run, Jefferson worried most about New Orleans, the only port available for the $3 million in annual produce of farmers along the Ohio and Mississippi river system. The Spanish had temporarily granted Americans the right to park their produce there while awaiting transfer to seagoing vessels. But in 1802, the Spanish colonial administrator in New Orleans issued an order revoking this right. The order had originated in Spain, but most Americans assumed it had come from Bonaparte who, although he now owned Louisiana, had yet to take possession of it. An alarmed Jefferson described New Orleans as the "one single spot" on the globe whose possessor "is our natural and habitual enemy." "The day that France takes possession of N. Orleans," he added, "we must marry ourselves to the British fleet and nation."

The combination of France's failure to subdue Saint Domingue and the termination of American rights to deposit produce in New Orleans led to the American purchase of Louisiana. Jefferson dispatched James Monroe and Robert R. Livingston to Paris to buy New Orleans from France. Meanwhile, Bonaparte had concluded that his Caribbean empire was not worth the cost. In addition, he planned to resume war in Europe and needed cash. So he decided to sell *all* of Louisiana. The American commissioners and the French government settled on a price of $15 million. Thus, the United States gained an immense, uncharted territory between the Mississippi River and the Rocky Mountains (see Map 8.1). No one knew its exact size. Bonaparte's minister merely observed that the bargain was noble. But the **Louisiana Purchase** virtually doubled the area of the United States at a cost, omitting interest, of thirteen and one-half cents an acre.

Jefferson found himself caught between his ideals and reality. No provision of the Constitution explicitly authorized the government to acquire new territory. Jefferson believed in strict construction—the doctrine that the Constitution should be interpreted according to its letter—but he recognized that doubling the size of the republic would guarantee land for American farmers, the backbone of the nation and the true guardians of liberty. Strict construction was not an end in itself but a means to promote republican liberty. If that end could be achieved in some way other than by strict construction, so be it. Jefferson was also alert to practical considerations. Most Federalists opposed the Louisiana Purchase because it would decrease the relative importance of their strongholds on the eastern seaboard. As the leader of the Democratic-Republican Party, Jefferson saw no reason to hand the Federalists an issue by dallying over ratification of the treaty to reconcile constitutional issues.

8-1.5 The Election of 1804

Jefferson's acquisition of Louisiana left the Federalists dispirited and without a popular national issue. As the election of 1804 approached, the main threat to Jefferson was not the Federalist Party but his own vice president, Aaron Burr. In 1800, Burr had tried

> **Louisiana Purchase**
> The United States bought the Louisiana Territory (the area from the Mississippi River to the Rocky Mountains) from France in 1803 for $15 million. The purchase virtually doubled the area of the United States at a cost, omitting interest, of thirteen and one-half cents an acre.

MAP 8.1 THE LOUISIANA PURCHASE AND THE EXPLORATION OF THE WEST The explorations of Lewis and Clark demonstrated the vast extent of the area purchased from France.

to take advantage of a tie in the Electoral College to gain the presidency, a betrayal in the eyes of most Democratic-Republicans who assumed he had been nominated for the vice presidency. The adoption in 1804 of the Twelfth Amendment, which required separate and distinct ballots in the Electoral College for the presidential and the vice-presidential candidates, clarified the electoral process, but did not end Burr's conniving. He had spent much of his vice presidency in intrigues with the Federalists. The Democratic-Republicans dumped him from their ticket in 1804 in favor of George Clinton. In the election, the Federalist nominees Charles C. Pinckney and Rufus King carried only two states, failing to hold even Massachusetts. Jefferson's overwhelming victory brought his first term to a fitting close. Between 1801 and 1804, the United States had doubled its territory and started to pay off its debt.

8-1.6 Exploring the Land: The Lewis and Clark Expedition

Louisiana dazzled Jefferson's imagination. Americans knew virtually nothing about the immense territory, not even its western boundary. A case could be made for the Pacific Ocean, but Spain claimed part of the Pacific coast. Jefferson was content to claim that Louisiana extended at least to the mountains west of the Mississippi, which few citizens of the United States had ever seen. Thus, the Louisiana Purchase was both a bargain and a surprise package.

Even before the acquisition of Louisiana, Jefferson had planned an exploratory expedition; picked its leader, his personal secretary and fellow Virginian Lieutenant Meriwether Lewis; and sent him to Philadelphia for a crash course in sciences such as zoology, astronomy, and botany that were relevant to exploration. Jefferson was genuinely interested in gathering scientific information. His instructions to Lewis cited the need to learn about Indian languages and customs, climate, plants, birds, reptiles, and insects. Above all, Jefferson hoped the **Lewis and Clark expedition** would find a water route across the continent to the Pacific Ocean. The potential economic benefits from such a route included diverting the lucrative fur trade from Canadian to American hands and boosting trade with China.

Setting forth from St. Louis in May 1804, Lewis, his second-in-command William Clark, and about fifty others followed the Missouri River and then the

Lewis and Clark expedition
Expedition led by Meriwether Lewis and William Clark to explore the Louisiana Territory. Jefferson instructed Lewis to trace the Missouri River to its source, cross the western highlands, and follow the best water route to the Pacific. He ordered Lewis to learn about Indian languages and customs, climate, plants, birds, reptiles, and insects.

Snake and Columbia rivers (see Going to the Source). In the Dakota country, Lewis and Clark hired a French-Canadian fur trader, Toussaint Charbonneau, as a guide and interpreter. Slow-witted and inclined to panic, Charbonneau proved to be a mixed blessing, but his wife, **Sacajawea**, who accompanied him on the trip, made up for his failings and served as a guide. A Shoshone and probably no more than sixteen years old in 1804, Sacajawea had been stolen by a rival tribe and then claimed by Charbonneau. When first encountered by Lewis and Clark, she had just given birth to a son; indeed, the infant's presence helped reassure Native American tribes of the expedition's peaceful intent.

Still, Lewis and Clark faced obstacles. The expedition brought them in contact with numerous tribes, most importantly the powerful Sioux but also Mandans, Hidatsas, and Arikaras, each with a history of warring on other tribes and of its own internal feuds. Reliant on Indians for guides, packers, and interpreters, Lewis and Clark had to become instant diplomats. Jefferson had told them to assert American sovereignty over the Purchase. This objective led them to distribute medals and uniforms to chiefs ready to support American authority and to stage periodic military parades and displays of their weapons, which included cannons. But no tribe had a single chief; rather, different tribal villages had different chiefs. At times, Lewis and Clark miscalculated, for example, when they treated an Arikara chief as the "grand chief," to the outrage of his rivals. Yet their diplomacy generally was successful because they avoided violence.

The group finally reached the Pacific Ocean in November 1805 and then returned to St. Louis, but not before collecting a mass of scientific information, including the disturbing fact that more than three hundred miles of mountains separated the Missouri from the Columbia. The expedition's drawings of the geography of the region led to more accurate maps and heightened interest in the West.

LEWIS AND CLARK WITH SACAJAWEA. Artist's rendering of Sacajawea serving as a guide for Meriwether Lewis and William Clark on their exploration of the territory acquired in the Louisiana Purchase. *(Lewis and Clark with Sacagawea (colour litho) (detail), Paxson, Edgar Samuel (1852–1915) / Private Collection / Peter Newark American Pictures / The Bridgeman Art Library International)*

8-2 The Gathering Storm

What challenges to American government and national sovereignty did the United States face in the early decades of the nineteenth century?

In gaining control of Louisiana, the United States had benefited from the preoccupation of European powers with their own struggles. But between 1803 and 1814, the renewal of the Napoleonic Wars in Europe turned the United States into a pawn in a chess game played by others and helped make Jefferson's second term far less successful than his first.

Europe was not Jefferson's only problem. He had to deal with a conspiracy to dismantle the United States, the product of the inventive and perverse mind of Aaron Burr, and to face down challenges within his own party, led by John Randolph.

8-2.1 Challenges on the Home Front

Aaron Burr suffered a string of reverses in 1804. After being denied renomination as vice president, he entered into a series of intrigues with a faction of despairing and extreme

> **Sacajawea**
> Indian girl who accompanied Lewis and Clark during their expedition and served as their guide.

(or "High") Federalists in New England. Led by Senator Timothy Pickering of Massachusetts, these High Federalists plotted to sever the Union by forming a pro-British Northern Confederacy composed of Nova Scotia (part of British-owned Canada), New England, New York, and even Pennsylvania. Although most Federalists disdained the plot, Pickering and others settled on Burr as their leader and helped him gain the Federalist nomination for the governorship of New York. Alexander Hamilton, who had thwarted Burr's grab for the presidency in 1800 by throwing his weight behind Jefferson, now foiled Burr a second time by allowing publication of his "despicable opinion" of Burr. Defeated in the election for New York's governor, Burr challenged Hamilton to a duel and mortally wounded him at Weehawken, New Jersey, on July 11, 1804.

Indicted in two states for murdering Hamilton, Burr—still vice president—now hatched a scheme so bold that not even his political opponents could believe him capable of such treachery. He allied himself with the unsavory military governor of the Louisiana Territory, General James Wilkinson, who had been on Spain's payroll intermittently as a secret agent since the 1780s. Their plot had several dimensions: they would create an independent confederacy of western states, conquer Mexico, and invade West Florida. The scheming duo presented the plot imaginatively. To westerners, they said it had the covert support of the Jefferson administration; to the British, that it was a way to attack Spanish lands; and to the Spanish, that it would open the way to dividing up the United States.

By the fall of 1806, Burr and about sixty followers were making their way down the Ohio and Mississippi rivers to join Wilkinson at Natchez. In October 1806, Jefferson denounced the conspiracy. Wilkinson abandoned the plot and proclaimed himself the most loyal of Jefferson's followers. Burr tried to escape to West Florida but was intercepted. Brought back to Richmond, he was put on trial for treason. Chief Justice Marshall presided at the trial and instructed the jury that the prosecution had to prove actual treasonable acts—an impossible task because the conspiracy had never reached fruition. Jefferson was furious, but Marshall was merely following the clear wording of the Constitution, which deliberately made treason difficult to prove. The jury returned a verdict of not proved, which Marshall entered as "not guilty." Still under indictment for his murder of Hamilton, Burr fled to Europe where he tried to interest Napoleon in making peace with Britain as a prelude to a proposed Anglo-French invasion of the United States and Mexico.

PLAINS PIPE BOWL Instructed by Jefferson to acquaint themselves with the Indians' "ordinary occupations in the arts," Lewis and Clark collected this Lakota sacred pipe, whose red stone symbolized the flesh and blood of all people and whose smoke represented the breath that carries prayers to the Creator. Considering pipes sacred objects, Indians used them to seal contracts and treaties and to perform ceremonial healing. *(Gift of the Heirs of David Kimball. (c) President and Fellows of Harvard College, Peabody Museum of Archaeology and Ethnology, PM# 99-12-10/53106.1 (T3038).)*

Besides the Burr conspiracy, Jefferson faced a challenge from a group of Democratic-Republicans led by the president's fellow Virginian, John Randolph, a man of abounding eccentricities and acerbic wit. Like many propertied Americans of the 1770s, Randolph believed that governments always menaced popular liberty. Jefferson had originally shared this view, but he recognized it as an ideology of opposition, not power; once in office, he compromised. In contrast, Randolph remained frozen in the 1770s, denouncing every government action as decline and proclaiming that he would throw all politicians to the dogs except that he had too much respect for dogs.

Randolph turned on Jefferson, most notably, for backing a compromise in the Yazoo land scandal. In 1795, the Georgia legislature had sold the huge Yazoo tract (35 million acres—most of present-day Alabama and Mississippi) for a fraction of its value to land companies that had bribed virtually the entire legislature. The next legislature canceled the sale, but many investors, knowing nothing of the bribery, had already bought land in good faith. In 1803, a federal commission compromised with an award of 5 million acres to Yazoo investors. For Randolph, the compromise was itself a scandal—further evidence of the decay of republican virtue.

Meriwether Lewis's Journal

President Jefferson had instructed Meriwether Lewis and William Clark to trace the Missouri River to its source. Friendly Indians told them that the river originated in great falls in the mountains. Lewis and Clark knew they were near the source, but on June 3, 1805, they came to a fork in the Missouri. Scouting parties briefly followed each fork, but without conclusive results. The right (north) fork, now the Marias River, looked exactly like the Missouri River that Lewis and Clark had followed for a thousand miles, but taking it would have led them to oblivion. Against the opinion of most members of their expedition, Lewis and Clark chose the left (south) fork and two days later came upon great falls, the source of the Missouri. Lewis described the choice in his journal.

This morning early we passed over and formed a camp on the point formed by the junction of the two large rivers. . . . An interesting question was now to be determined; which of these rivers was the Missouri. . . . To mistake the stream at this period of the season, two months of the traveling season having now elapsed, and to ascend such stream . . . and then be obliged to return and take the other stream would not only loose us the whole of this season but would probably so dishearten the party that it might defeat the expedition altogether. . . . The no[r]th fork is deeper than the other but it's courant not so swift; it's waters run in the same boiling and roling manner which has uniformly characterized the Missouri throughout it's whole course so far; it's waters are of a whitish brown colour[,] very thick and t[u]rbid, also characteristic of the Missouri; while the South fork is perfectly transparent [and] runs very rappid but with a smooth unriffled surface[,] it's bottom composed of round and flat smooth stones like most rivers issuing from a mountainous country. The bed of the N[orth] fork [is] composed of some gravel but principally mud; in short the air & character of this river is so precisely that of the Missouri below that the party with very few exceptions have already pronounced the N[orth] fork to be the Missouri; myself and Capt. C[lark] not quite so precipitate have not yet decided but if we were to give our opinions I believe we should be in the minority, certain it is that the North fork gives the colouring matter and character which is retained from hence to the gulph of Mexico. . . . Convinced I am that if [the North fork] penetrated the Rocky Mountains to any great extent it's waters would be clearer unless it should run an immence distance indeed after leaving those mountains through those level plains in order to acquire its turbid hue. What astonishes us a little is that the Indians who appeared to be so well acquainted with the geography of this country should not have mentioned this river on [the] [r]ight hand if it not be the Missouri; *the river that scolds all others* as they call it if there is in reality such an one, ought agreeably to their account to have fallen in a considerable distance below, and on the other hand if this right hand or N[orth] fork be the Missouri I am equally astonished at their not mentioning the S[outh] fork which they must have passed to get to those large falls which they mention on the Missouri. Thus have our cogitating faculties been busily employed all day.

Source: *Reuben Gold Thwaites, ed.,* Original Journals of the Lewis and Clark Expedition, 1804–1806, *volume 2 [1904].*

QUESTIONS

1. Which fork would you have taken?
2. Why did President Jefferson think it was important to American strategic interests that Lewis and Clark find the source of the Missouri river?

8-2.2 The Suppression of American Trade and Impressment

Burr's acquittal and Randolph's taunts shattered the aura of invincibility surrounding Jefferson. Now foreign affairs posed an even sharper challenge. As Britain and France resumed their war in Europe, U.S. merchants prospered by carrying sugar and coffee from the French and Spanish Caribbean colonies to Europe. This trade not only provided Napoleon with supplies but also drove down the price of sugar and coffee from British colonies by adding to the glut of these commodities on the world market. The British concluded that their economic problems stemmed from American prosperity.

For Americans, this boom depended on the re-export trade, which evaded British regulations. According to the British Rule of 1756, any trade closed during peacetime could not be opened during war; if it was, the British would stop it. For example, France usually restricted the sugar trade with Europe to French ships during peacetime and thus could not open it to American ships during war. The U.S. response to the Rule of 1756 was the "broken voyage," by which U.S. ships carried French sugar or coffee to American ports, unloaded it, passed it through customs, and then re-exported it as *American* produce. Britain tolerated this dodge for nearly a decade but in 1805 initiated a policy of total war toward France, including the strangulation of French trade. In 1805, a British court declared broken voyages illegal.

Next came a series of British trade decrees ("Orders in Council") that established a blockade of French-controlled ports on the coast of Europe. Napoleon responded with his so-called Continental System, a series of counter-proclamations that ships obeying British regulations would be subject to seizure by France. In effect, this Anglo-French war of decrees outlawed virtually all U.S. trade; if an American ship complied with British regulations, it became a French target, and vice versa.

Both Britain and France seized American ships, but British seizures were far more humiliating to Americans. Because France was a weaker naval power than Britain, most of France's seizures of American ships occurred in European ports where American ships had been lured by Napoleon's often inconsistent enforcement of his Continental System. In contrast, British warships hovered just beyond the American coast. The Royal Navy stopped and searched virtually every American vessel off New York, for example. At times, U.S. ships had to line up a few miles from the American coast to be searched by the Royal Navy.

To these provocations, the British added **impressment**. Royal Navy press gangs had long scoured the docks and taverns of British ports and forced ("pressed") civilians into service. As war with France intensified Britain's need for sailors, Britain increasingly extended the practice to seizing alleged Royal Navy deserters on American merchant ships. British sailors had good reason to be discontented with their navy. Discipline on the Royal Navy's "floating hells" was often brutal and the pay low; sailors on American ships made up to five times more than those on British ships. Consequently, the Royal Navy suffered a high rate of desertion to American ships. In 1807, for example, 149 of the 419 sailors on the American warship *Constitution* were British subjects. Although less damaging to the American economy than the seizure of ships, impressment was equally galling. Even American-born seamen, six thousand between 1803 and 1812, were impressed into the Royal Navy. British arrogance peaked in June 1807. A British warship, HMS *Leopard*, patrolling off Virginia, attacked an unsuspecting American frigate, USS *Chesapeake*, and forced it to surrender. The British then boarded the vessel and seized four supposed deserters. One, a genuine deserter, was later hanged; the other three, former Britons, had "deserted" only from impressments and were now American citizens. The so-called *Chesapeake-Leopard* Affair enraged the country. Jefferson remarked that he had not seen so belligerent a spirit in America since 1775.

8-2.3 The Embargo Act of 1807

Yet while making some preparations for war, Jefferson adopted "peaceable coercion" by suspending trade with Britain and France to gain respect for neutral rights. By far the most controversial legislation of either of Jefferson's terms, the **Embargo Act of 1807** prohibited vessels from leaving American ports for foreign ports. Technically, it prohibited only exports, but its practical effect was to stop imports as well, for few foreign ships would venture into American ports if they had to leave without cargo. Amazed by the boldness of the act, a British newspaper described the embargo as "little short of an absolute secession from the rest of the civilized world." Just as in the pre-Revolutionary rebellion against Britain, American women answered the call to support the embargo by boycotting British goods.

The embargo did not have the intended effect. Although British sales to the United States dropped 50 percent between 1807 and 1808, the British quickly found new markets in South America, where rebellions against Spanish rule had flared up. Furthermore, the Embargo Act contained some loopholes. For example,

Impressment
The practice of forcing civilians into military service. It was used widely by the British, and antagonized Americans, in the years leading up to the War of 1812.

Embargo Act of 1807
This law prohibited vessels from leaving American ports for foreign ports. Technically, it prohibited only exports, but its practical effect was to stop imports as well, for few foreign ships would venture into American ports if they had to leave without cargo.

"PERRY'S VICTORY AT PUT-IN-BAY, 1813" After four-fifths of his crew on the brig *Lawrence* had been killed or wounded, Commandant Oliver H. Perry transferred his flag to the brig *Niagara*. It bore the words "Don't give up the Ship," the last reported words of Captain James Lawrence on the USS *Chesapeake* in 1807. After the battle, Perry sent a message to General William Henry Harrison: "We have met the enemy and they are ours. Two ships, two brigs, one schooner and one sloop." *(The Art Archive at Art Resource, NY)*

it allowed American ships blown off course to put in at European ports if necessary; suddenly, many captains were reporting that adverse winds had forced them across the Atlantic. Treating the embargo as a joke, Napoleon seized any American ships he could lay hands on and then informed the United States that he was only helping to enforce the embargo. The British were less amused, but the embargo confirmed their view that Jefferson was an ineffectual philosopher, an impotent challenger compared with Napoleon.

The United States itself felt the harshest effects of the embargo. Some thirty thousand American seamen found themselves out of work. Hundreds of merchants went into bankruptcy, and jails swelled with debtors. A New York City newspaper noted that the only activity still flourishing in the city was prosecution for debt. Farmers were devastated. Unable to export their produce or sell it at a decent price to hard-pressed urban dwellers, many farmers could not pay their debts. In desperation, one farmer in Schoharie County, New York, sold his cattle, horses, and farm

implements, worth eight hundred dollars before the embargo, for fifty-five dollars. Speculators who had purchased land, expecting to sell it later at a higher price, also took a beating because cash-starved farmers stopped buying land. "I live and that is all," wrote one New York speculator. "I am doing no business, cannot sell anybody property, nor collect any money."

The embargo fell hardest on New England, especially Massachusetts, which in 1807 had twice the ship tonnage per capita of any other state and more than a third of the entire nation's ship tonnage in foreign trade. For a state so dependent on foreign trade, the embargo was a calamity.

The situation was not entirely bleak. The embargo forced a diversion of merchants' capital into manufacturing. Before 1808, the United States had only fifteen mills for fashioning cotton into textiles; by the end of 1809, an additional eighty-seven mills had been constructed (as discussed in Chapter 9). But none of this comforted merchants already ruined or mariners driven to soup kitchens. Nor could New

Englanders forget that the source of their misery was a policy initiated by one of the "Virginia lordlings," "Mad Tom" Jefferson, who knew little about New England and who had a dogmatic loathing of cities, the very foundations of New England's prosperity. A Massachusetts poet wrote,

Our ships all in motion once whitened the ocean,
They sailed and returned with a cargo
Now doomed to decay they have fallen a prey
To Jefferson, worms, and embargo

8-2.4 James Madison and the Failure of Peaceable Coercion

Even before the Embargo Act, Jefferson had announced that he would not be a candidate for reelection. With his blessing, the Democratic-Republican congressional caucus nominated **James Madison** and George Clinton for the presidency and vice presidency. The Federalists countered with Charles C. Pinckney and Rufus King, the same ticket that had made a negligible showing in 1804. In 1808, the Federalists staged a modest comeback, gaining twenty-four congressional seats. Still, Madison won 122 of 175 electoral votes for president, and the Democratic-Republicans retained control of Congress.

The Federalist revival, modest as it was, rested on two factors. First, Federalist opposition to the Embargo Act gave the party a national issue it had long lacked. Second, younger Federalists had abandoned their elders' gentlemanly disdain for campaigning and deliberately imitated vote-winning techniques such as barbecues and mass meetings that had worked for the Democratic-Republicans.

To some contemporaries, "Little Jemmy" Madison, five feet, four inches tall, seemed a weak and shadowy figure compared to Jefferson. In fact, Madison's intelligence and capacity for systematic thought matched Jefferson's. He had the added advantage of being married to Dolley Madison. A striking figure in her turbans and colorful dresses, Dolley arranged receptions at the White House in which she charmed Democratic-Republicans, and even some Federalists, into sympathy with her husband's policies.

Madison continued the embargo with minor changes. Like Jefferson, he reasoned that Britain was "more vulnerable in her commerce than in her armies." The American embargo, however, was coercing no one, and on March 1, 1809, Congress replaced the Embargo Act with the weaker, face-saving Non-Intercourse Act. This act opened trade to all nations except

James Madison
Elected president of the United States in 1808; was the nation's leader during the War of 1812.

war hawks
Militant Democratic-Republicans who demanded more aggressive policies.

Britain and France and then authorized the president to restore trade with either of those nations if it stopped violating neutral rights. But neither complied. In May 1810, Congress substituted a new measure, Macon's Bill No. 2. This legislation opened trade with Britain and France, and then offered each a clumsy bribe: If either nation repealed its restrictions on neutral shipping, the United States would halt trade with the other.

None of these steps had the desired effect. While Jefferson and Madison lashed out at France and Britain as moral demons ("The one is a den of robbers and the other of pirates," snapped Jefferson), the belligerents saw the world as composed of a few great powers and many weak ones. When great powers went to war, there were no neutrals. Weak nations like the United States should stop babbling about moral ideals and seek the protection of a great power. Neither Napoleon nor the British intended to accommodate the Americans.

As peaceable coercion became a fiasco, Madison came under fire from militant Democratic-Republicans, known as **war hawks**, who demanded more aggressive policies. Coming mainly from the South and West, regions where "honor" was a sacred word, the militants were infuriated by insults to the American flag. In addition, economic recession between 1808 and 1810 had convinced the firebrands that British policies were wrecking their regions' economies. The election of 1810 brought several war hawks to Congress. Led by thirty-four-year-old Henry Clay of Kentucky, who preferred war to the "putrescent pool of ignominious peace," the war hawks included John C. Calhoun of South Carolina, Richard M. Johnson of Kentucky, and William King of North Carolina, all future vice presidents. Clay was elected Speaker of the House.

8-2.5 Tecumseh and the Prophet

More emotional and pugnaciously nationalistic than Jefferson and Madison, the war hawks called for the expulsion of the British from Canada and the Spanish from the Floridas. Their demands merged with western settlers' fears that the British in Canada were actively recruiting the Indians to halt the march of American settlement. In reality, American policy, not meddling by the British, was the source of bloodshed on the frontier.

In contrast to his views about blacks, Jefferson believed that Indians and whites could live peacefully together if the Indians abandoned their hunting and nomadic ways and took up farming. If they farmed, they would need less land. Jefferson and Madison insisted that the Indians be compensated fairly for ceded land and that only those Indians with a claim to the land they were ceding be allowed to conclude treaties with whites. Reality conflicted with Jefferson's ideals (see Chapter 7). The march of white settlement was steadily shrinking Indian hunting grounds, while some Indians themselves were becoming more willing to sign away land in payment to whites for blankets, guns, and the liquor that transported them into a daze even as their culture collapsed.

In 1809, no American was more eager to acquire Indian lands than William Henry Harrison, the governor of the Indiana Territory. The federal government had just divided Indiana, splitting off the present states of Illinois and Wisconsin into a separate Illinois Territory. Harrison recognized that, shorn of Illinois, Indiana would not achieve statehood unless it could attract more settlers by offering them land currently owned by Indians. Disregarding instructions from Washington to negotiate only with Indians who claimed the land they were ceding, Harrison rounded up a delegation of half-starved Indians, none of whom lived on the rich lands along the Wabash River that he craved. By the Treaty of Fort Wayne in September 1809, these Indians ceded millions of acres along the Wabash at a price of two cents an acre.

This treaty outraged the numerous tribes that had not been party to it. Among the angriest were **Tecumseh**, the Shawnee chief, and his brother, Lalawéthica. Late in 1805, Lalawéthica had had a frightening dream in which he saw drunken Indians tormented for eternity. Overnight, Lalawéthica was transformed from a drunken misfit into a preacher. He gave up liquor and began pleading with Indians to return to their traditional ways and to avoid contact with whites. He quickly became known as the Prophet. Soon, he would take a new name, **Tenskwatawa**, styling himself the "Open Door" through which all Indians could revitalize their culture. Shawnees listened to his message.

In the meantime, Tecumseh sought to build a coalition of several tribes to stem the tide of white settlement. He insisted that Indian lands belonged collectively to all the tribes and hence could not be sold by splinter groups. Failing to reach a settlement with Tecumseh or the Prophet, Harrison concluded that it was time to attack the Indians. His target was a Shawnee encampment called Prophetstown near the mouth of the Tippecanoe River. With Tecumseh away recruiting southern Indians to his cause, Tenskwatawa ordered an attack on Harrison's encampment, a mile from Prophetstown, in the predawn hours of November 7, 1811. Outnumbered two to one and short of ammunition, Tenskwatawa's force was beaten off after inflicting heavy casualties.

Although it was a small engagement, the Battle of Tippecanoe had several large effects. It made Harrison a national hero, and the memory of the battle would contribute to his election as president three decades later. It discredited Tenskwatawa, whose conduct during the battle drew criticism from his followers. It elevated Tecumseh into a position of recognized leadership

PORTRAIT OF TECUMSEH Also known as the Prophet a Shawnee leader who sought to unite Indian groups and stop the spread of white settlement and influence. *(ClassicStock.com/Superstock)*

among the western tribes. Finally, it persuaded Tecumseh, who long had distrusted the British as much as the Americans, that alliance with the British was the only way to stop the spread of American settlement.

8-2.6 Congress Votes for War

By spring 1812, President Madison had decided that war with Britain was inevitable. On June 1, he sent his war message to Congress. Meanwhile, an economic depression struck Britain, partly because the American policy of restricting trade

Tecumseh
The Shawnee leader who sought to unite several tribes in Ohio and the Indiana Territory against American settlers.

Tenskwatawa
Tecumseh's brother who was looked down on by fellow Shawnees as a drunken mischief. Later on, he gave up liquor and began tearful preaching to surrounding tribes to return to their old ways and to avoid contact with whites. He quickly became known as the Prophet.

with that country had finally started to work. Under pressure from its merchants, Britain suspended the Orders in Council on June 23. But Congress had already passed the declaration of war. Furthermore, Britain's suspension failed to meet Madison's demand that Britain unilaterally pledge to respect the rights of neutrals.

Neither war hawks nor westerners held the key to the vote in favor of war. The West was still too sparsely settled to have many representatives in Congress. Rather, the votes of Democratic-Republicans in populous states like Pennsylvania, Maryland, and Virginia were the main force propelling the war declaration through Congress. Opposition to war came mostly from the Northeast, with its Federalist strongholds in Massachusetts, Connecticut, and New York. Congressional opposition to war thus revealed a sectional as well as a party split. In general, however, southern Federalists opposed the war declaration, and northern Democratic-Republicans supported it. In other words, the vote for war followed party lines more closely than sectional lines. Much like James Madison himself, the typical Democratic-Republican advocate of war had not wanted war in 1810, or even in 1811, but had been led by the accumulation of grievances to demand it in 1812.

In his war message, Madison had listed impressment, the continued presence of British ships in American waters, and British violations of neutral rights as grievances that justified war. None of these complaints fully explains why Americans went to war in 1812 rather than earlier—for example, in 1807 after the *Chesapeake-Leopard* Affair. Madison also listed British incitement of the Indians as a stimulus for war. This grievance contributed to war feeling in the West, but the West had too few American inhabitants to drive the nation into war. A more important underlying cause was the economic recession that affected the South and West after 1808, as well as the conviction, held by John C. Calhoun and others, that British policy was damaging America's economy.

Finally, it was vitally important that Madison rather than Jefferson was president in 1812. Jefferson had believed Britain was motivated primarily by its desire to defeat Napoleon and that once the war in Europe ended, the provocations would stop. Madison held that Britain's real motive was to strangle American trade once and for all and thereby

"A SCENE FROM THE FRONTIER AS PRACTICED BY THE HUMANE BRITISH AND THEIR WORTHY ALLIES" In his 1812 War Message to Congress, President James Madison accused British traders and garrisons on the frontier of encouraging the sort of warfare practiced by the "Savages," "peculiarly shocking to humanity." Here, an Indian scalps a white while a British officer promises another Indian a reward for scalps. *(Library of Congress Prints and Photographs Division)*

eliminate the United States as a trading rival. In his war message, he stated flatly that Britain was meddling with American trade not because trade interfered with Britain's "belligerent rights" but because it "frustrated the monopoly which she covets for her own commerce and navigation."

8-3 The War of 1812

What is the best way to understand the War of 1812 and its place in U.S. history?

Although American cruisers, notably the *Constitution*, would win a few sensational duels with British warships, the U.S. Navy could not prevent the British from clamping a naval blockade on the American coast. Canada, which Madison viewed as a key prop of the British Empire, became the principal target. With their vastly larger population and resources, few Americans expected a long or difficult struggle. To Jefferson, the conquest of Canada seemed "a mere matter of marching."

Little justified this optimism. Although many Canadians were immigrants from the United States, to the Americans' surprise they fought to repel the invaders. Many of the best British troops were in Europe fighting Napoleon, but the British enlisted Native Americans—and used fear of these "uncontrollable savages" to force American surrenders. The American state militias were filled with Sunday soldiers who "hollered for water half the time, and whiskey the other." Few militiamen understood the goals of the war. In fact, outside Congress there was not much blood lust in 1812. Opposition to the war ran strong in New England; and even in Kentucky, the home of war hawk Henry Clay, only four hundred answered the first call to arms. For many Americans, local attachments were still stronger than national ones.

8-3.1 On to Canada

From the summer of 1812 to the spring of 1814, the Americans launched a series of unsuccessful attacks on Canada (see Map 8.2). In July 1812, General William Hull led an American army from Detroit into Canada, quickly returned when Tecumseh cut his supply line, and surrendered Detroit and two thousand men to thirteen hundred British and Indian troops. In the fall of 1812, the British and their Mohawk allies crushed a force of American regulars at the Battle of Queenston, near Niagara Falls, while New York militiamen, contending that they had volunteered only to protect their homes and not to invade Canada, looked on from the New York side of the border. A third American offensive in 1812, a projected attack on Montreal via Lake Champlain, fell apart when the militia again refused to advance into Canada.

Renewed American offensives and subsequent reverses in 1813 convinced the Americans that they could not retake Detroit while the British controlled Lake Erie. During the winter of 1812–1813, Captain Oliver H. Perry constructed a little fleet of vessels; on September 10, 1813, he destroyed a British squadron at Put-in-Bay on the western end of the lake. The British then pulled out of Detroit, but American forces under General William Henry Harrison overtook and defeated a combined British and Indian force at the Battle of the Thames on October 5, where Tecumseh died. These victories by Perry and Harrison cheered Americans, but efforts to invade Canada continued to falter. In June 1814, American troops crossed into Canada on the Niagara front but withdrew after fighting two bloody but inconclusive battles at Chippewa (July 5) and Lundy's Lane (July 25).

FIRST LADY DOLLEY MADISON BY REMBRANDT PEALE, CIRCA 1809 As the attractive young wife of Secretary of State James Madison, Dolley Madison acted virtually as the nation's First Lady during the administration of Jefferson, a widower. Friendly, tactful, and blessed with an unfailing memory for names and events, she added to her reputation as an elegant hostess after her husband became president. *(Rembrandt Peale/Bettmann/CORBIS)*

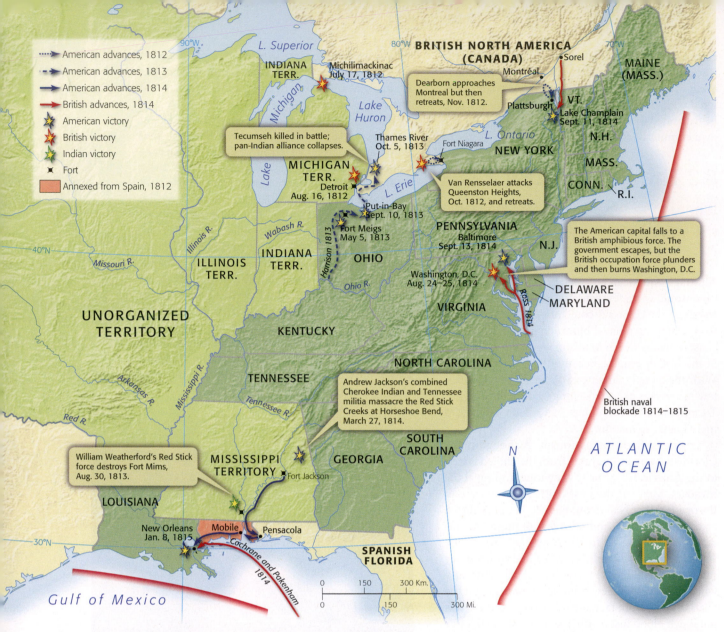

MAP 8.2 THE THREE U.S. INVASIONS OF 1812 Most of the war's major engagements occurred on or near the northern frontier of the United States, but the Royal Navy blockaded the entire Atlantic coast, and the British army penetrated as far south as Washington and New Orleans.

Legend:
- American advances, 1812
- American advances, 1813
- American advances, 1814
- British advances, 1814
- American victory
- British victory
- Indian victory
- Fort
- Annexed from Spain, 1812

Map labels:
- L. Superior
- BRITISH NORTH AMERICA (CANADA)
- Sorel
- MAINE (MASS.)
- INDIANA TERR.
- Michilimackinac July 17, 1812
- Montréal
- Lake Huron
- Dearborn approaches Montreal but then retreats, Nov. 1812.
- VT.
- Plattsburgh
- Lake Champlain Sept. 11, 1814
- N.H.
- Lake Michigan
- Tecumseh killed in battle; pan-Indian alliance collapses.
- Thames River Oct. 5, 1813
- L. Ontario
- Fort Niagara
- NEW YORK
- MASS.
- CONN.
- R.I.
- Lake Huron
- MICHIGAN TERR.
- Detroit Aug. 16, 1812
- L. Erie
- Put-in-Bay Sept. 10, 1813
- Van Rensselaer attacks Queenston Heights, Oct. 1812, and retreats.
- The American capital falls to a British amphibious force. The government escapes, but the British occupation force plunders and then burns Washington, D.C.
- Fort Meigs May 5, 1813
- PENNSYLVANIA
- Baltimore Sept. 13, 1814
- N.J.
- DELAWARE
- MARYLAND
- Illinois R.
- Wabash R.
- Harrison 1813
- OHIO
- Ohio R.
- Washington, D.C. Aug. 24–25, 1814
- Ross 1814
- 40°N
- Missouri R.
- ILLINOIS TERR.
- INDIANA TERR.
- VIRGINIA
- UNORGANIZED TERRITORY
- KENTUCKY
- NORTH CAROLINA
- British naval blockade 1814–1815
- Arkansas R.
- Mississippi R.
- TENNESSEE
- Tennessee R.
- Andrew Jackson's combined Cherokee Indian and Tennessee militia massacre the Red Stick Creeks at Horseshoe Bend, March 27, 1814.
- SOUTH CAROLINA
- Red R.
- William Weatherford's Red Stick force destroys Fort Mims, Aug. 30, 1813.
- MISSISSIPPI TERRITORY
- Fort Jackson
- GEORGIA
- ATLANTIC OCEAN
- N
- LOUISIANA
- New Orleans Jan. 8, 1815
- Mobile
- Pensacola
- Cochrane and Pakenham 1814
- SPANISH FLORIDA
- Gulf of Mexico
- 30°N
- 0 150 300 Km.
- 0 150 300 Mi.
- 90°W 80°W 70°W

8-3.2 The British Offensive

With fresh reinforcements from Europe, where Napoleon had abdicated as emperor after his disastrous invasion of Russia, the British took the offensive in the summer of 1814. General Sir George Prevost led a force of ten thousand British veterans in an offensive meant to split the New England states, where opposition to the war was strong, from the rest of the country. The British advanced down Lake Champlain until meeting the well-entrenched American forces at Plattsburgh. After his fleet met defeat on September 11, Prevost abandoned the campaign.

Ironically, the British achieved a far more spectacular success in an operation originally designed as a diversion from their main thrust down Lake Champlain. In 1814, a British army landed near Washington and met a larger American force, composed mainly of militia, at Bladensburg, Maryland, on August 24. The Battle of Bladensburg quickly became the "Bladensburg races" as the American militia fled, almost without firing a shot. The British then descended on Washington. Madison, who had witnessed the Bladensburg fiasco, escaped into the Virginia hills. His wife, Dolley, pausing only long enough to load her silver, a bed, and a portrait of George Washington onto her carriage, hastened to join her husband, while British troops ate the supper prepared for the Madisons at the presidential mansion. Then they burned the mansion and other public buildings in Washington. A few weeks later, the British attacked Baltimore, but after failing to crack its defenses, they broke off the operation.

8-3.3 The Treaty of Ghent, 1814

In August 1814, negotiations to end the war commenced between British and American commissioners at Ghent, Belgium. News of the American naval victory at Plattsburgh and Prevost's retreat to Canada brought home to the British that after two years of fighting, they controlled neither the Great Lakes nor Lake Champlain. The final **Treaty of Ghent**, signed on Christmas Eve 1814, restored the *status quo ante bellum* (the state of things before the war); neither side gained or lost territory. Several additional issues, including fixing a boundary between the United States and Canada, were referred to joint commissions for future settlement. Nothing was done about impressment, but the end of the war in Europe made neutral rights a dead issue.

Ironically, America's most dramatic victory came on January 8, 1815, two weeks after the treaty had been signed but before word of it had reached America. A British army had descended on New Orleans and attacked the city's defenders. The U.S. troops, commanded by General

WASHINGTONIANS FLEEING THE CITY AS THE BRITISH INVADE ON AUGUST 24, 1814 As the British approached Washington, Margaret Bayard Smith wrote, "a universal confidence reign'd among our citizens. Few doubted our conquering." When American resistance crumbled, she was stunned. After viewing the blackened ruins of the Capitol and the president's mansion, she concluded that Americans must "learn the dreadful[,] horrid trade of war." *(Granger, NYC)*

Andrew ("Old Hickory") Jackson, legendary as a fierce Indian fighter, shredded the line of advancing redcoats, inflicting more than two thousand casualties while losing only thirteen of their own.

8-3.4 The Hartford Convention

Although it meant nothing in terms of the war, the Battle of New Orleans had a devastating effect on the Federalist Party. The Federalist comeback in the election of 1808 had continued into the election of 1812, when their candidate DeWitt Clinton, an antiwar Democratic-Republican, had lost the electoral vote but carried all of New England except Vermont, as well as New York and New Jersey. American military setbacks in the war intensified Federalist disdain for the Madison administration. He seemed to epitomize over a decade of Democratic-Republican misrule at Federalist expense. Jefferson's attack on the judiciary had seemed to threaten the rule of law. The Louisiana Purchase, constitutionally dubious, had reduced the relative importance of Federalist New England. Now "Mr. Madison's War" brought fresh misery in the form of the British blockade. A few Federalists began to talk of New England's secession from the Union.

In late 1814, a Federalist convention met in Hartford, Connecticut. Although some advocates of secession were present, moderates took control and passed a series of resolutions summarizing New England's grievances. At the root of these grievances lay the belief that New Englanders were becoming a permanent minority in a nation dominated by southern Democratic-Republicans who failed to understand New England's commercial interests. The convention proposed to amend the Constitution to abolish the three-fifths clause (which gave the South a disproportionate share of votes in Congress by allowing it to count slaves as a basis of representation), to require a two-thirds vote of Congress to declare war and admit new states into the Union, to limit the president to a single term, to prohibit the election of two successive presidents from the same state, and to bar embargoes lasting more than sixty days.

News of the Treaty of Ghent and Jackson's victory at New Orleans dashed the Federalists' hopes of gaining broad popular support. The goal of the Hartford Convention had been to assert states' rights rather than disunion, but to many the proceedings smelled of a traitorous plot. The restoration of peace, moreover, stripped the Federalists of the primary grievance that had fueled the convention. In the election of 1816, Democratic-Republican James Monroe, Madison's hand-picked successor and a fellow Virginian, swept the nation over negligible Federalist opposition. He

> **Andrew ("Old Hickory") Jackson**
> American general, and later president, who was known for his ferocity as an Indian fighter. He and his men defeated the British in the Battle of New Orleans.

would win reelection in 1820 with only a single dissenting electoral vote. As a force in national politics, the Federalists were finished.

8-4 The Awakening of American Nationalism

Why is the "Era of Good Feelings" largely a misnomer for the Monroe years?

The United States emerged from the War of 1812 bruised but intact. In its first major war since the Revolution, the Republic had demonstrated not only that it could fight on even terms against a major power but also that republics could fight wars without turning to despotism. The war produced more than its share of symbols of American nationalism. Whitewash cleared the smoke damage to the presidential mansion; thereafter, it became known as the White House. The British attack on Fort McHenry, guarding Baltimore, prompted a young observer, Francis Scott Key, to compose "The Star-Spangled Banner."

The Battle of New Orleans boosted Andrew Jackson onto the stage of national politics and became a source of legends about American military prowess. It appears to most contemporary scholars that the British lost because as they advanced within range of Jackson's riflemen and cannon, they unaccountably paused and became sitting ducks. But in the wake of the battle, Americans spun a different tale. The legend arose that Jackson owed his victory not to Pakenham's blundering tactics but to hawk-eyed Kentucky frontiersmen whose rifles picked off the British with unerring accuracy. In fact, many frontiersmen in Jackson's army had not carried rifles; even if they had, gunpowder smoke would have obscured the enemy. But none of this mattered at the time. Just as Americans preferred militia to professional soldiers, they chose to believe that their greatest victory of the war had been the handiwork of amateurs.

8-4.1 Madison's Nationalism and the Era of Good Feelings, 1817–1824

The War of 1812 had two major political consequences. First, it eliminated the Federalists as a national political force. Second, with the Federalists no longer a force, Democratic-Republicans increasingly embraced doctrines long associated with the Federalists. For example, the expiration of the charter of the first Bank of the United States in 1811 had forced the government to plead with private bankers for wartime loans.

In a message to Congress in December 1815, Madison called for creation of a new national bank, federal support for internal improvements such as roads and canals, and tariff protection for the new industries that had sprung up during the embargo. In Congress, another Democratic-Republican, Henry Clay of Kentucky, proposed similar measures, which he called the American System, with the aim of making the young nation economically self-sufficient and free from dependence on Europe. In 1816, Congress chartered the Second Bank of the United States and enacted a moderate tariff. Federal support for internal improvements proved to be a thornier problem. Madison favored federal aid in principle but believed that a constitutional amendment was necessary to authorize it. Accordingly, just before leaving office in 1817, he vetoed an internal-improvements bill.

As so-called **National Republicans** adopted positions they had once disdained, an **"Era of Good Feelings"** dawned on American politics. A Boston newspaper, impressed by the warm reception accorded President James Monroe while touring New England, coined the phrase in 1817. It has stuck as a description of Monroe's two administrations from 1817 to 1825.

But the good feelings were paper-thin. Madison's 1817 veto of the internal-improvements bill revealed the persistence of disagreements about the role of the federal government under the Constitution. Furthermore, the continuation of slavery was arousing sectional animosities that a journalist's phrase about good feelings could not dispel. Not surprisingly, the postwar consensus began to unravel almost as soon as Americans recognized its existence.

BATTLE OF NEW ORLEANS.

GENERAL ANDREW JACKSON. LEADING TROOPS IN A BATTLE AGAINST THE BRITISH IN NEW ORLEANS. Occuring two weeks after the War of 1812 ended, this battle sealed Jackson's place as a war hero. *(Library of Congress Prints and Photographs Division Washington, D.C. [LC-DIG-pga-01838])*

8-4.2 John Marshall and the Supreme Court

In 1819, Jefferson's old antagonist John Marshall, who was still chief justice, issued two opinions that stunned Democratic-Republicans. In the first case, *Dartmouth College* v. *Woodward*, Marshall concluded that the college's original charter, granted to its trustees by George III in 1769, was a contract. Because the Constitution specifically forbade states to interfere with contracts, an effort by New Hampshire to turn Dartmouth into a state university was unconstitutional. The implications of Marshall's ruling were far-reaching for businesses as well as colleges. In effect, Marshall said that once a state had chartered a college or a business, it surrendered both its power to alter the charter and, in large measure, its authority to regulate the beneficiary.

A few weeks later, the chief justice handed down an even more momentous decision in *McCulloch v. Maryland*. Reflecting popular outrage at the disclosure that managers of the Baltimore branch of the Second Bank of the United States had embezzled $1.5 million, Maryland had imposed a tax on the branch and sued McCulloch, one of the embezzlers, when the Bank refused to pay. These events raised two issues. First, did Congress have the power to charter a national bank? Speaking for a unanimous Court, Marshall conceded that nothing in the Constitution explicitly granted this power. But the broad sweep of enumerated powers, he reasoned, implied the power to charter a bank. Marshall was clearly engaging in a broad, or "loose," rather than strict, construction (interpretation) of the Constitution. Second, could a state tax an agency of the federal government that lay within its borders? Marshall argued that any power of the national government, enumerated or implied, was supreme within its sphere. States could not interfere with the exercise of federal powers. Maryland's tax was such an interference because "the power to tax involves the power to destroy," and was plainly unconstitutional.

Marshall's decision in the *McCulloch* case dismayed many Democratic-Republicans, especially strict Jeffersonians who revered John Randolph and who were coming to be known as **Old Republicans**. Although Madison had supported the establishment of the Second Bank of the United States, the bank had made itself unpopular by tightening its loan policies during the summer of 1818. This contraction of credit triggered the Panic of 1819, a severe depression that gave rise to considerable distress throughout the country, especially among western farmers. At a time when the bank was widely blamed for the panic, Marshall's ruling stirred controversy by placing the bank beyond the regulatory power of any state government. His decision, indeed, was as much an attack on state sovereignty as it was a defense of the bank. The Constitution, Marshall argued, was the creation not of state governments but of the people of all the states, and thus was more fundamental than state laws. His reasoning assailed the Democratic-Republican theory, best expressed in the Virginia and Kentucky Resolutions of 1798–1799 (see Chapter 7), that the Union was essentially a compact among states, which were more immediately responsive to the people's will than the federal government. Old Republicans regarded the compact theory of the Union as a guarantor of popular liberty. As they saw it, Marshall's *McCulloch* decision, along with his decision in the *Dartmouth College* case, stripped state governments of the power to impose the will of their people on corporations.

8-4.3 The Missouri Compromise, 1820–1821

The fragility of the Era of Good Feelings became even more apparent in the two-year-long controversy over statehood for Missouri. Slavery as an institution continued to expand in the South after the 1793 invention of the cotton gin. Although the international trade would legally end in 1808 as outlined in the Constitution, the trade would continue illegally as the reliance on slave labor escalated. From 1790 to 1810, the slave population increased roughly seventy percent to 1.2 million, a figure that continued to rise in subsequent years (see Chapter 12). Carved from the Louisiana Purchase, Missouri attracted slaveholders. In 1819, when the House of Representatives was considering a bill to admit Missouri as a state, 16 percent of the territory's inhabitants were slaves. Then a New York Democratic-Republican offered an amendment that prohibited the further introduction of slaves and provided for the emancipation, at age twenty-five, of all slave offspring born after Missouri's admission as a state. Following rancorous debate, the House accepted the amendment, and the Senate rejected it. Both chambers voted along sectional lines.

Prior to 1819, slavery had not been the primary source of the nation's sectional divisions. For example, Federalists' opposition to the embargo and the War of 1812 had sprung from their fear

McCulloch v. Maryland
The court case that ruled that States could not interfere with the exercise of federal powers. A tax by Maryland on the Baltimore branch of the Second Bank of the United States was plainly unconstitutional, according to this rule.

Old Republicans
Strict Jeffersonians who revered John Randolph and regarded the compact theory of the Union as a guarantor of popular liberty.

that the dominant Democratic-Republicans were sacrificing New England's commercial interests to those of the South and West—not from hostility to slavery. The Missouri question, which Jefferson compared to "a fire bell in the night, [which] awakened me and filled me with terror," now thrust slavery into the center of long-standing sectional divisions.

In 1819, the Union had eleven free and eleven slave states. The admission of Missouri as a slave state would upset this balance to the advantage of the South. Equally important, Missouri was on the same latitude as the free states of Ohio, Indiana, and Illinois, and northerners worried that admitting Missouri as a slave state would set a precedent for the extension of slavery into the northern part of the Purchase. Finally, the disintegration of the Federalists as a national force reduced the need for unity among Democratic-Republicans, and they increasingly heeded sectional pressures more than calls for party loyalty.

Virtually every issue that was to wrack the Union during the next forty years was present in the controversy over Missouri: southern charges that the North was conspiring to destroy the Union and end slavery; accusations by northerners that southerners were conspiring to extend the institution. Southerners openly proclaimed that antislavery northerners were kindling fires that only "seas of blood" could extinguish. Such threats of civil war persuaded some northern congressmen who had originally supported the restriction of slavery in Missouri to back down. A series of congressional agreements known collectively as the **Missouri Compromise** resolved the crisis.

To balance the number of free and slave states, Congress in 1820 admitted Maine as a free state and Missouri as a slave state; to forestall a further crisis, it also prohibited slavery in the remainder of the Louisiana Purchase north of 36°30'—the southern boundary of Missouri (see Map 8.3). But compromise did not come easily. The individual components of the eventual compromise passed by close and ominously sectional votes.

No sooner had the compromise been forged than it nearly fell apart. As a prelude to statehood, Missourians drafted a constitution that prohibited free blacks, whom some eastern states viewed as citizens, from entering their territory. This provision clashed with the federal Constitution's provision that citizens of one state were entitled to the same rights as citizens of other states. Balking at Missourians' exclusion of free blacks, antislavery northerners barred Missouri's admission into the Union until 1821, when Henry Clay engineered a new agreement. This second Missouri Compromise prohibited Missouri from discriminating against citizens

JAMES MONROE BY SAMUEL F. B. MORSE The last member of the generation active in the Revolution to occupy the presidency, Monroe was loyal to Jefferson's principles but sought to rise above partisanship. His two terms (1817–1825) became known as the Era of Good Feeling. *(GL Archive/Alamy)*

of other states but left open the issue of whether free blacks were citizens.

The Missouri Compromise was widely viewed as a southern victory. The South had gained admission of Missouri, whose acceptance of slavery was controversial, while the North had merely gained Maine, whose rejection of slavery inspired no controversy. Yet the South had conceded to freedom a vast block of territory north of 36°30'. Although much of this territory was unorganized Indian country that some viewed as unfit for white habitation, seven states eventually would be formed out of it. Also, to the dismay of southern Old Republicans, already alarmed by the Marshall Court's restrictions on state powers, the Missouri Compromise reinforced the principle, originally set down by the Northwest Ordinance of 1787, that Congress had the right to prohibit slavery in some territories.

Missouri Compromise
This stated that in order to balance the number of free and slave states, Congress in 1820 would admit Maine as a free state and Missouri as a slave state; to forestall a further crisis, it also prohibited slavery in the remainder of the Louisiana Purchase north of 36°30'—the southern boundary of Missouri.

MAP 8.3 **THE MISSOURI COMPROMISE, 1820–1821** The Missouri Compromise temporarily quelled controversy over slavery by admitting Maine as a free state and Missouri as a slave state, and by prohibiting slavery in the remainder of the Louisiana Purchase north of 36°30'.

8-4.4 Foreign Policy Under Monroe

American foreign policy between 1816 and 1824 reflected more consensus than conflict. The end of the Napoleonic Wars and the signing of the Treaty of Ghent had removed most of the foreign-policy disagreements between Federalists and Democratic-Republicans. Moreover, Monroe was fortunate to have as his secretary of state an extraordinary diplomat, **John Quincy Adams**. The son of the last Federalist president, Adams had been the only Federalist in the Senate to support the Louisiana Purchase, and he later became an ardent Democratic-Republican. An austere and scholarly man whose library equaled his house in monetary value, Adams was a tough negotiator and a fervent nationalist.

As secretary of state, Adams moved quickly to strengthen the peace with Great Britain. During his tenure, the United States and Britain signed the Rush-Bagot Treaty of 1817, which effectively demilitarized the Great Lakes by severely restricting the number of ships the two powers could maintain there. Next, the British-American Convention of 1818 restored to

John Quincy Adams
The Secretary of State under James Monroe who helped strengthen ties with Great Britain. He was the son of former president John Adams, and he became president in 1825.

Americans the same fishing rights off Newfoundland they had enjoyed before the War of 1812 and fixed the boundary between the United States and Canada from the Lake of the Woods west to the Rockies. Beyond the Rockies, the vast country known as Oregon was declared "free and open" to both American and British citizens. As a result of these two agreements, the United States had a secure border with British-controlled Canada for the first time since independence, and a claim to the Pacific.

The nation now turned its attention to dealing with Spain, which still owned East Florida and claimed West Florida. No one was certain whether the Louisiana Purchase included West Florida. Acting as if it did, the United States in 1812 had simply added a slice of West Florida to the state of Louisiana and another slice to the Mississippi Territory. Using the pretext that it was a base for Seminole Indian raids and a refuge for fugitive slaves, Andrew Jackson, now the military commander in the South, invaded East Florida in 1818. He hanged two British subjects and captured Spanish forts. Jackson had acted without explicit orders, but Adams supported the raid, guessing correctly that it would panic the Spanish into further concessions.

In 1819, Spain agreed to the **Adams-Onís (Transcontinental) Treaty**. By its terms, Spain ceded East Florida to the United States, renounced its claims to West Florida, and agreed to a southern border of the United States west of the Mississippi, by which the United States conceded that Texas was not part of the Louisiana Purchase, while Spain agreed to a northern limit to its claims to the West Coast (see Map 8.3). It thereby left the United States free to pursue its interests in Oregon.

8-4.5 The Monroe Doctrine, 1823

John Quincy Adams had long believed that God and nature had ordained that the United States would eventually span the entire continent of North America. Throughout his negotiations leading up to the Adams-Onís Treaty, he made it clear to Spain that if the Spanish did not concede some of their territory in North America, the United States might seize all of it, including Texas and even Mexico. Yet Spain was concerned with larger issues than American encroachment. Its primary objective was to suppress the revolutions against Spanish rule that had broken out in South America. To accomplish this goal, Spain sought support from the European monarchs who had organized the Holy Alliance in 1815. The brainchild of the tsar of Russia, the Holy Alliance aimed to quash revolutions everywhere in the name of Christian and monarchist principles. Britain, whose trading interests in South America were hampered by Spanish restrictions, refused to join the Holy Alliance. British foreign minister George Canning proposed that the United States and Britain issue a joint statement opposing any European interference in South America, while pledging that neither would annex any part of Spain's old empire in the New World.

While sharing Canning's opposition to European intervention in the New World, Adams preferred that the United States make a declaration of policy on its own rather than "come in as a cock-boat in the wake of the British man-of-war." Adams flatly rejected Canning's insistence on a joint pledge never to annex Spain's former territories, for Adams wanted the freedom to annex Texas or Cuba, should their inhabitants one day "solicit a union with us."

This was the background of the **Monroe Doctrine**, as President Monroe's message to Congress on December 2, 1823, later came to be called. The message, written largely by Adams, announced three key principles: that unless American interests were involved, U.S. policy was to abstain from European wars; that the "American continents" were not "subjects for future colonization by any European power"; and that the United States would construe any attempt at European colonization in the New World as an "unfriendly act."

Europeans widely derided the Monroe Doctrine as an empty pronouncement. Fear of the British navy, not the Monroe Doctrine, prevented the Holy Alliance from intervening in South America. With hindsight, however, the Europeans might have taken the doctrine more seriously, for it had important implications. First, by pledging itself not to interfere in European wars, the United States was excluding the possibility that it would support revolutionary movements in Europe. For example, Adams opposed U.S. recognition of Greek patriots fighting for independence from the Ottoman Turks. Second, by keeping open its options to annex territory in the Americas, the United States was using the Monroe Doctrine to claim a preeminent position in the New World.

Adams-Onís (Transcontinental) Treaty
The agreement in 1819 between Spain and the United States where Spain ceded East Florida to the United States, renounced its claims to West Florida, and agreed to a southern border of the United States west of the Mississippi that ran north along the Sabine River (separating Texas from Louisiana) and then westward along the Red and Arkansas Rivers to the Rocky Mountains, finally following the forty-second parallel to the Pacific. In effect, the United States conceded that Texas was not part of the Louisiana Purchase, while Spain agreed to a northern limit to its claims to the West Coast. It thereby left the United States free to pursue its interests in Oregon.

Monroe Doctrine
The doctrine that proclaimed three key principles: that unless American interests were involved, U.S. policy was to abstain from European wars; that the "American continents" were not "subjects for future colonization by any European power"; and that the United States would construe any attempt at European colonization in the New World as an "unfriendly act."

The Whole Vision

■ *Was Jefferson's election truly the "revolution" he claimed it to be?*

Jefferson was only narrowly elected to office in 1800, so he was not referring to the vote count when he described his presidency as a revolution. And certainly, his views on race were anything but revolutionary. Jefferson was a major figure of the American Revolution and he embraced a distinctive view of the role of government and the people in a republic. His vision was for a nation built on the strength of independent farmers, who he saw as the true bastions of liberty. As such, his "revolution" was to implement those policies that would secure this vision and eliminate anything he saw as a threat to liberty. Topping the list was reversing several of the Federalist economic policies advocated by Treasury Secretary Alexander Hamilton and others, as well as those regarding the judiciary. He also sought to enlarge the physical size and scope of the United States and to secure its borders via the Louisiana Purchase, even if that decision challenged his views on the constitutional powers of the presidency. Such moves did indeed boost Jefferson's popularity and aided his reelection bid.

■ *What challenges to American government and national sovereignty did the United States face in the early decades of the nineteenth century?*

During the presidencies of both Thomas Jefferson and James Madison, the United States faced both internal and external challenges to its authority as an independent nation. Internally, growing factionalism and political discord led to plots against the government from those on the inside. Internally, too, the problems wrought by the Louisiana Purchase and white expansionism led to new tensions with Native Americans. After the Battle of Tippecanoe, Native Americans would again reconsider whether their needs were best served by allying with the Americans or the British. Externally, as Britain and France waged war against each other, U.S. leaders faced constant challenges and ongoing affronts to the nation's neutrality, prompting new (and often unsuccessful) foreign policy initiatives. As tensions escalated, so did Madison's concerns about Britain's larger agenda, which for the president made war inevitable as a means to preserve American autonomy.

■ *What is the best way to understand the War of 1812 and its place in U.S. history?*

As a battle, the War of 1812 holds little military significance. It lasted just two years, and effectively neither side "won," choosing instead to sign a treaty that would restore relations to their prewar status. The neutrality the U.S. sought to have respected by other international powers became a mute point; impressment was not addressed; and other treaty issues were sent to committees for resolution. Instead, the war is best understood for its symbolic value and for its enduring impact on the U.S. political landscape. Symbolically, the war mattered for two reasons. First, it marked the end of conflicts with Britain and resolved boundary disputes in the West. Second, the war resulted in the demise of the Federalist party, seen as traitors for their role at the Hartford Convention and the policies advocated there. But the issues Federalists embraced did not vanish, and instead found a new home in a divided Democratic-Republican party.

■ *Why is the "Era of Good Feelings" largely a misnomer for the Monroe years?*

While the immediate postwar era did bring a sense of national pride and political unity that inspired the moniker "Era of Good Feelings," it was soon supplanted by deeper tensions. The Federalists were no longer a force in national politics, but new political rifts appeared. Questions emerged about federal versus state powers, for example, and Old Republicans challenged others' interpretations of the Union and the Constitution. The prospect of slavery's expansion into Louisiana Purchase territories caused concerns about political and sectional balance in Congress. Despite the agreement reached in the Missouri Compromise, the conflict in some ways proved a harbinger of sectionalism as a new national political force. Externally, "bad feelings" continued with some European countries, resulting in foreign policy initiatives and, most dramatically, the Monroe Doctrine.

9 The Transformation of American Society, 1815–1840

THE OLD SLATER MILL, PAWTUCKET, RHODE ISLAND. Artist rendering of the Slater Mill, which, when it opened in 1793, became the first successful cotton textile mill in the United States. Located along the river, the mill relied on water to power the machines that transformed raw cotton into cloth. It marks the beginning of industrialization in the U.S. *(Randy Duchaine/Alamy)*

CHRONOLOGY 1815–1840

1790	Samuel Slater opens his first Rhode Island mill for the production of cotton yarn.
1793	Eli Whitney invents the cotton gin.
1807	Robert R. Livingston and Robert Fulton introduce the steamboat *Clermont* on the Hudson River.
1811	Construction of the National Road begins at Cumberland, Maryland.
1813	Incorporation of the Boston Manufacturing Company.
1816	Second Bank of the United States chartered.
1817–1825	Construction of the Erie Canal started. Mississippi enters the Union.
1819	Economic panic, ushering in four-year depression. Alabama enters the Union.
1820–1850	Growth of female moral-reform societies.

1820s	Expansion of New England textile mills.
1824	*Gibbons* v. *Ogden*.
1828	Baltimore and Ohio Railroad chartered.
1830	Indian Removal Act passed by Congress.
1831	*Cherokee Nation* v. *Georgia*. Alexis de Tocqueville begins visit to the United States to study American penitentiaries.
1832	*Worcester* v. *Georgia*.
1834	First strike at the Lowell mills.
1835	Treaty of New Echota.
1837	Economic panic begins a depression that lasts until 1843.
1838	The Trail of Tears.
1840	System of production by interchangeable parts perfected.

The life of Harriet Jane Hanson Robinson (1825–1911) intersected some of the most important changes in American society between 1820 and the Civil War. As one of the "operatives" in the Lowell, Massachusetts, textile mills, she was on the front lines of the industrial revolution and an active participant in early labor organization. Though she entered factory work at the age of ten, she managed to acquire a decent education in one of Massachusetts's rapidly proliferating public high schools. Her young adulthood was shaped by the new importance of peer-group relationships because she worked and lived with other young women. Her marriage to William Stevens Robinson, editor of an antislavery newspaper in Lowell, marked her elevation to middle-class standing. It also confirmed her involvement in the antislavery movement and subsequent women's suffrage movement, as well as her support for the new Whig Party (discussed in Chapter 10). In all these areas of her life, Harriet Robinson was very much a girl—and then a woman—of her times.

The success of the industrial experiment at Lowell was in part the result of hard times in rural New England. By 1820, the region's small, rock-strewn farms could no longer support its rural population. Many young men were moving west or to northeastern cities, while young women sought work in the new textile mills. In 1830, more than 70 percent of the female workers in Lowell were between the ages of fifteen and nineteen. The city's mill girls of the 1830s and early 1840s constituted a self-conscious group, the most concentrated group of teenage women anywhere in the United States. When she was eleven, Harriet led her young coworkers in a "turn-out" (strike) to protest a reduction in wages.

But native-born, Protestant girls like Harriet did not see themselves as part of a permanent working class. The mill girls sought "betterment," which included both the independence provided by wages and the educational opportunities offered by Lowell's numerous schools, libraries, and churches. The owners of the eight industrial corporations in Lowell built these cultural institutions to attract "respectable" operatives, but the mill girls used them to expand their own opportunities. Between 1840 and 1845, the girls edited their own literary monthly, the *Lowell Offering*, which gained international attention. Most mill women, like Harriet, contracted more advantageous marriages than they would

HARRIET JANE HANSON ROBINSON *(Courtesy of the Trustees of the Boston Public Library/Rare Books)*

237

have had they remained in isolated New England villages. These upwardly mobile farmers' daughters became part of the "middling classes" in antebellum America. They came to see themselves as individuals who could make deliberate choices that would shape the course of their lives. For example, they controlled the size of their families. Whereas Harriet's maternal grandfather had sired fifteen children, Harriet gave birth to only four. Many of them came to treat their religious affiliation as a matter of choice, attending worship services at more than one of the twenty-six churches built in Lowell before 1860. Harriet, who was raised a Congregationalist, became a Universalist.

Harriet was part of the broader shift in the United States toward a market economy as well as other notable transformations in the first half of the nineteenth century. The market revolution, for example, fueled a complementary revolution in the available modes of transportation, enabling goods to reach a wider swath of the nation much faster. The move west onto the lands acquired by the Louisiana Purchase expanded the size of the nation. The number of cities increased as well. Not all groups benefited by such transformations, especially people of color. Such changes led to new dynamics in social relationships across class, race, and gender lines and even within families.

9-1 Westward Expansion

What is the best way to understand westward expansion in the early nineteenth century?

In 1790, the vast majority of the nearly 4 million non-Indian people of the United States lived east of the Appalachian Mountains. But half a century later, in 1840, one-third of the 17 million non-Indian people lived west of the Appalachians and east of the Mississippi River. That area, which Americans of the time called the West, historians refer to as the **Old Northwest** and the **Old Southwest**.

Traveling as families rather than as individuals, most migrants went west in search of a better version of the life they had known in the East: more land and bountiful crops. Several factors nurtured their high expectations: the growing power of the federal government; its ruthless removal of the Indians from the path of white settlement; and a boom in the prices of agricultural commodities after the War of 1812.

Americans moved west in a series of bursts. The first occurred after 1791, when four new states joined the Union—Vermont, Kentucky, Tennessee, and Ohio—by 1803. The second burst occurred between 1816 and 1821, with the addition of another six states: Indiana, Mississippi, Illinois, Alabama, Maine, and Missouri. And settlers continued to pour farther west into Michigan. Ohio's population jumped from 45,000 in 1800 to 581,000 by 1820 and 1,519,000 by 1840; Michigan's expanded from 5,000 in 1810 to 212,000 by 1840.

To reach markets with their produce, most migrants clustered near the navigable rivers of the West, especially the magnificent system created by the Ohio and Mississippi rivers. Only with the spread of canals in the 1820s and 1830s, and later of railroads, did westerners venture far from rivers.

9-1.1 Western Society and Customs

Migrants to the West brought with them values and customs peculiar to the regions they had left behind. Migrants from New England or upstate New York, who settled the northern areas of Ohio, Indiana, and Illinois, grew wheat, supplemented by dairying and fruit orchards. These "Yankees" valued public schools; lived in houses made of sod, stone, or clapboard; and quickly formed towns.

In contrast, emigrants from the Upland South settled the southern parts of Ohio, Indiana, and Illinois, where they raised corn and hogs. Called "Butternuts" after the color of their homespun clothing, they lived in log cabins on isolated farmsteads. Because they came from less densely populated regions, they were slower to form towns and public schools. Though some Butternuts, like Abraham Lincoln's father Thomas, opposed slavery, many more supported it, and little love was lost between antislavery Yankees and proslavery Butternuts. In 1824, an attempt to legalize slavery in Illinois was barely defeated at the polls.

Regardless of their origins, most westerners craved sociability. Rural families joined with their neighbors in group sports and festivities. Men met for games that tested their strength or agility, such as wrestling, weightlifting, and a variant of the modern hammer toss. Some games were brutal by our present standards. In gander pulling, horseback riders competed to pull the head off a duck whose neck had been plucked and greased. Women usually combined household work with recreation at quilting and sewing

Old Northwest
The northern part of the area between the Appalachian and the Mississippi River.

Old Southwest
The southern part of the area between the Appalachian and the Mississippi River.

parties, carpet tackings, and poultry pluckings. But social activities often brought the genders together. Group corn huskings usually ended with dances, and "hoedowns" and "frolics" were widely popular.

Before 1840, few westerners could afford elegant living. Arriving on the Michigan frontier from New York City in 1835, the well-bred Caroline Kirkland quickly discovered that her neighbors thought they had a right to borrow anything she owned with no more than a blunt declaration that "you've got plenty." "For my own part," Kirkland related, "I have lent my broom, my thread, my tape, my spoons, my cat, my thimble, my scissors, my shawl, my shoes, and have been asked for my comb and brushes." Westerners' relative lack of refinement made them easy targets for easterners' contempt.

Westerners responded to such contempt by saying that at least they were honest democrats, not soft would-be aristocrats. They showed little tolerance for social pretensions. On one occasion, a woman who improvised a privacy screen in a crowded room was dismissed as "stuck up." A politician who rode to a public meeting in a buggy instead of on horseback lost votes.

9-1.2 The Far West

Exploration carried some Americans even farther west. Zebulon Pike was exploring the Spanish Southwest in 1806 when he sighted the Colorado peak that was later named after him. In 1811, after the Lewis and Clark expedition, New York merchant John Jacob Astor founded the fur-trading post of Astoria at the mouth of the Columbia River in the Oregon Country. In the 1820s and 1830s, fur traders operated along the Missouri River from St. Louis to the Rocky Mountains and beyond. At first, whites relied on Native Americans to bring them furs, but during the 1820s white trappers or "mountain men"—among them, Kit Carson and Jim Bridger—battled danger and harsh conditions to gather furs on their own. Jim Beckwourth, son of a white man and a slave woman in Virginia, was a legendary mountain man who lived for a time with the Crow Indians and who established the route through the Sierras taken by many easterners to the gold fields of California after 1848.

Jedediah Smith was representative of these men. Born in New York's Susquehanna Valley in 1799, Smith moved west with his family to Pennsylvania and Illinois and signed on with an expedition bound for the upper Missouri River in 1822. In the course of his explorations, he was almost killed by a grizzly bear in the Black Hills of South Dakota, crossed the Mojave Desert into California, explored the San Joaquin Valley, and hiked back across the Sierras and the Great Basin to the Great Salt Lake. The exploits of Smith and other mountain men were celebrated in popular biographies, and they became legends in their own day.

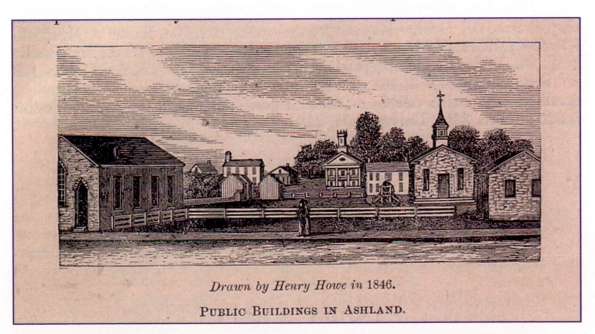

Drawn by Henry Howe in 1846.

PUBLIC BUILDINGS IN ASHLAND.

ASHLAND, OHIO, IN 1846 Historian Henry Howe sketched this image of Ashland, Ohio (which had been laid out under the name "Uniontown" in 1815). As a native of Connecticut, Howe focused on the town center with its public buildings—including several churches, an academy, and an open site for a planned courthouse—to emphasize how quickly pioneers from the Northeast formed orderly towns in the Northwest. *(Henry Howe, Historical Collections of Ohio, Cincinnati: Derby, Bradley, and Co., 1847)*

9-1.3 The Federal Government and the West

The most important cause of expansion to the Mississippi from 1790 to 1840 was the growing strength of the federal government. Even before the Constitution was ratified, several states had ceded their western land claims to the national government, thereby creating the bountiful public domain. The Land Ordinance of 1785 provided for the survey and sale of these lands, and the Northwest Ordinance of 1787 established procedures for transforming them into states. The Louisiana Purchase of 1803 brought the entire Mississippi River under American control, and the Transcontinental Treaty of 1819 wiped out the last vestiges of Spanish power east of the Mississippi.

The federal government directly stimulated settlement of the West by promising land to men who enlisted during the War of 1812. With 6 million acres allotted to these military bounties, many former soldiers and their families pulled up roots and moved west. To facilitate westward migration, Congress authorized funds in 1816 for the extension of the National Road, a highway begun in 1811 that reached Wheeling, Virginia, on the Ohio River in 1818 and Vandalia, Illinois, by 1838. Soon settlers thronged the road. "Old America seems to be breaking up," a traveler on the National Road wrote in 1817. "We are seldom out of sight, as we travel on this grand track towards the Ohio, of family groups before and behind us."

The same government power that aided whites brought misery to the Indians. Virtually all the foreign policy successes during the Jefferson, Madison, and Monroe administrations worked to Native Americans' disadvantage. In the wake of the Louisiana Purchase, Lewis and Clark bluntly commanded the Indians to "shut their ears to the counsels of bad birds" and listen henceforth only to the "Great Father" in Washington. In the stalemate that ended the War of 1812, the only real losers were the Indians. Early in the negotiations leading to the Treaty of Ghent, the British had insisted on the creation of an Indian buffer state between the United States and Canada in the Old Northwest. But the British eventually abandoned their former allies to the policies of land-hungry Americans.

9-1.4 The Removal of the Indians

White settlers moving west encountered sizable numbers of Native Americans in their paths, particularly in the South, home to the so-called **Five Civilized Tribes**: the Cherokees, Choctaws, Creeks, Chickasaws, and Seminoles. Years of commercial dealings and intermarriage with whites had created in these tribes, especially the Cherokees, an influential minority who embraced Christianity, practiced agriculture, built gristmills, and owned slaves. One of their chiefs, Sequoyah, devised a written form of their language; other Cherokees published a bilingual newspaper, the *Cherokee Phoenix*.

The "civilization" of southern Indians impressed New England missionaries more than southern whites, who viewed the Civilized Tribes with contempt and coveted their land. Presidents James Monroe and John Quincy Adams had concluded several treaties with Indian tribes, providing for their voluntary removal to public lands west of the Mississippi River. Although some assimilated mixed-bloods sold their tribal lands to the government, others resisted because their prosperity depended on trade with neighboring whites. Full-bloods, the majority even in the "civilized" tribes, clung to their land and customs. They wanted to remain near the burial grounds of their ancestors, and they condemned anyone who bartered away tribal lands to whites. When the Creek mixed-blood chief William McIntosh sold all Creek lands in Georgia and two-thirds of Creek lands in Alabama to the government in the Treaty of Indian Springs (1825), a Creek tribal council executed him.

During the 1820s, whites in Alabama, Georgia, and Mississippi intensified pressure on the Indians by surveying tribal lands and squatting on them (setting up residence without permission). Southern legislatures, reluctant to restrain white settlers, moved to expropriate Indian lands unless the Indians moved west. State laws extended jurisdiction over the tribes, effectively outlawing tribal government. The states even excluded Indians from serving as witnesses in court cases involving whites—a practice that made it difficult for Indians to collect debts owed them by whites.

These measures delighted that old Indian-fighter-turned-president, Andrew Jackson. Reared on the frontier and sharing its contempt for Indians, Jackson believed that Indian tribes should not be treated as independent nations; instead, they should be subject to the laws of whatever state they occupied. This position spelled doom for the Indians, who could not vote or hold state office. In 1834, Cherokee chief John Ross got a taste of what state jurisdiction meant when Georgia put his house up as a prize in the state lottery.

In 1830, President Jackson secured passage of the **Indian Removal Act**, which authorized him to exchange public lands in the West for Indian

---

Five Civilized Tribes
The Cherokees, Choctaws, Creeks, Chickasaws, and Seminoles.

Indian Removal Act
This law authorized Andrew Jackson to exchange public lands in the West for Indian territories in the East and appropriated $500,000 to cover the expenses of removal.

territories in the East. The act appropriated $500,000 to cover the expenses of removal. But the real costs of removal, both human and monetary, were vastly greater. During Jackson's eight years in office, the federal government forced Indians to exchange 100 million acres of their own lands for only 32 million acres of public lands. In the late 1820s and early 1830s, the Choctaws, Creeks, and Chickasaws started their "voluntary" removal to the West. In 1836, Creeks who had clung to their homes were removed by force, many of them in chains. Seminoles in Florida resisted, fighting a bitter war between 1835 and 1842 that cost the federal government $20 million. More than a decade later, most of the Seminoles would agree to move west to Indian territory, though some stayed in Florida.

Ironically, the Cherokees, often considered the most "civilized" tribe because of their efforts to assimilate to white ways, suffered the worst fate. The Cherokee had proclaimed themselves an independent nation, established a government with a bicameral legislature, and in 1827 adopted a constitution and economy much like that of the United States, including slaveholding. They petitioned the U.S. Supreme Court for an injunction against Georgia's assertion of state jurisdiction over their "nation." In the case of *Cherokee Nation* v. *Georgia* (1831), Chief Justice John Marshall denied the Cherokees' claim to status as a republic within Georgia and identified them instead as a "domestic dependent nation" within the United States. But Marshall added that prolonged occupancy had given the Cherokees a legitimate claim to their lands within Georgia. A year later, in *Worcester* v. *Georgia*, he clarified the Cherokees' legal position by holding that they were a "distinct" political community entitled to federal protection from Georgia's claims.

President Jackson's reported response was, "John Marshall has made his decision; now let him enforce it." Jackson simply ignored the ruling. Then federal agents persuaded some minor Cherokee chiefs to sign the Treaty of New Echota (1835), which ceded all Cherokee lands in the United States for $5.6 million and free passage west. Congress ratified this treaty (by a single vote). But the vast majority of Cherokees denounced it, and in 1839, a Cherokee party murdered its three principal signers, including a former editor of the *Cherokee Phoenix*.

The end of the story was simple and tragic. In 1838, thousands of Cherokees were removed by force to the new Indian Territory in what is now Oklahoma. They traveled west along what became known as the **"Trail of Tears"** (see Map 9.1). A young man who would become a colonel in the Confederate Army participated in the forced removal. He later recollected: "I fought through the civil war and have seen men shot to pieces and slaughtered by the thousands, but the Cherokees removal was the cruelest work I ever knew." Perhaps as many as eight thousand Cherokees, more than one-third of the entire nation, died during and just after the removal.

Indians living in the Northwest Territory fared no better. A series of treaties extinguished their land titles, and most moved west of the Mississippi. The removal of the northwestern Indians prompted two uprisings. The first, led by Red Bird, a Winnebago chief, began in 1827 but was quickly crushed. The second, led by a Sac and Fox chief named Black Hawk, raged along the Illinois frontier until 1832, when federal troops and Illinois militia

POLITICAL CARTOON OF JACKSON AND NATIVE AMERICANS This cartoon, which depicts Native Americans as children or dolls subject to father Andrew Jackson, was intended as a satire on Jackson's policy of forcibly removing the Indians to reservations. The painting in the upper right corner pointedly depicts the goddess Liberty trampling a tyrant. (*William L. Clements Library, University of Michigan*)

"Trail of Tears"
The forced migration in 1838 of Cherokee Indians from their Georgia homelands to what is now Oklahoma.

virtually annihilated Black Hawk's followers. Black Hawk's downfall persuaded the other Old Northwest tribes to cede their lands. Between 1832 and 1837, the United States acquired nearly 190 million acres of Northwest Indian land for $70 million in gifts and annual payments.

9-1.5 Working the Land: The Agricultural Boom

After the War of 1812, the rising prices of agricultural commodities such as wheat, corn, and cotton sharpened white land hunger. Several factors accounted for the skyrocketing farm prices. During the Napoleonic Wars, the United States quickly captured former British markets in the West Indies and former Spanish markets in South America. After the wars ended, American farmers found brisk demand for their wheat and corn in Britain and France, both exhausted by two decades of warfare. In addition, demand within the United States for western farm commodities intensified after 1815 as industrialization and urbanization in the East drew workers into nonagricultural employment. Finally, the West's splendid river systems made it possible for farmers to ship wheat and corn downriver to New Orleans. There, wheat and corn were either sold or transshipped to the beckoning markets. Just as government policies made farming in the West possible, high prices for foodstuffs made it attractive.

As the prospect of raising wheat and corn pulled eastern farmers toward the Old Northwest, Eli Whitney's invention of the cotton gin in 1793 (see Chapter 7) stimulated settlement of the Old Southwest, particularly Alabama and Mississippi. As cotton clothing came into fashion around 1815, the British textile industry provided a seemingly inexhaustible demand for raw cotton. With its warm climate, wet springs and summers, and relatively dry autumns, the Old Southwest was well suited to cotton cultivation. The explosion of small farmers and planters

MAP 9.1 THE REMOVAL OF THE NATIVE AMERICANS TO THE WEST, 1820–1840 The so-called Trail of Tears, followed by the Cherokees, was one of several routes along which various tribes migrated on their forced removal to reservations west of the Mississippi.

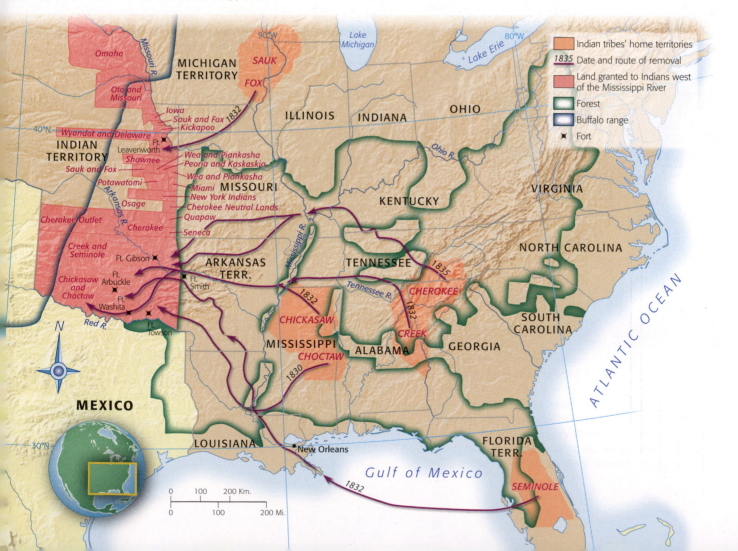

out of the seaboard South into the Old Southwest resembled a gold rush. By 1817, "Alabama fever" gripped the South; settlers were bidding the price of good land up to thirty to fifty dollars an acre. Cotton, which had accounted for less than a quarter of all American exports between 1802 and 1807, comprised just over half by 1830 and nearly two-thirds by 1836.

9-2 The Growth of the Market Economy

What was the impact of the shift to a market economy in the early nineteenth century?

Many farmers traditionally had grown only enough food to feed their families (subsistence agriculture) and engage in small-scale local exchange. With agricultural commodities like wheat and cotton commanding high prices, a growing number of farmers added a cash crop (commercial agriculture) to participate in the emerging **market economy**. In the South, slaves became an increasingly valuable commodity; after 1815, the sale of slaves from declining agricultural states in the Southeast to planters and farmers migrating to the Southwest grew into a huge business. "Virginia," an observer stated in 1832, "is, in fact, a *negro* raising State for other States; she produces enough for her own supply and six thousand a year for sale."

The unprecedented scale of commercial agriculture after 1815 exposed farmers to new economic risks. Farmers had no control over prices in distant markets. Furthermore, the time lapse between harvesting a cash crop and selling it forced farmers to borrow money to sustain their families. Thus, the market economy forced farmers into short-term debt in pursuit of long-term profit. In addition, many western farmers had to borrow money to buy their land, due to the federal government's failure to devise an effective policy for transferring the public domain directly into the hands of small farmers.

9-2.1 Federal Land Policy, Speculators, and Squatters

Early federal land policy attempted to ensure the orderly settlement of the public domain. To this end, the Ordinance of 1785 divided public lands into sections of 640 acres (see Chapter 6). The architects of the ordinance realized that most farmers could not afford such large lots on their own; they assumed that farmers who shared ties based on religion or geographic origin would band together to purchase sections. The goal was for compatible settlers to live on adjoining lots in what amounted to rural neighborhoods, thus making the task of government easier than if settlers lived in isolation on widely scattered homesteads.

Political developments in the 1790s undermined the expectations of the ordinance's framers. Federalists, who were based in the East, were reluctant to encourage western settlement but still eager to raise revenue for the federal government from land sales. They reconciled their conflicting goals by encouraging the sale of huge tracts to wealthy speculators, investors who would wait for land values to rise and then sell off parcels to farmers. For example, in the 1790s the Holland Land Company, composed mainly of Dutch investors, bought up much of western New York and western Pennsylvania. Federalists passed a law in 1796 that maintained the minimum purchase size of 640 acres

> **market economy**
> An economic system in which goods and services are produced for sale rather than for personal consumption; market economies are driven by supply and demand as well as the incentive to earn a profit.

THE SQUATTERS, BY GEORGE CALEB BINGHAM (1850). As the Missouri painter explained to his New York City viewers, "The Squatters as a class, are not fond of the toil of agriculture, but erect their rude cabins upon those remote portions of the national domain, when the abundant game supplies their phisical [sic] wants. When this source of subsistence becomes diminished in consequence of increasing settlements around they usually sell out their slight improvement, with their 'preemption title' to the land, and again follow the receding footsteps of the Savage." *(Photograph © 2012 Museum of Fine Arts, Boston)*

at a minimum price of $2 an acre and allowed only one year for complete payment. Few small farmers could afford to buy that much land at that price.

Convinced that the small farmer was the backbone of the republic, Jefferson and the Republicans took a different tack. Their land law of 1800 dropped the minimum purchase to 320 acres at a minimum of $2 an acre and allowed up to four years for full payment. By 1832, the minimum purchase had shrunk to 40 acres and the price to $1.25 an acre.

Although Congress steadily liberalized federal land policy, speculators always remained one step ahead. Long before 1832, speculators were selling forty-acre lots to farmers. Farmers preferred small lots (rarely buying more than 160 acres) because the lands they purchased were typically wooded, and a new landowner could clear no more than ten to twelve acres of trees in a year. All land in the public domain was sold at auction, usually for much more than the minimum price set by law. With agricultural prices soaring, speculators assumed that land would continue to rise in value and accordingly were willing to bid high on new land, which they resold to farmers at hefty profits.

The growing availability of credit after the War of 1812 encouraged speculation. The chartering of the Second Bank of the United States in 1816 increased the amount of money in circulation and stimulated the chartering of private banks within individual states (state banks). In just five years, between 1812 and 1817, the value of all bank notes in circulation soared from $45 million to $100 million. Stockholders and officers saw banks as agencies that could lend them money for land speculation. The result was an orgy of land speculation; by 1819, the dollar value of public land sales was more than 1,000 percent greater than the average between 1800 and 1814.

Despite the dominant role played by speculators, most of the public domain eventually found its way into the hands of small farmers. Speculators gained nothing by holding land for prolonged periods and were only too happy to sell it when the price was right. The activities of the speculators were also constrained by a familiar frontier figure called the squatter.

Even before the creation of the public domain, **squatters** had simply helped themselves to western land. Even George Washington had been unable to drive squatters off lands he owned in the West. Squatters were an independent and proud lot, scornful of their fellow citizens who they saw as "softened by Ease, enervated by Affluence and Luxurious Plenty, & unaccustomed to Fatigues, Hardships, Difficulties or dangers." But squatters especially hated speculators and formed claims associations to monitor auctions and prevent speculators from bidding up land prices. Squatters also pressured Congress to allow them preemption rights—that is, the right to purchase at the minimum price land they had already settled on and improved. Seeking to undo the damaging effects of its own laws, Congress responded by passing special preemption laws for squatters in specific areas and finally, in 1841, acknowledged a general right of preemption.

But preemption laws were of no use to farmers who arrived after speculators had already bought up the land. These later settlers, having exhausted their small savings on livestock, seed, and tools, had to buy land from speculators on credit at interest rates ranging as high as 40 percent. Many western farmers, drowning in debt, had to skimp on subsistence crops while expanding cash crops in the hope of paying off their creditors.

Countless farmers who had carried basically conservative expectations to the West quickly became economic risk-takers. Forced to raise cash crops in a hurry, many worked their acreage to exhaustion and then moved on in search of new land. On the "moving frontier," not only did the line of settlement shift farther west with each passing decade, but the same people moved repeatedly. Abraham Lincoln's parents typified this westward trek, migrating from the East through several farms in Kentucky and then further west to Indiana.

9-2.2 The Panic of 1819

The land boom collapsed in the financial **Panic of 1819**. The loose financial practices of state banks contributed significantly to the panic. State banks issued their own bank notes, which were promises to pay the bearer ("redeem") a certain amount of specie (gold or silver coinage) on demand. State banks had long issued far more bank notes than they could redeem—notes that fueled the land boom after 1815. Farmers also borrowed to buy more land and plant more crops and planned to repay their loans by selling their crops to Europe. But after 1817, the combination of bumper crops in Europe and a recession in Britain trimmed foreign demand for U.S. wheat, flour, and cotton.

In the summer of 1818, reacting to the uncontrolled flood of state bank notes, the Bank of the United States began to insist that state banks offer specie to redeem notes now held by the Bank of the United States. State bank notes were often presented for redemption to the Bank of the United States because it had more branches than any state bank. And whenever the Bank of the United States redeemed a state bank note in specie, it became a creditor of the state bank. When the Bank of the United States demanded redemption in specie of its

squatters
People who occupied land that they did not own and did not have permission to occupy.

Panic of 1819
A major financial collapse that brought on a lot of bank failures and unemployment.

state bank notes, the state banks had to force farmers and land speculators to repay loans.

The result was a cascade of economic catastrophes. The biggest losers were the land speculators. Land that had once sold for as much as sixty-nine dollars an acre plummeted to two dollars an acre. Land prices fell because the credit squeeze drove down the market prices of staples like wheat, corn, cotton, and tobacco. Cotton, which had sold for thirty-two cents a pound in 1818, sank as low as seventeen cents a pound in 1820. Because farmers could not get much cash for their crops, they could not pay the debts they owed on their land. Because speculators could not collect money owed them by farmers, the value of land they still held for sale collapsed.

The Panic left behind a bitter public animosity toward banks, particularly the Bank of the United States, which was widely blamed for the hard times. The Panic also demonstrated just how dependent farmers had become on distant markets. One response was the acceleration of the search for better, cheaper ways to get crops to market.

9-2.3 The Transportation Revolution

Despite the large scale of western settlement in the first few decades of the nineteenth century, the transportation system in the United States remained limited. The great rivers west of the Appalachians could not connect western farmers to eastern markets because, by nature's decree, they flowed north to south. Roads were notoriously poor and expensive to maintain, and horse-drawn wagons had limited capacity. How were western farmers going to turn a profit from their cash crops if they could not transport them to eastern markets? Without major changes in the transportation network, the market economy would remain local and regional rather than national. In the early decades of the nineteenth century, Americans began to address this problem, initiating the **transportation revolution**.

In 1807, Robert R. Livingston and Robert Fulton introduced the steamboat *Clermont* on the Hudson River. They soon gained a monopoly from the New York legislature to run a ferry service between New York and New Jersey. Spectacular profits lured competitors, who secured a license from Congress and then filed suit to break the Livingston-Fulton monopoly. After a long court battle, the Supreme Court decided unanimously against the monopoly in the case of **Gibbons v. Ogden** (1824). Led by Chief Justice John Marshall, the Court ruled that Congress's constitutional power to regulate interstate commerce applied to navigation and thus had to prevail over New York's power to license the Livingston-Fulton monopoly. In the aftermath of this decision, other state-granted monopolies collapsed, and steamboat traffic increased rapidly. The number of steamboats operating on western rivers jumped from seventeen in 1817 to 727 by 1855.

Steamboats quickly assumed a vital role along the Mississippi–Ohio river system. Before the coming of the steamboat, the keelboat (a covered flatboat pushed by oars or poles) ruled the western rivers. But the keelboat took three or four months to complete the 1,350-mile voyage from New Orleans to Louisville. A steamboat, by contrast, could make the trip in twenty-five days. The development of long, shallow hulls enabled steamboats to navigate the Mississippi-Ohio system even when river levels dropped during the summer. To compete for passengers, steamboats began to offer luxurious cabins and lounges, called saloons. The saloon of the steamboat *Eclipse* was the length of a football field and featured skylights, chandeliers, and velvet-upholstered furniture.

While steamboats were proving their value, canals were replacing roads and turnpikes as the focus of investment. Although the cost of canal construction was mind-boggling—Jefferson dismissed the idea as little short of madness—canals offered the prospect of connecting the Mississippi-Ohio river system with the Great Lakes, and the Great Lakes with eastern markets.

Constructed between 1817 and 1825, New York's **Erie Canal**, connecting the Hudson River with Lake Erie, enabled produce from Ohio to reach New York City along a continuous stretch of waterways (see Map 9.2). Completion of the Erie Canal started a canal boom during the late 1820s and 1830s. Ohio constructed a network of canals for carrying wheat by water to Lake Erie. After transport across Lake Erie, the wheat was milled into flour in Rochester, New York, then shipped on the Erie Canal to Albany and down the Hudson River to New York City. Throughout the nation, canals reduced shipping costs from twenty to thirty cents a ton per mile in 1815 to two to three cents a ton per mile by 1830.

When another economic depression hit in the late 1830s, many states responded by scrapping their costly canal projects. As the canal boom was

---

transportation revolution
When attention and investment shifted to improving transportation on waterways.

Gibbons v. Ogden
Chief Justice John Marshall ruled that Congress's constitutional power to regulate interstate commerce applied to navigation and thus had to prevail over New York's power to license the Livingston-Fulton monopoly. In the aftermath of this decision, other state-granted monopolies collapsed, and steamboat traffic increased rapidly. The number of steamboats operating on western rivers jumped from 17 in 1817 to 727 by 1855.

Erie Canal
It connected the Hudson River with Lake Erie and enabled produce from Ohio to reach New York City by a continuous stretch of waterways.

STEAMSHIP *BEN CAMPBELL* AT LANDING, 1852 By the time the steamship *Ben Campbell* was built around 1852, steamboats had gotten a lot faster. *(Library of Congress Prints and Photographs Division [LC-USZ6-2054])*

ending, an entirely new form of transportation was being introduced: the railroad. In 1825, the world's first commercial railroad began operation in England, and by 1840 Americans had laid some three thousand miles of track—roughly equivalent to total canal mileage. During the 1830s, railroad investment surpassed canal investment. Cities like Baltimore and Boston, which lacked connections with major inland waterways, turned to railroads to enlarge their share of the western market.

Railroads had obvious advantages over canals: they were cheaper to build, achieved faster speeds, and were able to reach more places. But the potential of the railroads was only slowly realized. Most early railroads ran between cities in the East, rather than from east to west, and carried more passengers than freight. Not until 1849 did freight revenues exceed passenger revenues, and not until 1850 was the East Coast connected by rail to the Great Lakes.

Two factors explain the relatively slow spread of interregional railroads. First, unlike canals, which were built by state governments, most railroads were constructed by private corporations seeking quick profits. To minimize their original investment, railroad companies resorted to cost-cutting measures such as covering wooden rails with iron bars. As a result, American railroads, though relatively cheap to build, proved expensive to maintain—in contrast to canals, which, while expensive to construct, proved relatively cheap to maintain and often lasted decades after railroads appeared. A second reason for the slow spread of interregional railroads was that canal prices for shipping bulky commodities such as iron ore, coal, and nonperishable agricultural produce remained lower than railroad prices.

9-2.4 The Growth of the Cities

The transportation revolution sped the growth of towns and cities. Canals and railroads vastly increased business opportunities: for banks to lend money, insurers to cover risks of transport, warehouses and brokers to store and sell goods. In relative terms, the most rapid urbanization in American history occurred between 1820 and 1860. The Erie Canal turned New York City into the nation's largest city; its population rose from 124,000 in 1820 to 800,000 by 1860. An even more revealing change was the transformation of sleepy

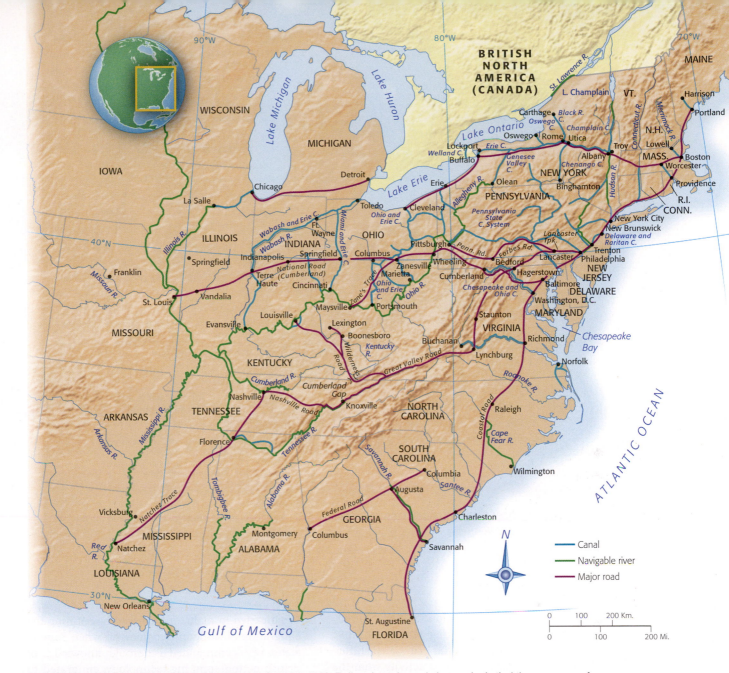

MAP 9.2 **MAJOR RIVERS, ROADS, AND CANALS, 1825–1860** Railroads and canals increasingly tied the economy of the Midwest to that of the Northeast.

villages of a few hundred people into thriving towns of several thousand. For example, the Erie Canal grew Rochester, New York, from a small village in 1817 into Flour City with nine thousand residents by 1830.

Cities and towns grew with dramatic speed, especially in the West (see Map 9.3). Pittsburgh, Cincinnati, and St. Louis were little more than hamlets in 1800, occupied by transient populations of hunters, traders, and soldiers. But between 1815 and 1819, the agricultural boom and the steamboat transformed all three places into bustling cities. Cincinnati's population

nearly quadrupled between 1810 and 1820, then doubled in the 1820s. Prominent western cities were river ports: Pittsburgh, Cincinnati, and Louisville on the Ohio; St. Louis and New Orleans on the Mississippi. With the exception of Pittsburgh, these cities were commercial hubs rather than manufacturing centers, and they were flooded with people eager to make money. In 1819, land speculators in St. Louis were bidding as much as a thousand dollars an acre for lots that had sold for thirty dollars an acre in 1815. Waterfronts endowed with natural beauty were swiftly overrun by stores and docks.

MAP 9.3 POPULATION DISTRIBUTION, 1790 AND 1850 By 1850, high population density characterized parts of the Midwest as well as the Northeast.

Source: 1900 Census of Population, *Statistical Atlas,* plates 2 and 8.

The transportation revolution selected some cities for growth while sentencing others to relative decline. The completion of the Erie Canal shifted the center of western economic activity from the river cities toward such Great Lakes cities as Buffalo, Cleveland, Detroit, Chicago, and Milwaukee. In 1830, nearly 75 percent of all western city-dwellers lived in the river ports of New Orleans, Louisville, Cincinnati, and Pittsburgh; by 1840, as new cities sprang up, that proportion had dropped to just 20 percent (see Map 9.4).

9-3 Industrial Beginnings

What were the causes and effects of early industrialization?

Industrialization gave an added boost to the growth of cities and towns. The United States lagged a generation behind Britain in building factories, and Britain tried to maintain that lead by banning the emigration of skilled mechanics. So when Samuel Slater, who commanded a thorough knowledge of British cotton-spinning technology, emigrated to the United States in 1789, he passed himself off as a farm laborer. The following year, he helped design and build the country's first cotton mill, at Pawtucket, Rhode Island. Slater's workforce quickly grew from nine workers to one hundred, and his mills multiplied. After Slater's pioneering work, the pace of industrialization quickened in the 1810s and 1820s, especially in the production of cotton textiles and shoes.

The commitment to industrialization varied by region. Southern planters invested in land and slaves rather than machines. In contrast, New England's depleted soil stimulated investment in factories. Industrialization was a gradual process that involved a reorganization of labor, with each worker fabricating only a part of the final product. Often, but not always, the industrial process gathered workers into large factories. Finally, high-speed machines

MAP 9.4 AMERICAN CITIES, 1820 AND 1860 In 1820, most cities were seaports. By 1860, however, cities dotted the nation's interior and included San Francisco on the West Coast. This change occurred in large measure because of the transportation revolution.

replaced skilled handwork. In some industries, these elements occurred simultaneously, but more often they took place over several years.

Industrialization changed lives. Most workers in the early factories were recruited from farms. Farming men and women had worked hard from sunrise to sunset, but they had set their own pace and taken periodic breaks between tasks. Factory workers, operating machines that ran continuously, encountered the new discipline of industrial time, regulated by clocks rather than tasks. Industrialization also encouraged a focus on more specialized production beyond the factories. During the colonial era, most farm families had made their own clothes and often their shoes. With industrialization, they began to concentrate on farming, while purchasing factory-made clothes and shoes.

9-3.1 Causes of Industrialization

A host of factors stimulated industrialization. The Embargo Act of 1807 prompted merchants barred from foreign trade to redirect their capital into factories. The tariffs passed during the Era of Good Feelings protected American industries from foreign competition, and New England's output of cotton cloth rose from 4 million yards in 1817 to 323 million yards by 1840. The many cascading rivers that flowed from the Appalachian Mountains to the Atlantic Ocean provided abundant waterpower for mills. The transportation revolution opened new markets for manufactured products in the South and West.

Industrialization was also driven by problems with the rural economy. In New England in the late eighteenth century, the population had grown beyond the land's ability to support it. Farm families adopted new strategies to survive. For example, a farmer would decide to grow flax, which his wife and daughters would make into linen for sale; or he would plant broomcorn, and he and his sons would spend the winter months making brooms for local sale. In time, he would form a partnership to manufacture brooms on a larger scale and for more-distant markets. At some point, he would cease to be a farmer, purchasing his broomcorn from farmers and, with hired help, concentrating on the manufacturing process. Other merchants would provide him with broom handles and twine and would purchase and sell all the brooms he could make.

The comparatively high wages paid to unskilled laborers in the United States encouraged employers to replace them with machines. Because of Britain's head start in developing industrial technology, some American entrepreneurs simply copied British designs. While ostensibly on vacation in England, a wealthy Boston merchant, Francis Cabot Lowell, charmed information about British textile machinery out of his hosts; later he engaged an American mechanic to construct machines from drawings he had made each night in his hotel room. The United States benefited from the absence of craft organizations (called guilds in Britain) that tied artisans to a single trade. In the absence of guilds, American artisans experimented freely with machines outside their own area of training. In the 1790s, Oliver Evans, a wagon-maker from Delaware, built an automated

flour mill that required only a single supervisor, who merely watched grain pour into one side of the machine and flour emerge from the other.

Even in the absence of new technology, Americans searched for new cost-cutting methods of production. After inventing the cotton gin, **Eli Whitney** won a government contract in 1798 to produce ten thousand muskets by 1800. Whitney planned to meet this seemingly impossible deadline by using unskilled workers to make interchangeable parts that could be used in any of his factory's muskets. Whitney promised much more than he could deliver (as discussed in Chapter 11) and missed his deadline. But within a few decades, his idea would transform American manufacturing.

9-3.2 Women and Textile Towns in New England

New England became America's first industrial region (see Map 9.5). The crises in foreign trade that led to the War of 1812 had devastated the region's commercial economy and stimulated capital investment in manufacturing. New England's swift rivers were ideal sources of waterpower for mills.

Cotton textiles led the way. In 1813, a group of Boston merchants called the Boston Associates, who included Francis Cabot Lowell, incorporated the Boston Manufacturing Company. With ten times the capital of any previous American cotton mill, this company quickly built textile mills in the Massachusetts towns of Waltham and Lowell. By 1836, the Boston Associates controlled eight companies employing more than six thousand workers.

The **Waltham and Lowell textile mills** differed in two ways from the earlier Rhode Island mills established by Samuel Slater. Slater's mills performed only two of the operations needed to turn raw cotton into clothing: carding (separating raw cotton into fine strands) and spinning these strands into yarn. The weaving process he contracted out to women working in their homes. Unlike Slater's mills, the Waltham and Lowell mills turned out finished fabrics that required only one additional step, stitching fabric into clothing.

In addition, the Waltham and Lowell mills upset the traditional, family-based order of New England society. Slater tried to support traditional family structure not only by contracting weaving to farm families but also by hiring entire families to work in his mill complexes. The men in Slater's employ raised crops on nearby company lands, while the women and children tended the machines in his factories. By contrast, 80 percent of the employees in Waltham and Lowell were young unmarried women (many in their teens) who had been lured from farms by the promise of wages, just as Alexander

Eli Whitney
Inventor of the cotton gin.

Waltham and Lowell textile mills
These mills turned out finished fabrics that required only one additional step, stitching into clothes. In contrast to other New England mills, 80 percent of the workers in Waltham and Lowell, places that had not even existed in the eighteenth century, were young unmarried women who had been lured from farms by the promise of wages.

MAP 9.5 COTTON MILLS IN THE NORTHEAST In 1820, manufacturing employment was concentrated mostly in the Northeast, where the first textile mills appeared. By 1850, the density of manufacturing in the Northeast had increased, but new manufacturing centers arose in Baltimore, Pittsburgh, and Cincinnati.

Source: Historical Atlas of the United States, 2nd ed. (Washington, DC: National Geographic Society, 1993), p. 148.

Hamilton envisioned as Secretary of the Treasury in the 1790s (see Chapter 7).

Initially, parents were uncomfortable with sending their young daughters far from home to work in the mills and away from the watchful eyes of parents who could ensure their moral values and behavior. In England, factories had been associated with poverty and rumors that low-paid female workers were enticed to prostitution, which was worrisome to New Englanders. At the same time, the shift to a market economy meant families bought more of the items they—especially women—once produced in the home; as such, farm families were in greater need of the potential income daughters could provide and had far less need for their household or farm labor. Daughters, too, understood that they were at the cusp of an important transition, and they enthusiastically embraced the opportunity to both assist their families and potentially enjoy a modicum of independence. Mary Paul, a Vermont teenager, settled her doubts about leaving home for Lowell by concluding that "I … must work where I can get more pay."

To assuage parental concerns about morality, mill owners established supervised living arrangements and a highly structured work life. In place of traditional family discipline, the workers ("operatives") had to live either in company boardinghouses or in licensed private dwellings, attend church on the Sabbath, observe a 10:00 P.M. curfew, and comply with the company's moral regulations. The girls typically roomed together in groups of four to six, where they ultimately formed strong friendships. During their limited leisure time, they produced a literary magazine, *The Lowell Offering*, the cost of which was paid by factory owners. Boardinghouse chaperones ensured that the girls obeyed house rules, which were designed to give the mills a good reputation so that New England farm daughters would continue to be attracted to factory work. Daughters used some of their earnings for small purchases, but most of it went back to their families.

MILL GIRL AROUND 1850 This girl most likely worked in a Massachusetts textile mill, at either Lowell or Waltham. Her swollen and rough hands suggest that she was a "warper," one of the jobs usually given to children. Warpers were responsible for constantly straightening out the strands of cotton or wool as they entered the loom. *(Jack Naylor Collection/Picture Research Consultants and Archives)*

The major social groups that contributed to the Lowell system lived in separate worlds. The Boston Associates provided capital but rarely visited the factories. Their agents, all men, gave orders to the operatives, mainly women. The girls worked long days, and conditions in the factories could be harsh. To provide the humidity necessary to keep the threads from snapping, overseers nailed factory windows shut and sprayed the air with water. The air was filled with cotton dust and the deafening roar of the machines.

In the late 1830s, mill owners reduced wages and speeded up work schedules in response to growing competition and an economic depression. They counted on notions of gender when they made such moves, expecting that the female operatives would passively accept these new directives. Instead, the girls had developed a proud identity as workers, and the bonds they formed in the boardinghouses and factory empowered some eight hundred Lowell mill women to defy norms about women's submissiveness and quit work in 1834, protesting the wage cuts. Two years later, another "turnout" involved fifteen hundred to two thousand women. These were the largest strikes in American history to that date, noteworthy as strikes not only of employees against employers but also of women against men. In striking the girls challenged notions of women's subordination to men and defied social sanctions against women speaking in public.

But the Panic of 1837 led to a layoff and factory shutdown. When the factories reopened, managers had new demands for longer hours and increased production. By the 1840s, factory workers across Massachusetts—female and male—banded together in seeking a law limiting the work day to ten hours. The factory world the women first entered decades earlier was changing in other ways, too. In the early years, labor shortages benefitted workers, but by the 1840s, the reverse (a surplus of workers) was true. A new generation of mill workers, many of them Irish immigrants, was forming a permanent industrial working class. Founded as a pastoral "mill village," Lowell was turning into a city sharply divided between the native-born and the Irish, Protestants and Catholics, and rich and poor—a mirror of a changing America.

The Waltham and Lowell mills were much larger than most factories. As late as 1860, the average industrial establishment employed only eight workers. Outside of textiles, many industries continued to depend on industrial **"outwork."** For example, in the 1830s, more than fifty thousand New England farmwomen earned wages in their homes by making hats out of straw and palm leaves provided by merchant capitalists. Similarly, before the new sewing machine made possible the concentration of all aspects of shoe manufacture in large factories in the 1850s, women often sewed parts of shoes at home and sent the piecework to factories for finishing.

9-3.3 Artisans and Workers in Mid-Atlantic Cities

New York City and Philadelphia also became industrial centers dependent on outwork. Lured by the prospect of distant markets, some urban artisans and merchants began to travel throughout the country to drum up orders for manufactured goods. They hired unskilled workers, often women, to work in small shops or homes fashioning parts of shoes or saddles or dresses. A New York reporter wrote,

We have been in some fifty cellars in different parts of the city, each inhabited by a shoemaker and his family. The floor is made of rough plank laid loosely down, and the ceiling is not quite so high as a tall man. The walls are dark and damp and . . . the

"outwork"
Collaboration between households and factories in producing industrial goods—for instance, the sewing of shoe parts at home to be sent to the factory for finishing.

miserable room is lighted only by . . . the little light that struggles from the steep and rotting stairs. In this apartment often lives the man and his work-bench, the wife, and five or six children of all ages; and perhaps a palsied grandfather or grandmother and often both. . . . Here they work, here they cook, they eat, they sleep, they pray.

New York and Philadelphia were home to artisans with strong craft traditions who valued their independence. Those with highly marketable skills like cutting leather or clothing patterns continued to earn good wages. A minority grew rich by turning themselves into businessmen who spent less time making products than traveling to obtain orders. But artisans lacking the capital to become businessmen found themselves on the downslide in the face of competition from cheap, unskilled labor.

In the late 1820s, skilled male artisans in New York, Philadelphia, and other cities began to form trade unions and workingmen's political parties to protect their interests. Disdaining association with unskilled workers, most of these groups initially sought to restore privileges and working conditions that skilled artisans had once enjoyed. But the steady deterioration of working conditions in the early 1830s demonstrated that skilled and unskilled workers were in the same boat. In 1835 in Philadelphia, the two groups united to create the first general strike: unskilled coal haulers struck for a ten-hour day in 1835, and skilled carpenters, shoemakers, leather workers, and other artisans quickly joined them. With so many workers facing economic decline by the 1830s, many white Americans began to wonder whether their nation was truly a land of equality.

9-4 The Revolution in Social Relationships

How and why were older systems of power and authority transformed in the first half of the nineteenth century?

Following the War of 1812, the growth of interregional trade, commercial agriculture, and manufacturing disrupted traditional social relationships and forged new ones. Two broad changes took place. First, more Americans questioned authority, even that of their parents, and embraced individualism. That term had once meant nothing more than selfishness; now it connoted positive qualities such as self-reliance and each person's ability to judge his or her own best interests. Individualism made ordinary Americans less likely to defer to the opinions

DAGUERREOTYPE OF A BLACKSMITH This blacksmith holds a horseshoe and pliers in one hand and a hammer in the other. Shoeing horses kept blacksmiths busy but they also forged iron into rails and gates. Every village had its blacksmith in the decades before the Civil War. *(Library of Congress Prints and Photographs Division [LC_USZC4-3948])*

of people with superior wealth, education, or social position. That was especially important in an era when the gulf widened between those at the top economic rungs of society and those at the bottom.

Second, even as Americans began to question the traditional basis of authority, they sought to construct new sources of authority. For example, middle-class men and women came to embrace the idea that men held sway over the public world of business and politics while women wielded special powers of moral influence from their "separate sphere" in the home. In addition, individuals increasingly banded together with others to form voluntary associations whose purpose was to influence the direction of society.

9-4.1 Urban Inequality: The Rich and the Poor

The gap between the rich and the poor widened in the first half of the nineteenth century. In cities, a small fraction of residents owned a huge share of the wealth. For example, in New York City, the richest 4 percent owned nearly half the wealth in 1828 and more than two-thirds by 1845. Splendid residences, elite neighborhoods, and social clubs set the rich apart. In 1828, more than half of the five hundred wealthiest families in New York City lived on just eight of its more than 250 streets. By the late 1820s, the city had a club so exclusive that it was called simply The Club.

According to the popular myth of the self-made man, any man could choose to rise from "rags to riches." In reality, less than 5 percent of the wealthy had started life poor, and almost 90 percent were born rich. The usual way to acquire wealth was to inherit it, increase it by marrying well, then expand it through wise investment. Occasional rags-to-riches stories like that of John Jacob Astor and his fur-trading empire sustained the myth of the self-made man, but it remained mainly a myth.

By today's standards, most antebellum Americans were poor. They lived close to the edge of misery and depended on their children's labor just to meet expenses. For example, Harriet Hanson Robinson's widowed mother ran a boardinghouse in Lowell where she shopped, cooked, and did the laundry for forty-five people each day; her daughter Harriet washed dishes at the boardinghouse before entering the mills. But when antebellum Americans spoke of poverty, they were not thinking of the ordinary hardships that affected most people. The greater specter haunting them was "pauperism," a state of severe economic dependency created by all sorts of misfortunes. Epidemics of yellow fever and cholera could devastate families. A frozen canal or harbor brought unemployment to boatmen and dock workers; a frozen river forced layoffs in factories that depended on waterpower. Even ordinary illness and old age, in the absence of health insurance and pensions, condemned many people to pauperism.

Middle-class moralists liked to distinguish the "deserving" poor from the "undeserving" poor, assigning indolent loafers and drunkards to the latter category and blaming their poverty on their own life choices. Most moralists comforted themselves with the belief that pauperism would not pass from one generation to another. The "deserving" poor, they believed, were poor due to circumstances beyond anyone's control, such as old age and disease, while the "undeserving" poor were poor due to decisions to squander money on liquor.

This assumption was ill-founded. In reality, a class of people who could not escape poverty was emerging in the major cities during the first half of the nineteenth century. A major source of such entrenched poverty was immigration. As early as 1801, a New York newspaper called attention to the arrival of boatloads of immigrants with large families, people without money or health who were "expiring from the want of sustenance."

The poorest white immigrants were from Ireland, where English landlords had been evicting peasants from the land in order to convert it to commercial use. Severed from the land, the Irish became a nation of wanderers, scrounging for wages wherever they could. "The poor Irishman," it was said, "the wheelbarrow is his country." By the early 1830s, the great majority of canal workers in the North were Irish immigrants. Without the backbreaking labor of the Irish, the Erie Canal would never have been built. Many Irish congregated in the infamous Five Points district in New York City. After a neighborhood brewery was converted into housing for hundreds of people in 1837, Five Points quickly emerged as the worst slum in America.

The Irish were not only poor, they were Catholics—a faith despised by the Protestant majority in the United States. But even the Protestant poor came in for rough treatment in the years between 1815 and 1840. Middle-class Americans were increasingly convinced that success lay within everyone's grasp. The poor, they believed, were responsible for their own misery. Ironically, even as many Americans blamed the poor for being poor, they practiced discrimination that kept some groups mired in enduring poverty. Northern free blacks were a major target of such discrimination.

9-4.2 Free Blacks in the North

Racial prejudice against black Americans was deeply ingrained in white society throughout the nation. Although slavery had largely disappeared in the North by 1820, northern whites passed laws to restrict black voting rights even as they expanded them for white men. In New York State, for example, a constitutional revision of 1821 eliminated property requirements for white voters but kept them for blacks (see Chapter 8). Rhode Island and Pennsylvania banned all blacks from voting. Throughout the half-century after 1800, only one major city, Boston, permitted blacks to vote on equal terms with whites.

Some laws barred free blacks from migrating across city or state borders. Missouri's original constitution authorized the state legislature to prevent blacks from entering the state "under any pretext whatsoever." Municipal ordinances often barred free blacks from using public conveyances and facilities and either excluded them from public schools or forced them into segregated schools. Northern jails, almshouses, and hospitals also practiced racial segregation.

Employment practices forced free blacks into the least-skilled and lowest-paying occupations throughout the northern cities. Recollecting his youthful days in Providence, Rhode Island, in the early 1830s, William J. Brown wrote: "To drive carriages, carry a market basket after the boss, and brush his boots, or saw wood and run errands was as high as a colored man could rise." Although a few urban free blacks became successful entrepreneurs and achieved moderate wealth, as a group they were only half as likely as city-dwellers in general to own real estate.

PORTRAIT OF A BLACK MAN At a time when job opportunities for African Americans were limited, the attire of this black man and the presence of the steamboat *New Philadelphia* in the background make it likely that he was the ship's steward or head waiter. The *New Philadelphia* was the first Hudson River steamboat to introduce "colored waiters." Its reputation for speed and innovation was a source of great pride to its officers and crew. *(2006 Board of Trustees, National Gallery of Art, Washington, D.C)*

Just as northern African Americans formed their own churches, they gradually acquired some control over the education of their children. The 1820s and 1830s witnessed an explosion of black self-help societies like New York City's Phoenixonian Literary Society, devoted to encouraging black education and run by such black leaders as Samuel Cornish and Henry Garnett.

9-4.3 The "Middling Classes"

The majority of antebellum Americans lived neither in splendid wealth nor in grinding poverty. Most belonged to what men and women of the time called the middling classes. Even though the rich owned an increasing proportion of all wealth, most people's standard of living rose between 1800 and 1860, particularly between 1840 and 1860 when per capita income grew at an annual rate of around 1.5 percent.

Americans applied the term *middling classes* to families headed by professionals, small merchants and manufacturers, landowning farmers, and self-employed artisans. Commentators portrayed these people as living stable and secure lives. In reality, life in the middle often proved unpredictable. The commercializing economy created greater opportunities for both rising and falling on the social scale. An enterprising import merchant, Allan Melville, the father of novelist Herman Melville, prospered until the late 1820s, when his business sagged. By 1830, he was "destitute of resources and without a shilling." Despite loans of $3,500, Melville's downward spiral continued until he died in 1832, broken in spirit and nearly insane.

In the emerging market economy, occupational categories such as farmer and artisan often conveyed little useful information about how someone actually made his living. Asa G. Sheldon, born in Massachusetts in 1788, called himself a farmer, offered advice on growing corn and cranberries, and gave speeches about the glories of agriculture. But Sheldon actually spent little time tilling the soil. In 1812, he began transporting hops from New England to breweries in New York City, and soon extended this business to Philadelphia and Baltimore. The profits he invested in land, not to farm it but to sell its timber. When a business setback forced him to sell his property, he was soon back in

White churches also discriminated against free blacks by confining them to separate benches or galleries. A black walkout from a Methodist church in Philadelphia prompted the formation of the first black-run Protestant denomination, called the **African Methodist Episcopal Church**. When some black worshipers mistakenly sat in the church's whites-only gallery, they were ejected. Then, as their leader **Richard Allen** reported, "we all went out of the church in a body, and they were no longer plagued by us." In 1816, Allen, a former slave, initiated the African Methodist Episcopal, or AME Church, of which he would become a bishop. By 1822, the AME Church had active congregations in Washington, D.C., Pittsburgh, New York City, and throughout the mid-Atlantic states. Its members campaigned against slavery, boycotting produce grown by slaves.

African Methodist Episcopal Church
The first black-run Protestant denomination.

Richard Allen
A former slave who was ejected from the Methodist church of Philadelphia for mistakenly sitting in the gallery designed for whites. He eventually became a bishop of the African Methodist Episcopal Church.

operation "through the disinterested kindness of friends" who lent him money. Sheldon used the loans to purchase carts and oxen for a new company that filled swamps and cleared and graded land for railroads, employing Irish immigrants to do the shoveling. Through such diversified businesses as these, "farmer" Asa Sheldon grew prosperous.

The emerging market economy also transformed what it meant to be an "artisan." During the colonial period, artisans had formed a proud and cohesive group whose members often attained the goal of self-employment. They owned their own tools, made their own products on order from customers, and boarded their labor force of apprentices and journeymen in their homes. But by 1840, artisans had entered a new world of economic relationships shaped not only by new industrial technology but by the reorganization of production. The work lives of carpenters, for example, were transformed by the new demand for housing generated by town and city growth. Some carpenters, usually those with access to capital, became contractors. They took orders for more houses than they could build themselves and hired large numbers of journeymen to do the construction work. Similarly, some shoemakers spent less time crafting shoes than making trips to obtain orders, then hired other workers to fashion the shoes. In effect, the older artisanal class was splitting into two new groupings: some became self-employed entrepreneurs, while others became wage-earning journeymen who worked for others.

The middling classes experienced a high degree of spatial mobility. The transportation revolution, by making it easier for Americans to purchase services as well as goods, spurred many young men to enter the professions. The number of medical schools rose from one in 1765 to twenty in 1830 and sixty-five in 1860. Frequently, the new men who crowded into medicine and into the ministry and law were forced into incessant motion. Physicians rode from town to town looking for patients. The itinerant clergyman riding an old nag to visit the faithful or conduct revivals became a familiar figure in newly settled areas. Even well-established lawyers and judges spent part of each year riding from one county courthouse to another, bunking (usually two to a bed) in rough country inns.

Transience affected the lives of most Americans. Farmers exhausted their land by intensively cultivating cash crops and then moved on. City dwellers moved frequently as they changed jobs. A survey by the Boston police on Saturday, September 6, 1851, when Boston's population was 145,000, showed that from 6:30 A.M. to 7:30 P.M., 41,729 people entered the city and 42,313 left. At a time when there were few suburbs, it is safe to say that these people were not commuters. Most likely, they were moving in search of work, as much a necessity for many in the middling classes as for the poor.

The commercialization of the economy increased both the numbers of professionals and the frequency of attacks on them. Newly minted lawyers and doctors seldom had deep roots in the towns they served or convincing claims to social superiority. "Men dropped down into their places as from clouds," one critic wrote. "Nobody knew who or what they were, except as they claimed." A horse doctor one day would the next day hang up his sign as "Physician and Surgeon" and "fire at random a box of his pills into your bowels, with a vague chance of hitting some disease unknown to him, but with a better prospect of killing the patient, whom or whose administrator he charged some ten dollars a trial for his marksmanship."

Westerners were particularly well known for questioning authority. Eastern travelers sneered that every westerner they met claimed to be a "judge," "general," "colonel," or "squire." In a society in which everyone was new, such titles were easily adopted and just as easily challenged. In the West, where neither law nor custom sanctioned claims of superiority, would-be gentlemen substituted an exaggerated sense of personal honor. Obsessed with their fragile status, many reacted testily to the slightest insult. Dueling became a widespread frontier practice. At a Kentucky militia parade in 1819, an officer's dog jogged onto the field and sat at his master's knee. Enraged by this breach of military decorum, another officer ran the dog through with his sword. A week later, both officers met with pistols at ten paces. One was killed, the other maimed for life.

Intense criticism of lawyers, physicians, and ministers exemplified the assault on traditional authority. Some complained that lawyers needlessly prolonged and confused court cases so that they could charge high fees. These jabs at the learned professions peaked between 1820 and 1850. Samuel Thomson, a farmer's son with little formal education, led a successful movement to eliminate all barriers to entering the medical profession, including educational requirements. By 1845, every state had repealed laws that required licenses and education to practice medicine. Meanwhile, relations between ministers and their parishioners grew acrimonious. In colonial New England, ministers had usually served a single parish for life, but by the 1830s rapid turnover was becoming the norm as parishioners grew more willing to dismiss clergymen whose theology displeased them. Ministers themselves were becoming more ambitious—more inclined to leave small, poor congregations for large, wealthy ones.

9-4.4 The Challenge to Family Authority

At the same time as adults were attacking the learned professions, children were questioning parental authority. Young people were faced with a choice between staying at home to help their parents or venturing out on their own. Writing to her parents in Vermont shortly before taking a job in a Lowell textile mill, eighteen-year-old Sally Rice quickly got to the point. "I must of course have something of my own before many more years have passed over my head and where is that something coming from if I go home and earn nothing. I have but one life to live and I want to enjoy myself as I can while I live."

A similar desire for independence tempted young men to leave home at earlier ages than in the past. Although the great migration to the West was primarily a movement of entire families, movement within regions—especially from farms to towns and cities—was frequently spearheaded by restless and single young people. Two young men in Virginia put it succinctly. "All the promise of life seemed to us to be at the other end of the rainbow—somewhere else—anywhere else but on the farm. . . . And so all our youthful plans had as their chief object the getting away from the farm."

Courtship and marriage patterns also changed. Many young people who could no longer depend on their parents for land began to decide for themselves when and whom to marry. Whereas American colonists had advised young people to choose marriage partners whom they could learn to love, by the early 1800s young men and women viewed romantic love as indispensable to a successful marriage. "In affairs of love," a young lawyer in Maine wrote, "young people's hearts are generally much wiser than old people's heads."

One sign of young people's increasing autonomy in courtship and marriage was the declining likelihood that daughters would marry in their exact birth order. Traditionally, fathers had wanted their daughters to marry in the order of their birth to avoid planting the suspicion that something was wrong with the ones passed over. Toward the end of the eighteenth century, however, as daughters began to make their own marital decisions, that practice ceased to be customary. Long engagements also became more common. Some young women delayed tying the knot, fearing that marriage would snuff out their independence. New Yorkers Caroline and William Kirkland were engaged for seven years before their marriage in 1828. Equally striking was the increasing number of young women who chose not to marry. **Catharine Beecher**, a popular writer and the daughter of prominent minister Lyman Beecher, broke off her engagement during the 1820s despite her father's pressure to marry the young man. She later renewed the engagement, but after her fiancé's death in a shipwreck, she remained single for the rest of her life.

Moralists, alarmed at the signs that young people were living in a world of their own, flooded the country with advice books stressing the same message: young men and women no longer subject to parental authority should develop self-control and

that internalized system of government called "character." The self-made adult, they instructed their readers, began with the self-made youth.

9-4.5 Wives and Husbands

Relations between spouses, too, were changing. Of course, wives remained unequal to their husbands in many ways. With few exceptions, the law did not allow married women to own property; divorce law favored husbands; and battered women received no legal protection. But the ideology about the roles wives and husbands should play in a marriage was shifting during the 1820s and 1830s.

One source of the change, zealously advocated by Catharine Beecher, was the doctrine of **separate spheres**, or what historians have called the ideology or "cult" of true womanhood. Emerging amid the changes of the early nineteenth century, this white, middle class ideology divided men's and women's roles into distinct realms, with men's sphere defined as the public worlds of work and politics and women's as the private world of home and family. In this view, men were to be providers, dealing with the harsh realities of business, where "true" women were to shun paid labor and put their energies into making the home a sanctuary for their families. In truth, many women's lives bore little resemblance to these ideals; poor and slave women could hardly avoid work the way middle- and upper-class white women might. Still, the ideology served as a powerful force about idealized womanhood. Moreover, in the context of a market revolution in which work increasingly became equated with its ability to generate cash (a salary), the work women did at home was no longer considered work; instead, it was seen as a "natural" extension of femininity, something women did simply because they were women.

One of the most important duties assigned to women was raising children. In the immediate aftermath of the American Revolution, motherhood took on a social and moral function under the banner of "Republican Motherhood" (Chapter 7), as women were charged with educating children to become virtuous citizens. Women gained a foothold in the teaching profession—previously dominated by men—because teaching was seen as an extension of their gender roles.

But the notion of motherhood inherent in the nineteenth-century ideology of true womanhood had a religious component, influenced by the religious revivals known as the Second Great Awakening that began in the 1810s and 1820s (see Chapter 10). Women were an important force in

Catharine Beecher
A leading author and the daughter of prominent minister Lyman Beecher.

separate spheres
An ideology about gender roles that emerged in the nineteenth century, which defined men's roles as in the public worlds of work and politics, and women's roles within the private realms of home and family.

the new religiosity of the revival movement. As such, prescriptions for idealized motherhood were infused with Christian piety. Good Christian women were depicted not only as morally superior but as charged with safeguarding their children's and family's morals. Where men were encouraged to pursue selfish interests in the public worlds of business and politics, women were expected to be selfless, sacrificing their own wants for the greater good of their families. Additionally, they were, by virtue of their alleged moral virtue, supposed to be pure, lacking in sexual desire. During the eighteenth century, church sermons emphasized the father's duty to govern the family; by the 1830s, childrearing manuals were addressed to mothers rather than to fathers. "How entire and perfect is this dominion over the unformed character of your infant," proclaimed Lydia Sigourney in her popular *Letters to Mothers* (1838). Women's publications such as *Godey's Lady's Book* in the mid-nineteenth century would further perpetuate this image of middle-class, Christian piety within true womanhood.

The idea of women's sphere complemented the image of the home as a haven or refuge from a society marked by turmoil and disorder. The popular culture of the 1830s and 1840s painted an alluring portrait of home life through songs like "Home, Sweet Home" and poems such as Henry Wadsworth Longfellow's "The Children's Hour." Clement Moore's poem "A Visit from St. Nicholas" was part of the growing popularity of Christmas as a holiday season when family members gathered to exchange warm affection. Even the physical appearance of houses changed. Architect Andrew Jackson Downing published plans for cottage-like single-family homes that he hoped would offset the "spirit of unrest" and the feverish pace of American life. In the ideal home, he wrote, "There should be something to love. There must be nooks about it, where one would love to linger; windows, where one can enjoy the quiet landscape at his leisure; cozy rooms, where all fireside joys are invited to dwell."

Downing deserves credit as a prophet because one of the motives that impelled later Americans to flee cities for suburbs was the desire to own their own homes. In the 1820s and 1830s, this ideal was beyond the reach of most people—not only blacks, immigrants, and sweatshop workers but also most members of the middle class. In the countryside, although middle-class farmers still managed productive households, these were anything but tranquil; wives milked cows and bled hogs, and children fetched wood, drove cows to pasture, and chased blackbirds from cornfields. In the cities, middle-class families often had to sacrifice their privacy by taking in boarders to supplement family income.

THE COUNTRY PARSON DISTURBED AT BREAKFAST This young couple's decision to wed seems to have been on the spur of the moment. As young men and women became more independent of parental control, they gave their impulses freer play. *(Courtesy Childs Gallery, Boston)*

SOURCE

Tocqueville on American Democracy

In 1831, Alexis de Tocqueville, a twenty-five-year-old French aristocrat, arrived in the United States. Officially, Tocqueville and his traveling companion, Gustave de Beaumont, were here to study American prisons. But Tocqueville's real interest lay in investigating American "democracy." His two-volume *Democracy in America* (1835, 1840) is widely considered the keenest analysis of the United States ever written by a foreigner.

Tocqueville associated democracy with government by the people and an increasing "equality of condition." In Europe, constant political turmoil battered progress toward equality.

In contrast, the United States had enjoyed a half-century of political stability as a republic.

Tocqueville knew that some white Americans were rich and others poor, and that many blacks were enslaved. Still, he found in the United States more equality of condition than in France. Above all, American citizens *thought* they were equal to each other. They were unaccustomed to giving, or taking, orders. Tocqueville attributed their ability to build so many roads, canals, factories, model towns, churches, and schools to their penchant for "public associations in civil life."

Americans of all ages, all conditions, and all dispositions constantly form associations. They have not only commercial and manufacturing companies, in which all take part, but associations of a thousand other kinds, religious, moral, serious, futile, general or restricted, enormous or diminutive. The Americans make associations to give entertainments, to found seminaries, to build inns, to construct churches, to diffuse books, to send missionaries to the antipodes; in this manner, they found hospitals, prisons, and schools. If it is proposed to inculcate some truth or to foster some feeling by the encouragement of a great example, they form a society. Wherever at the head of some new undertaking you see the government in France or a man of rank in England, in the United States you will be sure to find an association. . . . The English often perform great things singly, whereas the Americans form associations for the smallest undertakings. It is evident that the former people consider association as a powerful means they have of acting. . . .

Aristocratic communities always contain, among a multitude of persons who by themselves are powerless, a small number of powerful and wealthy citizens, each of whom can achieve great undertakings single-handed. In

aristocratic societies, men do not need to combine in order to act, because they are strong held together. Every wealthy and powerful citizen constitutes the head of a permanent and compulsory association, composed of all those who are dependent on him or whom he makes subservient to the execution of his designs.

Among democratic nations, on the contrary, all the citizens are independent and feeble; they can hardly do anything by themselves, and none of them can oblige his fellow men to lend him their assistance. They all, therefore, become powerless if they do not learn voluntarily to help one another. If men living in democratic countries had no right and no inclination to associate for political purposes, their independence would be in great jeopardy, but they might long preserve their wealth and their cultivation: whereas if they never acquired the habit of forming associations in ordinary life, civilization itself would be endangered. A people among whom individuals lost the power of achieving great things single-handed, without acquiring the means of producing them by united exertions, would soon relapse into barbarism.

Source: Alexis de Tocqueville, *Democracy in America [1840] (vol. 2, New York, Vintage, 1972), 106–107.*

QUESTIONS

1. List some examples of the sorts of organizations that Tocqueville would have viewed as "public associations in civil life."

2. What did Tocqueville mean when he said that in democratic nations all citizens are "independent and feeble"?

A subtle implication of the doctrine of separate spheres was that women should wield control not only over childrearing, but family planning—how many children they would bear. In 1800, the United States had one of the highest birthrates ever recorded. The average American woman bore 7.04 children. In the preindustrial farming economy, children were vital to a labor source that carried out essential tasks in the household economy and, when grown, took care of their aging parents. But with the spread of a commercial economy, for urban middling-class parents, children were no longer economic assets who could make a significant contribution to the family economy. Rather, they were economic deficits requiring education for a rapidly changing industrial economy. By 1850, the average woman was bearing only 5.02 children; by 1900, that number had dipped to 3.98. The birthrate remained high among blacks and many immigrant groups, but it fell drastically among native-born whites, particularly in towns and cities.

For the most part, the decline in the birthrate was accomplished by abstinence from sexual intercourse, *coitus interruptus* (withdrawal before ejaculation), or abortion. By the 1840s, abortionists were advertising remedies for "female irregularities," a common euphemism for unwanted pregnancies. No available birth-control devices were foolproof, and much misinformation circulated about birth-control techniques. Nonetheless, interest in birth-control devices was intensifying. In 1832, Dr. Charles Knowlton of Massachusetts described the procedure for vaginal douching in his book *Fruits of Philosophy*. Although Knowlton was repeatedly prosecuted and once jailed for obscenity, efforts to suppress his ideas succeeded only in generating further publicity. By 1865, popular tracts had familiarized Americans with a wide range of birth-control methods, including the condom and the diaphragm. The decision to limit family size was usually reached jointly by wives and husbands. Husbands emphasized that the economic value of children was declining, while wives argued that having fewer children would give mothers more time to nurture and cherish each one.

Supporters of the ideal of separate spheres did not advocate legal equality for women. Indeed, the ideal of separate spheres was an explicit alternative to legal equality. But in addition to enhancing women's roles within marriage, separate spheres allowed some women a measure of independence from the home. For example, the ideal sanctioned the travels of domestic reformer Catharine Beecher to lecture women on better ways to raise children and manage their households. Married women, too, found they could capitalize on notions of women's nurturing roles to extend their influence beyond the home, to charitable or **voluntary associations** seeking to improve society. Young men formed debating societies to sharpen their wits and enhance their economic prospects. **Alexis de Tocqueville**, a brilliant French observer, described men's and women's voluntary endeavors as "public associations in civil life" (see Going to the Source).

Voluntary associations encouraged sociability. As transients and newcomers flocked into towns and cities, they sought out others with similar characteristics, experiences, or interests. Gender was the basis of many voluntary societies. Of twenty-six religious and charitable associations in Utica, New York, in 1832, for instance, one-third were exclusively for women. Race was still another basis for voluntary associations. Two Boston organizations—Thompson Literary and Debating Society and the Philomathean Adelphic Union for the Promotion of Literature and Science—were groups for free blacks.

Voluntary associations also enhanced their members' public influence. At a time when state legislatures showed little interest in regulating the sale of alcoholic beverages, men and women joined in temperance societies to promote voluntary abstinence. To combat prostitution, women formed moral-reform societies, which sought to shame men into chastity by publishing the names of brothel patrons in newspapers. Moral-reform societies also gave some women influence over men. Here, as elsewhere, the tendency of the times was to forge new ties between like-minded Americans.

The Whole Vision

■ *What is the best way to understand westward expansion in the early nineteenth century?*

Americans surged westward in the early nineteenth century, and several factors enticed them to do so. The seeming availability of land, especially after the Louisiana Purchase, encouraged many people to head west, as did an evolving array of policies by the U.S. government designed to promote westward expansion and development of the lands acquired from France. That Native Americans already occupied these lands seemed of little concern; in fact, U.S. policies worked to the disadvantage of native peoples to move them off the lands they owned that whites desired. Economic forces also played a role in stimulating westward expansion. As demand for farm products within and beyond the United States increased in the early nineteenth century, many would-be farmers hoped to benefit from this booming market by starting farms in the West. Market forces led others west, too—squatters, who could ill afford to purchase land; slaves, who were taken west by masters to cultivate cotton; and investors who hoped to tap the promise of the West by buying up land at cheap prices and reselling it.

■ *What was the impact of the shift to a market economy in the early nineteenth century?*

The move from a subsistence-based economy to production for market produced pro-found changes throughout the United States. For farmers, it meant their fate was more directly tied to the ups and downs of the economy; that, of course, meant greater financial risks. For slaves, it meant that in regions based on staple crops throughout the South, the institution was not only here to stay but also that slavery was expanding. Ever-evolving federal land policies may have been designed to make land more affordable to farmers, but they also stimulated speculative investments that ultimately had dire consequences for the U.S. economy. Efforts to move goods faster and to newly settled regions of the West spurred a transportation revolution, which in turn helped fuel the rapid growth of cities, including those in newer, more remote locations. What was absolutely clear about the growth of a market economy was that the U.S. would increasingly find itself facing cycles of boom and bust, and farmers as well as businesspeople would now find themselves at the whims of the economy.

KEY TERMS

Old Northwest (p. 238)

Old Southwest (p. 238)

Five Civilized Tribes (p. 240)

Indian Removal Act, 1830 (p. 240)

"Trail of Tears" (p. 241)

market economy (p. 243)

squatters (p. 244)

Panic of 1819 (p. 244)

transportation revolution (p. 245)

Gibbons v. *Ogden* (p. 245)

Erie Canal (p. 245)

Eli Whitney (p. 250)

Waltham and Lowell textile mills (p. 250)

"outwork" (p. 252)

African Methodist Episcopal Church (p. 255)

Richard Allen (p. 255)

Catharine Beecher (p. 257)

separate spheres (p. 257)

voluntary associations (p. 260)

Alexis de Tocqueville (p. 260)

What were the causes and effects of early industrialization?

Various factors inspired the shift to industrialization, among them trade and foreign policy decisions in the years before the War of 1812. New technologies, along with improvements in transportation, also played a role. Population growth and improvements in wages similarly contributed to the growth of industrialization. The impact of industrialization depended on the region and its economy. Some regions moved toward industrialization sooner—partly due to economic necessity—while others continued to focus on more traditional means of production. For those regions that did engage in early industrialization, the shift altered how people worked and structured their daily lives. Some people in the early years of industrialization were able to engage in outwork done at home, while others moved to factories. To protect their interests, artisans began to form trade unions and alliances with other workers. Factory owners, in their quest for more and more workers, turned to a new group: young, New England farm girls, whose role as workers would prove transformative for them and for society. Finally, even regions that did not industrialize were affected by industrialization in terms of demand for agricultural products such as cotton that were the raw materials of early industrial output.

How and why were older systems of power and authority transformed in the first half of the nineteenth century?

The transformations wrought by industrialization, urbanization, and the transportation revolution greatly affected the way people related to each other. Older systems of deference broke down, as did other forms of authority in the workplace, the family, marital relationships, and between the social classes. While most people saw their standard of living rise, in truth, the rich got richer and the poor got poorer. Those in the middle were ultimately divided into self-employed businessmen or laborers who worked for others. Relationships within the family changed as young people left home in quest of jobs and other opportunities. Gender roles between spouses were similarly altered by the market revolution, as new ideologies emerged about men's and women's proper spheres. Even as opportunities increased for whites, race continued to prove restrictive for free blacks in the new industrializing economy, and in many cases, their political rights diminished as those for white men expanded. Such discrimination, however, helped fuel the rise of separate black institutions.

10 Democratic Politics, Religious Revival, and Reform, 1824–1840

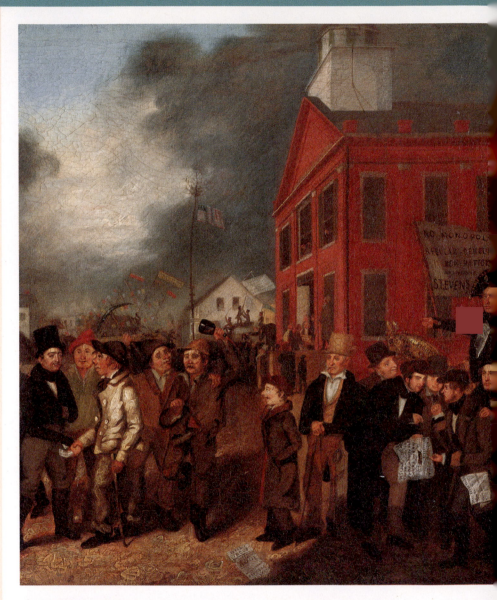

FIRST STATE ELECTION IN MICHIGAN Michigan's early elections were rowdy. Here, Detroit voters cast ballots in the state's first gubernatorial election in 1837. Democrat Stevens Mason, shown on the left backed by a "no monopoly" banner, defeated the Whig candidate. *(Gift of Mrs. Samuel T. Carson photograph @ 1991 The Detroit Institute of Arts (detail). Bridgeman Art Library Ltd.)*

CHRONOLOGY 1824–1840

1824	John Quincy Adams elected president by the House of Representatives.
1826	American Temperance Society organized.
1828	Andrew Jackson elected president.
	"Tariff of Abominations."
	John Calhoun anonymously writes *South Carolina Exposition and Protest*.
1830	Jackson's Maysville Road Bill veto.
	Indian Removal Act.
1830–1831	Charles G. Finney's Rochester revival.
1831	William Lloyd Garrison starts *The Liberator*.
1832	Jackson vetoes recharter of the Bank of the United States.
	Jackson reelected president.
	South Carolina Nullification Proclamation.
1833	Force Bill.
	Compromise Tariff.
	American Anti-Slavery Society founded.
	South Carolina nullifies the Force Bill.

1834	Whig Party organized.
1836	Specie Circular.
	Martin Van Buren elected president.
1837	Horace Mann becomes secretary of the Massachusetts Board of Education.
	Elijah Lovejoy murdered by proslavery mob.
	Grimké sisters set out on lecture tour of New England.
1837–1843	Economic depression.
1838	Garrison's New England Non-Resistance Society founded.
	Sarah Grimké's *Letters on the Condition of Women and the Equality of the Sexes* and Angelina Grimké's *Letters to Catharine E. Beecher*.
1840	Independent Treasury Act passed.
	William Henry Harrison elected president.
	First Washington Temperance Society started.
1841	Dorothea Dix begins exposé of prison conditions.
	Brook Farm community founded.
1848	Seneca Falls convention.

One cold Sunday in March 1841, educator Dorothea Dix was teaching a religious class for women prisoners in the House of Corrections at East Cambridge, Massachusetts. After class, she was shocked to discover a number of insane inmates shivering in unheated cells. When she confronted the jailer, he explained that providing stoves for "lunatics" was not only dangerous but unnecessary because they did not suffer from cold. The outraged Dix went to court and successfully petitioned to have stoves provided for the jail's insane inmates. With this action, she launched her career as an advocate for humanitarian treatment of the mentally ill.

Dix hatched a bold plan. She would personally visit jails and almshouses throughout Massachusetts to study the living conditions of the insane, then present evidence of their abuse to the state legislature. For two years, Dix documented the conditions of the mentally ill, which were far worse than she had anticipated. When jailers and almshouse keepers tried to deny her access, she replied, "I cannot adopt description of the condition of the insane secondarily; what I assert for fact, I must see for myself." In 1843, she presented to the legislature a report or "memorial" describing the insane confined "in cages, closets, cellars, stalls, pens! Chained, naked, beaten with rods, and lashed into obedience." The Massachusetts legislature responded by funding an expansion of the state's mental hospital. Encouraged by her success, Dix spent the next 15 years traveling throughout the nation, documenting abuses and presenting her memorials, filled with statistics and moral outrage, to state legislatures, which then allocated funds for twenty new insane "asylums" or havens. By the time of the Civil War, twenty-eight states, four cities, and the federal government had constructed public mental institutions.

What drove this sickly woman to endure dangerous travel, confront the terrible living conditions of the mentally ill, and endure the ridicule of those

DOROTHEA DIX (*National Portrait Gallery, Smithsonian Institution/Art Resource, NY*)

who found her crusade "unladylike"? Like many other women and men of the period, Dorothea Dix's reform impulse drew from a deep well of religious conviction. The two religions that shaped her Christian beliefs were seemingly at odds. The Methodist revivalism of her childhood was emotional and demanded a dramatic conversion experience. But the Unitarianism of her young adulthood was rationalistic and emphasized gradual spiritual improvement. What the two religions shared, however, was theological perfectionism: the belief in the innate moral capacities of all men and women and their ability to strive toward spiritual perfection. "Raise up the fallen," she wrote, "console the afflicted, defend the helpless, minister to the poor, reclaim the transgressor, be benefactors of mankind!" Even the raving lunatic, in Dix's eyes, carried a spark of inner divinity that should be nurtured in a properly controlled moral environment.

Dorothea Dix's perfectionist faith in the powers of moral institutions was shared by other reformers who regarded asylums—such as penitentiaries, almshouses, and orphan homes—as the solution for many of society's ills. If humankind was fundamentally good, they reasoned, poor environments must be at fault when people went wrong. The solution was to place deviants in specially designed environments that imposed order on their disorderly lives and minds. Asylums subjected inmates to regimented schedules, controlling social interaction, and sometimes—especially in the new penitentiaries—dictating forced isolation and physical punishment. Though reformers such as Dix certainly aimed at genuinely humanitarian reform, their strategies actually generated new forms of social control over the criminal, the poor, and the mentally ill.

Spread primarily by the wave of religious revivals known as the Second Great Awakening, theological perfectionism shaped a host of reforms that swept the United States after 1820, including temperance, antislavery, public education, women's rights, and utopian communitarianism. Most of these movements, like Dix's crusade for the mentally ill, raised fundamental questions about the proper balance of order and freedom in the new American democracy. Were temperance reformers justified in passing legislation that prohibited liquor sales? Did solitary confinement promote self-government among criminal offenders or impose a new form of governmental tyranny over them? These questions of order versus freedom also lay at the heart of the new two-party system that would reshape American political life during the presidential terms of Andrew Jackson. Jacksonian Democrats rallied to the cause of freedom, so long as freedom was largely restricted to adult white men. By contrast, Whigs—the party more likely to support the work of Dorothea Dix—were quick to take up the cause of moral order and to fill the ranks of the era's many reform movements.

10-1 The Rise of Democratic Politics, 1824–1832

How was the election process and the presidency increasingly transformed in the early nineteenth century?

Whatever their differences, all politicians in the 1820s and 1830s had to adapt to the emerging democratic view of politics as a forum for expressing the will of the common people. Gentlemen could still be elected to office, but their political success now depended less on their education and wealth and more on their ability to win the battle over public opinion.

The Republican (or Democratic-Republican) party of Thomas Jefferson was also unraveling, paving the way for the beginning of a two-party system in American politics. Pressures generated by industrialization in New England, the spread of cotton cultivation in the South, and westward expansion all contributed to a split among Republicans into two new parties: the Democrats and the National Republicans, later the Whigs. In general, Republicans who retained Jefferson's preference for states' rights became Democrats; Republicans who believed that the national government should actively encourage economic development, the so-called National Republicans, ultimately became Whigs.

10-1.1 Democratic Ferment

Political democratization took several forms. Beginning in the West, one state after another abolished the requirement that voters own property (also discussed in Chapter 8). By 1840, property ownership was a requirement in only seven of the twenty-six states. The total number of voters skyrocketed, with 2.4 million men voting in 1840, more than double

political democratization
The rising democratic idea of politics as a forum for the expression of the will of the common people rather than as an activity that gentlemen conducted for the people. One of the most common forms of this was the abolition of the requirement that voters own property. Moreover, written ballots replaced the custom of voting aloud, which had enabled so-called superiors to influence their inferiors at the polls. Appointive office increasingly became elective.

that of 1828. Private, written ballots replaced the custom of voting aloud, which had enabled elites to influence their subordinates at the polls. Formerly appointed offices became elected offices. Though the Electoral College survived, the choice of presidential electors by state legislatures gave way to direct election by the voters. In 1800, a supporter of Thomas Jefferson could only vote for the men who would vote for the men who would vote for Jefferson. By 1824, however, only six state legislatures continued to choose presidential electors, and by 1832, only one.

The fierce battles between the Republicans and the Federalists beginning in the 1790s had taught both parties how to court voters. At grand, party-run barbecues from Maine to Maryland, potential voters happily washed down free clams and oysters with free beer and whiskey. Republicans sought to expand suffrage in the North, and Federalists did the same in the South, each in the hope of becoming the majority party in that section. Democratization was also advanced by the transportation and communications revolutions that helped distribute newspapers and political materials, creating a more politically informed public.

Political democratization had its limitations. In 1820, both Federalists and Republicans were still organized from the top down, relying on a caucus to nominate candidates rather than on popularly elected nominating conventions. Women and free blacks remained disfranchised. Nevertheless, open opposition to the "common people" (meaning adult white males) was becoming a formula for political suicide. The people, one Federalist complained, "have become too saucy and are really beginning to fancy themselves equal to their betters."

10-1.2 The Election of 1824 and the Adams Presidency

In 1824, five Democratic-Republican candidates vied for the presidency. John Quincy Adams emerged as New England's favorite. South Carolina's brilliant John C. Calhoun competed with Georgia's William Crawford for southern support. (Calhoun would ultimately opt to run for vice president instead.) From the West marched the ambitious **Henry Clay** of Kentucky, confident that his American System of protective tariffs and federally supported internal improvements would win votes from both eastern manufacturing interests and western agriculturalists.

The fifth candidate was Andrew Jackson of Tennessee. Already popular on the frontier and in the South, he quickly won additional support from opponents of the American System in Pennsylvania and northern states. As the only presidential candidate in the election of 1824 not linked to the Monroe administration, Jackson gained popularity after the

Panic of 1819, which, as Calhoun commented, had left people with "a general mass of disaffection to the Government" and "looking out anywhere for a leader." The Panic also led to more successful public demands for the franchise. To Thomas Jefferson, however, Jackson was "one of the most unfit men I know of for such a place" as the presidency.

In the election, Jackson won more popular and electoral votes than any other candidate but failed to gain the majority required by the Constitution. Adams came in second place, while Crawford's presidential hopes were dashed by a paralyzing stroke. Clay lagged far behind. So the election was thrown into the House of Representatives, whose members had to choose a president from the top three candidates—Jackson, Adams, and Crawford. Hoping to forge an alliance between the West and Northeast for a future presidential bid, Clay threw his support to New Englander John Quincy Adams, who won. When the new president appointed Clay his secretary of state, Jackson's supporters accused Adams of stealing victory by entering a "corrupt bargain" with Clay, an allegation that formed a dark cloud over Adams's presidency. The move also divided Democratic-Republicans into the National Republicans, supporting Adams, and the Democrats, who backed Jackson, as they geared up for the 1828 presidential race.

As president, Adams focused on strengthening the national government. In his eyes, the American republic was the culmination of human progress, and he intended to further that progress through a broad-gauged program for American development. He embraced Clay's American System, which included protective tariffs and a national bank. In his First Annual Message to Congress, he laid out his plans to improve public education, expand communications and commerce, and launch an ambitious program of federal internal improvements. In foreign policy, he proposed that the United States participate in the first pan-American conference to promote commerce with Latin America. Condemning what he called "the baneful weed of party strife," Adams sought to remain aloof from partisan politics, leaving most of Monroe's officeholders in place and even appointing his own opponents to high office.

But Adams's ambitions met with growing political opposition. Those who still stung from the Panic of 1819 rejected his tariff and national bank programs. Strict constructionists opposed internal improvements on constitutional grounds.

Henry Clay
Politician from Kentucky who was one of the leaders of the Whig party. He ran against Andrew Jackson in 1824 and threw in his votes with John Quincy Adams's when Jackson failed to capture the majority as required by the Constitution. His action secured the presidency for Adams, but when Adams promptly appointed him his secretary of state, Jackson's supporters raged that a "corrupt bargain" had cheated Jackson of the presidency.

Southerners protested U.S. participation in the pan-American conference because it included regimes that had abolished slavery, including the black republic of Haiti, created by slave revolutionaries. At the midterm congressional elections of 1826 and 1827, Adams's opponents took control of both houses of Congress. While Adams continued to practice a time-honored politics of courting regional leaders so they would deliver the votes of their followings, his opponents—most important, Martin Van Buren of New York—were inventing a new grassroots politics based on organization and partisan loyalty.

10-1.3 The Rise of Andrew Jackson and the Election of 1828

As President Adams's popularity declined, Andrew Jackson's rose. While seasoned politicians distrusted his notoriously hot temper and his penchant for duels, Jackson was still a popular hero for his victory over the British in the Battle of New Orleans. And because he had fought in the American Revolution as a boy, Jackson seemed to many Americans a living link to a more virtuous past.

The presidential campaign of 1828 began almost as soon as Adams was inaugurated in 1824. The Democratic-Republicans began amassing support for Jackson for president and Calhoun for vice president. By the 1828 election, the party would rename itself simply the **Democratic Party**. Its opponents, the National Republicans, rallied behind Adams and his running mate, treasury secretary Richard Rush. Jackson's supporters began to put together a modern political machine based on local committees and state conventions, partisan newspapers, and public rallies. Two years before the election of 1828, towns and villages across the United States were buzzing with political activity and debate between "Adams men" and "Jackson men." The second American party system was beginning to take shape.

The 1828 campaign was a vicious, mudslinging affair. The National Republicans called Jackson a murderer for killing several men in duels and military executions and charged him with adultery for living with Rachel Robards—who later became his wife—when she was still married to another man. Jackson's supporters responded by accusing Adams of spending public funds on a billiard table for the White House and offering a beautiful American prostitute to the Russian tsar.

Although both sides slung mud, Jackson's men had better aim. Charges by Adams's supporters that Jackson was an illiterate backwoodsman backfired, increasing his popularity

by casting him as a common man. Jackson's supporters explained that the people's choice was between "the democracy of the country, on the one hand, and a lordly purse-proud aristocracy on the other." Though Jackson was actually a wealthy slaveholder, people wanted to see in him the idealized common man: uncorrupt, natural, and plain.

Jackson won the election with more than twice the electoral vote of Adams (see Map 10.1). Yet the popular vote was much closer and reflected the sectional bases of the new parties. Adams's voter support in New England was twice that of Jackson's, while Jackson received double his opponent's vote in the South and nearly triple in the Southwest.

10-1.4 Jackson in Office

Although he advocated limited government, Jackson solidified the power of the presidency. As a vocal opponent of privilege, President Jackson made the federal civil service his first target. Many officeholders, he believed, regarded their jobs as entitlements. Jackson, by contrast, supported "rotation in office," which gave a wider array of people an opportunity to work for the government and which he believed might also make government more representative of the people's interests. Jackson did not invent rotation, but he applied it more thoroughly than his predecessors by firing nearly half the higher civil service, especially postmasters and customs officers.

Although Jackson defended these dismissals on democratic grounds, he also had a partisan motive. The firings were concentrated in the Northeast, the stronghold of his defeated presidential opponent. Instead, he filled these and other positions with his most loyal supporters. Among Jackson's new appointments was Martin van Buren, former senator and by 1828 governor of New York—who helped secure Jackson's election and found the Democratic Party—as his Secretary of State. Jackson also appointed his devotee Samuel Swartwout. Unfortunately, as the chief customs officer for the port of New York, Swartwout embarrassed Jackson by running off with millions of dollars of customs receipts. Critics dubbed the practice of basing appointments on party loyalty the **spoils system**.

Jackson's positions on internal improvements and tariffs sparked even more controversy. He did not oppose all federal aid for internal improvements. But Jackson suspected that public officials used such aid to win political support by handing out favors. To end such corruption, he flatly rejected federal support for roads within states. In 1830, when a bill came before him that would have provided federal money for a 60-mile road between Maysville and Lexington, Kentucky, Jackson vetoed it on the grounds of its "purely local character." In doing so, however, he seemed to back away from his earlier support for Clay's American System.

Democratic Party
A new political party that emerged in the 1820s.

spoils system
The practice of basing appointments on party loyalty.

entered Congress in 1811 as a war hawk, supported the protectionist tariff of 1816, and dismissed strict construction of the Constitution as philosophical nonsense. During the late 1820s, however, Calhoun the nationalist became Calhoun the states' rights sectionalist. The reasons for his shift were complex. He had supported the tariff of 1816 to encourage fledgling industries and provide revenue for military preparedness. By 1826, however, national defense was no longer a priority, and the infant industries of 1816 had grown into troublesome adolescents demanding even higher tariffs.

Calhoun also burned with ambition to be president. Jackson had stated that he would serve for only one term, and Calhoun planned to succeed him. To become president, the one-time protectionist knew he had to maintain the support of the South, which was growing opposed to tariffs. Calhoun's own home state of South Carolina, suffering economically from the migration of cotton cultivation into Alabama and Mississippi, blamed its troubles on tariffs. Tariffs, according to Calhoun's constituents, not only drove up the price of manufactured goods, they also threatened to damage the American market for British textiles

JOHN QUINCY ADAMS President Adams is pictured here in his study. A map of the Chesapeake and Ohio Canal conveys his support for internal improvements, and his many books demonstrate the commitment to learning that Andrew Jackson's supporters successfully used against him in the election of 1828. *(Everett Historical/Shutterstock.com)*

The tariff issue tested Jackson's support even in the South. In 1828, while Adams was still president, some of Jackson's supporters in Congress had helped pass a high protective tariff that strongly favored western agriculture and New England manufacturing to the disadvantage of the South, which had few industries to protect and would now face higher prices for manufactured goods. Taking for granted southern support, which Jackson seemed to have clinched with the Indian Removal Act of 1830 (see Chapter 9), Jackson's supporters calculated that southerners would blame the Adams administration for this "Tariff of Abominations." Instead, southerners leveled their fury directly at Jackson.

10-1.5 Nullification

The tariff of 1828 opened a major rift between Jackson and his vice president, John C. Calhoun, which would shake the foundations of the Republic. Early in his career, Calhoun had been an ardent nationalist. He

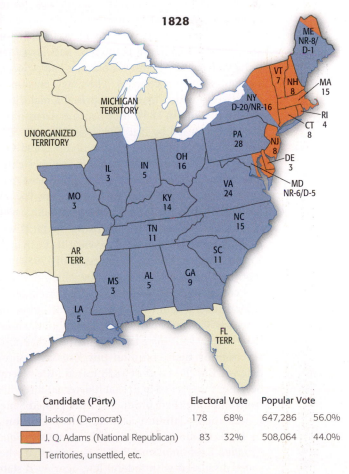

Candidate (Party)	Electoral Vote		Popular Vote	
■ Jackson (Democrat)	178	68%	647,286	56.0%
■ J. Q. Adams (National Republican)	83	32%	508,064	44.0%
■ Territories, unsettled, etc.				

MAP 10.1 **THE ELECTION OF 1828**

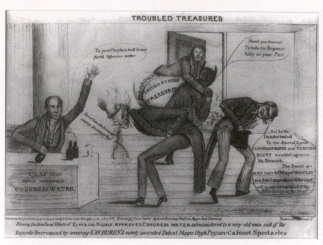

JACKSON AND THE BANK. This political cartoon satirized Jackson's attack on the Bank of the United States and hailed Henry's Clay's efforts to mount Congressional resistance. *(Library of Congress Prints and Photographs Division Washington, D.C.[LC-USZ62-19667])*

and thus reduce British demand for southern cotton. The more New England industrialized, the more protectionist its congressmen became. And the more the South came to rely on King Cotton, the more vigorously southerners opposed the tariff.

Opposition to tariffs in the South was not just economic. Many southerners feared that if the federal government could pass tariff laws favoring one section over another, it could also pass laws meddling with slavery. South Carolinians had especially strong reasons for concern. Their state was one of only two in which blacks comprised a majority of the population. In 1831, they became alarmed over a slave revolt led by Nat Turner in Virginia. That same year in Massachusetts, William Lloyd Garrison launched an abolitionist newspaper called *The Liberator*. These developments convinced many South Carolinians that a line had to be drawn against tariffs and any future federal interference with slavery.

Calhoun's grounds for opposing the tariff were constitutional. He embraced the view, set forth in the Virginia and Kentucky Resolutions of 1798–1799, that the Union was a compact by which the states had conferred limited and specified powers on the federal government. Although the Constitution did empower Congress to levy tariffs, Calhoun insisted that the only legitimate tariffs were those that raised revenue for such common purposes as national defense. But the tariff of 1828 raised little revenue because it was set so high that it deterred foreigners from shipping their products to the United States. It was thus, Calhoun argued, unconstitutional. In 1828, Calhoun anonymously wrote the *South Carolina Exposition and Protest*, arguing that when states disagreed with federal law, aggrieved states had the right to nullify the law within their borders.

A southerner, Calhoun had tried to steer clear of the issue during the 1828 election.

Like Calhoun, Jackson was strong-willed and proud. And while he supported states' rights and feared the growth of a powerful federal government, he disavowed the notion that state sovereignty could supercede that of the national government. Unlike Calhoun, he was already president and the leader of a national party that included supporters in such pro-tariff states as Pennsylvania. To retain key northern support while soothing the South, Jackson devised two policies.

The first was to distribute surplus federal revenue to the states. In the years before federal income taxes, tariffs on foreign imports were a major source of federal revenue. Jackson hoped these funds, fairly distributed among the states, would remove the taint of sectional injustice from the tariff, while forcing the federal government to restrict its own spending. Jackson's second policy was to reduce tariffs from the sky-high levels of 1828. Calhoun, reluctant to break openly with Jackson, muffled his protest, hoping that Jackson would lower the tariff and thus protect Calhoun's presidential hopes. In 1832, Congress did pass slightly reduced tariff rates, but these did not satisfy South Carolinians.

Meanwhile, two personal issues further damaged relations between Calhoun and Jackson. In 1829, Jackson's secretary of war, John H. Eaton, had married the widowed daughter of a Washington tavern keeper. By her own account, Peggy O'Neale Timberlake was "frivolous, wayward, [and] passionate." While still married to a naval officer away on duty, Peggy had openly flirted with Eaton, a boarder at her father's tavern. After her husband died and she married Eaton, the newlyweds were snubbed socially by Calhoun's wife and his friends in the cabinet. Jackson, who blamed his wife Rachel's recent death on the campaign mudslinging against her, befriended the Eatons. The Calhouns, he decided, had snubbed the Eatons to discredit Jackson and advance Calhoun's own presidential aspirations.

To make matters worse, in 1830 Jackson received conclusive evidence supporting his long-time suspicion that in 1818, then-secretary of war Calhoun had supported Jackson's punishment for his unauthorized raid into Spanish Florida. This confirmation combined with the Eaton affair to convince Jackson that he had to "destroy [Calhoun] regardless of what injury it might do me or my administration." At a Jefferson Day dinner in April 1830, when Jackson proposed the toast, "Our Union: It must be preserved," Calhoun pointedly responded, "The Union, next to our liberty, most dear. May we always remember that it can only be preserved by distributing equally the benefits and burdens of the Union."

WHIG POLITICAL BANNER, CA. 1840 This banner makes clear that the central objective of the Whig Party was national economic development. The American eagle presides over a busy landscape of commerce and industry, featuring (from left to right) a clipper ship, steamboat, railroad, and canal lock. In the foreground lies a plow, an anvil, and a weaver's shuttle. *(Fenimore Art Museum, Cooperstown, New York/New York State Historical Association)*

The stage was now set for the **nullification crisis**, a direct clash between the president and vice president. In 1831, Calhoun acknowledged authorship of the *South Carolina Exposition and Protest*. In November 1832, a South Carolina convention nullified the tariffs of 1828 and 1832 and forbade the collection of customs duties within the state. Jackson moved quickly to label nullification an "abominable doctrine" that would reduce the government to anarchy, and berated the nullifiers as "unprincipled men who would rather rule in hell, than be subordinate in heaven." Jackson even sent weapons to loyal Unionists in South Carolina. In December 1832, he issued a proclamation that, while promising South Carolinians further tariff reductions, condemned nullification as itself unconstitutional. The Constitution, he emphasized, had established "a single nation," not a league of states.

The crisis eased in March 1833 when Jackson signed into law two measures, called by one historian "the olive branch and the sword." The olive branch was the Compromise Tariff of 1833, which provided for a gradual reduction of duties between 1833 and 1842. The sword was the Force Bill, authorizing the president to use arms to collect customs duties in South Carolina. Although South Carolina promptly nullified the Force Bill, it construed the Compromise Tariff as a concession and rescinded its nullification of the tariffs of 1828 and 1832.

The Compromise of 1833 was one of the many accommodations by which the Union lurched from one sectional crisis to the next in the decades before the Civil War. Like most of those compromises, it mixed partisanship with statesmanship. The man largely responsible was Kentucky senator Henry Clay. Clay had long favored high tariffs as part of his American System, but he supported tariff reduction in 1833 for two reasons. First, he feared that without some concessions to South Carolina, the Force Bill would result in civil war. Second, he feared that without compromise, the basic principle of protective tariffs would be destroyed. Clay preferred to take responsibility for lowering tariffs himself, rather than pass the responsibility to the Jacksonians.

For their part, the nullifiers sarcastically toasted, "Andrew Jackson: On the soil of South Carolina he received an humble birthplace. May he not find in it a traitor's grave!" Although recognizing that South Carolina had failed to gain broad southern support for nullification and that they would have to bow to pressure, the nullifiers preferred to make Clay, not Jackson, the hero of the hour. So they supported Clay's Compromise Tariff. Everywhere Americans hailed Clay as the Great Compromiser. Even Martin Van Buren acknowledged that Clay had "saved the country."

10-1.6 The Bank Veto and the Election of 1832

Andrew Jackson recognized that the gap between rich and poor was widening during the 1820s and 1830s (see Chapter 9). He did not object to wealth acquired by hard work. But he disapproved of the wealthy growing wealthier by securing favors or "privileges" from corrupt legislatures. In addition, his own disastrous financial speculations early in his career had left him with a deep suspicion of all banks, paper money, and monopolies. The Bank of the United States was, in his eyes, guilty on every count.

The **Second Bank of the United States** had received a twenty-year charter from Congress in 1816. As a creditor to state banks, with the authority to demand repayment in specie (gold or silver coinage), the Bank of the United States held the power to restrain state banks from excessively printing and lending money. Such power provoked hostility. Many Americans blamed the bank for precipitating the Panic of 1819. Furthermore, as the official depository for federal revenue, the bank's capital of $35 million was

nullification crisis
Direct clash between the president and his vice president.

Second Bank of the United States
Received a twenty-year charter from Congress in 1816. However, it was located in Philadelphia, not Washington, and its directors enjoyed considerable independence. Its president, the aristocratic Nicholas Biddle, viewed himself as a public servant, duty-bound to keep it above politics.

more than double the annual expenditures of the federal government, yet it was only distantly controlled by the government. Its stockholders were private citizens. Although chartered by Congress, the bank was located in Philadelphia. Its directors enjoyed considerable independence, and its president, the aristocratic Nicholas Biddle, viewed himself less as a government employee than as a public servant, duty-bound to keep the bank above politics.

Encouraged by Henry Clay, who hoped that supporting the bank would help carry him into the White House in 1832, Biddle secured congressional passage of a bill to recharter the bank. Jackson vetoed it, denouncing the bank as a private and privileged monopoly that drained the West of specie, eluded state taxation, and made "the rich richer and the potent more powerful." Failing to persuade Congress to override Jackson's veto, Clay pinned his hopes on gaining the presidency himself.

By 1832, Jackson had made his views on major issues clear. He was simultaneously a staunch defender of states' rights and a staunch Unionist. Although he cherished the Union, he believed the states were too diverse to accept strong direction from Washington. The safest course was to allow the states considerable freedom so they would remain content within the Union and not pursue dangerous doctrines like nullification.

Breaking his earlier promises to retire, Jackson again ran for president in 1832, replacing Calhoun with Martin Van Buren as his running mate. Henry Clay ran on the National Republican ticket, touting his American System of protective tariffs, national banking, and federal support for internal improvements. Jackson won. Secure in office for another four years, he was ready to finish dismantling the Bank of the United States.

10-2 The Bank Controversy and the Second Party System, 1833–1840

How did the bank controversy and emergence of the Whigs solidify the two-party system?

Jackson's bank veto ignited a searing controversy. His efforts to destroy the bank gave rise to the opposition Whig Party, stimulated popular interest in politics, and contributed to the severe economic downturn known as the Panic of 1837. By 1840, the bank controversy had fundamentally divided the Whig and Democratic parties into the second party system.

In part, tempers flared over banking because the U.S. government issued no official paper currency. Instead, money took the form of notes (promises to redeem in specie) dispensed by banks. These IOUs fueled economic development by making it easier for businesses and farmers to acquire loans for building factories or buying land. But when notes depreciated because of public doubts about a bank's solvency, wage earners who had been paid in paper rather than specie suffered. Furthermore, paper money encouraged economic speculation. Farmers who bought land on credit in the expectation of rising values could be left mired in debt when agricultural prices dropped. Would the United States embrace swift economic development at the price of allowing some speculators to fail dramatically while others got rich? Or would the nation opt for more modest growth based on "honest" manual work and frugality? Between 1833 and 1840 these questions dominated American politics.

10-2.1 The War on the Bank

Jackson could have allowed the bank to die quietly when its charter ran out in 1836. But Jackson and some of his followers feared the bank's power too much to wait. When Biddle, anticipating further attacks, began to call in the bank's loans and contract credit during the winter of 1832–1833, Jacksonians saw their darkest fears confirmed. The bank, Jackson assured Van Buren, "is trying to kill me, but I will kill it." Jackson retaliated by removing federal deposits from the Bank of the United States and placing them in state banks, called "pet banks" by their critics because they were usually selected for loyalty to the Democratic Party.

But Jackson's redistribution of federal deposits backfired. He himself opposed paper money and easy credit, which encouraged ordinary Americans to undertake risky get-rich-quick schemes. But as state banks became depositories for federal revenue, they began to print more paper money and extend more loans to farmers and speculators eager to buy public lands in the West. Government land sales rose from $6 million in 1834 to $25 million in 1836. Jackson's policy was producing exactly the kind of economy he was trying to suppress.

Jackson had hoped to limit the number of state banks that would receive federal deposits. But all demanded a piece of the action, and the number of state-bank depositories grew to twenty-three by the end of 1833. Jackson was caught between crosswinds. Some Democrats resented the Bank of the United States because it periodically contracted credit and restricted lending by state banks. Western Democrats, in particular, had long viewed the Cincinnati branch of the Bank of the United States as inadequate to supply their credit needs. Advocating

GENERAL JACKSON SLAYING THE MANY HEADED MONSTER.

JACKSON VERSUS THE BANK Andrew Jackson, aided by Martin Van Buren (center), attacks the Bank of the United States, which, like the monstrous Hydra of Greek mythology, keeps sprouting new heads. The largest head belongs to Nicholas Biddle, the bank's president. *(Jackson slaying the many headed monster', 1828 (colour litho), American School, (19th century) / Private Collection / Peter Newark American Pictures / Bridgeman Images)*

"soft" or paper money, these Democrats in 1836 pressured a reluctant Jackson to sign the Deposit Act, which increased the number of deposit banks and loosened federal control over them. But Jackson continued to believe that paper money sapped "public virtue" and "robbed honest labour of its earnings to make knaves rich, powerful and dangerous." Seeking to reverse the damaging effects of the Deposit Act, in 1836 Jackson issued the Specie Circular, which provided that payment for public lands must be made in specie.

Prior to the depression of 1837, most Democrats favored soft money. The hard-money (specie) view was advocated within Jackson's inner circle and by a faction of the New York Democratic Party called the Locofocos. The Locofocos grew out of several different "workingmen's" parties that called for free public education, the abolition of imprisonment for debt, and a reduced ten-hour workday. Most of these parties proved short-lived, but in New York the "workies" were gradually absorbed by the Democratic Party. A mixture of intellectuals, small artisans, and journeymen, they worried about inflation, demanded payment in specie, and distrusted banks and paper money. In 1835, a faction of workingmen broke away from Tammany Hall, the main Democratic Party organization in New York City, and met in a hall whose candles were lit by a newfangled invention called the "locofoco," or match. Thereafter, these radical workingmen were called Locofocos.

10-2.2 The Rise of Whig Opposition

Jackson's magnetic personality had swept him to victory in 1828 and 1832. But his opposition to federal measures for stimulating economic development—internal improvements, protective tariffs, and the Bank of the United States—prompted his opponents to form a new opposition party called the **Whig Party**. Jacksonian Democrats generally feared that federal efforts

> **Whig Party**
> The main opponent of Andrew Jackson's Democratic Party.

to stimulate the national economy would weaken states' rights and strengthen the "moneyed aristocracy." By contrast, the Whigs supported those economic measures—the basic components of Henry Clay's American System—and an activist federal government in pursuit of a stronger and more regionally interdependent national economy. Whereas the Democrats' vision for future growth favored simple geographic expansion, the Whigs' vision was tied to the market revolution and rested on the belief that manufacturing and agricultural interests should work together toward national prosperity.

Though the South remained the Democrats' strongest base, the Whigs made some inroads into that region. Jackson's victory over nullification drove some southerners into the Whig Party simply because they opposed Jackson. His policy of redistributing federal deposits pleased some southerners but dismayed others who did not need cheaper and easier credit. The president's suspicion of federal aid for internal improvements also alienated some southerners who feared that the South would lag behind the North if it failed to improve its transportation networks. Because so much southern capital was tied up in slavery, southerners looked to the federal government for funding, and when rebuffed, they drifted into the Whig Party. The Whigs made the greatest progress in southern market towns and among planters with close ties to southern bankers and merchants.

Meanwhile, northern social reformers were strengthening the opposition to Jackson. These reformers wanted to improve American society by ending slavery and liquor consumption, improving public education, and elevating public morality. Most reformers were drawn to the Whig Party because its acceptance of government intervention to improve society could apply to moral as well as economic issues; Democrats resisted reforms, which they thought undermined American freedom by imposing a uniform standard of conduct. Middle-class reformers won additional Whig support from some native-born Protestant workers through their shared contempt for Irish-Catholic immigrants. The two groups disliked the Irish for different reasons. The reformers distrusted them because they drank liquor, opposed public education (which promoted Protestantism), and, once admitted to citizenship, tended to vote Democratic. Native-born Protestant workers disliked Irish immigrants as competitors in the labor force. As a result, some native-born working men allied politically with Whig reformers in common opposition to the Irish.

No source of Whig strength, however, was more remarkable than Anti-Masonry. Freemasonry had long provided prominent men, including George Washington, with fraternal fellowship based in exotic, secret rituals. What sparked the Anti-Masonic crusade was the abduction and disappearance in 1826 of William Morgan, a Mason who had threatened to publish a book exposing the order's secrets. Efforts to solve the mystery of Morgan's disappearance failed because local officials who were themselves Masons kept obstructing the investigation. In response, public opposition to the Masons began to form. Rumors spread throughout the Northeast that Masonry was a powerful, anti-Christian conspiracy to suppress popular liberty and provide a safe haven for wealthy drunkards. Many northeastern farmers and artisans were drawn into the Whig Party by their opposition to Masonry.

By 1836, the Whigs had become a national party with widespread appeal. Nationwide, the Whig Party attracted those with close ties to the market economy—commercial farmers, planters, merchants, and bankers. In the North, the Whigs picked up additional support from reformers, evangelical clergymen (especially Presbyterians and Congregationalists), Anti-Masons, and manufacturers. In the South, they appealed to some former nullificationists including, briefly, Calhoun himself. Everywhere, the Whigs attacked Jackson as "King Andrew I"; they strategically named their party after that of the American patriots who opposed King George III in 1776. The Whigs wanted to convince the American people that they, not the Democrats, were the true heirs to the Revolution.

10-2.3 The 1836 Election and the Panic of 1837

Jackson's popularity was a tough act to follow. In 1836, the Democrats ran Martin Van Buren, Jackson's vice president and hand-picked successor for president. Party leaders reminded voters that the real heir to Jackson was the Democratic Party itself because it perfectly embodied the popular will. The less cohesive Whig Party produced three candidates: William Henry Harrison of Ohio, Daniel Webster of Massachusetts, and W. P. Mangum of North Carolina. Democrat Hugh Lawson White of Tennessee also ran against Van Buren, whom he distrusted, then defected to the Whigs after the election. Democrats responded to this proliferation of Van Buren opponents by accusing the Whigs of a plot to divide the vote so that no candidate would receive the required majority in the Electoral College. The election would then be thrown into the House of Representatives, where once again, as in 1824, they feared corrupt bargains would be struck. In reality, the Whigs were simply divided, and Van Buren won a clear majority. But there were signs of trouble ahead for the Democrats. The popular vote was close. In the South, where four years earlier the Democrats had won two-thirds of the votes, they now won barely half. Jackson left office and returned to Nashville in a burst of glory. But the public's mood quickly darkened, for no sooner was Van Buren in office than a severe depression, called the **Panic of 1837**, struck.

In the speculative boom of 1835 and 1836, the total number of banks doubled, the value of bank notes in circulation nearly tripled, and commodity and land prices soared. The states, encouraged by easy money and high commodity prices, made new commitments to build canals. Then in May 1837, prices began to tumble, and bank after bank suspended specie payments. After a short rally, the economy crashed again in 1839. The Bank of the United States, which had continued to operate as a state bank with a Pennsylvania charter, failed. Nicholas Biddle was charged with fraud and theft. Once again, banks throughout the nation suspended specie payments.

The ensuing depression was far more severe than the economic downturn of 1819. Those lucky enough to find work saw their wage rates drop by roughly one-third. In despair, many workers turned to the prophecies of William Miller, a New England religious enthusiast convinced that the end of the world was imminent. Dressed in black coats and stovepipe hats, Miller's followers roamed urban sidewalks and rural villages in search of converts. Many sold their possessions and purchased white robes to ascend into heaven on October 22, 1843, the day the world was supposed to end. By then, the worst of the depression was over; but at its depths, the economic slump made despairing people receptive to Miller's predictions.

"Little Magician" Martin Van Buren needed all his political skills to confront the depression that was damaging not only ordinary citizens but the Democratic Party itself. Whigs dubbed him "Martin Van Ruin," and in 1838 succeeded in sweeping the governorship and most legislative seats in Van Buren's home state of New York. To seize the initiative, Van Buren called for the creation of an independent Treasury. The idea was simple: The federal government, instead of depositing its money in banks that would use it as the basis for speculative loans, would hold onto its revenues and keep them from the grasp of corporations. When Van Buren finally signed the Independent Treasury Bill into law on July 4, 1840, his supporters hailed it as America's second Declaration of Independence.

The independent Treasury reflected the deep Jacksonian suspicion of an alliance between government and banking. But the Independent Treasury Act failed to address the banking issue on the state level, where newly chartered state banks—over nine hundred of them by 1840—lent money to farmers and businessmen. The Whigs, who blamed the depression on Jackson's Specie Circular rather than on the banks, continued to encourage bank charters as a way to spur economic development. In contrast, growing numbers of Democrats blamed the depression on banks and paper money, and swung toward the hard-money stance long favored by Jackson and his inner circle. In Louisiana and Arkansas, Democrats prohibited banks altogether, and elsewhere they imposed severe restrictions—banning, for example, the issuing of paper money in small denominations. After 1837, the Democrats became an antibank, hard-money party.

10-2.4 Log Cabins, Hard Cider, and a Maturing Second Party System

Despite the depression, the Democrats renominated Van Buren for president. The Whigs avoided their mistake of 1836 by settling on a single candidate, Ohio's William Henry Harrison, and ran former Senator John Tyler of Virginia as vice president. Harrison, who at age sixty-seven was barely eking out a living as a farmer, was picked because he had few enemies. Early in the campaign, the Democrats made a fatal mistake by ridiculing Harrison as "Old Granny," a man who desired only to spend his declining years sipping cider in a log cabin. Unwittingly, the Democrats had handed their opponents the most famous campaign symbol in American history. The Whigs immediately praised Harrison as a rugged frontiersman, the hero of the Battle of Tippecanoe, and a defender of all western settlers living in log cabins.

Refusing to publish a platform, the Whigs ran a "hurrah" campaign, trumpeting "Tippecanoe and Tyler too." They used log cabins for headquarters, sang log-cabin songs, passed around log-cabin cider, and called their newspaper *Log Cabin*. Van Buren, they charged, was a soft aristocrat who lived in "regal splendor," drinking fine wines from silver goblets while people went hungry in the streets. Harrison, by contrast, was content to drink hard cider from a plain mug. Just twelve years after Jackson's triumph over the "purse-proud aristocrat" Adams, the Whigs were effectively using Democratic tactics against the Democratic candidate.

The election results gave Harrison a clear victory (see Map 10.2). Van Buren carried only seven states, even failing to hold his home state of New York. The depression would probably have made it impossible for any Democrat to have triumphed in 1840, but Van Buren had additional problems. Unlike Harrison and Jackson, he wore no halo of military glory. He also ran a surprisingly old-fashioned campaign, sitting at his desk writing encouraging letters to key supporters, while Harrison traveled by railroad around the country to appeal directly to the people. Van Buren, the master politician, was beaten at his own game.

> **Panic of 1837**
> A severe depression that struck the United States beginning in May 1837. Prices began to tumble, and bank after bank suspended specie payments.

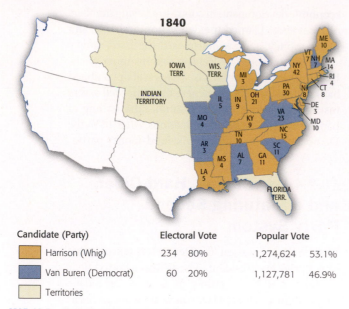

1840

Candidate (Party)	Electoral Vote		Popular Vote	
Harrison (Whig)	234	80%	1,274,624	53.1%
Van Buren (Democrat)	60	20%	1,127,781	46.9%
Territories				

MAP 10.2   THE ELECTION OF 1840

In addition to electioneering tactics like log cabins and hard cider, the 1840 election ushered in a significant long-term trend in voting. Between 1836 and 1840, the popular vote expanded by 60 percent, the greatest proportional jump between consecutive elections in American history; since 1828, the total number of votes cast in presidential elections had doubled, rising from 1.2 million to 2.4 million. Neither reduced suffrage requirements nor population growth was the main cause of this increase. Rather, it resulted from a jump in voter turnout. In 1828, 1832, and 1836, the proportion of white males who voted had fluctuated between 55 percent and 58 percent. In 1840, it shot to 80 percent.

What brought voters to the polls was a combination of severe economic depression and the noisy log-cabin campaign of 1840. Yet voter turnout remained high even after prosperity returned during the following decade. The second party system, which had been developing slowly since 1828, reached a high plateau in 1840 and remained there for more than a decade. Politicians increasingly presented clear alternatives to voters. The gradual hardening of the line dividing the two parties stimulated enduring popular interest in politics.

"THE NEW ERA WHIG TRAP SPRUNG," NEW YORK, 1840 This Whig cartoon from the election of 1840 shows Democrat Martin Van Buren trapped inside the Whig campaign symbol, a log cabin. Andrew Jackson is desperately trying to pry him out. *(Library of Congress Prints and Photographs Division)*

Another major current feeding partisan passions in American life were the social and moral reform movements that burst onto the national scene in the 1830s. Those movements originated in religious developments.

10-3 The Rise of Popular Religion

What does the advent of new religious movements reveal about nineteenth-century American society?

In *Democracy in America*, Alexis de Tocqueville pointed out an important difference between his country and the United States: "In France I had almost always seen the spirit of religion and the spirit of freedom pursuing courses diametrically opposed to each other; but in America I found that they were intimately united, and that they reigned in common over the same country." From this observation, Tocqueville drew a startling conclusion: religion was "the foremost of the political institutions" of the United States.

In calling religion a political institution, Tocqueville did not mean that Americans gave special political privileges to any particular denomination. He meant that in America, religion and democracy were compatible rather than antagonistic: religion reinforced democracy, even as democracy reshaped religious practice. Just as Americans expected their politicians to address the common man, they insisted that ministers preach to ordinary people. The most successful ministers were those who used plain words to move the heart, not theological complexities to impress the mind. Increasingly, too, Americans demanded religious doctrines that put individuals in charge of their own spiritual destiny. They moved away from the Calvinist conviction that God had predetermined who would be saved and who would be damned and toward the belief that anyone who tried could attain heaven.

Americans were democratizing heaven itself. The harmony between religious and democratic impulses owed much to a series of religious revivals known as the Second Great Awakening.

10-3.1 The Second Great Awakening

The **Second Great Awakening** ignited in Connecticut during the 1790s and swept the country during the half-century that followed. At first, educated Congregationalists and Presbyterians such as Yale president Timothy Dwight dominated the revivals. But as revivalism spread to frontier states like Tennessee and Kentucky, it underwent striking changes typified by the rise of camp meetings. These were gigantic, prolonged revivals in which members of several denominations gathered into sprawling open-air camps to hear energetic preachers proclaim that the Second Coming of Jesus was near and the time for repentance was now. All people were welcome and attended, regardless of race, class, or gender, and even in the South blacks and whites were together at revival meetings.

The most famous camp meeting occurred at Cane Ridge, Kentucky, in August 1801, when a huge crowd assembled to hear thunderous sermons, sing hymns, and experience the influx of divine grace. One eyewitness described the meeting:

At night, the whole scene was awfully sublime. The ranges of tents, the fires, reflecting light amidst the branches of the towering trees; the candles and lamps illuminating the encampment; hundreds moving to and fro, with lights or torches, like Gideon's army; the preaching, praying, singing, and shouting, all heard at once, rushing from different parts of the ground, like the sound of many waters, was enough to swallow up all the powers of contemplation.

Among the more extreme features of frontier revivals were the "exercises" in which men and women rolled around like logs, jerked their heads furiously, and barked like dogs. Critics blasted the frontier frenzy for encouraging more lust than spirituality and complained that "more souls were begot [meaning conceived] than saved." The early frontier revivals fundamentally challenged traditional religious customs. The most successful revivalists were not college graduates but ordinary farmers and artisans who had themselves experienced powerful religious conversions and regarded learned ministers with contempt for their dry expositions of theology.

No religious denomination proved more successful on the frontier than the Methodists. With fewer than seventy thousand members in 1800, the Methodists quickly became America's largest Protestant denomination, claiming more than a million members by 1844. In contrast to New England Congregationalists and Presbyterians, Methodists emphasized that religion was a matter of the heart rather than the head. The frontier Methodists disdained "settled" ministers tied to fixed parishes. They preferred itinerant circuit riders—young, often unmarried men who traveled from place

Second Great Awakening
A religious revival movement that began in Connecticut in the 1790s. It featured gigantic revival meetings in many parts of the country in which members of several denominations gathered together in sprawling open-air camps for up to a week to hear revivalists proclaim that the Second Coming of Jesus was near and that the time for repentance was now.

Charles G. Finney
Began his career as a lawyer, but after a religious conversion in 1821, he became a Presbyterian minister and conducted revivals in towns such as Rome and Utica along the Erie Canal. Although he also found time for trips to New York and Boston, his greatest "harvest" came in the thriving canal city of Rochester in 1830–1831.

to place on horseback and preached in houses and open fields. As circuit rider Peter Cartwright explained, it was his mission to "carry the gospel to destitute souls that had, by their removal into some new country, been deprived of the means of grace."

Although the frontier revivals disrupted religious custom, they also promoted social and moral order on the frontier. After Methodist circuit riders left an area, their converts formed weekly "classes" that served as the grassroots structure for Methodist churches. The classes established the Methodist code of behavior, called the Discipline, which reinforced family and community values amidst the disorder of frontier life. Class members not only worshiped together, they provided mutual religious and moral encouragement and reprimanded one another for drunkenness, fighting, fornication, even sharp business practices.

10-3.2 The Burned-Over District

By the 1820s, the center of the Second Great Awakening had shifted into western New York, a region that came to be known as the "Burned-Over District" because the fires of revival blazed so hot there. This region was filling with descendants of Puritans who hungered for religious experience and with enterprising people drawn by dreams of wealth along the Erie Canal. The Burned-Over District offered a fertile field for both high expectations and bitter discontent.

The man who harnessed these social forces to religion was **Charles G. Finney**. In 1821, while studying to become a lawyer, Finney experienced a powerful religious conversion. When a church deacon arrived at his office to remind him that he had retained Finney's legal services for a trial, Finney replied, "I have a retainer from the Lord Jesus Christ to plead his cause, and I cannot plead yours." He became a Presbyterian minister and conducted dozens of revivals in towns along the canal, as well as in New York City and Boston. But his greatest "harvest" of souls was gathered in the thriving canal city of Rochester in 1830–1831.

The Rochester revival justified Finney's reputation as the "father of modern revivalism." First, it was a citywide revival in which all denominations participated. Finney was a pioneer of cooperation among Protestant denominations. Second, Finney employed new devices for speeding conversions, such as the "anxious

seat," where those ready for conversion were placed so they could be made objects of special prayer, and the "protracted meeting," which went on nightly for up to a week.

Finney's emphasis on special techniques distinguished him from eighteenth-century revivalists such as Jonathan Edwards. Whereas Edwards had portrayed revivals as the miraculous work of divine grace, Finney understood them to be human creations. Although a Presbyterian, Finney rejected the Calvinist doctrine of innate depravity—the belief that humans had an inborn, irresistible inclination to sin. Sin, according to Finney, was a voluntary act, and sinners could will themselves out of sin just as readily as they had chosen it. They even exercised the power to lead perfect lives free from all sin, on

LORENZO DOW AND THE JERKING EXERCISE Lorenzo Dow (1777–1834) was a spellbinding Methodist revivalist who preached throughout the United States early in the Second Great Awakening. His unkempt appearance, harsh voice, and jerky physical movements earned him a reputation for eccentricity. But his success in winning souls demonstrated the democratic appeal of revivalism. (*Picture Research Consultants & Archives*)

the model of Christ—a doctrine called **theological perfectionism**. Finney's converts left his meetings convinced that all their past guilt had been washed away and they were beginning a new life. "I have been born again," a young convert wrote. "I am three days old when I write this letter."

Originally controversial, Finney's ideas came to dominate "evangelical" Protestantism, which focused on the need for an emotional conversion experience. He was successful because he told nineteenth-century Americans what they wanted to hear: that their destinies lay in their own hands. A society that celebrated the self-made man embraced Finney's assertion that, even in religion, people could make of themselves what they chose. As a frontier revivalist with a relatively dignified style, Finney's appeal extended to merchants, lawyers, and small manufacturers in the towns and cities of the Northeast.

A major source of Finney's success was his recognition that revivals seldom succeeded without the active participation of women. During the Second Great Awakening, female converts outnumbered male converts by about two to one. Finney encouraged women to give public testimonies of their religious experiences and often succeeded in converting men by first converting their wives and daughters. After a visit from Finney, Melania Smith, the religiously inactive wife of a Rochester physician, greeted her husband with a blunt reminder of "the woe which is denounced against the families which call not on the Name of the Lord." Dr. Smith soon joined one of Rochester's Presbyterian churches.

10-3.3 Critics of Revivals: The Unitarians

Along with supporters, the revivals had their critics. Some people openly doubted that revivals produced permanent changes in behavior. Critics condemned revivalists for encouraging "such extravagant and incoherent expressions, and such enthusiastic fervor, as puts common sense and modesty to the blush."

One small but influential group of critics was the Unitarians. Their basic doctrine—that Jesus was not divine, but rather a human model for the moral life—had gained acceptance among religious rationalists during the eighteenth-century Enlightenment. Only in the early nineteenth century did Unitarianism emerge as a separate denomination. In New England, hundreds of Congregational churches were divided by the departure of Unitarians and ensuing legal battles over which group held legitimate claim to the church property. Although Unitarianism won relatively few converts outside New England, its tendency to attract the wealthy and educated gave Unitarians influence beyond their numbers.

Unitarians criticized revivals as uncouth emotional exhibitions. They argued that moral goodness should be cultivated, not through a dramatic conversion experience, but through a gradual process of "character building" in which believers modeled their behavior on Jesus. Yet both Unitarians and revivalists rejected the Calvinist emphasis on innate depravity and shared the belief that human behavior could be changed for the better. William Ellery Channing, the Unitarian leader who most influenced Dorothea Dix, claimed that all Christianity had but one purpose: "the perfection of human nature, the elevation of men into nobler beings."

10-3.4 Mormonism

The Unitarian denial of Christ's divinity challenged a fundamental doctrine of orthodox Christianity. Yet Unitarianism proved far less controversial than another new denomination—the Church of Jesus Christ of Latter-Day Saints, or **Mormons**. Its founder, Joseph Smith, grew to manhood in a family that moved constantly to and fro, but never up. His ne'er-do-well father moved his family nearly twenty times in ten years before settling in Palmyra, New York, in the heart of the Burned-Over District. As a boy, Smith dreamed of finding buried treasure and wrestled with religious uncertainty created by the conflicting claims of the Methodists, Presbyterians, and Baptists around him. Who was right and who was wrong, he wondered, or were they "all wrong together"?

Smith's religious perplexity was common in the Burned-Over District, but his solution was unique. An angel named Moroni, he reported, led him to a buried book of revelation and special seer stones to help with its translation, which he completed in 1827. The Book of Mormon tells the story of the ancient Hebrew prophet Lehi whose descendants came to America and created a prosperous civilization to await Jesus as its savior. Jesus had actually appeared and performed miracles in the New World. But the American descendants of Lehi had departed from the Lord's ways. As punishment, God cursed some with dark skin— thus creating the American Indians who, by the time of Columbus's arrival, had forgotten their history. Mormonism—one of the few major religions to originate in the United States—placed America at the center of religious history.

> **theological perfectionism**
> The belief that human beings have the power to lead perfect lives free from all sin, on the model of Christ; it grew in popularity during the early nineteenth century and was widely touted by revivalist ministers such as Charles G. Finney.
>
> **Mormons**
> Members of the Church of Jesus Christ of Latter-Day Saints. It emerged in the 1820s, and was very controversial. They believe that Jesus had actually appeared and performed miracles in America, but the American descendants of the ancient Hebrew prophet Lehi had departed from the Lord's ways and quarreled among themselves.

Smith quickly gathered followers. For some believers, the Book of Mormon resolved the turmoil created by conflicting Protestant interpretations of the Bible. But Smith's claim to a new revelation guaranteed a hostile response from many American Protestants, who believed he had undermined the authority of their Scripture. To escape persecution, and move closer to the Indians whose conversion was one of their goals, Smith and his followers began relocating westward from New York. In Illinois, they built a model city called Nauvoo and a magnificent temple supported by thirty huge pillars (see Map 10.3). But in 1844, a group of dissident Mormons accused Smith and his inner circle of practicing plural marriage. When Smith destroyed the group's newspaper press, militias moved in to restore law and order. They arrested Smith and his brother Hirum and threw them into jail in Carthage, Illinois, where a lynch mob killed them both. One of Joseph's plural wives wrote, "Never, since the Son of God was slain / Has blood so noble flow'd from human vein."

Joseph Smith had once hoped that Americans would fully embrace Mormonism. But persecution gradually convinced him that the Mormons' survival required separation from American society. In removing from the larger society of "Gentiles," the Mormons mirrored the efforts of many other religious communities during the 1830s and 1840s.

One in particular, the Shakers, has held an enduring fascination for Americans.

10-3.5 The Shakers

The Shakers were founded by Mother Ann Lee, the illiterate daughter of an English blacksmith, who came to America in 1774. Mother Ann's followers believed she was the second incarnation of God: as Jesus had been the Son of God, she was God's Daughter. Called "Shakers" for their convulsive dancing at worship services, the group established tightly knit agricultural-artisan communities whose purpose was the pursuit of religious perfection. "Hands to work, and hearts to God" was their guiding motto. Shaker artisans produced furniture renowned for its beauty and strength and invented such conveniences as the clothespin and the circular saw.

For all their material achievements as artisans, the Shakers were fundamentally otherworldly. Mother Ann, who had lost four infant children, had a religious vision of God expelling Adam and Eve from the Garden of Eden for their sin of sexual intercourse. Shaker communities practiced celibacy and carefully separated the sleeping and working quarters of men and women to discourage contact. To maintain their membership, Shakers relied on new converts and the adoption of orphans, and at

MAP 10.3 **RELIGIOUS AND UTOPIAN COMMUNITIES, 1800–1845** The desire to construct a perfect society gave rise to hundreds of utopian communities between 1800 and 1845. Some, like the Shaker and Mormon communities, arose from religious motives. Others, as discussed later in this chapter, were more secular in origin, attempting to allay the selfish excesses of social and economic competition.

their peak in the 1830s and 1840s they numbered about six thousand members in eight states. As part of their pursuit of religious perfection, they practiced Christian socialism, pooling their land and implements to create remarkably prosperous villages. A British visitor observed that "the earth does not show more flourishing fields, gardens, and orchards than theirs."

While the Shakers chose to separate themselves from the competitive individualism of the larger society, the message of most evangelical Protestants, including Charles G. Finney, was that religion was compatible with economic self-advancement. Most revivalists taught that the pursuit of wealth was acceptable as long as people were honest, temperate, and bound by conscience. But many of them believed that the world was in serious need of improvement and that converts had a religious responsibility to pursue moral and social reform.

10-4 The Age of Reform

In what ways were the reform movements an extension of the democratic impulses of the nineteenth century?

The heart of religious revival was the democratic belief that individual men and women could take charge of their own spiritual destinies and strive toward personal perfection. Many converts extended similar expectations to society. Saved souls, they believed, could band together to stamp out the many evils that plagued the American republic. Like John Quincy Adams, they embraced "the spirit of improvement," forming a wide range of voluntary associations whose purpose was to improve society. Reformers tackled such social problems as slavery, sexual inequality, intemperance, and the inhumane treatment of criminals and the insane. Armed with the moralism of revival, they tended to view all social issues as matters of good versus evil and to assume that God was on their side.

But not all reformers were converts of revival. Many school reformers and women's rights advocates were religious liberals—either hostile or indifferent to revivals. Dorothea Dix's work on behalf of the mentally ill drew more power from her involvement in Boston Unitarianism than from the Methodism of her childhood. Abolitionists openly criticized the churches for condoning slavery and often separated themselves from denominational bodies that refused to condemn the institution. But by portraying slaveholding as a sin that called for immediate repentance, even religiously liberal

abolitionists borrowed their language and their psychological appeal from revivalism. Whatever a reformer's personal relationship to the revivals of the Second Great Awakening, the Age of Reform drew much of its fuel from that evangelical movement.

10-4.1 The War on Liquor

Early nineteenth-century Americans were heavy drinkers. In 1825, the average adult male drank about seven gallons of alcohol annually (mostly whiskey and hard cider), in contrast to less than two gallons in our own time (mostly beer and wine). One reason for this heavy consumption was the state of western agriculture. Before the transportation revolution, western farmers could not make a profit by shipping grain in bulk to eastern markets. But they could profit by distilling their corn and rye into whiskey, which poured out of the West in large quantities. Drunkenness pervaded all social classes and occupations. Heavy drinking generated a host of social problems, including domestic violence, economic failure, and disease, as well as the new medical diagnosis of delirium tremens.

Before 1825, temperance reformers advocated moderation in consuming alcohol. But in that year, Connecticut revivalist Lyman Beecher delivered six widely acclaimed lectures that condemned all use of alcoholic beverages. A year later, evangelical Protestants created the **American Temperance Society**, the first national temperance organization, which demanded total abstinence. By 1834, some five thousand state and local temperance societies were affiliated with the American Temperance Society. Their membership was between one-third and one-half women, who, along with their children, endured the bulk of the domestic violence and poverty created by excessive drinking.

The primary strategy of the American Temperance Society was to use "moral suasion" to persuade people to "take the pledge"—the promise never to consume alcohol. To that end, temperance reformers flooded the country with tracts denouncing the "amazing evil" of strong drink, paid reformed drunkards to deliver public lectures, and produced temperance plays. They even formed a children's organization called the "Cold Water Army." Its small members pledged, "We, Cold Water Girls and Boys, / Freely renounce the treacherous joys / Of Brandy, Whiskey, Rum and Gin; / The Serpent's lure to death and sin."

Among the main targets of temperance reformers were the laboring classes. In the small workshops of the preindustrial era, passing the jug every few hours throughout the workday was a time-honored practice. But early factories demanded a more disciplined, sober workforce, so industrial employers were quick

> **American Temperance Society**
> The first national temperance organization, committed to ending alcohol consumption.

to embrace temperance reform. In East Dudley, Massachusetts, three manufacturers refused to sell liquor in their factory stores, calculating that any profits from the sale would be wiped out by lost work time and "the scenes of riot and wickedness thus produced." Industrial employers in Rochester, New York, invited Charles G. Finney to preach up a revival in their city as part of an effort to convince their workers to abstain from alcohol.

Workers themselves initially showed little interest in temperance. But after the Panic of 1837, some grew convinced that their economic survival depended on a commitment to sobriety. In 1840, they formed the Washington Temperance Society in Baltimore, with a branch for women called the Martha Washingtonians. Drawing more mechanics (workingmen) than ministers or manufacturers, the Washington Societies offered mutual self-help. Many members were themselves reformed drunkards, like Boston baker Charles Woodman, who blamed his business collapse on his return to his "old habit" of excessive drinking. Men like Woodman reasoned that while the forces of economic dislocation were beyond their control, sobriety lay within their control. Take care of temperance, one Washingtonian assured his audience, and the Lord will take care of the economy.

The Washingtonians' debt to religious revivalism was actually greater than that of the American Temperance Society. Washingtonians viewed drinking as sinful and held "experience meetings" in which members testified to their "salvation" from liquor and their "regeneration" through total abstinence or "teetotalism" (an emphatic form of the word *total*). Martha Washingtonians pledged to smell their husbands' breath each night, and paraded with banners that read "Teetotal or No Husband." The Washington Societies spread farther and faster than any other antebellum temperance organization.

As the temperance movement won new supporters, some crusaders began to demand legal prohibition—the banning of liquor traffic at the local and state level. In 1838, Massachusetts prohibited the sale of distilled spirits in amounts less than fifteen gallons, thereby restricting small purchases by individual drinkers. In 1851, Maine

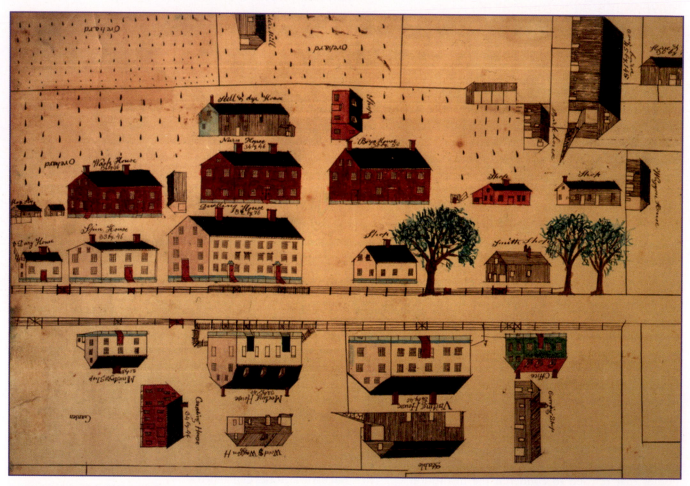

SHAKER VILLAGE AT ALFRED, MAINE, 1845 A Shaker cobbler named Joshua Bussell created this illustrated map of the Shaker Village at Alfred, Maine. It documents the Shakers' belief that spatial organization was an important part of the pursuit of spiritual perfection. *(Library of Congress Prints and Photographs Division)*

banned the manufacture and sale of all intoxicating beverages. Prohibition was controversial, even within the movement. But taken together, the two central strategies of the temperance movement—moral suasion and legal prohibition—scored remarkable success. Per capita consumption of distilled spirits, which had risen steadily between 1800 and 1830, began to fall during the 1830s. By the 1840s, consumption had dropped to less than half its peak rate in the 1820s.

10-4.2 Public-School Reform

In the early nineteenth century, the typical American school was a rural one-room schoolhouse. Here, students ranging in age from three to twenty or older sat on benches learning little more than reading and counting and spending only a few months in school each year. Their teachers were typically recent college graduates who took teaching jobs temporarily before pursuing other professions. Students never forgot the primitive conditions and harsh discipline of these schools, especially the floggings until "the youngster vomited or wet his breeches."

Rural parents, who expected little more than basic literacy for their children, were generally content with these schools. But reformers wanted education to equip students for an increasingly competitive industrial economy. **Horace Mann**, the first secretary of the Massachusetts board of education, created in 1837, pursued a range of strategies for achieving this goal: shifting the burden of financial support for schooling from parents to the state, extending the school term to as many as ten months each year, standardizing textbooks, dividing students into grades based on their age and achievements, and compelling attendance. Within Mann's educational vision, school should occupy the bulk of every child's time and energy.

School reformers sought to spread industrial values as well as combat ignorance. Requiring students to arrive on time, they believed, would teach workplace punctuality, and matching students against their peers would stimulate competitiveness. School textbooks taught such lessons as "Idleness is the nest in which mischief lays its eggs." The McGuffey readers, which sold 50 million copies between 1836 and 1870, preached industry, honesty, sobriety, and patriotism.

Success did not come easily. Educational reformers faced challenges from rural parents who were satisfied with the district schools and reluctant to lose their children's agricultural labor for most of the year. Urban Catholics, led by the bishop of New York City, objected to the anti-Catholic and anti-Irish biases of standard textbooks. In both rural and urban areas, the laboring poor opposed compulsory education because their family economy depended on children's wage-earning.

Yet school reformers prevailed, at least in the North, in part because their opponents failed to unify (schooling in the South is discussed in Chapter 12). Education reform also enlisted influential allies. Urban workingmen's parties were drawn to the cause by the prospect of free, tax-supported schools. Industrial employers were won over by the hope that public schools would create a disciplined workforce. Women recognized that dividing students into different grade levels would improve their own opportunities to become teachers. Though women were believed to be incapable of controlling one-room schools, whose pupils included rambunctious young men, few people doubted their ability to manage classes of eight-year-olds. As predicted by educational reformer Catharine Beecher (Lyman's daughter), school reform opened the teaching profession to women. By 1900, about 70 percent of the nation's schoolteachers were women.

School reform also appealed to native-born Americans alarmed by the influx of immigrants. The public school was coming to be seen as the best mechanism for creating a common American culture out of an increasingly diverse society. As one reformer observed, "We must decompose and cleanse the impurities which rush into our midst" through the "one infallible filter—the SCHOOL." Very few educational reformers, however, called for racially integrated schools. The few black children who tried to attend public school were greeted with open hostility and sometimes violence.

10-4.3 Abolition

Antislavery sentiment flourished in the Revolutionary era, encouraging northerners to establish emancipation schemes within their state borders. Free blacks, too, established some of the earliest abolitionist efforts in the North, writing essays that described the worst aspects of slavery and appealing to local legislatures in their quest to end the practice. There were roughly fifty African American antislavery groups by the 1830s.

But among whites, opposition to slavery declined in the first two decades of the nineteenth century. The American Colonization Society (founded in 1816) did propose a limited plan for emancipation, under which slaveholders would be compensated for voluntarily freeing their slaves and free blacks would be

> **Horace Mann**
> Became the first secretary of the newly created Massachusetts board of education in 1837 and presided over sweeping reforms to transform schools into institutions that occupied most of a child's time and energy. His goals included shifting financial support from parents to the state, extending the school term from two or three to as many as ten months, standardizing textbooks, classifying students into grades based on their age and attainment, and compelling attendance.

"colonized" in Liberia in West Africa. But some slaveholders became colonizationists, not to support emancipation but to remove free blacks from their vicinity. And colonization had virtually no hope of succeeding because of the South's growing dependence on slavery. In addition, the Society never had enough funds to buy freedom for significant numbers of slaves. Between 1820 and 1830—a period when the slave population nearly doubled in size—only 1,400 blacks migrated to Liberia, and most of them were not recently manumitted slaves.

Most African Americans opposed colonization. As native-born Americans, they asked, how could they be sent back to a continent they had never known? "We are natives of this country," one black pastor proclaimed. "We only ask that we be treated as well as foreigners." In opposition to colonization, blacks formed their own abolition societies. David Walker, a North Carolina-born free black who owned a used clothing store in Boston, smuggled antislavery tracts into the South by stuffing them into the pockets of clothes he shipped there. In 1829, Walker published an *Appeal . . . to the Colored Citizens of the World*, urging slaves to rise up and murder their masters if slavery were not abolished. He warned whites that "your DESTRUCTION is at hand, and will be speedily consummated unless you REPENT." In 1830, black leaders began holding annual conventions devoted to abolishing slavery in the South and repealing discriminatory black codes in the North.

Some white abolitionists also began to move toward more radical positions. In 1821, Quaker Benjamin Lundy began a newspaper, the *Genius of Universal Emancipation*, which proposed that no new slave states be admitted to the Union, the internal slave trade should be outlawed, the three-fifths clause of the Constitution repealed, and Congress should abolish slavery wherever it had the authority to do so. In 1828, Lundy hired a young New Englander, **William Lloyd Garrison**, as his assistant editor. With his premature baldness and steel-rimmed glasses, Garrison looked more like a schoolmaster than a revolutionary. But in 1831, when he launched his newspaper, *The Liberator*, he quickly established himself as the most prominent and provocative white abolitionist. "I am in earnest," Garrison wrote. "I will not equivocate—I will not excuse—I will not retreat a single inch—AND I WILL BE HEARD." He filled the pages of *The Liberator* with gruesome stories of slaves beaten to death or burned alive by their masters, and appealed to the humanity of his readers to abolish the institution.

In 1833, Garrison gathered about sixty delegates, black and white, men and women, to form the American Antislavery Society. His battle cry was "immediate emancipation" without compensation to slaveholders. Free blacks should not be shipped to Africa, but granted full equality with whites. He pointedly greeted slaves as "a Man and a Brother," "a Woman and a Sister." Garrison quickly gained support from black abolitionists, who made up three-fourths of his newspaper subscribers in the early years. One black barber in Pittsburgh sent Garrison sixty dollars to support *The Liberator*.

Fugitive slaves played a central role in the abolitionist movement. The foremost of these was Frederick Douglass, who escaped from slavery in Maryland in 1838 and condemned the institution in his autobiography, his newspaper the *North Star*, and his public lectures. Douglass could rivet an audience with an opening line. "I appear before the immense assembly this evening as a thief and

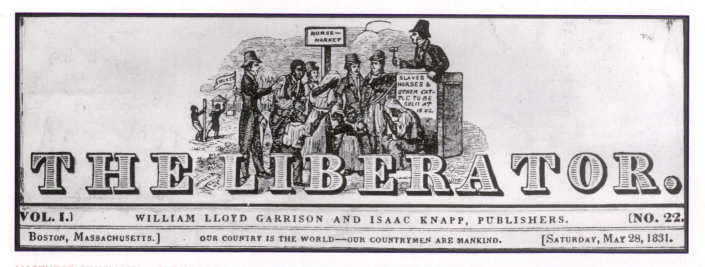

MASTHEAD OF WILLIAM LLOYD GARRISON'S ANTISLAVERY NEWSPAPER, *THE LIBERATOR*. The image above the title shows the inhumanity of a slave auction, which equated the sale of black slaves with that of horses and other animals. *(Hulton Archive/Stringer/ Getty Images)*

a robber," he proclaimed. "I stole this head, these limbs, this body from my master, and ran off with them." Other fugitive slaves—including William Wells Brown and Harriet Tubman—served the cause by publicizing the horrors of slavery, telling tales of brutal treatment and families separated by sale.

Relations between black and white abolitionists were not always harmonious. Many white abolitionists opposed social equality for blacks, favored lighter-skinned Negroes, and sometimes excluded black abolitionists from their meetings. Yet the racial prejudice of white abolitionists was mild compared to that of most whites, some of whom transferred their hatred of blacks to abolitionists. Mobs led by local elites attacked the homes and businesses of black and white abolitionists, destroyed their printing presses, and disrupted their meetings. In 1834, an anti-abolitionist mob destroyed forty-five homes in Philadelphia's black community. In 1835, a Boston mob dragged Garrison through town with a hanging noose around his neck. And in 1837, a mob in Alton, Illinois, destroyed the printing press of antislavery editor Elijah P. Lovejoy, then shot him and dragged his mutilated corpse through the streets.

Abolitionists, like temperance reformers, drew on the language of revivals in condemning slavery as sin. But Protestant churches did not rally behind abolition as they rallied behind temperance. The Rev. Lyman Beecher roared against the evils of strong drink but merely whispered about those of slavery. In 1834, he tried to suppress abolitionists at Cincinnati's Lane Theological Seminary where he was president. In response, a student named Theodore Dwight Weld, who was a follower of Charles G. Finney, led the "Lane rebels" out of Beecher's seminary to the more radical Oberlin College.

Issues of strategy and tactics divided abolitionists during the 1830s. For some, the legal and political arena seemed to offer the best opportunities for ending slavery. But Garrison and his followers were beginning to reject all participation in party politics—and even government itself. In 1838, they founded the New England Non-Resistance Society, based on Garrison's radical new doctrine of non-resistance. According to that doctrine, the fundamental evil of slavery was its reliance on force, the opposite of Christian love. And government, like slavery, ultimately rested on coercion; even laws passed by elected legislatures required police enforcement. True Christians, Garrison concluded, should refuse to vote, hold office, or have anything to do with government.

The second major issue dividing abolitionists was the role of women in the movement. From the outset, women had actively participated in antislavery, working separately from men in female auxiliaries. Then in 1837, **Angelina and Sarah Grimké**, daughters of a South Carolina slaveholder, undertook an antislavery lecture tour of New England, speaking in public before mixed audiences of men and women and sharing the horrors of slavery that they witnessed firsthand. Critics said such conduct was indelicate; women should obey men, not lecture them. The Grimkés responded in 1838 by writing two classics of American feminism: Sarah Grimké's *Letters on the Condition of Women and the Equality of the Sexes*, and Angelina Grimké's *Letters to Catharine E. Beecher* (who opposed female equality). Some abolitionists dismissed their efforts; women's grievances, said poet John Greenleaf Whittier, were "paltry" compared to the "great and dreadful wrongs of the slave." Even Angelina's husband, "Lane Rebel" Theodore Dwight Weld, thought women's rights should be subordinated to antislavery.

In 1840, abolitionist Abby Kelley was elected to a previously all-male committee, and the resulting battle split the American Antislavery Society. Garrison, who strongly supported women's rights, won control of the organization, and his antifeminist opponents—including New York philanthropists Arthur and Lewis Tappan and former slaveholder James G. Birney of Alabama—walked out. Some of them flocked to the new Liberty Party, which nominated Birney for president in 1840 on a platform that called on Congress to abolish slavery in the District of Columbia, end the interstate slave trade, and stop admitting new slave states to the Union. Others followed Lewis Tappan into the new American and Foreign Anti-Slavery Society.

But the break-up of the American Anti-Slavery Society did not significantly damage the larger movement. By 1840, more than fifteen hundred local antislavery societies were busy circulating abolitionist tracts, newspapers, and even chocolates wrapped in antislavery messages. Local societies pursued a grassroots campaign to flood Congress with petitions calling for an end to slavery in the District of Columbia. When exasperated southerners in 1836 adopted a "gag rule" automatically tabling these petitions without discussion, they triggered a debate that shifted public attention from abolitionism to the constitutional rights of free expression and Congressional petition—a debate that further served the antislavery cause. And the split between moderates and radicals actually helped the antislavery movement by giving northerners

Angelina and Sarah Grimké
Daughters of a South Carolina slaveholder; they embarked on an antislavery lecture tour of New England in 1837. What made them so controversial was that they drew mixed audiences of men and women to their lectures at a time when it was thought indelicate for women to speak before male audiences.

a choice between different levels and strategies of commitment.

10-4.4 Woman's Rights

When Sarah and Angelina Grimké took up the cause of woman's rights in 1838, they were not merely defending their right to participate in the antislavery movement. They were responding to similarities between the conditions of black slaves and women of all races. Garrison himself stressed the special degradation and sexual vulnerability of women under slavery, denouncing the slaveholding South as one vast brothel. Early issues of *The Liberator* contained a "Ladies' Department" illustrated with a kneeling slave woman imploring, "Am I Not a Woman and a Sister?" When abolitionists such as Philadelphia Quaker **Lucretia Mott**, Lucy Stone, and Abby Kelley embraced women's rights, they were acknowledging a sisterhood in oppression with female slaves.

In the early nineteenth century, American women were prohibited from voting or holding public office and denied access to higher education and the professions. Married women had no legal identity apart from their husbands: they could not own property or control their own earnings, sue or be sued, or enter a contract. Divorced women could not gain custody of their children. And in the midst of many humanitarian efforts to eradicate violence—including movements against dueling and war, military flogging, and capital punishment—domestic violence went virtually unchallenged, except as a side issue within the temperance movement. According to the popular idea of separate spheres, women's place was in the home, and even in their proper sphere their legal rights were severely limited.

But reform movements provided middle-class women with unprecedented opportunities to work in public without openly rejecting the domestic sphere. When women left their homes to distribute religious tracts, battle intemperance, or work for peace, they could claim they were transforming wretched homes into nurseries of happiness. It was a tricky argument to make: justifying reform activities on behalf of family protection could undercut women's demands for legal equality. But the experiences acquired in a range of reform activities provided invaluable skills for women to take up the cause of their own rights.

At its most radical, the woman's rights movement openly challenged gender-based double standards. "Men and women," Sarah Grimké wrote, "are CREATED EQUAL! They are both moral and accountable beings, and whatever is right for man to do, is right for woman." Even well beyond antislavery leadership circles, ordinary women were beginning to claim a woman's right to full equality with men. In 1846, six farm women from rural Jefferson County, New York, petitioned the state constitutional convention to demand "equal, and civil and political rights with men." Significantly, they declined to invoke the cult of domesticity to make their case, proclaiming that "a self evident truth is sufficiently plain without argument." Sexual equality, which most Americans still regarded as unthinkable, was for some beginning to seem a matter of common sense.

The discrimination encountered by women in the antislavery movement drove them to make woman's rights a separate cause. In the 1840s, Lucy Stone became the first abolitionist to give a lecture devoted entirely to woman's rights. When Lucretia Mott arrived at the World's Anti-Slavery Convention in London in 1840, and was seated in a screened-off section for women, her own allegiance to woman's rights was sealed. So was that of **Elizabeth Cady Stanton**, who attended the London meeting with her abolitionist husband on their honeymoon. In 1848, Mott and Stanton together organized the **Seneca Falls Convention** for woman's rights at Seneca Falls, New York. More than 300 men and women attended, among them noted abolitionist and former slave Frederick Douglass, affirming his commitment to racial and gender equality. That convention's Declaration of Sentiments, modeled on the Declaration of Independence, began with the assertion that "all men and women are created equal." The convention passed twelve resolutions, eleven of them unanimously, and the twelfth, woman's right to vote, over a minority opposition (see Going to the Source). After the Civil War, woman suffrage became the main demand of woman's rights advocates.

Woman's rights advocates won a few notable victories. In 1860, Stanton's lobbying helped secure passage of a New York law allowing married women to own property—not the first such law, but the most comprehensive to that date. But woman's rights had less short-run impact

---

Lucretia Mott
A Quaker from Philadelphia who became a leader in advocating for women's rights.

Elizabeth Cady Stanton
One of the leading women's rights activists in the 1840s and the decades that followed; among the authors of the Delcaration of Sentiments.

Seneca Falls Convention
Women's rights convention in 1848. The convention's Declaration of Sentiments, modeled on the Declaration of Independence, began with the assertion that "all men and women are created equal." The convention passed twelve resolutions, and only one, a call for the right of women to vote, failed to pass unanimously; but it did pass. Ironically, after the Civil War, the call for woman suffrage became the main demand of women's rights advocates for the rest of the century.

The Declaration of Sentiments

The Declaration of Sentiments, drafted by Elizabeth Cady Stanton, was passed at the Woman's Rights Convention held at Seneca Falls, New York, on July 20, 1848. Modeled on the Declaration of Independence and drawing on principles of human freedom developed in the antislavery movement, the Declaration of Sentiments offered a systematic statement of the sexual inequalities pervading American society and politics and was a powerful demand for woman's rights. This document represented a watershed moment in the broader history of human rights in the United States.

When, in the course of human events, it becomes necessary for one portion of the family of man to assume among the people of the earth a position different from that which they have hitherto occupied, but one to which the laws of nature and of nature's God entitle them, a decent respect to the opinions of mankind requires that they should declare the causes that impel them to such a course.

We hold these truths to be self-evident: that all men and women are created equal; that they are endowed by their Creator with certain inalienable rights; that among these are life, liberty, and the pursuit of happiness; that to secure these rights governments are instituted, deriving their just powers from the consent of the governed. Whenever any form of government becomes destructive of these ends, it is the right of those who suffer from it to refuse allegiance to it, and to insist upon the institution of a new government, laying its foundation on such principles, and organizing its powers in such form, as to them shall seem most likely to effect their safety and happiness. Prudence, indeed, will dictate that governments long established should not be changed for light and transient causes . . . But when a long train of abuses and usurpations, pursuing invariably the same object, evinces a design to reduce them under absolute despotism, it is their duty to throw off such government, and to provide new guards for their future security. Such has been the patient sufferance of the women under this government, and such is now the necessity which constrains them to demand the equal station to which they are entitled.

The history of mankind is a history of repeated injuries and usurpations on the part of man toward woman, having in direct object the establishment of an absolute tyranny over her . . .

He has never permitted her to exercise her inalienable right to the elective franchise . . .

He has made her, if married, in the eyes of the law, civilly dead.

He has taken from her all right to property, even to the wages she earns . . .

In the covenant of marriage, she is compelled to promise obedience to her husband, he becoming, to all intents and purposes, her master—the law giving him the power to deprive her of her liberty, and to administer chastisement. ...

He has monopolized nearly all the profitable employments, and from those she is permitted to follow, she receives but a scanty remuneration . . .

He has denied her the facilities for obtaining a thorough education—all colleges being closed against her . . .

He has created a false public sentiment by giving to the world a different code of morals for men and women. . . .

He has endeavored, in every way that he could, to destroy her confidence in her own powers, to lessen her self-respect, and to make her willing to lead a dependent and abject life.

Now, in view of this entire disfranchisement of one-half the people of this country, their social and religious degradation,—in view of the unjust laws above mentioned, and because women do feel themselves aggrieved, oppressed, and fraudulently deprived of their most sacred rights, we insist that they have immediate admission to all the rights and privileges which belong to them as citizens of these United States.

QUESTIONS

1. Why, in your view, did Stanton decide to model the Declaration of Sentiments so closely on the Declaration of Independence?
2. Based on this document, what parallels do you see between the antislavery movement and the woman's rights movement during this period?

SOJOURNER TRUTH, 1864 Born into slavery in New York, the woman who named herself Sojourner Truth became a religious perfectionist, a powerful evangelical preacher, and one of the most influential abolitionists and feminists of her time. In the 1860s, she sold photographic portraits of herself printed on small cards, explaining, "I sell the shadow to support the substance." *(Schomburg Center, NYPL/Art Resource, NY.)*

than many other reforms, including temperance, school reform, and abolitionism. Women would not secure the national right to vote until 1920, fifty-five years after the Thirteenth Amendment abolished slavery. Nineteenth-century feminists had to content themselves with piecemeal gains. The cause of woman's rights suffered from its association with abolitionism and met resistance from advocates of separate spheres (see Chapter 9). Nevertheless, women made important strides toward equality.

10-4.5 Penitentiaries and Asylums

Beginning in the 1820s, reformers began to combat poverty, crime, and insanity by establishing new model institutions based on innovative theories about the roots of deviancy. As urban poverty and crime grew increasingly visible, investigators concluded that such problems arose not from innate sinfulness but from poor home environments, especially a failure of parental discipline. Both religious and secular reformers believed that human nature could be improved through placement in the proper moral environment. The reformers' model of the proper environment for paupers, criminals, and the mentally ill was the asylum, an institution that would remove deviants from corrupting influences by placing them in a controlled, orderly environment, and provide them with moral supervision and disciplined work.

Unitarian minister William Ellery Channing hoped that, "The study of the causes of crime may lead us to its cure." The colonial jail had been merely a temporary holding cell for offenders awaiting trial; early American criminals were punished by flogging, branding, or hanging rather than extended prison terms. By contrast, the nineteenth-century penitentiary was an asylum designed to lead criminals to "penitential" reformation by isolating them and encouraging them to contemplate their guilt for designated terms of incarceration. Two different models for the penitentiary emerged in the antebellum era. New York's "Auburn system" forbade prisoners to speak or look at one another as they worked together by day, and confined them in individual, windowless cells by night. Under the more extreme "Pennsylvania" or "separate system," each prisoner was confined day and night in a single cell with a walled courtyard for exercise, deprived of human contact within the prison, and permitted no news or visits from the outside.

Antebellum reformers also designed special asylums for the poor and the mentally ill. The prevailing colonial practice of poor relief was "outdoor relief," supporting the poor by placing them in other people's households. The new "indoor relief" confined the infirm poor in almshouses, and the able-bodied poor in workhouses. Once again, reformers believed that removing the poor from their demoralizing surroundings and subjecting them to institutional regimentation and disciplined labor would transform them into virtuous, productive citizens. A parallel movement shaped new approaches to treating the mentally ill, as illuminated in the work of humanitarian reformer Dorothea Dix. Instead of imprisoning the insane in jails and sheds, she argued, society should house them in orderly hospitals where they should receive proper medical and moral care.

Penitentiaries, almshouses and workhouses, and insane asylums all reflected the same optimistic belief that the solution for deviancy lay in

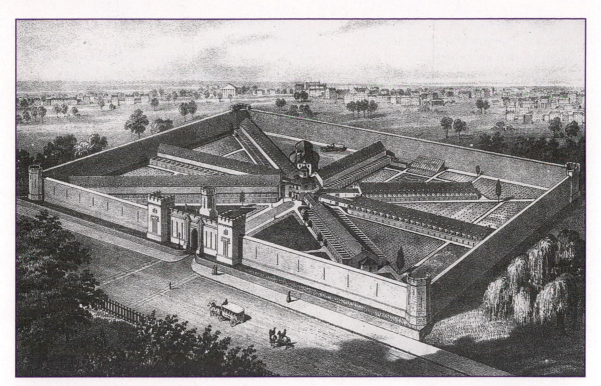

PENNSYLVANIA'S EASTERN STATE PENITENTIARY Established in 1822, this penitentiary was the showcase of the Pennsylvania or "separate" system of prison discipline. Each inmate was confined to a single cell and denied all contact with other inmates. This sketch was done by inmate 2954 in 1855. *(The state penitentiary, for the eastern district of Pennsylvania, printed by P.S. Duval & Co, c.1855 (litho)/Cowperthwaite, Samuel (fl.1855)/LIBRARY COMPANY OF PHILADELPHIA/Library Company of Philadelphia, PA, USA/Bridgeman Images)*

proper moral environments. From one point of view, such efforts were humanitarian: they confined criminals rather than flogging them, offered relief to the poor, and provided shelter and medical care to the homeless insane. But from another point of view, the asylum reformers were practicing extreme forms of social control. Convinced that criminals, the poor, and the insane required regimentation, they incarcerated them, policed their social interaction, and controlled their every move. The idealism behind the new asylums was genuine, but utopian intentions did not protect asylum inmates from the sufferings of confinement and regimentation.

10-4.6 Utopian Communities

The reformist belief in the possibility of human perfection assumed purest expression in the **utopian communities** that first began to form in the 1820s and flourished during the next few decades (see Map 10.3). Among the hundreds of utopian experiments undertaken in the antebellum period, most aimed at offering alternatives to the selfish excesses of social and economic competition. Modern Times on Long Island and the North American Phalanx at Red Bank, New Jersey,

were influenced by the ideas of Frenchman Charles Fourier, who sought to eradicate the evils of economic competition by establishing a harmonious society whose members all pursued "attractive" labor.

In 1825, British industrialist Robert Owen founded the New Harmony community in Indiana. As a successful Scottish mill owner, Owen had improved his workers' living conditions and educational opportunities. If social arrangements could be perfected, he believed, then vice and misery would disappear because human character was formed entirely by environment. Owen proposed to create "Villages of Unity and Mutual Cooperation" where occupational, religious, and political groups would live together in perfect balance. Upon founding New Harmony, Owen confidently predicted that northerners would embrace its principles within two years. Instead, the community became a magnet for idlers and fanatics and failed within two years. But Owen's ideas survived the wreckage of New Harmony. His insistence that human character was formed by environment and that cooperation was superior to competition had an enduring

> **utopian communities**
> Experimental communities that sprang up in the 1820s as an alternative to the competitiveness of mainstream society.

impact on urban workers, who took up his cause of educational reform in the years to come.

Experimental communities multiplied rapidly during the economic crises of the late 1830s and 1840s. Brook Farm, near Boston, was the creation of a group of religious philosophers called transcendentalists, who sought to revitalize Christianity by proclaiming the infinite spiritual capacities of ordinary men and women. Convinced that the competitive commercial life of the cities was unnatural, and committed to balancing mental and manual labor in their own personal lives, Brook Farmers spent their days milking cows and mowing hay and their evenings contemplating philosophy. Brook Farm attracted several renowned writers, including Ralph Waldo Emerson and Nathaniel Hawthorne, and its literary magazine, *The Dial*, became an important forum for transcendentalist ideas about philosophy, art, and literature (as discussed further in Chapter 11). But its lifespan was brief.

The most controversial utopian experiment was the Oneida Community, established in 1848 in New York by John Humphrey Noyes. A convert of Charles Finney, Noyes too became a theological perfectionist. At Oneida, he advocated a form of Christian communism that challenged conventional notions of religion, property, gender roles, and even clothing and childrearing. The Oneidans renounced private property, put men to work in kitchens, and adopted the radical new bloomer costume for women. But what most upset their critics was the application of communism to marriage. In place of conventional marriage, which Noyes regarded as profoundly selfish, he advocated "complex marriage," in which every member of the community was married to every other member of the opposite sex. Oneida did not promote a sexual free-for-all: couplings were arranged through an intermediary, in part to track paternity. Contemporaries dismissed Noyes as a licentious crackpot. Yet Oneida achieved considerable prosperity and was attracting new members long after other utopias had failed.

Despite the ridicule of many of their contemporaries, utopian communities exemplified the idealism and hopefulness that permeated nearly all reform movements in the antebellum period.

The Whole Vision

■ *How was the election process and the presidency increasingly transformed in the early nineteenth century?*

Simply stated, the political system in America was becoming more democratized, more politicized, and in some ways, more complicated. The old system of electoral politics re-quired that only property-owning men could vote and that candidates for the presidency be chosen not by the public, but by state legislators. That would fade quickly as more states removed property requirements for voting and made the nomination of candidates a public decision. While the seeds of the two-party system can be traced further back than the emergence of Andrew Jackson on the national political scene, the disputed 1824 election and subsequent 1828 election marked the rise of the Democratic Party and the advent of the American two-party system. But the two-party system would also reveal sectional differences and rifts that would come to increasingly shape political debates and controversies during Jackson's years in office and beyond. Leaders in this era faced new challenges: how to balance sectional interests while maintaining the loyalty of supporters in each region and how to limit the size of the federal government while asserting its preeminence over state authority. These concerns would plague the Jackson administration throughout his two terms in office, as manifested in the nullification crisis and bank controversy.

■ *How did the bank controversy and emergence of the Whigs solidify the two-party system?*

The controversy over the bank not only further stimulated public interest in politics, it was the final straw in a coming division between the political parties that led to the emergence of the Whig Party. With the arrival of the Whigs in the 1830s (and solidly by 1840), the nation's shift to a two-party system was complete. The heated nature of the bank controversy assured that party lines were firmly drawn in terms of the important issues of the day. While both Whigs and Democrats would find adherents in all regions, each would gain their own strongholds in the pivotal regions of the Northeast and the South. More important than region, the parties' positions on key issues would determine their base of support. People lined up for one party or the other according to their class, ethnicity and religious beliefs, as well as their desire for an activist national government. They similarly sided with the Whigs or Democrats based on visions of economic growth via expanding the physical size of the nation or via the market economy. Finally, beliefs about the perfectibility of society through reform efforts had voters allying with one party or the other. The Panic of 1837 and the election of 1840 not only solidified party loyalties, but also the trend toward rising voter participation.

KEY TERMS

political democratization (p. 266)

Henry Clay (p. 267)

Democratic Party (p. 268)

spoils system (p. 268)

nullification crisis (p. 271)

Second Bank of the United States (p. 271)

Whig Party (p. 273)

Panic of 1837 (p. 275)

Second Great Awakening (p. 277)

Charles G. Finney (p. 278)

theological perfectionism (p. 279)

Mormons (p. 279)

American Temperance Society (p. 281)

Horace Mann (p. 283)

William Lloyd Garrison (p. 284)

Angelina and Sarah Grimké (p. 285)

Lucretia Mott (p. 286)

Elizabeth Cady Stanton (p. 286)

Seneca Falls Convention (p. 286)

utopian communities (p. 289)

■ *What does the advent of new religious movements reveal about nineteenth-century American society?*

In a nutshell, the Second Great Awakening, religious revivalism, and the emergence of new religious sects in America during this time period demonstrates the extension of democratizing influences beyond politics into social and cultural life. Americans increasingly moved away from a top-down or authoritarian structure in all of their institutions, abandoning the notion of "betters" and deference for a more egalitarian approach. The preachers of the Second Great Awakening made listeners responsible for their individual spiritual destiny, rather than entrusting that power exclusively to ministers. Revivals were open to all people, regardless of class, race, or gender. Religious denominations that embraced theological perfectionism gained adherents, as did those that relied on emotions or an emotional conversion experience. But groups that were critical of the highly charged evangelical revivals also found a new base of support among those who took a more rational approach. Some, too, depicted Jesus more as a man—much like the common men and women of the nineteenth century—and less as a god. Such positions, however, would, in turn, spark the emergence of other religions such as the Mormons and the Shakers, each with their own views about divinity and human responsibility.

■ *In what ways were the reform movements an extension of the democratic impulses of the nineteenth century?*

The notion that human beings were capable of improvement and responsible for their own destiny was embedded in the revival movement and part of the reason the revivals were so popular. Many people then sought to take the ideas of perfectibility and extend them to improving their society. As they looked around, they could easily see areas and issues that, if properly addressed, would lead to the betterment of the country. Even those who were not involved in the revival movements could still share the desire to improve society, albeit drawing their inspiration from different sources. Reformers addressed a host of issues, from those calling for changes in personal behavior, such as temperance, to those seeking greater social change, such as ending slavery, promoting public education, or advocating for increased rights for women. Some movements were driven by quests for greater control over workers, immigrants, and society; others sought to expand democracy to groups that had been left beyond its reach. The reform fervor drew in new activists, too, among them women, though that sometimes provoked debates about women's proper gender roles. Strategies for reform also changed, as groups moved from efforts to convince people of the error of their ways to seeking new laws that would mandate such changes. When reform seemed impossible, some opted out, seeking to achieve human perfection and cooperation in their own separate, utopian societies.

11 Technology, Culture, and Everyday Life, 1840–1860

STEAM LOCOMOTIVE CROSSING THE NIAGARA RAILWAY SUSPENSION BRIDGE, 1860s Suspension bridges like this were developed in the 1850s to bear the great weight of locomotives and railroad cars. *(From The New York Public Library)*

CHRONOLOGY 1840–1860

1820	Washington Irving, *The Sketch Book*.
1823	Philadelphia completes the first urban water-supply system.
	James Fenimore Cooper, *The Pioneers*.
1826	Cooper, *The Last of the Mohicans*.
1831	Mount Auburn Cemetery opens.
1832	A cholera epidemic strikes the United States.
1833	The *New York Sun*, the first penny newspaper, is established.
1834	Cyrus McCormick patents the mechanical reaper.
1835	James Gordon Bennett establishes the *New York Herald*.
1837	Ralph Waldo Emerson, "The American Scholar."
1841	P.T. Barnum opens the American Museum.
	Edgar Allan Poe, "The Murders in the Rue Morgue."
1844	First telegraph message transmitted.
1846	W. T. G. Morton successfully uses anesthesia. Elias Howe, Jr. patents the sewing machine.
1849	Second major cholera epidemic.
	Astor Place theater riot leaves twenty-two dead.
1850	Nathaniel Hawthorne, *The Scarlet Letter*.
1851	Hawthorne, *The House of the Seven Gables*.
	Herman Melville, *Moby-Dick*.
	Erie Railroad completes its line to the West.
1853	Ten small railroads are consolidated into the New York Central Railroad.
1854	Henry David Thoreau, *Walden*.
1855	Walt Whitman, *Leaves of Grass*.
1856	Pennsylvania Railroad completes Chicago link.
1857	Baltimore–St. Louis rail service completed.
1858	Frederick Law Olmsted is appointed architect in chief for Central Park.

In 1850, Isaac M. Singer's life was not going well. Thirty-nine and often penniless, he had been an unsuccessful actor, carpenter, and inventor. His early inventions had been clever, but not commercially successful. Having deserted his wife and children, he lured Mary Ann Sponslor into living with him by promising marriage. Sponslor nursed him when he was sick, but instead of marrying her, Singer beat her and had affairs with other women. Then in 1850, Singer made significant improvements on a sewing machine similar to one patented in 1846 by Elias Howe, Jr., and within ten years, he was a wealthy man.

Here was a machine everyone wanted. New England's textile mills had initially mechanized the production of cloth, but not the transformation of fabric into clothing. Instead, factories hired young women to stitch fabric by hand in their homes. Where it took a single woman three hours to hand-stitch a pair of pants, a sewing machine could do the job in thirty-eight minutes. Once the proper machine tools had been designed for manufacturing sewing machines, they became widely available to factories eager to purchase them. By saving time, sewing machines made clothing cheaper, which was a major boost to the ready-made clothing industry. Contemporaries could not praise the new machines enough. The *New York Tribune* predicted that, with the spread of sewing machines, people "will dress better, change oftener, and altogether grow better looking." Sewing machines would create a nation "without spot or blemish."

This optimistic response to technological change was typical of the 1850s. The term *technology* had been coined in 1829 to indicate the application of science to improving life's conveniences. Many Americans believed that technology was God's instrument of progress. Some predicted that the telegraph, another invention of the age, would usher in world peace. The cotton gin, the steam engine, and the mechanical reaper prompted similarly utopian hopes for the future. For New Englander Edward Everett in 1852, the locomotive was "a miracle of science, art, and capital, a magic power . . . by which the forest is thrown open, the lakes and rivers are bridged, the valleys rise, and all Nature yields to man."

Yet progress had a darker side. As Ralph Waldo Emerson bluntly observed, "Machinery is dangerous. The weaver becomes the web, the machinist the machine. If you do not use the tools, they use you." The newly invented revolver was useless

ISAAC SINGER (*National Portrait Gallery, Smithsonian Institution/Art Resource, NY*)

for hunting and not much good in battle, but excellent for violently settling private disputes. The farmwomen who had once earned money sewing by hand in their homes were displaced by working-class women who sewed by machine in small urban sweatshops. Philosophers and artists began to worry about the despoliation of the landscape by factories, and some urban Americans launched efforts to preserve natural enclaves as retreats from the evils of progress.

11-1 Technology and Economic Growth

Was technology truly a democratizing force in the mid-nineteenth century?

Among the major technological improvements that transformed life in antebellum America were the steam engine, the cotton gin, the mechanical reaper, the sewing machine, and the telegraph. Some of these originated in Europe, but Americans had a flair for investing in others' inventions and perfecting their own. Widely hailed as democratic, technology drew praise from all sides. Conservative statesman Daniel Webster praised machines for doing the work of people without requiring food or clothing. Radical labor organizer Sarah Bagley, a textile worker, traced the improvement of society to new technology. American schoolboys, according to a Swedish tourist in 1849–1851, constantly drew pictures on their slates of steamboats, engines, and other forms of "locomotive machinery."

Of course, along with its beneficial aspects, technology had a negative side. For example, improvements in Eli Whitney's cotton gin between 1793 and 1860 increased eightfold the amount of cotton that could be cleaned in a day. But it also entrenched slavery by intensifying southern dependence on cotton. Machine manufacture undercut the position of artisans by rendering many traditional skills obsolete. Nevertheless, by increasing productivity, technology lowered commodity prices and raised living standards for substantial numbers of free Americans between 1840 and 1860.

11.1-1 Agricultural Advancement

After 1830, American settlers were edging westward from the woodlands of Ohio and Kentucky into the prairie lands of Indiana, Michigan, Illinois, and Missouri, where flat grasslands alternated with forests. Prairie soil, though richly fertile, was matted with thick roots and resistant to plowing. But in 1837, John Deere invented a steel-tipped plow that cut in half the labor required to till for planting. Timber for houses and fencing was available in nearby woods, and settlements developed and spread rapidly.

Wheat became to midwestern farmers what cotton was to the South. "The wheat crop is the great crop of the North-west," an agricultural journal noted in 1850. "It pays debts, buys groceries, clothing and lands, and answers more emphatically the purposes of trade among farmers than any other crop." Technological advances sped the harvesting as well as the planting of wheat. The traditional hand sickle had consumed huge amounts of time and labor, and the cut wheat had to be picked up and bound by hand. But in 1834, Cyrus McCormick of Virginia patented a horse-drawn mechanical reaper that harvested grain seven times faster with half the workforce. In 1847, he opened a factory in Chicago, and by 1860 he had sold 80,000 reapers. The mechanical reaper guaranteed that wheat would dominate the midwestern prairies.

Ironically, McCormick, a proslavery southerner, would see his invention aid the North during the Civil War. The North provided the main market for the **McCormick reaper** and its many competitors; the South, with its reliance on unpaid slave labor, had little incentive to invest in labor-saving agricultural machinery. During the Civil War, McCormick sold more than a quarter of a million reapers, which helped keep northern agricultural production high at a time when many farmers were off fighting the war.

Even as Americans were mechanizing agriculture, they tended to farm wastefully, preferring to seek "virgin" soil rather than improve "worn-out" soil. But some eastern farmers, confronted by competition from the West, began to experiment with improved agricultural techniques. By fertilizing their fields with plaster left over from canal construction, Virginia wheat growers raised their average yield from six bushels per acre in 1800 to fifteen bushels by the 1850s. American cotton planters in the Southeast began to import guano (sea bird droppings) from Peru to fertilize their fields in an effort to compete successfully with the fertile soil of the Old Southwest. In Orange County, New York, dairy farmers fed their cows the best clover and bluegrass and undertook cleaner dairy processing. The result was a superior butter that sold at more than double the price of ordinary butter.

McCormick reaper
Mechanical reaper invented by Cyrus McCormick in 1847.

11-1.2 Technology and Industrial Progress

Industrial advances between 1840 and 1860 owed an immense debt to the development of effective machine tools, power-driven machines that cut and shaped metal to precise specifications. In the early 1800s, Eli Whitney's plan to manufacture muskets by using interchangeable parts actually awaited the development of the machine tools essential to the system. After 1830, American manufacturers began to import machine-tool technology from Britain. By the 1840s, machine tools had greatly reduced the need to hand-file parts to make them fit, and they were applied to the manufacture of firearms, clocks, and sewing machines. After midcentury, Europeans began to call this system of manufacturing interchangeable parts the **"American System of Manufacturing"** and to import machine tools manufactured in the United States. After touring American factories in 1854, a British engineer concluded that Americans "universally and willingly" resorted to machines as a substitute for manual labor.

The American manufacturing system had several distinct advantages. Traditionally, damage to any part of a mechanical contrivance rendered the whole machine useless. The perfection of interchangeable parts made replacement parts possible, so machines could be repaired and maintained. In addition, improved machine tools enabled entrepreneurs to push inventions or products into mass production quickly, which attracted investors. Sophisticated machine tools, according to one manufacturer, increased production "by confining a worker to one particular limb of a pistol until he had made two thousand." Such advantages were spectacular in terms of growth and profit for business owners; for workers, it meant the end of their roles as skilled producers who could manufacture an item from start to finish. Instead, they were increasingly being redefined as laborers, and the work they did in factories was marked by specific and finite tasks.

Along with machine tools and interchangeable parts, the telegraph proved an important innovation for communication, as well as for economic and new business growth. After the transmission of the first telegraph message in 1844, Americans seized enthusiastically on the telegraph's promise to eliminate the constraints of time and space. The speed with which

> **"American System of Manufacturing"**
> System of manufacturing that used interchangeable parts.

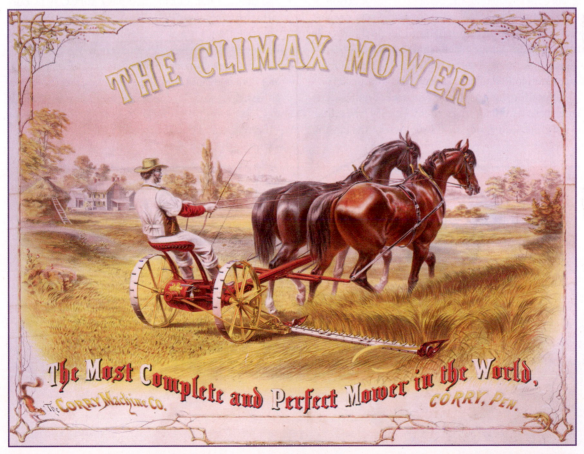

THE CLIMAX MOWER The United States became the leading manufacturer of agricultural implements in the nineteenth century. The Pennsylvania company that manufactured this mowing device proudly called it "the most complete and perfect mower in the world." *(Library of Congress Prints and Photographs Division [LC-USZC4-2340])*

Americans formed telegraph companies and strung their lines stunned a British engineer, who noted in 1854 that "no private interests can oppose the passage of a line through any property." Boston developed an elaborate system of telegraph stations that could alert fire companies throughout the city when a blaze broke out in any neighborhood. By 1852, more than fifteen thousand miles of telegraph lines connected cities as distant as Quebec, New Orleans, and St. Louis.

11-1.3 The Railroad Boom

Even more than the telegraph, the railroad dramatized the democratic promise of technology. In 1790, travel by horse averaged fourteen miles an hour. By 1850, an ordinary American could travel three times faster—by train.

Americans' love of early railroad travel had a lot to overcome. Sparks from locomotives showered passengers riding in open cars, and discouraged passengers in closed coaches from opening the windows. (Frontier hero Davy Crockett was an exception; he explained that "I can only judge of the speed by putting my head out to spit, which I did, and overtook it so quick, that it hit me smack in the face.") Brakes were difficult and dangerous to operate. Trains rarely ran at night because they lacked lights. Before the introduction of standard time zones in 1883, scheduling was a nightmare and delays were frequent. Individual railroads used different-gauge track, making frequent train changes necessary; even in the 1850s, a journey from Charleston to Philadelphia required eight transfers.

Yet nothing hampered the advance of railroads or Americans' enthusiasm for them. In 1851, the editor of the *American Railroad Journal* wrote that in the previous twenty years, the locomotive had become "the great agent of civilization and progress, the most powerful instrument for good the world has yet reached." Between 1840 and 1860, the size of the rail network and the power and convenience of trains underwent a stunning transformation. Track mileage increased from three thousand to thirty thousand miles; closed coaches replaced open cars; kerosene lamps made night travel possible; and increasingly powerful engines enabled trains to climb steep hills. Fifty thousand miles of telegraph wire enabled dispatchers to communicate with trains en route and thus reduce delays. By 1860, the United States had more track than all the rest of the world combined.

Railroads represented the second major phase of the transportation revolution. Canals remained in use—the Erie Canal did not reach its peak volume until 1880—but the railroads gradually overtook them, first in passengers and then in freight. By 1860, the value of goods transported by railroads greatly surpassed that carried by canals.

By 1860, railroads had spread like vast spider webs east of the Mississippi River. They transformed southern cities like Atlanta and Chattanooga into thriving commercial hubs. Most important, the railroads linked the East and the Midwest. The New York Central and the Erie Railroads joined New York City to Buffalo; the Pennsylvania Railroad connected Philadelphia to Pittsburgh; and the Baltimore and Ohio linked Baltimore to Wheeling, Virginia (now West Virginia). Simultaneously, intense construction in Ohio, Indiana, and Illinois created trunk lines that tied these routes to cities farther west. By 1860, rail lines ran from Buffalo to Chicago, from Pittsburgh to Fort Wayne, and from Wheeling to St. Louis (see Map 11.1).

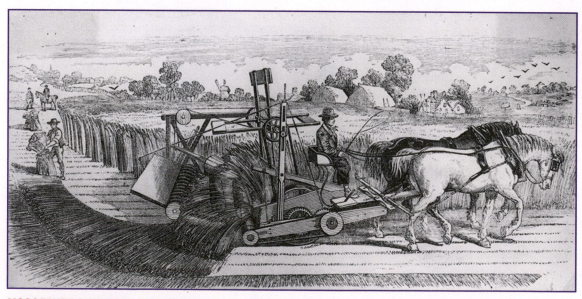

MCCORMICK'S REAPER Cyrus McCormick's mechanical reaper, patented in 1834, won the most prestigious medal at London's Crystal Palace Exhibition in 1851. That same year, McCormick licensed the British company of Burgess and Key to produce his reapers in England. *(Hulton Archive/Getty Images)*

GEORGE INNES, THE LACKAWANNA VALLEY, CA. 1856. This landscape painting was commissioned by the Delaware, Lackawanna, and Western Railroad to celebrate the railroad's growth—specifically, the construction of the line's first roundhouse, just outside Scranton, Pennsylvania. But the tree stumps littering the foreground suggest the painter's concerns over the impact of industrial progress on the American landscape. *(Courtesy of National Gallery of Art, Washington)*

The dramatic growth of Chicago illustrates the impact of expanding rail links. In 1849, Chicago was just a village of a few hundred people with virtually no rail service. By 1860, it had become a city of one hundred thousand served by eleven railroads. Farmers in the Upper Midwest, who had once shipped their grain, livestock, and dairy products down the Mississippi River to New Orleans, could now send products directly east by railroad. Chicago thus supplanted New Orleans as the main commercial hub of the continental interior.

Rail lines stimulated the settlement of the Midwest. By 1860 Illinois, Indiana, and Wisconsin had replaced Ohio, Pennsylvania, and New York as the leading wheat-growing states. Railroads increased the value of farmland and promoted additional settlement. In turn, population growth triggered industrial development in cities such as Chicago, Davenport, and Minneapolis because the new settlers needed lumber for fences and houses, and gristmills to grind wheat into flour.

Railroads also encouraged the growth of small towns along their routes. The Illinois Central, which had more track than any other railroad in 1855, made money not only from carrying passengers and freight but from investing in real estate along its route. After purchasing land for stations, the Illinois Central laid out towns around the stations. In 1854 Manteno, Illinois, was just a vacant crossroads, but after becoming a railroad stop, it grew into a bustling town with hotels, lumberyards, grain elevators, and gristmills. The Illinois Central even dictated the naming of streets. Those running east and west were named after trees, while those running north and south were given numbers. By the Civil War, the railroad-linked Midwest was no longer considered a frontier region.

As the nation's first big business, the railroads transformed the way business was conducted. During the early 1830s railroads, like canals, depended on state funding. With the onset of depression in the late 1830s, however, state governments scrapped many railroad projects. Convinced that railroads burdened them with high taxes and blasted hopes, voters in several states amended their constitutions to bar state funding for railroads and canals. Federal aid would not become widely available until the

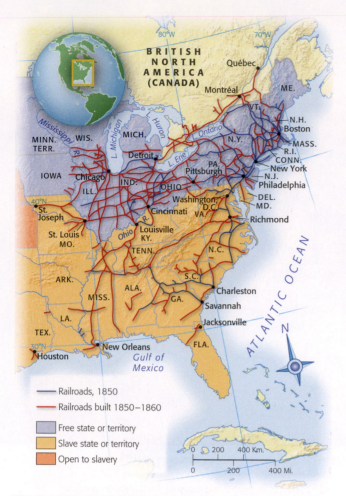

MAP 11.1 **RAILROAD GROWTH, 1850–1860** Rail ties between the East and the Midwest greatly increased during the railroad "boom" of the 1850s.

A Wall Street analyst noted that railroad men seeking financing "must remember that money is power, and that the [financier] can dictate to a great extent his own terms."

11-1.4 Rising Prosperity

Technological advances improved the lives of consumers by reducing prices on many commodities. For example, clocks that had cost $50 to make by hand in 1800 could be produced by machine for fifty cents in 1850. At the same time, the widening use of steam power contributed to a 25 percent rise in the average worker's real income (actual purchasing power) between 1840 and 1860. Earlier factories, which relied on water power, had to shut down when rivers or streams froze. With the spread of steam engines, factories stayed open longer and thus increased workers' annual wages. For example, although hourly wages for textile workers showed little gain, their average annual wages rose from $163 in 1830 to $201 by 1859 due largely to factories' more continuous operation.

The growth of towns and cities also contributed to an increase in incomes. Densely populated towns and cities offered many opportunities for year-round work, sometimes by shifting from one type of employment to another. The urban dock worker thrown out of work by frozen waterways might find employment as a hotel porter or an unskilled indoor laborer.

Towns and cities also provided women and children with new opportunities for paid labor. The wages of children between the ages of ten and eighteen came to play an integral role in the family economy. Family heads who earned more than six hundred dollars a year could afford to keep their children in school. But many breadwinners made less than three hundred dollars a year. Budgets of working-class families in New York City and Philadelphia during the early 1850s reveal annual expenditures of five hundred to six hundred dollars, with more than 40 percent spent on food, 25–30 percent on rent, and most of the remainder on clothing and fuel. Such a family needed the wages of the children and sometimes the wife, as well as the male head of the household, just to stay afloat.

Some farming families enjoyed a better quality of life than urban wage-earning families. A farmer who owned land, livestock, and a house did not have to worry about paying rent or buying fuel and rarely ran short of food. Still, to purchase, clear, and stock a farm could cost as much as five hundred dollars and promised no financial return for a few years. The majority of agricultural workers did not own farms and were exposed to seasonal fluctuations in demand for labor. "A year in some farming states such as Pennsylvania," a traveler commented in 1823, "is only of eight months duration, four months

Civil War, and local and county governments could not keep up with the funding needed for the dramatic expansion of the railroad network in the 1850s. Aware of the economic benefits of railroads, people living near them had long purchased government-issued railroad securities and railroad stock. But the large railroads of the 1850s needed more capital than small investors could generate.

Gradually, the center of railroad financing shifted to New York City, where the railroad boom of the 1850s helped make Wall Street the nation's greatest capital market. The securities of all the leading railroads were traded on the floor of the **New York Stock Exchange**. Railroad expansion also turned New York City into the center of modern investment firms. Investment firms evaluated the securities of railroads in Davenport or Chattanooga, then found purchasers for these securities in New York, Paris, or Hamburg. Controlling the flow of funds to railroads, investment bankers began to exert influence over the railroads' internal affairs.

New York Stock Exchange
New York City's center of financing where leading railroads were traded in the 1850s.

being lost to the laborer, who is turned away as a useless animal." So urban wage earners were sometimes better off than agricultural workers.

The economic advantages of urban living help explain why so many Americans were moving to cities. During the 1840s and 1850s, American cities provided some residents with an unprecedented range of comforts and conveniences.

11-2 The Quality of Life

Were all of the changes affecting daily life in the mid-nineteenth century for the better?

"Think of the numberless contrivances and inventions for our comfort and luxury," exclaimed poet Walt Whitman, "and you will bless your star that Fate has cast your lot in the year of Our Lord 1857." Improvements in the quality of life affected such mundane activities as eating, drinking, and even washing. The patent office in Washington was flooded with sketches of reclining seats, washing machines, mechanical street sweepers, and fly traps. Machine-made furniture began to transform house interiors. New stoves revolutionized heating and cooking.

Yet change occurred unevenly. Technology enabled the middle class to enjoy luxuries formerly reserved for the rich but widened the distance between the middle class and the poor. As middle-class homes became increasingly lavish, the urban poor lived in cramped tenements. Some critical elements of daily comfort such as medicine lagged behind the curve of progress. Nevertheless, the benefits of progress impressed Americans more than its limitations.

11-2.1 Dwellings

During the early 1800s, the randomly sited wood frame houses that had dotted colonial cities began to yield to more orderly brick row houses. Row houses, which were practical responses to rising land values (Manhattan values rose by as much as 750 percent between 1785 and 1815), drew criticism for their "extreme uniformity." But they were not all alike. Middle-class row houses, with their cast iron balconies, curved staircases, and beautifully finished interiors, were larger and more elaborate than working-class row houses and less likely to be subdivided for occupancy by several families. The worst of the subdivided row houses, called tenements, were often inhabited by Irish immigrants and free blacks.

Home furnishings also revealed the widening gap between the prosperous and the poor. Middle- and upper-class families decorated their houses with fine furniture in the ornate, rococo style, along with wool carpeting, wallpaper, pianos, pictures, and gilt-framed mirrors. The mass production of furniture reduced prices and tended to level taste between the middle and upper classes, while still setting those classes off from everyone below them. Some members of the middle class took pains to decorate the public areas of their houses, especially the parlor, as lavishly as possible to impress visitors, while furnishing the rest of the house sparsely.

In rural areas, the quality of housing depended largely on the age of the settlement. In new settlements, the standard dwelling was a rude log cabin with planked floors, clay chimneys, and windows covered by oiled paper or cloth. As rural communities matured, log cabins gave way to insulated balloon-frame houses of two or more rooms. Instead of thick posts and beams laboriously fitted together, a balloon-frame house had a skeleton of two-by-fours spaced at eighteen-inch intervals. The balloon-frame was lighter and stronger than the older post-and-beam method and required no technical knowledge of joinery. The simplicity and cheapness of such houses endeared them to western builders.

11-2.2 Conveniences and Inconveniences

By today's standards, everyday life in the 1840s and 1850s was primitive. But contemporaries were struck by how much better it was becoming. In urban areas, coal-burning stoves were rapidly displacing open hearths for heating and cooking. Stoves made it possible to cook several dishes at once and thus helped diversify the American diet, while railroads brought in fresh vegetables that, a century earlier, could not be found on even elite dinner tables.

Contemporaries were also grateful for the new urban waterworks—systems of pipes and aqueducts that brought fresh water from rivers or reservoirs to street hydrants. In the 1840s, New York City completed the Croton aqueduct, which carried water into the city from reservoirs to the north. By 1860, sixty-eight public water systems operated in the United States.

Despite these improvements, home comforts remained limited. Coal left a dirty residue that polluted the air, and faulty stoves could emit carbon monoxide. One architect called stoves "the national curse," "secret poisoners" that were "more insidious" than "slavery, socialism, Mormonism . . . tobacco, patent medicines, or coffee." The American diet continued to be affected by seasonal fluctuations. Only the rich could afford fruit out of season. Home iceboxes were rare before 1860, so salt remained the most widely used preservative. One reason antebellum

Americans ate more pork than beef was that salt pork was marginally less bad-tasting than salt beef.

Although public waterworks were among the most impressive engineering feats of the age, only a fraction of the urban population lived near water hydrants. So most houses still had no running water, and taking a bath still required heating the water on a stove. A New England physician reported that not one in five of his patients took even one bath a year.

Infrequent bathing added pungent body odors to the many strong smells of urban life. In the absence of municipal sanitation, street cleaning was done by private contractors with a reputation for slack performance. Hogs were allowed to roam freely and scavenge (and hogs that turned down the wrong street often landed in the dinner pots of the poor).

Mounds of stable manure and outdoor privies added to the stench. Flush toilets were rare, and sewer systems lagged behind water-supply systems. In 1860, Boston—which boasted more flush toilets than most other cities—still had only five thousand for a population of 178,000. Conveniences such as running water and flush toilets became one more way for progress to divide the upper and middle classes from the poor.

Conveniences also sharpened gender differences. Technological improvements combined with the ideology of true womanhood to put greater pressure on women to keep even cleaner homes. In her popular *Treatise on Domestic Economy* (1841), Catharine Beecher told women that technological progress made it their duty to maintain every house as a "glorious temple" by keeping carpets clean and

FAMILY GROUP This daguerreotype, taken about 1852, reveals the domestic details so essential to claiming middle-class social status: curtains, a wall hanging, a piano with scrolled legs, a family pet, ladies engaged in music and reading, and a young man staring into space—perhaps pondering how to pay for it all. *(Courtesy of George Eastman House, International Museum of Photography and Film)*

furniture polished. Skeptical of this trend toward fastidiousness, another writer cautioned women in 1857 against "ultra-housewifery." What's more, work previously done by women within and for the household—making soap or weaving textiles—was now purchased in the marketplace. As such, there was increasing need for the money needed to buy goods, money typically earned by men, and the work women did—which was not cash based—became increasingly devalued in comparison.

11-2.3 Disease and Medicine

Despite their improving standard of living, Americans remained vulnerable to disease. **Epidemics** swept through cities and felled thousands. Yellow fever and cholera together killed one-fifth of New Orleans' population in 1832–1833, and cholera alone carried off 10 percent of the St. Louis population in 1849. Life expectancy for newborns in New York and Philadelphia during the 1830s and 1840s averaged only twenty-four years.

The transportation revolution actually increased the peril from epidemics by spreading them from one community to the next. The cholera epidemic of 1832, which was the first truly national epidemic, followed transportation networks out of New York City: one disease route ran up the Hudson River across the Erie Canal to Ohio and down the Ohio and Mississippi Rivers to New Orleans; the other route followed shipping lines up and down the East Coast.

The failure of physicians to explain epidemic diseases reinforced hostility toward their profession. No one understood that cholera and yellow fever were caused by bacteria. Physicians argued with each other over whether epidemic diseases were spread by human touch or by "miasmas," gases arising from rotten vegetation or dead animals. Neither theory worked. Quarantines failed to prevent the spread of epidemics (an argument against the contagion theory), and many residents of swampy areas contracted neither yellow fever nor cholera (a refutation of the miasma theory). Understandably, municipal leaders declined to delegate more than advisory powers to boards of health, which were dominated by physicians.

Although epidemic disease baffled physicians, surgery made major progress with the discovery of anesthesia. Prior to 1840, young people sometimes entertained themselves at parties by inhaling nitrous oxide or "laughing gas," which suppressed pain and produced giddiness. But few recognized its surgical possibilities. Then in 1842, Crawford Long, a Georgia physician who had attended laughing-gas frolics in his youth, employed sulfuric ether (a liquid with the same properties as nitrous oxide) during a surgical operation. Dr. Long failed to follow up on his discovery, but four years later William T. G. Morton, a Boston dentist, successfully administered sulfuric ether during an operation at Massachusetts General Hospital. Within a few years, ether came into wide surgical use.

The discovery of anesthesia improved the public image of surgeons, long viewed as brutes who liked to torture their patients. It also permitted longer and more careful operations. Nevertheless, physicians' ignorance of the importance of clean hands and sterilized instruments continued to harm patients. In 1843, Boston physician and poet Oliver Wendell Holmes, Sr. published a paper blaming the spread of puerperal (childbed) fever on the failure of obstetricians to disinfect their hands between one delivery and the next. But doctors only gradually accepted the importance of disinfection. As a result, operations remained as dangerous as the diseases or wounds they tried to heal. The mortality rate for amputations hovered around 40 percent.

11-2.4 Popular Health Movements

Suspicious of orthodox medicine, antebellum Americans turned to a variety of alternative therapies and regimens that promised longer and healthier lives. One popular treatment was hydropathy, or the "water cure," which arrived from Europe during the 1840s. By the mid-1850s, the United States had twenty-seven hydropathic sanatoriums, which used cold baths and wet packs to provide "an abundance of water of dewy softness and crystal transparency, to cleanse, renovate, and rejuvenate the disease-worn and dilapidated system." The water cure held a special attraction for women because hydropathy promised to relieve the pains of childbirth and menstruation, and sanatoriums proved to be congenial gathering places for middle-class women.

Sylvester Graham, a former temperance reformer, propounded a more affordable health system than the water cure. In response to the 1832 cholera epidemic, Graham urged Americans to eat vegetables, fruits, and whole-grain bread (called Graham bread) and abstain from meat and spices, coffee and tea, and alcohol. Soon he added to his list of forbidden indulgences "sexual excess"—which he defined as marital intercourse more than once a month. Many of Graham's disciples were moral and social reformers. Grahamites had a special table at the Brook Farm community. Like other reformers, Grahamites traced the evils of American society to unnatural cravings. Just as temperance reformers blamed the craving for alcohol, and abolitionists blamed the craving for illicit power, Graham blamed most social ills on the craving for meat, stimulants, and sex.

Graham was dismissed by Ralph Waldo Emerson as "the prophet of

epidemics
Diseases in a human population during a certain period of time.

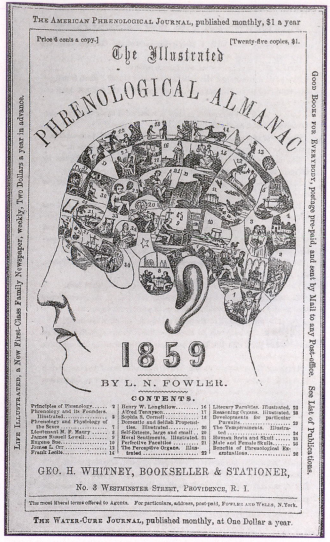

"THE ILLUSTRATED PHRENOLOGICAL ALMANAC, 1859" Phrenologists like Lorenzo Fowler, editor of the *Phrenological Almanac*, divided the brain into distinct "faculties" and argued that each could be improved through proper exercise. *(Historic Cherry Hill Collections, Albany, NY)*

health reform but also the popular fad of **phrenology**. Phrenology rested on the idea that the human mind comprised thirty-seven distinct faculties, or "organs," each located in a different part of the brain. The strength of each faculty was indicated by its size. Therefore, phrenologists believed, a person's character could be assessed through an examination of the bumps and depressions of the skull. They also believed that anyone could improve her or his character by properly managing each organ: by exercising underdeveloped faculties (for example, too little Benevolence) and suppressing overdeveloped faculties (for example, too much Amorousness).

In the United States two brothers, Orson and Lorenzo Fowler, became the chief promoters of phrenology in the 1840s. Orson originally planned to be a Protestant missionary but instead became a phrenology missionary, opening a publishing house in New York City that mass-marketed books on the subject. When criticized for godlessness, the Fowlers pointed to a huge organ called "Veneration" to prove that people were naturally religious. When criticized for pessimistic determinism, Lorenzo proudly reported that several of his own organs had been expanded through exercise. As Orson liked to say, "Self-Made, or Never-Made."

Americans were drawn to the practicality of phrenology. In a mobile, individualistic society, it promised practitioners a quick way to size up other people's characters and improve their own. Some merchants used phrenological charts to pick suitable clerks, and some women asked their fiancés to undergo phrenological examination before the wedding. More important, phrenology's promise of universal improvement was irresistible to antebellum Americans. Just as they had invented machines to better their lives, they invented scientific strategies that promised personal improvement.

11-3 Commercializing Leisure

What were the hallmarks and significance of mass entertainment in the mid-nineteenth century?

Americans had long found ways to enjoy themselves. Even New England Puritans had indulged in games and sports. After 1830, however, the initiative for providing entertainment began to shift from ordinary people to entrepreneurs who used technology to supply new ways to entertain the public. Between 1830 and 1860, technology commercialized American entertainment, making Americans more dependent on recreations that were manufactured

bran bread and pumpkins," and even threatened by mobs, including a crowd of angry butchers and commercial bakers whose businesses were jeopardized by his reform program. But Graham's doctrines attracted a broad audience. Boardinghouses began to offer Grahamite menus. His books sold well, and his lectures drew large crowds. His regime addressed the popular desire for better health at a time when orthodox medicine still seemed to do more damage than good.

11-2.5 **Phrenology**

The belief that each person was master of his or her own destiny underlay not only evangelical religion and

phrenology
The idea that the human mind comprised thirty-seven distinct faculties, or "organs," each located in a different part of the brain. Phrenologists thought that the degree of each organ's development determined skull shape, so that they could analyze a person's character by examining the bumps and depressions of the skull.

and sold. Entertainment became something to be purchased, in the form of cheap newspapers and novels as well as affordable tickets to plays, museums, and lectures.

Technology encouraged individuals to become spectators rather than creators of their own amusements. Just as the Boston Associates adopted new technology to produce textiles, men such as James Gordon Bennett, one of the founders of the penny press in America, and P. T. Barnum, the greatest showman of the nineteenth century, amassed fortunes by making and selling entertainment. Widely popular, this mass, commercial entertainment also encouraged the passivity of those who consumed it.

11-3.1 Newspapers

In 1830, the typical American newspaper was only four pages long. Its front and back pages were devoted to advertisements, and the two middle pages contained editorials, details of ship arrivals and cargoes, reprints of political speeches, and notices of political events. Fortunately, such papers did not rely on sales but on subsidies from the political groups with which they allied. They could profit without offering the exciting news stories and eye-catching illustrations that later generations of newspaper readers would take for granted.

The 1830s witnessed the beginnings of a stunning transformation in the American newspaper. Technological innovation increased both the supply of paper and the speed of production. The new steam-driven cylindrical presses led to a tenfold increase in the number of printed pages that could be produced in an hour. Enterprising journalists, among them the Scottish-born James Gordon Bennett, responded by introducing the **penny press**, which relied on mass circulation to turn a profit. In 1833, the *New York Sun* became America's first penny newspaper, and Bennett's *New York Herald* followed in 1835. The lower prices of these new penny newspapers made them affordable to wider and more diverse groups of people. By June 1835, the combined daily circulation of New York's three penny papers reached forty-four thousand, almost twenty thousand higher than the combined circulation of the city's eleven dailies before 1833. From 1830 to 1840, the total circulation of American newspapers rose from roughly seventy-eight thousand to 300,000 and the number of weekly newspapers more than doubled.

The penny press revolutionized the marketing and contents of newspapers as well as their production. Earlier six-cent papers had been purchased at the printer's office, but the new penny papers were hawked by newsboys on busy street corners. The penny papers reduced political and commercial coverage and expanded human-interest stories of

robberies, murders, and abandoned children. They printed courtroom transcripts of sensational trials, such as that of Richard Robinson for the hatchet-murder of the beautiful prostitute Helen Jewett in a New York brothel in 1836. Charles Dickens parodied such coverage by naming one fictional American newspaper the *New York Stabber*.

But despite such limitations, as sociologist Michael Schudson observes, "The penny press invented the modern concept of 'news'"—employing their own correspondents and using the telegraph to speed the communications process. The best penny papers, including Bennett's *New York Herald* and Horace Greeley's *New York Tribune*, pioneered modern financial and political reporting. From its inception, the *Herald* contained a daily "money article" that analyzed financial events. As Bennett observed, "The spirit, pith, and philosophy of commercial affairs is what men of business want." Snooping reporters outraged Washington politicians. In 1848, *Tribune* correspondents were temporarily barred from the House of Representatives for reporting that an Ohio Congressman ate sausage and bread every day in the House chamber, picked his teeth with a jack-knife, and wiped his greasy hands on his clothing.

11-3.2 The Theater

Theaters, like newspapers, increasingly appealed to a mass audience. Antebellum theaters were large (sometimes seating twenty-five hundred to four thousand people) and drew all social classes. With seat prices ranging from twelve to fifty cents, the typical theater audience included lawyers and merchants and their wives, artisans and clerks, sailors, apprentices, African Americans, and prostitutes. Prostitutes usually sat in the top gallery or third tier, "that dark, horrible, guilty" place. Their presence in theaters was taken for granted, though the public sometimes grumbled when they solicited customers in the more expensive seats.

Theater audiences, according to critics, were notoriously ill-behaved. The lower orders of patrons cracked peanuts, spat tobacco, got drunk, and talked loudly throughout the performance. They stamped their feet, hooted at villains, and threw garbage at characters or performances they disliked. Contributing to such rowdiness was the animosity between the fan bases of different theatrical stars. In 1849, a long-running feud between leading American actor Edwin Forrest and popular British actor William Macready culminated in the Astor Place riot in New York City, which left twenty-two people dead. The Astor Place riot demonstrated the broad popularity of the theater, and the cross-class clashes that might ensue. Forrest's

penny press
Inexpensive newspapers that were produced in the 1830s.

supporters included Irish workers who loathed the British and appealed to "working men" to rally against the "aristocrat" Macready. Macready, who projected a polished and intellectual image, attracted the better-educated classes.

The most popular plays were emotionally charged melodramas in which virtue was rewarded, vice punished, and the hero won the beautiful heroine. Melodramas offered theatergoers such sensational features as volcanic eruptions, staged battles, even live horses on stage. Yet the single most popular dramatist in the antebellum theater was William Shakespeare. In 1835, Philadelphians witnessed sixty-five performances of Shakespeare's plays. Americans who never read a line of Shakespeare grew familiar with Othello, Juliet, and King Lear. Theatrical managers adapted Shakespeare to a popular audience by highlighting sword fights and assassinations, cutting some speeches, and occasionally substituting happy endings for sad ones. And they entertained audiences between acts with jugglers and acrobats, impersonations of Tecumseh or Aaron Burr, or the exhibition of a three-year-old child who weighed one hundred pounds.

11-3.3 Minstrel Shows

A stock character in antebellum plays was the Yankee or "Brother Jonathan" figure who idealized the American as a rustic but clever patriot who routinely outsmarted city slickers and decadent aristocrats. In a different way, the popular minstrel shows of the 1840s and 1850s forged enduring racial stereotypes that buttressed white Americans' sense of superiority by diminishing black Americans.

Minstrel shows featured white performers in burnt-cork blackface who entertained their audiences with songs, dances, and humorous sketches pretending to mimic black culture. But while minstrelsy did borrow a few elements of African American culture, most of its contents were white inventions, aimed both at expressing and reinforcing the prejudices of the working-class whites who dominated the audience. Minstrel shows depicted blacks as stupid, clumsy, and absurdly musical, and parodied African culture by naming their performances the

THE CROW QUADRILLES. Published in 1837, this 10-page sheet music collection of minstrel songs was produced by Baltimore journalist-poet John H. Hewitt. The song titles, listed on the front, include "Jim Crow", which would come to serve as a term for racial discrimination. The booklet cover (shown here) featured performers in blackface in various – typically mocking – scenarios. (Library of Congress Prints and Photographs Division Washington, D.C.[LC-USZ62-109807])

"Nubian Jungle Dance" and the "African Fling." At a time of intensifying political conflict over slavery, minstrel shows used stock characters to ridicule African Americans. These characters included Uncle Ned, the tattered and docile slave, and Zip Coon, the arrogant urban freeman who paraded around in high hat and long-tailed coat and lived off his girlfriends.

By the 1850s, major cities from New York to San Francisco had several minstrel theaters. Touring professionals and local amateurs brought minstrelsy to small towns and villages. Mark Twain later recalled how minstrelsy had burst upon Hannibal, Missouri, in the early 1840s as "a glad and stunning surprise." Minstrel troupes even entertained a succession of presidents in the antebellum White House.

11-3.4 P. T. Barnum

P. T. Barnum has been considered the father of mass entertainment in the United States because he thoroughly understood how to profit from the public's demand for stimulation and excitement. As a young man in Bethel, Connecticut, he started a newspaper, the *Herald of Freedom*, which assailed wrongdoing in high places, and throughout his life, he thought of himself as a public benefactor. Yet honesty was never his strong suit. As a small-town grocer in Connecticut, he regularly cheated his customers on the dubious premise that they were trying to cheat him. Barnum, in short, was a Yankee hustler and idealist rolled into one.

After moving to New York City in 1834, Barnum launched his career as an entertainment entrepreneur. He got his start exhibiting a black woman named Joice Heth, whom he billed (implausibly enough) as the 169-year-old former slave nurse of George Washington. When audiences began to dwindle, Barnum wrote anonymously to a newspaper saying that "Joice Heth is not a human being [but] an automaton, made up of whalebone, india-rubber, and numberless springs." In response, hundreds of people who had already paid to see Heth returned to determine whether she was machine or living woman. Suspicions of fraud, Barnum knew, only sold more tickets. He was playing a game with the public, and the public played right back.

In 1841, Barnum purchased a rundown museum in New York City, renamed it the American Museum, and opened a new chapter in the history of popular entertainment. Earlier museums had exhibited stuffed birds and animals, rock specimens, and portraits of famous people—largely for educational purposes. Barnum, who cared less for education than entertainment, drew throngs of customers by stimulating curiosity. Visitors to the American Museum could see ventriloquists, magicians, albinos, a 25-inch-tall five-year-old whom Barnum named General Tom Thumb, and the "Feejee Mermaid," billed by Barnum as "positively asserted by its owner to have been taken alive in the Feejee Islands." By 1850, the American Museum had become the best-known museum in the nation.

Blessed with a genius for publicity, Barnum recognized that newspapers could invent news as well as report it. One of his favorite tactics was to write letters to newspapers (under various names) reporting that the scientific world was agog over some astonishing natural curiosity that the public could see for itself at the American Museum. He also marketed his museum as respectable family entertainment by providing regular lectures on the evils of alcohol and the benefits of Christian religion. Barnum thus helped break down barriers between the pastimes of husbands and wives, parents and children.

Finally, Barnum successfully tapped the public's insatiable curiosity about natural wonders. In 1835, the editor of the *New York Sun* boosted his circulation by claiming that a famous astronomer had discovered pelicans and winged men on the moon. At a time when each passing year brought new technological wonders, the public was ready to believe in anything.

P. T. BARNUM AND TOM THUMB When P. T. Barnum posed with his protégée—whose real name was Charles Sherwood Stratton—sometime around 1850, the twelve-year-old "human curiosity" stood a little over two feet in height. Barnum and Stratton enjoyed a long partnership that brought considerable wealth to both of them. *(National Portrait Gallery, Smithsonian Institution/Art Resource, NY)*

11-4 The American Renaissance in Literature and Art

What fueled the American Renaissance in literature and art?

In the early nineteenth century, Europeans took little notice of American literature. "Who ever reads an American book?" taunted one British critic. Americans responded defensively by pointing to Washington Irving, author of *Rip Van Winkle* and *The Legend of Sleepy Hollow*. Irving's readers showered him with praise, even naming hotels and steamboats after him, but they had to concede that Irving had done much of his best writing while living in England.

After 1820, the United States experienced a flowering of literature and art called the **American Renaissance**. Its leading literary figures included James

> **American Renaissance**
> A flowering of art and literature in the United States that began in the 1820s. Not only were Americans writing more books; increasingly, they sought to depict the features of their nation in literature and art.

Fenimore Cooper, Ralph Waldo Emerson, Henry David Thoreau, Margaret Fuller, Walt Whitman, Nathaniel Hawthorne, Herman Melville, and Edgar Allan Poe. Its leading artists included Thomas Cole, Asher Durand, Frederick Church, and George Catlin. In 1800, American authors accounted for a negligible proportion of the output of American publishers. But by 1830, 40 percent of the books published in the United States were written by Americans; by 1850, that proportion had increased to 75 percent.

American writers and artists often sought to depict the national features of the United States—its land and its people—in their work. The quest for a distinctively American culture shaped the writings of Cooper, Emerson, and Whitman. The celebration of the American landscape appeared in the majestic paintings of the Hudson River school—the first homegrown American movement in painting—and the landscape architecture of Frederick Law Olmsted, designer of New York's Central Park.

11-4.1 Roots of the American Renaissance

Two broad developments, one economic and the other philosophical, contributed to the cultural efflorescence of the American Renaissance. First, the transportation revolution created a national market for books, especially fiction. Initially, this market worked to the advantage of British authors, especially Sir Walter Scott, whose historical novel *Waverley* (1814) made him a literary star in the American market. American readers gobbled up his books and gratefully named more than a dozen towns Waverley. Scott's success demonstrated that the public hungered for fiction and prompted Americans like James Fenimore Cooper to write fiction for the growing literary market.

Second, the American Renaissance reflected the rise of a philosophical movement known as romanticism. In contrast to eighteenth-century classicism, which had regarded standards of beauty as universal, romanticism insisted that literature reveal the longings of the individual author's soul. Whereas classicists valued the writer's learning—especially of ancient Greek and Roman civilization—romantics valued the emotional expressiveness of literature and its truthfulness to its creator's inner feelings.

The emergence of a national book market and the romantic movement combined to make American literature more democratic. Romanticists accepted the production of books for a national market and embraced fiction for its wide popular appeal and its emphasis not on classical learning, but on shared human feelings and experiences. One sign of the democratic turn in literature was that many of the best-selling novels of the antebellum period—such as Harriet Beecher Stowe's *Uncle Tom's Cabin*—were written by women. And one response to Stowe's book came from an African American woman, who produced the semi-autobiographical work, *Our Nig; Or, Sketches from the Life of a Free Black* (1859). This book was rediscovered by historians in the 1980s and is now regarded as a vital African American contribution to American literature.

Fiction had a subversive quality that contributed to its popularity. Authors could create unconventional characters, situations, and outcomes. Whereas essays usually developed unmistakable conclusions, novels left more room for interpretation by the reader. Even when a novel had a lesson to teach, the reader's interest was likely to be aroused less by the moral of the story than by the development of characters and plot.

11-4.2 Cooper, Emerson, Thoreau, Fuller, and Whitman

James Fenimore Cooper was the first important figure in this literary upsurge. He introduced an enduringly influential fictional character, the frontiersman Natty Bumppo ("Leatherstocking"). In *The Pioneers* (1823), Natty is an old man settled on the shores of Lake Otsego in upstate New York. A spokesman for nature against the relentless advance of civilization, Natty blames farmers for wantonly destroying game and reducing majestic forests to wastelands. Natty immediately became a popular figure, and in subsequent novels such as *The Last of the Mohicans* (1826), *The Pathfinder* (1840), and *The Deerslayer* (1841), Cooper unfolded the frontier hero's earlier life for a reading public eager for what we'd now call the prequel.

Ralph Waldo Emerson emerged in the late 1830s as the most influential spokesman for American literary nationalism. As the leading light of the movement known as transcendentalism, an American expression of romanticism, Emerson believed that our ideas of God and freedom are not learned, but inborn. Knowledge, like sight, involves an instantaneous and direct perception of truth. So learned people, Emerson concluded, enjoyed no special advantage in pursuing truth. All persons can glimpse the truth by simply trusting the promptings of their hearts.

This basic premise of transcendentalism posed the exciting possibility that the raw young democracy of the United States could produce as noble a literature and art as Old World cultures. "Our day of dependence, our long apprenticeship to the learning

James Fenimore Cooper
The first important figure of the American Renaissance. His most significant innovation was to introduce a distinctively American fictional character, frontiersman Natty Bumppo ("Leatherstocking").

Ralph Waldo Emerson
The most influential spokesman for American literary nationalism. As the leading light of the movement known as transcendentalism, an American offshoot of romanticism, he contended that our ideas of God and freedom are inborn; knowledge resembles sight—an instantaneous and direct perception of truth. That being so, he concluded, learned people enjoy no special advantage in pursuing truth. All persons can glimpse the truth if only they trust the promptings of their hearts.

of other lands draws to a close," Emerson announced in his address "The American Scholar" (1837). The time had come for Americans to trust themselves. Let "the single man plant himself indomitably on his instincts and there abide," he proclaimed, and "the huge world will come around to him."

Emerson's literary nationalism was expressed mainly in his essays (he disliked fiction), which explored broad themes—"Beauty," "Wealth," and "Representative Men"—in vivid, fresh language. For example, he praised independent thinking by saying the scholar should not "quit his belief that a popgun is a popgun, though the ancient and honorable of the earth affirm it to be the crack of doom." Believing that knowledge reflected God's voice within each individual and that truth was intuitive, Emerson did not present systematic arguments backed by evidence to prove his point. Rather, he relied on a sequence of vivid if unconnected assertions whose truth the reader was supposed to see instantly.

From his home in Concord, Massachusetts, Emerson exercised a magnetic attraction for young intellectuals who were social misfits, including **Henry David Thoreau**. A crucial difference, however, separated the two men. Though intellectually adventurous, Emerson was not a man of action. By contrast, Thoreau fully lived his ideas. When war with Mexico broke out, he went to jail rather than pay his poll tax, refusing to support a war he believed would extend slavery further west. This experience led Thoreau to write his abidingly influential essay on "Civil Disobedience" (1849), in which he defended a citizen's right to disobey unjust laws.

On July 4, 1845, in a personal declaration of independence, Thoreau moved a few miles from Concord Center to the woods surrounding Walden Pond. He spent two years there living in a small cabin he constructed and providing for his own wants as simply as possible. His purpose in retreating to Walden was to write an account of a river trip he had taken with his brother in 1839—later published as *A Week on the Concord and Merrimack Rivers*. But he wrote a more important book, *Walden* (1854), described by a contemporary as "the logbook of his woodland cruise." Thoreau filled it with day-to-day descriptions of hawks and the pond, his invention of raisin bread, and his trapping of the woodchucks that ravaged his vegetable garden. But *Walden* had a larger transcendentalist message. Thoreau's retreat taught him that anyone could satisfy his material wants with only a few weeks' work each year and preserve the remainder of his time for examining life's purpose. The problem with Americans, he said, was that they turned themselves into "mere machines" to acquire pointless wealth. For Thoreau, material and moral progress were not as intimately related as most Americans liked to think (see Going to the Source).

Among the most remarkable figures in Emerson's circle was **Margaret Fuller**, whose status as an intellectual woman distanced her

MARGARET FULLER Disappointed that his first child was a girl, Margaret Fuller's father decided to educate her as if she were a boy, and she wrecked her health studying Latin, English, and French classics. As an adult, she joined Ralph Waldo Emerson's transcendentalist circle. In 1846, she went to Europe as the *Tribune's* foreign correspondent. There she met artists and writers, observed the Revolutions of 1848, and married an Italian nobleman. On her return to America in 1850, she, her husband, and their infant son died in a shipwreck off Long Island. *(Constance Fuller Threinen/Picture Research Consultants and Archive)*

Henry David Thoreau
American writer who shared Emerson's intellectual pursuit. However, he was more of a doer than Emerson was. At one point he went to jail rather than pay his poll tax. This revenue, he knew, would support the war with Mexico, which he viewed as part of a southern conspiracy to extend slavery. The experience led him to write "Civil Disobedience" (1849), in which he defended a citizen's right to disobey unjust laws. He also wrote *Walden*, where he argued that he (and by implication, others) could satisfy material wants with only a few weeks' work each year and thereby leave more time for reexamining life's purpose. The problem with Americans, he said, was that they turned themselves into "mere machines" to acquire wealth without asking why.

Margaret Fuller
One of the most remarkable figures of the Transcendentalist movement, she contended that no woman could achieve the kind of personal fulfillment lauded by Emerson unless she developed her intellectual abilities and overcame her fear of being called masculine.

Henry David Thoreau, "Walking" (1862)

In the early 1850s, Henry David Thoreau (1817–1862) developed two lectures for the lyceum circuit, titled "The Wild" and "Walking." He later merged them into the single essay "Walking" that was published one month after his death. "Walking," a companion essay to his most famous work *Walden*, expressed his views on natural wildness, the American West, and the need for an American literature rooted in nature. Thoreau's line, "in Wildness is the preservation of the World," has become a touchstone of modern environmentalism.

I wish to speak a word for Nature, for absolute freedom and wildness, as contrasted with a freedom and culture merely civil—to regard man as an inhabitant, or a part and parcel of Nature, rather than a member of society. I wish to make an extreme statement, if so I may make an emphatic one, for there are enough champions of civilization: the minister and the school committee and every one of you will take care of that. . . .

Nowadays almost all man's improvements, so called, as the building of houses and the cutting down of the forest and of all large trees, simply deform the landscape, and make it more and more tame and cheap. . . .

We go eastward to realize history and study the works of art and literature, retracing the steps of the race; we go westward as into the future, with a spirit of enterprise and adventure. The Atlantic is a Lethean stream,* in our passage over which we have had an opportunity to forget the Old World and its institutions. . . .

The West of which I speak is but another name for the Wild; and what I have been preparing to say is, that in Wildness is the preservation of the World. Every tree sends its fibers forth in search of the Wild. The cities import it at any price. Men plow and sail for it. From the forest and wilderness come the tonics and barks which brace mankind.

Our ancestors were savages. The story of Romulus and Remus being suckled by a wolf is not a meaningless fable.** The founders of every state which has risen to eminence have drawn their nourishment and vigor from a similar wild source. It was because the children of the Empire were not suckled by the wolf that they were conquered and displaced by the children of the northern forests who were. . . .

Where is the literature which gives expression to Nature? He would be a poet who could impress the winds and streams into his service, to speak for him; who nailed words to their primitive senses, as farmers drive down stakes in the spring, which the frost has heaved; who derived his words as often as he used them—transplanted them to his page with earth adhering to their roots; whose words were so true and fresh and natural that they would appear to expand like the buds at the approach of spring, though they lay half smothered between two musty leaves in a library—aye, to bloom and bear fruit there, after their kind, annually, for the faithful reader, in sympathy with surrounding Nature.

Source: Henry David Thoreau, "Walking," *Atlantic Monthly,* vol. 9, no. 56 (June 1862): [657]–674.

* In the underworld of Greek mythology, Lethe was the river of forgetfulness.

** Romulus and Remus, the mythical founders of Ancient Rome, were abandoned as infants in the wilderness but saved by a wolf that fed and protected them.

QUESTIONS

1. What were Thoreau's views on the ideal relationship between Nature and civilization, and between Nature and the individual? What sorts of "improvements" in his lifetime do you think were shaping his ideas?

2. How was Thoreau responding to Emerson's call for a distinctively American literature?

from conventional society. Disappointed that his first child was not a boy, Fuller's father, a prominent Massachusetts politician, determined to give Margaret the sort of education young men could acquire at Harvard. First drilled in Latin and Greek, she then turned to the German romantics and English literary classics. Her exposure to Emerson's ideas during a stay at Concord in 1836 drew her toward transcendentalism, with its vindication of the free life of the spirit over formal doctrines and its insistence on the need for each person to discover truth on her own.

Ingeniously, Fuller managed to turn transcendentalism into a profession. Between 1839 and 1844, she conducted "Conversations" for fee-paying participants drawn from Boston's elite. Transcendentalism influenced her feminist classic, *Woman in the Nineteenth Century* (1845). Breaking with the prevailing notion of separate spheres for men and women, Fuller contended that no woman could achieve the intellectual fulfillment promoted by Emerson unless she devoted herself to developing her mental abilities without fear of being called "masculine." Fuller asserted that "What Woman needs is not as a woman to act or rule, but as a nature to grow, as an intellect to discern, as a soul to live freely and unimpeded, to unfold such powers as were given to her when we left our common home."

Emerson had an ability to sympathize with a wide range of people, including not only the prickly Thoreau and the scholarly Fuller but the outgoing and earthy **Walt Whitman**. Whitman had left school at age eleven and worked his way up from printer's apprentice to journalist and then editor for various newspapers in Brooklyn, Manhattan, and New Orleans. A familiar figure at Democratic Party functions, he marched in party parades and put his pen to the service of its antislavery wing.

Journalism and politics, in addition to his own rough-and-tumble life, gave Whitman an intimate knowledge of ordinary Americans. The more he came to know them, the more he loved them. Reading Emerson nurtured his own belief that America would be the cradle of a new man in whom natural virtue would flourish untainted by European corruption—a man like Andrew Jackson, that "massive, yet most sweet and plain character." The threads of Whitman's early life and career came together in his major work *Leaves of Grass*, a book of poems first published in 1855 and reissued with additions in subsequent years.

Leaves of Grass shattered poetic conventions. Whitman wrote in free verse, meaning that most of his poems had neither rhyme nor meter. His poems were passionate and earthy at a time when delicacy reigned in the literary world. To the dismay of critics, he wrote of "the scent of these armpits finer than prayer" and "winds whose soft-tickling genitals rub against me." Whitman also introduced himself into his poems, most explicitly in "Song of Walt Whitman" (later retitled "Song of Myself"). He wrote of himself because he viewed himself—crude and plain, self-taught and passionately democratic—as the personification of the American people:

Comrade of raftsmen and coalmen, comrade of all who shake hands and welcome to drink and meat, A learner with the simplest, a teacher of the thought-fullest.

By 1860, Whitman had acquired a considerable reputation as a poet. Nevertheless, the small original edition of *Leaves* was ignored or even ridiculed. One reviewer called it a "heterogeneous mass of bombast, egotism, vulgarity, and nonsense"; another suggested that it was the work of an escaped lunatic. But within two weeks of its publication, Emerson, who had never met Whitman, wrote, "I find it the most extraordinary piece of wit and wisdom that America has yet contributed." Emerson had long called for the appearance of "the poet of America" and his transcendental intuition told him that Whitman was that poet.

11-4.3 Hawthorne, Poe, and Melville

None of the major contributors to the American Renaissance actually heeded Emerson's call to write about the everyday experiences of ordinary Americans—what Emerson called "the meal in the firkin [bucket]; the milk in the pan; the ballad in the street." **Nathaniel Hawthorne** set *The Scarlet Letter* (1850) in Puritan New England, *The House of the Seven Gables* (1851) in a mansion haunted by memories of the colonial past, and *The Marble Faun* (1859) in Rome. **Edgar Allan Poe** chose Europe as the setting for several of his short stories, including "The Murders in the Rue Morgue" (1841) and "The Cask of Amontillado" (1846). **Herman Melville**'s sea-going novels *Typee* (1846) and *Omoo* (1847) took place among exotic South Sea islands, and his masterpiece *Moby-Dick* (1851) was set on a whaling ship at sea. If the only surviving documents from the 1840s and 1850s were its major novels, historians would face an impossible task in trying to understand daily life in antebellum America.

The unusual settings favored by these three writers reflected

Walt Whitman
Well-known author of *Leaves of Grass*, which shattered most existing poetic conventions. Not only did he write in free verse, but the poems were also lusty and blunt at a time when delicacy reigned in the literary world.

Nathaniel Hawthorne
Well-known author of *The Scarlet Letter*.

Edgar Allan Poe
Famous American writer who wrote short stories such as "The Murders in the Rue Morgue" (1841) and "The Cask of Amontillado" (1846).

Herman Melville's
Famous author of *Moby Dick*.

their view that American life lacked the stuff of great fiction. Hawthorne bemoaned the difficulty of writing about a country "where there is no shadow, no antiquity, no mystery, no picturesque and gloomy wrong, nor anything but a commonplace prosperity in broad and simple daylight." In addition, all three writers were more interested in probing the depths of human psychology than the intricacies of social relationships. Their preoccupation with the mental states of their characters grew out of their underlying pessimism about the human condition. Whereas Emerson, Fuller, and Whitman had faith in the promptings of people's better selves, Hawthorne, Poe, and Melville saw individuals as bundles of dark, internal conflicts.

The pessimism of these dark romantics led them to create characters obsessed by pride and guilt, and driven by a desire for revenge or an unnatural quest for perfection. They set their stories on the margins of society, where they were free to explore the complexities of human motivation without dealing with the mundane realities of everyday life. For example, in *The Scarlet Letter*, Hawthorne turned to the Puritan past to examine the psychological and moral consequences of adultery. So intensely did Hawthorne focus on the moral dilemmas of his central characters, Hester Prynne and the Rev. Arthur Dimmesdale, that he conveyed little sense of the social life of the Puritan village surrounding them. Melville, who dedicated *Moby-Dick* to Hawthorne, shared the latter's dark imagination. Captain Ahab's relentless and futile pursuit of the white whale that had cost him his leg fails to fill the chasm in his soul and brings death to all his mates except the novel's narrator, Ishmael. Poe also channeled his pessimism—and possibly his madness—into dark romantic achievements. In perhaps his finest short story, "The Fall of the House of Usher" (1839), he employed the Gothic setting of a nightmarish, crumbling mansion to convey the moral agony of a decaying, incestuous family.

Hawthorne, Melville, and Poe deliberately ignored Emerson's call to write about the everyday experiences of Americans. And they refused to follow Cooper's lead by creating distinctively American heroes. Yet each contributed to an indisputably American literature. Ironically, their conviction that the lives of ordinary Americans provided inadequate materials for fiction led them to create a uniquely American fiction marked less by the description of ordinary life than by the analysis of psychological states. In this way, they fulfilled a prediction made by Alexis de Tocqueville: that writers in democratic nations, while rejecting many of the traditional sources of fiction, would explore abstract and universal questions of human nature.

11-4.4 Literature in the Marketplace

Despite the democratic tendencies of romanticism, some writers worried that commercialism corrupted art. Reclusive poet Emily Dickinson, for example, refused to publish her work. She lived all of her fifty-six years on the same street in Amherst, Massachusetts ("I do not go from home," she said), writing exquisite poems that examined, in her words, every splinter in the groove of the brain. But in an age that offered few university professorships or artists' fellowships, writers were often compelled to write for profit. Poe, a notoriously heavy drinker always pressed for cash, scratched out a meager living writing short stories for popular magazines. Thoreau, despite his reputation for aloof self-reliance, craved public recognition. Only after trying and failing to market his poems in 1843 did he turn to the detailed accounts of nature that won him a readership.

Emerson, too, wanted to reach a broader public. After abandoning his first vocation as a Unitarian minister, he reached for a new sort of audience and a new source of income: the lyceum. Lyceums—local organizations for sponsoring lectures—spread throughout the northern tier of states after the late 1820s to meet popular demands for entertainment and self-improvement. Most of Emerson's published essays originated as lyceum lectures delivered throughout the Northeast and Midwest, including some sixty speeches in Ohio alone between 1850 and 1867. Thanks to newly built railroads and the cheap newspapers that publicized lyceum programs, many speakers followed in Emerson's path. Thoreau presented a digest of *Walden* as a lyceum lecture before the book was published. One stalwart of the lyceum circuit said that he lectured in exchange for "F-A-M-E—Fifty and My Expenses." As Herman Melville pledged, "If they will pay my expenses and give a reasonable fee, I am ready to lecture in Labrador or on the Isle of Desolation off Patagonia."

As the Grimké sisters had discovered, women enjoyed few opportunities for public speaking, and most lyceum lecturers were men. But women were tapping into the growing market for literature. Fiction-writing became the most lucrative occupation open to women before the Civil War. Novelist Susan Warner's *The Wide, Wide World*, published in 1850, went through fourteen editions by 1852. Maria Cummins's *The Lamplighter*, published in 1854, sold forty thousand copies in eight weeks. Harriet Beecher Stowe's *Uncle Tom's Cabin*, published in 1852, exceeded all previous sales by selling 100,000 copies in just five months. Nathaniel Hawthorne,

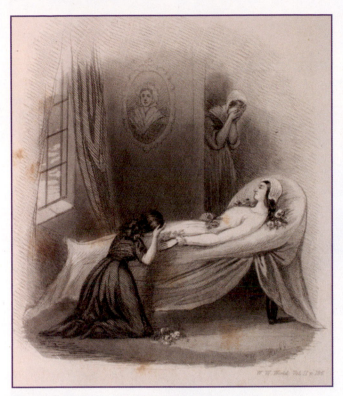

"DEATHBED OF ALICE HUMPHREYS" from Susan Warner's popular novel, *The Wide, Wide World* (1850). Deathbed scenes were an important convention in sentimental fiction, designed to evoke a powerful emotional response from the reader. In this one, Alice Humphreys dies, leaving her beloved friend Ellen Montgomery, who had been abandoned by her parents to the unloving care of her stern Aunt Fortune, even lonelier and more bereft. *(American Antiquarian Society)*

whose own works sold modestly, bitterly condemned what he called the "d—d mob of scribbling women" who were outselling and outearning him.

Susan Warner and others benefited from advances in printing technology that significantly reduced the price of books. Before 1830, Sir Walter Scott's novels had been issued in three-volume sets that retailed for as much as thirty dollars. As canals and railroads began to carry new books to general stores across the land, publishers in New York and Philadelphia competed with one another to stock those stores with inexpensive novels. By the 1840s, cheap paperbacks costing as little as seven cents were flooding the market. Those who did not purchase books could read fiction in "story newspapers" such as the weekly *New York Ledger*, which was devoted mainly to serializing novels; the *Ledger*'s subscribers numbered four hundred thousand in 1860. In addition, the spread of public schools and academies contributed to higher literacy and a widening audience for fiction, especially among women.

The most popular form of fiction in the 1840s and 1850s was the sentimental or domestic novel, written mostly by women for women. The typical plot centers on a young girl who is either a poor and friendless orphan or a wealthy heiress suddenly faced with the necessity of making her own way in the world. In either case, the girl's situation awakens her to inner resources she hadn't previously recognized and instills in her a new sense of her value and strength. The moral of *The Wide, Wide World* was that women had the power and authority to clean up the messes left by men.

Another popular genre in the antebellum reading market was sensationalist fiction, which drew on such dark romantic themes as criminality, mystery, and horror, but took them to extremes unknown in the works of Hawthorne, Melville, or even Poe. The best-selling novel in America before *Uncle Tom's Cabin* was George Lippard's *The Quaker City; or The Monks of Monk Hall, A Romance of Philadelphia Life, Mystery, and Crime*, published in 1845. Based loosely on a real Philadelphia murder, it told the story of Monk Hall, a six-story structure (three floors above ground, three below) filled with secret passageways and trapdoors, where outwardly respectable Philadelphians gathered nightly to carouse, consume drugs, and rape young virgins. Works such as this tapped into the market for sensationalism created by the penny press.

Authors such as Hawthorne, Poe, and Melville thus had to compete with story newspapers, sentimental fiction, and sensationalism. The philosopher Emerson shared the lecture circuit with the showman P. T. Barnum. Poe sneered that the public's judgment of a writer's merits was nearly always wrong. By and large, however, the major writers of the American Renaissance (with the exception of Melville, whose critical acclaim was delayed to the twentieth century) were not overlooked by their society. Emerson's lectures were highly successful, Hawthorne's *The Scarlet Letter* enjoyed respectable sales, and Poe's "The Raven" (1844) was extremely popular. But the writers most likely to achieve commercial success were those who met popular expectations for moral and spiritual uplift, horror and mystery, or love stories and happy endings.

11-4.5 American Landscape Painting

At the same time as American writers were trying to create a distinctly American literature, American painters were searching for a national style in art. European classicists had devoted much attention to the ancient and medieval past, painting historical scenes and portraits that celebrated the antiquity of

THOMAS COLE, *THE LAST OF THE MOHICANS, CORA KNEELING AT THE FEET OF TAMENUND*, 1827 One year after James Fenimore Cooper's novel *The Last of the Mohicans* was published, Thomas Cole painted the white captive Cora pleading with Tamenund, Chief of the Delaware, not to be forced into marriage with an evil Indian warrior. In Cole's painting, this human drama is dwarfed by the sublime beauty of the American wilderness. *(akg-images)*

their civilizations. In the absence of such traditions, American artists turned to landscape painting. Just as Hawthorne had complained about the lack of shadow and antiquity in American society, American painters sometimes lamented that the American landscape had no "poetry of decay" in the form of ruined castles and crumbling temples. Nevertheless, they found abundant subject matter in the natural history and grandeur of their own land.

The center of American landscape painting in the nineteenth century was the **Hudson River School**, which flourished from the 1820s to the 1870s. Numbering more than fifty painters, it was best represented by Thomas Cole, Asher Durand, and Frederick Church. None was exclusively a landscapist. Some of Cole's most popular paintings were allegories, including *The Course of Empire*, a sequence of five canvases depicting the rise and fall of an ancient city, which warned its viewers that luxurious living would doom their republic. Nor did these artists paint only the Hudson River. Cole's student Frederick Church, who was internationally the best known of the three, painted the Andes Mountains during an extended trip to South America in 1853. After the Civil War, German-born Albert Bierstadt adapted Hudson River school conventions to his monumental canvases of the Rocky Mountains.

But landscape artists did paint countless scenes of the Hudson River region, which captured their attention in part through the folkloric writings of Washington Irving, and the completion of the Erie Canal. What Hudson River painters contributed to American art was a romantic emphasis on emotional effect over illustrative accuracy. Thomas Cole's dramatic treatments of towering peaks and massive gnarled trees prompted poet William Cullen Bryant to compare them to "acts of religion." Similar motifs marked Frederick Church's paintings of the Andes

Hudson River School
American art movement in the mid-1800s. The artists primarily painted scenes of the region around the Hudson River, a waterway that Americans compared in majesty to the Rhine.

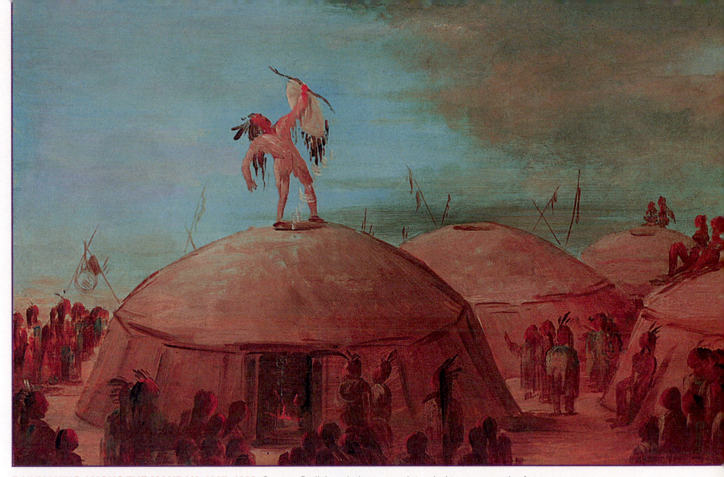

RAINMAKING AMONG THE MANDAN, 1837–1839 George Catlin's paintings were intended to preserve the faces, customs, and habitats of the Indian tribes who were thought to be going extinct due to advancing civilization. *(Smithsonian American Art Museum, Washington, DC/Art Resource, NY)*

Mountains, which used erupting volcanoes and thunderstorms to evoke dread and a sense of majesty.

After 1830, the writings of Emerson and Thoreau along with the paintings of the Hudson River School popularized a new view of nature that challenged the environmental devastation taking place all around them. Western pioneers were cutting down forests to plant vast fields with cash crops, while easterners were clear-cutting their own forests to fuel the new steam engines of railroads and industrial factories. One traveler complained that Americans would rather view a wheat field or a cabbage patch than a virgin forest. But romantic writers and artists glorified pristine nature; "in wildness is the preservation of the world," Thoreau wrote. Their outlook blended with growing popular fears that, as one contemporary wrote in 1847, "The axe of civilization is busy with our old forests." As the "wild and picturesque haunts of the Red Man" became "the abodes of commerce and the seats of civilization," this writer concluded, "it behooves our artists to rescue from its grasp the little that is left before it is too late." Cole and other landscape painters often used the motif of the felled tree to express their concern about the encroachments of civilization on American nature.

Like Cole, painter **George Catlin** also tried to preserve a vanishing America, but his main concern was the native peoples of the land. Observing an Indian delegation passing through Philadelphia in 1824, Catlin resolved that his life's work would be to paint Native Americans in their pure and "savage" state. Journeying up the Missouri River in 1832 he sketched at a feverish pace, and in 1837 exhibited his "Indian gallery" of faces and customs from nearly fifty tribes. Catlin viewed the Indian as a noble savage whose mind, in his words, was "a beautiful blank." His paintings, though intended to preserve what he and his contemporaries called the "vanishing Indian," actually encouraged viewers to believe that Indians were doomed to extinction by the encroachment of civilization—an attitude that justified further white expansion and conquest.

By the 1830s, romantic city-dwellers were creating little enclaves of nature as spiritual antidotes to sprawling urban development. Some enclaves were the so-called rural cemeteries. Starting with Mount Auburn Cemetery near Boston in 1831, landscaped cemeteries

George Catlin
American painter whose main goal was to paint as many Native Americans as possible in their pure and "savage" state.

MT. AUBURN CEMETERY, 1847 This "rural" or "garden" cemetery outside Boston was designed to express a romantic view of nature, with its beautiful trees planted along winding lanes. The figures of the man and child indicate the landscape designers' belief in the educational value of the rural cemetery. Among the many prominent Bostonians buried here was humanitarian reformer Dorothea Dix. *(Mount Auburn Cemetery)*

with names such as "Harmony Grove" and "Greenwood" sprang up near major cities, offering curving tree-lined lanes and artificial ponds for the enjoyment of strolling city-dwellers. Designed for the living rather than the dead, they quickly became tourist attractions.

Other natural enclaves were urban parks carefully crafted to resemble the countryside. In 1858 New York City chose a plan drawn by landscape architect

Frederick Law Olmsted
Chief architect of New York City's Central Park.

Frederick Law Olmsted and Calvert Vaux for its proposed Central Park. Olmsted and Vaux designed the park to screen out the surrounding city, planting bordering trees to conceal nearby buildings, and constructing four sunken thoroughfares to carry traffic unobtrusively across the park. The effect was to make Central Park "picturesque," meaning that its manmade woods, meadows, and lake reminded visitors of natural landscapes they had seen in pictures. Thus nature was made to mirror art.

The Whole Vision

■ *Was technology truly a democratizing force in the mid-nineteenth century?*

The short answer: yes and no. The impact of technology would depend on whether one was free or enslaved, a worker or employer, a farmer or laborer. Yes, technology revolutionized transportation, communication, farming, and commercial production by making all of these faster, easier, and more affordable. Technologically improved implements gave midwestern farmers a profitable staple crop, and advances in railroad development not only facilitated further westward expansion but the rise of cities and towns in previously remote areas. Machine tool technology and factory production simplified and shortened work, which saved time and money, allowed for mass production, and lowered the cost of goods. Wages increased, due in part to work becoming less seasonal and to longer shifts. But the nature and value of worked changed; skilled work formerly done by artisans was replaced by factory production and divided into pieces. Cotton farming in the South became easier via technology, which was not good news for slaves. And as investment in technology became big business, money—and the power that came with it—would increasingly be in fewer and fewer hands.

■ *Were all of the changes affecting daily life in the mid-nineteenth century for the better?*

The obvious answer, of course, is no, not all of the changes that affected daily life in the nineteenth century proved to be beneficial—and even those that were did not necessarily improve life for all people. Technology certainly changed all aspects of daily life from housework to household construction and conveniences. But some of the new devices came with negative and dangerous side effects, and there were gender implications, too, as women faced more demanding expectations and new associations with the work they did at home. Even as technology made some things easier, some aspects of life remained unchanged such as personal hygiene. Medical advances were slow, though there were some important breakthroughs, and new alternative therapies focused on helping people live healthier lives, with varying degrees of success. Most important, there were class implications for all of the technological changes; the middle class benefitted far more from improvements than did the poor, further widening the class divide.

■ *What were the hallmarks and significance of mass entertainment in the mid-nineteenth century?*

Like other areas of life, technology and innovation transformed what constituted entertainment in this era. Where people formerly created their own leisure activities, they increasingly began to purchase them, becoming consumers and spectators of all kinds of entertainment. Diverse groups and classes often mingled and clashed at various events such as theater, sometimes violently. While the widespread availability of entertainment might be seen as a democratizing trend, the era's forms of entertainment reflected the competing tastes of different groups as much as it did the need of one group to convey their superiority over others, as in the racial stereotypes portrayed in minstrel shows. Newspapers became more affordable, too, and what constituted news was dramatically altered by the advent of the penny press with its ability to reach wider and more diverse audiences. Entrepreneurs who understood how to capture the desires of mass audiences, such as P. T. Barnum, not only led new trends in entertainment but became wealthy doing so.

KEY TERMS

McCormick reaper (p. 296)

"American System of Manufacturing" (p. 297)

New York Stock Exchange (p. 300)

epidemics (p. 303)

phrenology (p. 304)

penny press (p. 305)

minstrel shows (p. 306)

P. T. Barnum (p. 306)

American Renaissance (p. 307)

James Fenimore Cooper (p. 308)

Ralph Waldo Emerson (p. 308)

Henry David Thoreau (p. 309)

Margaret Fuller (p. 309)

Walt Whitman (p. 311)

Nathaniel Hawthorne (p. 311)

Edgar Allan Poe (p. 311)

Herman Melville (p. 311)

Hudson River School (p. 314)

George Catlin (p. 315)

Frederick Law Olmsted (p. 316)

■ *What fueled the American Renaissance in literature and art?*

In a nutshell, the American Renaissance was driven by a quest for a truly American art and literary form, something that reflected the American character and landscape and was distinct from European forms. Here, too, technological innovation coupled with economic imperatives, national pride, and new schools of philosophical thought helped to facilitate the emergence of the American Renaissance. Romanticism, and later transcendentalism, with its focus on the individual as author and creator, made a wider array of topics acceptable in literary circles, a decided democratic trend. This included both a celebration of America as well as critiques and questions about the advance of American society and the course it was taking. Some authors celebrated America's potential; others were more cynical and pessimistic. Painters, too, sought to capture both the essence of the American landscape—including its Native American inhabitants—and to lament its passing. Inexpensive printing techniques also made reading more democratic. Books became more affordable and widely read, which in some ways created a seeming class divide between authors of literature versus those of new popular or mass forms of fiction, such as the sentimental novels often written by women.

12 The Old South and Slavery, 1830–1860

FAMILY GROUP The African American woman shown here was probably a slave mammy who may have substituted for the absent mother of the children. That she was included in the family photo indicates her role as caregiver, though as the children incline toward the father, her status and distance is apparent. It is unknown whether the slave owner included her in the photo as part of the southern paternalistic defense of slavery; it is also unknown whether he engaged in a sexual relationship—forcible or otherwise—with this slave. *(J. Paul Getty Museum)*

1790s	Methodists and Baptists start to make major strides in converting slaves to Christianity.		**1832**	Virginia legislature narrowly defeats a proposal for gradual emancipation.
1793	Eli Whitney invents the cotton gin.			Virginia's Thomas R. Dew writes an influential defense of slavery.
1800	Gabriel Prosser leads a slave rebellion in Virginia.		**1835**	Arkansas admitted to the Union.
1808	Congress prohibits the external slave trade.		**1837**	Economic panic begins, lowering cotton prices.
1812	Louisiana, the first state formed out of the Louisiana Purchase, is admitted to the Union.		**1844–1845**	Methodist Episcopal and Baptist churches split into northern and southern wings over slavery.
1816–1819	Boom in cotton prices stimulates settlement of the Old Southwest.		**1845**	Florida and Texas admitted to the Union.
1819–1820	Missouri Compromise.		**1849**	Sugar production in Louisiana reaches its peak.
1822	Denmark Vesey's conspiracy uncovered in South Carolina.		**1849–1860**	Period of high cotton prices.
1831	William Lloyd Garrison starts *The Liberator*.		**1857**	Hinton R. Helper, *The Impending Crisis of the South*.
	Nat Turner rebellion in Virginia.		**1859**	John Brown's raid on Harpers Ferry.
			1860	South Carolina secedes from the Union.

Slipping through the swampy woodlands of Southampton County, Virginia, in the early morning of August 22, 1831, **Nat Turner** and six other slaves embarked on a grisly campaign of liberation. Turner had been preparing for this moment since February, when he had interpreted a solar eclipse as a long-awaited sign from God for him to lead his people against slavery by killing slaveholders. Employing hatchets and axes, Nat and his band quickly slaughtered Joseph Travis, his wife Sally, and two other whites in the house. The Turner band then moved through the countryside; by noon more than sixty slaves had taken up hatchets and more than sixty whites had been shot, clubbed, or hacked to death.

As word of the violence spread, thousands of militia and vigilantes poured into Southampton from other Virginia counties and from across the border in North Carolina. Shocking destruction greeted them; dismembered bodies and fresh blood testified to the rage unleashed by the rebels.

Now it was the whites' turn for vengeance. In their rage and terror, they killed scores of blacks, including many who had taken no part in the rebellion. Turner's band was overpowered, and those not shot on sight were jailed, tried and then hanged. Turner himself slipped away and hid in the woods until his capture on October 30. After a trial, he too was hanged.

Before his execution, Turner explained his actions in his "Confessions," recorded by his court-appointed lawyer and subsequently published. In them, Turner did not claim that he had been personally mistreated by his owners. Instead, he set forth his religious conviction that all slavery was evil, an offense against God. Turner was a religious mystic, who had seen heavenly visions of white and black spirits fighting each other. He was one of many slaves converted to Christianity in the decades before and after 1800 by white Baptist and Methodist preachers, many of whom later hoped that Christianity would make slaves more docile. But Turner's ability to read had enabled him to find biblical passages that threatened death to anyone who "stealeth" a man, a fair description of slavery. Asked by his lawyer if he now understood his mistake, the rebel leader defiantly replied, "Was not Christ crucified?" A niece of George Washington voiced the fear of many whites by saying that she and other white Virginians were now living on a "smothered volcano."

> **Nat Turner**
> A slave who led a bloody rebellion in Southampton County, Virginia, in 1831. Before that, white Virginians had worried little about a slave rebellion.

NAT TURNER *(The Granger Collection)*

Upper South
Consisted of Virginia, North Carolina, Tennessee, and Arkansas.

Lower, or Deep, South
Consisted of South Carolina, Georgia, Florida, Alabama, Mississippi, Louisiana, and Texas.

Old South
Consisted of Virginia, North Carolina, Tennessee, Arkansas, South Carolina, Georgia, Florida, Alabama, Mississippi, Louisiana, and Texas.

Before Turner, white Virginians had spent little time worrying about slave rebellion. They experienced a brief scare in 1800 when a plot led by the slave Gabriel Prosser was discovered and nipped in the bud. But generally, white Virginians thought they had little to fear. They believed that their form of slavery was relatively mild, in contrast to the harsh regimen of the new cotton-growing areas in Alabama and Mississippi. In fact, when they first heard that some trouble had erupted in Southampton County, many whites jumped to the conclusion that the British were invading. Only gradually did they absorb the more menacing possibility that slaves were rebelling.

In the wake of Turner's insurrection, many Virginians, especially nonslaveholding whites in the western part of the state, urged Virginia to follow the lead of northern states and emancipate its slaves. During the winter of 1831–1832, the Virginia legislature wrangled over various proposals for emancipation. But those proposals were narrowly defeated, and afterward, opposition to slavery steadily weakened not only in Virginia but throughout the Old South.

Before the American Revolution, when slavery was still practiced throughout all thirteen colonies, the term *south* referred more to a direction on the compass than to a living place. But after the Revolution, as one northern state after another embraced emancipation, *the South* emerged as a distinctive region of the new nation, distinguished above all by its "peculiar institution" of slavery.

Not all states of the Old South were equally dependent on slave labor. The **Upper South** (including Virginia, North Carolina, Tennessee, and Arkansas) practiced a diversified agriculture of wheat, tobacco, hemp, vegetables, and livestock, which did not necessarily rely on slave labor. By contrast, the **Lower, or Deep, South** (including South Carolina, Georgia, Florida, Alabama, Mississippi, Louisiana, and Texas) pursued the two great cash crops of cotton and sugar, which depended heavily on slave labor. As a result, in the political crisis of 1861, the Upper South would approach secession more reluctantly than the Deep South. Despite their differences, however, their shared institution of slavery forged the Upper and Lower South into a single **Old South** where the "peculiar institution" scarred all social relationships: between blacks and whites, among whites, and between blacks. Without slavery, the region known as the Old South would not have come into being.

12-1 King Cotton

What made the South distinctive from the North?

In 1790, the southern economy was stagnating. Tobacco, once its primary cash crop, had exhausted the soil and lost profitability on the market. Alternative cash crops, such as rice and cotton, could only be grown near the Atlantic coast. As a result, three out of four southerners still lived along the Atlantic seaboard, mostly in the Chesapeake Bay area (Virginia and Maryland) and the Carolinas.

The contrast between that stagnant South of 1790 and the dynamic South of 1850 was stunning. By 1850, the southern population had shifted hundreds of miles further south and west. Cotton reigned as king, as growers worked to meet new demands for the crop created by the booming British textile industry. Indian removal (see Chapter 9) had made way for southern expansion into the **"Cotton Kingdom,"**

"Cotton Kingdom,"
A broad swath of territory that stretched from South Carolina, Georgia, and northern Florida in the east through Alabama, Mississippi, central and western Tennessee, and Louisiana, and from there on to Arkansas and Texas.

stretching from South Carolina, Georgia, and northern Florida in the east; through Alabama, Mississippi, central and western Tennessee, and Louisiana in the west; and further westward into Arkansas and Texas (see Map 12.1). As cotton cultivation spread west, so would slavery.

12-1.1 The Lure of Cotton

According to one British traveler, southern life was completely dominated by cotton: "Every flow of wind from the shore wafted off the smell of that useful plant; at every dock or wharf we encountered it in huge piles or pyramids of bales, and our decks were soon choked with it. All day, and almost all night long, the captain, pilot, crew, and passengers were talking of nothing else."

The Lower South, with its warm climate, wet springs and summers, and relatively dry autumns, was ideal for cultivating cotton. A small-scale cotton farmer needed neither slaves nor cotton gins nor the capital required for sugar cultivation. Perhaps 50 percent of the farmers in the "Cotton Belt" owned no slaves and hired commercial cotton gins to process

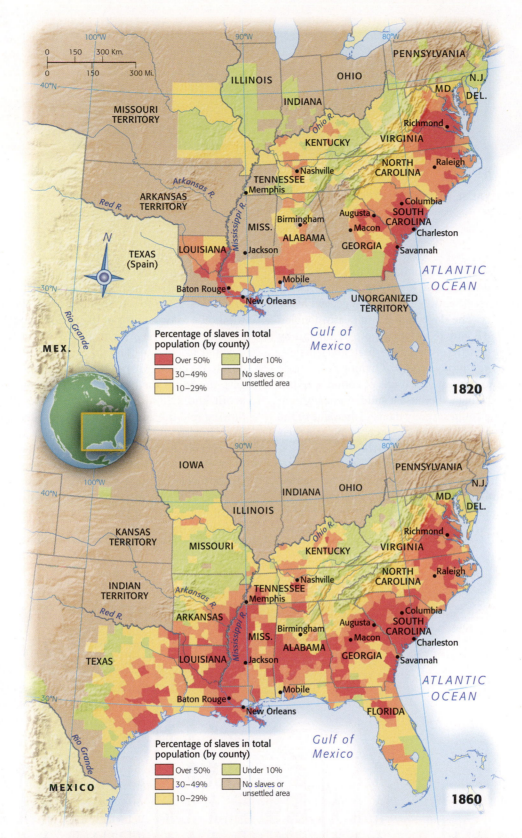

MAP 12.1 DISTRIBUTION OF SLAVES, 1820 AND 1860 In 1820, the majority of slaves resided along the southeastern seaboard. By 1860, however, slavery had spread throughout the South, and slaves were most heavily concentrated in the Deep South states.

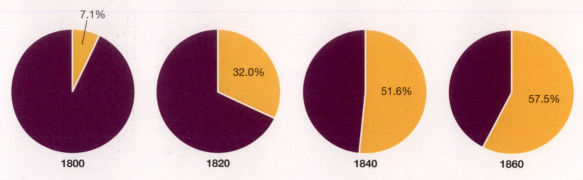

FIGURE 12.1 VALUE OF COTTON EXPORTS AS A PERCENTAGE OF ALL U.S. EXPORTS, 1800–1860
By 1840, cotton accounted for more than half of all U.S. exports.

their harvest. Cotton promised to make poor men prosperous and rich men kings (see Figure 12.1).

Yet large-scale cotton growing did depend heavily on slavery. The slave population nearly doubled between 1810 and 1830 (see Figure 12.2), and by 1830, three-fourths of all slaves—male and female—worked in the cotton economy. Owning slaves made it possible to harvest vast tracts of cotton speedily, a crucial advantage because a sudden rainstorm at harvest time could severely damage the value of the crop. Farmers who owned slaves could increase their cotton acreage and hence their profits.

Adding to the value of cotton agriculture was corn production. Because corn could be planted earlier and harvested later than cotton, slaveholders could maximize the value of their slave labor by shifting workers from corn to cotton and back

again over the course of the agricultural year. Corn provided the southern diet with an important grain and, when fed to hogs (in 1860, the region was home to two-thirds of the nation's hogs), with a major source of protein. By 1860, the acreage devoted to corn in the Old South *exceeded* that devoted to cotton. Grown together, cotton and corn gave the South the best of two economic worlds: profit and self-sufficiency. Cotton kept money flowing into the South, as intense market demand from British and New England textile mills kept prices high. And corn helped that money remain in the South because the region's dietary self-sufficiency made it unnecessary to import much food. As a result of this successful partnership, in 1860, the twelve wealthiest counties in the United States were all in the South.

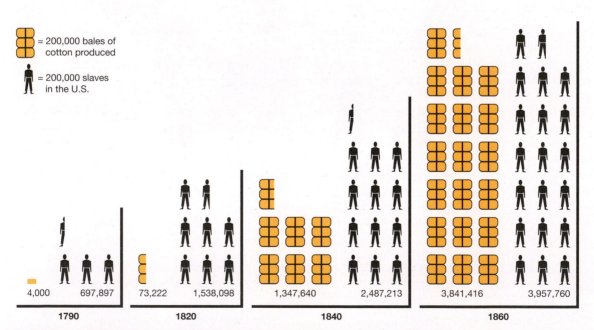

FIGURE 12.2 GROWTH OF COTTON PRODUCTION AND THE SLAVE POPULATION, 1790–1860 Cotton and slavery rose together in the Old South.

MAP 12.2 THE INTERNAL SLAVE TRADE, 1810–1860 An internal slave trade developed after the slave trade with Africa ended in 1808. With the growth of cotton production, farmers in the Upper South found it profitable to sell their slaves to planters in the Lower South.

12-1.2 Ties Between the Lower and Upper South

In the Lower South, two giant cash crops—sugar and cotton—dominated the agricultural scene. In the Upper South, a more diversified agriculture of tobacco, vegetable, hemp, and wheat prevailed. Despite these differences, the Upper South identified with the states of the Lower South rather than with the agricultural regions of the free states lying to the north.

A range of social, political, and economic factors promoted this regional identification. First, many settlers in the Lower South had originally lived in the Upper South and maintained family and other social ties to that area. Second, all white southerners benefited politically from the three-fifths clause of the Constitution, which enabled them to count slaves as a basis for congressional representation. Third, all white southerners were stung by abolitionist criticisms of slavery, which drew no distinction between the treatment of slaves in the Upper versus Lower South. Economic ties also helped bind the entire South together. The profitability of cotton and sugar increased the value of slaves throughout the entire region,

prompting Virginians in particular to take up slave-breeding to supply the **internal slave trade**. Without the sale of its slaves to the Lower South, an observer wrote, "Virginia will be a desert" (see Map 12.2).

12-1.3 The North and South Diverge

The changes responsible for the dynamic growth of the Old South widened the divergence between that region and the North. The South remained predominantly rural at a time when the North was growing increasingly urban. In 1820, the proportion of the South's population living in urban areas was one-half that of New England and the mid-Atlantic states, and by 1860, that proportion had dipped even lower, to one-third.

The South was also more resistant to industrialization than the North. By 1860, although the South had one-third of the nation's population, it accounted for only one-tenth of the nation's manufacturing. The industrial output of the entire South in 1850 was less than one-third that of the single northern state of Massachusetts.

> **internal slave trade**
> Slave trade within the Upper and Lower South.

Industry was not entirely absent from the South, however. A few southerners advocated industrialization to reduce the South's dependency on northern manufactured products. After touring northern textile mills, William Gregg established a company town for textiles at Graniteville, South Carolina, in 1845. By 1860, Richmond, Virginia, was home to the nation's fourth-largest producer of iron products, the **Tredegar Iron Works** (which would soon be supplying the Confederate Army with artillery). But these few industrial operations were the exception, not the rule.

Compared to factories in the North, most southern factories were small and oriented to nearby markets. Southern factories also remained more closely tied to agriculture. The leading northern factories turned animal hides into tanned leather and leather into shoes, or cotton into threads and threads into suits. In contrast, southern factories remained just one step removed from agriculture, turning grain into flour, corn into meal, and logs into lumber.

Slavery posed a major obstacle to southern industrialization, but not because slaves were unfit for factory labor. The Tredegar Iron Works, for example, employed slaves in skilled positions. But industrial slavery troubled southerners. Away from the strict supervision of plantations, slaves sometimes behaved like free laborers, shifting jobs, working overtime, even negotiating better working conditions. A Virginia planter who rented his slaves to an iron manufacturer complained that they "got the habit of roaming about and *taking care of themselves*."

Nevertheless, the chief brake on southern industrialization was not labor, but money. Southern capital was largely invested in slaves. To raise the money needed to build factories, southerners would have to sell their slaves. They had little incentive to do so. Cash crops like cotton and sugar were proven winners, whereas the benefits of industrialization were remote and uncertain. As long as southerners believed that an economy founded on cash crops would remain profitable, they had little reason to gamble on industrialization.

Another major divergence between the South and the North concerned education. White southerners rejected compulsory education and opposed taxing property to support schools. Some public aid flowed to state universities, but for most whites the only available schools were private. As the result of such policies, white illiteracy remained high in the South even as it declined in the North. For example, nearly 60 percent of the North Carolinians who enlisted in

CHARLESTON, SOUTH CAROLINA Merchants and planters erected mansions along Charleston's waterfront, but the majority of the city's people were black. Below its placid surface, Charleston seethed with rage at northern interference with slavery. In 1860, South Carolina would become the first state to secede from the United States. *(Image Courtesy of the Gibbes Museum of Art/Carolina Art Association, Gift of Victor A. Morawetz)*

the U.S. army before the Civil War were illiterate, compared to 30 percent of northern enlistees.

White southern indifference to public education crossed class lines. Agricultural, self-sufficient, and independently minded, the middling and poor whites of the South remained unconvinced of the need for public education. They had little use for the printed word, engaged in few complex economic transactions, and dealt infrequently with urban people. At the other end of the social spectrum, planters purchased private educations for their children and felt no need for an educated white workforce. Their workforce was predominantly black, and they were determined to keep their slaves illiterate lest they follow in the footsteps of rebels such as Nat Turner and acquire ideas of freedom from their reading.

Because the South diverged so sharply from the North, outsiders often dismissed the region as economically and socially backward. Northerners, who increasingly associated progress with the spread of cities and factories, concluded that the South was stuck in the past. In the 1850s, a northern journalist wrote of white southerners that "[t]hey work little, and that little, badly; they earn little, they sell little; they buy little, and they have little—very little—of the common comforts and consolations of civilized life." Visitors to the South sometimes felt as though they were traveling backward in time. "It seems as if everything had stopped growing, and was growing backwards," wrote antislavery novelist Harriet Beecher Stowe of the region. Such judgments betrayed northern regional prejudices. Although in 1840 southern per capita income was slightly below the national average, by 1860 it exceeded the national average. Southerners shared certain economic traits with northerners: they too were restless, eager to make money, skillful at managing complex commercial enterprises, and, when they chose, capable of becoming successful industrialists. Thus the white South was not economically backward so much as it was merely different. Cotton was a wonderful crop, and southerners could hardly be blamed for accepting its sway. As a southern senator wrote in 1858, "You dare not make war upon cotton; no power on earth dares to make war upon it. Cotton is king."

12-2 The White South

How did slavery shape the social and class dynamics of the South, even for those without slaves?

Considerable diversity shaped white social structure both within and between the slaveholding and non-slaveholding classes. At the wealthy extreme were those slaveholders who owned hundreds of slaves

and led lives of luxury; at the other extreme were those nonslaveholders who barely scraped by from one day to the next. In 1860, only one-quarter of all white families in the South owned slaves (see Figure 12.3). Of these, nearly half owned fewer than five, and nearly three-quarters had fewer than ten. Only 12 percent owned twenty or more slaves, and only 1 percent had a hundred or more. Large slaveholders were clearly a minority within a minority. Nonslaveholders also formed a diverse group. Most owned farms and drew on the labor of family members. But some were squatters living in the pine barrens and scratching out minimal livelihoods by raising livestock, hunting and fishing, and planting corn, oats, or sweet potatoes on land they did not own. Despite their lowly economic status, that their race meant they had the potential to own slaves made poorer whites inclined to see their identities more aligned with the planter class than that of slaves.

The four main social groups among southern whites were planters (owners of twenty slaves or more), small slaveholders (owners of fewer than twenty slaves), yeomen (family farmers), and pine barrens folk. Lawyers, physicians, merchants, and artisans did not fall into any of these agricultural groups, but tended to identify their interests with one or another of them. Rural artisans and merchants dealt primarily with yeomen farmers. Urban merchants and lawyers depended on the planters and adopted their viewpoint on most issues. Similarly, slave traders identified with the planters on whom they relied for their livelihood. Nathan Bedford Forrest, the uneducated son of a Tennessee blacksmith, made a fortune as a slave trader in Natchez, Mississippi. When the Civil War broke out, Forrest enlisted in the Confederate army as a private

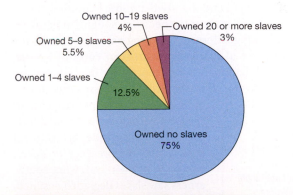

FIGURE 12.3 SLAVE OWNERSHIP IN THE SOUTH, 1860 In combination with the impact of Hinton R. Helper's *The Impending Crisis of the South* (1857), which called on nonslaveholders to abolish the institution of slavery in their own interest, the large number who owned no slaves left slaveholders worried about the loyalty of nonslaveholders to slavery.

and rose swiftly to become the South's greatest cavalry general. Plantation slavery directed Forrest's allegiances as surely as it did those of planters like Jefferson Davis, president of the Confederacy.

12-2.1 Planters and Plantation Mistresses

With its porticoed white mansion and vast fields teeming with slaves, the large plantation still dominates the popular image of the Old South. Though heavily romanticized, this image does have some basis in reality. **Plantation agriculture**, whether devoted to cotton, tobacco, rice, or sugar, was characterized by a high degree of division of labor. In the 1850s, Bellmead, a tobacco plantation on Virginia's James River, was the agricultural equivalent of a factory village. Its more than one hundred slaves were divided into the domestic staff (butlers, waiters, seamstresses, laundresses, maids, and gardeners), the pasture staff (shepherds, cowherds, and hog drivers), outdoor artisans (stonemasons and carpenters), indoor artisans (blacksmiths, carpenters, shoemakers, spinners, and weavers), and field hands. Such a division of labor required an abundance of both slaves and land. With such resources, large plantations could generate immense incomes by contemporary standards ($20,000 to $30,000 a year).

In the eighteenth century, during the first flush of settlement in the Piedmont and trans-Appalachian South, most planters had been content to live in simple log cabins. By contrast, in the decades after 1810, many elite planters vied with one another to build stately mansions. Lyman Hardy of Mississippi hired an architect to design his home near Natchez, which featured Ionic columns and a generous portico thirty-one feet long. They similarly embraced the role of social aristocrat, complete with the airs of refinement and dignity that those beneath them on the socioeconomic spectrum sought to emulate. Among gentlemen, an exaggerated pride took the form of a distinctive **southern code of honor**, which had men use violence—the duel—to defend their honor against even the slightest insult or dispute. At the root of most violence in the white South lay intensified feelings of personal pride that reflected the inescapable presence of slaves. Every day of their lives, white southerners saw slaves degraded, insulted, and powerless to resist. This experience encouraged white men to react violently to even seemingly trivial verbal insults in order to demonstrate that they had nothing in common with lowly slaves.

Slaves, however, especially in states such as Alabama and Mississippi, comprised the majority of planters' wealth. A field hand was worth as much as $1,700 in the 1850s. Planters could convert their wealth into luxuries only by selling their slaves and thus forfeiting their elite status as planters. Not surprisingly, most planters clung to large-scale slaveholding, even at the cost of scrimping on their lifestyles. A northern journalist observed that in the Southwest, men worth millions of dollars lived as if they were not worth hundreds.

Despite their wealth and social status, planters worried constantly about their financial position. High fixed costs—for housing and feeding slaves, maintaining cotton gins, hiring overseers—kept them searching for more and better land, higher efficiency, and greater self-sufficiency. Because cotton prices fluctuated seasonally, planters often assigned their cotton to commercial agents, who held onto the cotton until they could get the best price. In return, the agents extended credit so that planters could pay their bills until the cotton was sold. Chronic debt

CHARLOTTE HELEN AND HER NURSE LYDIA, 1857 Ten days after Charlotte's birth, which occurred when the family sought refuge on Sullivan's Island, South Carolina, during a yellow fever epidemic, a terrible storm swamped the beaches. Lydia refused the aid of a soldier, trusting no one but herself, and waded through the swirling waters to carry Charlotte Helen to safety. *(Image Courtesy of the Gibbes Museum of Art/Carolina Art Association, Gift of Alicia Hopton Middleton)*

plantation agriculture
Characterized by a high degree of division of labor, and dependence on the large-scale production of a staple crop.

southern code of honor
An extraordinary sensitivity to one's reputation; a belief that one's self-esteem depends on the judgment of others.

thus became intrinsic to the plantation economy and intensified the planters' quest for profitability.

Women of the planter class faced dual obligations that were sometimes at odds with each other. On the one hand, they were expected to occupy a pedestal of womanly virtues and gentility. That meant remaining above doing physical work, since labor was associated with slaves. On the other hand, once they married, they became, in effect, overseers and managers of their homes, raising children, supervising house slaves, making clothes and carpets, looking after smokehouses and dairies, planting gardens, and keeping accounts. They also handled the discipline of slaves, which at times included brutal physical punishments that northerners saw as a further corrupting influence of slavery on womanhood. Marriage also meant that, like northern women, any property or slaves they brought into the marriage were now the property and control of husbands. Southern fathers, concerned that their daughters' inheritance might be squandered by sons-in-law, sought to protect it legally via married women's property acts. In 1839, Mississippi passed the first law granting wives the right to retain control of their property; a year later, Arkansas followed suit. But in every other way, wives were to be submissive to husbands, and with few economic alternatives for women aside from marriage, many women remained silent about husbands' activities—even those they disagreed with—for fear they might be turned out of their homes.

Along with ongoing economic worries, planter couples faced psychological strains. Frequent moves disrupted circles of friends and relatives, especially as migration to the Old Southwest (Alabama, Mississippi, and eastern Texas) carried families into less settled, more desolate areas. Migration to the Southwest was particularly hard on plantation women. Those who migrated to the Old Southwest found themselves living in distant frontier regions, surrounded by slaves and missing the companionship of family and friends. "I am sad tonight, sickness preys on my frame," wrote a bride who moved to Mississippi in 1833. "I am alone and more than 150 miles from any near relative in the wild woods of an Indian nation." Planter wives were often deprived even of their husbands' companionship. Plantation agriculture kept men on the road, scouting new land for purchase, supervising outlying holdings, and transacting business in New Orleans or Memphis. During such absences, planter women worked with overseers to run their plantations.

Planters and their wives found various ways to cope with their isolation. Some left their plantations in the hands of an overseer and settled their families for extended periods in cities. In 1850, fully one-half the planters in the Mississippi Delta were absentees living in Natchez or New Orleans rather than on their plantations. But many planters acted as their own overseers and kept their families in residence on the plantation. They dealt with social isolation primarily by opening their homes to visitors. The responsibility for such hospitality fell heavily on wives, who might have to entertain as many as fifteen people for breakfast and serve the needs of visitors who sometimes stayed for weeks on end.

Even as they insisted on sexual purity for white women, southern men set decidedly looser standards for themselves. White male privilege extended itself to sexual relationships with female slaves—sometimes consensual but often the product of exploitation and rape. Elite women, especially widows, sometimes engaged in typically secret, often coerced, sexual relationships with male slaves, too, though they risked their social status and safety in doing so.

Among the greatest sorrows of planter women were the many mulatto children who stood as daily reminders of their husbands' sexual infidelities. Mary Boykin Chesnut, a South Carolina planter's wife, observed pointedly that "Any lady is ready to tell you who is the father of all the mulatto children in everybody's household but her own. These, she seems to think, drop from clouds." The brother of the abolitionist Grimké sisters of South Carolina fathered three mulatto children after the death of his wife. The gentlemanly code of white southerners usually tolerated such transgressions as long as they were not paraded in public—and sometimes even if they were. Richard M. Johnson of Kentucky, the man who allegedly killed Tecumseh during the War of 1812, lived openly for years with his black mistress, but still managed to get himself elected vice president of the United States in 1836.

White women who complained to husbands about their sexual indiscretions would find their concerns often fell on deaf ears, or worse, could result in wives being put out of their homes. Instead of forging unity between mistresses and victimized slave women, planters' sexual improprieties only divided these women further. Helpless to stop husbands, white women often took their anger and jealousy out on slave women and the children they produced, sometimes with violence. In her slave narrative, Harriet Jacobs wrote about hoping for protection from her mistress as she tried to elude her master's sexual advances, but Jacobs experienced harassment and taunting instead. Jacobs also recounted that Sarah Wilson, the daughter of a slave woman and her white master, remembered that as a child, she was "picked on" by her mistress until the master ordered his wife to let Sarah alone because she "got big, big blood in her."

The drudgery, isolation, and humiliation experienced by planters' wives turned surprisingly few of them against the system of slavery. At the outbreak

COLONEL AND MRS. JAMES A. WHITESIDE, SON CHARLES, AND SERVANTS, BY JAMES A. CAMERON, CA. 1858–1859 This portrait captures the patriarchy as well as the graciousness that whites associated with the ideal plantation. Not only the slave waiter and nurse but the planter's wife appear overshadowed by the master's presence. *(Hunter Museum of American Art, Chattanooga, Tennessee, Gift of Mr. and Mrs. Thomas B. Whiteside, 1975.7)*

of the Civil War, they supported the Confederacy as enthusiastically as any other group. However much they hated leading lonely lives surrounded by slaves, they (like their husbands) recognized that their wealth and position depended on the South's "peculiar institution" of slavery.

12-2.2 The Small Slaveholders

The great planters, who occupy pride of place in the popular mythology of the Old South, actually represented a small minority of slaveholders. A substantial majority of slaveholders—88 percent in 1860—owned fewer than twenty slaves, and most of these possessed fewer than ten. Like the planters, most small slaveholders were agriculturalists; but unlike the planters, small slaveholders often worked side-by-side with their slaves.

Small slaveholders experienced conflicting loyalties and ambitions, depending on their geographic location in the South. In the upland regions, where yeomen (nonslaveholding family farmers) were the dominant group, small slaveholders rarely aspired to become large planters. But in the low country and delta regions, where planters dominated, small slaveholders often aspired to planter status, and someone with ten

slaves could realistically hope to own thirty. The deltas were filled with ambitious small slaveholders striving to acquire more slaves. Whether a slaveholder owned ten slaves or fifty, the logic of the system was basically the same: the investment in slaves could be justified only by setting them to work raising profitable crops. Profitable crops demanded, in turn, more and better land. So the small slaveholders of the low country and delta areas were, much like the planters they emulated, restless and footloose.

The social structure of the deltas was fluid. In the 1810s and 1820s, small slaveholders led the initial push into the Cotton Belt because large planters were reluctant to risk transporting hundreds of valuable slaves into an unstable frontier region. But once the small slaveholders had paved the way westward, large planters gradually followed, buying up the land that the small slave owners had developed and carving large plantations out of the territory along the Mississippi River between Vicksburg and Natchez. Small slaveholders then used their profits from selling their land to buy more slaves and move on. They gradually transformed the region from Vicksburg to Tuscaloosa, Alabama, into a belt of medium-sized farms with a dozen or so slaves on each.

12-2.3 The Yeomen and Pine Barrens Whites

Nonslaveholding family farmers, or yeomen, comprised the largest single group of southern whites. Most yeomen owned their land, and many hired slaves at harvest time to help in the fields. Where the land was poor, as in eastern Tennessee, the landowning yeomen were typically subsistence farmers, but most grew some crops for the market. Whether they engaged in subsistence or commercial agriculture, they controlled landholdings far more modest than those of the planters—in the range of fifty to two hundred acres rather than the planter's five hundred or more acres.

Yeomen could be found anywhere in the South, but they tended to congregate in the upland regions. In the Southeast, they populated the Piedmont region running through Georgia, South Carolina, North Carolina, and Virginia; in the Southwest, they usually lived in the hilly upcountry far from the rich alluvial soil of the deltas. A minority of yeomen—most of them young men—did not own land, but lived with and worked for landowning relatives.

The leading characteristic of the yeomen was the value they attached to self-sufficiency. As nonslaveholders, they were not carried along by the logic that impelled slaveholders constantly to acquire more land and plant more cash crops. Although most yeomen raised cash crops, they devoted much of their acreage to subsistence crops such as corn, sweet potatoes, and oats. Whereas planters strived to achieve the ideal of profit with modest self-sufficiency, yeomen worked toward self-sufficiency with modest profit. To do so required the work of all family members. Yeomen's wives worked hard, managing the household, producing cloth for their family's clothes, and selling produce to raise money for items they could not make themselves. For yeomen with few or no slaves, the subordinate position of wives was especially important to their sense of power and status.

In contrast to the far-flung commercial transactions of planters, the economic exchanges of yeomen usually occurred within their immediate neighborhoods. Yeomen exchanged cotton, wheat, or tobacco for goods and services from local artisans and merchants. In some areas, they sold their surplus corn to the herdsmen and drovers who specialized in raising hogs. Along the French Broad River in eastern Tennessee, some twenty to thirty thousand hogs were fattened for market each year; at peak season, a traveler would see a thousand hogs a mile. When driven to market, the hogs were quartered at night in huge stock stands, veritable hog "hotels," and fed with corn supplied by the local yeomen.

Yeomen had a mixed reputation within the Old South. Those who lived in the low country and delta regions dominated by planters were often dismissed as "poor white trash." But those who lived in the upland areas, where they themselves were the dominant group, enjoyed the social respect of their fellow yeomen. Even the upland slaveholders were not inclined to insult the social standing of yeomen farmers because they too were essentially family farmers.

Beneath the yeoman and at the bottom of the social scale was one of the most controversial groups in the Old South: independent whites who lived in the pine barrens. Making up about 10 percent of southern whites, they usually squatted on the land, built crude cabins, planted corn between the tree stumps on partially cleared land, and grazed hogs and cattle in the piney woods. They did not raise cash crops, nor did they engage in the daily routine of orderly work that characterized family farmers. With their ramshackle houses and stump-strewn acreage, they appeared lazy and shiftless.

Antislavery northerners sometimes pointed to the **pine barrens people** as living proof that slavery degraded poor whites. But southerners shot back that the impoverished pine barrens people could at least feed themselves, unlike the starving paupers of northern cities. In general, the people of the pine barrens were self-reliant and fiercely independent. One reason they were regarded as lazy and shiftless was that the men often refused to hire themselves out for what they called "slave" labor, and the women similarly refused to work as servants. Neither victimized nor oppressed, these people generally lived in the pine barrens by choice.

12-2.4 Conflict and Consensus in the White South

A curious mix of aristocratic and democratic, premodern and modern features marked social relations in the white South. Although considerable class inequality was evident throughout the region, property ownership was relatively widespread. And though wealthy planters occupied a disproportionate number of seats in southern state legislatures, they did not necessarily get their way, nor did their political agenda always differ from that of other whites.

Planters and yeomen tangled on several major issues in the Old South and divided along party lines. Planters and their urban commercial allies inclined toward the Whig party because of their extensive

> **pine barrens people**
> Making up about 10 percent of southern whites, they usually squatted on the land, put up crude cabins, cleared some acreage on which they planted corn between tree stumps, and grazed hogs and cattle in the woods. They neither raised cash crops nor engaged in the daily routine of orderly work that characterized family farmers. With their ramshackle houses and handful of stump-strewn acres, they appeared lazy and shiftless.

MindTap

Beyond
America
Slavery as
a Global
Institution

economic dealings, reliance on banking, and constant need for credit. Yeomen farmers tended to be Democrats because of their intense commitment to self-sufficiency and economic independence.

But actual occasions for conflict between these groups were minimal, and an underlying political unity reigned. Especially in the Lower South, each of the four main social groups—planters, small slaveholders, yeomen, and pine barrens people—tended to cluster in different geographic areas. Planters dominated the delta. Small slave-owning families with ten to fifteen slaves clustered in other areas. Yeomen congregated in the upland areas far from the deltas. The people of the pine barrens lived in a world of their own. Though the Upper South saw more geographical intermingling of groups than the Lower, throughout the South each group attained a significant degree of independence from the others. Due to widespread landownership and the scarcity of factories, relatively few whites worked for other whites in the Old South, a situation that tended to minimize class conflict.

In addition, the political structure of the Old South was sufficiently democratic to prevent any one social group from gaining exclusive control over politics. In both the Upper and Lower Souths, the majority of state legislators were planters. Yet these same planters owed their election to the popular vote. The white South was affected by the same democratic currents that swept northern politics between 1815 and 1860, and the newer states of the South usually entered the Union with democratic constitutions that included universal white manhood suffrage—the right of all adult white males to vote.

Although yeomen often voted for planters, they did not issue their elected representatives a blank check to govern as they pleased. During the 1830s and 1840s, Whig planters who favored banks faced strong opposition from Democratic yeomen who blamed banks for the Panic of 1837. On banking issues, nonslaveholders got their way often enough to nurture their belief that they ultimately controlled politics and that slaveholders could not block their goals.

Nevertheless, nonslaveholders had ample grounds for resenting slaveholders. The white carpenter who complained in 1849 that "unjust, oppressive, and degrading" competition from slave labor depressed his wages surely had a point. Between 1830 and 1860, slaveholders gained an increasing proportion of the South's wealth while declining as a proportion of its white population. The proportional size of the slaveholding class shrank from 36 percent of the white population

in 1831, to 31 percent in 1850, then 25 percent in 1860. A Louisiana editor warned in 1858 that "the present tendency of supply and demand is to concentrate all the slaves in the hands of the few, and thus excite the envy rather than cultivate the sympathy of the people." Some southerners began to support the congressional reopening of the African slave trade to reduce the price of slaves by increasing the supply, thus giving more whites a stake in the institution.

As the proposed **Virginia emancipation legislation** in 1831–1832 (see this chapter's introduction) attests, slaveholders had some reason to question the allegiance of nonslaveholders to the "peculiar institution" of slavery. In 1857, Hinton R. Helper's ***The Impending Crisis of the South*** revealed the persistence of white opposition to slavery by calling on nonslaveholders to abolish slavery in defense of their own self-interest. On balance, however, slavery did not create deep divisions between the South's slaveholders and nonslaveholders. Although antagonism to slavery flourished in parts of Virginia up to 1860, proposals for emancipation dropped from the state's political agenda after 1832. In Kentucky, calls for emancipation were revived in 1849 in a popular referendum. But the pro-emancipation forces went down to crushing defeat. Thereafter, the continuation of slavery ceased to be a political issue in Kentucky and elsewhere in the South.

The repeated defeat of pro-emancipation sentiment in the South raises a key question. The majority of white southerners were not slaveholders, so why did they generally accept the institution? To look ahead, why did so many of them fight ferociously during the Civil War in defense of an institution whose benefits they did not directly enjoy? First, some nonslaveholders hoped eventually to become slaveholders themselves. Second, most accepted the racial assumptions upon which slavery rested, which rendered even the lowest-ranking whites superior to black slaves. Nonslaveholders as well as slaveholders dreaded the likelihood that emancipation might encourage "impudent" blacks to entertain ideas of social equality with whites. Blacks might demand the right to sit next to whites in railroad cars and even make advances to white women. "Now suppose they [the slaves] was free," a white southerner told a northern journalist in the 1850s; "you see they'd all think themselves just as good as we; of course they would if they was free. Now just suppose you had a family of children, how would you like to hev a niggar steppin' up to your darter?" Slavery, in short, appealed to whites as a time-honored and foolproof way to enforce the social subordination of blacks and guarantee white supremacy.

Finally, all white southerners feared the chaos and violence they believed would be unleashed by emancipation. Where would former slaves go, and what would they do? Colonizing freed blacks in Africa was unrealistic, southerners concluded, but without

Virginia emancipation legislation

A debate by the Virginia legislature over whether to abolish slavery following Nat Turner's revolt; ended by narrow defeat and abandoned as support for emancipation dwindled.

The Impending Crisis of the South

Written by Hinton R. Helper, it called upon nonslaveholders to abolish slavery in their own interest, and revealed the persistence of a degree of white opposition to slavery.

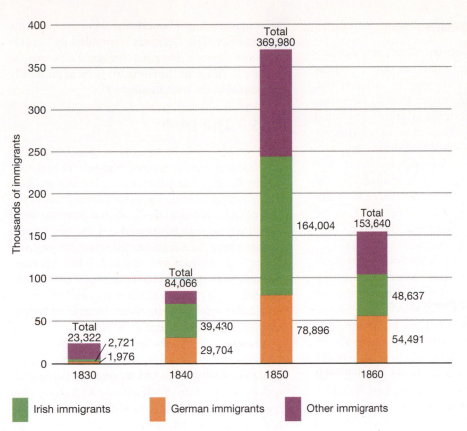

FIGURE 13.1 GERMAN, IRISH, AND TOTAL IMMIGRATION, 1830–1860 Irish and German immigrants led the more than tenfold growth of immigration between 1830 and 1860.

Source: *U.S. Bureau of the Census,* Historical Statistics of the United States, Colonial Times to 1970, Bicentennial Edition I *(Washington, DC, 1975).*

great plans for their future, all of which vanished quickly after landing," wrote a young German from Frankfurt in 1840. Immigrants quickly discovered that farming in America differed radically from European farming. Unlike the compact farming villages of Europe, American agricultural areas featured scattered farms. Although meeting occasionally for revivals or militia musters, American farmers lived in relative isolation, and they possessed an individualistic psychology that led them to speculate in land and to move frequently.

Clear patterns emerged amid the shocks and dislocations of immigration. Most of the Irish settlers before 1840 departed from Liverpool on sailing ships that carried English manufactures to eastern Canada and New England in return for timber. On arrival in America, few of these Irish had the capital to become farmers, so they crowded into the urban areas of New England, New York, Pennsylvania, and New Jersey, where they could more easily find jobs. In contrast, German emigrants usually left from continental ports on ships engaged in the cotton trade with New Orleans. Deterred from settling in the South by the presence of slavery, the oppressive climate, and the lack of economic opportunity, the Germans congregated in the upper Mississippi and Ohio valleys, especially in Illinois, Ohio, Wisconsin, and Missouri. Geographical concentration also

characterized most of the smaller groups of immigrants. More than half of the Norwegian immigrants, for example, settled in Wisconsin, where they typically became farmers.

Cities, rather than farms, attracted most antebellum immigrants. By 1860, **German and Irish immigrants** formed more than 60 percent of the population of St. Louis; nearly half the population of New York City, Chicago, Cincinnati, Milwaukee, Detroit, and San Francisco; and well over a third that of New Orleans, Baltimore, and Boston. These fast-growing cities created an intense demand for the labor of people with strong backs and a willingness to work for low wages. Irish construction gangs built the houses, new streets, and aqueducts that were changing the face of urban America and dug the canals and railroads that linked these cities. Urban areas provided the sort of community life that seemed lacking in farming settlements. Immigrant societies like the Friendly Sons of St. Patrick took root in cities and combined with associations like the Hibernian Society for the Relief of Emigrants from Ireland to welcome the newcomers.

> **German and Irish immigrants**
> The largest immigrant groups to come to the U.S. between 1840 and 1860. They formed more than 60 percent of the population of St. Louis; nearly half the population of New York City, Chicago, Cincinnati, Milwaukee, Detroit, and San Francisco; and well over a third of New Orleans, Baltimore, and Boston by 1860.

13-1.2 The Germans

In 1860, there was no German nation, only a collection of principalities and small kingdoms. German immigrants thought of themselves as Bavarians, Westphalians, or Saxons rather than as Germans. Moreover, the German immigrants included Catholics, Protestants, and Jews as well as a sprinkling of freethinkers who denounced the ritual, clergy, and doctrines of all religions. Although few in number, these critics were vehement in their attacks on the established churches. A pious Milwaukee Lutheran complained in 1860 that he could not drink a glass of beer in a saloon "without being angered by anti-Christian remarks or raillery against preachers."

German immigrants spanned a wide spectrum of social classes and occupations. Most were farmers, but a sizable minority were professionals, artisans, and tradespeople. Heinrich Steinweg, an obscure piano maker from Lower Saxony, arrived in New York City in 1851, anglicized his name to Henry Steinway, and in 1853 opened the firm of Steinway and Sons, which quickly achieved international acclaim for the quality of its pianos. Levi Strauss, a Jewish tailor from Bavaria, migrated to the United States in 1847. On hearing of the discovery of gold in California in 1848, Strauss gathered rolls of cloth and sailed for San Francisco. When a miner told him of the need for durable work trousers, Strauss fashioned a pair of overalls from canvas. To meet a quickly skyrocketing demand, he opened a factory in San Francisco; his cheap overalls, later known as blue jeans or Levi's, made him rich and famous.

For all their differences, the Germans were bound together by their common language, which induced recent immigrants to the United States to congregate in German neighborhoods. Even prosperous Germans bent on climbing the social ladder usually did so within their ethnic communities. Germans formed their own militia and fire companies, sponsored parochial schools in which German was the language of instruction, started German-language newspapers, and organized their own balls and singing groups. The range of voluntary associations among Germans was almost as broad as among native-born Americans.

Other factors beyond their common language brought unity to the German immigrants. Ironically, the Germans' diversity also promoted their solidarity. For example, because they supplied their own doctors, lawyers, teachers, journalists, merchants, artisans, and clergy, the Germans had little need to go outside their own neighborhoods. Native-born Americans simultaneously admired Germans' industriousness and resented German self-sufficiency, which they interpreted as clannishness. German refugee Moritz Busch complained that "the great mass of Anglo-Americans" held the Germans in contempt. The Germans responded by becoming more clannish. Their psychological separateness made it difficult for the Germans to be as politically influential as the Irish immigrants.

13-1.3 The Irish

Between 1815 and the mid-1820s, most Irish immigrants were Protestants, small landowners, and merchants in search of better economic opportunity. Many were drawn by enthusiastic veterans of the War of 1812, who had reported that America was a paradise filled with fertile land and abundant game, a place where "all a man wanted was a gun and sufficient ammunition to be able to live like a prince." From the mid-1820s to the mid-1840s, Irish immigrants became poorer and more frequently Catholic, primarily comprising tenant farmers whom Protestant landowners had evicted as "superfluous."

Protestant or Catholic, rich or poor, nearly 1 million Irish immigrants entered the United States between 1815 and 1844. Then, between 1845 and the early 1850s, blight destroyed harvest after harvest of Ireland's potatoes, virtually the only food of the peasantry, and created one of the most devastating famines in history. The Great Famine killed a million people. One landlord characterized the surviving tenants on his estate as no more than "famished and ghastly skeletons." To escape the ravages of famine, 1.8 million Irish migrated to the United States in the decade after 1845.

Overwhelmingly poor and Catholic, these newest Irish immigrants usually entered the workforce at or near the bottom. The popular image of Paddy with his pickax and Bridget the maid contained some truth. Irish men dug canals and railroad beds. Compared to other immigrant women, a high proportion of Irish women entered the workforce, if not as maids then often as textile workers. By the 1840s, Irish women were displacing native-born women in the textile mills of Lowell and Waltham. Poverty drove Irish women to work at an early age, and the outdoor, all-season work performed by their husbands turned many of them into working widows. Winifred Rooney became a nursemaid at the age of seven and an errand girl at eleven. She then learned needlework, a skill that helped her support her family after her husband's early death. Because the Irish usually married late, almost half the Irish immigrants were single, adult women, many of whom never married. For Irish women to become self-supporting was only natural.

Most Irish people lived a harsh existence. One immigrant described the life of the average Irish laborer in America as "despicable, humiliating, [and] slavish"; there was "no love for him—no protection

JOHN FALTER, THE FAMISHED Fearing being engulfed by a flood of Irish immigrants fleeing the potato famine in the mid-1840s, the United States insisted that some Irish be diverted to Canada. By the spring of 1847, the St. Lawrence River was filled with immigrants like this group disembarking at Grosse Isle in Canada. Some of these immigrants eventually made it to the United States. *(© Bettmann/CORBIS)*

of life—[he] can be shot down, run through, kicked, cuffed, spat upon—and no redress, but a response of 'served the damn son of an Irish b—right, damn him.' " Yet some Irish struggled up the social ladder. In Philadelphia, which had a more varied industrial base than Boston, Irish men made their way into iron foundries, where some became foremen and supervisors. Other Irish rose into the middle class by opening grocery and liquor stores.

Irish immigrants often conflicted with two quite different groups. The poorer Irish who dug canals and cellars, worked on the docks, took in laundry, and served white families competed directly with equally poor free blacks. This competition stirred up Irish animosity toward blacks and a hatred of abolitionists. At the same time, the Irish who secured skilled or semiskilled jobs clashed with native-born white workers.

13-1.4 Anti-Catholicism, Nativism, and Labor Protest

The surge of Irish immigration revived anti-Catholic fever, long a latent impulse among American Protestants. For example, in 1834 a mob, fueled by rumors

that a Catholic convent in Charlestown, Massachusetts, contained dungeons and torture chambers, burned the building to the ground. In 1835, the combative evangelical Protestant Lyman Beecher issued *A Plea for the West,* a tract in which he warned faithful Protestants of an alleged Catholic conspiracy to send immigrants to the West in sufficient numbers to dominate the region. A year later, the publication of Maria Monk's best-selling *Awful Disclosures of the Hotel Dieu Nunnery in Montreal* rekindled anti-Catholic hysteria. Although Maria Monk was actually a prostitute who had never lived in a convent, she professed to be a former nun. In her book, she described how the mother superior forced nuns to submit to the lustful advances of priests who entered the convent by a subterranean passage.

As Catholic immigration swelled in the 1840s, Protestants mounted a political counterattack. It took the form of nativist (anti-immigrant) societies with names like the American Republican party and the United Order of Americans. Although usually started as secret or semisecret fraternal orders, most of these societies developed political offshoots. One, the Order of the Star-Spangled Banner, would evolve by 1854 into the "Know-Nothing," or American, party and would become a major political force in the 1850s.

During the 1840s, however, nativist parties enjoyed only brief moments in the sun. These occurred mainly during flare-ups over local issues, such as whether students in predominantly Catholic neighborhoods should be allowed to use the Catholic Douay rather than Protestant King James version of the Bible for the scriptural readings that began each school day. In 1844, after the American Republican party won some offices in Philadelphia, fiery Protestant orators mounted soapboxes to denounce "popery," and Protestant mobs descended on Catholic neighborhoods. Before the militia quelled these "Bible Riots," thirty buildings lay in charred ruins, and at least sixteen people had been killed.

Nativism fed on an explosive mixture of fears and discontents. Protestants thought that their doctrine that each individual could interpret the Bible was more democratic than Catholicism, which made doctrine the province of the pope and bishops. In addition, at a time when the wages of native-born artisans and journeymen were depressed by the subdivision of tasks and by the aftermath of the Panic of 1837 (see Chapter 10), many Protestant workers concluded that Catholic immigrants, often desperately poor and willing to work for anything, were threats to their jobs.

Demand for land reform joined nativism as a proposed solution to workers' economic woes. Land reformers argued that workers' true interests could never be reconciled with an economic order in which factory workers sold their labor for wages and became "wage slaves." In 1844, English-born radical George Henry Evans organized the National Reform Association and rallied supporters with the slogan "Vote Yourself a Farm." Evans advanced neo-Jeffersonian plans for the establishment of "rural republican townships" composed of 160-acre plots for workers. Land reform offered little to factory operatives and wage-earning journeymen who completely lacked economic independence. In an age when a horse cost the average worker three months' pay and most factory workers dreaded "the horrors of wilderness life," the idea of solving industrial problems by resettling workers on farms seemed a pipe dream.

Labor unions appealed to workers left cold by the promises of land reformers. For example, desperately poor Irish immigrants, refugees from an agricultural society, believed they could gain more by unions and strikes than by plowing and planting. Even women workers organized unions in these years. The leader of a seamstresses' union

proclaimed, "Too long have we been bound down by tyrant employers."

Probably the most important development for workers in the 1840s was a state court decision. In ***Commonwealth v. Hunt*** (1842), the Massachusetts Supreme Judicial Court ruled that labor unions were not illegal monopolies that restrained trade. But because less than 1 percent of the workforce belonged to labor unions in the 1840s, this decision initially had little impact. Massachusetts employers brushed aside the *Commonwealth* decision, firing union agitators and replacing them with cheap immigrant labor. "Hundreds of honest laborers," a labor paper reported in 1848, "have been dismissed from employment in the manufactories of New England because they have been suspected of knowing their rights and daring to assert them." This repression effectively blunted demands for a ten-hour workday in an era when the twelve- or fourteen-hour day was typical.

Ethnic and religious tensions also split the working class during the 1830s and 1840s. Friction between native-born and immigrant workers inevitably became intertwined with the political divisions of the second party system.

13-1.5 Immigrant Politics

Few immigrants had ever cast a vote in an election prior to their arrival in America, and even fewer were refugees from political persecution. Political upheavals had erupted in Austria and several German states in the turbulent year of 1848 (the so-called Revolutions of 1848), but among the million German immigrants to the United States, only about ten thousand were political refugees, or "Forty-Eighters."

Once they had settled in the United States, however, many immigrants became politically active. They quickly found that urban political organizations would help them to find lodging and a job, in return for votes. Both the Irish and the Germans identified overwhelmingly with the Democratic Party. An obituary of 1837 that described a New Yorker as a "warm-hearted Irishman and an unflinching Democrat" could have been written of millions of other Irish. Similarly, the Germans became stalwart supporters of the Democrats in cities like Milwaukee and St. Louis.

Immigrants' fears about jobs partly explain their widespread support of the Democrats. Former president Andrew Jackson had given the Democratic Party an anti-aristocratic coloration, making the Democrats seem more sympathetic than the Whigs to the common people. In addition, antislavery was linked to the Whig party, and the Irish loathed abolitionism because they feared that freed slaves

---

nativism
Anti-immigrant policy.

Commonwealth v. Hunt
A court case in 1842 where the Massachusetts Supreme Judicial Court ruled that labor unions were not illegal monopolies that restrained trade.

would become their economic competitors. Moreover, the Whigs' moral and religious values seemed to threaten those of the Irish and Germans. Hearty-drinking Irish and German immigrants shunned temperance-crusading Whigs, many of whom were also rabid anti-Catholics. Even public-school reform, championed by the Whigs, was seen as a menace to the Catholicism of Irish children and as a threat to German language and culture.

Although liquor regulations and school laws were city or state concerns rather than federal responsibilities, the Democratic Party schooled immigrants in broad, national principles. It taught them to venerate George Washington, to revere Thomas Jefferson and Andrew Jackson, and to view "monied capitalists" as parasites who would tremble when the people spoke. It introduced immigrants to Democratic newspapers, Democratic picnics, and Democratic parades. The Democrats, by identifying their party with all that they thought best about the United States, helped give immigrants a sense of themselves as Americans. By the same token, the Democratic Party redirected immigrant political loyalties that often had been forged on local issues into the arena of national politics. During the 1830s, the party had persuaded immigrants that national measures like the Bank of the United States and the tariff, seemingly remote from their daily lives, were vital to them. Now, in the 1840s, the Democrats would try to convince immigrants that national expansion likewise advanced their interests.

13-2 The West and Beyond

What shaped U.S. settlement of the West in the mid-nineteenth century?

As late as 1840, Americans who referred to the West still meant the area between the Appalachian Mountains and the Mississippi River or just beyond. West of that lay the inhospitable Great Plains, a semiarid plateau with few trees. Winds sucked the moisture from the soil. Bands of nomadic Indians—including the Pawnees, Kiowas, and Sioux—roamed this territory and gained sustenance mainly from the buffalo. They ate its meat, wore its fur, and covered their dwellings with its hide. Aside from some well-watered sections of northern Missouri and eastern Kansas and Nebraska, the Great Plains presented would-be farmers with massive obstacles.

The formidable barrier of the Great Plains did not stop settlement of the West in the long run. Temporarily, however, it shifted public interest toward the verdant region lying beyond the Rockies, the Far West (see Map 13.1).

13-2.1 The Far West

By the Transcontinental (or Adams-Onís) Treaty of 1819, the United States had given up its claims to Texas west of the Sabine River and in return had received Spanish claims to the **Oregon country** north of California. Two years later, Mexico won its independence from Spain and took over all North American territory previously held by Spain. Then in 1824 and 1825, Russia abandoned its claims to Oregon south of 54°40′ (the southern boundary of Alaska). In 1827, the United States and Britain, each of which had claims to Oregon based on discovery and exploration, revived an agreement (originally signed in 1818) for joint occupation of the territory between 42° and 54°40′—a colossal area that contemporaries could describe no more precisely than the "North West Coast of America, Westward of the Stony [Rocky] Mountains" and that included all of modern Oregon, Washington, and Idaho as well as parts of present-day Wyoming, Montana, and Canada.

Despite these agreements and treaties, the vast Far West remained a remote and shadowy frontier during the 1820s. By 1820, the American line of settlement had reached only to Missouri, well over two thousand miles (counting detours for mountains) from the West Coast. El Paso on the Rio Grande and Taos in New Mexico lay, respectively, twelve hundred and fifteen hundred miles north of Mexico City. Britain, of course, was many thousands of miles from Oregon.

13-2.2 Far Western Trade

After sailing around South America and up the Pacific, early merchants had established American and British outposts on the West Coast. Between the late 1790s and the 1820s, for example, Boston merchants had built a thriving trade, exchanging eastern goods for western sea otter fur, cattle, hides, and tallow (rendered from cattle fat and used for making soap and candles). Between 1826 and 1828 alone, Boston traders took more than 6 million cattle hides out of California; in the otherwise undeveloped California economy, these hides, called "California bank-notes," served as the main medium of exchange. During the 1820s, the British Hudson's Bay Company developed a similar trade in Oregon and northern California.

The California trade created little friction with Mexico. Hispanic people born in California (called *Californios*) were as eager to buy as the traders were to sell. Traders who settled in California, like the Swiss-born John Sutter,

Oregon country
The land north of the forty-second parallel (the northern boundary of California), south of 54°40′ (the southern boundary of Alaska), and west of the Rocky Mountains.

Californios
People born in California.

MAP 13.1 **TRAILS TO THE WEST, 1840** By 1840, several trails carried pioneers from Missouri and Illinois to the West.

learned to speak Spanish and became assimilated into Mexican culture.

Farther south, trading links developed during the 1820s between St. Louis and Santa Fe along the famed **Santa Fe Trail**. Each spring, midwesterners loaded their wagons with tools, clothing, and household sundries and rumbled westward to Santa Fe, where they traded their merchandise for mules and New Mexican silver. Mexico welcomed this trade. By the 1830s, more than half the goods entering New Mexico by the Santa Fe Trail trickled into the mineral-rich interior provinces of Mexico, with the result that the Mexican silver peso, which midwestern traders brought back with them, quickly became the principal medium of exchange in Missouri.

The profitability of the beaver trade also prompted Americans to venture west from St. Louis to trap beaver in what is today western Colorado and eastern Utah. There they competed with agents of the Hudson's Bay Company. In

1825, on the Green River in Mexican territory, the St. Louis-based trader William Ashley inaugurated an annual encampment where traders exchanged beaver pelts for supplies, thereby saving themselves the trip to St. Louis. Although silk hats had become more fashionable than beaver hats by 1854, over a half-million beaver pelts were auctioned off in London alone that year.

For the most part, American traders and trappers operating on the northern Mexican frontier in the 1820s and 1830s posed more of a threat to the beaver than to Mexico's provinces. The Mexican people of California and New Mexico depended on the American trade for manufactured goods, and Mexican officials in both provinces relied on customs duties to support their governments. In New Mexico, the government often had to await the arrival of the annual caravan of traders from St. Louis before it could pay its officials and soldiers.

Although the relations between Mexicans and Americans were mutually beneficial during the 1820s, the potential for conflict was always present.

Santa Fe Trail
Trading route from St. Louis to Santa Fe.

SUNSET: CALIFORNIA SCENERY, BY ALBERT BIERSTADT German-born, Bierstadt became famous and wealthy for his paintings of the western mountains, which sacrificed accuracy for awe and majesty. *(Library of Congress Prints and Photographs Division [LC-DIG-pga-07915])*

Spanish-speaking, Roman Catholic, and accustomed to a more hierarchical society, the Mexicans formed a striking contrast to the largely Protestant, individualistic Americans. Furthermore, American traders returned with glowing reports of the climate and fertility of Mexico's northern provinces. By the 1820s, American settlers were already moving into eastern Texas. At the same time, the ties that bound the central government of Mexico to its northern frontier provinces were starting to fray.

13-2.3 Mexican Government in the Far West and the Texas Revolution of 1836

Spain, and later Mexico, recognized that the key to controlling the frontier provinces lay in promoting their settlement by civilized Hispanic people—Spaniards, Mexicans, and Indians who had embraced Catholicism and agriculture. The key instruments of Spain's expansion on the frontier had long been the Spanish missions. Paid by the government, the Franciscan priests who staffed the missions endeavored to convert Native Americans and settle them as farmers on mission lands. To protect the missions, the Spanish often had constructed forts, or presidios, near them. San Francisco was the site of a mission and a presidio founded in 1776 and did not develop as a town until the 1830s.

Dealt a blow by the successful struggle for Mexican independence, Spain's system of missions began to decline in the late 1820s. The Mexican government gradually "secularized" the missions by distributing their lands to ambitious government officials and private ranchers who turned the mission Indians into forced laborers. As many Native Americans fled the missions, returned to their nomadic ways, and joined with Indians who had always resisted the missions, lawlessness surged on the Mexican frontier, and few Mexicans ventured into the undeveloped territory.

To bring in settlers and to gain protection against Indian attacks, in 1824 the Mexican government began to encourage Americans to settle in the eastern part of the Mexican state known as Coahuila-Texas by bestowing generous land grants on agents known as *empresarios* to recruit American settlers. Initially, most Americans, like the *empresario* Stephen F. Austin, were content to live in Texas as naturalized Mexican citizens. But trouble brewed quickly. Most of the American settlers were southern farmers, often slaveholders. Having emancipated its own slaves in 1829, Mexico closed Texas to further American immigration in 1830 and forbade the introduction of more slaves. But the Americans, white and black, kept coming, and in 1834 Austin secured repeal of the 1830 prohibition on American immigration. Two years later, Mexican general Manuel Mier y Téran ran a sword through his heart

ENTIRRO DE UN ANGEL (FUNERAL OF AN ANGEL), BY THEODORE GENTILZ Protestant Americans who ventured into Texas came upon a Hispanic culture unlike anything they had seen. Here, a San Antonio procession follows the coffin of a baptized infant, who, in Catholic belief, will become an angel in heaven. *(Daughters of the Republic of Texas Library, Gift of the Tanaguana Society)*

in despair over Mexico's inability to stem and control the American advance. By 1836, Texas contained some thirty thousand white Americans, five thousand black slaves, and four thousand Mexicans.

As American immigration swelled, Mexican politics (which Austin compared to the country's volcanic geology) grew increasingly unstable. In 1834, Mexican president Antonio López de Santa Anna instituted a policy of restricting the powers of the regimes in Coahuila-Texas and other Mexican states. His actions ignited a series of rebellions in those regions, the most important of which became known as the Texas Revolution. Alarmed by Santa Anna's brutality, when Santa Anna invaded Texas in the fall of 1835, Austin cast his lot with the more radical Americans who wanted independence.

Santa Anna's army initially met with success. In February 1836, his force of four thousand men laid siege to San Antonio, whose two hundred defenders, including some *Tejanos*,

Alamo
An abandoned mission where 200 defenders of San Antonio retreated in February 1836 after Santa Anna's army of 4,000 men defeated them.

Sam Houston
Military leader and president of the Republic of Texas who defeated Santa Anna's men in 15 minutes.

retreated into an abandoned mission, the **Alamo**. On March 6, four days after Texas had declared its independence, the defenders of the Alamo were overwhelmed by Mexican troops. Most were killed in the final assault. A few, including famed frontiersman Davy Crockett, surrendered. Crockett then was executed on Santa Anna's orders. A few weeks later, Mexican troops massacred some 350 prisoners taken from an American settlement at Goliad.

Meanwhile, the Texans had formed an army, with **Sam Houston** as their leader. A giant man who wore leopard-skin vests, Houston retreated east to pick up recruits (mostly Americans who crossed the border to fight Santa Anna). Once reinforced, Houston turned and surprised the complacent Mexicans at San Jacinto, just east of what is now the city of Houston. Shouting "Remember the Alamo," Houston's army of eight hundred tore through the Mexican lines, killing nearly half of Santa Anna's men in fifteen minutes and taking Santa Anna prisoner. Houston then forced Santa Anna to sign a treaty (which the Mexican government never ratified) recognizing the independence of Texas (see Map 13.2).

13-2.4 The Overland Trail to California, New Mexico, and Oregon

Before 1840, California and New Mexico, both less accessible than Texas, exerted no more than a mild attraction for American settlers. Only a few hundred Americans resided in New Mexico in 1840 and perhaps four hundred in California. A contemporary observed that the Americans living in California and New Mexico "are scattered throughout the whole Mexican population, and most of them have Spanish wives. . . . They live in every respect like the Spanish."

Yet the beginnings of change were already evident. During the 1840s, Americans streamed into the Sacramento Valley, welcomed by California's Hispanic population as a way to encourage economic development and lured by favorable reports of the region. One tongue-in-cheek story told of a 250-year-old man who had to leave the idyllic region in order to die. For these land-hungry settlers, no sacrifice seemed too great if it led to California.

To the north, Oregon's abundant farmland beckoned settlers from the Mississippi Valley. During the 1830s, missionaries like the Methodist Jason Lee moved into Oregon's Willamette Valley, and by 1840 the area contained some five hundred Americans. Enthusiastic reports sent back by Lee piqued interest about Oregon. An orator in Missouri described Oregon as a "pioneer's paradise" where "the pigs are running around under the great acorn trees, round and fat and already cooked, with knives and forks sticking in them so that you can cut off a slice whenever you are hungry." To some, Oregon seemed even more attractive than California, especially because the joint American–British occupation seemed to herald better prospects for eventual U.S. annexation than California's.

Whether bound for California or Oregon, emigrants faced a four-month journey across terrain little known in reality but vividly depicted in fiction as an Indian killing ground. Assuming that they would have to fight their way across the Plains, settlers prepared for the trip by buying enough guns for an army from merchants in the rival jump-off towns of Independence and St. Joseph, Missouri. In reality, the pioneers were more likely to shoot themselves or each other by accident than to be shot by the usually cooperative Indians, and much more likely to be scalped by the inflated prices charged by merchants in Independence or "St. Joe."

Once embarked, the emigrants faced new hardships and hazards: kicks from mules, oxen that collapsed from thirst, overloaded wagons that broke down. Trails were difficult to follow—at least

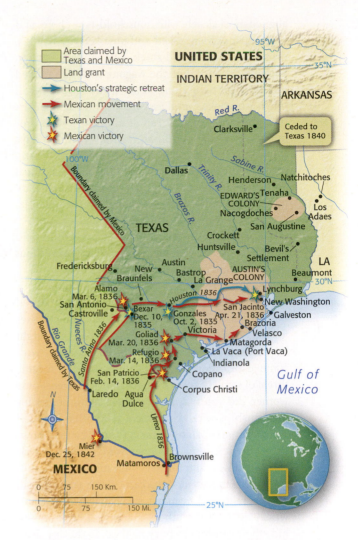

MAP 13.2 MAJOR BATTLES IN THE TEXAS REVOLUTION, 1835–1836 Sam Houston's victory at San Jacinto was the decisive action of the war and avenged the massacres at the Alamo and Goliad.

until they became littered by the debris of broken wagons and by the bleached bones of oxen. Guidebooks to help emigrants chart their course were more like guessbooks. The Donner party, which set out from Illinois in 1846, lost so much time following the advice of one such book that its members became snowbound in the High Sierras and reached California only after its survivors had turned to cannibalism.

Emigrants responded to the challenges of the overland trails by close cooperation with one another, traveling in huge wagon trains rather than alone. The earliest migrants tended to travel in family groups and sought to retain the gender relationships and ideology of true womanhood that marked their lives in the East (see Chapter 9). Men typically made the decision about whether or not to make the journey, and once on the trail, men performed the outside work while women did tasks that aligned most closely with household-type chores and childrearing. Men yoked and unyoked the wagons, drove the wagons and stock, and hunted. Women packed and unpacked the wagons each day, milked the cows brought along to stock the new farms in the West, cooked, and assisted with the childbirths that occurred on the trail at about the same frequency as in the nation as a whole. Women's days were typically far longer than their spouses', rising before their families to prepare the morning meal and continuing well into the evening getting ready for the next day's journey. Aside from the potential accidents—especially for women and children—posed by wagon travel, the journey proved stressful in other ways, as women completed chores without the household technology they once knew.

As whites trekked west, they did so across lands often occupied by Native Americans, which produced mutual fears and tensions, as well as distinct losses for Indian peoples. Migrants worried that they might be attacked by Indians, while Indians feared—with some justification—that white men posed a specific threat of sexual exploitation for native women. Some women did voluntarily leave their communities for relationships with white men, who often later left them to marry white women. Once deserted, however, Native American women were not always welcomed back to their former communities. In another example, Sarah Winnemucca, a Paiute woman, told of rumors that white men were slaughtering Indians, which led fearful mothers—including her own—to hide their children by burying them in the dirt, leaving only their heads above ground, camouflaged by sage brush. Native Americans suffered in other ways, too, from the spread of white illnesses to the increased starvation caused by the disappearance of the buffalo and other food shortages that accompanied American settlement. Some tried to resist white encroachment by attempting to charge passersby a toll.

Between 1840 and 1848, an estimated 11,500 emigrants followed an overland trail to Oregon, and some 2,700 reached California. Such numbers made a difference, for the British did not settle Oregon at all, and the Mexican population in California was small and scattered. By 1845, California clung to Mexico by the thinnest of threads. The territory's Hispanic population, the *Californios*, felt little allegiance to Mexico, which they contemptuously referred to as the "other shore." Some *Californios* wanted independence from Mexico; others looked to the day when California might become a protectorate of Britain or perhaps even France. But these *Californios*, with their shaky allegiances, now faced a growing number of American settlers with definite political allegiances.

13-3 The Politics of Expansion, 1840–1846

How did national politics influence debates and actions regarding westward expansion?

Westward expansion prompted the question of whether the United States should annex the independent Texas republic. In the mid-1840s, the Texas-annexation issue generated the kind of political passions that banking questions had ignited in the 1830s and became entangled with equally unsettling issues relating to California, New Mexico, and Oregon. Between 1846 and 1848, a war with Mexico and a dramatic confrontation with Britain settled all these questions on terms favorable to the United States.

At the start of the 1840s, western issues received little attention in a nation concerned with matters relating to economic recovery—notably, banking, the tariff, and internal improvements. Only after politicians failed to address the economic issues coherently did opportunistic leaders thrust issues relating to expansion to the top of the political agenda.

13-3.1 The Whig Ascendancy

The election of 1840 brought Whig candidate William Henry Harrison to the presidency and installed Whig majorities in both houses of Congress. The Whigs had proposed to replace Van Buren's darling, the Independent Treasury (see Chapter 10), with a national "fiscal agent," which, like the defunct Bank of the United States, would be a private corporation chartered by Congress and charged with regulating the currency. The Whigs also favored a revised tariff that would increase government revenues but remain low enough to permit the importation of foreign goods. According to the Whig plan, the states would then receive tariff-generated revenues for internal improvements.

The Whig agenda might have breezed into law. But Harrison died after one month in office, and his successor, Vice President **John Tyler**, an upper-crust Virginian added to the ticket in 1840 for his southern appeal, assumed the presidency. A former Democrat, Tyler had broken with Jackson over nullification, but he favored the Democratic philosophy of states' rights. As president, he repeatedly vetoed Whig proposals, including a bill to create a new national bank.

Tyler also played havoc with Whig tariff policy. The Compromise Tariff of 1833 had provided for a gradual scaling-down of tariff duties, until none was to exceed 20 percent by 1842. Amid the depression of the early 1840s, however, the provision for a 20 percent maximum tariff appeared too low to generate revenue. Without revenue, the Whigs would have no money to distribute among the states for internal improvements and no program with national appeal. In response, the Whig congressional majority passed two bills in the summer of 1842 that simultaneously postponed the final reduction of tariffs to 20 percent and ordered distribution to the states to proceed. Tyler promptly vetoed both bills. Tyler's mounting vetoes infuriated Whig leadership. "Again has the imbecile, into whose hands accident has placed the power, vetoed a bill passed by a majority of those legally authorized to pass it," screamed the *Daily Richmond Whig*. Some Whigs talked of impeaching Tyler. Finally, in August, needing revenue to run the government, Tyler signed a new bill that maintained some tariffs above 20 percent but abandoned distribution to the states.

Tyler's erratic course confounded and disrupted his party. By maintaining some tariffs above 20 percent, the tariff of 1842 satisfied northern manufacturers, but by abandoning distribution, it infuriated many southerners and westerners. In the congressional elections of 1842, the Whigs paid a heavy price for failing to enact their program. Although retaining a slim majority in the Senate, they lost control of the House to the Democrats. Now the nation had one party in control of the Senate, its rival in control of the House, and a president who appeared to belong to neither party.

13-3.2 Tyler and the Annexation of Texas

Although disowned by his party, Tyler ardently desired a second term as president. Domestic issues offered him little hope of building a popular following, but foreign policy was another matter. In 1842, Tyler's secretary of state, Daniel Webster, concluded a treaty with Great Britain, represented by Lord Ashburton, that settled a long-festering dispute over the boundary between Maine and the Canadian province of New Brunswick. Awarding more than half of the disputed territory to the United States, the Webster-Ashburton Treaty was popular in the North. Tyler reasoned that if he could now arrange for the **annexation of Texas**, he would build a national following.

The issue of slavery, however, clouded every discussion of Texas. Antislavery northerners viewed proposals to annex Texas as part of an elaborate southern conspiracy to extend slavery because Texas would certainly enter the Union as a slave state. In fact, some southerners dreamed of creating four or five slave states from Texas' vast area.

Nevertheless, in the summer of 1843, Tyler launched a propaganda campaign for Texas annexation. He alleged that Britain had designs on Texas,

which Americans would be prudent to forestall. Tyler's campaign was fed by reports from his unofficial agent in London, Duff Green, a protégé of John C. Calhoun and a man whom John Quincy Adams contemptuously dismissed as an "ambassador of slavery." Green assured Tyler that, as a prelude to undermining slavery in the United States, the British would pressure Mexico to recognize the independence of Texas in return for the abolition of slavery there. Calhoun, who became Tyler's secretary of state early in 1844, embroidered these reports with fanciful theories about British plans to use abolition as a way to destroy rice, sugar, and cotton production in the United States and gain for itself a monopoly on all three staples.

In the spring of 1844, Calhoun and Tyler submitted for Senate ratification a treaty annexing Texas to the United States. Among the supporting documents accompanying the treaty was a letter from Calhoun to the British minister in Washington, defending slavery as beneficial to blacks, the only way to protect them from "vice and pauperism." Abolitionists now had evidence that the annexation of Texas was linked to a conspiracy to extend slavery. Both Martin Van Buren, the leading northern Democrat, and Henry Clay, the most powerful Whig, came out against immediate annexation on the grounds that annexation would provoke the kind of sectional conflict that each had sought to bury, and the treaty went down to crushing defeat in the Senate. However decisive it appeared, this vote only postponed the final decision on annexation to the upcoming election of 1844.

13-3.3 The Election of 1844

Tyler's ineptitude turned the presidential campaign into a free-for-all. The president lacked a base in either party, and after testing the waters as an independent, he was forced to drop out of the race.

Henry Clay had a secure grip on the Whig nomination. Martin Van Buren appeared to have an equally firm grasp on the Democratic nomination, but the issue of Texas annexation split his party. Trying to appease all shades of opinion within his party, Van Buren stated that he would abide by whatever Congress might decide on the annexation issue. Van Buren's attempt to evade the issue succeeded only in alienating the modest number of northern annexationists, led by Michigan's former governor Lewis Cass, and the much larger group of southern annexationists. At the Democratic convention, Van Buren and Cass effectively blocked each other's nomination. The resulting deadlock was broken by the nomination of **James K. Polk** of

annexation of Texas
A foreign policy initiative that ignited debate between pro-slaveryites and abolitionists, eroded Tyler's base of support, and became the sole issue of the election of 1844.

James K. Polk
The first "dark-horse" presidential nominee in American history and a supporter of immediate annexation.

JAMES K. POLK Lacking charm, Polk bored even his friends, but few presidents could match his record of acquiring land for the United States. *(James K. Polk Memorial Association, Columbia, Tennessee)*

nothing against annexation as long as it would not disrupt sectional harmony. In September 1844, he came out against annexation. Clay's shifts on annexation alienated his southern supporters and prompted a small but influential body of northern antislavery Whigs to desert to the Liberty party, which had been organized in 1840. Devoted to the abolition of slavery by political action, the Liberty party nominated Ohio's James G. Birney for the presidency.

Annexation was not the sole issue of the campaign. The Whigs infuriated Catholic immigrant voters by nominating Theodore Frelinghuysen as Clay's running mate. A supporter of temperance and other Protestant causes, Frelinghuysen confirmed the image of the Whigs as the orthodox Protestant party and roused the largely Catholic foreign-born voters to turn out in large numbers for the Democrats.

On the eve of the election in New York City, so many Irish marched to the courthouse to be qualified for voting that the windows had to be left open for people to get in and out. "Ireland has reconquered the country which England lost," an embittered Whig moaned. Polk won the electoral vote 170 to 105, but his margin in the popular vote was only 38,000 out of 2.6 million votes cast, and he lost his own state of Tennessee by 113 votes (see Map 13.3). A shift of six thousand votes in New York, where the immigrant vote and Whig defections to the Liberty party had hurt Clay, would have given Clay the state and the presidency.

13-3.4 Manifest Destiny, 1845

The election of 1844 demonstrated that the annexation of Texas had more national support than Clay had realized. The surging popular sentiment

Tennessee, the first "dark-horse" presidential nominee in American history and a supporter of immediate annexation .

Jeering "Who is James K. Polk?" the Whigs derided the nomination. Polk was little known outside the South, and he had lost successive elections for the governorship of Tennessee. Yet Polk persuaded many northerners that annexation of Texas would benefit them. Conjuring an imaginative scenario, Polk and his supporters argued that if Britain succeeded in abolishing slavery in Texas, slavery would not be able to move westward; racial tensions in existing slave states would intensify; and the chances of a race war, which might spill over into the North, would increase. However far-fetched, this argument played effectively on northern racial phobias and helped Polk detach annexation from Calhoun's narrow, prosouthern defense of it.

In contrast to the Democrats, whose position was clear, Clay kept muddying the waters. First he told his followers he had

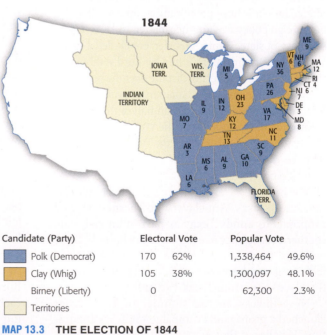

Candidate (Party)	Electoral Vote		Popular Vote	
Polk (Democrat)	170	62%	1,338,464	49.6%
Clay (Whig)	105	38%	1,300,097	48.1%
Birney (Liberty)	0		62,300	2.3%
Territories				

MAP 13.3 THE ELECTION OF 1844

for expansion that made the underdog Polk rather than Clay the man of the hour reflected a growing conviction among the people that America's natural destiny was to expand into Texas and all the way to the Pacific Ocean.

Expansionists emphasized extending the "area of freedom" and talked of "repelling the contaminating proximity of monarchies upon the soil that we have consecrated to the rights of man." For young Americans like Walt Whitman, such restless expansionism knew few limits. "The more we reflect upon annexation as involving a part of Mexico, the more do doubts and obstacles resolve themselves away," Whitman wrote. "Then there is California, on the way to which lovely tract lies Santa Fe; how long a time will elapse before they shine as two new stars in our mighty firmament?"

Americans awaited only a phrase to capture this ebullient spirit. In 1845, John L. O'Sullivan, a New York Democratic journalist, supplied that phrase when he wrote of "our **manifest destiny** to overspread and to possess the whole of the continent which Providence has given us for the development of the great experiment of liberty and federated self-government entrusted to us."

Advocates of Manifest Destiny used lofty language and invoked God and Nature to sanction expansion. Inasmuch as most proponents of Manifest Destiny were Democrats who favored annexing Texas, northern Whigs frequently dismissed Manifest Destiny as a smoke screen aimed at concealing the evil intent of expanding slavery. In reality, many expansionists were neither supporters of slavery nor zealous annexationists. Most had their eyes not on Texas but on Oregon and California. Despite their flowery phrases, these expansionists rested their case on hard material calculations. Blaming the post-1837 depression on the failure of the United States to acquire markets for its agricultural surplus, they saw the acquisition of Oregon and California as solutions. A Missouri Democrat observed that "the ports of Asia are as convenient to Oregon as the ports of Europe are to the eastern slope of our confederacy, with an infinitely better ocean for navigation." An Alabama Democrat praised California's "safe and capacious harbors," which, he assured, "invite to their bosoms the rich commerce of the East."

Expansionists desired more than profitable trade routes, however. At the heart of their thinking lay an impulse to preserve the predominantly agricultural character of the American people and thereby to safeguard democracy. Fundamentally, most expansionists were Jeffersonians. They equated cities and factories with class strife. After a tour of New England mill towns in 1842, John L. O'Sullivan warned Americans that should they fail to encourage alternatives to factories, the United States would sink to the level of Britain, a nation that the ardent

Democratic expansionist James Gordon Bennett described as a land of "bloated wealth" and "terrible misery."

Most Democratic expansionists linked the acquisition of new territory to their party's policies of low tariffs and decentralized banking. Where tariffs and banks tended to "favor and foster the factory system," expansion would provide farmers with land and with access to foreign markets for their produce. The acquisition of California and Oregon would provide enough land and harbors to sustain not only the 20 million Americans of 1845 but the 100 million that some expansionists projected for 1900 and the 250 million that O'Sullivan predicted for 1945.

Trumpeted by the penny press, this message made sense to the laboring poor of America's cities, many of them Irish immigrants. Expansion would open economic opportunities for the common people and thwart British plans to free American slaves, whom the poor viewed as potential competitors for scarce jobs.

Expansionism drew ideas from Thomas Jefferson, John Quincy Adams, and other leaders of the early Republic who had proclaimed the American people's right to displace both "uncivilized" and European people from the path of their westward movement. Early expansionists, however, had feared that overexpansion might create an ungovernable empire. Jefferson, for example, had proposed an indefinite restriction on the settlement of Louisiana. In contrast, the expansionists of the 1840s, citing the virtues of the telegraph and the railroad, believed that the problem of distance had been "literally annihilated."

13-3.5 Polk and Oregon

The growing spirit of Manifest Destiny escalated the issue of Oregon. To soften northern criticism of the still-pending annexation of Texas, the Democrats had included in their 1844 platform the assertion that American title "to the whole of the Territory of Oregon is clear and unquestionable." Taken literally, this statement, which Polk later repeated, pressed an unprecedented American claim to the entire Oregon Territory between California and 54°40′, the southern boundary of Alaska.

Polk's objectives in Oregon were more subtle than his language. He knew that the United States could never obtain all of Oregon without a war with Britain, and he wanted to avoid that. He proposed to use the threat of hostilities to persuade the British to accept what they had repeatedly rejected in the past—a division of Oregon at the forty-ninth parallel. Such a

> **manifest destiny**
> Coined by journalist John L. O'Sullivan, it was the belief that it was the United States' mission to expand its territorial and social reach.

division, extending the existing boundary between the United States and Canada from the Rockies to the Pacific, would give the United States both the excellent deep-water harbors of Puget Sound and the southern tip of British-controlled Vancouver Island. For their part, the British had long held out for a division along the Columbia River, which entered the Pacific Ocean far south of the forty-ninth parallel (see Map 13.4).

Polk's position aroused American support for acquiring the whole territory. Mass meetings adopted such resolutions as "We are all for Oregon, and *all* Oregon in the West" and "The Whole or None!" Furthermore, each passing year brought new American settlers into Oregon. John Quincy Adams, no supporter of the annexation of Texas or the 54°40′ boundary for Oregon, believed that the American settlements gave the United States a far more reasonable claim to Oregon than mere exploration and discovery gave the British. The United States, not Britain, Adams preached, was the nation bound "to make the wilderness blossom as the rose, to establish laws, to increase, multiply, and subdue the earth," all "at the first behest of God Almighty."

MAP 13.4 OREGON BOUNDARY DISPUTE Although demanding that Britain cede the entire Oregon Territory south of 54°40′, the United States settled for a compromise at the forty-ninth parallel.

In April 1846, Polk forced the issue by notifying Britain that the United States was terminating joint British-American occupation of Oregon. In effect, his message was that Britain could either go to war over American claims to 54°40′—or negotiate. Britain chose to negotiate. Although the British raged against "that ill-regulated, overbearing, and aggressive spirit of American democracy," they had too many domestic and foreign problems to welcome a war over what Lord Aberdeen, the British foreign secretary, dismissed as "a few miles of pine swamp." The ensuing treaty provided for a division at the forty-ninth parallel, with some modifications. Britain retained all of Vancouver Island as well as navigation rights on the Columbia River. On June 15, 1846, the Senate ratified the treaty, stipulating that Britain's navigation rights on the Columbia were merely temporary.

13-4 The U.S. War with Mexico and Its Aftermath, 1846–1848

What were the short- and long-term implications of the U.S. war with Mexico?

Between 1846 and 1848, the United States successfully fought a war with Mexico that led Mexico to renounce all claims to Texas and to cede its provinces of New Mexico and California to the United States. Many Americans rejoiced in the stunning victory. But some recognized that deep divisions over the status of slavery in New Mexico and California boded ill for their nation's future.

13-4.1 The Origins of the U.S. War with Mexico

While Polk was challenging Britain over Oregon, the United States and Mexico moved toward war. The impending conflict had both remote and immediate causes. One long-standing grievance lay in the failure of the Mexican government to pay some $2 million in debts owed to American citizens. Bitter memories of the Alamo and the Goliad massacre reinforced American loathing of Mexico. Above all, the issue of Texas poisoned relations between the two nations. Mexico still hoped to regain Texas or at least to keep it independent of the United States. Beset by internal strife—Mexico's presidency changed hands twenty times between 1829 and 1844—Mexico feared that, once in control of Texas, the "Colossus of the North" might seize other provinces, perhaps even Mexico itself, and treat Mexicans much as it treated its slaves.

Polk's election increased the strength of the pro-annexationists because his campaign had persuaded many northerners that enfolding Texas would bring national benefits. In February 1845, both houses of Congress responded to popular sentiment by passing a resolution annexing Texas. Texans, however, balked, in part because some feared that union with the United States would provoke a Mexican invasion and war on Texas soil.

Confronted by Texan timidity and Mexican belligerence, Polk moved on two fronts. To sweeten the pot for the Texans, he supported their claim that the Rio Grande constituted Texas's southern boundary, despite Mexico's contention that the Nueces River, a hundred miles north of the Rio Grande, bounded Texas. The area between the Nueces and the Rio Grande was largely uninhabited, but the stakes were high. Although only a hundred miles south of the Nueces at its mouth on the Gulf of Mexico, the Rio Grande meandered west and then north for nearly two thousand miles and encompassed a huge territory, including part of modern New Mexico. The Texas that Polk proposed to annex thus encompassed far more land than the Texas that had gained independence from Mexico in 1836. On July 4, 1845, reassured by Polk's largesse, a Texas convention overwhelmingly voted to accept annexation. In response to Mexican war preparations, Polk then made a second move, ordering American troops under General **Zachary Taylor** to the edge of the disputed territory. Taylor took up a position at Corpus Christi, a tiny Texas outpost situated just south of the Nueces and hence in territory still claimed by Mexico.

One reason for Polk's insistence on the Rio Grande boundary for Texas was to provoke a war with Mexico. Then, the United States could seize California for its fine harbors of San Diego and San Francisco. In fact, Polk had entered the White House with the firm intention of extending American control over California. By the summer of 1845, his followers were openly proclaiming that, if Mexico went to war with the United States over Texas, "the road to California will be open to us." Reports from American agents persuaded Polk that California might be acquired by the same methods as Texas: revolution followed by annexation.

Continued turmoil in Mexico further complicated the situation. In early 1845, a new Mexican government agreed to negotiate with the United States, and Polk, locked into a war of words with Britain over Oregon, decided to give negotiations a chance. In November 1845, he dispatched John Slidell to Mexico City with instructions to gain Mexican recognition of the annexation of Texas

with the Rio Grande border. In exchange, the U.S. government would assume the debt owed by Mexico to American citizens. Polk also authorized Slidell to offer up to $25 million for California and New Mexico. But by the time Slidell reached Mexico City, the government there had become too weak to make concessions to the United States, and its head, General José Herrera, refused to receive Slidell. Polk then ordered Taylor to move southward to the Rio Grande, hoping to provoke a Mexican attack and unite the American people behind war.

The Mexican government dawdled. Polk was about to send a war message to Congress when word finally arrived that Mexican forces had crossed the Rio Grande and ambushed two companies of Taylor's troops. Now the prowar press had its martyrs. *"American blood has been shed on American soil!"* one of Polk's followers proclaimed. On May 11, Polk informed Congress that war "exists by the act of Mexico herself" and called for $10 million to fight the war.

Polk's disarming assertion that the United States was already at war provoked furious opposition in Congress, where antislavery Whigs protested the president's high-handedness. For one thing, the Mexican attack on Taylor's troops had occurred on land never before claimed by the United States. By announcing that war already existed, moreover, Polk seemed to be undercutting Congress's power to declare war and using a mere border incident as a pretext to acquire more slave territory. The pro-Whig *New York Tribune* warned its readers that Polk was "precipitating you into a fathomless abyss of crime and calamity." Antislavery poet James Russell Lowell of Massachusetts wrote of the Polk Democrats,

They just want this Californy
So's to lug new slave-states in
To abuse ye, an' to scorn ye,
An' to plunder ye like sin.

But Polk had maneuvered the Whigs into a corner. Few Whigs could forget that the Federalists' opposition to the War of 1812 had wrecked the Federalist Party, and few wanted to appear unpatriotic by refusing to support Taylor's beleaguered troops. Swallowing their outrage, most Whigs backed appropriations for war against Mexico.

Polk's single-minded pursuit of his goals had prevailed. A humorless, austere man who banned dancing and liquor at White House receptions, Polk inspired little personal warmth. But he had clear objectives and pursued them unflinchingly. At every point, he had encountered opposition on the home front: from Whigs who saw him as a reckless adventurer; from northerners of both parties opposed to any

Zachary Taylor
Victorious military leader in the Mexican-American war who became the president of the United States in 1848. He was a member of the Whig Party.

expansion of slavery; and from John C. Calhoun, who despised Polk for his high-handedness and fretted that a war with Britain would strip the South of its market for cotton. Even freshman Congressman Abraham Lincoln challenged the war, delivering what became known as his "Spot Resolutions" to Congress in 1847. In them, he questioned Polk's claim that the land where American blood had been shed actually belonged to the U.S. at that time. Yet Polk triumphed over all opposition, in part because of his opponents' fragmentation, in part because of expansion's popular appeal, and in part because of the weakness of his foreign antagonists. Reluctant to fight over Oregon, Britain had negotiated. Too weak to negotiate, Mexico chose to fight over territory that it had already lost (Texas) and for territories over which its hold was feeble (California and New Mexico). And Congress failed to act on Lincoln's resolutions.

13-4.2 The U.S. War with Mexico

Most European observers expected Mexico to win the war. Its regular army was four times the size of the American forces, and it was fighting on home ground. The United States, having botched its one previous attempt to invade a foreign nation—Canada in 1812—now had to sustain offensive operations in an area remote from American settlements. American expansionists, however, hardly expected the Mexicans to fight at all. Racism and arrogance persuaded many Americans that the Mexicans, degraded by their mixed Spanish and Indian population, were "as sure to melt away at the approach of [American] energy and enterprise as snow before a southern sun."

In fact, the Mexicans fought bravely and stubbornly, although unsuccessfully. In May 1846, Taylor, "Old Rough and Ready," routed the Mexican army in Texas and pursued it across the Rio Grande, eventually capturing the major city of Monterrey. War enthusiasm surged in the United States. Recruiting posters blared, "Here's to old Zach! Glorious Times! Roast Beef, Ice Cream, and Three Months' Advance." Taylor's conspicuously ordinary manner—he went into battle wearing a straw hat and a plain brown coat—endeared him to the public, which kicked up its heels in celebration to the "Rough and Ready Polka" and the "General Taylor Quick Step."

After taking Monterrey, Taylor, starved for supplies, halted and granted Mexico an eight-week armistice. Eager to undercut Taylor's popularity—the Whigs were already touting him as a presidential candidate—Polk stripped him of half his forces and reassigned them to General Winfield Scott. Scott was to mount an amphibious attack on Vera Cruz and proceed to Mexico City, following the path of Cortés and his conquistadors. Events outstripped Polk's scheme, however, when Taylor defeated a far larger Mexican army at the Battle of Buena Vista, on February 22–23, 1847.

While Taylor was winning fame in northern Mexico, and before Scott had launched his attack on Vera Cruz, American forces farther north were dealing decisive blows to the remnants of Mexican rule in New Mexico and California. In the spring of 1846, Colonel Stephen Kearny marched an army from Fort Leavenworth, Kansas, toward Santa Fe. Reaching New Mexico, Kearny took the territory by a combination of bluff, bluster, and perhaps bribery, without firing a shot. The Mexican governor, following his own advice that "it is better to be thought brave than to be so," fled at Kearny's approach. After suppressing a brief rebellion by Mexicans and Indians, Kearny sent a detachment of his army south into Mexico. There, having marched fifteen hundred miles from Fort Leavenworth, these troops joined Taylor in time for the Battle of Buena Vista.

California also fell easily into American hands. In 1845, Polk had ordered the Pacific Squadron under Commodore John D. Sloat to occupy California's ports in the event of war with Mexico. To ensure victory, Polk also dispatched a courier overland with secret orders for one of the most colorful and important actors in the conquest of California, John C. Frémont. A Georgia-born adventurer, Frémont had married Jesse Benton, the daughter of powerful Senator Thomas Hart Benton of Missouri. Benton used his influence to have accounts of Frémont's explorations in the Northwest (mainly written by Jesse Benton Frémont) published as government documents. All of this earned glory for Frémont as "the Great Pathfinder." Finally overtaken by Polk's courier in Oregon, Frémont was dispatched to California to "watch over the interests of the United States." In June 1846, he rounded up a small force of American settlers, seized the village of Sonoma, and proclaimed the independent "Bear Flag Republic." The combined efforts of Frémont, Sloat, his successor David Stockton, and Stephen Kearny (who arrived in California after capturing New Mexico) quickly established American control over California.

The final and most important campaign of the war saw the conquest of Mexico City itself. In March 1847, Winfield Scott landed near Vera Cruz and quickly pounded that city into submission. Moving inland, Scott encountered Santa Anna at the seemingly impregnable pass of Cerro Gordo, but a young captain in Scott's command, Robert E. Lee, helped find a trail that led around the Mexican flank to a small peak overlooking the pass. There Scott planted howitzers and, on April 18, stormed the pass and routed the Mexicans. Scott now moved directly on Mexico City. Taking the key fortresses of Churubusco and Chapultepec (where another young captain,

THOMAS JONATHAN JACKSON Along with George B. McClellan and Robert E. Lee, the future "Stonewall" Jackson of Civil War fame first saw action in the Mexican-American War. A graduate of West Point, Jackson served as a lieutenant of artillery, rising to major after seeing action in the battles of Veracruz, Cerro Gordo, and Chapultepac. (© Bettmann/Corbis)

Ulysses S. Grant, was cited for bravery), Scott took the city on September 13, 1847 (see Map 13.5).

Although the Mexican army outnumbered the Americans in virtually every battle, they could not match the superior artillery or the logistics and organization of the "barbarians of the North." The Americans died like flies from yellow fever, and they carried into battle the agonies of venereal disease, which they picked up (and left) in many of the Mexican towns they took. But the Americans benefited from the unprecedented quality of their weapons, supplies, and organization.

By the **Treaty of Guadalupe Hidalgo** (February 2, 1848), Mexico ceded Texas with the Rio Grande boundary, New Mexico, and California to the United States. In return, the United States assumed the claims of American citizens against the Mexican government and paid Mexico $15 million (see Going to the Source). Although the United States gained the present states of California, Nevada, New Mexico, Utah, most of Arizona, and parts of Colorado and Wyoming, some rabid expansionists in the Senate denounced the treaty because it failed to include all of Mexico. But the acquisition of California ultimately satisfied Polk. Few senators, moreover, wanted to annex the mixed Spanish and Indian population

of Mexico. A writer in the Democratic Review expressed the prevailing view that "the annexation of the country [Mexico] to the United States would be a calamity," for it would incorporate into the United States "ignorant and indolent half-civilized Indians," not to mention "free negroes and mulattoes" left over from the British slave trade. The virulent racism of American leaders allowed the Mexicans to retain part of their nation. On March 10, 1848, the Senate ratified the treaty by a vote of 38 to 10.

13-4.3 The War's Effects on Sectional Conflict

Despite wartime patriotic enthusiasm, sectional conflict sharpened between 1846 and 1848. Territorial expansion sparked the Polk administration's major battles. To Polk, it mattered little whether new territories were slave or free. Expansion would serve the nation's interests by dispersing population and retaining its agricultural and democratic character. Focusing attention on slavery in the territories struck him as "not only unwise but wicked." The Missouri Compromise, prohibiting slavery north of 36°30′, impressed him as a simple and permanent solution to the problem of territorial slavery.

But many northerners were coming to see slavery in the territories as a profoundly disruptive issue that neither could nor should be solved simply by extending the 36°30′ line westward. Amounting to a small minority, abolitionists, who opposed any extension of slavery on moral grounds, posed a minor threat to Polk. More important were northern Democrats who feared that expansion of slavery into California and New Mexico (parts of each lay south of 36°30′) would deter free laborers from settling those territories. These Democrats argued that competition with slaves degraded free labor, that the westward extension of slavery would check the westward migration of free labor, and that such a barrier would aggravate the social problems already beginning to plague the East: class strife, social stratification, and labor protest

13-4.4 The Wilmot Proviso and the Election of 1848

A young Democratic congressman from Pennsylvania, David Wilmot, became the spokesman for these disaffected northern Democrats. In August 1846, he introduced an amendment to an appropriations bill. This amendment, known as the **Wilmot Proviso**, stipulated that

> **Treaty of Guadalupe Hidalgo**
> Mexico ceded Texas with the Rio Grande boundary, New Mexico, and California to the United States. In return, the United States assumed the claims of American citizens against the Mexican government and paid Mexico $15 million. It was signed on February 2, 1848.
>
> **Wilmot Proviso**
> The proposed amendment that stipulated that slavery be prohibited in any territory acquired by the negotiations.

slavery be prohibited in any territory acquired by the war with Mexico. Neither an abolitionist nor a critic of Polk on tariff policy, Wilmot spoke for those loyal Democrats who had supported the annexation of Texas on the assumption that Texas would be the last slave state. Wilmot's intention was not to split his party along sectional lines but instead to hold Polk to what Wilmot and other northern Democrats took as an implicit understanding: Texas for the slaveholders, California and New Mexico for free labor.

With strong northern support, the proviso passed in the House but stalled in the Senate. Polk refused to endorse it, and most southern Democrats opposed any barrier to the expansion of slavery south of the Missouri Compromise line. They believed that the westward extension of slavery would reduce the concentration of slaves in the older regions of the South and thus lessen the chances of a slave revolt.

The proviso raised unsettling constitutional issues. Calhoun and fellow southerners contended that since slaves were property, the Constitution protected slaveholders' right to carry their slaves wherever they chose. This position led to the conclusion (drawn explicitly by Calhoun) that the Missouri Compromise of 1820, prohibiting slavery in the territories north of 36°30′, was unconstitutional. On the other side were many northerners who cited the Northwest Ordinance of 1787, the Missouri Compromise, and the Constitution itself, which gave Congress the power to "make all needful rules and regulations respecting the territory or other property belonging to the United States," as justification for congressional legislation on slavery in the territories. With the election of 1848 approaching, politicians of both sides, eager to hold their parties together and avert civil war, frantically searched for a middle ground.

MAP 13.5   MAJOR BATTLES OF THE MEXICAN-AMERICAN WAR The Mexican War's decisive campaign began with General Winfield Scott's capture of Vera Cruz and ended with his conquest of Mexico City.

Polk on Texas and Oregon

President Polk delivered his inaugural address a few days after Congress had voted to admit Texas to the Union. By adopting a bellicose tone on the Oregon issue, Polk was seeking to keep expansionist sentiment alive and put the rival Whigs, who opposed expansion, in the uncomfortable position of seeming to ally with the hated British.

The Republic of Texas has made known her desire to come into our Union, to form part of our Confederacy and enjoy with us the blessings of liberty secured and guaranteed by our Constitution. Texas was once a part of our country—was unwisdely ceded away to a foreign power—is now independent and possesses an undoubted right to dispose of a part or the whole of her territory and to merge her sovereignty as a separate and independent state in ours. . . .

I regard the question of annexation as belonging exclusively to the United States and Texas, They are independent powers competent to contract, and foreign nations have no right to interfere with them or take exception to their reunion. Foreign powers do not seem to appreciate the true character of our Government. Our Union is a confederation of independent States, whose policy is peace with each other and all the world. To enlarge its limits is to extend the dominions of peace over additional territories and increasing millions. The world has nothing to fear from military ambition in our Government. While the chief magistrate and the popular branch in Congress are elected for short terms by the suffrages of those millions who must in their own persons bear all the burdens and miseries of war, our Government cannot be otherwise than pacific. Foreign powers therefore should look on the annexation of Texas to the United States not as the conquest of a nation seeking to extend her dominions by arms and violence, but as the peaceful acquisition of a territory once her own, by adding another member to our confederation, with the consent of that member, thereby diminishing the chances of war and opening to them new and ever increasing markets for their commerce. . . .

Nor will it become in a less degree my duty to assert and maintain by all constitutional means the right of the United States to that portion of our territory which lies beyond the Rocky Mountains. Our title to the country of Oregon is "clear and unquestionable," and already are our people preparing to perfect that title by occupying it with their wives and children. But eighty years ago our population was confined on the west by the ridge of the Alleghanies. Within that period—within the lifetime, I might say, of some of my hearers—our people, increasing to many millions, have filled the eastern valley of the Mississippi, adventurously ascended the Missouri to its headsprings, and are already engaged in establishing the blessings of self-government in valleys of which the rivers flow to the Pacific. The world beholds the peaceful triumphs of the industry of our emigrants. To us belongs the duty of protecting them adequately wherever they may be upon our soil. The jurisdiction of our laws and the benefits of our republican institutions should be extended over them in the distant regions which they have selected for their homes. The increasing facilities of intercourse will easily bring the States, of which the formation in that part of our territory can not be long delayed, within the sphere of our federative Union.

Source: Polk's Inaugural Address, March 4, 1845.

QUESTIONS

1. Why did Polk maintain that the United States, by its nature as a democracy, was necessarily peaceful? In view of Polk's actions toward Mexico and Britain, do you agree?
2. On what grounds did Polk justify American expansion? Did these grounds place any limit on that expansion?

As the campaign season neared, the Whigs watched in dismay as prosperity returned under Polk's program of an independent treasury and low tariffs. Never before had Clay's American System seemed so irrelevant. But the Wilmot Proviso gave the Whigs a political windfall; originating in the Democratic Party, it enabled the Whigs to portray themselves as the South's only dependable friends.

These considerations inclined the majority of Whigs toward Zachary Taylor. As a Louisiana slave-holder, he had obvious appeal to the South. As a political newcomer, he had no loyalty to the discredited American System. As a war hero, he had broad national appeal. Nominating Taylor as their presidential candidate in 1848, the Whigs presented him as an ideal man "without regard to creeds or principles" and ran him without any platform.

The Democrats faced a greater challenge because David Wilmot was one of their own. They could not ignore the issue of slavery in the territories, but if they embraced the positions of either Wilmot or Calhoun, the party would split along sectional lines. When Polk declined to run for reelection, the Democrats nominated Lewis Cass of Michigan, who solved their dilemma by announcing the doctrine of "squatter sovereignty," or popular sovereignty as it was later called. Cass argued that Congress should let the question of slavery in the territories be decided by the settlers. Squatter sovereignty appealed to many because of its arresting simplicity and vagueness. It neatly dodged the divisive issue of whether Congress had the power to prohibit territorial slavery. In fact, few Democrats wanted a definitive answer to this question. As long as the doctrine remained ambiguous, northern and southern Democrats alike could interpret it to their respective benefit.

In the campaign, both parties tried to ignore the issue of territorial slavery, but neither succeeded. A faction of the Democratic Party in New York that favored the Wilmot Proviso, called the Barnburners, broke away from the party, linked up with former Liberty party abolitionists, and courted antislavery "Conscience" Whigs to create the **Free-Soil party**. Declaring their dedication to "Free Trade, Free Labor, Free Speech, and Free Men," the Free-Soilers nominated Martin Van Buren on a platform opposing any extension of slavery.

Zachary Taylor benefited from Democratic disunity over the Wilmot Proviso and from his war-hero stature. He captured a majority of electoral votes in both North and South. Although failing to carry any state, the Free-Soil party ran well enough in the North to demonstrate the grassroots popularity of opposition to slavery extension. Defections to the Free-Soilers, for example, probably cost the Whigs Ohio. By showing that opposition to the spread of slavery had far greater appeal than the staunch abolitionism of the old Liberty party, the Free-Soilers sent the Whigs and Democrats a message that they would be unable to ignore in future elections.

13-4.5 The California Gold Rush

When Wilmot announced his proviso, the issue of slavery in the Far West was more abstract than practical because Mexico had yet to cede any territory and relatively few Americans resided in either California or New Mexico. Nine days before the signing of the Treaty of Guadalupe Hidalgo, however, an American carpenter discovered gold in the foothills of California's Sierra Nevada range. The **California gold rush** began within a few months. A San Francisco newspaper complained that "the whole country from San Francisco to Los Angeles, and from the shore to the base of the Sierra Nevada, resounds with the sordid cry to *gold*, GOLD, GOLD! while the field is left half-planted, the house half-built, and everything neglected but the manufacture of shovels and pickaxes."

By December 1848, pamphlets with titles like *The Emigrant's Guide to the Gold Mines* had hit the streets of New York City. Arriving by sea and by land, gold-rushers drove up the population of California from around fifteen thousand in the summer of 1848 to nearly 250,000 by 1852. Miners came from every corner of the world. A female journalist reported walking through a mining camp in the Sierras and hearing English, Italian, French, Spanish, German, and Hawaiian. Conflicts over claims quickly led to violent clashes between Americans and Hispanics (mostly Mexicans, Chileans, and Peruvians). Americans especially resented the Chinese who flooded into California in the 1850s, most as contract laborers for wealthy Chinese merchants, and who struck Americans as slave laborers. Yet rampant prejudice against the Chinese did not stop some American businessmen from hiring them as contract workers for the American mining combinations that were forming in the 1850s.

Within a decade, the gold rush turned the sleepy Hispanic town of Yerba Buena, with 150 people in 1846, into "a pandemonium of a city" of 50,000 known as San Francisco. No other U.S. city contained people from more parts of the world. Many of the immigrants were Irish convicts who arrived by way of Australia, to which they had been exiled for their crimes. All the ethnic and racial tensions of the gold fields were evident in the city. A young clergyman confessed that he carried a harmless-looking

Free-Soil party

A faction of the Democratic Party in New York that favored the Wilmot Proviso, called the Barnburners, they broke away from the party, linked up with former Liberty Party abolitionists, and courted antislavery "Conscience" Whigs.

California gold rush

After an American carpenter discovered gold in the foothills of California's Sierra Nevada range in 1848, many Americans moved to California to look for gold.

"UNION" WOODCUT, BY THOMAS W. STRONG, 1848 This 1848 campaign poster for Zachary Taylor reminded Americans of his military victories, unmilitary bearing (note the civilian dress and straw hat), and deliberately vague promises. As president, Taylor finally took a stand on the issue of slavery in the Mexican cession, but his position angered the South. *(Library of Congress)*

cane, which "will be found to contain a sword two-and-a-half feet long." In 1851, San Francisco's merchants organized the first of several Committees of Vigilance, which patrolled the streets, deported undesirables, and tried and hanged alleged thieves and murderers.

With the gold rush, the issue of slavery in the Far West became practical as well as abstract, and immediate rather than remote. The newcomers attracted to California in 1849 included free blacks and slaves brought by planters from the South. White prospectors loathed the thought of competing with either of these groups and wanted to drive all blacks, along with California's Indians, out of the gold fields. Tensions also intensified between the goldrushers and the *Californios*, whose extensive (if often vaguely worded) land holdings were protected by the terms of the Treaty of Guadalupe Hidalgo. Spawned by disputed claims and prejudice, violence mounted, and demands grew for a strong civilian government to replace the ineffective military government in place in California since the war. Polk began to fear that without a satisfactory congressional solution to the slavery issue, Californians might organize a government independent of the United States. The gold rush thus guaranteed that the question of slavery in the Mexican cession would be the first item on the agenda for Polk's successor and, indeed, for the nation.

The Whole Vision

■ **What were the myths and realities about immigration and the immigrant experience in mid-nineteenth-century America?**

Immigrants came to the United States during this period for numerous reasons. Many were influenced by relatives' tales of American wealth—often greatly exaggerated—and the potential to live more comfortable lives. While there were a small percentage who sought religious freedom, in fact, the quest for upward mobility proved the most important motivation, especially for immigrants hit by hard times in their homelands. Some came to be farmers, lured by the idea of owning land; others transplanted professional and marketable skills; still others became laborers. For would-be farmers, their ability to achieve this vision was limited by lack of access to the capital necessary to purchase land and implements. Many immigrants had to find jobs and discovered that working and living in America did not match the idyllic picture created by earlier arrivals. Nor did they receive a warm welcome. Instead, clashes based on religion and socioeconomic class and nativist fears and perceptions of immigrants were often a feature of immigrant life for some groups. Immigrants developed strategies to deal with the realities they encountered, including forming their own organizations and ethnic neighborhoods and engaging in ethnically oriented politics and reform movements.

■ **What shaped U.S. settlement of the West in the mid-nineteenth century?**

Initially, settlement of the West was slow. Notions of what constituted the West—and ideas about western settlement—were in flux during the first half of the nineteenth century. Some of this was influenced by foreign policy and shifting claims to western lands, as well as the seemingly far reach of the lands themselves to potential settlers. Aside from a few small trade outposts on the West Coast, early in the century most settlement reached only as far as Missouri. Ultimately, economic and political push-pull factors would encourage settlement. The Mexican government, too, would see advantages to encouraging American settlement in the beginning. Although much of the settlement of the Far West began with peaceful coexistence between Mexicans and Americans in the region, as the decades and American appetites for land advanced, tensions mounted and rebellions ensued. The trek of white settlers west was difficult not only for the women and families who made the journey, but also for the Native Americans, whose land they trampled and sometimes claimed in the process.

KEY TERMS

Tejano (p. 349)

Stephen F. Austin (p. 349)

German and Irish immigrants (p. 351)

nativism (p. 354)

Commonwealth v. *Hunt* (p. 354)

Oregon country (p. 355)

Californios (p. 355)

Santa Fe Trail (p. 356)

Alamo (p. 358)

Sam Houston (p. 358)

John Tyler (p. 360)

annexation of Texas (p. 361)

James K. Polk (p. 361)

manifest destiny (p. 363)

Zachary Taylor (p. 365)

Treaty of Guadalupe Hidalgo (p. 367)

Wilmot Proviso (p. 367)

Free-Soil party (p. 370)

California gold rush (p. 370)

■ *How did national politics influence debates and actions regarding westward expansion?*

The two dominant political parties in the 1840s—Whigs and Democrats—had differing views about expansion and the issues related to it. Much of that had to do with who each party thought would most benefit from such moves as well as regional concerns and sectional tensions. Texas triggered one of many political debates about expansion and the potential foreign policy and sectional issues that came with it. Slavery also contributed much to the debates both about Texas specifically and the nature of westward expansion generally. Americans—politicians and ordinary citizens—who supported annexation of Texas and further westward expansion embraced the ideology of Manifest Destiny as a justification. But leaders, aware of the risks involved in expanding into some territories, addressed each situation differently—even if the public made no such distinctions.

■ *What were the short- and long-term implications of the U.S. war with Mexico?*

In the short term, the road leading to war was paved with political differences between the U.S. and Mexico, some of them old wounds and some of them newer—arguably, at times fabricated—disputes about boundaries between the two countries. Changes within the leadership of both countries also fueled increased U.S. appetite for land and mounting tensions that ultimately led to war. The war forced the U.S. to form a stronger military, which included some future Civil War generals. In the short term, everyday Americans and politicians alike wondered about and vigorously debated the legitimacy of the war. But in the long term, the war and the territorial gains it brought the U.S. deepened rifts about the expansion of slavery and with it, the ability of one section to dominate the federal government and national policy. Sectional conflict escalated in the years after the war with Mexico, shaped in part by the expansion opportunities and territorial policies of the newly acquired lands. Political compromises would attempt to assuage the ever deepening regional divisions, but the stage was set in the years after the U.S. War with Mexico for the Civil War to come.

14 From Compromise to Secession, 1850–1861

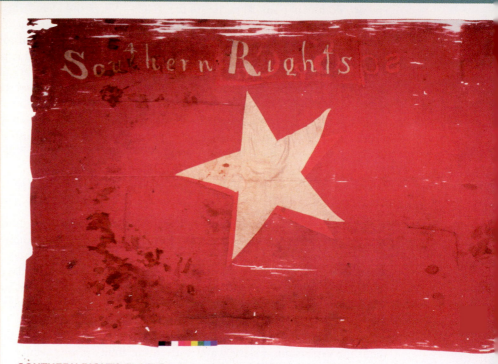

SOUTHERN RIGHTS FLAG Proslavery forces carried this flag while attacking the antislavery stronghold of Lawrence in the Kansas Territory. The raiders flew this flag over the local newspaper's offices and the Free State Hotel before burning each to the ground. *(Kansas State Historical Society)*

1848	Zachary Taylor elected president.		**1856**	"The sack of Lawrence."
1849	California seeks admission to the Union as a free state.			John Brown's Pottawatomie massacre.
				James Buchanan elected president.
1850	Nashville convention assembles to discuss the South's grievances.		**1857**	*Dred Scott* decision.
				President Buchanan endorses the Lecompton Constitution in Kansas.
	Compromise of 1850.			Panic of 1857.
1852	Harriet Beecher Stowe, *Uncle Tom's Cabin.*		**1858**	Congress refuses to admit Kansas to the Union under the Lecompton Constitution.
	Franklin Pierce elected president.			Lincoln-Douglas debates.
1853	Gadsden Purchase.		**1859**	John Brown's raid on Harpers Ferry.
1854	Ostend Manifesto.		**1860**	Abraham Lincoln elected president.
	Kansas-Nebraska Act.			South Carolina secedes from the Union.
	William Walker leads filibustering expedition into Nicaragua.		**1861**	The remaining Lower South states secede.
1854–1855	Know-Nothing and Republican parties emerge.			Confederate States of America established.
1855	Proslavery forces steal the election for a territorial legislature in Kansas.			Crittenden compromise plan collapses.
				Lincoln takes office.
	Proslavery Kansans establish a government in Lecompton.			Firing on Fort Sumter; Civil War begins.
	Free-soil government established in Topeka, Kansas.			Upper South secedes.

On April 12, 1861, Edmund Ruffin, a sixty-seven-year-old agricultural reformer and political pundit who had joined the Palmetto Guards, a volunteer military company, stood by a cannon on Morris Island in the bay of Charleston, South Carolina. Although young enough to be his grandchildren, many of the volunteers knew him as a champion of secession. The only way to save the South's civilization, he had argued for decades, was for the southern states to leave the United States and start a new nation.

Led by South Carolina, seven states in the Lower South had already done so, and in February 1861, they had formed the Confederate States of America. Now, the question became, who would commit the first hostile act, Union or Confederacy? President Abraham Lincoln, whose election had triggered South Carolina's secession, had vowed to defend federal property in the seceding states, including **Fort Sumter** in Charleston Bay. Gunfire had turned back one supply ship, and the fort would soon run out of food. Impatient Confederate leaders demanded its immediate surrender; the fort's commander refused. At 4:30 A.M., Ruffin pulled the cannon's lanyard and commenced the bombardment, which compelled the fort's surrender the next day. Lincoln responded by calling for 75,000 volunteers to suppress the rebellion. The Civil War had begun.

Four years later, Ruffin would take his own life, leaving a farewell note that expressed his extreme hatred for the North and his hope for "just retribution for Yankee usurpation, oppression, & atrocious outrages—& for deliverance and vengeance for the now ruined, subjugated, & enslaved Southern States." Before 1860, few listened to his ranting, less because of his defense of slavery as the finest labor system for both whites and blacks than because of his insistence that northerners, regardless of what they said, were hell-bent on destroying slavery.

Fort Sumter
Located in Charleston, South Carolina, this was where the shots that began the Civil War were fired.

EDMUND RUFFIN (Library of Congress Prints and Photographs Division [LC-DIG-cwpbh-00486])

Other southerners, more willing to take northerners at their word, felt considerably less threatened, even by the purely northern Republican Party. Formed in the mid-1850s, the Republican Party dedicated itself to stopping the extension of slavery into the territories, but the party's leaders insisted that they lacked constitutional authority to interfere with slavery in the southern states. Most white southerners trusted their influence in national institutions, especially the Democratic Party, to secure slavery.

However, sectional conflicts over slavery's extension eroded the appeal of national parties to the South during the 1850s. Then, in October 1859, a fanatical abolitionist named **John Brown** led a small band in seizing the federal arsenal at Harpers Ferry, Virginia, in the hope of igniting a slave insurrection. An abject failure, Brown's raid nevertheless brought to the surface all the white South's doubts about the "real" intentions of the North. Ruffin, long the prophet without honor in his own country, became the man of the hour and secession a bright star on the horizon.

14-1 The Compromise of 1850

Why was the Compromise of 1850 ultimately unsuccessful in resolving sectional divisions?

When the U.S. war with Mexico ended in 1848, the United States contained an equal number of free and slave states (fifteen each), but the vast territory acquired by the war threatened to upset this balance. Any solution to the question of slavery in the Mexican cession ensured controversy. The doctrine of **free soil**, which insisted that Congress prohibit slavery in the territories, horrified southerners. The idea of extending the Missouri Compromise line of 36°30' to the Pacific made no one happy: it angered free-soilers because it would allow slavery in New Mexico and southern California, and it infuriated southern proslavery extremists because it conceded that Congress could bar slavery in some territories. A third solution, **popular sovereignty**, which promised to ease the slavery extension issue out of national politics by allowing each territory to decide the matter for itself, pleased neither free-soilers nor proslavery extremists.

As the rhetoric escalated, events plunged the nation into crisis. Utah and then California, both acquired from Mexico, sought admission to the Union as free states. Texas, admitted as a slave state in 1845, aggravated matters by claiming the eastern half of New Mexico, where the Mexican government had abolished slavery.

By 1850, these territorial issues had become intertwined with two other concerns. Northerners increasingly attacked slavery in the District of Columbia, within the shadow of the Capitol; southerners complained about lax enforcement of the Fugitive Slave Act of 1793. Any broad compromise would have to take both troublesome matters into account.

14-1.1 Taylor's and Clay's Strategies for Compromise

President Zachary Taylor believed that the South must not kindle the issue of slavery in the territories because neither New Mexico nor California was suited to slavery. In 1849, Taylor asserted that "the people of the North need have no apprehension of the further extension of slavery."

Taylor's position differed significantly from the thinking behind the still controversial Wilmot Proviso, which insisted that Congress bar slavery from territories ceded by Mexico. Taylor's plan, in contrast, left the decision to new states. He prompted California to apply for admission as a free state, bypassing the territorial stage, and he strongly hinted that New Mexico do the same. Taylor's strategy appeared to guarantee a quick, practical solution to the problem of slavery extension. It would give the North two new free states. At the same time, it would acknowledge a position upon which all southerners agreed: a state could bar or permit slavery as it chose.

But southerners rejected Taylor's plan. It rested on what many considered a shaky assumption that slavery could never take root in California or New Mexico, and worse, it would effectively ban slavery in the Mexican cession. Both areas already contained slaves, who could be employed profitably in mining gold and silver. "California is by nature," a southerner proclaimed, "peculiarly a slaveholding State." South Carolina senator and former vice president John C. Calhoun trembled at the thought of adding more free states. "If this scheme excluding slavery from California and New Mexico should be carried out—if we are to be reduced to a mere handful . . . wo, wo, I say to this Union." Disillusioned with Taylor, nine southern states agreed to send delegations to a southern convention that was scheduled to

John Brown
Famous white abolitionist who was wanted for the massacre of white southerners in Kansas in 1856. He believed that God had ordained him "to purge this land with blood" of the evil of slavery.

free soil
The doctrine that insisted that Congress prohibit slavery in the territories.

popular sovereignty
Promised to ease the slavery extension issue out of national politics by allowing each territory to decide the question of slavery for itself.

meet in Nashville in June 1850. Taylor might have been able to contain mounting southern opposition if he had held a secure position in the Whig Party. But such leading Whigs as Daniel Webster of Massachusetts and Henry Clay of Kentucky, each of whom had presidential aspirations, never reconciled themselves to Taylor, a political novice. Early in 1850, Clay boldly challenged Taylor's leadership by forging a set of compromise proposals to resolve the range of contentious issues. In an omnibus bill, Clay proposed (1) the admission of California as a free state; (2) the division of the remainder of the Mexican cession into two territories, New Mexico and Utah (formerly Deseret), without federal restrictions on slavery; (3) the settlement of the Texas–New Mexico boundary dispute on terms favorable to New Mexico; (4) as an incentive for Texas, an agreement that the federal government would assume the considerable public debt of Texas; (5) the continuance of slavery in the District of Columbia but the abolition of the slave trade there; and (6) a more effective fugitive slave law.

The debates over Clay's bill during the late winter and early spring of 1850 witnessed the last major appearances on the public stage of Clay, Webster, and Calhoun—the trio of distinguished senators whose lives had mirrored every public event of note since the War of 1812. Clay played the role of the conciliator, as he had during the controversy over Missouri in 1820 and again during the nullification crisis in the early 1830s. Warning the South against secession, he assured the North that nature would check the spread of slavery more effectively than a thousand Wilmot Provisos. Gaunt and gloomy, a dying Calhoun listened as another senator read his address for him, a repetition of what he had been saying for years: The North's growing power, enhanced by protective tariffs and by the Missouri Compromise's exclusion of slaveholders from the northern part of the Louisiana Purchase, had created an imbalance between the sections. Only a decision by the North to treat the South as an equal could now save the Union. Three days later, Daniel Webster, who believed that slavery, "like the cotton-plant, is confined to certain parallels of climate," delivered his memorable "Seventh of March" speech. Speaking not "as a Massachusetts man, nor as a Northern man, but as an American," Webster chided the North for trying to "reenact the will of God" by legally excluding slavery from the Mexican cession and declared himself a forthright proponent of compromise.

However eloquent, the conciliatory voices of Clay and Webster made few converts. Strident voices countered them at every turn. The antislavery New York Whig William Seward, for example, enraged southerners by talking of a **"higher law"** than the Constitution—namely, the will of God against the extension of slavery. Clay's compromise faltered as Clay broke with President Taylor, who attacked Clay as a glory-hunter.

As the crisis worsened, a series of events in the summer of 1850 eased the way toward a resolution. When the Nashville convention assembled in June, the nine of fifteen slave states that sent delegates were primarily in the Lower South. Despite the reckless pronouncements of the "fire-eaters" (extreme advocates of "southern rights"), moderates dominated. Then Zachary Taylor, after eating and drinking too much at an Independence Day celebration, fell ill with gastroenteritis and died on July 9. His successor, Vice President Millard Fillmore of New York, supported Clay's compromise. Finally, Illinois Democrat **Stephen A. Douglas** took over the floor leadership from the exhausted Clay. Recognizing that Clay's "omnibus" lacked majority support in Congress, Douglas chopped it into a series of separate measures and sought to secure passage of each bill individually. To secure support from Democrats, he included the principle of popular sovereignty in the bills organizing New Mexico and Utah. By summer's end, Congress had passed each component of the **Compromise of 1850**: statehood for California; territorial status for Utah and New Mexico, allowing popular sovereignty; resolution of the Texas–New Mexico boundary disagreement; federal assumption of the Texas debt; abolition of the slave trade in the District of Columbia; and a new fugitive slave law (see Map 14.1).

14-1.2 Assessing the Compromise and the Fugitive Slave Act

President Fillmore hailed the compromise as a "final settlement" of sectional divisions, and Clay's reputation for conciliation reached new heights. Yet the compromise did not bridge the underlying differences between the two sections. Far from leaping forward to save the Union, Congress had backed into the Compromise of 1850; the majority of congressmen in one or another section opposed virtually all of the specific bills that made up the compromise. Most southerners, for example, voted against the admission of California and the abolition of the slave trade in the District of Columbia; the majority of northerners opposed the Fugitive Slave Act and the organization of New Mexico and Utah without a forthright congressional prohibition of slavery. These measures passed only because the minority of congressmen who genuinely desired compromise

"higher law"
The will of God.

Stephen A. Douglas
Politician from Illinois who was one of the nominees of the Democratic Party for president in 1860. He was the main advocate of the Compromise of 1850.

Compromise of 1850
Statehood for California; territorial status for Utah and New Mexico, allowing popular sovereignty; resolution of the Texas–New Mexico boundary disagreement; federal assumption of the Texas debt; abolition of the slave trade in the District of Columbia; and a new fugitive slave law.

combined with the majority in either the North or the South who favored each specific bill.

Each section both gained and lost from the Compromise of 1850. The North won California as a free state, New Mexico and Utah as likely future free states, a favorable settlement of the Texas–New Mexico boundary (most of the disputed area was awarded to New Mexico, a probable free state), and the abolition of the slave trade in the District of Columbia. The South's benefits were cloudier. By stipulating popular sovereignty for New Mexico and Utah, the compromise, to most southerners' relief, had buried the Wilmot Proviso's insistence that Congress formally prohibit slavery in these territories. But to southerners' dismay, the compromise left open the question of whether Congress could prohibit slavery in territories outside of the Mexican cession.

The one clear advantage gained by the South, a more stringent fugitive slave law, quickly proved a mixed blessing. Because few slaves had been taken into the Mexican cession, the question of slavery there had a hypothetical quality. However, the new fugitive slave law authorized southerners to pursue real fugitives on northern soil. Here was a concrete issue to which the average northerner, who may never have seen a slave and who cared little about slavery a thousand miles away, would respond with fury. Northern moderates accepted the **Fugitive Slave Act** as the price of saving the Union. But the law contained features distasteful to moderates and outrageous to staunchly antislavery northerners. It denied alleged fugitives the right of trial by jury, did not allow them to testify in their own behalf, permitted their return to slavery merely on the testimony of the claimant, and enabled court-appointed commissioners to collect ten dollars if they ruled for the slaveholder but only five dollars if they ruled for the fugitive. In authorizing federal marshals to raise posses to pursue fugitives on northern soil, the law threatened to turn the North into "one vast hunting ground." In addition, the law targeted all runaways, putting at risk fugitives who had lived in the North for thirty years or more. Above all, the law brought home to northerners the uncomfortable truth that the continuation of slavery depended on their complicity. By legalizing the activities of slave-catchers on northern soil, the law reminded northerners that slavery was a national problem, not merely a peculiar southern institution.

Antislavery northerners assailed the law as the "vilest monument of infamy of the nineteenth

MAP 14.1 THE COMPROMISE OF 1850 The Compromise of 1850 admitted California as a free state. Utah and New Mexico were left open to slavery or freedom on the principle of popular sovereignty.

century." "Let the President . . . drench our land of freedom in blood," proclaimed Ohio Whig congressman Joshua Giddings, "but he will never make us obey that law." His support for the law turned Senator Daniel Webster of Massachusetts into a villain in the eyes of the very people who for years had revered him as the "godlike Daniel." Abolitionist poet John Greenleaf Whittier wrote of his fallen idol,

All else is gone; from those giant eyes
The soul has fled:
When faith is lost, when honor dies,
The man is dead

Efforts to catch and return fugitive slaves inflamed feelings in both the North and the South. In 1854, a Boston mob, aroused by antislavery speeches, broke into a courthouse and killed a guard in an abortive effort to rescue fugitive slave Anthony Burns. Determined to prove that the law could be enforced "even in Boston," President Franklin Pierce sent a detachment of federal troops to escort Burns to the harbor, where a ship carried him back to slavery. As five platoons of troops marched with Burns to the ship, some fifty thousand people lined the streets. One Bostonian hung from his window a black coffin bearing the words "THE FUNERAL OF LIBERTY." Another draped an American flag upside down as a symbol that "my country is eternally disgraced by this day's proceedings."

The Burns incident shattered the complacency of conservative supporters of the Compromise of 1850. "We went to bed one night old fashioned conservative Compromise Union Whigs," textile manufacturer Amos A. Lawrence wrote, "and waked up stark mad Abolitionists." A Boston committee later successfully purchased Burns's freedom, but other fugitives had worse fates. Margaret Garner, about to be captured and sent back to Kentucky as a slave, slit her daughter's throat and tried to kill her other children rather than witness their return to slavery. This attempt to kill her children was for Garner a desperate form of resistance to slavery.

In response to the Fugitive Slave Act, "vigilance" committees spirited endangered blacks to Canada. Lawyers dragged out legal proceedings to raise slave-catchers' expenses, and nine northern states passed

A MODERN MEDEA To escape slavery, Margaret Garner fled from Kentucky to Ohio in 1856. Tracked down by a posse of slave-catchers acting under the authority of the Fugitive Slave Law, she killed her daughter with a butcher knife and was preparing to kill her other children and herself when she was subdued. Her experience reminded Americans of Medea, who in Greek legend murders her children to punish her husband Jason for leaving her for another woman. *(Picture Research Consultants & Archives)*

personal-liberty laws. By such techniques as forbidding the use of state jails to incarcerate alleged fugitives, these laws aimed to preclude state officials from enforcing the law.

The frequent cold stares, obstructive legal tactics, and occasional violence encountered by slaveholders who ventured north to capture runaway slaves helped demonstrate to southerners that opposition to slavery boiled just beneath the surface of northern opinion. In the eyes of most southerners, the South had gained little more from the Compromise of 1850 than the Fugitive Slave Act, and now even that northern concession seemed a phantom. After witnessing riots against the Fugitive Slave Act in Boston in 1854, a young Georgian studying law at Harvard wrote to his mother, "Do not be surprised if when I return home you find me a confirmed disunionist."

14-1.3 *Uncle Tom's Cabin*

The publication in 1852 of Harriet Beecher Stowe's novel **Uncle Tom's Cabin** aroused wide northern sympathy for fugitive slaves. Stowe, the daughter of famed evangelical Lyman Beecher and the younger sister of Catharine Beecher, stalwart advocate of domesticity for women, greeted the Fugitive Slave Act with horror. In a memorable scene from the novel, she depicted the slave Eliza, clutching her infant son, bounding across ice floes on the Ohio River to freedom.

Slavery itself was Stowe's main target. Much of her novel's power derives from its view that good intentions mean little against so evil an institution. The good intentions of a kindly slaveowner die with him, and Uncle Tom is sold to the vicious Yankee Simon Legree, who whips him to death.

The book was an instant best-seller. Three hundred thousand copies of *Uncle Tom's Cabin* were sold in 1852, and 1.2 million by the summer of 1853. Stage dramatizations, which added dogs to chase Eliza across the ice, eventually reached perhaps fifty times the number of people as the novel itself. As a play, *Uncle Tom's Cabin* enthralled working-class audiences normally indifferent, if not hostile, to abolitionism. A reviewer of one stage performance observed that the gallery was filled with men "in red woollen shirts, with countenances as hardy and rugged as the implements of industry employed by them in the pursuit of their vocations." At the point when Eliza escapes across the river, the reviewer was surprised to discover that many of the men in the audience were in tears.

Although *Uncle Tom's Cabin* hardly lived up to a proslavery lawyer's prediction that it would convert 2 million people to abolitionism, it did push many waverers to an aggressive antislavery stance. Indeed, fear of its effect inspired a host of southerners to pen

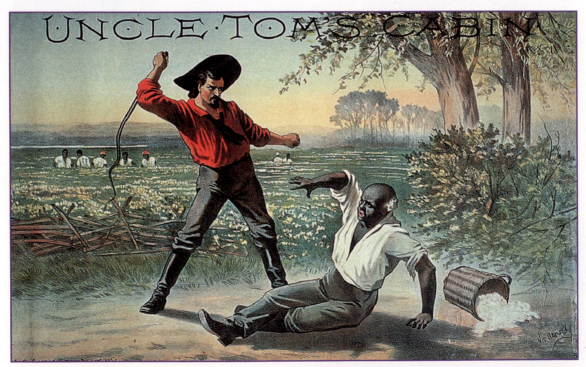

UNCLE TOM'S CABIN THEATER POSTER With its vivid word pictures of slavery, Harriet Beecher Stowe's *Uncle Tom's Cabin* translated well to the stage. Stowe herself was among the many who wrote dramatizations of the novel. Scenes of Eliza crossing the ice of the Ohio River with bloodhounds in pursuit and the evil Simon Legree whipping Uncle Tom outraged northern audiences and turned many against slavery. Southerners damned Mrs. Stowe as a "vile wretch in petticoats." *(National Museum of American History, Smithsonian Institution, Behring Center)*

anti–Uncle Tom novels. As historian David Potter concluded, the northern attitude toward slavery "was never quite the same after *Uncle Tom's Cabin*."

The book also sparked anger and apprehension in the South. To defend its peculiar institution, dozens of books emerged during the 1850s, countering the portrait offered in Stowe's book—even some children's books. Southern authors such as Mary Henderson Eastman, who wrote *Aunt Phillis's Cabin; or, Southern Life As It Is*, sought to portray the virtues of the slave system and paint an idyllic portrait of the South. While many of these books sold well, none came anywhere close to the literary achievement and public reach of Stowe's work.

14-2 The Collapse of the Second Party System, 1853–1856

What ultimately fueled the collapse of the second party system?

The Fugitive Slave Act fragmented the Whig Party. By masterminding defiance of the law, northern Whigs put southern Whigs, who long had come before the southern electorate as the party best able to defend slavery within the Union, on the spot.

In 1852, the Whigs' nomination of Mexican War hero Winfield Scott as their presidential candidate widened the sectional split within the party. Although a Virginian, Scott owed his nomination to the northern free-soil Whigs. His endorsement of the Compromise of 1850 undercut southern Whigs' effort to portray the Democrats as the party of disunion and themselves as the party of both slavery and the Union.

The Democrats bridged their own sectional division by nominating **Franklin Pierce** of New Hampshire, a dark-horse candidate whose chief attraction was that no faction of the party strongly opposed him. North and South, the Democrats rallied behind both the Compromise and the idea of applying popular sovereignty to the territories. In the most one-sided election since 1820, Pierce swept to victory. In state elections during 1852 and 1853, moreover, the Whigs were devastated in the South; one Whig stalwart lamented "the decisive breaking-up of our party."

Franklin Pierce had the dubious distinction of being the last presidential candidate for eighty years to win the popular and electoral vote in both the North and the South. Within the four years of Pierce's administration, the Whig Party disintegrated. In its place two new parties, first the American (Know-Nothing) Party, then the Republican Party, arose. Unlike the Whig Party, the Republican Party was a purely sectional, northern party. The Democrats survived as a national party, but

with a base so shrunken in the North that the Republican Party swept two-thirds of the free states in 1856.

For decades, the second party system had kept the conflict over slavery in check by giving Americans other issues—banking, internal improvements, tariffs, and temperance—to argue about. By the 1850s, the debate over slavery extension was pushing such issues into the background and exposing raw divisions in each party. Of the two parties, the Whigs had the larger, more aggressive free-soil wing, and hence they were more vulnerable than the Democrats. When Stephen A. Douglas put forth a proposal in 1854 to organize the vast Nebraska territory without restrictions on slavery, he ignited a firestorm that consumed the Whig party.

14-2.1 The Kansas-Nebraska Act

Signed by President Pierce at the end of May 1854, the **Kansas-Nebraska Act** shattered the already weakened second party system and triggered renewed sectional strife. The origins of the act lay in the seemingly uncontroversial desire of farm families to establish homesteads west of Iowa and Missouri. Bills to organize this area to extinguish Indian land titles and to provide a basis of government also had the backing of railroad enthusiasts, who dreamed of a rail line linking the Midwest to the Pacific.

In January 1854, Senator Stephen A. Douglas of Illinois proposed a bill to organize Nebraska as a territory. An ardent expansionist, Douglas had formed his political ideology in the heady atmosphere of Manifest Destiny during the 1840s. Although he preferred a railroad from his hometown of Chicago to San Francisco, Douglas dwelled on the national benefits that would attend construction of a railroad from anywhere in the Midwest to the Pacific. A railroad would enhance the importance of the Midwest, which could then hold the balance of power between the older sections of the North and South, and possibly promote unity rather than disruption. In addition, westward expansion through Nebraska with the aid of a railroad struck Douglas as an issue, comparable to Manifest Destiny, around which the splintering factions of the Democratic Party would unite.

Two sources of potential conflict loomed. First, some southerners advocated a rival route for the Pacific railroad that would start at either New Orleans or Memphis. Second, Nebraska lay within the Louisiana Purchase and north of the Missouri Compromise line of 36°30', a region closed to slavery (see Map 14.2). Under Douglas's bill, the South would lose the Pacific rail route *and* face the possibility of more free territory in the

Franklin Pierce
Democrat from New Hampshire who won the presidential election in 1848.

Kansas-Nebraska Act
Signed by President Pierce at the end of May 1854, it made it possible for settlers in the new states of Kansas and Nebraska to decide whether or not slavery would be allowed in their home states.

MAP 14.2   **THE KANSAS-NEBRASKA ACT, 1854** Kansas and Nebraska lay within the Louisiana Purchase, north of 36°30', and hence were closed to slavery until Stephen A. Douglas introduced his bills in 1854.

Union. To placate southerners and win their votes, Douglas made two concessions. He stated publicly that the Nebraska bill "superseded" the Missouri Compromise and rendered it "void." Next, he agreed to a division of Nebraska into two territories: Nebraska to the west of Iowa, and Kansas to the west of Missouri. Because Missouri was a slave state, most congressmen assumed that the division aimed to secure Kansas for slavery and Nebraska for free soil.

The modifications of Douglas's original bill set off a storm of protest. Congress quickly tabled the Pacific railroad (which, in the turn of events, would not be built until after the Civil War) and focused on the issue of slavery extension. Antislavery northerners assailed the bill as "an atrocious plot" to violate the "sacred pledge" of the Missouri Compromise and to turn Kansas into a "dreary region of despotism, inhabited by masters and slaves." Their rage electrified southerners, many of whom initially had reacted indifferently to the Nebraska bill. Some southerners had opposed an explicit repeal of the Missouri Compromise, from fear of stimulating sectional discord; others doubted that Kansas would attract many slaveholders. But the furious assault of antislavery northerners united the South behind the Kansas-Nebraska bill by turning the issue into one of sectional pride as much as slavery extension.

Despite the uproar, Douglas successfully guided the Kansas-Nebraska bill through the Senate, where it passed by a vote of 37 to 14. In the House of Representatives, where the bill passed by little more than a whisker, 113 to 100, the true dimensions of the conflict became apparent. Not a single northern Whig representative in the House voted for the bill, whereas the northern Democrats divided evenly, 44 to 44.

14-2.2 The Surge of Free Soil

Amid the clamor over his bill, Douglas ruefully observed that he could now travel to Chicago by the light of his own burning effigies. Neither a fool nor a political novice, he was the victim of a political bombshell—free soil—that exploded under his feet.

Support for free soil united northerners who agreed on little else. Some free-soilers opposed slavery on moral grounds and rejected racist legislation, but others were racists who opposed allowing any African Americans, slave or free, into the West. An abolitionist traced the free-soil convictions of many westerners to a "perfect, if not supreme" hatred of blacks. Racist free-soilers in Iowa and Illinois secured laws prohibiting settlement by black people.

One opinion shared by free-soilers of all persuasions was that slavery impeded whites' progress. Because a slave worked for nothing, the argument ran, no free laborer could compete with a slave. A territory might contain only a handful of slaves or none at all, but as long as Congress refused to prohibit slavery in the territories, the institution would gain a foothold and free laborers would flee. Wherever slavery appeared, a free-soiler proclaimed, "labor loses its dignity; industry sickens; education finds no schools; religion finds no churches; and the whole land of slavery is impoverished." Free-soilers also blasted the idea that slavery had natural limits. One warned that "slavery is as certain to invade New Mexico and Utah as the sun is to rise"; others predicted that if slavery gained a toehold in Kansas, it would soon invade Minnesota.

To free-soilers, the Kansas-Nebraska Act, with its erasure of the Missouri Compromise, was the last straw, for it revealed, one wrote, "a continuous movement by slaveholders to spread slavery over the entire North." For a Whig congressman from Massachusetts who had voted for the Compromise of 1850 and opposed abolitionists, the Kansas-Nebraska Act, "that most wanton and wicked act, so obviously designed to promote the extension of slavery," was too much to bear. "I now advocate the freedom of Kansas under all circumstances, and the prohibition of slavery in all territories now free." The uproar over the Kansas-Nebraska Act embarrassed the Pierce administration and doomed Manifest Destiny, as did increasing sectional rivalries. In 1853, his emissary James Gadsden negotiated the purchase from Mexico of a strip of land south of the Gila River (now southern Arizona and part of southern New Mexico), an acquisition favored by advocates of a southern railroad route to the Pacific. Fierce opposition to the Gadsden Purchase revealed mounting free-soilers' suspicion of expansion, and the Senate approved the treaty only after slashing nine thousand square miles from the parcel. The sectional rivalries beginning to engulf the Nebraska bill threatened any proposal to gain new territory.

Cuba provided vivid proof of the change in public attitudes about expansion. In 1854, a former Mississippi governor, John A. Quitman, planned a filibuster (an unofficial military expedition) to seize Cuba from Spain. Pierce forced Quitman to scuttle the expedition when faced with intense opposition from antislavery northerners who saw filibusters as another manifestation of the **Slave Power**—the conspiracy of slaveholders and their northern dupes to grab more territory for slavery.

In October 1854, American ambassadors to Great Britain, France, and Spain, two of them southerners, met in Belgium and issued the unofficial Ostend Manifesto, calling on the United States to acquire Cuba by any means, including force. Beset by the storm over the Kansas-Nebraska Act and the furor over Quitman's proposed filibuster, Pierce rejected the mandate.

Still, the idea of expansion into the Caribbean continued to attract southerners. Between 1853 and 1860, the year a firing squad in Honduras executed Tennessee-born adventurer William Walker, he led a succession of filibustering expeditions into Central America. Taking advantage of civil chaos in Nicaragua, he made himself the chief political force there, reinstituted slavery, and talked of making Nicaragua a U.S. colony.

Some southerners were against expansion, among them Louisiana sugar planters who opposed acquiring Cuba because Cuban sugar would compete with their own. But expansionists stirred enough commotion to worry antislavery northerners that the South was conspiring to establish a Caribbean slave empire. As long as the debate on the extension of slavery focused on the continental United States, prospects for expansion were limited. However, adding Caribbean territory to the pot changed all calculations.

14-2.3 The Whigs and the Know-Nothings, 1853–1856

While straining Democratic unity, the Kansas-Nebraska Act wrecked the Whig Party. In the law's immediate aftermath, most northern Whigs hoped to blame the Democrats for the act and to entice free-soil Democrats to their side. In the state and congressional elections of 1854, the Democrats were decisively defeated. But the Whig Party failed to benefit from the backlash against the Democrats. However furious at Douglas for initiating the act, free-soil Democrats could not forget that the southern Whigs had supported Douglas. In addition, the northern Whigs themselves were deeply divided between antislavery "Conscience" Whigs, led by Senator William Seward of New York, and conservatives, led by former president Millard Fillmore. The conservatives believed that the Whig Party had to adhere to the Compromise of 1850 to maintain itself as a national party.

Divisions within the Whig Party repelled antislavery Democrats from affiliating with it and prompted many antislavery Whigs to look for an alternative party. By 1856, the new Republican Party would become the home for most of these northern refugees from the traditional parties; but in 1854 and 1855, when the Republican Party was only starting to organize, the American, or Know-Nothing, party emerged as the principal alternative.

Slave Power
The conspiracy of slaveholders and their northern dupes to grab more territory for slavery.

One of a number of nativist societies that mushroomed in opposition to the massive immigration of the 1840s, the **Know-Nothings** originated in the secret Order of the Star-Spangled Banner. The party's popular name, Know-Nothing, derived from the standard response of its members to inquiries about its activities: "I know nothing." The Know-Nothings' core purpose was to rid the United States of immigrant and Catholic political influence. To this end, they pressured the existing parties to nominate and appoint only native-born Protestants to office and advocated an extension of the naturalization period before immigrants could vote.

Throughout the 1840s, nativists usually voted Whig, but their allegiance to the Whigs started to buckle during Winfield Scott's campaign for the presidency in 1852. In an attempt to revitalize his party, which was badly split over slavery, Scott had courted the traditionally Democratic Catholic vote. But Scott's tactic backfired. Most Catholics voted for Franklin Pierce. Nativists, meanwhile, felt betrayed, and after Scott's defeat, many gravitated toward the Know-Nothings. The Kansas-Nebraska Act cemented their allegiance to the Know-Nothings, who in the North opposed both the extension of slavery and Catholicism. An obsessive fear of conspiracies unified the Know-Nothings. They simultaneously denounced a papal conspiracy against the American republic and a Slave Power conspiracy spreading its tentacles throughout the United States. The Know-Nothings' surge was truly stunning. In 1854, they captured the governorship, all the congressional seats, and almost all the seats in the state legislature in Massachusetts.

After rising spectacularly between 1853 and 1855, the star of Know-Nothingism plummeted and gradually disappeared below the horizon after 1856. The Know-Nothings proved as vulnerable as the Whigs to sectional conflicts over slavery. Although primarily a force in the North, the Know-Nothings had a southern wing, comprised mainly of former Whigs who loathed both the antislavery northerners who were abandoning the Whig Party and the southern Democrats, whom they viewed as disunionist firebrands. In 1855, these southern Know-Nothings combined with northern conservatives to make acceptance of the Kansas-Nebraska Act part of the Know-Nothing platform, and thus they blurred the attraction of Know-Nothingism to those northern voters who were more antislavery than anti-Catholic.

One such Whig refugee, Illinois congressman Abraham Lincoln, asked pointedly: "How can anyone who abhors the oppression of negroes be in favor of degrading classes of white people?" "We began by declaring," Lincoln continued, "that 'all men are created equal.' We now practically read it 'all men are created equal except negroes.' When the Know-Nothings get control, it will read 'all men are created equal, except Negroes and foreigners and Catholics.'" Finally, even most Know-Nothings eventually came to conclude that, as one observer put it, "neither the Pope nor the foreigners ever can govern the country or endanger its liberties, but the slavebreeders and slavetraders do govern it, and threaten to put an end to all government but theirs." Consequently, the Know-Nothings proved vulnerable to the challenge posed by the emerging Republican Party, which did not officially embrace nativism and which had no southern wing to blunt its antislavery message.

14-2.4 The Republican Party and the Crisis in Kansas, 1855–1856

Born in the chaotic aftermath of the Kansas-Nebraska Act, the **Republican Party** sprang up in several northern states in 1854 and 1855. With the Know-Nothings' demise after 1856, the Republicans would become the main opposition to the Democratic Party. But few in 1855 would have predicted this. While united by opposition to the Kansas-Nebraska Act, the Republicans held various shades of opinion in uneasy balance. At one extreme were conservatives who merely wanted to restore the Missouri Compromise; at the other was a small faction of former Liberty Party abolitionists; and the middle held a sizable body of free-soilers.

Faced with these diverse constituencies, Republican leaders became political jugglers. To maintain internal harmony, the party's leaders avoided potentially divisive national issues such as the tariff and banking. Even so, Republican leaders recognized that they and the Know-Nothings were competing for many of the same voters. Believing that addiction to alcohol and submission to the pope were forms of enslavement, these voters often were pro-temperance, anti-Catholic, *and* antislavery.

The Republicans had clearer antislavery credentials than the Know-Nothings, but this fact alone did not guarantee that voters would respond more to antislavery than to anti-Catholicism or temperance. The Republicans needed a development that would make voters worry more about the Slave Power than about rum or Catholicism. Violence in Kansas, which quickly became known as Bleeding Kansas, united the party around its free-soil center, intensified antislavery feelings, and boosted Republican fortunes.

In the wake of the Kansas-Nebraska Act, Boston-based abolitionists had organized the New England

Know-Nothings
Founded in 1850, this party was one of many such societies that mushroomed in response to the unprecedented immigration of the 1840s. It had sought to rid the United States of immigrant and Catholic political influence by pressuring the existing parties to nominate and appoint only native-born Protestants to office and by advocating an extension of the naturalization period before immigrants could vote.

Republican Party
The political party that sprang up in several northern states in 1854 and 1855. After the Know-Nothings' demise in 1856, this party became the major opposition to the Democratic Party.

Emigrant Aid Company to send antislavery settlers into Kansas. The abolitionists' aim was to stifle efforts to turn Kansas into a slave state. But antislavery New Englanders arrived slowly in Kansas; the bulk of the territory's early settlers came from Missouri or elsewhere in the Midwest. Very few of these early settlers opposed slavery on moral grounds. Some, in fact, favored slavery; others wanted to keep all blacks, whether slave or free, out of Kansas.

Despite most settlers' racist leanings and utter hatred of abolitionists, Kansas became a battleground between proslavery and antislavery forces. In March 1855, thousands of proslavery Missourian "border ruffians," led by Senator David R. Atchison, crossed into Kansas to vote illegally in the first election for a territorial legislature. Drawing and cocking their revolvers, they quickly silenced any judges who questioned their right to vote in Kansas. These proslavery advocates probably would have won an honest election because they would have been supported by the votes both of slaveholders and of nonslaveholders horrified at rumors that abolitionists planned to use Kansas as a colony for fugitive slaves. But by stealing the election, the proslavery forces committed a grave tactical blunder. A cloud of fraudulence thereafter hung over the proslavery legislature subsequently established at Lecompton, Kansas. "There is not a proslavery man of my acquaintance in Kansas," wrote the wife of an antislavery farmer, "who does not acknowledge that the Bogus Legislature was the result of a gigantic and well planned fraud, that the elections were carried by an invading mob from Missouri." This legislature then further darkened its image by passing a succession of outrageous laws, limiting officeholding to individuals who would swear allegiance to slavery, punishing the harboring of fugitive slaves by ten years' imprisonment, and making the circulation of abolitionist literature a capital offense.

The territorial legislature's actions set off a chain reaction. Free-staters, including many settlers enraged by the proceedings at Lecompton, organized a rival government at Topeka in the summer and fall of 1855. In response, the Lecompton government in May 1856 dispatched a posse to Lawrence, where free-staters, heeding the advice of antislavery minister Henry Ward Beecher that rifles would do more than Bibles to enforce morality in Kansas, had taken up arms and dubbed their guns "Beecher's Bibles." Bearing banners emblazoned "southern rights" and "let yankees tremble and abolitionists fall," the proslavery posse tore through Lawrence, burning several buildings and destroying two free-state presses. There were no deaths, but Republicans immediately dubbed the incident "the sack of Lawrence."

The next move was made by John Brown. The sack of Lawrence convinced Brown that God now beckoned him "to break the jaws of the wicked." In late May, Brown led seven men, including his four sons and his son-in-law, toward the Pottawatomie Creek near Lawrence. Setting upon five men associated with the Lecompton government, they shot one to death and hacked the others to pieces with broadswords. Brown's "Pottawatomie massacre" struck terror into the hearts of southerners and completed the transformation of Bleeding Kansas into a battleground between the South and the North (see Map 14.3). A month after the massacre, a South Carolinian living in Kansas wrote to his sister,

I never lie down without taking the precaution to fasten my door and fix it in such a way that if it is forced open, it can be opened only wide enough for one person to come in at a time. I have my rifle, revolver, and old home-stocked pistol where I can lay my hand on them in an instant, besides a hatchet and an axe. I take this precaution to guard against the midnight attacks of the Abolitionists, who never make an attack in open daylight, and no Proslavery man knows when he is safe in this Ter[ritory.]

MAP 14.3   BLEEDING KANSAS Kansas became a battleground between free-state and slave-state factions in the 1850s.

Popular sovereignty had failed in Kansas. Instead of resolving the issue of slavery extension, popular sovereignty merely institutionalized the division over slavery by creating rival governments in Lecompton and Topeka. The Pierce administration then shot itself in the foot by denouncing the Topeka government and recognizing only its Lecompton rival. Pierce had forced northern Democrats into the awkward position of appearing to ally with the South in support of the "Bogus Legislature" at Lecompton.

Nor did popular sovereignty keep the slavery issue out of national politics. On the day before the sack of Lawrence, Republican senator **Charles Sumner** of Massachusetts delivered a bombastic and wrathful speech, "The Crime Against Kansas," in which he verbally whipped most of the U.S. Senate for complicity in slavery. Sumner singled out Senator Andrew Butler of South Carolina for making "the harlot, slavery" his mistress and for the "loose expectoration" of his speech (a nasty reference to the aging Butler's tendency to drool). Two days later, a relative of Butler, Democratic representative Preston Brooks of South Carolina, strode into the Senate chamber, found Sumner at his desk, and struck him repeatedly with a cane. The hollow cane broke after five or six blows, but Sumner required stitches, experienced shock, and did not return to the Senate for three years. Brooks became an instant hero in the South, and the fragments of his weapon were "begged as sacred

> **Charles Sumner**
> Republican senator from Massachusetts who opposed slavery.

relics." A new cane, presented to Brooks by the city of Charleston, bore the inscription "Hit him again."

Now Bleeding Kansas and Bleeding Sumner united the North. The sack of Lawrence, Pierce's recognition of the proslavery Lecompton government, and Brooks's actions seemed to clinch the Republican argument that an aggressive "slaveocracy" held white northerners in contempt. Abolitionists remained unpopular in northern opinion, but southerners were becoming even less popular. Northern migrants to Kansas coined a name reflecting their feelings about southerners: "the pukes." By denouncing the Slave Power more than slavery itself, Republican propagandists sidestepped the issue of slavery's morality, which divided their followers, and focused on portraying southern planters as arrogant aristocrats and the natural enemies of the laboring people of the North.

14-2.5 The Election of 1856

The election of 1856 revealed the scope of the political realignments of the preceding few years. In this, its first presidential contest, the Republican Party nominated John C. Frémont, the famed "pathfinder" who had played a key role in the conquest of California during the Mexican War. The Republicans then maneuvered the northern Know-Nothings into endorsing Frémont. The southern Know-Nothings picked the last Whig president, Millard Fillmore, as their candidate, and the Democrats dumped the battered Pierce for James Buchanan of Pennsylvania. A four-term congressman

ADMIT ME FREE FLAG In 1856, this flag was used at a rally at Pittsburgh, Pennsylvania, for Republican presidential nominee John C. Frémont. The oversized thirty-fourth star and the words "Admit Me Free" in the upper left part of the flag are in support of Kansas's admittance as a free state. *(Kansas State Historical Society)*

and long an aspirant to the presidency, Buchanan finally secured his party's nomination because he had the good luck to be out of the country (as minister to Great Britain) during the furor over the Kansas-Nebraska Act. As a signer of the Ostend Manifesto, he was popular in the South: virtually all of his close friends in Washington were southerners.

The campaign quickly turned into two separate races—Frémont versus Buchanan in the free states and Fillmore versus Buchanan in the slave states. In the North, the candidates divided clearly over slavery extension; Frémont's platform called for congressional prohibition of slavery in the territories, whereas Buchanan pledged congressional "noninterference." In the South, Fillmore appealed to traditionally Whig voters and called for moderation in the face of secessionist threats. But by nominating a well-known moderate in Buchanan, the Democrats undercut some of Fillmore's appeal. Although Fillmore garnered more than 40 percent of the popular vote in ten of the slave states, he carried only Maryland. In the North, Frémont outpolled Buchanan in the popular vote and won eleven of the sixteen free states; if Frémont had carried Pennsylvania and either Illinois, Indiana, or New Jersey, he would have won the election. As it turned out, Buchanan, the only truly national candidate in the race, secured the presidency.

The election yielded three clear conclusions. First, the American party was finished as a major national force. Having worked for the Republican Frémont, most northern Know-Nothings now joined that party, and southern Know-Nothings gave up on their party and sought new political affiliations. Second, although in existence scarcely more than a year, lacking any base in the South, and running a political novice, the Republican Party did very well. A purely sectional party had come within reach of capturing the presidency. Finally, as long as the Democrats could unite behind a single national candidate, they would be hard to defeat. To achieve such unity, however, the Democrats would have to find more James Buchanans—"doughface" moderates who would be acceptable to southerners and who would not drive even more northerners into Republican arms.

14-3 The Crisis of the Union, 1857–1860

What drove the North and South further apart in the mid-1850s?

No one ever accused James Buchanan of impulsiveness or fanaticism. Although a moderate eager to avoid controversy, he presided over one of the most controversy-ridden administrations in American history. Trouble arose first over the famed *Dred Scott* decision of the Supreme Court, then over the proslavery Lecompton Constitution in Kansas, next following the raid by John Brown on Harpers Ferry, and finally concerning secession itself.

The forces driving the nation apart were already spinning out of control by 1856. By the time of Buchanan's inauguration, southerners who looked north saw creeping abolitionism in the guise of free soil, whereas northerners who looked south saw an insatiable Slave Power. Once these images had taken hold in the minds of the American people, politicians like James Buchanan had little room to maneuver.

14-3.1 The Dred Scott Case, 1857

Pledged to congressional "noninterference" with slavery in the territories, Buchanan had long looked to the courts for a nonpartisan resolution of the vexing issue of slavery extension. A case that appeared to promise such a solution had been wending its way through the courts for years; and on March 6, 1857, two days after Buchanan's inauguration, the Supreme Court handed down its decision in *Dred Scott* v. *Sandford*.

During the 1830s, Dred Scott, a slave, had been taken by his master from the slave state of Missouri into Illinois and the Wisconsin Territory, areas respectively closed to slavery by the Northwest Ordinance of 1787 and the Missouri Compromise. After his master's death, Scott sued for his freedom on the grounds of his residence in free territory. In 1856, the case finally reached the Supreme Court.

The Court faced two key questions. Did Scott's residence in free territory during the 1830s make him free? Regardless of the answer to this question, did Scott, again enslaved in Missouri, have a right to sue in the federal courts? The Court could have resolved the case on narrow grounds by answering the second question in the negative, but Buchanan wanted a far-reaching decision that would deal with the broad issue of slavery in the territories.

In the end, Buchanan got the broad ruling that he sought, but one so controversial that it settled little. In the most important of six separate majority opinions, Chief Justice Roger B. Taney, a seventy-nine-year-old Marylander whom Andrew Jackson had appointed to succeed John Marshall in 1835, began with the narrow conclusion that Scott, a slave, could not sue for his freedom. Then the thunder started. No black, whether a slave or a free person descended from a slave, could become a citizen of the United States, Taney continued. Even if Scott had been a legal

> **Dred Scott v. Sandford**
> Court case in 1857 when a former slave, Dred Scott, sued for his own freedom after his master died on the grounds of his residence in free territory. In the end, Chief Justice Roger B. Taney decided that Scott could not sue for his own freedom. His ruling: No black, whether a slave or a free person descended from a slave, could become a citizen of the United States.

plaintiff, Taney ruled, his residence in free territory years earlier did not make him free because the Missouri Compromise, whose provisions prohibited slavery in the Wisconsin Territory, was itself unconstitutional. The compromise, declared Taney, violated the Fifth Amendment's protection of property (including slaves).

Contrary to Buchanan's hopes, the decision touched off a new blast of controversy over slavery in the territories. The antislavery press flayed it as a "willful perversion" filled with "gross historical falsehoods." Taney's ruling gave Republicans more evidence that a fiendish Slave Power conspiracy gripped the nation. Although the Kansas-Nebraska Act had effectively repealed the Missouri Compromise, the Court's majority now rejected even the principle behind the compromise, the idea that Congress could prohibit slavery in the territories. Five of the six justices who rejected this principle were from slave states. The Slave Power, a northern paper bellowed, "has marched over and annihilated the boundaries of the states. We are now one great homogenous slaveholding community." Like Stephen Douglas after the Kansas-Nebraska Act, President Buchanan now appeared to be a northern dupe of the "slaveocracy." Republicans restrained themselves from open defiance of the decision only by insisting that it did not bind the nation; Taney's comments on the constitutionality of the Missouri Compromise, they contended, amounted merely to *obiter dicta*, opinions superfluous to settling the case.

Reactions to the decision underscored the fact that by 1857 no "judicious" or nonpartisan solution to slavery extension was possible. Anyone who still doubted this needed only to read the fast-breaking news from Kansas.

14-3.2 The Lecompton Constitution, 1857

In Kansas, the free-state government at Topeka and the officially recognized proslavery government at Lecompton viewed each other with profound distrust. Buchanan's plan for Kansas looked simple: an elected territorial convention would draw up a constitution that would either permit or prohibit slavery; Buchanan would submit the constitution to Congress; Congress would then admit Kansas as a state.

Unfortunately, the plan exploded in Buchanan's face. Popular sovereignty, the essence of Buchanan's plan, demanded fairplay, a scarce commodity in Kansas. The territory's history of fraudulent elections left both sides reluctant to commit their

Lecompton Constitution
A frame of government that protected the rights of those slaveholders already living in Kansas to their slave property and provided for a referendum in which voters could decide whether to allow in more slaves.

fortunes to the polls. An election for a constitutional convention took place in June 1857, but free-staters, by now a majority in Kansas, boycotted the election on the grounds that the proslavery side would rig it. Dominated by proslavery delegates, a constitutional convention then met and drew up a frame of government, the **Lecompton Constitution**, that protected the rights of those slaveholders already living in Kansas to their slave property and provided for a referendum in which voters could decide whether to allow in more slaves.

The Lecompton Constitution created a dilemma for Buchanan. A supporter of popular sovereignty, he had gone on record in favor of letting the voters in Kansas decide the slavery issue. Now he was confronted by a Constitution drawn up by a convention that had been elected by less than 10 percent of the eligible voters, by plans for a referendum that would not allow voters to remove slaves already in Kansas, and by the prospect that the proslavery side would conduct the referendum no more honestly than it had other ballots. Yet Buchanan had compelling reasons to accept the Lecompton Constitution as the basis for the admission of Kansas as a state. The South, which had provided him with 112 of his 174 electoral votes in 1856, supported the constitution. Buchanan knew, moreover, that only about two hundred slaves resided in Kansas, and he believed that the prospects for slavery in the remaining territories were slight. The contention over slavery in Kansas struck him as another example of how extremists could turn minor issues into major ones. To accept the constitution and speed the admission of Kansas as either a free state or a slave state seemed the best way to pull the rug from beneath the extremists and quiet the ruckus in Kansas. Accordingly, in December 1857, Buchanan endorsed the Lecompton Constitution.

Stephen A. Douglas and other northern Democrats broke with Buchanan. To them, the Lecompton Constitution, in allowing voters to decide only whether more slaves could enter Kansas, violated the spirit of popular sovereignty. "I care not whether [slavery] is voted down or voted up," Douglas declared. But to refuse to allow a vote on the constitution itself, with its protection of existing slave property, smacked of a "system of trickery and jugglery to defeat the fair expression of the will of the people."

Even as Douglas broke with Buchanan, events in Kansas took a new turn. A few months after electing delegates to the convention that drew up the Lecompton Constitution, Kansans had gone to the polls to elect a territorial legislature. So flagrant was the fraud in this election—one village with thirty eligible voters returned more than sixteen hundred proslavery votes—that the governor disallowed enough proslavery returns to give free-staters a majority in the legislature. This territorial legislature then called for a referendum on the Lecompton Constitution and thus slavery itself. Whereas the Kansas constitutional convention had restricted the choice of voters to the narrow issue of the future introduction of slaves, the territorial legislature sought a referendum that would allow Kansans to vote against the protection of existing slave property as well.

In December 1857, the referendum called earlier by the constitutional convention was held. Boycotted by free-staters, the constitution with slavery passed overwhelmingly. Two weeks later, in the election called by the territorial legislature, the pro-slavery side abstained, and the constitution went down to crushing defeat. Buchanan tried to ignore this second election, but when he attempted to bring Kansas into the Union under the Lecompton Constitution, Congress blocked him and forced yet another referendum. This time, Kansans were given the choice between accepting or rejecting the entire constitution, with the proviso that rejection would delay statehood. Despite the proviso, Kansans overwhelmingly voted down the constitution.

Buchanan had simultaneously failed to tranquilize Kansas and alienated northerners in his own party. His support for the Lecompton Constitution confirmed the suspicion of northern Democrats that the southern Slave Power pulled all the important strings in their party. Douglas became the hero of the hour for northern Democrats. "The bone and sinew of the Northern Democracy are with you," a New Yorker wrote to Douglas. Yet Douglas himself could take little comfort from the Lecompton fiasco, as his cherished formula of popular sovereignty increasingly looked like a prescription for civil strife rather than harmony.

14-3.3 The Lincoln-Douglas Debates, 1858

Despite the acclaim he gained in the North for his stand against the Lecompton Constitution, Douglas faced a stiff challenge in Illinois for reelection to the U.S. Senate. Of his Republican opponent, Abraham Lincoln, Douglas said: "I shall have my hands full. He is the strong man of his party—full of wit, facts, dates—and the best stump speaker with his droll ways and dry jokes, in the West."

Physically as well as ideologically, the two men formed a striking contrast. Tall (6'4") and gangling, ambition and a passion for self-education had carried **Abraham Lincoln** from the Kentucky log cabin in which he was born in 1809 through a youth filled with various occupations (farm laborer, surveyor, rail-splitter, flatboatman, and storekeeper) into law and politics in his adopted Illinois. There he had capitalized on westerners' support for internal improvements to gain election to Congress in 1846 as a Whig. Having opposed the Mexican-American

War and the Kansas-Nebraska Act, he joined the Republican Party in 1856.

Douglas was fully a foot shorter than the towering Lincoln. Born in New England, Douglas appealed primarily to the small farmers of southern origin who populated the Illinois flatlands. To these and others, he was the "little giant," the personification of the Democratic Party in the West. The campaign quickly became more than just another Senate race because it pitted the Republican Party's rising star against the Senate's leading Democrat and, thanks to the railroad and the telegraph, received unprecedented national attention.

Although some Republicans extolled Douglas's stand against the Lecompton Constitution, to Lincoln, Douglas was still Douglas, the author of the infamous Kansas-Nebraska Act and a man who

> **Abraham Lincoln**
> Illinois lawyer who joined the Republican Party in 1856 and ran for president in 1860. He became one of the most important presidents of the United States.

STEPHEN A. DOUGLAS Douglas's politics were founded on his unflinching conviction that most Americans favored national expansion and would support popular sovereignty as the fastest and least controversial way to achieve it. Douglas's self-assurance blinded him to rising northern sentiment for free soil. *(National Portrait Gallery, Smithsonian Institution, Washington, DC/Art Resource, NY)*

cared not whether slavery was voted up or down as long as the vote was honest. Opening his campaign with the "House Divided" speech ("this nation cannot exist permanently half slave and half free"), Lincoln reminded his Republican followers of the gulf that still separated his doctrine of free soil from Douglas's popular sovereignty. Douglas dismissed the house-divided doctrine as an invitation to secession. What mattered to him was not slavery, which he viewed as merely an extreme way to subordinate a supposedly inferior race, but the continued expansion of white settlement. Like Lincoln, he wanted to keep slavery out of the path of white settlement. But unlike his rival, Douglas believed popular sovereignty was the surest way to attain this goal without disrupting the Union.

The high point of the campaign came in a series of seven debates held from August to October 1858. The Lincoln-Douglas debates mixed political drama with the atmosphere of a festival. At the debate in Galesburg, for example, dozens of horse-drawn floats descended on the town from nearby farming communities. One bore thirty-two girls dressed in white, one for each state, and a thirty-third who dressed in black with the label "Kansas" and carried a banner proclaiming "they won't let me in."

Douglas used the debates to portray Lincoln as a virtual abolitionist and advocate of racial equality. Both charges were calculated to doom Lincoln in the eyes of the intensely racist Illinois voters. In response, Lincoln affirmed that Congress had no constitutional authority to abolish slavery in the South, and in one debate he asserted bluntly that "I am not, nor ever have been in favor of bringing about the social and political equality of the white, and black man." However, fending off charges of extremism was getting Lincoln nowhere; so in order to seize the initiative, he tried to maneuver Douglas into a corner.

In view of the *Dred Scott* decision, Lincoln asked in the debate at Freeport, could the people of a territory lawfully exclude slavery? In essence, Lincoln was asking Douglas to reconcile popular sovereignty with the *Dred Scott* decision. Lincoln had long contended that the Court's decision rendered popular sovereignty as thin as soup boiled from the shadow of a pigeon that had starved to death. If, as the Supreme Court's ruling affirmed, Congress had no authority to exclude slavery from a territory, then it seemingly followed that a territorial legislature created by Congress also lacked power to do so. To no one's surprise, Douglas replied that notwithstanding the *Dred Scott* decision, the voters of a territory could effectively exclude slavery simply by refusing to enact laws that gave legal protection to slave property.

Douglas's "Freeport doctrine" salvaged popular sovereignty but did nothing for his reputation among southerners, who preferred the guarantees of the *Dred Scott* ruling to the uncertainties of popular

ABRAHAM LINCOLN Clean-shaven at the time of his famous debates with Douglas, Lincoln would soon grow a beard to give himself a more distinguished appearance. *(Library of Congress Prints and Photographs Division)*

sovereignty. Whereas Douglas's stand against the Lecompton constitution had already tattered his reputation in the South ("he is already dead there," Lincoln affirmed), his Freeport doctrine stiffened southern opposition to his presidential ambitions.

Lincoln faced the problem throughout the debates that free soil and popular sovereignty, although distinguishable in theory, had much the

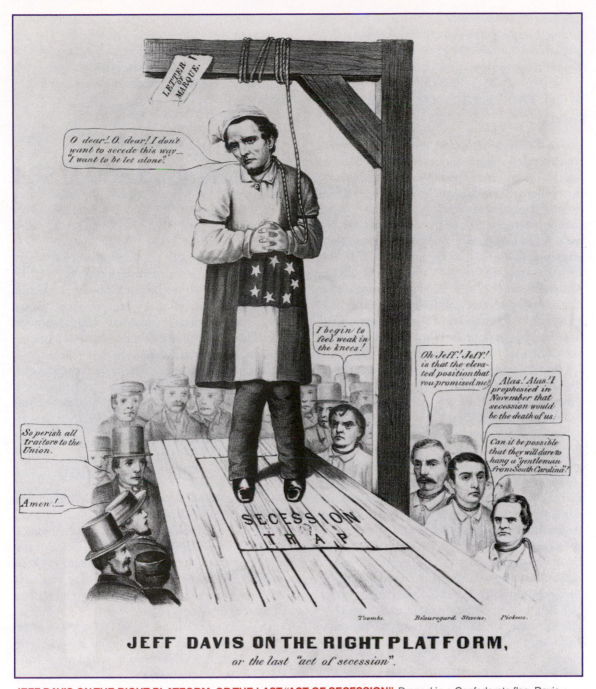

JEFF DAVIS ON THE RIGHT PLATFORM, OR THE LAST "ACT OF SECESSION" Draped in a Confederate flag, Davis, the elected president of the Confederacy, stands on a gallows and pleads, "I don't really want to secede this way." Prominent secessionists with nooses around their necks stand below Davis. Although many northerners expected high Confederate officials to be hanged for treason, none ever were. *(Library of Congress Prints and Photographs Division [LC-USZ62-89719])*

same practical effect. Neither Lincoln nor Douglas doubted that popular sovereignty, if fairly applied, would keep slavery out of the territories. In the closing debates, to keep the initiative and sharpen their differences, Lincoln shifted toward attacks on slavery as "a moral, social, and political evil." He argued that Douglas's view of slavery as merely an eccentric and unsavory southern custom would dull the nation's conscience and facilitate the legalization of slavery everywhere. But Lincoln compromised his own position by rejecting both abolition and equality for blacks.

Neither man scored a clear victory in argument, and the senatorial election itself settled no major issues. Douglas's supporters captured a majority of the seats in the state legislature, which at the time was responsible for electing U.S. senators. But despite the racist leanings of most Illinois voters, Republican candidates for the state legislature won a slightly larger share of the popular vote than did their Democratic rivals. Moreover, in its larger significance, the contest solidified the sectional split in the national Democratic Party and made Lincoln famous in the North and infamous in the South.

14-3.4 The Legacy of Harpers Ferry

Although Lincoln rejected abolitionism, he called free soil a step toward the "ultimate extinction" of slavery. Similarly, New York Republican senator William H. Seward spoke of an "irrepressible conflict" between slavery and freedom. Predictably, many white southerners ignored the distinction between free soil and abolition and concluded that Republicans and abolitionists were joined in an unholy alliance against slavery. To many in the South, the North seemed to be controlled by demented leaders bent on civil war. One southern defender of slavery equated the doctrines of the abolitionists with those of "Socialists, of Free Love and Free Lands, Free Churches, Free Women and Free Negroes-of No-Marriage, No-Religion, No-Private Property, No-Law and No-Government."

Nothing did more to freeze this southern image of the North than the evidence of northern complicity in John Brown's raid on the federal arsenal at Harpers Ferry, Virginia, on October 16, 1859. Brown and his followers were quickly overpowered; Brown himself was tried, convicted, and hanged. Lincoln and Seward condemned the raid. But some northerners turned Brown into a martyr; Ralph Waldo Emerson exulted that Brown's execution would "make the gallows as glorious as the cross." Furthermore, captured correspondence disclosed that Brown had received financial support from northern abolitionists. His objective, to inspire an armed slave insurrection, rekindled the deepest fears of white southerners.

In the wake of Brown's raid, rumors flew around the South, and vigilantes turned out to battle conspiracies that existed only in their minds. Volunteers, for example, mobilized to defend northeastern Texas against thousands of abolitionists supposedly on their way to pillage Dallas and its environs. In other incidents, vigilantes rounded up thousands of slaves, tortured some into confessing to nonexistent plots, and then lynched them. The hysteria fed by such rumors played into the hands of the extremists known as fire-eaters, who encouraged the witch hunt by spreading tales of slave conspiracies in the press so that southern voters would turn to them as alone able to "stem the current of Abolition."

More and more southerners concluded that the Republican Party itself directed abolitionism and deserved blame for Brown's raid. After all, had not influential Republicans spoken of an "irrepressible conflict" between slavery and freedom? The Tennessee legislature reflected southern views when it passed resolutions declaring that the Harpers Ferry raid was "the natural fruit of this treasonable 'irrepressible conflict' doctrine put forth by the great head of the Black Republican party and echoed by his subordinates."

14-4 The Union Fragments, 1860–1861

Was secession (and civil war) inevitable?

Although not all voters realized it, when they cast their ballots in the presidential election of 1860 they were deciding not just the outcome of an election but the fate of the Union. Lincoln's election initiated the process by which the southern states abandoned the United States for a new nation, the Confederate States of America. Initially, the Confederacy consisted only of states in the Lower South. As the Upper South hesitated to embrace secession, moderates searched frantically for a compromise that would save the Union. But they searched in vain. The time for compromise had passed.

14-4.1 The Election of 1860

As a single-issue, free-soil party, the Republicans had done well in the election of 1856. To win in 1860, however, they would have to broaden their appeal in the North, particularly in states like Pennsylvania and Illinois, which they had lost in 1856. To do so, Republican leaders had concluded, they needed to forge an economic program to complement their advocacy of free soil.

A severe economic slump following the so-called Panic of 1857 furnished the Republicans with a fitting opening. The depression shattered more than a decade of American prosperity and thrust economic concerns to the fore. In response, in the late 1850s the Republicans developed an economic program based on support for a protective tariff (popular in Pennsylvania) and on two issues favored in the Midwest, federal aid for internal improvements and the granting to settlers of free 160-acre homesteads out of publicly owned land. By proposing to make these homesteads available to immigrants who were not yet citizens, the Republicans went far in shedding the nativist image that lingered from their early association with the Know-Nothings. Carl Schurz, an 1848 German political refugee who had campaigned for Lincoln against Douglas in 1858, now labored mightily to bring his antislavery countrymen over to the Republican Party.

The Republicans' desire to broaden their appeal also influenced their choice of a candidate. At their convention in Chicago, they nominated Abraham Lincoln over the early front-runner, William H. Seward of New York. Although better known than Lincoln, Seward failed to convince his party that he could carry the key states of Pennsylvania, Illinois, Indiana, and New Jersey. Lincoln held the advantage not only of hailing from Illinois but also of projecting a more moderate image than Seward on the slavery issue—or so the party thought. Seward's penchant for controversial phrases like "irrepressible conflict" and "higher law" had given him a radical image. Lincoln, in contrast, had repeatedly affirmed that Congress had no constitutional right to interfere with slavery in the South and had explicitly rejected the "higher law" doctrine. The Republicans now needed only to widen their northern appeal.

The Democrats, still claiming to be a national party, had to bridge their own sectional differences. The *Dred Scott* decision and the conflict over the Lecompton constitution had weakened the northern Democrats and strengthened southern Democrats. While Douglas still desperately defended popular sovereignty, southern Democrats stretched *Dred Scott* to conclude that Congress now had to protect slavery in the territories.

The Democrats' internal turmoil boiled over at their Charleston convention in 1860. Failing to force acceptance of a platform guaranteeing federal protection of slavery in the territories, the delegates from the Lower South stalked out. The convention adjourned to Baltimore, where a new fight broke out over the question of seating hastily elected pro-Douglas slates of delegates from the Lower South states that had seceded from the Charleston convention. The decision to seat these pro-Douglas slates led to a walkout by delegates from Virginia and other states in the Upper South. The remaining delegates nominated Douglas; the seceders marched off to another hall in Baltimore and nominated Buchanan's vice president, John C. Breckinridge of Kentucky, on a platform calling for the congressional protection of slavery in the territories. Unable to rally behind a single nominee, the divided Democrats thus ran two candidates, Douglas and Breckinridge. The disruption of the Democratic Party was now complete.

The South still contained an appreciable number of moderates, often former Whigs who had joined with the Know-Nothings behind Fillmore in 1856. In 1860, these moderates, aided by former northern Whigs who opposed both Lincoln and Douglas, forged the new Constitutional Union Party and nominated John Bell, a Tennessee slaveholder who had opposed both the

Kansas-Nebraska Act and the Lecompton constitution. Calling for the preservation of the Union, the new party took no stand on the divisive issue of slavery extension.

With four candidates in the field, voters faced a relatively clear choice. Lincoln conceded that the South had a constitutional right to preserve slavery but demanded that Congress prohibit its extension. At the other extreme, Breckinridge insisted that Congress had to protect slavery in any territory that contained slaves. This left the middle ground to Bell and Douglas, the latter still committed to popular sovereignty but in search of a verbal formula that might reconcile it with the *Dred Scott* decision. Lincoln won a clear majority of the electoral vote, 180 to 123 for his three opponents combined. Although Lincoln gained only 39 percent of the popular vote, his popular votes were concentrated in the North, the majority section, and were sufficient to carry every free state. Douglas ran a respectable second to Lincoln in the popular vote but a dismal last in the electoral vote. As the only candidate to campaign in both sections, Douglas suffered from the scattered nature of his votes and carried only Missouri. Bell won Virginia, Kentucky, and Tennessee, and Breckinridge captured Maryland and the Lower South (see Map 14.4).

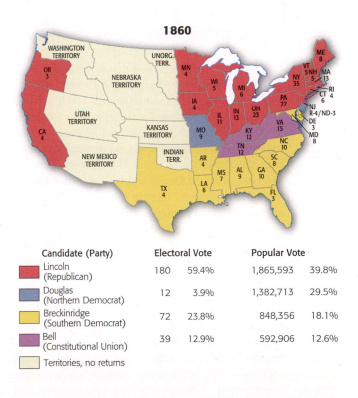

1860

Candidate (Party)	Electoral Vote		Popular Vote	
Lincoln (Republican)	180	59.4%	1,865,593	39.8%
Douglas (Northern Democrat)	12	3.9%	1,382,713	29.5%
Breckinridge (Southern Democrat)	72	23.8%	848,356	18.1%
Bell (Constitutional Union)	39	12.9%	592,906	12.6%
Territories, no returns				

MAP 14.4 THE ELECTION OF 1860 Having given the nation four of its first five presidents, the South confronted permanent minority status after the election of 1860. Despite receiving no votes in the South, Lincoln won the electoral vote easily. Even had the Democrats united behind a single candidate, Lincoln would have won the election.

14-4.2 The Gospel of Disunion

A pamphlet published in 1860 embodied in its title the growing conviction of southerners that *The South Alone Should Govern the South*. Lincoln's election struck most of the white South as a calculated northern insult. The North, a South Carolina planter told a visitor from England, "has got so far toward being abolitionized as to elect a man avowedly hostile to our institutions."

Few southerners believed Lincoln would fulfill his promise to protect slavery in the South, and most feared he would act as a mere front man for more John Browns. "Now that the black radical Republicans have the power I suppose they will Brown us all," a South Carolinian lamented (see Going to the Source). A Mississippian residing in Illinois expressed his reaction to the election more bluntly:

It seems the north wants the south to raise cotton and sugar rice tobacco for the northern states, also to pay taxes and fight her battles and get territory for the purpose of the north to send her greasy Dutch and free niggers into the territory to get rid of them. At any rate that was what elected old Abe President. Some professed conservative Republicans Think and say that Lincoln will be conservative also but sir my opinion is that Lincoln will deceive them. [He] will undoubtedly please the abolitionists for at his election they nearly all went into fits with Joy.

These fears help to explain why states in the Lower South seceded months before Lincoln took office on March 4, 1861. On December 20, 1860, a South Carolina convention voted unanimously for secession; in short order Alabama, Mississippi, Florida, Georgia, Louisiana, and Texas followed. On February 4, delegates from these seven states met in Montgomery, Alabama, and established the **Confederate States of America**. With their secession, most of these states dispatched commissioners to persuade other slave states to follow them in exiting the Union. These commissioners invariably made the same point: Lincoln's election left southerners with only one choice—to secede or to accept "negro equality" and the end of slavery.

Once in office, Lincoln certainly had the power to make life uncomfortable for slaveholders. Owing nothing to the South for his election, he could appoint antislavery northerners as governors of territories or as postmasters who might disseminate abolitionist pamphlets in the South. Some southerners contended that secession would make it easier for the South to acquire more territory for slavery in the Caribbean. Other southerners continued to complain that the North blocked the access of slaveholders to territories in the continental United States.

Nonetheless, these arguments alone did not clinch the case for secession. In his Inaugural Address, Lincoln stated that he did not object to a proposed constitutional amendment that would have prohibited any future amendment abolishing slavery in any state. Furthermore, the South was scarcely united in desiring additional slave territory in Mexico, Cuba, or Central America. States like Alabama, Mississippi, and Texas contained vast tracts of unsettled land that could be converted to cotton cultivation far more easily than the Caribbean. Nor would secession stop future John Browns from infiltrating the South to provoke slave insurrections.

Viewed as a practical tactic to secure concrete goals, secession did not make a great deal of sense. Yet to dwell on the impracticality of secession as a choice for the South is to miss the point. The events of the 1850s persuaded many southerners that the North had deserted the true principles of the Union. Southerners interpreted northern resistance to the Fugitive Slave Act and to slavery in Kansas as either illegal or unconstitutional, and they viewed headline-grabbing phrases such as "irrepressible conflict" and "a higher law" as virtual declarations of war on the South. To southerners, it was the North, not the South, that had grown peculiar.

More fundamentally, southerners believed that the North was treating the South as its inferior, as no more than a slave. "Talk of Negro slavery," exclaimed southern proslavery philosopher George Fitzhugh, "is not half so humiliating and disgraceful as the slavery of the South to the North." Having persuaded themselves that slavery made it possible for them to enjoy unprecedented freedom and equality, white southerners took great pride in their homeland. They bitterly dismissed Republican portrayals of the South as a region of arrogant planters and degraded white common folk. Submission to the Republicans, declared Democratic senator Jefferson Davis of Mississippi, "would be intolerable to a proud people."

14-4.3 The Upper South and the Coming of War

Despite the abruptness of the Lower South's withdrawal from the Union, uncertainty laced the movement for secession. Many southerners had resisted calls for immediate secession. Even after Lincoln's election, fire-eating secessionists had met opposition in the Lower South from so-called cooperationists, who called upon the South to act in unison or not at all. Many cooperationists had hoped to delay secession to wring concessions from the North that might remove the need for secession. Jefferson Davis, inaugurated in February 1861 as president of the Confederacy,

Confederate States of America Formed on February 4, 1861, and was made up of South Carolina, Alabama, Mississippi, Florida, Georgia, Louisiana, and Texas.

SOURCE

Lincoln at Cooper Union

Abraham Lincoln's Cooper Union speech, delivered in New York City on February 27, 1860, elevated him into the national spotlight. On the basis of his own extensive research, he established that in later votes in Congress, a clear majority of the thirty-nine signers of the Constitution demonstrated their view that the federal government had the power to restrict slavery in the territories. So much for the South's insistence that it was the true heir to the Founding generation. Lincoln then continued as follows.

Will they [southerners] be satisfied if the Territories be unconditionally surrendered to them? We know they will not. In all their present complaints against us, the Territories are scarcely mentioned. Invasions and insurrections are the rage now [a reference to John Brown's raid]. Will it satisfy them if in the future we have nothing to do with invasions and insurrections? We know it will not. We so know because we know we never had anything to do with invasions and insurrections; and yet this total abstaining does not exempt us from the charge and the denunciation.

The question recurs, what will satisfy them? Simply this: we must not only let them alone, but we must somehow convince them that we do let them alone. This, we know by experience, is no easy task. We have been trying to convince them from the very beginning of our organization [the Republican Party], but with no success. In all our platforms and speeches we have constantly protested our purpose to let them alone; but this has had no tendency to convince them. . . .

These natural, and apparently adequate means all failing, what will convince them? This, and this only: cease to call slavery *wrong* and join them in calling it *right*. And this must be done thoroughly—done in *acts* as well as *words*. Silence will not be tolerated. . . . We must arrest and return their fugitive slaves with greedy pleasure. We must pull down our free state constitutions. The whole atmosphere must be disinfected of all taint of opposition to slavery, before they will cease to believe that all their troubles proceed from us.

I am quite aware they do not state their case in precisely this way. Most of them would probably say to us, "Let us alone, do nothing to us, and say what you please about slavery." But we do let them alone—have never disturbed them—so that, after all, it is what we say, which dissatisfies them. They will continue to accuse us of doing, until we cease saying. . . . Holding, as they do, that slavery is morally right, and socially elevating, they cannot cease to demand a full national recognition of it, as a legal right, and a social blessing.

Source: Abraham Lincoln at Cooper Union, 1860.

QUESTIONS

1. Lincoln's mainly Republican audience included some prominent Democrats. What image of the Republican Party was he trying to counter?
2. Was Lincoln trying to conciliate the South, or unify the North? Explain your answer.

was a reluctant secessionist who remained in the U.S. Senate two weeks after his own state of Mississippi had seceded. Even zealous advocates of secession had a hard time reconciling themselves to secession and believing that they were no longer citizens of the United States. "How do you feel now, dear Mother," a Georgian wrote, "that *we* are in a foreign land?"

At first, the Upper South states of Virginia, North Carolina, Tennessee, and Arkansas flatly rejected secession (see Map 14.5). In contrast to the Lower South, which had a guaranteed export market for its cotton, the Upper South depended heavily on economic ties to the North that would be severed by secession. Furthermore, with proportionately far fewer slaves than the Lower South, the states of the Upper South doubted the loyalty of their sizable nonslaveholding populations to the idea of secession. Virginia, for example, had every reason to question the allegiance to secession of its nonslaveholding western counties, which would soon break away to form Unionist West Virginia. Few in the Upper South could forget the raw nerve touched by the publication in 1857 of Hinton R. Helper's *The Impending Crisis of the South*. A nonslaveholding North Carolinian, Helper had described slavery as a curse upon poor white southerners and thereby questioned one of the most sacred southern doctrines, the idea that slavery rendered all whites equal.

If secession were to spark a war between the states, moreover, the Upper South appeared to be the likeliest battleground. Whatever the exact weight assignable to each of these factors, one point is clear: the secession movement that South Carolina so boldly started in December 1860 seemed to be falling apart by March 1861.

The lack of southern unity confirmed the view of most Republicans that the secessionists were more bluster than substance. Seward described secession as the work of "a relatively few hotheads," and Lincoln believed that the loyal majority of southerners would soon wrest control from the fire-eating minority.

This perception stiffened Republican resolve to resist compromise. Moderate John J. Crittenden of Kentucky proposed compensation for owners of runaway slaves, repeal of northern personal-liberty laws, a constitutional amendment to prohibit the federal government from interfering with slavery in the southern states, and another amendment to restore the Missouri Compromise line for the remaining territories and protect slavery below it. But in the face of steadfast Republican opposition, the Crittenden plan collapsed.

Lincoln's faith in a "loyal majority" of southerners exaggerated both their numbers and their devotion to the Union. Many southern opponents of the

MAP 14.5 SECESSION Four key states—Virginia, Arkansas, Tennessee, and North Carolina—did not secede until after the fall of Fort Sumter. The border slave states of Maryland, Delaware, Kentucky, and Missouri stayed in the Union.

fire-eating secessionists were sitting on the fence and hoping for major concessions from the North; their allegiance to the Union thus was conditional. Lincoln can be faulted for misreading southern opinion, but even if his assessment had been accurate, it is unlikely that he would have accepted the Crittenden plan. The sticking point was the proposed extension of the Missouri Compromise line. To Republicans this was a surrender, not a compromise, because it hinged on the abandonment of free soil, the founding principle of their party. In addition, Lincoln well knew that some southerners still talked of seizing more territory for slavery in the Caribbean. In proposing to extend the 36°30' line, the Crittenden plan specifically referred to territories "hereafter acquired." Lincoln feared it would be only a matter of time "till we shall have to take Cuba as a condition upon which they [the seceding states] will stay in the Union."

Beyond these considerations, the precipitous secession of the Lower South changed the question that Lincoln faced. The issue was no longer slavery extension but secession. The Lower South had left the Union in the face of losing a fair election. For Lincoln to have caved in to such pressure would have violated majority rule, the principle upon which the nation, not just his party, had been founded.

By the time Lincoln took office in March 1861, little more than a spark was needed to ignite a war. William Seward, whom Lincoln had appointed secretary of state, now became obsessed with the idea of conciliating the Lower South in order to hold the Upper South in the Union. In addition to advising the evacuation of federal forces from Fort Sumter, Seward proposed a scheme to reunify the nation by provoking a war with France and Spain. But Lincoln brushed aside Seward's advice. Instead, the president informed the governor of South Carolina of his intention to supply Fort Sumter with much-needed provisions, but not with men and ammunition. To gain the dubious military advantage of attacking Fort Sumter before the arrival of relief ships, Confederate batteries began to bombard the fort shortly before dawn on April 12. The next day, the fort's garrison surrendered.

Lincoln's appeal for seventy-five thousand volunteers from the loyal states to suppress the rebellion pushed citizens of the Upper South off the fence upon which they had perched for three months. "I am a Union man," one southerner wrote, "but when they [the Lincoln administration] send men south it will change my notions. I can do nothing against my own people." In quick succession, Virginia, North Carolina, Arkansas, and Tennessee leagued with the Confederacy. After acknowledging that "I am one of those dull creatures that cannot see the good of secession," Robert E. Lee resigned from the army rather than lead federal troops against his native Virginia.

The North, too, was ready for a fight, less to abolish slavery than to punish secession. Worn out from his efforts to find a peaceable solution to the issue of slavery extension, and with only a short time to live, Stephen Douglas assaulted "the new system of resistance by the sword and bayonet to the results of the ballot-box" and affirmed: "I deprecate war, but if it must come I am with my country, under all circumstances, and in every contingency."

The Whole Vision

■ **Why was the Compromise of 1850 ultimately unsuccessful in resolving sectional divisions?**

Tensions mounted in the immediate aftermath of the U.S. war with Mexico over the fate of the newly acquired lands from Mexico and the broader implications of such decisions. At the core were concerns about interpretation and power—who in the U.S. would and should (and legally, had the right) to decide about the extension of slavery to the territories. There was also anxiety about what the addition of new slave or free states would mean for the balance of power in the U.S. Congress. Various competing political doctrines and ideals emerged, but there was little consensus. Passage of the Compromise of 1850 had more to do with party politics and the stature of those advocating for it—most notably Henry Clay and Stephen Douglas—than with what the compromise promised either side. Despite the hopes of its champions, the Compromise of 1850 did not resolve the issues or restore calm; rather, it fanned the flames of sectional divide. Part of the problem was the weak support behind passage of the compromise in the first place; the rest had to do with the specifics it outlined. Southerners disliked many aspects of the compromise. Northerners passed laws in their states to circumvent the portions of the compromise that they refused to enforce, and northern antislavery activism became more widespread and strident.

■ **What ultimately fueled the collapse of the second party system?**

Before the end of the second party system, Americans had multiple issues to consider when casting ballots or choosing a party affiliation. But as tensions over slavery and its expansion continued to divide the nation in the years after the war with Mexico, they also altered the state of political parties and the issues that forged party allegiance. Slavery became the single issue that dominated politics and party loyalties, and new political battles such as those around Kansas and Nebraska only further illustrated the growing regional nature of the existing parties. Divisions within the Whigs over this issue lent power to its opponents and contributed to the party's demise and its replacement first by the Know-Nothings and ultimately the Republicans. The battle over the fate of Kansas as slave or free-soil, dubbed "Bleeding Kansas," solidified the North–South political divide. The proof that regional alliances—rather than the two-party system—had come to dominate politics was evident in the presidential election of 1856.

What drove the North and South further apart in the mid-1850s?

The division between free-soilers and advocates of slavery continued to heat up during the latter part of the 1850s. Several key issues and milestones demonstrated just how wide the gap had become and at the same time fanned the flames of distrust and enmity. In each case, too, what became clear were the distinctly different visions of both the roles and rights of states and the place of slavery in the nation's future. While some hoped that the Dred Scott case of 1857 would have the courts solve the issue in a nonpartisan and mutually satisfactory way, that did not come to pass. In fact, the case only created new controversies over the meaning of slavery and freedom in the territories. Efforts such as the Lecompton Constitution that rested on popular sovereignty fared no better. The famous Lincoln-Douglas debates of 1858 only underscored the complexity of attempts to solve the slave question via popular sovereignty and at the same time foreshadowed the deep North–South political divisions that would mark the 1860 presidential election. John Brown's raid at Harpers Ferry fed southern suspicions and fear of the antislavery North and the Republican Party.

Was secession (and civil war) inevitable?

Historians continue to ask and debate this important question. By 1860, the divisions between the North and South were deep and profound. The political parties that had traditionally served as an outlet for safeguarding, expressing, and negotiating political views were no longer able to serve in that role. Sectionalism divided the parties, just as it split the nation. The election of Abraham Lincoln as president made that point all too clear. What had emerged by 1860 was an intense sense of distrust between the North and South and differences that were not only profound but increasingly irreconcilable. Aside from deep divisions in terms of the labor systems they embraced, the North and South vehemently disagreed on what constituted the Union, and especially, on the rights of states versus that of the national government. The southern states that seceded after Lincoln's election as president did not believe their vision, way of life, or autonomy could survive within the Union. Those that did not initially or ever secede weighed the value of both options as well as the potential for, and Lincoln's commitment to, compromise. But in a seceded South that believed it not only had a right to break away much as the colonies had during the American Revolution, stopping the Union from entering its territory and supplying Fort Sumter was deemed militarily necessary.

15 Crucible of Freedom: Civil War, 1861–1865

UNION SOLDIERS Soldiers of the 5th Ohio Cavalry moved through the South in 1864 with Union General William T. Sherman. *(Ronn Palm Museum of Civil War Images, Gettysburg, PA)*

CHRONOLOGY 1861–1865

1861
President Abraham Lincoln calls for volunteers to suppress the rebellion (April).

Virginia, Arkansas, Tennessee, and North Carolina join the Confederacy (April–May).

Lincoln imposes a naval blockade on the South (April).

U.S. Sanitary Commission formed (June).

First Battle of Bull Run (July).

First Confiscation Act (August).

1862
Legal Tender Act (February).

George B. McClellan's Peninsula Campaign (March–July).

Battle of Shiloh (April).

Confederate Congress passes the Conscription Act (April).

David G. Farragut captures New Orleans (April).

Homestead Act (May).

Seven Days' Battles (June–July).

Pacific Railroad Act (July).

Morrill Land Grant Act (July).

Second Confiscation Act (July).

Battle of Antietam (September).

Preliminary Emancipation Proclamation (September).

Battle of Fredericksburg (December).

1863
Emancipation Proclamation issued (January).

Lincoln suspends writ of *habeas corpus* nationwide (January).

1864
(cont.)
National Bank Act (February).

Congress passes the Enrollment Act (March).

Battle of Chancellorsville (May).

Woman's National Loyal League formed (May).

Battle of Gettysburg (July).

Surrender of Vicksburg (July).

New York City draft riots (July).

Battle of Chickamauga (September).

1864
Ulysses S. Grant given command of all Union armies (March).

Battle of the Wilderness (May).

Battle of Spotsylvania (May).

Battle of Cold Harbor (June).

Surrender of Atlanta (September).

Lincoln reelected (November).

William T. Sherman's march to the sea (November–December).

1865
Congress passes the Thirteenth Amendment (January).

Sherman moves through South Carolina (January–March).

Grant takes Richmond (April).

Robert E. Lee surrenders at Appomattox (April).

Lincoln dies (April).

Joseph Johnston surrenders to Sherman (April).

"Events transcending in importance anything that has ever happened within the recollection of any living person in *our* country, have occurred since I have written last in my journal," wrote Georgia matron Gertrude Clanton Thomas in July 1861. "*War has* been declared." Fort Sumter in South Carolina had surrendered; Lincoln had called for seventy-five thousand troops; four more southern states—Virginia, North Carolina, Arkansas, and Tennessee—had left the Union; and the newly formed Confederate government had moved from Montgomery, Alabama, to Richmond, Virginia.

At her marriage in 1852, Gertrude Thomas had become mistress of a small estate, Belmont, about six miles south of Augusta, Georgia. The estate and thirty thousand dollars' worth of slaves had been part of her dowry. While her husband, Jefferson Thomas, farmed plantation land he had inherited in a nearby county, Gertrude Thomas supervised the workforce at Belmont and wrestled with her position on slavery. "[T]he institution of slavery degrades the white man more than the Negro," she had declared in 1858. "All southern women are abolitionists at heart." After secession, her doubts about slavery persisted. "[T]he view has gradually become fixed

GERTRUDE CLANTON THOMAS IN THE 1850s *(Ronn Palm Museum of Civil War Images, Gettysburg, PA)*

401

in my mind that the institution of slavery is not right," she confided to her journal during the war. "[T]o hold men and women in *perpetual* bondage is wrong." Other times, more practical concerns about slaves emerged. "I do think that if we had the same [amount] invested in something else as a means of support," Gertrude Thomas wrote, "I would willingly, nay gladly, have the responsibility of them taken off my shoulders."

But slavery was the basis of Gertrude Thomas's wealth and social position. When war began, Gertrude and Jefferson Thomas fervently supported the newborn Confederacy. Jefferson Thomas enlisted in a cavalry company, and served until 1862, when, passed over for promotion, he hired a substitute. Gertrude Thomas loyally boosted the Confederate cause. "Our country is invaded—our homes are in danger—We are deprived . . . of that glorious liberty for which our Fathers fought and bled," she declared.

As war raged on, Gertrude Thomas longed for its end. The war transformed both societies in many ways. North and South, women took on more responsibilities and embraced opportunities that took them beyond what had been available to them at any time prior. Slaves fled or resisted complying with slaveholders as they had in the past. Both sides weathered hardships and shortages—though they were far worse for the South—and even peace came at a price. In the last year of war, Union invasions damaged the plantations run by Jefferson Thomas. The Thomas family lost a small fortune of fifteen thousand dollars in Confederate bonds and ninety slaves. One by one, the former slaves left the Belmont estate, never to return.

Neither side foresaw the carnage that war would bring; one out of every five soldiers who fought in the Civil War died in it. And no one anticipated a protracted war. Most northern estimates of the war's duration ranged from one month to a year; rebels, too, counted on a speedy victory. Partisans on both sides, like Gertrude Thomas, claimed the ideals of liberty, loyalty, and patriotism as their own. Once it became clear that war would extend beyond a few battles, leaders on both sides considered strategies once unpalatable or even unthinkable. The South had to defy its states' rights principles and form a central government to orchestrate the war and the objectives of the Confederacy, including imposing a draft and tax levies, as well as virtually extorting supplies from civilians. By the war's end, the Confederacy was even ready to arm its slaves in an ironically desperate effort to save a society founded on slavery. The North, which began the war with the limited objective of overcoming secession and explicitly disclaimed any intention of interfering with slavery, found that to win, it had to shred the fabric of southern society by destroying slavery.

15-1 Mobilizing for War

What challenges did each side— North and South—face in preparing for war?

North and South alike were unprepared for war. In April 1861, the Union had only a small army of sixteen thousand men scattered all over the country, mostly in the West. One-third of Union army officers had resigned to join the Confederacy. The nation's new president, Abraham Lincoln, struck many observers as a yokel. That such a government could marshal its people for war seemed doubtful. The federal government had levied no direct taxes for decades and had never imposed a draft. The Confederacy, even less prepared, had no tax structure, no navy, only two tiny gunpowder factories, and poorly equipped, unconnected railroad lines.

During the first two years of war, both sides would have to overcome these deficiencies, raise and supply large armies, and finance the war's heavy costs. In each region, mobilization expanded the powers of government to an extent that few had anticipated.

15-1.1 Recruitment and Conscription

The Civil War armies were the largest organizations ever created in America; by the war's end, more than 2 million men served in the Union army and 800,000 in the Confederate army (see Figure 15.1). In the first flush of enthusiasm, volunteers rushed to the colors. "We will be held responsible before God if we don't do our part," declared a New Jersey recruit. "I go for wiping them out," a Virginian told his governor.

At first, raising armies depended on local efforts rather than on national or even state direction. Citizens opened hometown recruiting offices, held rallies, and signed up volunteers; regiments usually consisted of soldiers from the same locale. Southern cavalrymen provided their own horses, and

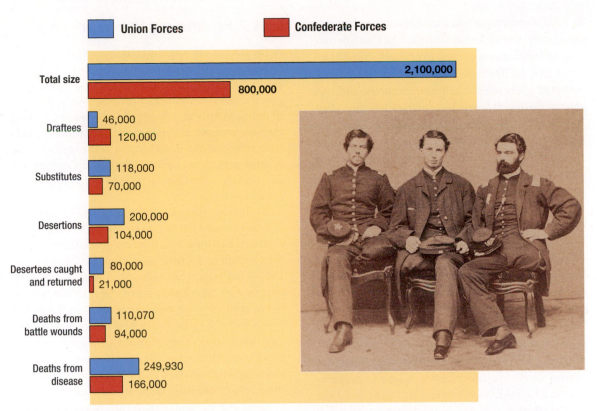

Union Forces   **Confederate Forces**

	Union	Confederate
Total size	2,100,000	800,000
Draftees	46,000	120,000
Substitutes	118,000	70,000
Desertions	200,000	104,000
Desertees caught and returned	80,000	21,000
Deaths from battle wounds	110,070	94,000
Deaths from disease	249,930	166,000

FIGURE 15.1 OPPOSING ARMIES OF THE CIVIL WAR "They sing and whoop, they laugh: they holler to de people on de ground and sing out 'Good bye,'" remarked a slave watching rebel troops depart. "All going down to die." As this graph shows (see also Figure 15.3), the Civil War had profound human costs. The total death count (620,000) represents a minimum estimate. North or South, hardly a family did not grieve for a lost relative or friend. Injured veterans became a common sight in cities, towns, and rural districts well into the twentieth century. This photograph shows Union volunteers with amputations performed by U.S. surgeons during the Civil War. *(William Gladstone/Picture Research Consultants & Archives)*

uniforms everywhere depended mainly on local option. In both armies, the troops elected officers up to the rank of colonel.

This informal and democratic way of raising and organizing soldiers could not long withstand the stress of war. As early as July 1861, the Union began examinations for officers. Also, as casualties mounted, military demand soon exceeded the supply of volunteers. The Confederacy felt the pinch first and in April 1862 enacted the first **conscription** law in American history. It required all able-bodied white men age eighteen to thirty-five to serve in the military for three years. Subsequent amendments made the age limits seventeen and fifty.

The Confederacy's Conscription Act antagonized southerners. Opponents charged that the draft was a despotic assault on state. Exemptions for many occupations, from religious ministry to shoemaking, aggrieved the nonexempt. So did a loophole, closed in 1863, that allowed the well-off to hire substitutes (at a cost that came to exceed $1,000). One amendment, the so-called 20-Negro law, exempted an owner or overseer of twenty or more slaves from service. Although southerners widely feared loss of control over slaves if all able-bodied white men were away in the army, the 20-Negro law led to complaints about "a rich man's war but a poor man's fight."

Despite opposition, the Confederate draft became increasingly hard to evade; this stimulated volunteering. Only one soldier in five was a draftee, but 70–80 percent of eligible white southerners served in the Confederate army. An 1864 law that required all soldiers then in the army to serve for the duration of the war ensured that a high proportion of Confederate soldiers would be battle-hardened veterans.

Once the army was raised, it needed supplies. At first, the South relied on arms and ammunition imported from Europe, weapons confiscated from federal arsenals, and guns captured on the battlefield. These stopgap measures bought time to develop an industrial base.

conscription
This required all able-bodied white men age eighteen to thirty-five to serve in the military for three years. Subsequent amendments raised the age limit to forty-five and then to fifty, and lowered it to seventeen.

By 1862, southerners had a competent head of ordnance (weaponry), Josiah Gorgas. The Confederacy assigned ordnance contracts to privately owned factories like the Tredegar Iron Works in Richmond, provided loans to establish new factories, and created government-owned industries like the giant Augusta Powder Works in Georgia. The South lost few, if any, battles for want of munitions.

Supplying troops with clothing and food proved more difficult. Southern soldiers often lacked shoes; when the South invaded Maryland in 1862, thousands of Confederate soldiers remained behind because they could not march barefoot on Maryland's gravel-surfaced roads. Late in the war, Robert E. Lee's Army of Northern Virginia ran out of food but never ammunition. Southern supply problems had several sources: railroads that fell into disrepair or were captured, an economy that relied more heavily on producing tobacco and cotton than growing food, and Union invasions early in the war that overran the livestock and grain-raising districts of central Tennessee and Virginia. Close to desperation, the Confederate Congress in 1863 passed the Impressment Act, an unpopular law that authorized army officers to take food from reluctant farmers at prescribed prices and to impress slaves into labor for the army, a provision that provoked even more resentment.

The industrial North had fewer supply problems. But recruitment was another matter. When the initial tide of enthusiasm for enlistment ebbed, Congress followed the Confederacy's example and turned to conscription with the Enrollment Act of March 1863; every able-bodied white male citizen age twenty to forty-five now faced the draft.

Like the Confederate conscription law of 1862, the Enrollment Act granted exemptions, although only to high government officials, ministers, and men who were the sole support of widows, orphans, or indigent parents. It also offered two means of escaping the draft: substitution, or paying another man who would serve instead; and commutation, paying a $300 fee to the government. Enrollment districts often competed for volunteers by offering cash payments (bounties); dishonest "bounty jumpers" repeatedly deserted after collecting payments. Democrats charged that conscription violated individual liberties and states' rights. Ordinary citizens resented the commutation and substitution provision and leveled their own "poor man's fight" charges. Still, as in the Confederacy, the law stimulated volunteering. Only 8 percent of Union soldiers were draftees or substitutes.

Legal Tender Act
Signed in 1862, it authorized the issue of $150 million of the so-called greenbacks.

15-1.2 Financing the War

At the start of the war, the recruitment and supply of huge armies lay far beyond the capacity of American public finance. In the 1840s and 1850s, the federal government met its meager revenue needs from tariff duties and income from public land sales. During the war, however, annual federal expenditures gradually rose, and the need for new sources of revenue became urgent. Yet neither Union nor Confederacy initially wished to impose taxes to which Americans were unaccustomed.

Both sides therefore turned to war bonds; that is, to loans from citizens to be repaid by future generations. Patriotic southerners quickly bought up the Confederacy's first bond issue ($15 million) in 1861. That same year, a financial wizard, Philadelphia banker Jay Cooke, urged the northern public to buy a much larger bond issue ($150 million). But bonds had to be paid for in gold or silver coin (specie), which was in short supply. Soaking up most of its available specie, the South's first bond issue threatened to be its last. In the North, many hoarded their gold rather than spend it on bonds.

Grasping the limits of taxes and bond issues, both sides began to print paper money. Early in 1862, Lincoln signed into law the **Legal Tender Act**, which authorized the issue of $150 million of so-called greenbacks. Christopher Memminger, the Confederacy's treasury secretary, and Salmon P. Chase, his Union counterpart, shared a distrust of paper money, but as funds dwindled each came to accept the idea. The availability of paper money made it easier to pay soldiers, levy taxes, and sell war bonds. Unlike gold and silver, which had established market values, the value of paper money depended mainly on public confidence in the government that issued it. To bolster that confidence, Union officials made the greenbacks legal tender (that is, acceptable in payment of most public and private debts).

In contrast, the Confederacy never made its paper money legal tender; suspicions arose that the southern government lacked confidence in it. To compound the problem, the Confederacy raised less than 5 percent of its wartime revenue from taxes (compared to 21 percent in the North). The Confederacy did enact a comprehensive tax measure in 1863, but Union invasions and the South's relatively undeveloped system of internal transportation made tax collection a hit-or-miss proposition.

Confidence in the South's paper money quickly evaporated, and the value of Confederate paper in relation to gold plunged. The Confederate response—printing more paper money, a billion dollars by 1865—merely accelerated southern inflation. Whereas prices in the North rose about 80 percent during the war, the Confederacy suffered an inflation rate of over 9,000 percent. What cost a southerner one dollar in 1861 cost forty-six dollars by 1864.

By raising taxes, floating bonds, and printing paper money, both North and South broke with the hard-money, minimal-government traditions of American public finance. For the most part, these changes were unanticipated and often reluctant adaptations to wartime conditions. But in the North, Republicans took advantage of the southern Democrats' departure from Congress to push through one measure that they and their Whig predecessors had long advocated: a system of national banking. Passed in February 1863 over Democratic opposition, the **National Bank Act** established criteria by which a bank could obtain a federal charter and issue national bank notes (notes backed by the federal government). It also gave private bankers an incentive to purchase war bonds. The North's ability to revolutionize its public finance system reflected both long experience with complex financial transactions and political cohesion in wartime.

15-1.3 Political Leadership in Wartime

The Civil War pitted rival political systems as well as armies and economies against each other. The South entered the war with several apparent political advantages. Lincoln's call for militiamen to suppress the rebellion had transformed Southern waverers into tenacious secessionists. "Never was a people more united or more determined," a New Orleans woman wrote in the spring of 1861. Southerners also claimed a strong leader. A former secretary of war and U.S. senator from Mississippi, President **Jefferson Davis** of the Confederacy possessed experience, honesty, courage, and what one officer described as "a jaw sawed in *steel*."

In contrast, the Union's list of political liabilities seemed long. Loyal but contentious, northern Democrats disliked conscription, the National Bank Act, and abolition of slavery. Among Republicans, Lincoln had trouble commanding respect. Unlike Davis, he had served in neither the cabinet nor the Senate; his informal western manners dismayed easterners. Northern setbacks early in the war convinced most Republicans in Congress that Lincoln was ineffectual. Criticism of Lincoln sprang from **Radical Republicans**, a group that included Secretary of the Treasury Salmon P. Chase, Senator Charles Sumner of Massachusetts, and Representative Thaddeus Stevens of Pennsylvania. On some issues, the Radicals cooperated with Lincoln. But they assailed him early in the war for failing to make emancipation a war goal and later for being too eager to readmit the conquered rebel states into the Union.

Lincoln's distinctive style of leadership at once encouraged and disarmed opposition among Republicans. Self-contained until ready to act, he met complaints with homespun anecdotes that caught opponents off guard. The Radicals often saw Lincoln as a prisoner of the party's conservative wing; conservatives complained he was too close to the Radicals. But Lincoln's cautious reserve left open his lines of communication with both wings of the party and fragmented his opposition. He also co-opted some of his critics, including Chase, by bringing them into his cabinet.

In contrast, Jefferson Davis had a knack for making enemies. A West Pointer, he would rather have led the army than the government. His cabinet endured frequent resignations; the Confederacy had five secretaries of war in four years. Davis's relations with his vice president, Alexander Stephens of Georgia, verged on disastrous. A wisp of a man, Stephens weighed less than a hundred pounds, but he compensated for his slight physique with an acidic tongue. Leaving Richmond,

National Bank Act
This established criteria by which a bank could obtain a federal charter and issue national bank notes (notes backed by the federal government). It also gave private bankers an incentive to purchase war bonds.

Jefferson Davis
President of the Confederacy.

Radical Republicans
A group of Republicans that included Secretary of the Treasury Salmon P. Chase, Senator Charles Sumner of Massachusetts, and Representative Thaddeus Stevens of Pennsylvania. They never formed a tightly knit unit; on some issues they cooperated with Lincoln. But they assailed him early in the war for failing to make emancipation a war goal and later for being too eager to readmit the conquered rebel states into the Union.

JEFFERSON DAVIS AND VARINA DAVIS Jefferson Davis and his wife, Varina Howell Davis, around the time of their marriage in the 1840s. (*Private Collection/Picture Research Consultants & Archives*)

ABRAHAM LINCOLN A portrait of Lincoln made in the Washington, D.C., studio of photographer Alexander Gardner in November 1863, eleven days before the president gave the Gettysburg Address. *(Library of Congress Prints and Photographs Division)*

the Confederate capital, in 1862, Stephens spent most of the war in Georgia, where he sniped at Davis as "weak and vacillating, timid, petulant, peevish, obstinate."

The clash between Davis and Stephens also involved an ideological division like that at the heart of the Confederacy. The Confederate Constitution, drafted in February 1861, explicitly guaranteed state sovereignty and prohibited the Confederate Congress from enacting protective tariffs or supporting internal improvements (measures long opposed by southern voters). For Stephens and other influential Confederates—among them the governors of Georgia and North Carolina—the Confederacy existed not only to protect slavery but, equally important, to enshrine the doctrine of states' rights. In contrast, Davis's main objective was to secure the independence of the South from the North, if necessary at the expense of states' rights.

This difference between Davis and Stephens somewhat resembled the discord between Lincoln and northern Democrats. Like Davis, Lincoln believed that victory demanded a strong central government; like Stephens, northern Democrats resisted governmental centralization. But Lincoln could control his foes more skillfully than Davis because, by temperament, he was more suited to conciliation and also because the nature of party politics in the two sections differed.

In the South, the Democrats and the remaining Whigs agreed to suspend party rivalries for the duration of the war. Although intended to promote southern unity, this decision actually encouraged disunity. Without the organization that party rivalry provided, southern politics disintegrated along personal and factional lines. Lacking a party system to back him, Davis could not mobilize votes to pass measures that he favored nor depend on the support of party loyalists.

In contrast, in the Union, northern Democrats' organized opposition to Lincoln tended to unify the Republicans. After Democrats won control of five states (including Lincoln's Illinois) in 1862, Republican leaders learned a lesson: no matter how much they disdained Lincoln, they had to rally behind him or risk losing office. Ultimately, the Union developed more political cohesion than the Confederacy, not because it had fewer divisions but because it managed its divisions more effectively.

15-1.4 Securing the Union's Borders

Even before large-scale fighting began, Lincoln moved to safeguard Washington, which was bordered by two slave states (Virginia and Maryland) and filled with Confederate sympathizers. A week after Fort Sumter, a Baltimore mob attacked a Massachusetts regiment bound for Washington, but enough troops slipped through to protect the capital. Lincoln then dispatched federal troops to Maryland, where he suspended the writ of *habeas corpus* (a court order requiring that the detainer of a prisoner bring that person to court and show cause for his or her detention); federal troops could now arrest pro-secession Marylanders without formally charging them with specific offenses. Cowed by Lincoln's bold moves, the legislatures of Maryland and Delaware (another border slave state) rejected secession.

Next, Lincoln authorized the arming of Union sympathizers in Kentucky, a slave state with a Unionist legislature, a secessionist governor, and a thin chance of staying neutral. Lincoln also stationed troops under General Ulysses S. Grant just across the Ohio River from Kentucky, in Illinois. When a Confederate army invaded Kentucky early in 1862, Grant's soldiers drove it out. Officially, at least, Kentucky became the third slave state to declare for the Union. The fourth, Missouri, faced four years of fighting between Union and Confederate troops, and between bands of guerrillas and bushwhackers, a name for Confederate guerrillas who lurked in the underbrush. These included William Quantrill, a rebel desperado, and his murderous apprentices, Frank and Jesse James. Despite savage combat and the divided loyalties of its people, Missouri never left the Union. West Virginia, admitted to the Union in 1863, would become the last of five border slave states that remained in the Union. (West Virginia was established in 1861, when thirty-five counties in the mainly nonslaveholding region of Virginia west of the Shenandoah Valley refused to follow the state's leaders into secession.)

By holding the first four border slave states—Maryland, Delaware, Kentucky, and Missouri—in the Union, Lincoln kept open his routes to the free states and gained access to the river systems in Kentucky and Missouri that led into the heart of the Confederacy. Lincoln's firmness, particularly in Maryland, scotched charges that he was weak-willed. The crisis also forced the president to exercise long-dormant powers. In the case *Ex parte Merryman* (1861), Chief Justice Roger B. Taney ruled that Lincoln had exceeded his authority in suspending the writ of *habeas corpus* in Maryland. The president ignored Taney's ruling, citing the Constitution's authorization of the writ's suspension in "Cases of Rebellion" (Article I, Section 9). Lincoln insisted that he, rather than Congress, would determine whether a rebellion existed.

15-2 In Battle, 1861–1862

Is it accurate to claim that the Civil War was "the first modern war"?

The Civil War was the first war to rely extensively on railroads, the telegraph, mass-produced weapons, joint army-navy tactics, iron-plated warships, rifled guns and artillery, and trench warfare. All of this lends some justification to its description as the first modern war. But to the participants, slogging through muddy swamps and laden with equipment, the war hardly seemed modern. In many ways, the soldiers had the more accurate perspective because the new weapons did not always work, and both sides employed tactics that were more traditional than modern.

15-2.1 Armies, Weapons, and Strategies

Compared with the Confederacy's 9 million people (one-third of them slaves), the Union had 22 million people in 1861 (see Figure 15.2). The North also had 3.5 times as many white men of military age, 90 percent of all U.S. industrial capacity, and two-thirds

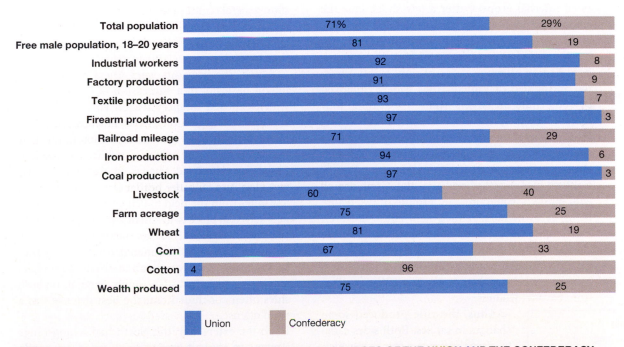

	Union	Confederacy
Total population	71%	29%
Free male population, 18–20 years	81	19
Industrial workers	92	8
Factory production	91	9
Textile production	93	7
Firearm production	97	3
Railroad mileage	71	29
Iron production	94	6
Coal production	97	3
Livestock	60	40
Farm acreage	75	25
Wheat	81	19
Corn	67	33
Cotton	4	96
Wealth produced	75	25

FIGURE 15.2 **COMPARATIVE POPULATION AND ECONOMIC RESOURCES OF THE UNION AND THE CONFEDERACY, 1861** At the start of the war, the Union enjoyed huge advantages in population, industry, railroad mileage, and wealth, and—as it would soon prove—a superior ability to mobilize its vast resources. The Confederacy, however, enjoyed the many advantages of fighting a defensive war.

of its railroad track. Yet the Union faced a daunting challenge: to force the South back into the Union. The South, in contrast, fought merely for its independence and largely on terrain it knew well. To subdue the Confederacy, the North would have to sustain offensive operations over a vast area.

Measured against this challenge, the Union's advantages in population and technology shrank. The North had more men, but needed to defend long supply lines and occupy captured areas; consequently, it could commit a smaller proportion to frontline duty. The South, which relied on slaves for labor, could assign a higher proportion of white men to combat. The North required, and possessed, superior railroads, though it had to move troops and supplies huge distances, and guerrillas could easily sabotage northern lines. The South could shift troops relatively short distances within its defensive arc without using railroads. Finally, southerners had an edge in soldiers' morale, for Confederate troops battled on home ground. "No people ever warred for independence," a southern general acknowledged, "with more relative advantages than the Confederates."

The Civil War witnessed experiments with various newly developed weapons, including the submarine, the repeating rifle, and the multibarreled Gatling gun, the forerunner of the machine gun. More important was the perfection in the 1850s of a bullet known as the minie ball (for inventor Claude Minie) whose powder would not clog a rifle's spiraled internal grooves after a few shots. Like the smoothbore muskets that both armies had employed at the start of the war, most improved rifles had to be reloaded after each shot. However, the smoothbore had an effective range of only eighty yards; the Springfield or Enfield rifles widely employed by 1863 could hit targets accurately at up to four hundred yards.

The rifle's development challenged long-accepted military tactics, which stressed the mass infantry charge against an opponent's weakest point. Prewar military manuals assumed that defenders armed with muskets would fire only a round or two before being overwhelmed. Armed with rifles, however, a defending force could fire several rounds before closing with the enemy. Attackers would now rarely get close enough to thrust bayonets; fewer than 1 percent of the casualties in the Civil War resulted from bayonet wounds.

Thus, the rifle produced some changes in tactics. Both sides came to grasp the value of trenches, which provided defenders protection against withering rifle fire. By 1865, trenches pockmarked the landscape in Virginia and Georgia. Also,

growing use of the rifle forced generals to rely less on cavalry. Traditionally, cavalry had ranked among the most prestigious components of an army, in part because cavalry charges were effective and in part because the cavalry helped maintain class distinctions within the army. More accurate rifles reduced cavalry effectiveness by increasing the firepower of foot soldiers. Thus, both sides relegated cavalry to reconnaissance missions and raids on supply trains.

Still, the introduction of the rifle did not totally invalidate traditional tactics. On the contrary, historians now contend, high casualties reflected the long duration of battles rather than the new efficacy of rifles. The attacking army still stood an excellent chance of success if it achieved surprise; the South's lush forests provided abundant opportunities for an army to sneak up on its foe. For example, at the Battle of Shiloh in 1862, Confederate attackers surprised and almost defeated a larger Union army despite the noise created by green rebel troops en route to the battle, many of whom fired their rifles into the air to see if they would work.

Lack of any element of surprise could doom an attacking army. At the Battle of Fredericksburg in December 1862, Confederate troops inflicted appalling casualties on Union forces attacking uphill over open terrain, and at Gettysburg in July 1863, Union riflemen and artillery shredded charging southerners. But generals might still achieve partial surprise by hitting an enemy before it had concentrated its troops. Because surprise often proved effective, most generals continued to believe their best chance of success lay in striking an unwary or weakened enemy with all the troops they could muster rather than in relying on guerrilla or trench warfare.

Much like previous wars, the Civil War was fought basically in a succession of battles during which exposed infantry traded volleys, charged, and countercharged. Whichever side withdrew from the field was usually considered the loser, though it frequently sustained lighter casualties than the supposed victor. Both sides had trouble exploiting their victories. As a rule, the beaten army moved back a few miles from the field to lick its wounds; the winners stayed in place to lick theirs. Politicians on both sides raged at generals for not pursuing a beaten foe, but it was difficult for a mangled victor to gather horses, mules, supply trains, and exhausted soldiers for a new attack. Not surprisingly, generals on both sides often concluded that the best defense was a good offense.

To the extent that the North had a long-range strategy in 1861, it lay in the so-called **Anaconda plan**. Devised by a hero of the Mexican-American War, General Winfield Scott, the plan called for the Union to blockade the southern coastline and to thrust, like a snake, down the Mississippi River.

Sealing off and severing the Confederacy, Scott expected, would make the South recognize the futility of secession and end the war quickly. However, although Lincoln quickly ordered a blockade of the southern coast, the North lacked the troops and naval flotillas to seize the Mississippi in 1861. So while the Mississippi remained an objective, northern strategy did not unfold according to a specific blueprint like the Anaconda plan.

Early in the war, the pressing need to secure the border slave states, particularly Kentucky and Missouri, dictated Union strategy west of the Appalachian Mountains. Once in control of Kentucky, northern troops plunged southward into Tennessee. The Appalachians tended to seal this western theater off from the eastern theater, where major clashes of 1861 occurred.

15-2.2 Stalemate in the East

The Confederacy's decision in May 1861 to move its capital from Montgomery, Alabama, to Richmond, Virginia, shaped Union strategy. "Forward to Richmond" became the Union's first war cry. Before they could reach Richmond, one hundred miles southwest of Washington, Union troops had to dislodge a Confederate army brazenly encamped at Manassas Junction, Virginia, only twenty-five miles from the Union capital (see Map 15.1). Lincoln ordered General Irvin McDowell to attack his former West Point classmate, Confederate general P. G. T. Beauregard. In the resulting **First Battle of Bull Run** (or First Manassas), amateur armies clashed in bloody chaos under a blistering July sun. Picnicking Washington dignitaries witnessed the carnage, as Beauregard routed the larger Union army.

After Bull Run, Lincoln replaced McDowell with General George B. McClellan as commander of the Army of the Potomac, the Union's main fighting force in the East. Another West Pointer, McClellan had served with distinction in the Mexican-American War. A master of administration and training, he could turn a ragtag mob into a disciplined fighting force. His soldiers adored him, but Lincoln quickly became disenchanted. Lincoln believed the key to a Union victory lay in simultaneous, coordinated attacks on several fronts so that the North could exploit its advantage in manpower and resources. McClellan, a proslavery Democrat, hoped for a relatively bloodless Southern defeat, followed by readmission of the Confederate states with slavery intact.

In the spring of 1862, McClellan got a chance to implement his strategy. After Bull Run, the Confederates had pulled back to block the Union onslaught against Richmond. Rather than directly attack the Confederate army, McClellan decided to move his army by water to the tip of the peninsula formed by the York and James Rivers and then move northwestward up the peninsula to Richmond. McClellan's plan had several advantages. Depending on water transport rather than on railroads exposed to Confederate cavalry, the McClellan strategy reduced the vulnerability of northern supply lines. Approaching Richmond from the southeast, it threatened the South's supply lines. By aiming for the Confederate capital rather than for the Confederate army stationed to its northeast, McClellan hoped to maneuver the southern troops into a futile attack on his army.

At first, the massive Peninsula Campaign unfolded smoothly. Three hundred ships transported seventy thousand men and huge stores of supplies to the tip of the peninsula. Reinforcements swelled McClellan's army to one hundred thousand. By late May, McClellan was within five miles of Richmond. But then he hesitated. Overestimating Confederate strength, he refused to launch a final attack without further reinforcements, which were turned back by Confederate general Thomas "Stonewall" Jackson in the Shenandoah Valley.

While McClellan delayed, General **Robert E. Lee** took command of the Confederacy's Army of Northern Virginia. A foe of secession and so courteous that at times

First Battle of Bull Run
The first major land battle in the Civil War. It was also known as First Manassas.

Robert E. Lee
Leader of the Confederate army.

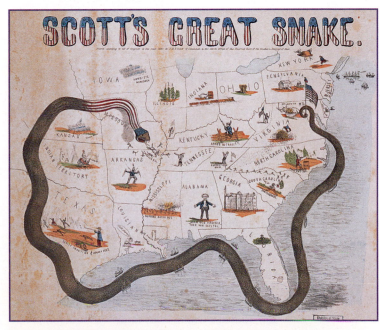

"SCOTT'S GREAT SNAKE," 1861 General Winfield Scott's scheme to surround the South and await a seizure of power by southern Unionists drew scorn from critics, who called it the Anaconda plan. In this lithograph, the "great snake" prepares to push down the Mississippi, seal off the Confederacy, and crush it. *(Library of Congress Prints and Photographs Division)*

MAP 15.1 THE WAR IN THE EAST, 1861–1862 Union advances on Richmond were turned back at Fredericksburg and the Seven Days' Battles, and the Confederacy's invasion of Union territory was stopped at Antietam.

he seemed too gentle, Lee possessed the qualities that McClellan most lacked: boldness and a willingness to accept casualties. Seizing the initiative, Lee attacked McClellan in late June 1862. The ensuing Seven Days' Battles, fought in the forests east of Richmond, cost the South nearly twice as many men as the North and ended in a virtual slaughter of Confederates. Unnerved by mounting casualties, McClellan sent increasingly panicky reports to Washington. Lincoln, who cared little for McClellan's peninsula strategy, ordered McClellan to call off the campaign and return to Washington.

With McClellan off the scene, Lee and his lieutenant, Stonewall Jackson, boldly struck north and, at the Second Battle of Bull Run (Second Manassas), routed a Union army under General John Pope. Lee's next stroke was even bolder. Crossing the Potomac River in early September 1862, he invaded western Maryland, where the forthcoming harvest could feed his troops. Lee

could now threaten Washington, indirectly relieve pressure on Richmond, improve the prospects of peace candidates in the North's fall elections, and possibly induce Britain and France to recognize Confederate independence. But McClellan met Lee at the **Battle of Antietam** (or Sharpsburg) on September 17. A tactical draw, Antietam proved a strategic victory for the North; Lee subsequently canceled his invasion and retreated south of the Potomac.

Heartened by Northern success, Lincoln then issued the Emancipation Proclamation, a war measure that freed all slaves under rebel control. The toll of 24,000 casualties at Antietam, however, made it the bloodiest day of the entire war. One part of the battlefield, a Union veteran recalled, contained so many bodies that a man could have walked through it without stepping on the ground.

Complaining that McClellan had "the slows," Lincoln faulted his commander for not pursuing Lee after Antietam. McClellan's replacement,

Battle of Antietam
First major battle on northern soil.

General Ambrose Burnside, thought himself unfit for high command. He was right. In December 1862, Burnside led 122,000 federal troops against 78,500 Confederates at the Battle of Fredericksburg. Burnside captured the town of Fredericksburg, northeast of Richmond, but then sacrificed his army in futile charges up the heights west of the town. Even Lee shuddered at the carnage. "It is well that war is so terrible, or we should grow too fond of it," he told an aide. Richmond remained, in the words of a southern song, "a hard road to travel." The war in the East had become a stalemate.

15-2.3 The War in the West

The Union fared better in the West. There, the war ranged over a vast terrain that provided access to rivers leading directly into the South. The West also spawned new leadership: In the war's first year, an obscure Union general, **Ulysses S. Grant**, won attention. A West Point graduate, Grant had fought in the Mexican-American War and retired from the army in 1854 with a reputation for heavy drinking. He then failed in farming and business. When the Civil War began, he gained an army commission through political pressure.

In 1861–1862, Grant retained control of two border states, Missouri and Kentucky. Moving into Tennessee, he captured two strategic forts, Fort Henry on the Tennessee River and Fort Donelson on the Cumberland. Grant then headed south to attack Corinth, Mississippi, a major railroad junction (see Map 15.2).

In early April 1862, to defend Corinth, Confederates under generals Albert Sidney Johnston and P. G. T. Beauregard surprised Grant's army, encamped near a church named Shiloh twenty miles north of the town, in southern Tennessee. Hoping to whip Grant before Union reinforcements arrived, Confederates exploded from the woods near Shiloh before breakfast and almost drove the federals into the Tennessee River. Beauregard cabled Richmond with news of Confederate triumph. But Grant and his lieutenant, **William T. Sherman**—a West Point graduate and Mexican-American war veteran who had most recently run a southern military academy—steadied the Union line. Union reinforcements arrived at night, and a federal counterattack drove the Confederates from the field the next day. Although Antietam would soon erase the distinction, the **Battle of Shiloh** was the bloodiest in American history to that date. Of the seventy-seven thousand men engaged, twenty-three thousand were killed or wounded, including Confederate general Albert Sidney Johnston, who bled to death from a leg wound. Defeated at Shiloh, the Confederates soon evacuated Corinth.

MAP 15.2 THE WAR IN THE WEST, 1861–1862 By the end of 1862, the North held New Orleans and the entire Mississippi River except for the stretch between Vicksburg and Port Hudson.

To attack Grant at Shiloh, the Confederacy had stripped the defenses of its largest city, New Orleans. A combined Union land-sea force under General Benjamin Butler, a Massachusetts politician, and Admiral David G. Farragut, a Tennessean loyal to the Union, seized the opportunity. Farragut took New Orleans in late April and soon conquered Baton Rouge and Natchez as well. Meanwhile, another Union flotilla moved down the Mississippi and captured Memphis in June. Now the North controlled the entire river, except for a two-hundred-mile stretch between Port Hudson, Louisiana, and Vicksburg, Mississippi.

Ulysses S. Grant
Leader of the Union army.

William T. Sherman
West Point graduate and Mexican-American war veteran who had most recently run a southern military academy. He led the Union troops and captured Atlanta.

Battle of Shiloh
The bloodiest in American history to that date. It happened in April 6–7, 1862.

THE BATTLE OF ANTIETAM A painting of the Antietam battlefield by James Hope, a Union soldier of the Second Vermont Infantry, shows three brigades of Union troops advancing under Confederate fire. In the photograph of Antietam, dead rebel gunners lie next to the wreckage of their battery. The building in both painting and photograph, a Dunker church, was the scene of furious fighting. *(Antietam National Battlefield, Sharpsburg, MD, and Library of Congress Prints and Photographs Division)*

Union and Confederate forces also clashed in 1862 in the trans-Mississippi West. On the banks of the Rio Grande, Union volunteers, joined by Mexican-American companies, drove a Confederate army from Texas out of New Mexico. A thousand miles to the east, in northern Arkansas and western Missouri, armies vied to secure the Missouri River, a crucial waterway that flowed into the Mississippi. In Pea Ridge, Arkansas, in March 1862, forewarned northern troops scattered a Confederate force of sixteen thousand that included three Cherokee regiments. (Indian units fought on both sides in Missouri, where guerrilla combat raged until the war's end.)

These Union victories changed the nature of the trans-Mississippi war. As the rebel threat faded, regiments of western volunteers that had mobilized to crush Confederates turned to fighting Indians. Conflict between Union forces and Native Americans erupted in Minnesota, Arizona, Nevada, Colorado,

and New Mexico, where California volunteers and the New Mexico cavalry, led by Colonel Kit Carson, overwhelmed the Apaches and Navajos. After 1865, federal troops moved west to complete the rout of the Indians that had begun in the Civil War.

15-2.4 The Soldiers' War

Civil War soldiers were typically volunteers from farms and small towns who joined companies of recruits from their locales. Many who enrolled in 1861 and 1862—those who served at Shiloh and Antietam—reenlisted when their terms expired and became the backbones of their respective armies. Local loyalties spurred enrollment, especially in the South; so did ideals of honor and valor. Soldiers on both sides envisioned military life as a transforming experience from citizen to warrior. Exultant after a victory, an Alabama volunteer told his father, "With your first shot you become a new man." Thousands of underage volunteers, that is, boys under eighteen, also served in the war; so did at least 250 women disguised as men.

Recruits were meshed into regiments and then sent to camps of instruction. Training was meager, and much of army life tedious and uncomfortable. Food was one complaint. Union troops ate beans, bacon, salt pork, pickled beef, and a staple called hardtack, square flour-and-water biscuits that were almost impossible to crack with a blow. Confederate diets featured bacon and cornmeal, and as a southern soldier summed it up, "Our rations is small." Rebel armies often ran out of food, blankets, clothes, socks, and shoes. On both sides, crowded military camps—plagued by poor sanitation and infested with lice, fleas, ticks, flies, and rodents—ensured soaring disease rates and widespread grievances. A sergeant from New York, only partly in jest, described his lot as "laying around in the dirt and mud, living on hardtack, facing death in bullets and shells, eat up by wood-ticks and body-lice."

Dreams of military glory swiftly faded. For most soldiers, Civil War battles meant inuring themselves to the stench and reality of death. "[E]very shot you fire into them sends some one to eternity," a New Jersey artilleryman recalled, "but still you are prompted by a terrible desire to kill all you can." The deadly cost of battle fell most heavily on the infantry, in which at least three out of four soldiers served. Although repeating rifles had three or four times the range of the old smoothbore muskets, a mix of inexperience, inadequate training, and barriers of terrain curbed their impact. Instead, masses of soldiers faced one another at close range for long periods, exchanging fire until one side or the other gave up and fell back. The high casualty figures at Shiloh and Antietam reflected not advanced technology but the armies' inability to use it effectively. "Our victories . . . seem to settle nothing," a southern officer wrote in 1862. "It is only so many killed or wounded, leaving the war of blood to go on." Armies gained efficiency in battle through experience, and only late in the war.

In their voluminous letters home (Civil War armies were the most literate armies that had ever existed), volunteers discussed their motives as soldiers. Some Confederates enlisted to defend slavery. "I choose to fight for southern rights and southern liberty" against the "vandals of the North" who were "determined to destroy slavery," a Kentucky Confederate announced. Among northern volunteers, concern for saving the Union prevailed. A small minority voiced antislavery sentiments early in the war: "I have no heart in this war if the slaves cannot go free," a soldier from Wisconsin declared. Few Union recruits, however, initially shared this antipathy to slavery. But as war went on, northern soldiers accepted the need to free the slaves, sometimes for humanitarian reasons. "Since I am down here I have learned and seen more of what the horrors of slavery was than I ever knew before," an Ohio officer wrote from Louisiana. Others had more practical goals. By the summer of 1862, Union soldiers in the South had become agents of liberation; many who once had damned the "abolitionist war" now endorsed emancipation as part of the Union war effort. As an Indiana soldier declared, "Every negro we get strengthens us and weakens the rebels."

15-2.5 Ironclads and Cruisers: The Naval War

By plunging its navy into the Confederacy like a dagger, the Union exploited a clear-cut advantage. The North began the war with more than forty active warships against none for the South, and by 1865 the United States had the largest navy in the world. Steamships could penetrate the South's excellent river system from any direction.

Yet the Union navy faced an extraordinary challenge: to blockade the South's thirty-five hundred miles of coast. Early in the war, small, sleek Confederate blockade-runners darted with impunity in and out

A UNION SOLDIER Sarah Rosetta Wakeman, alias Private Lyons Wakeman, served in the Union army disguised as a man. She joined the 153rd Regiment, New York State Volunteers. *(Russell Kasper)*

of southern harbors. The North gradually tightened the blockade by outfitting tugs, whalers, excursion steamers, and ferries as well as frigates to patrol southern coasts. The proportion of Confederate blockade-runners that made it through dropped from 90 percent early in the war to 50 percent by 1865. Northern seizure of rebel ports and coastal areas diminished the South's foreign trade even more. In daring amphibious assaults of 1861 and 1862, the Union captured the excellent harbor of Port Royal, South Carolina, the coastal islands off South Carolina (see Map 15.3 later in the chapter), and most of North Carolina's river outlets. Naval patrols and amphibious operations reduced the South's ocean trade to one-third its prewar level.

Despite meager resources, the South strove to offset the North's naval advantage. Early in the war, the Confederacy raised the scuttled Union frigate *Merrimac*, sheathed its sides with an armor of ironplate, rechristened it *Virginia*, and dispatched it to attack wooden Union ships in Hampton Roads, Virginia. The *Merrimac* destroyed two northern warships but met its match in the hastily built Union ironclad the *Monitor*. In the first engagement of ironclads in history, the two ships fought an indecisive battle on March 9, 1862. The South constructed other ironclads and even the first submarine, which dragged a mine through water to sink a Union ship off Charleston in 1864; the "fish" failed to resurface and went down with its prey. But the South never built enough ironclads to overcome Northern supremacy in home waters. Nor did Confederate success on the high seas—where wooden, steam-driven commerce raiders wreaked havoc on the Union's merchant marine—tip the balance of war in the South's favor: the North, unlike its foe, did not depend on imports for war materials. The South would lose the naval war.

15-2.6 The Diplomatic War

While armies and navies clashed in 1861–1862, conflict developed on a third front, diplomacy. At the war's start, the Confederacy sought European recognition of its independence. Southern confidence ran high. Planning to establish a colonial empire in Mexico, Napoleon III of France welcomed a permanent division of the United States. The French and British upper classes seemed sympathetic to the South and eager for the downfall of the brash Yankee republic. Furthermore, influential southerners contended, an embargo of cotton exports would bring Britain to its knees. Britain, dependent on the South for four-fifths of its cotton,

they reasoned, would break the Union blockade and provoke war with the North rather than endure an embargo.

Leaving nothing to chance, the Confederacy in 1861 dispatched emissaries James Mason to Britain and John Slidell to France to lobby for recognition of an independent South. But their ship, the *Trent*, fell into Union hands, and when the pair ended up in Boston as prisoners, British tempers exploded. Considering one war at a time enough, President Lincoln released Mason and Slidell. But settling the *Trent* affair did not eliminate friction between the United States and Britain. Union diplomats protested the construction in British shipyards of two Confederate commerce raiders, the *Florida* and the *Alabama*. In 1863, the U.S. minister to London, Charles Francis Adams (the son of former president John Quincy Adams), threatened war if two British-built ironclads commissioned by the Confederacy, the so-called Laird rams, were turned over to the South. Britain capitulated to Adams's protests and purchased the rams for its own navy.

On balance, the South fell far short of its diplomatic objectives. Although recognizing the Confederacy as a belligerent, neither Britain nor France ever recognized it as a nation. Basically, the Confederacy overestimated the power of its vaunted **"cotton diplomacy."** Southern threats to Britain about an embargo of cotton exports failed; planters conducted business as usual by raising cotton and trying to slip it through the blockade. Still, the South's share of the British cotton market slumped from 77 percent in 1860 to only 10 percent in 1865. Forces beyond Southern control had weakened British demand. Bumper cotton crops in the late 1850s had glutted the British market by the start of the war and Britain had found new suppliers in Egypt and India. Gradually, too, the North's tightened blockade restricted southern exports.

The South also exaggerated Britain's stake in helping the Confederacy. As a naval power that had frequently blockaded its own enemies, Britain's diplomatic interest lay in supporting the Union blockade in principle; from Britain's standpoint, to help the South break the blockade would set a precedent that could easily boomerang. Finally, although France and Britain often considered recognizing the Confederacy, the timing never seemed quite right. Union success at Antietam in 1862 and Lincoln's subsequent issuance of the **Emancipation Proclamation** dampened Europe's enthusiasm for recognition at a crucial juncture. By transforming the war into a struggle to end slavery, the Emancipation Proclamation stirred pro-Union feeling in antislavery Britain, particularly among liberals and the working class. The proclamation, declared Henry Adams (diplomat Charles Francis Adams's son) from London, "has done more for us here than all of our former victories and all our diplomacy."

PUNCH, OR THE LONDON CHARIVARI.—JULY 6, 1861.

NAUGHTY·JONATHAN.

"YOU SHAN'T INTERFERE, MOTHER—AND YOU OUGHT TO BE ON MY SIDE—AND IT'S A GREAT SHAME—AND I DON'T CARE—AND YOU SHALL INTERFERE—AND I WON'T HAVE IT."

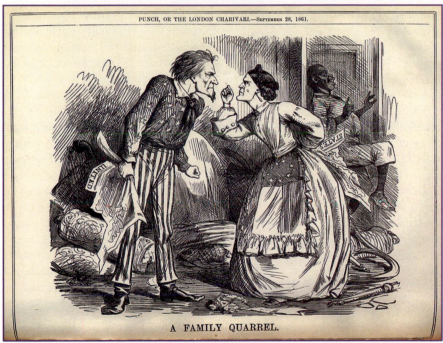

PUNCH, OR THE LONDON CHARIVARI.—September 28, 1861.

A FAMILY QUARREL.

BRITAIN VIEWS THE CIVIL WAR

British illustrator and political cartoonist John Tenniel assessed the American Civil War for British readers in *Punch* magazine. Tenniel's commentary featured domestic disputes and family feuds, as in these two cartoons from the war's first year. In "Naughty Jonathan" (July 1861), a petulant brat, the United States, whines at his parent, the matron Britannia ("You shan't interfere, Mother—and you ought to be on my side—and it's a great shame—and I don't care—and you shall interfere—and I won't have it."). Britannia, aloof, is unbothered. In "A Family Quarrel" (September 1861), two enraged spouses—the furious North and belligerent South (each currently vying for British favor)—rip up the map of the United States along with the rest of their household possessions. A delighted slave, in a minstrel-like prance, listens in at the doorway. By 1863 the Union had gained the lead in the rivalry for British support. *(Library of Congress Prints and Photographs Division and Library of Congress Prints and Photographs Division)*

15-3 Emancipation Transforms the War, 1863

How did the Emancipation Proclamation transform the war?

"I hear old John Brown knocking on the lid of his coffin and shouting 'Let me out! Let me out!'" abolitionist Henry Stanton wrote to his wife after the fall of Fort Sumter. "The Doom of Slavery is at hand." In

1861, this prediction seemed wildly premature. In his inaugural that year, Lincoln had stated bluntly, "I have no purpose, directly or indirectly, to interfere with the institution of slavery in the states where it exists." Yet in two years, a mix of necessity and conviction thrust emancipation to the forefront of northern war goals.

The rise of emancipation as a war objective reflected the changing character of the war. As the struggle dragged on, demands intensified in the North for the prosecution of "total war"—a war that would shatter the social and economic foundations of the Confederacy. Even northerners who saw no moral value in abolishing slavery started to recognize the military value of emancipation as a tactic to cripple the South.

15-3.1 From Confiscation to Emancipation

Union policy on emancipation developed in stages. As soon as northern troops began to invade the South, questions arose about the disposition of captured rebel property, including slaves. Slaves who fled behind the Union lines were sometimes considered "contraband"—enemy property liable to seizure—and were put to work for the Union army. Some commanders viewed this practice as a useful tool of war; others did not, and the Lincoln administration was evasive. To establish an official policy, Congress in August 1861 passed the first Confiscation Act, which authorized the seizure of all property used in military aid of the rebellion, including slaves. Under this act, slaves who had been employed directly by the Confederate armed forces and who later fled to freedom became "captives of war." But nothing in the act actually freed these individuals, nor did the law apply to fugitive slaves who had not worked for the Confederate military.

Several factors underlay the Union's cautious approach to the confiscation of rebel property. Officially maintaining that the South could not legally secede, Lincoln argued that southerners were still entitled to the Constitution's protection of property. The president also had practical reasons to walk softly. He did not want to alienate slaveholders in the border states or proslavery Democrats in the North. If the Union tampered with slavery, these Democrats feared, southern blacks might come north and compete with white workers. Aware of such fears, Lincoln assured Congress in December 1861 that the war would not become a "remorseless revolutionary struggle."

From the start of the war, however, Radical Republicans pushed Lincoln to adopt a policy of emancipation. Radicals agreed with black abolitionist Frederick Douglass that "to fight against slaveholders without fighting against slavery, is but a half-hearted business." Each Union defeat, moreover, reminded northerners that the Confederacy, with a slave labor force in place, could commit a higher proportion of its white men to battle. The idea of emancipation as a military measure thus gained increasing favor in the North, and in July 1862 Congress passed the second Confiscation Act. This law authorized the seizure of the property of all persons in rebellion and stipulated that slaves who came within Union lines "shall be forever free." The law also authorized the president to employ blacks as soldiers.

Nevertheless, Lincoln continued to stall, even as pressure for emancipation rose. "My paramount object in this struggle is to save the Union, and is not either to save or destroy slavery," Lincoln told antislavery journalist Horace Greeley. "If I could save the Union without freeing *any* slave, I would do it; and if I could save it by freeing *all* the slaves, I would do it; and if I could do it by freeing some and leaving others alone, I would also do that."

Lincoln had always loathed slavery but was not an abolitionist, and he worried about the Constitutional implications of any moves on the institution. Still, by the spring of 1862, he had accepted the Radical position that the war must lead to slavery's abolition. He held back mainly because he did not want to be pushed by Congress into a step that might disrupt northern unity nor to press the issue while Union armies reeled in defeat. After failing to persuade the Union slave states to emancipate slaves with compensation, Lincoln drafted a proclamation of emancipation, circulated it within his cabinet, and waited for the right moment to announce it. Finally, after the Union victory in September 1862 at Antietam, Lincoln issued the preliminary Emancipation Proclamation, which declared all slaves under rebel control free as of January 1, 1863. Announcing the plan in advance softened the surprise, tested public opinion, and gave the states still in rebellion an opportunity to preserve slavery by returning to the Union—an opportunity that none, however, took. The final Emancipation Proclamation, issued on January 1, 1863, declared "forever free" all slaves in areas in rebellion.

The proclamation had limited practical impact. Applying only to rebellious areas where the Union had no authority, it exempted the Union slave states and those parts of the Confederacy then under Union control (Tennessee, West Virginia, southern Louisiana, and sections of Virginia). Moreover, it mainly restated what the second Confiscation Act had already stipulated: if rebels' slaves fell into Union hands, those slaves would be free. Yet the proclamation was a brilliant political stroke. By issuing it as a military measure in his role as commander-in-chief, Lincoln pacified northern conservatives. Its aim, he stressed, was to injure the Confederacy, threaten its property, heighten its dread, sap its morale, and hasten its demise. By issuing the proclamation himself, Lincoln stole the initiative from the Radicals in Congress and inspired some support for the Union among European liberals.

Furthermore, the proclamation pushed the border states toward emancipation: By the end of the war, Maryland and Missouri would abolish slavery. Significantly, it increased slaves' incentives to escape as northern troops approached. Fulfilling the worst of Confederate fears, it enabled blacks to join the

Union army. And it galvanized activists such as Elizabeth Cady Stanton, Susan B. Anthony, and Lucy Stone to push for more definitive and far-reaching legislation ending slavery. Forming the **Woman's National Loyal League** with other activists, they amassed 260,000 signatures—the majority from women—on a petition to free all slaves, not just those in rebel territory. This initiative played an important role in the Thirteenth Amendment (1865) abolishing slavery.

The Emancipation Proclamation did not end slavery everywhere or free "*all* the slaves." But it changed the war. From 1863 on, the war for the Union would also be a war against slavery.

15-3.2 Crossing Union Lines

The attacks and counterattacks of opposing armies turned many slaves into pawns of war. Some slaves became free when Union soldiers overran their areas. Others fled their plantations as federal troops approached to take refuge behind Union lines. A few were freed by northern assaults, only to be re-enslaved by Confederate counterthrusts. One North Carolina slave celebrated liberation on twelve occasions, as often as Union soldiers marched through his locale. By 1865, about half a million slaves were in Union hands.

In the first year of the war, when the Union had not yet established a policy toward "contrabands" (fugitive slaves), masters could retrieve them from the Union army. After 1862, however, slaves who crossed Union lines were considered free. Many freedmen served in army camps as cooks, teamsters, and laborers. Some worked for pay on abandoned plantations or were leased out to planters who swore allegiance to the Union. In camps or outside them, freedmen had cause to question the value of liberation. Deductions for clothing, rations, and medicine ate up most of their earnings. Labor contracts often tied them to their employers for long periods. Moreover, freedmen encountered fierce prejudice among Yankee soldiers, many of whom feared that emancipation would propel postwar blacks north. The best solution to the "question of what to do with the darkies," wrote one northern soldier, "would be to shoot them."

But this was not the whole story. Fugitive slaves who aided the Union army as spies and scouts helped to break down ingrained bigotry. "The sooner we get rid of our foolish prejudice the better for us," a Massachusetts soldier wrote. Before the war's end, northern missionary groups and freedmen's aid societies sent agents south to work among freed slaves, distribute relief, and organize schools. In March 1865, just before hostilities ceased, Congress created the **Freedmen's Bureau**, an agency responsible for the relief, education, and employment of former slaves. The Freedmen's Bureau law also stipulated that forty acres of abandoned or confiscated land could be leased to each freedman or southern Unionist, with an option to buy after three years. This was the first and only time that Congress provided for the redistribution of confiscated Confederate property.

15-3.3 The Black Experience: Union Soldiers and Wartime Slavery

In the war's first year, the Union had rejected African American soldiers. After the second Confiscation Act, Union generals formed black regiments in occupied New Orleans and on the Sea Islands off the coasts of South Carolina and Georgia. Only after the Emancipation Proclamation did large-scale enlistment begin. Prominent African Americans such as Frederick Douglass worked as recruiting agents in northern cities. Douglass linked black military service to black claims as citizens. "Once let the black man get . . . an eagle on his button, and a musket on his shoulder and bullets in his pocket, and there is no power on earth which can deny that he has earned the right to citizenship." Union drafts now included blacks, and freedmen in refugee camps throughout the occupied South enlisted. By the war's end, 186,000 African Americans had served in the Union army, one-tenth of all Union soldiers. Fully half came from the Confederate states (see Going to the Source).

White Union soldiers often objected to black recruits on racial grounds, and blacks knew they had to prove their manhood and their military capabilities. But some whites, including Colonel Thomas Wentworth Higginson, a liberal minister and former John Brown supporter who led a black regiment, welcomed black soldiers. "Nobody knows anything about these men who has not seen them in battle," Higginson exulted after a successful raid in Florida in 1863. "There is a fierce energy about them…." Even Union soldiers who held blacks in contempt came to approve of "anything that will kill a rebel." All blacks served in separate regiments under white officers. Colonel Robert Gould Shaw of the 54th Massachusetts Infantry, an elite black regiment, died in combat—as did half his troops—in an attack on Fort Wagner in Charleston harbor in July 1863.

Woman's National Loyal League
An organization that called for a constitutional amendment to abolish slavery founded by women active in the suffrage movement.

Freedmen's Bureau
Created by Congress in March 1865, it had responsibility for the relief, education, and employment of former slaves.

Frederick Douglass Calls for Black Troops

Reformer Frederick Douglass (1818–1895), who escaped from slavery in 1838, became an author, orator, and avid abolitionist. As soon as the Civil War began, Douglass urged the Union to declare emancipation and to accept black soldiers in the Union army. As he later stated in his autobiography, "I preached that the Union cause would never prosper until the war assumed an anti-slavery attitude and the Negro was allowed to fight on the loyal side." Eventually, by 1863, the Union adopted the policies that Douglass espoused. Douglass explained his rationale in a column of May 1861 on "How to End the War."

[T]here is but one easy, short and effectual way to suppress and put down the desolating war which the slaveholders and their rebel minions are now waging. . . . Fire must be met with water, darkness with light, and war for the destruction of liberty must be met with war for the destruction of slavery. *The simple way, then, to put an end to the savage and desolating war now waged by the slaveholders, is to strike down slavery itself, the primal cause of that war.* . . .

Freedom to the slave should now be proclaimed from the Capitol. . . . The time for mild measures is past. . . . A lenient war is a lengthy war, and therefore the worst kind of war. Let us stop it, and stop it effectually. . . . This can be done at once. . . . *Let the slaves and free colored people be called into service, and formed into a liberating army*, to march into the South and raise the banner of emancipation among the slaves. The South having brought revolution and war upon the country, and having elected and consented to play at that fearful game, she has no right to complain if some good as well as calamity shall result from her own act and deed.

The slaveholders have not hesitated to employ the sable arms of the Negroes at the South in erecting the fortifications which silenced the guns of Fort Sumter, and brought the star-spangled banner to the dust. They often boast, and not without cause, that their negroes will fight for them against the North. They have no scruples against employing the Negroes to exterminate freedom, and in overturning the government. . . . Oh! That this Government would only now be as true to liberty as the rebels, who are attempting to batter it down, are true to slavery. We have no hesitation in saying that ten thousand black soldiers might be raised in the next thirty days to march upon the South. One black regiment alone would be, in such a war, the full equal of two white ones. The very fact of color in this case would be more powerful than powder and balls. The slaves would learn more as to the nature of the conflict from the presence of one such regiment, than from a thousand preachers. Every consideration of justice, humanity, and sound policy confirms the wisdom of calling upon black men just now to take up arms in behalf of their country.

We are often asked by persons in the street as well as by letter, what our people will do in the present solemn crisis. . . . Our answer is, would to God you would let us do something! We lack nothing but your consent. We are ready and would go, counting ourselves happy in being permitted to serve and suffer for the cause of freedom and free institutions. But you won't let us go. . . . Until the nation shall repent of this weakness and folly, until they shall make the cause of their country the cause of freedom, until they shall strike down slavery, the source and center of this gigantic rebellion, they don't deserve the support of a single sable arm, nor will it succeed in crushing the cause of our present troubles.

Source: *Douglass Monthly,* May 1861, in Philip S. Foner, ed., *Frederick Douglass: Selected Speeches and Writings* (Chicago: Lawrence Hill Books, 1999), 448–449.

QUESTIONS

1. What arguments does Douglass offer in support of Union use of African American troops?
2. In Douglass's view, what would Union acceptance of black soldiers signify to wartime slaves and to the Confederates?

Black soldiers suffered a far higher mortality rate than white troops. Typically assigned to labor detachments or garrison duty, blacks were less likely than whites to be killed in action but more likely to die of illness in bacteria-ridden garrisons. The Confederacy refused to treat captured black soldiers as prisoners of war, a policy that prevented their exchange for Southern prisoners. Instead, Jefferson Davis ordered all blacks taken in battle to be sent back to the states from which they came, to be re-enslaved or executed. In a notorious incident, when Confederate troops under General Nathan Bedford Forrest captured Fort Pillow, Tennessee, in 1864, they massacred many black soldiers who had surrendered—an act that provoked outcries but no retaliation from the North.

Well into the war, African American soldiers faced inequities in pay. White soldiers earned $13 a month plus a $3.50 clothing allowance; black privates received only $10 a month, with clothing deducted. "We have come out like men and we Expected to be Treated as men but we have bin Treated more Like Dogs then men," a black soldier complained to Secretary of War Edwin Stanton. In June 1864, Congress belatedly equalized the earnings of black and white soldiers.

Although fraught with hardships and inequities, military service became a symbol of citizenship for blacks. It proved that "black men can give blows as well as take them," Frederick Douglass declared. "Liberty won by white men would lose half its lustre." Above all, the use of black soldiers, especially former slaves, struck a telling blow against the Confederacy. "They will make good soldiers," General Grant wrote to Lincoln in 1863, "and taking them from the enemy weakens him in the same proportion they strengthen us."

Meanwhile, anxious white southerners on the home front feared slave revolts. "We should be practically helpless should the negroes rise," declared a Louisiana planter's daughter, "since there are so few men left at home." To control 3 million slaves, white southerners tightened slave patrols, moved entire plantations to relative safety from Union troops in Texas or in upland regions of the coastal South, and spread fear among slaves. "The whites would tell the colored people not to go to the Yankees, for they would harness them to carts . . . in place of horses," reported Susie King Taylor, a fugitive slave from Savannah.

Some slaves remained faithful to their owners and helped hide family treasures from marauding Union soldiers. Others wavered between loyalty and hunger for freedom: one slave accompanied his master to war, rescued him when he was wounded, and then escaped on his master's horse. Given a choice between freedom and bondage, slaves usually chose freedom. Few slaves helped the North as dramatically as Robert

Smalls, a hired-out slave boatman who turned over a Confederate steamer to the Union navy, but most who had a chance to flee to Union lines did so. The idea of freedom was irresistible. On learning of his freedom from a Union soldier, a Virginia coachman dressed in his master's clothes, "put on his best watch and chain, took his stick, and . . . told him [the master] that he might for the future drive his own coach."

Most slaves, however, lacked means of escape and remained under their owners' nominal control. Despite fears of southern whites, no general uprising of slaves occurred; the Confederacy continued to impress thousands of slaves to toil in war plants, army camps, and field hospitals. But even slaves with no chance of flight were alert to the opportunity that war provided and swiftly tested the limits of enforced labor. As a Savannah mistress noted as early as 1861, the slaves "show a very different face from what they have had heretofore." Moreover, wartime conditions reduced slave productivity. With most white men off at war, the master-slave relationship weakened. White women and boys left to manage plantations complained of their difficulty in controlling slaves, who commonly refused to work, labored inefficiently, or destroyed property. A Texas wife contended that her slaves were "trying all they can, it seems to me, to aggravate me" by neglecting the stock, breaking plows, and tearing down fences. "You may give your Negroes away," she finally wrote despairingly to her husband in 1864.

Whether southern slaves fled to freedom or merely stopped working, they acted effectively to defy slavery, liberate themselves from its regulations, and undermine the plantation system. Thus

FORDING THE RAPPAHANNOCK RIVER When federal troops came within reach, those slaves who could do so liberated themselves by fleeing behind Union lines. These Virginia fugitives, lugging all their possessions, move toward freedom in the summer of 1862, after the Second Battle of Bull Run. *[Library of Congress Prints and Photographs Division Washington, D.C.(LC-DIG-cwpb-00218)]*

southern slavery disintegrated even as the Confederacy fought to preserve it. Hard-pressed by Union armies and short of manpower, the Confederate Congress, late in the war in 1864, considered the drastic step of impressing slaves into its army as soldiers in exchange for their freedom at the war's end. Robert E. Lee favored the policy, believing that if the Confederacy did not arm its slaves, the Union would. Others were adamantly opposed. "If slaves will make good soldiers," a Georgia general argued, "our whole theory of slavery is wrong." Originally against arming slaves, Jefferson Davis changed his mind in 1865. In March 1865, the Confederate Congress narrowly passed a bill to arm three hundred thousand slave soldiers, although it omitted any mention of emancipation. Because the war ended a few weeks later, however, the plan was never put into effect.

Although the Confederacy's decision to arm the slaves came too late to affect the war, debate over arming them hurt southern morale. By then, the South's military position had started to deteriorate.

15-3.4 The Turning Point of 1863

In the summer and fall of 1863, Union fortunes dramatically improved in every theater of war. Yet the year began badly. The Northern slide, which had started with Burnside's defeat at Fredericksburg, Virginia, in December 1862, persisted into the spring of 1863. Burnside's successor, General Joseph "Fighting Joe" Hooker, a windbag fond of issuing pompous proclamations to his troops, suffered a crushing defeat in May 1863 at Chancellorsville, Virginia, where he was routed by Lee and Stonewall Jackson. Chancellorsville proved

costly for the South—Confederate sentries accidentally killed Stonewall Jackson—but it humiliated the North; Hooker had twice as many men as Lee. Reports from the West brought no better news. Repulsed at Shiloh in western Tennessee, the Confederates still had a powerful army in central Tennessee under General Braxton Bragg. Furthermore, despite repeated efforts, Grant was unable to take Vicksburg; the two-hundred-mile stretch of the Mississippi between Vicksburg and Port Hudson remained in rebel hands.

Union fortunes rose after Chancellorsville when Lee decided to invade the North. Lee needed supplies that war-wracked Virginia could no longer provide; he also hoped to draw Northern troops from besieged Vicksburg to the eastern theater. Lee envisioned a major Confederate victory on northern soil that would increase the sway of pro-peace Democrats and gain European recognition of the Confederacy. Moving his seventy-five thousand men down the Shenandoah Valley, Lee pressed into southern Pennsylvania. Lincoln, rejecting Hooker's plan to attack an unprotected Richmond, replaced Hooker with the more reliable George G. Meade.

Early in July 1863, Lee's offensive ground to a halt at a Pennsylvania road junction, Gettysburg (see Map 15.4). Confederates foraging for shoes in the town stumbled into some Union cavalry. Soon both sides called for reinforcements, and the war's

SEA ISLAND WAGE LABOR The arrival of the Union navy on the Sea Islands off the coast of Georgia and South Carolina in November 1861 liberated some ten thousand slaves, the first large group of enslaved people freed by the Civil War. The site of pioneer ventures in freedmen's education, black wage labor, and land redistribution, the Sea Islands served as a wartime testing ground for new social policies. Here, the manager of a plantation near Beaufort, South Carolina, on the island of Port Royal, shares the terms of a labor contract with former slaves, now free laborers, in 1863. *(From the Collections of the South Carolina Historical Society)*

MAP 15.3 THE SEA ISLANDS The island chain was the site of unique wartime experiments in new social policies.

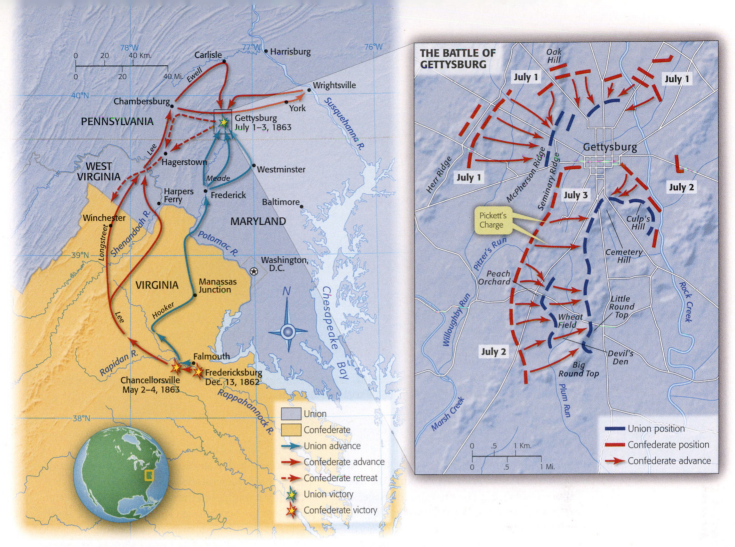

MAP 15.4 GETTYSBURG, 1863 The failure of Pickett's charge against the Union center on July 3 was the decisive action in the war's greatest battle.

greatest battle, the **Battle of Gettysburg**, began. On July 1, Meade's troops installed themselves in hills south of town along a line: the shank ran along Cemetery Ridge and a northern hook encircled Culp's Hill. By the end of the first day, Meade's army outnumbered the Confederates ninety thousand to seventy-five thousand. On July 2, Lee rejected advice to plant his army in a defensive stance between Meade's forces and Washington and instead attacked the Union flanks, with some success. But because Confederate assaults were uncoordinated, and some southern generals disregarded orders and struck where they chose, the Union moved in reinforcements and regained its earlier losses.

By the afternoon of July 3, believing that the Union flanks had been weakened, Lee attacked Cemetery Ridge in the center of the North's defensive line. After southern cannon shelled the line, a massive infantry force of fifteen thousand Confederates, Pickett's charge, moved in. But as Confederate cannon sank into the ground and fired too high, Union fire wiped out the rebel charge; rifled

weapons proved their deadly effectiveness. More than half of Pickett's troops were dead, wounded, or captured. When Lee withdrew to Virginia on July 4, he had lost seventeen generals and over one-third of his army. Total Union and Confederate casualties numbered almost fifty thousand. Although Meade failed to pursue and destroy the retreating rebels, he had halted Lee's foray into the North; the Union rejoiced.

Almost simultaneously, the North won a strategic victory in the West, at the **Battle of Vicksburg**; here, Grant finally pierced Vicksburg's defenses (see Map 15.5). Situated on a bluff on the east bank of the Mississippi, Vicksburg was protected on the west by the river and on the north by hills, forests, and swamps. It could be attacked only over a thin strip of dry land to its east and south. Positioned to the north of Vicksburg, Grant moved his troops far to the west of the city and down to a point on the river south of Vicksburg.

Battle of Gettysburg
The greatest battle and the turning point of the Civil War.

Battle of Vicksburg
Strategic victory in the West. It gave the Union the control of the Mississippi River.

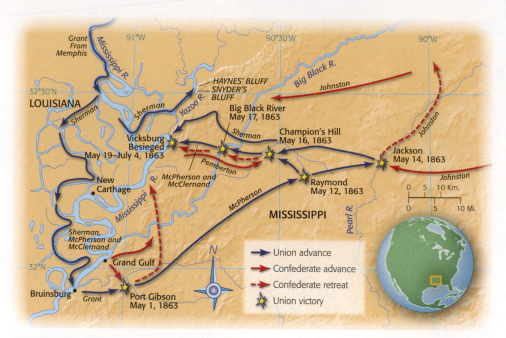

MAP 15.5 **THE WAR IN THE WEST, 1863: VICKSBURG** Grant first moved his army west of Vicksburg to a point on the Mississippi south of the town. Then he marched northeast, taking Jackson, and finally west to Vicksburg.

Meanwhile, Union gunboats and supply ships ran past the Confederate batteries overlooking the river at Vicksburg (sustaining considerable damage) to transport Grant's army across to the east bank.

Grant then swung in a large semicircle, first northeastward to capture Jackson, the capital of Mississippi, and then westward back to Vicksburg. After a six-week siege, in which famished soldiers and civilians in Vicksburg survived by eating mules and even rats, General John C. Pemberton surrendered his thirty-thousand-man garrison to Grant on July 4, the day after Pickett's charge at Gettysburg. Port Hudson, the last Confederate holdout on the Mississippi, soon surrendered to another Union army. "The Father of Waters flows unvexed to the sea," Lincoln declared.

A second crucial Union victory in the West soon followed. General William S. Rosecrans fought and maneuvered Braxton Bragg's Confederate army out of central Tennessee and into Chattanooga, in the southeastern tip of the state. Forced to evacuate Chattanooga, Bragg defeated the pursuing Rosecrans at the bloody Battle of Chickamauga (September 19–20, 1863) and drove him back into Chattanooga. The arrival of Grant and reinforcements from the Army of the Potomac broke Bragg's siege of Chattanooga in November. With Chattanooga secure, the way lay open for a Union strike into Georgia.

Union successes in the second half of 1863 stiffened northern will to keep fighting and plunged some rebel leaders into despair. Hearing of Vicksburg's fall, Confederate ordnance chief Josiah Gorgas lamented, "Yesterday we rode the pinnacle of success—today absolute ruin seems our portion. The Confederacy totters to its destruction."

Totter it might, but the South was far from beaten. Although the outcome at Gettysburg quashed southerners' hopes for victory on northern soil, Lee could still defend Virginia. The loss of Vicksburg and the Mississippi cut the Confederacy in half but the rebel states west of the river—Arkansas, Louisiana, and Texas—could still provide soldiers. Even with the loss of Chattanooga, the Confederacy retained most of the Carolinas, Georgia, Florida, and Mississippi. Few thought the fate of the Confederacy had been sealed.

15-4 War and Society, North and South

How did the war alter both northern and southern societies?

Extending beyond battlefields, the Civil War engulfed two economies and societies. By 1863, stark contrasts emerged: superior resources enabled the Union to meet wartime demand as the imperiled Confederacy could not. But both regions experienced labor shortages and inflation; both confronted problems of disunity and dissent. In both societies, war impinged on everyday life. Families were disrupted and dislocated, especially in the South. Women on both sides assumed new roles at home, in the workplace, and in both war and relief efforts.

15-4.1 The War's Economic Impact: The North

War affected the Union's economy unevenly. Some industries fared poorly: deprived of raw cotton, the cotton-textile industry went into a tailspin. But industries directly linked to the war effort, such as the manufacture of arms, shoes, and clothing, profited from huge government contracts; the Union army needed a million uniforms a year. Railroads flourished. Some privately owned lines, which had overbuilt before the war, doubled their volume of traffic. In 1862, the federal government itself went into the railroad business; it established the United States Military Railroads (USMRR) to carry troops and supplies to the front. By 1865, the USMRR was the world's largest railroad.

Republicans in Congress, now a big majority, actively promoted business growth. Overriding Democratic foes, they hiked the tariff in 1862 and again in 1864 to protect domestic industries. The Republican-sponsored Pacific Railroad Act of 1862 provided for the development of a transcontinental railroad, an idea that had foundered before the war on feuds over which route such a railroad should follow. With the South out of the picture and unable to demand a southern route, Congress chose a northern route from Omaha to San Francisco. Chartering the Union Pacific and Central Railroad corporations, Congress gave each large land grants and generous loans: more than 60 million acres and $20 million. Issuance of greenbacks and the creation of national banking rules brought a measure of uniformity to the nation's financial system.

Republicans designed these measures to benefit all social classes, and partially succeeded. The **Homestead Act**, passed in 1862, embodied the party's ideal of "free soil, free labor, free men." It granted 160 acres of public land to settlers after five years of residence on the land. By 1865, twenty thousand homesteaders occupied new land in the West under the Homestead Act. Republicans also sponsored the **Morrill Land Grant Act** of 1862, which gave the states proceeds of public lands to fund the start of universities that offered "such branches of learning as are related to agriculture and mechanic arts." The law spurred the growth of large state universities, mainly in the Midwest and West, including Michigan State, Iowa State, and Purdue, among many others.

In general, however, the war benefited wealthy citizens more than others. Corrupt contractors grew rich by selling the government substandard merchandise such as the notorious "shoddy" clothing made from compressed rags, which quickly disintegrated. Speculators made millions in the gold market. Because the price of gold in relation to greenbacks rose whenever public confidence in the government fell, gold speculators gained from Union defeats. Businessmen with access to scarce commodities also reaped astounding profits. Manpower shortages stimulated wartime demand for the mechanical reaper that Cyrus McCormick had patented in 1834. Paid for reapers in greenbacks, which he distrusted, McCormick at once reinvested them in pig iron and watched in glee as wartime demand almost doubled its price.

Ordinary Americans suffered. Higher protective tariffs, wartime excise taxes, and inflation bloated the prices of finished goods, while wages lagged 20 percent or more behind cost increases. Lagging wages became severe as boys and women replaced army-bound men in government offices and factories. For women employees, entry into government jobs—even at half the pay of male clerks—represented a major advance. But employers' access to low-paid labor undercut the bargaining power of men who remained in the workforce.

Many workers decried low wages, and some, such as cigar makers and locomotive engineers, formed national unions, a process that would accelerate after the war. Employers denounced worker complaints as unpatriotic hindrances to the war effort, and in 1864, the government diverted troops from combat to put down protests in war industries from New York to the Midwest.

15-4.2 The War's Economic Impact: The South

The war shattered the South's economy. Indeed, if both regions are considered together, the war retarded *American* economic growth. For example, American commodity output, which had registered huge increases of 51 percent and 62 percent in the 1840s and 1850s, respectively, rose only 22 percent in the 1860s. This modest gain depended wholly on the North, for in the 1860s commodity output in the South actually *declined* 39 percent.

While the South sought to spur industrial production, multiple factors offset the region's wartime industrial growth. War wrecked the South's railroads; invading Union troops tore up tracks, twisted rails, and burned railroad cars. Cotton production, once the foundation of southern prosperity, sank from more than 4 million bales in 1861 to three hundred thousand bales in 1865; Union invasions took their toll on production, particularly in Tennessee and Louisiana.

Homestead Act
Passed in 1862, embodied the Republican party's ideal of "free soil, free labor, free men" by granting 160 acres of public land to settlers after five years of residence on the land.

Morrill Land Grant Act
This gave to the states proceeds of public lands to fund the establishment of universities emphasizing "such branches of learning as are related to agriculture and mechanic arts." It spurred the growth of large state universities, mainly in the Midwest and West. Michigan State, Iowa State, and Purdue universities, among many others, profited from the law.

Union invaders also occupied the South's food-growing regions, and in areas under Confederate control, the manpower drain cut yields per acre of crops like wheat and corn; scarcities abounded. Agricultural shortages compounded severe inflation. By 1863, salt selling for $1.25 a sack in New York City cost $60 in the Confederacy. Food riots erupted in 1863 in Mobile, Atlanta, and Richmond; in Richmond ironworkers' wives paraded to demand lower food prices.

Part of the blame for Southern food shortages rested with planters. Despite government pleas to grow more food, many planters continued to raise cotton. To feed hungry armies, the Confederacy had to impress food from civilians, a policy that evoked resentment and spurred military desertions. Food-impressment agents usually concentrated on the easiest targets—farms run by the wives of active soldiers. "I don't want you to stop fighting them Yankees," wrote the wife of an Alabama soldier, "but try and get off and come home and fix us all up some and then you can go back." By the end of 1864, half of the Confederacy's soldiers were absent from their units.

The manpower drain that hampered food production reshaped the lives of southern white women. With three out of four white men in the military over the course of the war, Confederate women found their locales transformed. "There is a vacant chair in every house," mourned a Kentucky Confederate girl. Left in charge of farms and plantations, women faced new challenges and chronic shortages. As manufactured goods became scarce, southern homemakers wove cloth and devised replacements for goods no longer attainable, including inks, dyes, coffee, shoes, and wax candles.

The war's proximity made many Confederate women into refugees. Property destruction or even the threat of Union invasions drove families away from their homes; those with slave property to preserve, in particular, sought to flee before Union forces arrived. Areas remote from military action, especially Texas, were favored destinations. Disorienting and disheartening, the refugee experience sapped morale. "I will never feel like myself again," a Georgia woman who had escaped from the path of Union troops wrote to her husband in 1864.

In one respect, the persistence of cotton growing helped the South: Cotton became the basis for the Confederacy's flourishing trade with the enemy. The U.S. Congress virtually legalized this trade in July 1861 by allowing northern commerce

SIX NORTH CAROLINA WOMEN The departure of most men of military age to serve in the Confederate army reshaped southern households and the experience of family members. The faces of these young North Carolina women, in a portrait titled "Confederate Belles," reflect hardship, resolution, and no doubt changed expectations. *(Museum of the Confederacy, Richmond, Virginia)*

with southerners loyal to the Union. In practice, of course, it proved impossible to tell loyalists from rebels; northern traders happily swapped bacon, salt, blankets, and other products for southern cotton. By 1864, traffic through the lines provided enough food for Lee's Army of Northern Virginia. A northern congressman lamented that the Union's policy was "to feed an army and fight it at the same time."

Trading with the enemy alleviated southern food shortages but damaged morale. The prospect of traffic with Yankees gave planters an incentive to keep growing cotton, and fattened middlemen. "Oh! the extortioners," complained a Confederate war office clerk in Richmond. "Our patriotism is mainly in the army and among the ladies of the South. The avarice and cupidity of men at home could only be exceeded by ravenous wolves."

Prisoners of war also came with economic costs. Prisoner exchanges between North and South, at first common, collapsed by midwar, partly because the South refused to exchange black prisoners and partly because the North gradually concluded that exchanges benefited the manpower-short Confederacy more than the Union. Both sides consequently had more prisoners than they could handle. Miserable conditions plagued southern camps. Squalor and insufficient rations turned the Confederate prison camp at Andersonville, Georgia, into a virtual death camp; three thousand prisoners a month (out of a total of thirty-two thousand) were dying there by August 1864. After the war an outraged northern public secured the execution of Andersonville's commandant. Though camps were not much better, they had lower mortality rates. Deterioration of the southern economy contributed massively to the wretched state of southern prison camps.

15-4.3 Dealing with Dissent

Both wartime governments faced mounting dissent and disloyalty. Among Confederates, dissent took two basic forms. First, a vocal group of states' rights activists, notably Vice President Alexander Stephens and governors Zebulon Vance of North Carolina and Joseph Brown of Georgia, persistently attacked Jefferson Davis's government as despotic. Second, pro-Union sentiment flourished among a segment of Confederate common people, particularly those in the Appalachian Mountain region that ran from western North Carolina through Tennessee into northern Georgia and Alabama. Nonslaveholding small farmers who predominated here saw Confederate rebellion as a slave owners' conspiracy. Resentful of such measures as the 20-Negro exemption from conscription, they voiced reluctance to fight for what a North Carolinian called "an adored

trinity," of cotton, slaves, and "chivalry." "All they want," an Alabama farmer complained of the planters, "is to get you pupt up and to fight for their infurnal Negroes and after you do there fighting you may kiss there hine parts for o they care."

On the whole, the Confederate government responded mildly to popular disaffection. In 1862, roughly a year after Lincoln made a similar move, the Confederate Congress gave Jefferson Davis the power to suspend the writ of *habeas corpus*, but Davis used his power only sparingly.

Lincoln faced similar challenges in the North, where the Democratic minority opposed both emancipation and wartime growth of centralized power. Although "War Democrats" conceded that war was necessary to preserve the Union, "Peace Democrats" (called "Copperheads" by their opponents, to suggest resemblance to a species of easily concealed poisonous snakes) demanded a truce and a peace conference. They charged that administration war policy would "exterminate the South," make reconciliation impossible, and spark "terrible social change and revolution."

Strongest in the border states, the Midwest, and the northeastern cities, the Democrats mobilized support among farmers of southern background in the Ohio Valley and urban workers, especially recent immigrants, who feared job loss to free blacks. In 1863, this volatile brew of antagonisms exploded into antidraft protests in several cities. Most violent were the **New York City Draft Riots** in July. Enraged by the first drawing of names under the Enrollment Act and by a longshoremen's strike in which blacks had been used as strikebreakers, mobs of Irish working-class men and women roamed the streets for four days until suppressed by federal troops. The city's Irish loathed the idea of being drafted to fight a war on behalf of the slaves who, once free, might migrate north to compete for jobs, and they resented the provision of the draft law that allowed the rich to purchase substitutes. Workers also had contempt for laws that allowed the wealthy to hire a substitute rather than serve when drafted. The rioters lynched at least a dozen blacks, injured hundreds more, and burned draft offices, the homes of wealthy Republicans, and the Colored Orphan Asylum.

President Lincoln's dispatch of federal troops to quash these riots typified his forceful response to dissent. Lincoln imposed martial law with far less hesitancy than Davis. After suspending the writ of *habeas corpus* in Maryland in 1861, he barred it nationwide in 1863 and authorized the arrest of rebels, draft resisters, and those engaged in "any disloyal practice." Many saw it as a violation of civil liberties

New York City Draft Riots
Enraged by the first drawing of names under the Enrollment Act and by a longshoremen's strike in which blacks had been used as strikebreakers, mobs of Irish working-class men and women roamed the streets for four days until suppressed by federal troops.

United States Sanitary Commission

An organization that raised funds at "sanitary fairs," bought and distributed supplies, ran special kitchens to supplement army rations, tracked down the missing, and inspected army camps.

and an unprecedented extension of presidential power. Newspapers that disagreed with Lincoln's positions on the war were closed, and thousands of Americans faced arrest and imprisonment. The responses of Davis and Lincoln to dissent underscored the differences between the two regions' wartime political systems. As we have seen, Davis lacked the institutionalization of dissent provided by party conflict and had to tread warily, lest his foes brand him a despot. In contrast, Lincoln and other Republicans used dissent to rally patriotic fervor against the Democrats.

Forceful as he was, Lincoln did not unleash a reign of terror against dissent. In general, the North preserved freedom of the press, speech, and assembly. Of some fifteen thousand civilians arrested during the war, most were quickly released. A few cases aroused concern. In 1864, a military commission sentenced an Indiana man to be hanged for an alleged plot to free Confederate prisoners. The Supreme Court reversed his conviction two years later; it ruled that civilians could not be tried by military courts when the civil courts were

open (*Ex parte* Milligan, 1866). Of more concern were arrests of politicians, notably Clement L. Vallandigham, an Ohio Peace Democrat. Courting arrest, Vallandigham challenged the administration, denounced the suspension of *habeas corpus*, proposed an armistice, and in 1863 was sentenced to jail for the war's duration by a military commission. When Ohio Democrats then nominated him for governor, Lincoln changed the sentence to banishment. Escorted to enemy lines in Tennessee, Vallandigham was left in the hands of bewildered Confederates and eventually fled to Canada. The Supreme Court refused to review his case.

15-4.4 Women and the War

Wartime patriotism impelled civilians North and South, especially women, to work tirelessly to aid soldiers. Many volunteered to prepare bandages; others raised millions of dollars for the wounded. The **United States Sanitary Commission**, formed early in the war by civilians to help the Union's medical bureau, depended on women volunteers. Described by one woman as a "great artery that bears the people's love to the army," the commission raised funds at "sanitary fairs," bought and

ORGANIZERS OF THE NEW YORK SANITARY FAIR These imposing New York women of 1864 ran an exceptionally profitable "Sanitary Fair," under the auspices of the U.S. Sanitary Commission, that raised more than one million dollars for soldiers' relief. *(Western Reserve Historical Society, Cleveland, Ohio)*

distributed supplies, ran special kitchens to supplement army rations, tracked down the missing, and inspected army camps. They also played a huge part in the implementation of an ambulance corps for the Union side. The volunteers' exploits became legendary. One poor widow, Mary Ann "Mother" Bickerdyke, served sick and wounded Union soldiers. When a doctor asked by what authority she demanded supplies, she shot back: "From the Lord God Almighty. Do you have anything that ranks higher than that?"

Called "angels" of the battlefield, thousands of women served the Union and the Confederacy as nurses, often on the front lines. Famous for her campaigns on behalf of the insane, Dorothea Dix became head of the Union's nursing corps. Clara Barton, an obscure clerk in the U.S. Patent Office, found ingenious ways to channel medicine to the sick and wounded. Learning of Union movements before Antietam, Barton showed up at the battlefield on the eve of the clash with a wagonload of supplies. After the war, in 1881, she founded the American Red Cross. Confederate Sally Tompkins was commissioned a captain for her hospital work. Wherever they worked, nurses witnessed haunting sights. "About the amputating table," one reported, "lay large piles of human flesh . . . the stiffened membranes seemed to be clutching oftentimes at our clothing."

Pioneered by British reformer Florence Nightingale in the 1850s, nursing was a new vocation for women and to critics, a brazen departure from women's proper sphere. Male doctors were unsure how to react to women in the wards. Some saw the potential for mischief, but others viewed women nurses as potentially useful. Nursing was, like the military, segregated. Susie Taylor King, who in 1863 escaped slavery in Georgia to freedom in Union-occupied territory of South Carolina, cared for black soldiers in a segregated facility.

Black or white, the biggest risk for nurses in hospitals was disease. Author Louisa May Alcott, a nurse at the Union Hotel Hospital in Washington, D.C., contracted typhoid. Although the ratio of disease to battle deaths was much lower in the Civil War than in the U.S War with Mexico due partly to sanitary improvements (see Chapter 11), still, for every soldier killed during the Civil War, two died of disease. Scientific investigations that would lead to the germ theory of disease were only starting in the 1860s. Arm and leg wounds frequently led to gangrene or tetanus, and typhoid, malaria, diarrhea, and dysentery raged through army camps. While male soldiers were guaranteed a pension, it wasn't until 1890, that women—white and black—who had earned a salary as a nurse during the Civil War would receive a wartime pension.

Women also sought to aid the military more directly. Many followed husbands to the camps, working as laundresses and cooks, though even in those roles, they might be called upon to take up arms. Often, they juggled multiple roles. Belle Boyd, a nurse and spy, once dashed through a field, waving her bonnet, to give Stonewall Jackson information. Harriet Tubman, known for her work with the Underground Railroad, was a nurse, a military advisor, a scout, and a spy for the Union army. She posed as a slave to gain access to information about southern strategy, and organized her own troop of black male scouts. The information she provided Union troops led to the successful Combahee River raid in South Carolina in 1863, that blocked supplies from Confederates and sent hundreds of slaves fleeing to the Union. Despite the importance of her contributions and countless efforts by her and on her behalf, she never received a Union pension for her wartime contributions (though she did receive a widow's pension on behalf of her late husband's service). Confederate spy Rose Greenhow relied on her feminine charms to get behind enemy lines and garner vital military information. In fact, the spy secrets she passed on helped ensure a southern victory in the first battle of Bull Run.

Some women, too, sought to participate directly in the fighting, large numbers of them posing as men to do so. While most of the women who passed as men were on the Union side, one famous Confederate example was Loreta Velazquez, a Cuban immigrant whose husband supported her decision to pose as Harry T. Buford. Once discovered to be female—usually after being wounded—they were typically dismissed, though Velazquez somehow managed to avoid being found out. She later shared her story in her 1876 book *The Woman in Battle*.

Less dangerously though, North and South, thousands of women showed their patriotism by taking over jobs vacated by men in offices and mills. Home industry revived at all levels of society. In rural areas, where manpower dwindled, women often plowed, planted, and harvested. "Women were in the field everywhere," an Illinois woman recalled. "No rebuffs could chill their zeal; no reverses repress their ardor."

Few women worked more effectively for their region's cause than Philadelphia-born Anna E. Dickinson. After losing her job in the federal mint (for denouncing General George McClellan as a traitor), Dickinson threw herself into hospital volunteer work and public lecturing. Her lecture "Hospital Life," about soldiers' suffering, won attention among Republican politicians. In 1863, hard-pressed by the Democrats, they invited Dickinson, then scarcely twenty-one, to campaign for Republicans in New Hampshire and Connecticut. Articulate and poised, Dickinson captivated her listeners. Soon Republican

ANDERSONVILLE PRISON Started in early 1864, the overcrowded Andersonville prison in southwest Georgia provided no shelter for its inmates, who built tentlike structures out of blankets, sticks, or whatever they could find. Exposure, disease, and poor sanitation contributed to a mortality rate almost double that in other Confederate prison camps. The prisoners in this unusual image, made by a Confederate photographer, barely had room to stand. *(Massachusetts Commandery Military Order of the Loyal Legion and the U.S. Army Military History Institute)*

candidates who had dismissed the offer of aid from a woman begged her to campaign for them.

Northern women's rights advocates hoped that the war would yield equality for women as well as freedom for slaves. Not only should a grateful North reward women for their wartime services, these women reasoned, but it should recognize the link between black rights and women's rights. Elizabeth Cady Stanton and Susan B. Anthony used the Woman's National Loyal League they initially organized to abolish slavery as a vehicle for promoting women's suffrage as well.

Despite high expectations, the war brought women little closer to economic or political equality. Women in offices and factories continued to earn less than men. Sanitary Commission workers and most wartime nurses, as volunteers, earned nothing. Nor did the war alter the prevailing definition of woman's sphere. In 1860, that sphere already included charitable and benevolent activities; in wartime the scope of benevolence grew to embrace care for the wounded. Yet men continued to dominate the medical profession. The keenest disappointment of women's rights advocates lay in their failure to capitalize on rising abolitionist sentiment to secure the vote for women. Northern politicians saw little value in woman suffrage. The *New York Herald*, which supported the Loyal League's attack on slavery, dismissed its call for woman suffrage as "nonsense and tomfoolery." Stanton wrote bitterly, a few years later, "Women's cause is in deep water."

15-5 The Union Victorious, 1864–1865

To what can we attribute a Union victory in the Civil War?

Despite successes at Gettysburg and Vicksburg in 1863, the Union stood no closer to taking Richmond at the start of 1864 than in 1861; most of the Lower South still remained under Confederate control. Union invasion had taken a toll on the South, but inability to destroy the main Confederate armies eroded the Union's will to attack. War weariness strengthened northern Democrats and jeopardized Lincoln's prospects for reelection.

The year 1864 was crucial for the North. While Grant dueled with Lee in the East, a Union army under William T. Sherman attacked from Tennessee and captured Atlanta in early September. Atlanta's fall boosted northern morale and helped to reelect Lincoln. The curtain now rose on the last act of war: After taking Atlanta, Sherman marched across Georgia and on into South Carolina; in Virginia, Grant backed Lee into trenches around Petersburg and Richmond and brought on the Confederacy's collapse.

15-5.1 The Eastern Theater in 1864

Early in 1864, Lincoln made Grant commander of all Union armies and promoted him to lieutenant general. At first glance, the stony-faced, cigar-puffing Grant seemed an unlikely candidate for such an exalted rank, held previously only by George Washington. But Grant's success in the West had made him the Union's most popular general. With his promotion, Grant moved his headquarters to the Army of the Potomac in the East and mapped a strategy for final victory.

Like Lincoln, Grant believed that the Union had to coordinate its attacks on all fronts in order to exploit its numerical advantage and prevent the South from shifting troops between eastern and western theaters. Accordingly, Grant planned a sustained offensive against Lee in the East while sending Sherman to attack in Georgia. Sherman's mission was to break up the Confederate army and "to get into the interior of the enemy's country . . . inflicting all the damage you can."

The war's pace quickened dramatically. In early May 1864, Grant led 118,000 men against Lee's sixty-four thousand in a forested area near Fredericksburg, Virginia, called the Wilderness. Checked by Lee in a series of bloody engagements (the Battle of the Wilderness, May 5–7), Grant then suffered new reverses at Spotsylvania on May 12 and Cold Harbor on June 3. These engagements were fierce; at Cold Harbor, Grant lost seven thousand men in a single hour. Oliver Wendell Holmes, Jr., a Union lieutenant and later a Supreme Court justice, wrote home how "immense the butcher's bill has been." Instead of recoiling, Grant persisted; he forced Lee to pull back to the trenches guarding Petersburg and Richmond.

Once entrenched, Lee could no longer swing around to the Union rear, cut Yankee supply lines, or as at Chancellorsville, surprise the Union's main force. Lee dispatched General Jubal A. Early on raids down the Shenandoah Valley, which served Confederates as a granary and an indirect way to menace Washington. Grant countered by ordering General Philip Sheridan to march through the valley from the north and "lay it waste." By September 1864, Sheridan controlled the Shenandoah Valley.

While Grant and Lee grappled in the Wilderness, Sherman led ninety-eight thousand men into Georgia. Opposing him with fifty-three thousand Confederate troops (soon reinforced to sixty-five thousand), General Joseph Johnston retreated toward Atlanta. Johnston planned to conserve strength for a final defense of Atlanta while forcing Sherman to extend his supply lines. Dismayed by Johnston's defensive strategy, Jefferson Davis replaced him with the adventurous John B. Hood. Hood, who had lost the use of an arm at Gettysburg and a leg at Chickamauga, had to be strapped to his saddle; but for all his disabilities, he liked to take risks. In a prewar poker game, he had bet $2,500 with "nary a pair in his hand." Hood gave Davis what he wanted, a series of attacks on Sherman's army. But Sherman pressed forward against Hood's depleted army. Unable to defend Atlanta's supply lines, Hood evacuated the city, which Sherman took on September 2, 1864.

15-5.2 Lincoln's Reelection and Sherman's Total War

Atlanta's fall came at a timely moment for Lincoln, who faced a tough reelection campaign. Lincoln had secured the Republican renomination with difficulty. Radical Republicans, who had flayed Lincoln for delay in declaring emancipation a war goal, now spurned his plans to restore the occupied parts of the Confederacy to the Union. The Radicals insisted that only Congress, not the president, could set requirements for readmission of conquered areas. They found Lincoln's standards too lenient and endorsed treasury secretary Salmon P. Chase for the nomination. Democrats, meanwhile, had never forgiven Lincoln for making emancipation a war goal. Peace Democrats now demanded an immediate armistice, followed by negotiations between North and South.

Facing formidable challenges, Lincoln benefited from both his own resourcefulness and his foes' problems. Chase's challenge failed, and by the time of the Republican convention in July, Lincoln's managers held control. To isolate the Peace Democrats and attract prowar Democrats, Republicans formed a temporary organization, the National Union party, and replaced Lincoln's vice president, Hannibal Hamlin, with a prowar southern Unionist, Democratic Senator Andrew Johnson of Tennessee. This tactic helped exploit the widening split among the Democrats, who nominated George B. McClellan, former commander of the Army of the Potomac. But McClellan, saddled with a Copperhead platform, spent much of his campaign distancing himself from his party's peace-without-victory plank.

Despite disarray among Democrats, as late as August 1864, Lincoln doubted his reelection. Leaving little to chance, he arranged for furloughs so that Union soldiers, most of whom supported him, could vote in states lacking absentee ballots. But the timely fall of Atlanta punctured the northern antiwar movement and saved Lincoln's presidency. With 55 percent of the popular vote and 212 out of 233 electoral votes, Lincoln swept to victory. The convention that nominated Lincoln had endorsed a constitutional amendment to abolish slavery, which Congress passed early in 1865. The **Thirteenth Amendment** would be ratified by the end of the year (see Table 15.1).

Meanwhile, Sherman gave the South a new lesson in total war. After evacuating Atlanta, Hood led his Confederate army north toward Tennessee in the hope of luring Sherman out of Georgia. Refusing to chase Hood around Tennessee, Sherman proposed to abandon his supply lines, march his army across Georgia to Savannah, and live off the countryside. He would break the South's will to fight, terrify its people, and "make war so terrible . . . that generations would pass before they could appeal again to it."

Sherman began by burning much of Atlanta and forcing most of its civilian population to leave.

This harsh measure relieved him of the need to feed and garrison the city. Then, sending enough troops north to stop Hood in Tennessee, he led the bulk of his army, sixty-two thousand men, on a 285-mile trek to Savannah (see Map 15.6). Soon thousands of slaves followed the army. "Dar's de man dat rules the world," a slave cried on seeing Sherman.

Sherman's four columns of infantry, augmented by cavalry screens, moved on a front sixty miles wide and at a pace of ten miles a day. They destroyed everything that could aid southern resistance—arsenals, munitions plants, cotton gins, cotton stores, crops, livestock, and railroads. Ripping up tracks, Union soldiers heated rails in giant fires and twisted them into "Sherman neckties." Although told not to destroy civilian property, foragers ransacked and sometimes demolished homes. Indeed, havoc seemed a vital part of Sherman's strategy. By the time he reached Savannah, he estimated that his army had destroyed about a hundred million dollars' worth of property.

After taking Savannah in December 1864, Sherman's army wheeled north toward South Carolina, the first state to secede and, in Sherman's view, one "that deserves all that seems in store for her." His columns advanced unimpeded to Columbia, South Carolina's capital, where looters, slaves, and soldiers of both sides razed much of the city. Sherman then headed for North Carolina. By spring 1865, his army had left behind over four hundred miles of ruin. Other Union armies moved into Alabama and Georgia and took thousands of prisoners. Northern forces had penetrated the entire Confederacy, except

Table 15.1 Emancipation of Slaves in the Atlantic World: A Selective List

HAITI	1794	A series of slave revolts began in Saint-Domingue in 1791 and 1792, and spread under the leadership of Toussaint L'Ouverture. In 1794, the French Republic abolished slavery in all French colonies. In 1804, Saint-Domingue became the independent republic of Haiti.
BRITISH WEST INDIES	1834	Parliament in 1833 abolished slavery gradually in all lands under British control, usually with compensation for slave owners. The law affected the entire British Empire, including British colonies in the West Indies such as Barbados and Jamaica. It took effect in 1834.
MARTINIQUE AND GUADELOUPE	1848	Napoleon had restored slavery to these French colonies in 1800; the Second French Republic abolished it in 1848.
UNITED STATES	1865	The Thirteenth Amendment, passed by Congress in January 1865 and ratified in December 1865, freed all slaves in the United States. Prior to that, the second Confiscation Act of 1862 liberated those slaves who came within Union lines, and the Emancipation Proclamation of January 1, 1863, declared free all slaves in areas under Confederate control.
CUBA	1886	In the early 1880s, the Spanish Parliament passed a plan of gradual abolition, which provided an intermediate period of "apprenticeship." In 1886, Spain abolished slavery completely. Cuba remained under Spanish control until the end of the Spanish-American War in 1898.
BRAZIL	1888	Brazil, which had declared its independence from Portugal in 1822, passed a law to effect gradual emancipation in 1871, and in 1888, under the "Golden Law," abolished slavery completely.

15-5.3 Toward Appomattox

While Sherman headed north, Grant renewed his assault on the entrenched Army of Northern Virginia. His objective was Petersburg, a railroad hub south of Richmond (see Map 15.7). Although Grant had previously failed to overwhelm Confederate defenses in front of Petersburg, the devastation wrought by Sherman's army crippled Confederate morale: rebel desertions reached epidemic proportions. Late in March 1865 Grant, reinforced by Sheridan, swung his forces around the western flank of Petersburg's defenders. Lee could not stop him. On April 2, Sheridan smashed the rebel flank at the Battle of Five Forks. A courier bore the grim news to Jefferson Davis, attending church in Richmond: "General Lee telegraphs that he can hold his position no longer."

Davis left his pew, gathered his government, and fled the city. In the morning of April 3, Union troops entered Richmond, pulled down the Confederate flag, and ran up the Stars and Stripes over the capitol. Explosions set by retreating Confederates left the city "a sea of flames." Fires damaged the Tredegar Iron Works. Union troops liberated the town jail, which housed slaves awaiting sale, and its rejoicing inmates poured into the streets. On April 4, Lincoln toured the city and, for a few minutes, sat at Jefferson Davis's desk.

Lee made a last-ditch effort to escape Grant and reach Lynchburg, sixty miles west of Petersburg. He planned to use rail connections there to join General Joseph Johnston's army, which Sherman had pushed into North Carolina. But Grant and Sheridan choked off Lee's escape route, and on April 9 Lee

ATLANTA, GEORGIA General Sherman's campaign through Georgia and South Carolina in 1864 turned parts of the landscape into rubble. Before leaving Atlanta in flames, Union troops destroyed the railroad and blew up its depot. This photo of ruins, and many like it, suggests the crushing impact of war on the southern economy and environment. *(Library of Congress Prints and Photographs Division[LC-DIG-cwpb-02226])*

for Texas and Florida, and crushed its wealth. "War is cruelty and you cannot refine it," Sherman wrote. "Those who brought war into our country deserve all the curses and maledictions a people can pour out."

MAP 15.6 **SHERMAN'S MARCH THROUGH THE SOUTH, 1864–1865**

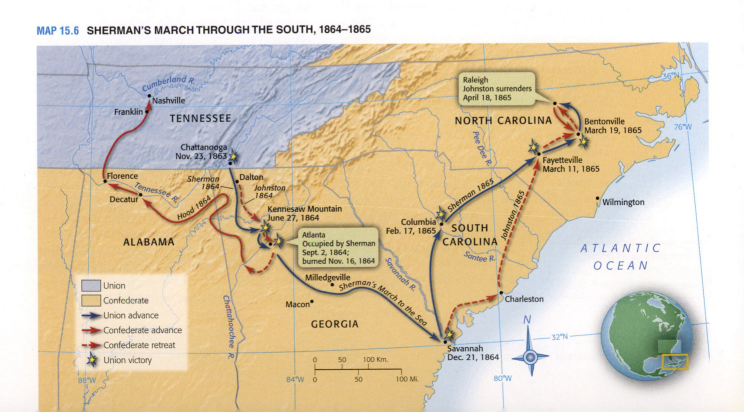

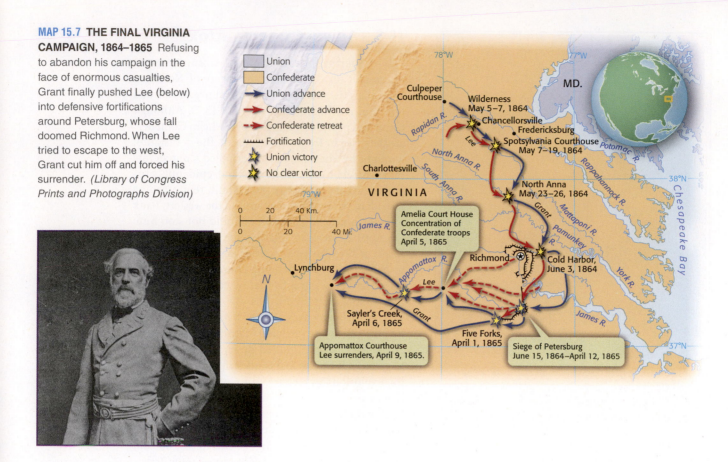

MAP 15.7 THE FINAL VIRGINIA CAMPAIGN, 1864–1865 Refusing to abandon his campaign in the face of enormous casualties, Grant finally pushed Lee (below) into defensive fortifications around Petersburg, whose fall doomed Richmond. When Lee tried to escape to the west, Grant cut him off and forced his surrender. *(Library of Congress Prints and Photographs Division)*

bowed to the inevitable. He asked for terms of surrender and met Grant in a private home in the village of **Appomattox Court House**, Virginia, east of Lynchburg. While stunned troops gathered outside, Lee appeared in full dress uniform, with a sword. Grant entered in his customary disarray, smoking a cigar. The final surrender occurred four days later: Lee's troops laid down their arms between federal ranks. "On our part," wrote a Union officer, "not a sound of trumpet . . . nor roll of drum; not a cheer . . . but an awed stillness rather." Grant paroled Lee's twenty-six thousand men and sent them home with their horses and mules "to work their little farms." Remnants of Confederate resistance collapsed within a month. Johnston surrendered to Sherman on April 18, and Davis was captured in Georgia on May 10.

Grant returned to a jubilant Washington, and on April 14 turned down a theater date with the Lincolns. That night at Ford's Theater, an unemployed pro-Confederate actor, John Wilkes Booth, entered Lincoln's box and shot him in the head. Waving a knife, Booth leaped onstage shouting the Virginia state motto, *"Sic semper tyrannis"* ("Such is always the fate of tyrants") and then fled, despite a broken leg. That same night, a Booth accomplice stabbed Secretary of State Seward, who later recovered; a third conspirator, assigned to Vice President Johnson, failed to attack. Union troops hunted down Booth in Virginia within two weeks and shot him to death. Of eight accused accomplices, four were hanged and the rest imprisoned. On April 15, Lincoln died, and Andrew Johnson became president. Six days later, Lincoln's funeral train departed on a mournful journey from Washington to Springfield, Illinois, with crowds of thousands gathering at stations to weep as it passed.

15-5.4 The Impact of the War

The Civil War took a larger human toll than any other war in American history. At least 620,000 soldiers lost their lives, and some scholars estimate even more. The death count—360,000 Union soldiers and 260,000 Confederates—nearly equaled the number of American soldiers killed in all the nation's earlier and later wars combined (see Figure 15.3). Most families suffered losses. Vivid reminders of the price of Union remained for many years; armless and legless veterans gathered at regimental reunions; and

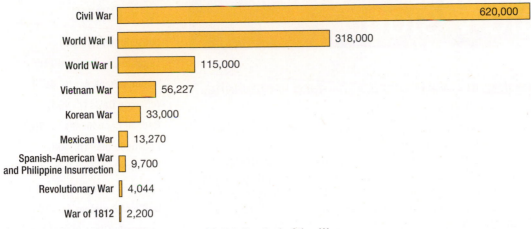

Total Civil War Deaths Compared to U.S. Deaths in Other Wars

Civil War	620,000
World War II	318,000
World War I	115,000
Vietnam War	56,227
Korean War	33,000
Mexican War	13,270
Spanish-American War and Philippine Insurrection	9,700
Revolutionary War	4,044
War of 1812	2,200

FIGURE 15.3 Civil War Deaths Compared with U.S. Deaths in Other Wars

monuments to the dead arose on village greens. Soldiers' widows collected pensions well into the twentieth century.

The war's costs were staggering, but war did not ruin the national economy, only the southern part of it. Vast Confederate losses, about 60 percent of southern wealth, were offset by northern advances. At the war's end, the North had almost all of the nation's wealth and capacity for production. Spurring economic modernization, the war provided a friendly climate for industrial development and capital investment. No longer the largest slave-owning power in the world, the United States would now become a major industrial nation.

The war had political as well as economic ramifications. It created a "more perfect Union" in place of the prewar federation of states. The doctrine of states' rights did not disappear, but talk of secession stopped; states would never again exercise their antebellum range of powers. The national banking system, created in 1863, gradually supplanted state banks. Greenbacks provided a national currency. The federal government had exercised powers that many in 1860 doubted it possessed. By ending slavery and imposing an income tax, it asserted power over kinds of private property once thought untouchable.

Finally, the Civil War fulfilled abolitionist prophecies as well as Unionist goals. Freeing 3.5 million slaves and expediting efforts by slaves to liberate themselves, the war produced the very sort of radical upheaval in southern society that Lincoln had originally said it would not induce.

GRANT IN 1864 Exuding determination and competence, General Ulysses S. Grant posed in front of his tent in 1864. Within a year, Grant's final assault on Petersburg and the Union army's triumphant march into Richmond would bring the war to an end. *(National Archives and Records Administration)*

The Whole Vision

KEY TERMS

■ *What challenges did each side—North and South—face in preparing for war?*

The challenges that each side faced had to do with politics, economics, and military preparedness. They also had to do with the goals of war and the region and terrain on which most battles would be fought, since that would offer advantages for one side over the other. Politically, the North had a central government in place; all it had to do was determine the necessary measures to fund and supply its war effort—and hope for Congressional approval and state compliance. The South, on the other hand, had the additional challenge of creating a central government—in the middle of states' rights territory and counter to the political imperatives around this that led to war—and garnering southern support for the measures it took. Both sides faced challenges in financing the war and staffing an army, especially the question of a draft. The state of each region's economy at the time of disunion also posed challenges in terms of generating food and other needed supplies, and there, one side would have a definite advantage as the war progressed. Rallying the public behind the war and national/military leaders proved far easier for one side than for the other, at least at the outset of the conflict.

■ *Is it accurate to claim that the Civil War was "the first modern war"?*

The answer, in short, is yes and no and depends on which aspects of the war being discussed. To conduct a war requires preparedness, military strategy, weaponry, and supplies. Even before battles begin—and during the course of war itself—nations make a host of behind-the-scenes decisions designed to position them well for what lay ahead. The Union and Confederacy made several such decisions, including where to locate the seat of government, that were not only meant to ensure its broader strategy but also influence that of its enemies. In terms of weaponry and naval vessels, the Civil War indeed had aspects of a modern war. But the ability to use weapons and other technology efficiently and effectively at times undermined their potential and left many battles fought in more traditional ways. Some generals, too, preferred traditional rather than modern approaches to formulating a strategy. On the other hand, as the war progressed, the measure of modernity may be evident in the body count. Soldiers might question just how modern the war was, especially with minimal and often dismal food and other supplies, as well as the nature of their camps.

■ *How did the Emancipation Proclamation transform the war?*

Lincoln held off taking a position on slavery in the early years of the war for several reasons, among them his fierce and primary objective to restore the Union at any cost. But as the battle raged on, issues of confiscation and contraband slaves put many more slaves under Union control. Military strategy also had some looking at the advantages slavery might have offered the South in terms of the number of white men available for service. Politically, Lincoln struggled with multiple issues from the constitutionality of attempts to interfere with slavery to appeasing conservatives and retaining the loyalty of border states to pressure from Radical Republicans in Congress. Militarily, however, the notion of emancipation proved an enticing means to injure the Confederacy on multiple levels. The proclamation itself had little immediate impact since it was limited to states within the rebellion. But symbolically, it officially linked the cause of war to more than just preserving the Union—it now included ending slavery. It also opened up a potential new cadre of potential Union soldiers among African Americans.

How did the war alter both northern and southern societies?

The war affected every aspect of society in both regions. It also gave the North a chance to make moves, unrestrained by southern interests or disagreements. Many of these moves had to do with development of the West, the railroads, and other commercial concerns and had long-term consequences for industrial development regionally and nationally. While American economic output was halted generally by war, Southern development was stunted and its economy declined and was ultimately upended. Tensions about the focus of southern agriculture production divided many Confederates. The war also widened class divisions in the North and made some people rich, albeit not always by legitimate means. War fed dissent and divisions on both sides, some of it violent, and raised questions about how best to deal with it. Similarly, the demands of war transformed gender roles by providing new opportunities for women in each region, on the home front and in the war effort itself. During the war, the behavior of slaves within slave states increasingly challenged slavery and made slaveholders concerned.

To what can we attribute a Union victory in the Civil War?

Both sides were war-weary by 1863, and although the Union had won a few pivotal battles, its ability to take control of the Deep South and win the war remained uncertain. Some crucial political and military decisions helped begin to turn the tide, among them Grant's promotion to lieutenant general. The move sped the pace of war and ushered in a more aggressive Union military strategy, some of which included vast destruction of key southern territory and cities. Sherman's strategy of total war not only eliminated supply stores and pummeled wide swaths of the South, it profoundly affected southern morale among both soldiers and the public. Union victories continued, and despite some last-ditch efforts by Lee's army, the war wound toward a close. But victory was not necessarily sweet. While it did lead to reunification of the nation, it came at a high cost in casualties—the largest number of any American war.

16 Reconstruction and Resistance, 1865–1877

THE DEVASTATED SOUTH After the Civil War, parts of the devastated Confederacy resembled a wasteland. Homes, crops, and railroads had been destroyed; farming and business had come to a standstill; and uprooted southerners wandered about. Here, ruins of homes in Baton Rouge, Louisiana. *(Archive Photos/Getty Images)*

CHRONOLOGY 1863–1879

1863	President Abraham Lincoln issues Proclamation of Amnesty and Reconstruction.
1864	Wade-Davis bill passed by Congress and pocket-vetoed by Lincoln.
1865	Freedmen's Bureau established.
	Civil War ends.
	Lincoln assassinated.
	Andrew Johnson becomes president.
	Johnson issues Proclamation of Amnesty and Reconstruction.
	Ex-Confederate states hold constitutional conventions (May–December).
	Black conventions begin in the ex-Confederate states.
	Thirteenth Amendment added to the Constitution.
	Presidential Reconstruction completed.
1866	Congress enacts the Civil Rights Act of 1866 and the Supplementary Freedmen's Bureau Act over Johnson's vetoes.
	Ku Klux Klan founded in Tennessee.
	Tennessee readmitted to the Union.
	Race riots in southern cities.
	Republicans win congressional elections.
	American Equal Rights Association formed.
1867	Reconstruction Act of 1867.
	William Seward negotiates the purchase of Alaska.
	Constitutional conventions meet in the ex-Confederate states.
	Howard University founded.
1868	President Johnson is impeached, tried, and acquitted.
	Omnibus Act.
	Fourteenth Amendment added to the Constitution.
	Ulysses S. Grant elected president.
1869	Transcontinental railroad completed.
1870	Congress readmits the four remaining southern states to the Union.
	Fifteenth Amendment added to the Constitution.
	Enforcement Act of 1870.
1871	Second Enforcement Act.
	Ku Klux Klan Act.
1872	Liberal Republican party formed.
	Amnesty Act.
	Alabama claims settled.
	Grant reelected president.
1873	Panic of 1873 begins (September–October), setting off a five-year depression.
1874	Democrats gain control of the House of Representatives.
1875	Civil Rights Act of 1875.
	Specie Resumption Act.
1876	Disputed presidential election: Rutherford B. Hayes versus Samuel J. Tilden.
1877	Electoral commission decides election in favor of Hayes.
	The last Republican-controlled governments overthrown in Florida, Louisiana, and South Carolina.
1879	"Exodus" movement spreads through several southern states.

Born at midcentury, Katie Rowe grew up on a cotton plantation with two hundred slaves near Washington, Arkansas. The slaves had "hard traveling" on her plantation, she told an interviewer in 1937. The owner, Dr. Isaac Jones, lived in town, and an overseer ran the place harshly. Dr. Jones was harsh, too. When Union and Confederate forces clashed nearby in 1862 at Pea Ridge, Arkansas, Dr. Jones announced that the enemy would never liberate his slaves because he would shoot them first ("line you up on de bank of Bois d' Arc Creek and free you wid my shotgun").

Emancipation in June 1865 inaugurated a moment of excitement and an era of transition for the former slaves. Hundreds of thousands of black soldiers, some of them liberated slaves, fought in the Union armies to speed the end of the war and end slavery forever. Finally, blacks possessed the freedom they had long sought, and they did not wait to use it. After emancipation, Katie Rowe and her family—knowing the market value of their labor—pushed back when an overseer tried to mete out tasks too harshly. A second supervisor offered somewhat better terms: "[W]e all got something left over after dat first go out," she noted.

Katie eventually married Billy Rowe, a Cherokee, and moved with him to Oklahoma. Interviewed decades later in Tulsa, Oklahoma, where she lived with her youngest daughter, Katie Rowe recalled the days of "hard traveling" and the joyful moment

KATIE ROWE IN 1937 *(Library of Congress Prints and Photographs Division)*

437

when slavery ended. "It was the fourth day of June in 1865 that I begins to live," Katie Rowe declared.

For the nation, as for Katie Rowe, the end of the Civil War was an instant of uncharted possibilities and a time of unresolved conflicts. While former slaves exulted over freedom, the postwar mood of ex-Confederates was often as grim as the wasted southern landscape. Unable to face "southern Yankeedom," some planters considered emigrating to the American West or to Europe, Mexico, or Brazil, and a few thousand did. The morale of the vanquished rarely concerns the victors, but the Civil War was a special case, for the Union had sought not merely military triumph but the return of national unity. The federal government in 1865 therefore faced unprecedented questions.

First, how could the Union be restored and the defeated South reintegrated into the nation? Would the Confederate states be treated as conquered territories, or would they quickly rejoin the Union with the same rights as other states? Who would set the standards for readmission—Congress or the president? Most important, what would happen to the more than 3.5 million former slaves? The future of the freedmen constituted the crucial issue of the postwar era, for emancipation had set in motion a profound upheaval. Before the war, slavery had determined the South's social, economic, and political structure. What would replace it? The end of the Civil War, in short, posed two problems that had to be solved simultaneously: how to readmit the South to the Union and how to define the status of free blacks in American society.

Between 1865 and 1877, the nation met these challenges, but not without discord and strife. Conflict prevailed in the halls of Congress as legislators debated plans to readmit the South to the Union; in the former Confederacy, where defeated southerners and newly freed former slaves faced an era of turbulence; and in the postwar North, where economic and political clashes arose. By 1877, ex-Confederate resistance had largely foiled northern plans for the postwar South. Indeed, the crises of Reconstruction—the restoration of the former Confederate states to the Union—reshaped the legacy of the Civil War.

16-1 Reconstruction Politics, 1865–1868

How did Radical Republicans gain control of Reconstruction politics?

At the end of the Civil War, President Johnson might have exiled, imprisoned, or executed Confederate leaders and imposed martial law indefinitely. Demobilized Confederate soldiers might have continued armed resistance to federal occupation forces. Freed slaves might have taken revenge on former owners and other white southerners. But none of this occurred. Instead, intense *political* conflict dominated the immediate postwar years. National politics produced new constitutional amendments, a presidential impeachment, and some of the most ambitious domestic legislation ever enacted by Congress, the Reconstruction Acts of 1867–1868. The major outcome of Reconstruction politics was the enfranchisement of black men, a development that few—black or white—had expected when Lee surrendered.

In 1865, only a small group of politicians supported black suffrage. All were Radical Republicans, a minority faction that had emerged during the war. Led by Senator

Charles Sumner
Senator from Massachusetts and key leader of the Radical Republicans, until his death in 1874.

Thaddeus Stevens
Congressman from Pennsylvania who led the fight for Radical Reconstruction in the House.

Charles Sumner of Massachusetts and Congressman Thaddeus Stevens of Pennsylvania, the Radicals had clamored for the abolition of slavery and a demanding reconstruction policy. But the Radicals, outnumbered in Congress, faced long odds. Still, they managed to win broad Republican support for parts of their Reconstruction program, including black male enfranchisement. Just as civil war had led to emancipation, a goal once supported by only a minority of Americans, so Reconstruction policy became bound to black suffrage, a momentous change that originally had only narrow political backing.

16-1.1 Lincoln's Plan

Conflict over Reconstruction began even before the war ended. In December 1863, President Lincoln issued the Proclamation of Amnesty and Reconstruction, which enabled southern states to rejoin the Union if at least 10 percent of those who had cast ballots in the election of 1860 would take an oath of allegiance to the Union and accept emancipation. This minority could then create a loyal state government. Lincoln's plan excluded some southerners from oath-taking, such as Confederate officials and military officers; they would have to apply for presidential pardons. Also excluded were blacks, who had not been voters in 1860. Lincoln hoped to undermine the Confederacy by fostering pro-Union governments within it and to build a southern Republican party.

Radical Republicans in Congress, however, envisioned a slower readmission process that would bar even more ex-Confederates from political life. The Wade-Davis bill, passed by Congress in July 1864, provided that a military governor would rule each former Confederate state; after at least half the eligible voters took an oath of allegiance to the Union, delegates could be elected to a state convention that would repeal secession and abolish slavery. To qualify as a voter or delegate, a southerner would have to take a second, "ironclad" oath, swearing that he had never voluntarily supported the Confederacy. Like the 10 percent plan, the congressional plan did not provide for black suffrage, a measure then supported by only some Radicals. Unlike Lincoln's plan, however, the Wade-Davis scheme would have delayed the readmission process almost indefinitely.

Claiming he did not want to bind himself to any single restoration policy, Lincoln pocket-vetoed the Wade-Davis bill (failed to sign the bill within ten days of the adjournment of Congress). The bill's supporters blasted Lincoln's act. By the war's end, the president and Congress had reached an impasse. Arkansas, Louisiana, Tennessee, and parts of Virginia under Union army control moved toward readmission under variants of Lincoln's plan. But Congress refused to seat their delegates, as it had a right to do. What Lincoln's ultimate policy would have been remains unknown. But after his assassination, on April 14, 1865, Radical Republicans turned with hope toward his successor, **Andrew Johnson** of Tennessee.

16-1.2 Presidential Reconstruction

The only southern senator to remain in Congress when his state seceded, Andrew Johnson had served as military governor of Tennessee from 1862 to 1864. Defying the Confederate stand, he had declared that "treason is a crime and must be made odious." Above all, Johnson had long sought the destruction of the planter aristocracy. A self-educated man of humble North Carolina origins, Johnson had moved to Greenville, Tennessee, in 1826. He had entered politics in the 1830s as a spokesman for non-slave-owning whites and rose rapidly from local official to congressman to governor to senator. Once the owner of eight slaves, Johnson reversed his position on slavery during the war. When emancipation became Union policy, he supported it. But Johnson neither adopted abolitionist ideals nor challenged racist sentiments. He hoped mainly that the fall of slavery would injure southern aristocrats. Johnson, in short, had his own political agenda. Moreover, he was a lifelong Democrat who had been added to the Republican, or National Union, ticket in 1864 to broaden its appeal and who had become president by accident.

In May 1865, with Congress out of session, Johnson shocked Republicans by announcing his own program to bring back into the Union the seven southern states still without reconstruction governments—Alabama, Florida, Georgia, Mississippi, North Carolina, South Carolina, and Texas. Almost all southerners who took an oath of allegiance would receive a pardon and amnesty; all their property except slaves would be restored. Oath takers could elect delegates to state conventions, which would have to proclaim secession illegal, repudiate state debts incurred under the Confederacy, and ratify the Thirteenth Amendment, which abolished slavery. (Proposed by an enthusiastic wartime Congress early in 1865, the amendment would be ratified in December of that year.) As under Lincoln's plan, Confederate civil and military officers would still be disqualified, as would well-off ex-Confederates—those with taxable property worth $20,000 or more. This purge of the plantation aristocracy, Johnson said, would benefit "humble men, the peasantry and yeomen of the South, who have been decoyed . . . into rebellion." Poorer whites would now be in control.

Presidential Reconstruction took effect in the summer of 1865, but with unforeseen consequences. Disqualified Southerners applied in droves for pardons, which Johnson handed out liberally—some thirteen thousand of them. Johnson also dropped plans to punish treason. By the end of 1865, all seven states had created new civil governments that, in effect, restored the status quo from before the war. Confederate army officers and large planters assumed state offices. Former Confederate generals and officials—including Alexander Stephens of Georgia, the former Confederate vice president—won election to Congress. Some states refused to ratify the Thirteenth Amendment or to repudiate their Confederate debts.

Most infuriating to Radical Republicans, all seven states took steps to ensure a landless, dependent black labor force: They passed **"black codes"** to replace the slave codes, state laws that had regulated slavery. Because Johnson's plan assured the ratification of the Thirteenth Amendment, all states guaranteed the freedmen some basic rights—to marry, own property, make contracts, and testify in court against other blacks—but the codes harshly restricted freedmen's behavior. Some established racial segregation in public places; most prohibited racial intermarriage, jury service by blacks, and court testimony by blacks against whites. All codes included

Andrew Johnson
Former slave owner and senator from Tennessee; as Lincoln's successor and seventeenth president, he lost control over Reconstruction policy and barely survived impeachment in 1868.

Presidential Reconstruction
Andrew Johnson's plan to pardon ex-Confederate leaders and readmit former Confederate states to the union on lenient terms.

"black codes"
Laws passed by southern states to limit the rights of freedmen.

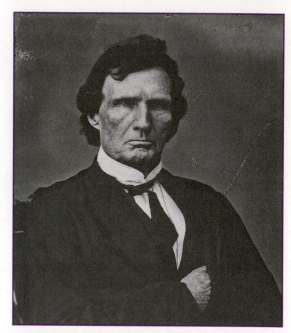

RADICAL REPUBLICAN LEADERS Charles Sumner, left, senator from Massachusetts, and Thaddeus Stevens, congressman from Pennsylvania, led the Radical Republican faction in Congress. *(Library of Congress Prints and Photographs Division)*

provisions that effectively barred former slaves from leaving the plantations. Mississippi prohibited blacks from buying and selling farmland. Most states required annual contracts between landowners and black agricultural workers; blacks without contracts risked arrest as vagrants and involuntary servitude.

The black codes left freedmen no longer slaves but not really liberated either. In practice, many clauses in the codes never took effect: The Union army and federal agents suspended the enforcement of racially discriminatory provisions of the new laws. But the black codes revealed white southern intentions. They showed what "home rule" would have been like without federal interference.

Many northerners denounced what they saw as southern defiance. "What can be hatched from such an egg but another rebellion?" asked a Boston newspaper. Republicans in Congress agreed. When Congress convened in December 1865, it refused to seat delegates of ex-Confederate states. Republicans prepared to dismantle the black codes and lock ex-Confederates out of power.

16-1.3 Congress versus Johnson

Southern blacks' status now became the major issue in Congress. Radical Republicans like Congressman Thaddeus Stevens—who hoped to impose black suffrage on the former Confederacy and delay southern

readmission—were still a minority in Congress. Conservative Republicans, who favored Johnson's plan, formed a minority too, as did the Democrats, who also supported the president. Moderate Republicans, the largest congressional bloc, agreed with Radicals that Johnson's plan was too feeble, but they wanted to avoid a dispute with the president. None of the four congressional blocs could claim the two-thirds majority needed to overturn a presidential veto. But ineptly, Johnson alienated a majority of moderates and pushed them into the Radicals' arms.

Two proposals to invalidate the black codes, drafted by a moderate Republican, Senator Lyman Trumbull of Illinois, won wide Republican support. Congress first voted to continue the Freedmen's Bureau, started in March 1865, whose term was ending (see "Freedmen's Bureau," Chapter 15, p. 417). This federal agency, headed by former Union general O. O. Howard and staffed mainly by army officers, provided relief, rations, and medical care; built schools for freed blacks; put them to work on abandoned or confiscated lands; and tried to protect their rights as laborers. Congress extended the bureau's life for three years and gave it new power to run special military courts, to settle labor disputes, and to invalidate labor contracts forced on freedmen by the black codes. In February 1866, Johnson vetoed the Supplementary Freedmen's Bureau bill.

In March 1866, Congress passed a second measure proposed by Trumbull, a bill that made blacks

U.S. citizens with the same civil rights as other citizens and authorized federal intervention in the states to ensure black rights in court. Johnson vetoed the civil rights bill also. He argued that it would "operate in favor of the colored and against the white race." In April, Congress overrode his veto; the **Civil Rights Act of 1866** was the first major law ever passed over a presidential veto. In July, Congress enacted the Supplementary Freedmen's Bureau Act over Johnson's veto as well. Johnson's vetoes puzzled many Republicans because the new laws did not undercut presidential Reconstruction. The president insisted, however, that both bills were illegitimate because southerners had been shut out of the Congress that passed them. Johnson won support in the South and from northern Democrats. But he had alienated moderate Republicans, who now joined Radicals to oppose him. Johnson had lost "every friend he has," one moderate declared.

Some historians view Andrew Johnson as a political incompetent who, at this crucial juncture, bungled both his readmission scheme and his political future. Others contend he was merely trying to forge a centrist coalition. In either case, Johnson underestimated the possibility of Republican unity. Once united, the Republicans took their next step: the passage of a constitutional amendment to prevent the Supreme Court from invalidating the new Civil Rights Act and block Democrats in Congress from repealing it.

16-1.4 The Fourteenth Amendment, 1866

In April 1866, Congress adopted the **Fourteenth Amendment**, proposed by the Joint Committee on Reconstruction. To protect blacks' rights, the amendment declared in its first clause that all persons born or naturalized in the United States were citizens of the nation and of their states and that no state could abridge their rights without due process of law or deny them equal protection of the law. This section nullified the *Dred Scott* decision of 1857, which had denied that blacks were citizens. Second, the amendment guaranteed that if a state denied suffrage to any of its male citizens, its representation in Congress would be proportionally reduced. This clause did not ensure black suffrage, but it threatened to deprive southern states of some legislators if black men were denied the vote. This was the first time that the word *male* was written into the Constitution; to the women's rights advocates, woman suffrage seemed a yet more distant prospect. Third, the amendment disqualified from state and national office *all* prewar officeholders—civil and military, state and federal—who had supported the Confederacy, unless Congress removed their disqualifications by a two-thirds vote. In so providing, Congress

KING ANDREW This Thomas Nast cartoon, published in *Harper's Weekly* just before the 1866 congressional elections, conveyed Republican antipathy to Andrew Johnson. The president is depicted as an autocratic tyrant. Radical Republican Thaddeus Stevens, upper right, has his head on the block and is about to lose it. The Republic sits in chains. *(Harper's Weekly, 1866)*

sought to invalidate Johnson's wholesale distribution of amnesties and pardons. Finally, the amendment repudiated the Confederate debt and maintained the validity of the federal debt.

The most ambitious step Congress had yet taken, the Fourteenth Amendment revealed growing Republican receptivity to Radical demands, including black male enfranchisement. The amendment's passage created a firestorm. Abolitionists decried the second clause as a "swindle" because it did not explicitly ensure black suffrage. Southerners and northern Democrats condemned the third clause as vengeful. Southern legislatures, except for Tennessee's, refused to ratify the amendment, and President Johnson denounced it. His defiance solidified the new alliance between moderate and Radical Republicans, and turned the congressional elections of 1866 into a referendum on the Fourteenth Amendment.

> **Civil Rights Act of 1866**
> Made blacks U.S. citizens; first major law ever passed over a presidential veto.
>
> **Fourteenth Amendment**
> Defined citizenship and guaranteed equal protection under the law.

Reconstruction Act of 1867
Imposed military rule on ten southern states and required them to ratify the Fourteenth Amendment.

Over the summer, Johnson set off on a whistlestop train tour from Washington to St. Louis and Chicago and back. But this innovative campaign tactic—the "swing around the circle," as Johnson called it—failed. Humorless and defensive, the president made fresh enemies and doomed his hope of sinking the Fourteenth Amendment, which moderate and Radical Republicans defended.

Republicans carried the congressional elections of 1866 in a landslide, winning almost two-thirds of the House and four-fifths of the Senate. They had secured a mandate for the Fourteenth Amendment and their own Reconstruction program, even if the president vetoed every part of it.

16-1.5 Congressional Reconstruction, 1866–1867

Congressional debate over reconstructing the South began in December 1866 and lasted three months. Radical Republican leaders called for black suffrage, federal support for public schools, confiscation of Confederate estates, and an extended period of military occupation in the South. Moderate Republicans accepted parts of the plan. In February 1867, Congress passed the **Reconstruction Act of 1867**. Johnson vetoed the law, and on March 2, Congress passed it over his veto. Later that year and in 1868, Congress passed three further Reconstruction acts, all enacted over presidential vetoes, to refine and enforce the first (see Table 16.1).

Table 16.1 Major Reconstruction Legislation

Law and Date of Congressional Passage	Provisions	Purpose
Civil Rights Act of 1866 (April 1866)[1]	Declared blacks citizens and guaranteed them equal protection of the laws.	To invalidate the black codes.
Supplementary Freedmen's Bureau Act (July 1866)[1]	Extended the life of the Freedmen's Aid Bureau and expanded its powers.	To invalidate the black codes.
Reconstruction Act of 1867 (March 1867)[1]	Invalidated state governments formed under Lincoln and Johnson. Divided the former Confederacy into five military districts. Set forth requirements for readmission of ex-Confederate states to the Union.	To replace presidential Reconstruction with a more stringent plan.
Supplementary Reconstruction Acts		To enforce the First Reconstruction Act.
Second Reconstruction Act (March 1867)[1]	Required military commanders to initiate voter enrollment.	
Third Reconstruction Act (July 1867)[1]	Expanded military commanders' powers.	
Fourth Reconstruction Act (March 1868)[1]	Provided that a majority of voters, however few, could put a new state constitution into force.	
Army Appropriations Act (March 1867)[1]	Declared in a rider that only the general of the army could issue military orders.	To prevent President Johnson from obstructing Reconstruction.
Tenure of Office Act (March 1867)[1]	Prohibited the president from removing any federal official without the Senate's consent.	To prevent President Johnson from obstructing Reconstruction.
Omnibus Act (June 1868)[2]	Readmitted seven ex-Confederate states to the Union.	To restore the Union, under the term of the First Reconstruction Act.
Enforcement Act of 1870 (May 1870)[3]	Provided for the protection of black voters.	To enforce the Fifteenth Amendment.
Second Enforcement Act (February 1871)	Provided for federal supervision of southern elections.	To enforce the Fifteenth Amendment.
Third Enforcement Act (Ku Klux Klan Act) (April 1871)	Strengthened sanctions against those who impeded black suffrage.	To combat the Ku Klux Klan and enforce the Fourteenth Amendment.
Amnesty Act (May 1872)	Restored the franchise to almost all ex-Confederates.	Effort by Grant Republicans to deprive Liberal Republicans of campaign issue.
Civil Rights Act of 1875 (March 1875)[4]	Outlawed racial segregation in transportation and public accommodations and prevented exclusion of blacks from jury service.	To honor the late senator Charles Sumner.

[1] Passed over Johnson's veto.

[2] Georgia was soon returned to military rule. The last four states were readmitted in 1870.

[3] Sections of the law declared unconstitutional in 1876.

[4] Invalidated by the Supreme Court in 1883.

MAP 16.1 THE RECONSTRUCTION OF THE SOUTH The Reconstruction Act of 1867 divided the former Confederate states, except Tennessee, into five military districts and set forth the steps by which new state governments could be created.

The Reconstruction Act of 1867 invalidated the state governments formed under the Lincoln and Johnson plans. Only Tennessee, which had ratified the Fourteenth Amendment and had been readmitted to the Union, escaped further reconstruction. The new law divided the other ten former Confederate states into five temporary military districts, each run by a Union general (see Map 16.1). Voters—all black men, plus those white men who had not been disqualified by the Fourteenth Amendment—could elect delegates to a state convention that would write a new state constitution granting black suffrage. When eligible voters ratified the new constitution, elections could be held for state officers. Once Congress approved the state constitution, once the state legislature ratified the Fourteenth Amendment, and once the amendment became part of the federal Constitution, Congress would readmit the state into the Union.

The Reconstruction Act of 1867 was far more radical than the Johnson program because it enfranchised blacks and disfranchised many ex-Confederates. It fulfilled a central goal of the Radical Republicans: to delay the readmission of former Confederate states until Republican governments could be established and thereby prevent an immediate rebel resurgence. But the new law was not as harsh toward ex-Confederates as it might have been. It provided for only temporary military rule; it did not prosecute Confederate leaders for treason, permanently bar them from politics, or provide for confiscation or redistribution of property.

During the congressional debates, Radical Republican congressman Thaddeus Stevens had argued for the confiscation of large Confederate estates to "humble the proud traitors" and to provide for former slaves. He had proposed subdividing such confiscated property into forty-acre tracts to be distributed among the freedmen and selling the rest to pay off war debts. Stevens's land-reform bill won Radical support but never made progress; most Republicans held property rights sacred. Tampering with such rights in the South, they feared, would jeopardize those rights in the North. Thus land reform never came about. The "radical" Reconstruction acts were a compromise.

Congressional Reconstruction took effect in the spring of 1867, but Johnson, as commander in chief, impeded its enforcement by replacing pro-Radical military officers with conservative ones. Republicans seethed. More suspicious than ever, congressional moderates and Radicals again joined forces to block Johnson from further obstructing Reconstruction.

16-1.6 The Impeachment Crisis, 1867–1868

In March 1867, Republicans in Congress passed two laws to curb presidential power. The **Tenure of Office Act** barred the president from removing civil officers without Senate consent. Cabinet members, the law stated, were to hold office "during the term of the president by whom they may have been appointed" and could be fired only with the Senate's approval. The goal was to bar Johnson from dismissing Secretary of War Edwin M. Stanton, a Radical ally. The other law,

> **Tenure of Office Act**
> Law requiring the president to seek Senate consent before removing civil officers.

a rider to an army appropriations bill, barred the president from issuing military orders except through the commanding general, Ulysses S. Grant, who could not be removed without the Senate's consent.

The Radicals' enmity toward Johnson, however, went further: they now sought grounds on which to impeach him. The House Judiciary Committee could at first find no valid charges against Johnson. But the president again rescued his foes by providing the charges they needed.

In August 1867, with Congress out of session, Johnson suspended Secretary of War Stanton; in early 1868, he replaced him with a general. Johnson's defiance forced Republican moderates, who had at first resisted impeachment, into yet another alliance with the Radicals: the president had "thrown down the gauntlet," a moderate charged. The House approved eleven charges of impeachment, nine based on violation of the Tenure of Office Act. The other charges accused Johnson of ignoring "the high duties of office," seeking to disgrace Congress, and not enforcing the Reconstruction acts.

Johnson's trial in the Senate, which began in March 1868, riveted public attention for eleven weeks. Seven congressmen, including leading Radical Republicans, served as prosecutors or "managers." Johnson's lawyers maintained that he was merely seeking a court test by violating the Tenure of Office Act, which he thought was unconstitutional. Furthermore, Johnson was guilty of no crime indictable in a regular court.

The congressional "managers" countered that impeachment was a political process, not a criminal trial, and that Johnson's "abuse of discretionary power" constituted an impeachable offense. Although Senate opinion split along party lines, some Republicans wavered, fearful that removal of a president would destroy the balance of power among the three branches of the federal government. They also distrusted Radical Republican Benjamin Wade, the president pro tempore of the Senate, who, because there was no vice president, would become president if Johnson were thrown out.

Late in May 1868, the Senate voted against Johnson 35 to 19, one vote short of the two-thirds majority needed for conviction. Despite intense pressure, seven Republicans had risked political suicide and sided with the twelve Senate Democrats against removal. In so doing, they set a precedent: their vote discouraged impeachment on political grounds for decades to come. But the anti-Johnson forces had also achieved their goal: Andrew Johnson would serve the rest of his term as a lame-duck president with little power or credibility. Republicans in Congress, meanwhile, pursued their last major Reconstruction objective: to guarantee black male suffrage.

16-1.7 The Fifteenth Amendment and the Question of Woman Suffrage, 1869–1870

Black suffrage was the linchpin of congressional Reconstruction. Only with the black vote could Republicans secure control of the ex-Confederate states. The Reconstruction Act of 1867 had forced southern states to enfranchise black men in order to reenter the Union, but much of the North rejected black suffrage. Congressional Republicans therefore had two aims. The **Fifteenth Amendment**, proposed by Congress in 1869, sought to protect black suffrage in the South. The amendment prohibited the denial of suffrage by the states to any citizen on account of "race, color, or previous condition of servitude."

Democrats argued that the proposed amendment violated states' rights by denying each state leverage over who would vote. But Democrats did not control enough states to defeat the amendment, and it was ratified in 1870. Four ex-Confederate states—Mississippi, Virginia, Georgia, and Texas—that had delayed the Reconstruction process were therefore forced to approve the Fifteenth Amendment, as well as the Fourteenth, in order to rejoin the Union. Some southerners appreciated the new amendment's omissions; as a Richmond newspaper pointed out, it had "loopholes through which a coach and four horses can be driven." What were these loopholes? The Fifteenth Amendment neither guaranteed black office-holding nor prohibited voting restrictions such as property requirements and literacy tests. Such restrictions might be used—and ultimately were used—to deny blacks the vote.

The debate over black suffrage drew new participants into the political fray. In 1866, when Congress debated the Fourteenth Amendment, women's rights advocates tried to join forces with abolitionist allies in the American Equal Rights Association, which (they hoped) would promote both black suffrage and woman suffrage. Most Radical Republicans, however, did not want to be saddled with the woman-suffrage plank; they feared it would impede their primary goal, black enfranchisement.

This defection provoked disputes among women's rights advocates. Some argued that black suffrage would pave the way for the women's vote and that black men deserved priority. "If the elective franchise is not extended to the Negro, he is dead," explained Frederick Douglass, a longtime women's rights supporter. "Woman has a thousand ways by which she can attach herself to the ruling power of

Fifteenth Amendment
Prevented states from denying the vote to any citizen on account of "race, color, or previous condition of servitude."

the land that we have not." But women's rights leaders Elizabeth Cady Stanton and **Susan B. Anthony** disagreed. In their view, the Fourteenth Amendment had disabled women by including the word *male*, and the Fifteenth Amendment failed to remedy this injustice. Instead, Stanton contended, the amendment established an "aristocracy of sex" and increased women's disadvantages.

The battle over black suffrage and the Fifteenth Amendment split women's rights advocates into two rival suffrage associations, formed in 1869. The Boston-based American Woman Suffrage Association, endorsed by reformers such as Julia Ward Howe and Lucy Stone, retained an alliance with male abolitionists and campaigned for woman suffrage in the states. The New York–based and more radical National Woman Suffrage Association, led by Stanton and Anthony, condemned its former male allies and promoted a federal woman suffrage amendment.

Throughout the 1870s, the rival woman suffrage associations vied for constituents. In 1869 and 1870, independent of the suffrage movement, two territories, Wyoming and Utah, enfranchised women. But suffragists failed to sway legislators elsewhere. When Susan B. Anthony mobilized about seventy women to vote nationwide in 1872, she was indicted, convicted, and fined. One woman who tried to vote, Missouri suffragist Virginia Minor, brought suit with her husband against the registrar who had excluded her. The Minors claimed that the Fourteenth Amendment enfranchised women. In *Minor* v. *Happersett* (1875), however, the Supreme Court declared that a state could constitutionally deny women the vote. Divided and rebuffed, woman suffrage advocates braced for a long struggle.

By 1870, when the Fifteenth Amendment was ratified, Congress could look back on five years of achievement. Since the start of 1865, three constitutional amendments had strengthened American democracy: the Thirteenth Amendment abolished

ANTHONY AND STANTON, CA. 1870 Women's rights advocates Susan B. Anthony (left) and Elizabeth Cady Stanton began to promote woman suffrage when the issue of black suffrage arose in 1866. They subsequently assailed the proposed Fifteenth Amendment for excluding women. "[I]n proportion as you multiply the rulers, the condition of the politically estranged is more hopeless and degraded," Stanton declared at a woman suffrage convention. By the end of the 1860s, activists had formed two competing suffragist organizations. *(Portrait of Elizabeth Cady Stanton (1815–1902) and Susan B. Anthony (1820–1906), c.1880 (b/w photo)/American Photographer, (19th century)/SCHLESINGER LIBRARY, RADCLIFFE INSTITUTE, HARVARD/ Schlesinger Library, Radcliffe Institute, Harvard University/Bridgeman Images)*

slavery, the Fourteenth expanded civil rights, and the Fifteenth barred the denial of suffrage on the basis of race (see Table 16.2). Congress had also readmitted the former Confederate states into the Union. But after 1868, congressional momentum slowed, and the theater of action shifted to the South, where tumultuous change occurred.

Susan B. Anthony
Women's rights advocate whose National Woman Suffrage Association called for a federal women suffrage amendment.

Table 16.2 The Reconstruction Amendments

Amendment and Date of Congressional Passage	Provisions	Ratification
Thirteenth (January 1865)	Prohibited slavery in the United States.	December 1865
Fourteenth (June 1866)	Defined citizenship to include all persons born or naturalized in the United States. Provided proportional loss of congressional representation for any state that denied suffrage to any of its male citizens. Disqualified prewar officeholders who supported the Confederacy from state or national office. Repudiated the Confederate debt.	July 1868, after Congress made ratification a prerequisite for readmission of ex-Confederate states to the Union
Fifteenth (February 1869)	Prohibited the denial of suffrage because of race, color, or previous condition of servitude.	March 1870; ratification required of Virginia, Texas, Mississippi, and Georgia for readmission to the Union

16-2 Reconstruction Governments

What impact did federal Reconstruction policy have on the Confederacy and on ex-Confederates?

During the unstable years of Presidential Reconstruction, 1865–1867, the southern states had to create new governments, revive the war-torn economy, and face the impact of emancipation. Crises abounded. War costs had devastated southern wealth, cities and factories lay in rubble, plantation labor systems disintegrated, and racial tensions flared. Beginning in 1865, freedmen organized black conventions, political meetings at which they protested ill treatment and demanded equal rights. A climate of violence prevailed. Race riots erupted in major southern cities, such as the events of May 1866 in Memphis, where black Union soldiers settled after the war. A fight between black veterans and white policemen sparked a citywide riot, with white mobs ransacking the homes of black families and killing indiscriminately. More than forty blacks were killed. Federal troops were required to quell the violence in Memphis, and again in response to another riot in New Orleans two months later. Even when Congress imposed military rule, ex-Confederates did not feel defeated. "Having reached bottom, there is hope now that we may rise again," a South Carolina planter wrote in his diary.

Congressional Reconstruction, supervised by federal troops, took effect in the spring of 1867. The Johnson regimes were dismantled, state constitutional conventions met, and voters elected new state governments, which Republicans dominated. In 1868, most former Confederate states rejoined the Union, and two years later, the last four states—Virginia, Mississippi, Georgia, and Texas—followed.

But Republican rule was brief, lasting less than a decade in all southern states, far less in most of them, and on average under five years. Opposition from southern Democrats, the landowning elite, thousands of vigilantes, and, indeed, most white voters proved insurmountable. Still, the governments formed under congressional Reconstruction were unique because black men, including ex-slaves, participated in them. In no other society where slaves had been liberated—neither Haiti, where slaves had revolted in the 1790s, nor the British Caribbean islands, where Parliament had ended slavery in 1833—had freedmen gained democratic political rights.

16-2.1 A New Electorate

The Reconstruction laws of 1867–1868 transformed the southern electorate by temporarily disfranchising 10–15 percent of potential white voters and by enfranchising more than seven hundred thousand freedmen. Outnumbering white voters by one hundred thousand, blacks held voting majorities in five states.

The new electorate provided a base for the Republican Party, which had never existed in the South. To scornful Democrats, southern Republicans comprised three types of scoundrels: northern "carpetbaggers," who had allegedly come south seeking wealth and power (with so few possessions that they could be stuffed into traveling bags made of carpet material); southern "scalawags," predominantly poor and ignorant whites, who sought to profit from Republican rule; and hordes of uneducated freedmen, who were ready prey for Republican manipulators. Although the "carpetbag" and "scalawag" labels were derogatory and the stereotypes they conveyed inaccurate, they remain in use as a form of shorthand. Crossing class and racial lines, the hastily established Republican Party was in fact a loose coalition of diverse factions with often contradictory goals.

To northerners who moved south after the Civil War, the former Confederacy was an undeveloped region, ripe with possibility. The carpetbaggers' ranks included many former Union soldiers who hoped to buy land, open factories, build railroads, or simply enjoy the warmer climate. Albion Tourgee, a young lawyer who had served with the New York and Ohio volunteers, for example, relocated in North Carolina after the war to improve his health; there he worked as a journalist, politician, and Republican judge. Perhaps no more than twenty thousand northern migrants like Tourgee—including veterans, missionaries, teachers, and Freedmen's Bureau agents—headed south immediately after the war, and many soon returned north. But those who remained held almost one out of three state offices and wielded disproportionate political power.

Scalawags, white southerners who supported the Republicans, included some entrepreneurs who applauded party policies such as the national banking system and high protective tariffs as well as some prosperous planters, former Whigs who had opposed secession. Their numbers included a few prominent politicians, among them Mississippi's governor James Alcorn, who became Republicans in order to retain influence and limit Republican radicalism. Most scalawags, however, were small farmers from the mountain regions of North Carolina, Georgia, Alabama, and Arkansas. Former Unionists who had owned no slaves and felt no loyalty toward the landowning elite, they sought to improve their economic position. Unlike carpetbaggers, they lacked commitment to black rights or black suffrage; most came from regions with few blacks and cared little whether blacks voted or not. Scalawags held the most political offices during Reconstruction, but they proved the least stable element of the southern Republican coalition; eventually, many drifted back to the Democratic fold.

Freedmen, the backbone of southern Republicanism, provided eight out of ten Republican votes. Republican rule lasted longest in states with the largest black populations—South Carolina, Mississippi, Alabama, and Louisiana. Introduced to politics in the black conventions of 1865–1867, the freedmen sought land, education, civil rights, and political equality, and they remained loyal Republicans. As an elderly freedman announced at a Georgia political convention in 1867, "We know our friends." Although Reconstruction governments depended on African American votes, freedmen held at most one in five political offices. Blacks served in all southern legislatures but constituted a majority only in the legislature of South Carolina, whose population was more than 60 percent black. In the House of Representatives, a mere 6 percent of southern members were black, and almost half of these came from South Carolina. No blacks were elected governor, and only two—Hiram Revels and Blanche K. Bruce, both of Mississippi—served in the U.S. Senate. (Still, the same number of African Americans served in the Senate throughout the entire twentieth century.)

Black officeholders on the state level formed a political elite. They often differed from black voters in background, education, and wealth. A disproportionate number were literate blacks who had been free before the Civil War. In the South Carolina legislature, most black members, unlike their constituents, came from large towns and cities; many had spent time in the North; and some were well-off property owners or even former slave owners. Color differences were evident, too: 43 percent of South Carolina's black state legislators were mixed-race, compared to only 7 percent of the state's black population.

Black officials and black voters often had different priorities. Most freedmen cared mainly about their economic future, especially about acquiring land; black officeholders cared most about attaining equal rights. Still, both groups shared high expectations and prized enfranchisement. "We'd walk fifteen miles in wartime to find out about the battle," a Georgia freedman declared. "We can walk fifteen miles and more to find how to vote."

16-2.2 Republican Rule

Large numbers of blacks participated in American government for the first time in the state constitutional conventions of 1867–1868. The South Carolina convention had a black majority, and in Louisiana half the delegates were freedmen. The conventions forged

REPUBLICANS IN THE SOUTH CAROLINA LEGISLATURE, CA. 1868 Only in South Carolina did blacks comprise a majority in the legislature and dominate the legislative process during Reconstruction. This photographic collage of "Radical" legislators, black and white, suggests the extent of black representation. "Now is the black man's day," declared a black politician. "[N]ow is *our time*." A northern reporter, in contrast, saw in the legislature "the spectacle of a society suddenly turned upside down." In 1874, African Americans won the majority of seats in South Carolina's state senate as well. *(Radical members of the So. Ca. Legislature, c.1868 (albumen photo)/ Gibbes, James G. (fl.1868)/Swann Auction Galleries/Private Collection/ Bridgeman Images)*

democratic changes in their state constitutions. Delegates abolished property qualifications for officeholding, made many appointive offices elective, and redistricted state legislatures more equitably. All states established universal manhood suffrage.

But no state instituted land reform. When proposals for land confiscation and redistribution arose at the state conventions, they fell to defeat, as they had in Congress. Hoping to attract northern investment to the reconstructed South, southern Republicans hesitated to threaten property rights or to adopt land-reform measures that northern Republicans had rejected. South Carolina did set up a commission to buy land and make it available to freedmen, and several states changed their tax structures to force uncultivated land onto the market, but in no case was ex-Confederate land confiscated.

ELECTIONEERING AT THE SOUTH A candidate for public office addresses a political meeting in the late 1860s. Such meetings attracted entire communities of freed people. Black women, though un-enfranchised, often attended political rallies and other events (as shown). They may have viewed the decision involved in voting as a household choice and the franchise as a collective possession. *(The Granger Collection)*

Once civil power shifted from the federal army to the new state governments, Republican governments began ambitious programs of public works. They built roads, bridges, and public buildings; approved railroad bonds; and funded institutions to care for orphans, the insane, and the disabled. They also expanded state bureaucracies, raised pay for state employees, and formed state militia, in which blacks were often heavily represented. Finally, they created public-school systems, almost nonexistent in the South until then.

These changes cost millions, and taxes skyrocketed. State legislatures increased poll taxes or "head" taxes (levies on individuals); enacted luxury, sales, and occupation taxes; and imposed new property taxes. Before the war, southern states had taxed property in slaves but had barely taxed landed property. Now state governments assessed even small farmers' holdings; propertied planters felt overburdened. Although northern tax rates still exceeded southern rates, southern landowners resented the new levies. In their view, Reconstruction punished the propertied, already beset by labor problems and falling land values, in order to finance the vast expenditures of Republican legislators.

To Reconstruction's foes, Republican rule was wasteful and corrupt, the "most stupendous system of organized robbery in history." A state like Mississippi, which had an honest government, provided little basis for such charges. But critics could justifiably point to Louisiana, where the governor pocketed thousands of dollars of state funds and corruption permeated all government transactions (as indeed it had before the war). Or they could cite South Carolina, where bribery ran rampant. Besides government officials who took bribes, postwar profiteers included the railroad promoters who doled them out. Not all were Republicans. Nor did the Republican regimes in the South hold a monopoly on corruption. After the war, bribery pervaded government transactions North and South, and far more money changed hands in the North. But critics assailed Republican rule for additional reasons.

16-2.3 Counterattacks

Ex-Confederates spoke with dread about black enfranchisement and the "horror of Negro domination." As soon as congressional Reconstruction took effect, former Confederates campaigned to undermine it. Democratic newspapers assailed delegates to North Carolina's constitutional convention as an "Ethiopian minstrelsy" and called Louisiana's constitution "the work of ignorant Negroes cooperating with a gang of white adventurers."

Democrats delayed mobilization until southern states were readmitted to the Union and then swung into action. At first, they sought to win black votes; but when that failed, they tried other tactics. In 1868–1869, Georgia Democrats challenged the eligibility of black legislators and expelled them from office. In response, the federal government reestablished military rule in Georgia, but determined Democrats still undercut Republican power. In every southern state, they contested elections, backed dissident Republican factions, elected some Democratic legislators, and lured scalawags away from the Republican Party.

Vigilante efforts to reduce black votes bolstered the Democrats' campaigns to win white ones. Antagonism toward free blacks, long a motif in southern life, resurged after the war. In 1865,

Freedmen's Bureau agents itemized outrages against blacks, including shooting, murder, rape, arson, and "inhuman beating." Vigilante groups sprang up spontaneously in all parts of the former Confederacy under names like moderators, regulators, and, in Louisiana, Knights of the White Camelia. One group rose to dominance. In the spring of 1866, six young Confederate war veterans in Tennessee formed a social club, the **Ku Klux Klan**, distinguished by elaborate rituals, hooded costumes, and secret passwords. By the election of 1868, when black men could first vote, Klan dens had spread to all southern states. Klansmen embarked on night raids to intimidate black voters. No longer a social club, the Ku Klux Klan was now a terrorist movement and a violent arm of the Democratic Party.

The Klan sought to suppress black voting, reestablish white supremacy, and topple Reconstruction governments. Its members attacked Freedmen's Bureau officials, white Republicans, black militia units, economically successful blacks, and black

Ku Klux Klan
Organization that used terrorism to prevent freedmen from voting and to reestablish white supremacy.

THE KU KLUX KLAN Disguised in long white robes and hoods, Ku Klux Klansmen sometimes claimed to be the ghosts of Confederate soldiers. The Klan, which spread rapidly after 1867, sought to end Republican rule, restore white supremacy, and obliterate, in one southern editor's words, "the preposterous and wicked dogma of Negro equality." *(Tennessee State Archives)*

voters. Concentrated in areas where black and white populations were most evenly balanced and racial tensions greatest, Klan dens adapted their tactics and timing to local conditions. In Mississippi, the Klan targeted black schools; in Alabama, it concentrated on Republican officeholders. In Arkansas, terror reigned in 1868; in Georgia and Florida, Klan strength surged in 1870. Klansmen included prominent ex-Confederates, among them General Nathan Bedford Forrest, the leader of the 1864 Fort Pillow massacre, in which Confederate troops who captured a Union garrison in Tennessee murdered black soldiers who had surrendered. Vigilantism united southern whites of different social classes and drew on Confederate veterans' energy. In areas where the Klan was inactive, other vigilante groups took its place.

Republican legislatures passed laws to outlaw vigilantism, but as state militia could not enforce them, state officials sought federal help. Between May 1870 and February 1871, Congress passed three **Enforcement Acts**, each progressively more stringent. The First Enforcement Act protected black voters, but witnesses to violations were afraid to testify against vigilantes, and local juries refused to convict them. The Second Enforcement Act provided for federal supervision of southern elections, and the Third Enforcement Act, or Ku Klux Klan Act, strengthened punishments for those who prevented blacks from voting. It also empowered the president to use federal troops to enforce the law and to suspend the writ of *habeas corpus* in areas that he declared in insurrection. (The writ of *habeas corpus* is a court order requiring that the detainer of a prisoner bring that person to court and show cause for his or her detention.) The Ku Klux Klan Act generated thousands of arrests; most terrorists, however, escaped conviction.

By 1872, the federal government had effectively suppressed the Klan, but vigilantism had served its purpose. Only a large military presence in the South could have protected black rights, and the government in Washington never provided it. Instead, federal power in the former Confederacy diminished. President Grant steadily reduced troop levels in the South; Congress allowed the Freedmen's Bureau to die in 1869; and the Enforcement acts became dead letters. White southerners, a Georgia politician told congressional investigators in 1871, could not discard "a feeling of bitterness, a feeling that the Negro is a sort of instinctual enemy of ours." The battle over Reconstruction was in essence a battle over the implications of emancipation, and it had begun as soon as the war ended.

> **Enforcement Acts**
> Series of laws to protect black voters passed in 1870 and 1871; banned the Klan and similar groups.

16-3 The Impact of Emancipation

How did the newly freed slaves reshape their lives after emancipation?

"The master he says we are all free," a South Carolina slave declared in 1865. "But it don't mean we is white. And it don't mean we is equal." Emancipated slaves faced daunting handicaps. They had no property, tools, or capital; they possessed meager skills; and more than 95 percent were illiterate. Still, the exhilaration of freedom was overwhelming, as slaves realized, "Now I am for myself" and "All that I make is my own." Emancipation gave them the right to their own labor and a new sense of autonomy. Under Reconstruction, they sought to cast off white control and shed the vestiges of slavery.

16-3.1 Confronting Freedom

For former slaves, liberty meant mobility. Some moved out of slave quarters and set up dwellings elsewhere on their plantations; others left their plantations entirely. Landowners found that one freed slave after another vanished, with house servants and artisans leading the way. "I have never in my life met with such ingratitude," one South Carolina mistress exclaimed when a former slave ran off. Field workers, who had less contact with whites, were more likely to stay behind. Still, flight remained tempting. "The moment they see an opportunity to improve themselves, they will move on," diarist Mary Chesnut observed.

Emancipation stirred waves of migration within the former Confederacy. Some freed slaves left the Upper South for the Deep South and the Southwest—Florida, Mississippi, Arkansas, and Texas—where planters desperately needed labor and paid higher wages. More left the countryside for towns and cities. Urban black populations sometimes doubled or tripled after emancipation; the number of blacks in small rural towns grew as well. Many migrants eventually returned to their old locales, but they tended to settle on neighboring plantations rather than with former owners. Freedom was the major goal. "I's wants to be a free man . . . and nobody say nuffin to me, nor order me roun,'" an Alabama freedman told a northern journalist.

Efforts to find lost family members prompted much movement. "They had a passion, not so much for wandering as for getting together," a Freedmen's Bureau official commented. Parents sought children who had been sold; husbands and wives who had been separated by sale, or who lived on different plantations,

FORMER SLAVES ON PLANTATION IN WARREN COUNTY, MISSISSIPPI Emancipation brought the possibility of movement. Some freed people on big plantations (like this one in Warren County, Mississippi) remained where they were; some moved off to find work on other plantations; and others gravitated toward towns and cities. "If I stay here I'll never know I'm free," a valued cook told her former owner. "They all want to go to the cities," a South Carolina planter observed. "The fields have no attractions." *(From the photo collection of the Old Court House Museum, Vicksburg, Ms)*

reunited; and family members sought extended networks of kin. The Freedmen's Bureau helped former slaves get information about missing relatives and travel to find them. Bureau agents also tried to resolve conflicts that arose when spouses who had been separated under slavery married other people.

Reunification efforts often failed. Some fugitive slaves had died during the war or were untraceable. Other ex-slaves had formed new relationships and could not revive old ones. Still, success stories abounded. "I'se hunted an' hunted till I track you up here," one freedman told his wife, whom he found in a refugee camp twenty years after their separation by sale. Once reunited, freed blacks quickly legalized unions formed under slavery, sometimes in mass ceremonies of up to seventy couples. Legal marriage affected family life. Men asserted themselves as household heads; wives of able-bodied men often withdrew from the labor force to care for homes and families. "When I married my wife, I married her to wait on me and she has got all she can do right here for me and the children," a Tennessee freedman explained.

Black women's desire for domestic life caused labor shortages. Before the war, at least half of field workers had been women; in 1866, a southern journal claimed, men performed almost all the field labor. Still, by Reconstruction's end, many black women had returned to agricultural work as part of sharecropper families. Others took paid work in cities, as laundresses, cooks, and domestic servants. (White women often sought employment, too, because the war had incapacitated many white breadwinners, reduced the supply of future husbands, and left families impoverished.) However, former slaves continued to view stable, independent domestic life—especially the right to bring up their own children—as a major blessing of freedom. In 1870, eight out of ten black families in the cotton-producing South were two-parent families, about the same proportion as among whites.

16-3.2 African American Institutions

Freed blacks' desire for independence also fostered growth of black churches. In the late 1860s, some freedmen congregated at churches operated by northern missionaries; others withdrew from white-run churches and formed their own. The African Methodist Episcopal church, founded by Philadelphia blacks in the 1790s, gained thousands of new southern members. Negro Baptist churches sprouted everywhere, often growing out of plantation "praise meetings," religious gatherings organized by slaves.

Black churches offered a fervent, participatory experience. They also provided relief, raised funds for schools, and supported Republican policies.

Black ministers assumed leading political roles, first in the black conventions of 1865–1866 and later in Reconstruction governments. After southern Democrats excluded most freedmen from political life at Reconstruction's end, ministers remained the main pillars of authority in black communities.

Black schools played a crucial role for freedmen, too; ex-slaves eagerly sought literacy for themselves and, above all, for their children. At emancipation, blacks organized their own schools, which the Freedmen's Bureau soon supervised. Northern philanthropic societies paid the wages of instructors, about half of them women. "Our work is just as much missionary work as if we were in India or China," a Sea Islands teacher commented. In 1869, the bureau reported more than four thousand black schools in the former Confederacy. Within three years, each southern state had a public school system, at least in principle, generally with separate schools for blacks and whites. Advanced schools for blacks opened to train tradespeople, teachers, and ministers. The Freedmen's Bureau and northern organizations like the American Missionary Association helped found Howard, Atlanta, and Fisk universities (1866–1867) and Hampton Institute (1868).

However, black education remained limited. Few rural blacks could reach freedmen's schools located in towns. Underfunded black public schools, similarly inaccessible to most rural black children, held classes only for short seasons and sometimes drew vigilante attacks. At the end of Reconstruction, more than 80 percent of the black population was still illiterate, though literacy rose steadily among youngsters (see Table 16.3).

School segregation and other forms of racial separation were taken for granted. Some black codes of

Table 16.3 Percentage of Persons Unable to Write, by Age Group, 1870–1890, in South Carolina, Georgia, Alabama, Mississippi, and Louisiana

Age Group	1870	1880	1890
10–14			
Black	78.9	74.1	49.2
White	33.2	34.5	18.7
15–20			
Black	85.3	73.0	54.1
White	24.2	21.0	14.3
Over 20			
Black	90.4	82.3	75.5
White	19.8	17.9	17.1

Source: Roger Ransom and Richard Smith, *One Kind of Freedom* (Cambridge, UK: Cambridge University Press, 1978), 30.

HAMPTON INSTITUTE Founded in 1868, Hampton Institute in southeastern Virginia welcomed newly freed African Americans to vocational programs in agriculture, teacher training, and homemaking. These students, photographed at the school's entrance around 1870, were among Hampton's first classes. *(Archival and Museum Collection, Hampton University)*

1865–1866 had segregated public transportation and public accommodations. Even after the invalidation of the codes, the custom of segregation continued on streetcars, steamboats, and trains as well as in churches, theaters, inns, and restaurants. In 1870, Senator Charles Sumner of Massachusetts, a steadfast Radical, began promoting a bill to desegregate schools, transportation facilities, juries, and public accommodations. After Sumner's death in 1874, Congress honored him by a new law, the **Civil Rights Act of 1875**, which included his proposals, save for the controversial school-integration provision. But in 1883, in the *Civil Rights Cases*, the Supreme Court invalidated the law; the Fourteenth Amendment did not prohibit discrimination by individuals, the Court ruled, only that perpetrated by the state.

White southerners rejected the prospect of racial integration, which they insisted would lead to racial amalgamation. "If we have social equality, we shall have intermarriage," one white southerner contended, "and if we have intermarriage, we shall degenerate." Urban blacks sometimes challenged segregation practices; black legislators promoted bills to desegregate public transit; and some black officeholders decried all forms of racial separatism. "The sooner we as a people forget our sable complexion," said a Mobile official, "the better it will be for us as a race." But most freed blacks were less interested in "social equality," in the sense of interracial mingling, than in black liberty and community. The new postwar elite—teachers, ministers, and politicians—served black constituencies and therefore had a vested interest in separate black institutions. Rural blacks, too, widely preferred all-black institutions. They had little desire to mix with whites. On the contrary, they sought freedom from white control. Above all, they wanted to secure personal independence by acquiring land.

16-3.3 Land, Labor, and Sharecropping

"The sole ambition of the freedman," a New Englander wrote from South Carolina in 1865, "appears to be to become the owner of a little piece of land, there to erect a humble home, and to dwell in peace and security, at his own free will and pleasure." Indeed, to freed blacks everywhere, landownership signified economic independence; "forty acres and a mule" (a phrase that originated in 1864 when Union general William T. Sherman set aside land on the South Carolina Sea Islands for black settlement) promised emancipation from plantation labor, white domination, and cotton, the "slave crop."

But freedmen's visions of landownership failed to materialize, for, as we have seen, neither Congress nor the southern states imposed large-scale land reform.

Some freedmen obtained land with the help of the Union army or the Freedmen's Bureau, and black soldiers sometimes pooled resources to buy land, as on the Sea Islands of South Carolina and Georgia. In 1866, Congress passed the Southern Homestead Act, which set aside 44 million acres of public land in five southern states for freedmen and loyal whites. This acreage contained poor soil, and few former slaves had the resources to survive even until their first harvest. About four thousand blacks resettled on homesteads under the law, but most were unable to establish farms (poor whites fared little better). By Reconstruction's end, only a small minority of former slaves owned working farms. In Georgia in 1876, for instance, blacks controlled a mere 1.3 percent of total acreage. Without large-scale land reform, obstacles to black landownership remained overwhelming.

What were these obstacles? First, most freedmen lacked the capital to buy land and the equipment needed to work it. Furthermore, white southerners generally opposed selling land to blacks. Most important, planters sought to preserve a black labor force. Freedmen, they insisted, would work only under coercion, and not at all if the possibility of landownership arose. As soon as the war ended, the white South took steps to ensure that black labor would remain available on plantations.

During Presidential Reconstruction, southern state legislatures had tried to curb black mobility and preserve a captive labor force through the black codes. Under labor contracts in effect in 1865–1866, freedmen received wages, housing, food, and clothing in exchange for fieldwork. With cash scarce, wages usually took the form of a very small share of the crop, often one-eighth or less, divided among the entire plantation workforce. Freedmen's Bureau agents promoted the new labor system; they saw black wage labor as an interim arrangement that would lead to economic independence. "You must begin at the bottom of the ladder and climb up," Freedmen's Bureau head O. O. Howard exhorted a group of Louisiana freedmen in 1865.

But freedmen disliked the new wage system, especially the use of gang labor, which resembled the work pattern under slavery. Planters had complaints, too. In some regions the black labor force had shrunk to half its prewar size or less, due to the migration of freedmen and to black women's withdrawal from fieldwork. Once united in defense of slavery, planters now competed for black workers. But the freedmen, whom planters often scorned as lazy or inefficient, did not intend to work as long or as hard as they had labored under slavery. One planter claimed that workers accomplished only "two-fifths of what they did under the old system."

> **Civil Rights Act of 1875**
> Called for the desegregation of transportation facilities, juries, and public accommodations; invalidated by the Supreme Court in 1883.

As productivity fell, so did land values. Plummeting cotton prices and poor harvests compounded planters' woes. By 1867, an agricultural impasse had been reached: landowners lacked labor, and freedmen lacked land. But free blacks, unlike slaves, had the right to enter into contracts—or to refuse to do so—and thereby gained some leverage.

Planters and freedmen began experimenting with new labor schemes, including the division of plantations into small tenancies (see Map 16.2). **Sharecropping**, the most widespread arrangement, evolved as a compromise. Under the sharecropping system, landowners subdivided large plantations into farms of thirty to fifty acres, which they rented to freedmen under annual leases for a share of the crop, usually half. Freedmen preferred sharecropping to wage labor because it represented a step toward independence. Household heads could use the labor of family members. Moreover, a half-share of the crop far exceeded the fraction that freedmen had received as wages under the black codes. Planters often spoke of sharecropping as a concession, but they benefited, too. They retained power over tenants because annual leases did not have to be renewed; they could expel undesirable tenants at the end of the year. Most important, planters retained control of their land and in some cases extended their holdings. The most productive land, therefore, remained in the hands of a small group of owners, as before the war. Sharecropping forced planters to relinquish daily control over the labor of freedmen but helped to preserve the planter elite (see Going to the Source).

Sharecropping arrangements varied widely. On sugar and rice plantations, the wage system continued; strong markets for those crops enabled planters to pay workers in cash—cash that cotton planters lacked. Some freedmen remained independent renters. Some landowners leased areas to white tenants, who then subcontracted with black labor. But by the end of the 1860s, sharecropping prevailed in the cotton South, and continued to expand. A severe depression in 1873 drove many black renters into sharecropping. Thousands of independent white farmers became sharecroppers as well. Stung by wartime losses and by the dismal postwar economy, they sank into debt and lost their land to creditors. At Reconstruction's end, one-third of white farmers in Mississippi, for instance, were sharecroppers.

By 1880, 80 percent of the land in the cotton-producing states had been subdivided into tenancies, most of it farmed by sharecroppers, white and black (see Map 16.3, page 457). Indeed, white sharecroppers now outnumbered black ones, although a higher proportion of southern blacks, about 75 percent, were involved in the system. Changes in

Sharecropping
System in which a tenant farmer paid a share of the crop as rent to the landowner.

marketing and finance, meanwhile, made the sharecroppers' lot increasingly precarious.

16-3.4 Toward a Crop-Lien Economy

Before the Civil War, planters had depended on factors, or middlemen, who sold them supplies, extended credit, and marketed their crops through urban merchants. These long-distance credit arrangements were backed by the high value and liquidity of slave property. When slavery ended, the factorage system collapsed. The postwar South, with hundreds of thousands of tenants and sharecroppers, needed a far more localized credit network.

Into the gap stepped the rural merchants (often themselves planters), who advanced supplies to tenants and sharecroppers on credit and sold their crops to wholesalers or textile manufacturers. Because renters had no property to use as collateral, the merchants secured their loans with a lien, or claim, on each farmer's next crop. Exorbitant interest rates of 50 percent or more quickly forced many tenants and sharecroppers into a cycle of indebtedness. Owing part of the crop to a landowner for rent, a sharecropper also owed a rural merchant a large sum (perhaps amounting to the rest of his crop, or more) for supplies. Illiterate tenants who lost track of their financial arrangements often fell prey to unscrupulous merchants. "A man that didn't know how to count would always lose," an Arkansas freedman later explained. Once a tenant's debts or alleged debts exceeded the value of his crop, he was tied to the land, to cotton, and to sharecropping.

By Reconstruction's end, sharecropping and crop liens had transformed southern agriculture. They bound the region to staple production and prevented crop diversification. Despite plunging cotton prices, creditors—landowners and merchants—insisted that tenants raise only easily marketable cash crops. Short of capital, planters could no longer invest in new equipment or improve their land by crop rotation and contour plowing. Soil depletion, land erosion, and agricultural backwardness soon locked much of the South into a cycle of poverty.

Trapped in perpetual debt, tenant farmers became the chief victims of the new agricultural order. Raising cotton for distant markets, for prices over which they had no control, remained the only survival route open to poor farmers, regardless of race. But low income from cotton locked them into sharecropping and crop liens, from which escape was difficult. African American tenants saw their political rights dwindle, too. As one southern regime after another returned to Democratic control, freedmen could look for protection to neither state governments nor the federal government; northern politicians were preoccupied with their own problems.

The Barrow Plantation

David Crenshaw Barrow (1852–1929), who grew up on his family's 2,000-acre plantation in Oglethorpe County, Georgia, described in an 1881 article the changes that occurred there after the Civil War, as former slaves became tenant farmers. His father, landowner David C. Barrow, Sr., once a slaveholder, now rented out plots of land to tenant families, with a total of 162 members, who raised cotton and other crops. The younger Barrow in 1881 taught mathematics at the University of Georgia; he later served for many years as chancellor. His article, aimed at a national audience, seeks to assure northern readers that postwar changes in southern labor worked "thoroughly well."

In Georgia, the Negro has adapted himself to his new circumstances, and freedom fits him as if it had been cut out and made for him. . . .

One of the first planters in Middle Georgia to divide his plantations into farms was Mr. Barrow of Oglethorpe. The plantation upon which he now lives . . . with the exception of a single acre, [used by tenants] for church and school purposes, is the same size it was before the war. Here, however, the similarity ceases. Before the war everything on the place was under the absolute rule of an overseer (Mr. Barrow living then on another place). . . . [A]ll the Negro houses were close together, forming "the quarter." The house in which the overseer lived was close to the quarter. . . . This all has been so changed that the place would now hardly be recognized by one who had not seen it during the past sixteen years.

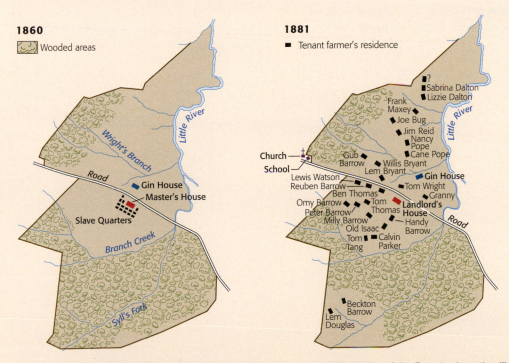

MAP 16.2 THE BARROW PLANTATION, 1860 AND 1881 The transformation of the Barrow plantation illustrates the striking changes in southern agriculture during Reconstruction. Before the Civil War, about 135 slaves worked on the plantation; after the war, the former slaves who remained signed labor contracts with owner David C. Barrow, Sr. Supervised by a hired foreman, the freedmen grew cotton for wages in competing squads, but disliked the new arrangement. In the late 1860s, Barrow subdivided his land into tenancies and freedmen moved their households from the old slave quarter to family farms. Among Barrow plantation tenants in 1881, one out of four families was named Barrow.

The transformation has been so gradual that almost imperceptibly a radical change has been effected. For several years after the war, the force on the plantation was divided into two squads.... Each of these squads was under the control of a foreman.... [T]he laborers were paid a portion of the crop as their wages, which did much toward making them feel interested in it....

This was the first change made, and for several years it produced good results. After a while, however, even the liberal control of the foremen grew irksome, each man feeling the very natural desire to be his own "boss" and farm to himself. As a consequence of this feeling, the two squads split into smaller and then still smaller squads, still working for part of the crop ... [but this system proved unsatisfactory].

[T]he present arrangement ... while it had difficulties in inception, has been found to work thoroughly well. Under it our colored farmers are tenants, who are responsible only for damage to the farms they work and for the prompt payment of their rent. [They] farm on a small scale, only two of them having more than one mule.... [T]he location of the houses caused considerable inconvenience and so it was determined to scatter them....

The labor of the farm is performed by the man, who usually does the plowing, and his wife and children, who do the hoeing, under his direction.... [T]heir landlord interferes only far enough to see that sufficient cotton is made to pay the rent.... The usual quantity of land planted is between twenty-five and thirty acres, about half of which is in cotton and the rest in corn and [vegetable] patches....

The slight supervision which is exercised over these tenants may surprise those ignorant of how completely the relations between the races at the South have changed. Mr. Barrow lives on his plantation, and yet there are some of his tenants' farms which he does not visit as often as once a month....

[The tenants] have become suited to their new estate, and it to them. I do not know of a single Negro who has swelled the number of the "exodus."

Source: David Crenshaw Barrow, "A Georgia Plantation," *Scribners Monthly* XXI (April 1881), pp. 830–836.

QUESTIONS

1. What changes in labor arrangements occurred on the Barrow plantation in the sixteen years after the Civil War? What remained the same?

2. Do you think Barrow's role as a member of landowning family shaped his account of postwar changes? If so, how?

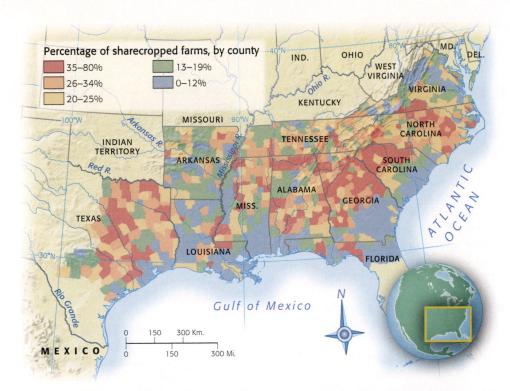

Percentage of sharecropped farms, by county

- 35–80%
- 26–34%
- 20–25%
- 13–19%
- 0–12%

MAP 16.3 SOUTHERN SHARECROPPING, 1880 The depressed economy of the late 1870s caused poverty and debt, increased tenancy among white farmers, and forced many renters, black and white, into sharecropping. By 1880, the sharecropping system pervaded most southern counties, with the highest concentrations in the cotton belt from South Carolina to eastern Texas. Sharecropping was most common, in short, in areas that had once had large numbers of slaves.

(*Source:* U.S. Census Office, *Tenth Census, 1880, Report of the Production of Agriculture* (Washington, DC: Government Printing Office, 1883), Table 5.)

16-4 New Concerns in the North, 1868–1876

Why did northern concern about Reconstruction begin to wane?

The nomination of Ulysses S. Grant for president in 1868 launched a chaotic era in national politics. Grant's two terms in office saw political scandals, a party revolt, massive depression, and steady retreat from Reconstruction policies. By the mid-1870s, northern voters cared more about the economic climate, unemployment, labor unrest, and currency problems than about the "southern question." Responsive to the shift in popular mood,

SHARECROPPERS DURING RECONSTRUCTION By the end of the 1870s, about three out of four African Americans in the cotton-producing states had become sharecroppers. Here, sharecroppers pick cotton in Aiken, South Carolina. (*Collection of the New York Historical Society*)

Republicans became eager to end sectional conflict and turned their backs on the freedmen of the South.

16-4.1 Grantism

Republicans had good reason to bypass party leaders and nominate the popular Grant. A war hero, Grant was endorsed by Union veterans and widely admired throughout the North. To oppose Grant, the Democrats nominated New York governor Horatio Seymour, arch-critic of the Lincoln administration in wartime and now a foe of Reconstruction. Grant ran on personal popularity more than issues. Although he carried all but eight states, the popular vote was close; in the South, newly enfranchised freedmen provided Grant's margin of victory.

A strong leader in war, Grant proved a passive president. Although he lacked Johnson's instinct for disaster, he had little political skill. Many of his cabinet appointees were mediocre if not unscrupulous; scandals plagued his administration. In 1869, financier Jay Gould and his partner Jim Fisk tried to corner the gold market with the help of Grant's brother-in-law, a New York speculator. When gold prices tumbled, investors were ruined and Grant's reputation suffered. Then, before the president's first term ended, his vice president, Schuyler Colfax, was found to be linked to the Crédit Mobilier, a fraudulent scheme to skim off the profits of the Union Pacific Railroad. Discredited, Colfax was dropped from the Grant ticket in 1872.

More trouble lay ahead. Grant's private secretary, Orville Babcock, was unmasked in 1875 after taking money from the "whiskey ring," distillers who bribed federal agents to avoid paying millions in taxes. In 1876, voters learned that Grant's secretary of war, William E. Belknap, had taken bribes to sell lucrative Indian trading posts in Oklahoma. Impeached and disgraced, Belknap resigned.

Although uninvolved in the scandals, Grant defended his subordinates. To his critics, "Grantism" came to stand for fraud, bribery, and political corruption—evils that spread far beyond Washington. In Pennsylvania, for example, the Standard Oil Company and the Pennsylvania Railroad controlled the legislature. Urban politics also provided rich opportunities for graft and swindles. The New York City press revealed in 1872 that Democratic boss William M. Tweed, the leader of Tammany Hall, led a ring that had looted the city treasury and collected millions in kickbacks and payoffs. When Mark Twain and coauthor Charles Dudley Warner

BOSS TWEED Thomas Nast's cartoons in *Harper's Weekly* helped topple New York Democratic boss William M. Tweed, who, with his associates, embodied corruption on a large scale. The Tweed Ring had granted lucrative franchises to companies they controlled, padded construction bills, practiced graft and extortion, and exploited every opportunity to plunder the city's funds. *(Harper's Weekly. 1871)*

published their satiric novel *The Gilded Age* (1873), readers recognized the book's speculators, self-promoters, and opportunists as familiar types in public life. (The term "Gilded Age" was subsequently used to refer to the decades from the 1870s to the 1890s.)

Grant had some success in foreign policy. In 1872, his administration engineered the settlement of the *Alabama* claims with Britain. To compensate for damage done by Confederate-owned but British-built ships, an international tribunal awarded the United States $15.5 million. But Grant's administration faltered when it tried to add nonadjacent territory to the United States. In 1867, Johnson's secretary of state, William H. Seward, had negotiated a treaty in which the United States bought Alaska from Russia at the bargain price of $7.2 million. Although the press mocked "Seward's Ice Box," the purchase kindled expansionists' hopes. In 1870, Grant decided to annex the eastern half of the Caribbean island of Santo Domingo (today called the Dominican Republic); the territory had been passed back and forth since the late eighteenth century among France, Spain, and Haiti. Annexation, Grant believed, would promote Caribbean trade and provide a haven for persecuted southern blacks. American speculators anticipated windfalls from land sales, commerce, and mining. But Congress disliked Grant's plan. Senator Charles Sumner denounced it as an imperialist "dance of blood." The Senate rejected the annexation treaty and further diminished Grant's reputation.

As the 1872 election approached, dissident Republicans voiced fears that "Grantism" at home and abroad would ruin the party. The dissidents took action. Led by a combination of former Radicals and other Republicans left out of Grant's "Great Barbecue" (a disparaging reference to profiteers who feasted at the public trough), the president's critics formed their own party, the **Liberal Republicans**.

16-4.2 The Liberals' Revolt

The Liberal Republican revolt split the Republican Party and undermined support for Republican southern policy. (The label "liberal" then meant support for economic doctrines such as free trade, the gold standard, and the law of supply and demand.) Denouncing "Grantism" and "spoilsmen" (political hacks who gained party office), Liberals urged civil service reform to bring the "best men" into government. Rejecting the "regular" Republicans' high-tariff policy, they espoused free trade. Most important, Liberals decried "bayonet rule" in the South. Even some one-time Radicals claimed that Reconstruction had achieved its goal: Blacks had been enfranchised and could now fend for themselves. Corruption in government, North and South,

posed greater danger than Confederate resurgence, Liberals claimed. In the South, they said, corrupt Republican regimes remained in power because the "best men"—the most capable politicians—were ex-Confederates barred from office-holding.

For president, the new party nominated *New York Tribune* editor Horace Greeley, who had inconsistently supported both a stringent reconstruction policy and leniency toward former rebels. The Democrats endorsed Greeley, too; their slogan was "Anything to Beat Grant." Horace Greeley campaigned so diligently that he worked himself to death making speeches from the back of a train, and died a few weeks after the election.

Grant, who won 56 percent of the popular vote, carried all the northern states and most of the sixteen southern and border states. But division among Republicans affected Reconstruction. To deprive the Liberals of a campaign issue, Grant Republicans in Congress, the "regulars," passed the Amnesty Act, which allowed most ex-Confederate officials to hold office. A flood of private amnesty acts followed. In Grant's second term, Republican desires to discard the "southern question" mounted as depression gripped the nation.

16-4.3 The Panic of 1873

The postwar years brought accelerated industrialization, rapid economic growth, and frantic speculation. Investors rushed to profit from rising prices, new markets, high tariffs, and seemingly boundless opportunities. Railroads led the speculative boom. In May 1869, railroad executives drove a golden spike into the ground at Promontory Point, Utah, joining the Union Pacific and Central Pacific lines. By 1873, almost four hundred railroad corporations crisscrossed the Northeast, consuming tons of coal and miles of steel rail from the mines and mills of Pennsylvania and neighboring states. Transforming the economy, the railroad boom led entrepreneurs to overspeculate, with drastic results.

Philadelphia banker Jay Cooke, who had helped finance the Union effort with his wartime bond campaign, had taken over a new transcontinental line, the Northern Pacific, in 1869. Northern Pacific securities sold briskly for several years, but in 1873 the line's construction costs outran bond sales. In September, Cooke defaulted on his obligations, and his bank, the largest in the nation, shut down. A financial panic began; other firms collapsed, as did the stock market. The Panic of 1873 triggered a five-year depression. Banks closed, farm prices plummeted, steel furnaces stood idle, and one out of four railroads failed. Within two years, eighteen thousand businesses went bankrupt; 3

> **Liberal Republicans**
> Dissident political faction that opposed Grant and called for civil service reform and an end to congressional Reconstruction in the South.

million were unemployed by 1878. Wage cuts struck those still employed; labor protests mounted; and industrial violence spread. The depression of the 1870s revealed that conflicts born of industrialization had replaced sectional divisions.

The depression also fed a dispute over currency that had begun in 1865. During the Civil War, Americans had used greenbacks, a paper currency not backed by a specific weight in gold. To stabilize the postwar currency, "sound money" supporters demanded withdrawal of greenbacks from circulation. Their opponents, "easy money" advocates, such as farmers and manufacturers dependent on easy credit, wanted an expanding currency (more greenbacks). Once depression began, demands for such "easy money" rose. The issue divided both major parties and was compounded by another one: how to repay the federal debt.

In wartime, the Union government had borrowed what were then astronomical sums, mainly by selling war bonds. Bondholders wanted repayment in coin, gold or silver, even though many had paid for bonds in greenbacks. To pacify bondholders, Senator John Sherman of Ohio and other Republicans pressed for the Public Credit Act of 1869, which promised repayment in coin. With investors reassured, Sherman guided legislation through Congress that swapped the old short-term bonds for new ones payable over the next generation. In 1872, another bill in effect defined "coin" as "gold coin" by dropping the silver dollar from the official coinage. Through a feat of compromise, which placated investors and debtors, Sherman preserved the public credit and Republican unity. His Specie Resumption Act of 1875 promised to put the nation on the gold standard in 1879.

But Sherman's measures did not satisfy the Democrats, who gained control of the House in 1875. Many Democrats and some Republicans demanded restoration of the silver dollar in order to expand the currency and relieve the depression. These "free-silver" advocates secured passage of the Bland-Allison Act of 1878, which partially restored silver coinage. In 1876, other expansionists formed the **Greenback Party**, which adopted the debtors' cause and fought to keep greenbacks in circulation, though with little success. As the depression receded in 1879, the clamor for "easy money" subsided, only to resurge in the 1890s with the emergence of the Populist Party (see Chapter 20). The controversial "money question" of the 1870s, never resolved, gave politicians and voters another reason to forget about the South.

Greenback Party
"Easy money" advocates who favored continued issuance of greenbacks and the free coinage of silver.

slaughterhouse cases
Supreme Court rulings that practically exempted state governments from the Fourteenth Amendment.

16-4.4 Reconstruction and the Constitution

The Supreme Court of the 1870s also played a role in weakening northern support for Reconstruction. In wartime, few cases of note had reached the Court. After the war, however, constitutional questions arose.

First, would the Court support congressional laws to protect freedmen's rights? The decision in *Ex parte* Milligan (1866) suggested not. In *Milligan*, the Court declared that a military commission established by the president or Congress could not try civilians in areas remote from war where the civil courts were functioning. Thus, special military courts to enforce the Supplementary Freedmen's Bureau Act were doomed. Second, would the Court sabotage the congressional Reconstruction plan, as Republicans feared? In *Texas* v. *White* (1869), the Court ruled that although the Union was indissoluble and secession was legally impossible, the process of Reconstruction was still constitutional. It was grounded in Congress's power to ensure each state a republican form of government and to recognize the legitimate government in any state.

But in the 1870s, the Court backed away from Reconstruction. In the **slaughterhouse cases** of 1873, the Supreme Court chipped away at the Fourteenth Amendment. The cases involved a business monopoly, not freedmen's rights, but provided an opportunity to interpret the amendment narrowly. In 1869, the Louisiana legislature had granted a monopoly over the New Orleans slaughterhouse business to one firm and closed down all other slaughterhouses in the interest of public health. The excluded butchers brought suit. The state had deprived them of their lawful occupation without due process of law, they claimed; such action violated the Fourteenth Amendment, which guaranteed that no state could "abridge the privileges or immunities" of U.S. citizens. The Supreme Court upheld the Louisiana legislature by issuing a doctrine of "dual citizenship." The Fourteenth Amendment, declared the Court, protected only the rights of *national* citizenship, such as the right of interstate travel, but not those rights that fell to citizens through *state* citizenship. The *Slaughterhouse* decision vitiated the intent of the Fourteenth Amendment—to secure freedmen's rights against state encroachment.

The Supreme Court again backed away from Reconstruction in two cases in 1876 involving the Enforcement Act of 1870, enacted to protect black suffrage. In *United States* v. *Reese* and *United States* v. *Cruikshank*, the Supreme Court undercut the act's effectiveness. Continuing its retreat from Reconstruction, the Supreme Court in 1883 invalidated both the Civil Rights Act of 1875 and the Ku Klux Klan Act of 1871. These decisions cumulatively dismantled the Reconstruction policies that Republicans had sponsored after the war and confirmed rising northern sentiment that Reconstruction's egalitarian goals could not be enforced.

16-4.5 Republicans in Retreat

The Republicans did not reject Reconstruction suddenly but rather disengaged from it gradually, a process that began with Grant's election to the presidency in 1868. Not an architect of Reconstruction policy, Grant defended it. But he believed in decentralized government and hesitated to assert federal authority in local and state affairs.

In the 1870s, as northern military force shrank in the South, Republican idealism waned in the North. The Liberal Republican revolt of 1872 eroded what remained of radicalism. Among "regular" Republicans, who backed Grant, many held ambivalent views. Commercial and industrial interests now dominated both wings of the party, and few Republicans wished to rekindle sectional strife. After the Democrats won the House in 1874, support for Reconstruction became a political liability.

By 1875, the Radical Republicans, so prominent in the 1860s, had vanished. Stevens and Sumner were dead. Other Radicals had lost office or conviction. "Waving the Bloody Shirt"—defaming Democratic opponents by reviving wartime animosity—now seemed counterproductive. Republican leaders reported that voters were "sick of carpetbag government" and tiring of both the "southern question" and the "Negro question." It seemed pointless to continue the unpopular and expensive policy of military intervention in the South to prop up Republican regimes that even President Grant found corrupt. Finally, few Republicans shared the egalitarian spirit that had animated Stevens and Sumner. Politics aside, Republican leaders and voters generally agreed with southern Democrats that blacks, although worthy of freedom, were inferior to whites. To insist on black equality would be thankless, divisive, politically suicidal—and would quash any hope of reunion between the regions. The Republicans' retreat from Reconstruction set the stage for its demise in 1877.

16-5 Reconstruction Abandoned, 1876–1877

What factors contributed to the end of Reconstruction in 1877?

"We are in a very hot political contest just now," a Mississippi planter wrote to his daughter in 1875, "with a good prospect of turning out the carpetbag thieves by whom we have been robbed for the past six to ten years." Similar contests raged through the South in the 1870s, as the white resentment grew and Democratic influence surged. By the end of 1872, the Democrats had regained power in Tennessee, Virginia, Georgia, and North Carolina. Within three years, they won control in Texas, Alabama, Arkansas, and Mississippi (see Table 16.4). By 1876, Republican rule survived in only three states—South Carolina, Florida, and Louisiana. Democratic victories in state elections of 1876 and

Table 16.4 The Duration of Republican Rule in the Ex-Confederate States

Former Confederate States	Readmission to the Union Under Congressional Reconstruction	Democrats (Conservatives) Gain Control	Duration of Republican Rule
Alabama	June 25, 1868	November 14, 1874	6½ years
Arkansas	June 22, 1868	November 10, 1874	6½ years
Florida	June 25, 1868	January 2, 1877	8½ years
Georgia	July 15, 1870	November 1, 1871	1 year
Louisiana	June 25, 1868	January 2, 1877	6½ years
Mississippi	February 23, 1870	November 3, 1875	6½ years
North Carolina	June 25, 1868	November 3, 1870	2 years
South Carolina	June 25, 1868	November 12, 1876	8 years
Tennessee	July 24, 1866[1]	October 4, 1869	3 years
Texas	March 30, 1870	January 14, 1873	3 years
Virginia	January 26, 1870	October 5, 1869[2]	0 years

Source: John Hope Franklin, *Reconstruction After the Civil War* (Chicago: University of Chicago Press, 1962), 231.

[1] Admitted before start of congressional Reconstruction.

[2] Democrats gained control before readmission.

political bargaining in Washington in 1877 abruptly ended what little remained of Reconstruction.

16-5.1 "Redeeming" the South

Republican collapse in the South accelerated after 1872. Congressional amnesty enabled ex-Confederate officials to regain office; divisions among the Republicans weakened their party's grip on the southern electorate; and attrition diminished Republican ranks. Carpetbaggers returned North or became Democrats. Scalawags deserted in even larger numbers. Tired of northern interference and finding "home rule" by Democrats a possibility, Scalawags concluded that staying Republican meant going down with a sinking ship. Scalawag defections ruined Republican prospects. Unable to win new white votes or retain the old ones, the always-fragile Republican coalition crumbled.

Meanwhile, Democrats mobilized once-apathetic white voters. The resurrected southern Democratic Party was divided: Businessmen who envisioned an industrialized "New South" opposed an agrarian faction called the Bourbons—the old planter elite. But Democrats shared one goal: to oust Republicans from office. Tactics varied by state. Alabama Democrats won by promising to cut taxes and by getting out the white vote. In Louisiana, the "White League," a vigilante organization formed in 1874, undermined Republicans. Intimidation also proved effective in Mississippi, where violent incidents—like the 1874 slaughter in Vicksburg of about three hundred blacks by rampaging whites—terrorized black voters. In 1875, the "Mississippi plan" took effect: local Democratic clubs armed their members, who dispersed Republican meetings, patrolled voter-registration places, and marched through black areas. "The Republicans are paralyzed through fear and will not act," the anguished carpetbag governor of Mississippi wrote to his wife. "Why should I fight a hopeless battle?" In 1876, South Carolina's "Rifle Clubs" and "Red Shirts," armed groups that threatened Republicans, continued the scare tactics that had worked so well in Mississippi.

Intimidation did not completely squelch black voting, but Democrats deprived Republicans of enough black votes to win state elections. In some counties, they encouraged freedmen to vote Democratic at supervised polls where voters publicly placed a card with a party label in a box. In other instances, economic pressure impeded black suffrage. Labor contracts included clauses barring attendance at political meetings; planters used eviction threats to keep sharecroppers in line. Together, intimidation and economic pressure succeeded.

"Redemption," the word Democrats used to describe their return to power, brought sweeping changes. Some states called constitutional conventions to reverse Republican policies. All cut back expenses, wiped out social programs, lowered taxes, and revised their tax systems to relieve landowners of large burdens. State courts limited the rights of tenants and sharecroppers. Most important, the Democrats, or "redeemers," used the law to ensure a stable black labor force. Legislatures restored vagrancy laws, revised crop-lien statutes to make landowners' claims superior to those of merchants, and rewrote criminal law. Local ordinances in heavily black counties often restricted hunting, fishing, gun carrying, and ownership of dogs and thereby curtailed freedmen's everyday activities. States passed severe laws against trespassing and theft; stealing livestock or wrongly taking part of a crop became grand larceny with a penalty of up to five years at hard labor. By Reconstruction's end, black convict labor was commonplace.

For the freedmen, whose aspirations rose under Republican rule, redemption was devastating. The new laws, Tennessee blacks contended at an 1875 convention, would impose "a condition of servitude scarcely less degrading than that endured before the late civil war." In the late 1870s, as the political climate grew more oppressive, an "exodus" movement spread through Mississippi, Tennessee, Texas, and Louisiana. Some African Americans became homesteaders in Kansas. After an outbreak of "Kansas fever" in 1879, four thousand **exodusters** from Mississippi and Louisiana joined about ten thousand who had reached Kansas earlier in the decade. But the vast majority of freedmen, devoid of resources, had no migration options or escape route. Mass movement of southern blacks to the North and Midwest would not gain momentum until the twentieth century.

16-5.2 The Election of 1876

By the autumn of 1876, with redemption almost complete, both parties sought to discard the heritage of animosity left by the war and Reconstruction. Republicans nominated Rutherford B. Hayes, three times Ohio's governor, for president. Untainted by the Grant-era scandals and popular with all factions in his party, Hayes presented himself as a "moderate" on southern policy. He favored "home rule" in the South and a guarantee of civil and political rights for all—two contradictory goals. The Democrats nominated Governor Samuel J. Tilden of New York, a millionaire corporate lawyer and political reformer, known for his assaults on the Tweed Ring that had plundered New York City's treasury. Both candidates favored sound money, endorsed civil-service reform, and decried corruption, an irony since the 1876 election would be extremely corrupt.

Tilden won the popular vote by a 3 percent margin and seemed destined to capture the 185 electoral votes needed for victory (see Map 16.4). But the Republicans challenged the pro-Tilden returns from South Carolina, Florida, and Louisiana. If they could deprive the Democrats of these nineteen electoral votes, Hayes would triumph. The Democrats, who needed only one of the disputed electoral votes for victory, challenged (on a technicality) the validity of Oregon's single electoral vote, which the Republicans had won. Twenty electoral votes, therefore, were in contention. But Republicans still controlled the electoral machinery in the three unredeemed southern states, where they threw out enough Democratic ballots to declare Hayes the winner.

The nation now faced an unprecedented dilemma. Each party claimed victory in the contested states, and each accused the other of fraud. In fact, both sets of southern results involved fraud: the Republicans had discarded legitimate Democratic ballots, and the Democrats had illegally prevented freedmen from voting. In January 1877, Congress created a special electoral commission—seven Democrats, seven Republicans, and one

THE WHITE LEAGUE Alabama's White League, formed in 1874, strove to oust Republicans from office by intimidating black voters. To political cartoonist Thomas Nast in *Harper's Weekly,* such vigilante tactics suggested an alliance between the White League and the outlawed Ku Klux Klan. *(Harper's Weekly. October 24, 1874)*

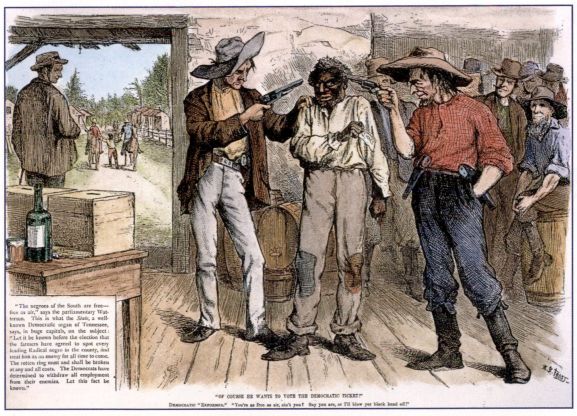

In another *Harper's Weekly* cartoon, published during the presidential campaign of 1876, White League vigilantes allied with Democrats assail a black voter in the polling place. Their goal: to topple the last Republican governments in the South. "You're free as air, ain't you?" declares one of the armed assailants. "Say you are or I'll blow your head off." *(Granger, NYC — All rights reserved)*

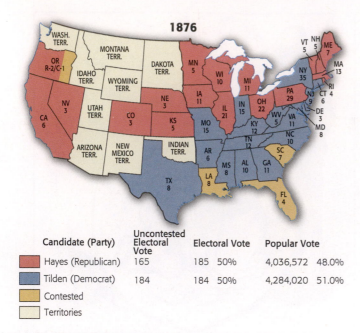

1876

Candidate (Party)	Uncontested Electoral Vote	Electoral Vote		Popular Vote	
Hayes (Republican)	165	185	50%	4,036,572	48.0%
Tilden (Democrat)	184	184	50%	4,284,020	51.0%
Contested					
Territories					

MAP 16.4 THE DISPUTED ELECTION OF 1876 Congress resolved the contested electoral vote of 1876 in favor of Republican Rutherford B. Hayes.

independent—to decide which party would get the contested electoral votes. When the independent resigned, Congress replaced him with a Republican, and the commission gave Hayes the election by a vote of 8 to 7.

Congress now had to certify the new electoral vote. But Democrats controlled the House, and some threatened to obstruct debate and delay approval of the electoral vote. Had they done so, the nation would have lacked a president on inauguration day, March 4. Room for compromise remained, for many southern Democrats accepted Hayes's election: former scalawags with commercial interests still favored Republican financial policies; railroad investors expected Republican support for a southern transcontinental line. Other southerners did not mind conceding the presidency as long as the new Republican administration would leave the South alone. Republican leaders, although sure of eventual triumph, were willing to bargain as well, for candidate Hayes desired not merely victory but southern approval.

Informal negotiations ensued, at which politicians exchanged promises. Ohio Republicans and southern Democrats, who met at a Washington hotel, agreed that if Hayes won the election, he would remove federal troops from South Carolina and Louisiana, and Democrats could gain control of those states. In other bargaining sessions, southern politicians asked for federal patronage, federal aid to railroads, and federal support for internal improvements. In return, they promised to drop the filibuster, to accept Hayes as president, and to treat freedmen fairly. With the threatened filibuster

THE EXODUS TO KANSAS Benjamin "Pap" Singleton, a one-time fugitive slave from Tennessee, returned there to promote the "exodus" movement of the late 1870s. Forming a real estate company, Singleton traveled the South recruiting parties of freed people who were disillusioned with the outcome of Reconstruction. These "exodusters," awaiting a Mississippi River boat, looked forward to political equality, freedom from violence, and homesteads in Kansas. *(Library of Congress Prints & Photographs Division/[LC-USZ62-26365])*

broken, Congress ratified Hayes's election. Once in office, Hayes fulfilled some of the promises his Republican colleagues had made. He appointed a former Confederate as postmaster general and ordered federal troops who guarded the South Carolina and Louisiana statehouses back to their barracks. Federal soldiers remained in the South after 1877 but no longer served a political function. Democrats, meanwhile, took over state governments in Louisiana, South Carolina, and Florida. When Republican rule toppled in these states, the era of Reconstruction finally ended.

But some of the bargains struck in the **Compromise of 1877**, such as Democratic promises to treat southern blacks fairly, were forgotten, as were Hayes's pledges to ensure freedmen's rights. "When you turned us loose, you turned us loose to the sky, to the storm, to the whirlwind, and worst of all . . . to the wrath of our infuriated masters," Frederick Douglass had charged at the Republican convention in 1876. "The question now is, do you mean to make good to us the promises in your Constitution?" The answer provided by the 1876 election and the 1877 Compromise was "No."

16-5.3 Reconstruction: Success or Failure?

In the end, was Reconstruction a success or a failure? Few historical questions have been more hotly debated. Reconstruction was no doubt a success for both political parties. Although unable to retain a southern constituency, the Republican Party no longer faced the unpopular "southern question." The Democrats, now empowered in the former Confederacy, remained entrenched there for over a century. "Home rule" was firmly in place. Reconstruction's end also signified a triumph for nationalism and reunion. As the nation applauded reconciliation of

South and North, Reconstruction's reputation sank. Looking back on the 1860s and 1870s, most late-nineteenth-century Americans dismissed the congressional effort to reconstruct the South as a fiasco—a tragic interlude of "radical rule" or "black reconstruction" fashioned by carpetbaggers, scalawags, and Radical Republicans.

With the hindsight of a century, historians continued to regard Reconstruction as a failure, though of a different kind. No longer viewed as a misguided scheme that collapsed because of Radical excess, Reconstruction is now widely seen as a democratic experiment that did not go far enough. Historians cite two main causes. First, Congress did not promote freedmen's independence through land reform; without property of their own, southern blacks lacked the economic power to defend their interests as free citizens. Second, the federal government neglected to back congressional Reconstruction with military force. Given the choice between protecting blacks' rights at whatever cost and promoting reunion, the government opted for reunion. As a result, the nation's adjustment to the consequences of emancipation would continue into the twentieth century.

The Reconstruction era left some significant legacies, including the Fourteenth and Fifteenth Amendments. Although neither amendment would be used to protect minority rights for almost a century, they remain monuments to the democratic zeal that swept Congress in the 1860s. The aspirations and achievements of Reconstruction also left an indelible mark on black citizens. After Reconstruction, many Americans turned to their economic futures—to railroads, factories, and mills, and to the exploitation of the country's bountiful natural resources.

Compromise of 1877
Deal that gave Republicans the presidency and restored Democrats to power in the South, ending Reconstruction.

The Whole Vision

■ *How did Radical Republicans gain control of Reconstruction politics?*

Between 1865 and 1877, the nation experienced a series of political crises. In Washington, conflict between President Johnson and Congress led to a stringent Republican plan for restoring the South, a plan that included the radical provision of black male enfranchisement. President Johnson ineptly abetted the triumph of his foes by his defiant stance, which drove moderate Republicans into an alliance against him with Radical Republicans. They even attempted to impeach the president for political reasons, but failed. The Fourteenth and Fifteenth Amendments, which Johnson opposed, were major triumphs for the Radicals. But the Fifteenth Amendment's restriction of voting rights to "males" led to a damaging split in the woman's suffrage movement.

■ *What impact did federal Reconstruction policy have on the former Confederacy and ex-Confederates?*

Democrats and ex-Confederates were largely excluded from political power in the South, which fell to Republicans and freedmen. The Reconstruction governments passed costly reform measures, most of which were later abandoned or scaled back. Terrorist organizations such as the Ku Klux Klan flourished briefly. They were outlawed by the federal government but had already intimidated freedmen.

■ *How did the newly freed slaves reshape their lives after emancipation?*

Emancipation reshaped black communities where former slaves sought new identities as free people. African Americans reconstituted their families; created black institutions, such as churches and schools; and participated in government for the first time in American history. They also took part in the transformation of southern agriculture. By Reconstruction's end, a new labor system, sharecropping, replaced slavery. Begun as a compromise between freedmen and landowners, sharecropping soon trapped African Americans and other tenant farmers in a cycle of debt; black political rights waned and Republicans lost control of the southern states.

■ *Why did northern concern about Reconstruction begin to wane?*

Other concerns soon began to preoccupy Republicans. The political scandals of the Grant administration and the impact of depression after the Panic of 1873 diverted northern attention from the South. By the mid-1870s, northern politicians were ready to discard the Reconstruction policies that Congress had imposed a decade before.

■ *What factors contributed to the end of Reconstruction in 1877?*

Republican control of the South began to collapse in the early 1870s. The Supreme Court threw out important measures intended to protect freedmen's rights. Simultaneously, the southern states returned to Democratic rule, as Republican regimes toppled one by one. Reconstruction's final collapse in 1877 reflected not only a waning of northern resolve but a successful ex-Confederate campaign of violence, intimidation, and protest that had started in the 1860s. By 1877, resistance had trumped Reconstruction. The price of the Republican victory in the disputed presidential election of 1876 was the end of Reconstruction and the return of the South to Democratic control.

Appendix

Declaration of Independence

IN CONGRESS, JULY 4, 1776
THE UNANIMOUS DECLARATION OF THE
THIRTEEN UNITED STATES OF AMERICA

When, in the course of human events, it becomes necessary for one people to dissolve the political bands which have connected them with another, and to assume, among the powers of the earth, the separate and equal station to which the laws of nature and of nature's God entitle them, a decent respect to the opinions of mankind requires that they should declare the causes which impel them to the separation.

We hold these truths to be self-evident: That all men are created equal; that they are endowed by their Creator with certain unalienable rights; that among these are life, liberty, and the pursuit of happiness; that, to secure these rights, governments are instituted among men, deriving their just powers from the consent of the governed; that whenever any form of government becomes destructive of these ends, it is the right of the people to alter or to abolish it, and to institute new government, laying its foundation on such principles, and organizing its powers in such form, as to them shall seem most likely to effect their safety and happiness. Prudence, indeed, will dictate that governments long established should not be changed for light and transient causes; and accordingly all experience hath shown that mankind are more disposed to suffer, while evils are sufferable, than to right themselves by abolishing the forms to which they are accustomed. But when a long train of abuses and usurpations, pursuing invariably the same object, evinces a design to reduce them under absolute despotism, it is their right, it is their duty, to throw off such government, and to provide new guards for their future security. Such has been the patient sufferance of these colonies; and such is now the necessity which constrains them to alter their former systems of government. The history of the present King of Great Britain is a history of repeated injuries and usurpations, all having in direct object the establishment of an absolute tyranny over these states. To prove this, let facts be submitted to a candid world.

He has refused his assent to laws, the most wholesome and necessary for the public good.

He has forbidden his governors to pass laws of immediate and pressing importance, unless suspended in their operation till his assent should be obtained; and, when so suspended, he has utterly neglected to attend to them.

He has refused to pass other laws for the accommodation of large districts of people, unless those people would relinquish the right of representation in the legislature, a right inestimable to them, and formidable to tyrants only.

He has called together legislative bodies at places unusual, uncomfortable, and distant from the depository of their public records, for the sole purpose of fatiguing them into compliance with his measures.

He has dissolved representative houses repeatedly, for opposing, with manly firmness, his invasions on the rights of the people.

He has refused for a long time, after such dissolutions, to cause others to be elected; whereby the legislative powers, incapable of annihilation, have returned to the people at large for their exercise; the state remaining, in the mean time, exposed to all the dangers of invasions from without and convulsions within.

He has endeavored to prevent the population of these states; for that purpose obstructing the laws of naturalization of foreigners; refusing to pass others to encourage their migration hither, and raising the conditions of new appropriation of lands.

He has obstructed the administration of justice, by refusing his assent to laws for establishing judiciary powers.

He has made judges dependent on his will alone, for the tenure of their offices, and the amount and payment of their salaries.

He has erected a multitude of new offices, and sent hither swarms of officers to harass our people and eat out their substance.

He has kept among us, in times of peace, standing armies, without the consent of our legislatures.

He has affected to render the military independent of, and superior to, the civil power.

He has combined with others to subject us to a jurisdiction foreign to our constitution, and unacknowledged by our laws, giving his assent to their acts of pretended legislation:

For quartering large bodies of armed troops among us;

For protecting them, by a mock trial, from punishment for any murders which they should commit on the inhabitants of these states;

For cutting off our trade with all parts of the world;

For imposing taxes on us without our consent;

For depriving us, in many cases, of the benefits of trial by jury;

For transporting us beyond seas, to be tried for pretended offenses;

For abolishing the free system of English laws in a neighboring province, establishing therein an arbitrary government, and enlarging its boundaries, so as to render it at once an example and fit instrument for introducing the same absolute rule into these colonies;

For taking away our charters, abolishing our most valuable laws, and altering fundamentally the forms of our governments;

For suspending our own legislatures, and declaring themselves invested with power to legislate for us in all cases whatsoever.

He has abdicated government here, by declaring us out of his protection and waging war against us.

He has plundered our seas, ravaged our coasts, burned our towns, and destroyed the lives of our people.

He is at this time transporting large armies of foreign mercenaries to complete the works of death, desolation, and tyranny already begun with circumstances of cruelty and perfidy scarcely paralleled in the most barbarous ages, and totally unworthy of the head of a civilized nation.

He has constrained our fellow-citizens, taken captive on the high seas, to bear arms against their country, to become the executioners of their friends and brethren, or to fall themselves by their hands.

He has excited domestic insurrection among us, and has endeavored to bring on the inhabitants of our frontiers the merciless Indian savages, whose known rule of warfare is an undistinguished destruction of all ages, sexes, and conditions.

In every stage of these oppressions we have petitioned for redress in the most humble terms; our repeated petitions have been answered only by repeated injury. A prince, whose character is thus marked by every act which may define a tyrant, is unfit to be the ruler of a free people.

Nor have we been wanting in our attentions to our British brethren. We have warned them, from time to time, of attempts by their legislature to extend an unwarrantable jurisdiction over us. We have reminded them of the circumstances of our emigration and settlement here. We have appealed to their native justice and magnanimity; and we have conjured them by the ties of our common kindred, to disavow these usurpations, which would inevitably interrupt our connections and correspondence. They, too, have been deaf to the voice of justice and of consanguinity. We must, therefore, acquiesce in the necessity which denounces our separation, and hold them, as we hold the rest of mankind, enemies in war, in peace friends.

We, therefore, the representatives of the United States of America, in General Congress assembled, appealing to the Supreme Judge of the world for the rectitude of our intentions, do, in the name and by the authority of the good people of these colonies, solemnly publish and declare, that these United Colonies are, and of right ought to be, FREE AND INDEPENDENT STATES; that they are absolved from all allegiance to the British crown, and that all political connection between them and the state of Great Britain is, and ought to be, totally dissolved; and that, as free and independent states, they have full power to levy war, conclude peace, contract alliances, establish commerce, and do all other acts and things which independent states may of right do. And for the support of this declaration, with a firm reliance on the protection of Divine Providence, we mutually pledge to each other our lives, our fortunes, and our sacred honor.

JOHN HANCOCK [President]
[and fifty-five others]

Constitution of the United States of America

Preamble

We the people of the United States, in order to form a more perfect union, establish justice, insure domestic tranquillity, provide for the common defense, promote the general welfare, and secure the blessings of liberty to ourselves and our posterity, do ordain and establish this CONSTITUTION for the United States of America.

Article I

SECTION 1. All legislative powers herein granted shall be vested in a Congress of the United States, which shall consist of a Senate and a House of Representatives.

SECTION 2. The House of Representatives shall be composed of members chosen every second year by the people of the several States, and the electors in each State shall have the qualifications requisite for electors of the most numerous branch of the State Legislature.

No person shall be a Representative who shall not have attained to the age of twenty-five years, and been seven years a citizen of the United States, and who shall not, when elected, be an inhabitant of that State in which he shall be chosen.

Representatives and direct taxes shall be apportioned among the several States which may be included within this Union, according to their respective numbers, *which shall be determined by adding to the whole number of free persons, including those bound to service for a term of years and excluding Indians not taxed, three-fifths of all other persons.* The actual enumeration shall be made within three years after the first meeting of the Congress of the United States, and within every subsequent term of ten years, in such manner as they shall by law direct. The number of Representatives shall not exceed one for every thirty thousand, but each State shall have at least one Representative; *and until such enumeration shall be made, the State of New Hampshire shall be entitled to choose three, Massachusetts eight, Rhode Island and Providence Plantations one, Connecticut five, New York six, New Jersey four, Pennsylvania eight, Delaware one, Maryland six, Virginia ten, North Carolina five, South Carolina five, and Georgia three.*

Note: Passages that are no longer in effect are printed in italic type.

When vacancies happen in the representation from any State, the Executive authority thereof shall issue writs of election to fill such vacancies.

The House of Representatives shall choose their Speaker and other officers; and shall have the sole power of impeachment.

SECTION 3. The Senate of the United States shall be composed of two Senators from each State, *chosen by the legislature thereof,* for six years; and each Senator shall have one vote.

Immediately after they shall be assembled in consequence of the first election, they shall be divided as equally as may be into three classes. The seats of the Senators of the first class shall be vacated at the expiration of the second year, of the second class at the expiration of the fourth year, and of the third class at the expiration of the sixth year, so that one-third maybe chosen every second year; and if vacancies happen by resignation or otherwise, during the recess of the legislature of any State, the Executive thereof may make temporary appointments until the next meeting of the legislature, which shall then fill such vacancies.

No person shall be a Senator who shall not have attained to the age of thirty years, and been nine years a citizen of the United States, and who shall not, when elected, be an inhabitant of that State for which he shall be chosen.

The Vice President of the United States shall be President of the Senate, but shall have no vote, unless they be equally divided.

The Senate shall choose their other officers, and also a President *pro tempore,* in the absence of the Vice President, or when he shall exercise the office of the President of the United States.

The Senate shall have the sole power to try all impeachments. When sitting for that purpose, they shall be on oath or affirmation. When the President of the United States is tried, the Chief Justice shall preside: and no person shall be convicted without the concurrence of two-thirds of the members present.

Judgment in cases of impeachment shall not extend further than to removal from the office, and disqualification to hold and enjoy any office of honor, trust or profit under the United States; but the party convicted shall nevertheless be liable and subject to indictment, trial, judgment and punishment, according to law.

SECTION 4. The times, places and manner of holding elections for Senators and Representatives shall be prescribed in each State by the legislature thereof; but the Congress may at any time by law make or alter such regulations, except as to the places of choosing Senators.

The Congress shall assemble at least once in every year, and such meeting *shall be on the first Monday in December, unless they shall by law appoint a different day.*

SECTION 5. Each house shall be the judge of the elections, returns and qualifications of its own members, and a majority of each shall constitute a quorum to do business; but a smaller number may adjourn from day to day, and maybe authorized to compel the attendance of absent members, in such manner, and under such penalties, as each house may provide.

Each house may determine the rules of its proceedings, punish its members for disorderly behavior, and with the concurrence of two-thirds, expel a member.

Each house shall keep a journal of its proceedings, and from time to time publish the same, excepting such parts as may in their judgment require secrecy; and the yeas and nays of the members of either house on any question shall, at the desire of one-fifth of those present, be entered on the journal.

Neither house, during the session of Congress, shall, without the consent of the other, adjourn for more than three days, nor to any other place than that in which the two houses shall be sitting.

SECTION 6. The Senators and Representatives shall receive a compensation for their services, to be ascertained by law and paid out of the treasury of the United States. They shall in all cases except treason, felony and breach of the peace, be privileged from arrest during their attendance at the session of their respective houses, and in going to and returning from the same; and for any speech or debate in either house, they shall not be questioned in any other place.

No Senator or Representative shall, during the time for which he was elected, be appointed to any civil office under the authority of the United States, which shall have been created, or the emoluments whereof shall have been increased, during such time; and no person holding any office under the United States shall be a member of either house during his continuance in office.

SECTION 7. All bills for raising revenue shall originate in the House of Representatives; but the Senate may propose or concur with amendments as on other bills.

Every bill which shall have passed the House of Representatives and the Senate, shall, before it become a law, be presented to the President of the United States; if he approve he shall sign it, but if not he shall return it with objections to that house in which it originated, who shall enter the objections at large on their journal, and proceed to reconsider it. If after such reconsideration two-thirds of that house shall agree to pass the bill, it shall be sent, together with the objections, to the other house, by which it shall likewise be reconsidered, and, if approved by two-thirds of that house, it shall become a law. But in all such cases the votes of both houses shall be determined by yeas and nays, and the names of the persons voting for and against the bill shall be entered on the journal of each house respectively. If any bill shall not be returned by the President within ten days (Sundays excepted) after it shall have been presented to him, the same shall be a law, in like manner as if he had signed it, unless the Congress by their adjournment prevent its return, in which case it shall not be a law.

Every order, resolution, or vote to which the concurrence of the Senate and House of Representatives may be necessary (except on a question of adjournment) shall be presented to the President of the United States; and before the same shall take effect, shall be approved by him, or being disapproved by him, shall be repassed by two-thirds of the Senate and House of Representatives, according to the rules and limitations prescribed in the case of a bill.

SECTION 8. The Congress shall have power

To lay and collect taxes, duties, imposts, and excises, to pay the debts and provide for the common defense and general welfare of the United States; but all duties, imposts and excises shall be uniform throughout the United States;

To borrow money on the credit of the United States;

To regulate commerce with foreign nations, and among the several States, and with the Indian tribes;

To establish an uniform rule of naturalization, and uniform laws on the subject of bankruptcies throughout the United States;

To coin money, regulate the value thereof, and of foreign coin, and fix the standard of weights and measures;

To provide for the punishment of counterfeiting the securities and current coin of the United States;

To establish post offices and post roads;

To promote the progress of science and useful arts by securing for limited times to authors and inventors the exclusive right to their respective writings and discoveries;

To constitute tribunals inferior to the Supreme Court;

To define and punish piracies and felonies committed on the high seas and offenses against the law of nations;

To declare war, grant letters of marque and reprisal, and make rules concerning captures on land and water;

To raise and support armies, but no appropriation of money to that use shall be for a longer term than two years;

To provide and maintain a navy;

To make rules for the government and regulation of the land and naval forces;

To provide for calling forth the militia to execute the laws of the Union, suppress insurrections, and repel invasions;

To provide for organizing, arming, and disciplining the militia, and for governing such part of them as may be employed in the service of the United States, reserving to the States respectively the appointment of the officers, and the authority of training the militia according to the discipline prescribed by Congress;

To exercise exclusive legislation in all cases whatsoever, over such district (not exceeding ten miles square) as may, by cession of particular States, and the acceptance of Congress, become the seat of government of the United States, and to exercise like authority over all places purchased by the consent of the legislature of the State, in which the same shall be, for erection of forts, magazines, arsenals, dock-yards, and other needful buildings;—and

To make all laws which shall be necessary and proper for carrying into execution the foregoing powers, and all other powers vested by this Constitution in the government of the United States, or in any department or officer thereof.

SECTION 9. *The migration or importation of such persons as any of the States now existing shall think proper to admit shall not be prohibited by the Congress prior to the year 1808; but a tax or duty may be imposed on such importation, not exceeding $10 for each person.*

The privilege of the writ of habeas corpus shall not be suspended, unless when in cases of rebellion or invasion the public safety may require it.

No bill of attainder or ex post facto law shall be passed.

No capitation, or other direct, tax shall be laid, unless in proportion to the census or enumeration herein before directed to be taken.

No tax or duty shall be laid on articles exported from any State.

No preference shall be given by any regulation of commerce or revenue to the ports of one State over those of another; nor shall vessels bound to, or from, one State, be obliged to enter, clear, or pay duties in another.

No money shall be drawn from the treasury, but in consequence of appropriations made by law; and a regular statement and account of the receipts and expenditures of all public money shall be published from time to time.

No title of nobility shall be granted by the United States: and no person holding any office of profit or trust under them, shall, without the consent of the Congress, accept of any present, emolument, office, or title, of any kind whatever, from any king, prince, or foreign state.

SECTION 10. No State shall enter into any treaty, alliance, or confederation; grant letters of marque and reprisal; coin money; emit bills of credit; make anything but gold and silver coin a tender in payment of debts; pass any bill of attainder, ex post facto law, or law impairing the obligation of contracts, or grant any title of nobility.

No State shall, without the consent of Congress, lay any imposts or duties on imports or exports, except what may be absolutely necessary for executing its inspection laws: and the net produce of all duties and imposts, laid by any State on imports or exports, shall be for the use of the treasury of the United States; and all such laws shall be subject to the revision and control of the Congress.

No State shall, without the consent of Congress, lay any duty of tonnage, keep troops or ships of war in time of peace, enter into any agreement or compact with another State, or with a foreign power, or engage in war, unless actually invaded, or in such imminent danger as will not admit of delay.

Article II

SECTION 1. The executive power shall be vested in a President of the United States of America. He shall hold his office during the term of four years, and, together with the Vice President, chosen for the same term, be elected as follows: Each state shall appoint, in such manner as the legislature thereof may direct, a number of electors, equal to the whole number of Senators and Representatives to which the State may be entitled in the Congress; but no Senator or Representative, or person holding an office of trust or profit under the United States, shall be appointed an elector.

The electors shall meet in their respective States, and vote by ballot for two persons, of whom one at least shall not be an inhabitant of the same State with themselves. And they shall make a list of all the persons voted for, and of the number of votes for each; which list they shall sign and certify, and transmit sealed to the seat of government of the United States, directed to the President of the Senate. The President of the Senate shall, in the presence of the Senate and the House of Representatives, open all the certificates, and the votes shall then be counted. The person having the greatest number of votes shall be the President, if such number be a majority of the whole number of electors appointed; and if there be more than one who have such majority, and have an equal number of votes, then the House of Representatives shall immediately choose by ballot one of them for President; and if no person have a majority, then from the five highest on the list said house shall in like manner choose the President. But in choosing the President the votes shall be taken by States, the representation from each State having one vote; a quorum for this purpose shall consist of a member or members from two-thirds of the States, and a majority of all the States shall be necessary to a choice. In every case, after the choice of the President, the person having the greatest number of votes of the electors shall be the Vice President. But if there should remain two or more who have equal votes, the Senate shall choose from them by ballot the Vice President.

The Congress may determine the time of choosing the electors and the day on which they shall give their votes; which day shall be the same throughout the United States.

No person except a natural-born citizen, or *a citizen of the United States at the time of the adoption of this Constitution,* shall be eligible to the office of President; neither shall any person be eligible to that office who shall not have attained to the age of thirty-five years, and been fourteen years a resident within the United States.

In case of the removal of the President from office or of his death, resignation, or inability to discharge the powers and duties of the said office, the same shall devolve on the Vice President, and the Congress may by law provide for the case of removal, death, resignation, or inability, both of the President and Vice President, declaring what officer shall then act as President, and such officer shall act accordingly, until the disability be removed, or a President shall be elected.

The President shall, at stated times, receive for his services a compensation, which shall neither be increased nor diminished during the period for which he shall have been elected, and he shall not receive within that period any other emolument from the United States, or any of them.

Before he enter on the execution of his office, he shall take the following oath or affirmation:—"I do solemnly swear (or affirm) that I will faithfully execute the office of the President of the United States, and will to the best of my ability preserve, protect and defend the Constitution of the United States."

SECTION 2. The President shall be commander in chief of the army and navy of the United States, and of the militia of the several States, when called into the actual service of the United States; he may require the opinion, in writing, of the principal officer in each of the executive departments, upon any subject relating to the duties of their respective offices, and he shall have power to grant reprieves and pardons for offenses against the United States, except in cases of impeachment.

He shall have power, by and with the advice and consent of the Senate, to make treaties, provided two-thirds of the Senators present concur; and he shall nominate, and by and with the advice and consent of the Senate, shall appoint ambassadors, other public ministers and consuls, judges of the Supreme Court, and all other officers of the United States, whose appointments are not herein otherwise provided for, and which shall be established by law: but Congress may by law vest the appointment of such inferior officers, as they think proper, in the President alone, in the courts of law, or in the heads of departments.

The President shall have power to fill up all vacancies that may happen during the recess of the Senate, by granting commissions which shall expire at the end of their next session.

SECTION 3. He shall from time to time give to the Congress information of the state of the Union, and recommend to their consideration such measures as he shall judge necessary and expedient; he may, on extraordinary occasions, convene both houses, or either of them, and in case of disagreement between them, with respect to the time of adjournment, he may adjourn them to such time as he shall think proper; he shall receive ambassadors and other public ministers; he shall take care that the laws be faithfully executed, and shall commission all the officers of the United States.

SECTION 4. The President, Vice President and all civil officers of the United States shall be removed from office on impeachment for, and on conviction of, treason, bribery, or other high crimes and misdemeanors.

Article III

SECTION 1. The judicial power of the United States shall be vested in one Supreme Court, and in such inferior courts as the Congress may from time to time ordain and establish. The judges, both of the Supreme and inferior courts, shall hold their offices during good behavior, and shall, at stated times, receive for their services a compensation which shall not be diminished during their continuance in office.

SECTION 2. The judicial power shall extend to all cases, in law and equity, arising under this Constitution, the laws of the United States, and treaties made, or which shall be made, under their authority;—to all cases affecting ambassadors, other public ministers and consuls;—to all cases of admiralty and maritime jurisdiction;—to controversies to which the United States shall be a party;—to controversies between two or more States;—*between a State and citizens of another State*;—between citizens of different States;—between citizens of the same State claiming lands under grants of different States, and between a State, or the citizens thereof, and foreign states, citizens or subjects.

In all cases affecting ambassadors, other public ministers and consuls, and those in which a State shall be party, the Supreme Court shall have original jurisdiction. In all the other cases before mentioned, the Supreme Court shall have appellate jurisdiction, both as to law and fact, with such exceptions, and under such regulations, as the Congress shall make.

The trial of all crimes, except in cases of impeachment, shall be by jury; and such trial shall be held in the State where said crimes shall have been committed; but when not committed within any State, the trial shall be at such place or places as the Congress may by law have directed.

SECTION 3. Treason against the United States shall consist only in levying war against them, or in adhering to their enemies, giving them aid and comfort. No person shall be convicted of treason unless on the testimony of two witnesses to the same overt act, or on confession in open court.

The Congress shall have power to declare the punishment of treason, but no attainder of treason shall work corruption of blood, or forfeiture except during the life of the person attainted.

Article IV

SECTION 1. Full faith and credit shall be given in each State to the public acts, records, and judicial proceedings of every other State. And the Congress may by general laws prescribe the manner in which such acts, records, and proceedings shall be proved, and the effect thereof.

SECTION 2. The citizens of each State shall be entitled to all privileges and immunities of citizens in the several States.

A person charged in any State with treason, felony, or other crime, who shall flee from justice, and be found in another State, shall on demand of the executive authority of the State from which he fled, be delivered up, to be removed to the State having jurisdiction of the crime.

No person held to service or labor in one State, under the laws thereof, escaping into another, shall, in consequence of any law or regulation therein, be discharged from such service or labor, but shall be delivered up on claim of the party to whom such service or labor may be due.

SECTION 3. New States may be admitted by the Congress into this Union; but no new State shall be formed or erected within the jurisdiction of any other State; nor any State be formed by the junction of two or more States, or parts of States, without the consent of the legislatures of the States concerned as well as of the Congress.

The Congress shall have power to dispose of and make all needful rules and regulations respecting the territory or other property belonging to the United States; and nothing in this Constitution shall be so construed as to prejudice any claims of the United States, or of any particular State.

SECTION 4. The United States shall guarantee to every State in this Union a republican form of government, and shall protect each of them against invasion; and on application of the legislature, or of the executive (when the legislature cannot be convened), against domestic violence.

Article V

The Congress, whenever two-thirds of both houses shall deem it necessary, shall propose amendments to this Constitution, or, on the application of the legislatures of two-thirds of the several States, shall call a convention for proposing amendments, which, in either case, shall be valid to all intents and purposes, as part of this Constitution, when ratified by the legislatures of three-fourths of the several States, or by conventions in three-fourths thereof, as the one or the other mode of ratification may be proposed by the Congress; provided *that no amendments which may be made prior to the year one thousand eight hundred and eight shall in any manner affect the first and fourth clauses in the ninth section of the first article*; and that no State, without its consent, shall be deprived of its equal suffrage in the Senate.

Article VI

All debts contracted and engagements entered into, before the adoption of this Constitution, shall be as valid against the United States under this Constitution, as under the Confederation. This Constitution, and the laws of the United States which shall be made in pursuance thereof; and all treaties made, or which shall be made, under the authority of the United States, shall be the supreme law of the land; and the judges in every State shall be bound thereby, anything in the Constitution or laws of any State to the contrary notwithstanding.

The Senators and Representatives before mentioned, and the members of the several State legislatures, and all executive and judicial officers, both of the United States and of the several States, shall be bound by oath or affirmation to support this Constitution; but no religious test shall ever be required as a qualification to any office or public trust under the United States.

Article VII

The ratification of the conventions of nine States shall be sufficient for the establishment of this Constitution between the States so ratifying the same.

Done in Convention by the unanimous consent of the States present, the seventeenth day of September in the year of our Lord one thousand seven hundred and eighty-seven and of the Independence of the United States of America the twelfth. In witness whereof we have hereunto subscribed our names.

[Signed by]
G° WASHINGTON
Presidt and Deputy from Virginia [and thirty-eight others]

Amendments to the Constitution

Amendment I*

Congress shall make no law respecting an establishment of religion, or prohibiting the free exercise thereof; or abridging the freedom of speech, or of the press; or the right of the people peaceably to assemble, and to petition the government for a redress of grievances.

Amendment II

A well-regulated militia being necessary to the security of a free State, the right of the people to keep and bear arms shall not be infringed.

Amendment III

No soldier shall, in time of peace, be quartered in any house without the consent of the owner, nor in time of war, but in a manner to be prescribed by law.

*The first ten amendments (Bill of Rights) were adopted in 1791.

Amendment IV

The right of the people to be secure in their persons, houses, papers, and effects, against unreasonable searches and seizures, shall not be violated, and no warrants shall issue but upon probable cause, supported by oath or affirmation, and particularly describing the place to be searched, and the persons or things to be seized.

Amendment V

No person shall be held to answer for a capital, or otherwise infamous crime, unless on a presentment or indictment of a grand jury, except in cases arising in the land or naval forces, or in the militia, when in actual service in time of war or public danger; nor shall any person be subject for the same offense to be twice put in jeopardy of life or limb; nor shall be compelled in any criminal case to be a witness against himself, nor be deprived of life, liberty, or property, without due process of law; nor shall private property be taken for public use without just compensation.

Amendment VI

In all criminal prosecutions, the accused shall enjoy the right to a speedy and public trial, by an impartial jury of the State and district wherein the crime shall have been committed, which district shall have been previously ascertained by law, and to be informed of the nature and cause of the accusation; to be confronted with the witnesses against him; to have compulsory process for obtaining witnesses in his favor, and to have the assistance of counsel for his defense.

Amendment VII

In suits at common law, where the value in controversy shall exceed twenty dollars, the right of trial by jury shall be preserved, and no fact tried by a jury shall be otherwise reexamined in any court of the United States, than according to the rules of the common law.

Amendment VIII

Excessive bail shall not be required, nor excessive fines imposed, nor cruel and unusual punishments inflicted.

Amendment IX

The enumeration in the Constitution, of certain rights, shall not be construed to deny or disparage others retained by the people.

Amendment X

The powers not delegated to the United States by the Constitution, nor prohibited by it to the States, are reserved to the States respectively, or to the people.

Amendment XI

[Adopted 1798]
The judicial power of the United States shall not be construed to extend to any suit in law or equity, commenced or prosecuted against one of the United States by citizens of another State, or by citizens or subjects of any foreign state.

Amendment XII

[Adopted 1804]
The electors shall meet in their respective States, and vote by ballot for President and Vice President, one of whom, at least, shall not be an inhabitant of the same State with themselves; they shall name in their ballots the person voted for as President, and in distinct ballots the person voted for as Vice President, and they shall make distinct lists of all persons voted for as President, and of all persons voted for as Vice President, and of the number of votes for each, which lists they shall sign and certify, and transmit sealed to the seat of government of the United States, directed to the President of the Senate;—the President of the Senate shall, in the presence of the Senate and House of Representatives, open all the certificates and the votes shall then be counted;—the person having the greatest number of votes for President shall be the President, if such number be a majority of the whole number of electors appointed; and if no person have such majority, then from the persons having the highest numbers not exceeding three on the list of those voted for as President, the House of Representatives shall choose immediately, by ballot, the President. But in choosing the President, the votes shall be taken by States, the representation from each State having one vote; a quorum for this purpose shall consist of a member or members from two-thirds of the States, and a majority of all the States shall be necessary to a choice. And if the House of Representatives shall not choose a President whenever the right of choice shall devolve upon them, before *the fourth day of March* next following, then the Vice President shall act as President, as in the case of the death or other constitutional disability of the President.

The person having the greatest number of votes as Vice President shall be the Vice President, if such a number be a majority of the whole number of electors appointed; and if no person have a majority, then from the two highest numbers on the list the Senate shall choose the Vice President; a quorum for the purpose shall consist of two-thirds of the whole number of Senators, and a majority of the whole number shall be necessary to a choice. But no person constitutionally ineligible to the office of President shall be eligible to that of Vice President of the United States.

Amendment XIII

[Adopted 1865]
SECTION 1. Neither slavery nor involuntary servitude, except as a punishment for crime whereof the party shall

have been duly convicted, shall exist within the United States, or any place subject to their jurisdiction.

SECTION 2. Congress shall have power to enforce this article by appropriate legislation.

Amendment XIV

[Adopted 1868]

SECTION 1. All persons born or naturalized in the United States, and subject to the jurisdiction thereof, are citizens of the United States and of the State wherein they reside. No State shall make or enforce any law which shall abridge the privileges or immunities of citizens of the United States; nor shall any State deprive any person of life, liberty, or property, without due process of law; nor deny to any person within its jurisdiction the equal protection of the laws.

SECTION 2. Representatives shall be apportioned among the several States according to their respective numbers, counting the whole number of persons in each State, excluding Indians not taxed. But when the right to vote at any election for the choice of Electors for President and Vice President of the United States, Representatives in Congress, the executive and judicial officers of a State, or the members of the legislature thereof, is denied to any of the male inhabitants of such State, being twenty-one years of age and citizens of the United States, or in any way abridged, except for participation in rebellion, or other crime, the basis of representation therein shall be reduced in the proportion which the number of such male citizens shall bear to the whole number of male citizens twenty-one years of age in such State.

SECTION 3. No person shall be a Senator or Representative in Congress or Elector of President and Vice President, or hold any office, civil or military, under the United States, or under any State, who, having previously taken an oath, as a member of Congress, or as an officer of the United States, or as a member of any State legislature, or as an executive or judicial officer of any State, to support the Constitution of the United States, shall have engaged in insurrection or rebellion against the same, or given aid and comfort to the enemies thereof. Congress may, by a vote of two-thirds of each house, remove such disability.

SECTION 4. The validity of the public debt of the United States, authorized by law, including debts incurred for payment of pensions and bounties for services in suppressing insurrection or rebellion, shall not be questioned. But neither the United States nor any State shall assume or pay any debt or obligation incurred in aid of insurrection or rebellion against the United States, or any claim for the loss or emancipation of any slave; but all such debts, obligations, and claims shall be held illegal and void.

SECTION 5. The Congress shall have the power to enforce, by appropriate legislation, the provisions of this article.

Amendment XV

[Adopted 1870]

SECTION 1. The right of citizens of the United States to vote shall not be denied or abridged by the United States or by any State on account of race, color, or previous condition of servitude.

SECTION 2. The Congress shall have power to enforce this article by appropriate legislation.

Amendment XVI

[Adopted 1913]

The Congress shall have power to lay and collect taxes on incomes, from whatever source derived, without apportionment among the several States, and without regard to any census or enumeration.

Amendment XVII

[Adopted 1913]

SECTION 1. The Senate of the United States shall be composed of two Senators from each State, elected by the people thereof, for six years; and each Senator shall have one vote. The electors in each State shall have the qualifications requisite for electors of [voters for] the most numerous branch of the State legislatures.

SECTION 2. When vacancies happen in the representation of any State in the Senate, the executive authority of such State shall issue writs of election to fill such vacancies: Provided, that the Legislature of any State may empower the executive thereof to make temporary appointments until the people fill the vacancies by election as the Legislature may direct.

SECTION 3. This amendment shall not be so construed as to affect the election or term of any Senator chosen before it becomes valid as part of the Constitution.

Amendment XVIII

[Adopted 1919; repealed 1933]

SECTION 1. *After one year from the ratification of this article the manufacture, sale, or transportation of intoxicating liquors within, the importation thereof into, or the exportation thereof from the United States and all territory subject to the jurisdiction thereof, for beverage purposes, is hereby prohibited.*

SECTION 2. *The Congress and the several States shall have concurrent power to enforce this article by appropriate legislation.*

SECTION 3. *This article shall be inoperative unless it shall have been ratified as an amendment to the Constitution by the legislatures of the several States, as provided by the Constitution, within seven years from the date of the submission thereof to the States by the Congress.*

Amendment XIX

[Adopted 1920]

SECTION 1. The right of citizens of the United States to vote shall not be denied or abridged by the United States or by any State on account of sex.

SECTION 2. The Congress shall have the power to enforce this article by appropriate legislation.

Amendment XX

[Adopted 1933]

SECTION 1. The terms of the President and Vice President shall end at noon on the 20th day of January, and the terms of Senators and Representatives at noon on the 3d day of January, of the years in which such terms would have ended if this article had not been ratified; and the terms of their successors shall then begin.

SECTION 2. The Congress shall assemble at least once in every year, and such meeting shall begin at noon on the 3d of January, unless they shall by law appoint a different day.

SECTION 3. If, at the time fixed for the beginning of the term of the President, the President-elect shall have died, the Vice President-elect shall become President. If a President shall not have been chosen before the time fixed for the beginning of his term, or if the President-elect shall have failed to qualify, then the Vice President-elect shall act as President until a President shall have qualified; and the Congress may by law provide for the case wherein neither a President-elect nor a Vice President-elect shall have qualified, declaring who shall then act as President, or the manner in which one who is to act shall be selected, and such persons shall act accordingly until a President or Vice President shall have qualified.

SECTION 4. The Congress may by law provide for the case of the death of any of the persons from whom the House of Representatives may choose a President whenever the right of choice shall have devolved upon them, and for the case of the death of any of the persons from whom the Senate may choose a Vice President whenever the right of choice shall have devolved upon them.

SECTION 5. Sections 1 and 2 shall take effect on the 15th day of October following the ratification of this article.

SECTION 6. This article shall be inoperative unless it shall have been ratified as an amendment to the Constitution by the Legislatures of three-fourths of the several States within seven years from the date of its submission.

Amendment XXI

[Adopted 1933]

SECTION 1. The eighteenth article of amendment to the Constitution of the United States is hereby repealed.

SECTION 2. The transportation or importation into any State, Territory, or Possession of the United States for delivery or use therein of intoxicating liquors, in violation of the laws thereof, is hereby prohibited.

SECTION 3. This article shall be inoperative unless it shall have been ratified as an amendment to the Constitution by conventions in the several States, as provided in the Constitution, within seven years from the date of submission thereof to the States by the Congress.

Amendment XXII

[Adopted 1951]

SECTION 1. No person shall be elected to the office of President more than twice, and no person who has held the office of President, or acted as President, for more than two years of a term to which some other person was elected President shall be elected to the office of President more than once. But this article shall not apply to any person holding the office of President when this article was proposed by the Congress, and shall not prevent any person who may be holding the office of President, or acting as President, during the term within which this article becomes operative from holding the office of President or acting as President during the remainder of such term.

SECTION 2. This article shall be inoperative unless it shall have been ratified as an amendment to the Constitution by the legislatures of three-fourths of the several States within seven years from the date of its submission to the States by the Congress.

Amendment XXIII

[Adopted 1961]

SECTION 1. The District constituting the seat of Government of the United States shall appoint in such manner as the Congress may direct:

A number of electors of President and Vice President equal to the whole number of Senators and Representatives in Congress to which the District would be entitled if it were a State, but in no event more than the least populous State; they shall be in addition to those appointed by the States, but they shall be considered for the purposes of the election of President and Vice President, to be electors appointed by a State; and they shall meet in the District and perform such duties as provided by the twelfth article of amendment.

SECTION 2. The Congress shall have the power to enforce this article by appropriate legislation.

Amendment XXIV

[Adopted 1964]

SECTION 1. The right of citizens of the United States to vote in any primary or other election for President or Vice President, for electors for President or Vice President, or for

Senator or Representative in Congress, shall not be denied or abridged by the United States or any State by reason of failure to pay any poll tax or other tax.

SECTION 2. The Congress shall have the power to enforce this article by appropriate legislation.

Amendment XXV

[Adopted 1967]
SECTION 1. In case of the removal of the President from office or of his death or resignation, the Vice President shall become President.

SECTION 2. Whenever there is a vacancy in the office of the Vice President, the President shall nominate a Vice President who shall take office upon confirmation by a majority vote of both Houses of Congress.

SECTION 3. Whenever the President transmits to the President pro tempore of the Senate and the Speaker of the House of Representatives his written declaration that he is unable to discharge the powers and duties of his office, and until he transmits to them a written declaration to the contrary, such powers and duties shall be discharged by the Vice President as Acting President.

SECTION 4. Whenever the Vice President and a majority of either the principal officers of the executive departments or of such other body as Congress may by law provide, transmit to the President pro tempore of the Senate and the Speaker of the House of Representatives their written declaration that the President is unable to discharge the powers and duties of his office, the Vice President shall immediately assume the powers and duties of the office as Acting President.

Thereafter, when the President transmits to the President pro tempore of the Senate and the Speaker of the House of Representatives his written declaration that no inability exists, he shall resume the powers and duties of his office unless the Vice President and a majority of either the principal officers of the executive department[s] or of such other body as Congress may by law provide, transmit within four days to the President pro tempore of the Senate and the Speaker of the House of Representatives their written declaration that the President is unable to discharge the powers and duties of his office. Thereupon Congress shall decide the issue, assembling within forty-eight hours for that purpose if not in session. If the Congress, within twenty-one days after receipt of the latter written declaration, or, if Congress is not in session, within twenty-one days after Congress is required to assemble, determines by two-thirds vote of both Houses that the President is unable to discharge the powers and duties of his office, the Vice President shall continue to discharge the same as Acting President; otherwise, the President shall resume the powers and duties of his office.

Amendment XXVI

[Adopted 1971]
SECTION 1. The right of citizens of the United States, who are eighteen years of age or older, to vote shall not be denied or abridged by the United States or by any State on account of age.

SECTION 2. The Congress shall have power to enforce this article by appropriate legislation.

Amendment XXVII[a]

[Adopted 1992]
No law, varying the compensation for services of the Senators and Representatives, shall take effect, until an election of Representatives shall have intervened.

---

[a]Originally proposed in 1789 by James Madison, this amendment failed to win ratification along with the other parts of what became the Bill of Rights. However, the proposed amendment contained no deadline for ratification, and over the years other state legislatures voted to add it to the Constitution; many such ratifications occurred during the 1980s and early 1990s as public frustration with Congress's performance mounted. In May 1992, the Archivist of the United States certified that, with the Michigan legislature's ratification, the article had been approved by three-fourths of the states and thus automatically became part of the Constitution.

THE AMERICAN LAND

ADMISSION OF STATES INTO THE UNION

STATE	DATE OF ADMISSION	STATE	DATE OF ADMISSION
1. Delaware	December 7, 1787	26. Michigan	January 26, 1837
2. Pennsylvania	December 12, 1787	27. Florida	March 3, 1845
3. New Jersey	December 18, 1787	28. Texas	December 29, 1845
4. Georgia	January 2, 1788	29. Iowa	December 28, 1846
5. Connecticut	January 9, 1788	30. Wisconsin	May 29, 1848
6. Massachusetts	February 6, 1788	31. California	September 9, 1850
7. Maryland	April 28, 1788	32. Minnesota	May 11, 1858
8. South Carolina	May 23, 1788	33. Oregon	February 14, 1859
9. New Hampshire	June 21, 1788	34. Kansas	January 29, 1861
10. Virginia	June 25, 1788	35. West Virginia	June 20, 1863
11. New York	July 26, 1788	36. Nevada	October 31, 1864
12. North Carolina	November 21, 1789	37. Nebraska	March 1, 1867
13. Rhode Island	May 29, 1790	38. Colorado	August 1, 1876
14. Vermont	March 4, 1791	39. North Dakota	November 2, 1889
15. Kentucky	June 1, 1792	40. South Dakota	November 2, 1889
16. Tennessee	June 1, 1796	41. Montana	November 8, 1889
17. Ohio	March 1, 1803	42. Washington	November 11, 1889
18. Louisiana	April 30, 1812	43. Idaho	July 3, 1890
19. Indiana	December 11, 1816	44. Wyoming	July 10, 1890
20. Mississippi	December 10, 1817	45. Utah	January 4, 1896
21. Illinois	December 3, 1818	46. Oklahoma	November 16, 1907
22. Alabama	December 14, 1819	47. New Mexico	January 6, 1912
23. Maine	March 15, 1820	48. Arizona	February 14, 1912
24. Missouri	August 10, 1821	49. Alaska	January 3, 1959
25. Arkansas	June 15, 1836	50. Hawaii	August 21, 1959

TERRITORIAL EXPANSION

TERRITORY	DATE ACQUIRED	SQUARE MILES	HOW ACQUIRED
Original states and territories	1783	888,685	Treaty of Paris
Louisiana Purchase	1803	827,192	Purchased from France
Florida	1819	72,003	Adams-Onís Treaty
Texas	1845	390,143	Annexation of independent country
Oregon	1846	285,580	Oregon Boundary Treaty
Mexican cession	1848	529,017	Treaty of Guadalupe Hidalgo
Gadsden Purchase	1853	29,640	Purchased from Mexico
Midway Islands	1867	2	Annexation of uninhabited islands
Alaska	1867	589,757	Purchased from Russia
Hawaii	1898	6,450	Annexation of independent country
Wake Island	1898	3	Annexation of uninhabited island
Puerto Rico	1899	3,435	Treaty of Paris
Guam	1899	212	Treaty of Paris
The Philippines	1899–1946	11 5,600	Treaty of Paris; granted independence
American Samoa	1900	76	Treaty with Germany and Great Britain
Panama Canal Zone	1904–1978	553	Hay-Bunau-Varilla Treaty
U.S. Virgin Islands	1917	133	Purchased from Denmark
Trust Territory of the Pacific Islands*	1947	717	United Nations Trusteeship

*A number of these islands have been granted independence: Federated States of Micronesia, 1990; Marshall Islands, 1991; Palau, 1994.

THE AMERICAN PEOPLE

POPULATION, PERCENTAGE CHANGE, AND RACIAL COMPOSITION FOR THE UNITED STATES, 1790–2010

CENSUS	POPULATION OF UNITED STATES	INCREASE OVER PRECEDING CENSUS		RACIAL COMPOSITION, PERCENT DISTRIBUTION*			
		NUMBER	PERCENTAGE	WHITE	BLACK	LATINO	ASIAN
1790	3,929,214			80.7	19.3	NA	NA
1800	5,308,483	1,379,269	35.1	81.1	18.9	NA	NA
1810	7,239,881	1,931,398	36.4	81.0	19.0	NA	NA
1820	9,638,453	2,398,572	33.1	81.6	18.4	NA	NA
1830	12,866,020	3,227,567	33.5	81.9	18.1	NA	NA
1840	17,069,453	4,203,433	32.7	83.2	16.8	NA	NA
1850	23,191,876	6,122,423	35.9	84.3	15.7	NA	NA
1860	31,433,321	8,251,445	35.6	85.6	14.1	NA	NA
1870	39,818,449	8,375,128	26.6	86.2	13.5	NA	NA
1880	50,155,783	10,337,334	26.0	86.5	13.1	NA	NA
1890	62,947,714	12,791,931	25.5	87.5	11.9	NA	NA
1900	75,994,575	13,046,861	20.7	87.9	11.6	NA	0.3
1910	91,972,266	15,997,691	21.0	88.9	10.7	NA	0.3
1920	105,710,620	13,738,354	14.9	89.7	9.9	NA	0.3
1930	122,775,046	17,064,426	16.1	89.8	9.7	NA	0.4
1940	131,669,275	8,894,229	7.2	89.8	9.8	NA	0.4
1950	150,697,361	19,028,086	14.5	89.5	10.0	NA	0.4
1960†	179,323,175	28,625,814	19.0	88.6	10.5	NA	0.5
1970	203,235,298	23,912,123	13.3	87.6	11.1	NA	0.7
1980	226,504,825	23,269,527	11.4	85.9	11.8	6.4	1.5
1990	248,709,873	22,205,048	9.8	83.9	12.3	9.0	2.9
2000	281,421,906	32,712,033	82.2	82.2	12.2	11.7	3.8
2010	308,745,538	27,323,632	9.7	72.4	12.6	16.3	4.8

*Not every racial group included (e.g., no Native Americans). Data for 1980, 1990, 2000, and 2010 add up to more than 100% because those who identify themselves as "Latino" may be of any race.

†First year for which figures include Alaska and Hawaii.

Source: *Census Bureau, Historical Statistics of the United States, updated by relevant Statistical Abstract of the United States and http://factfinder.census.gov.*

POPULATION DENSITY AND DISTRIBUTION, 1790–2010

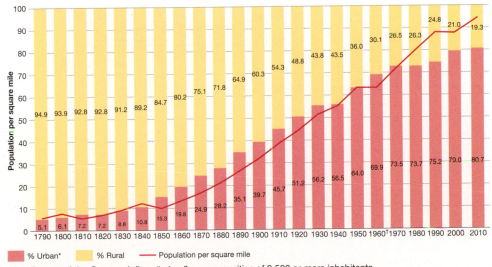

■ % Urban*   ■ % Rural   — Population per square mile

*The Bureau of the Census defines "urban" as communities of 2,500 or more inhabitants.
†First year for which figures include Alaska and Hawaii.

Source: *Census Bureau, Historical Statistics of the United States, updated by relevant Statistical Abstract of the United States.*

CHANGING CHARACTERISTICS OF THE U.S. POPULATION

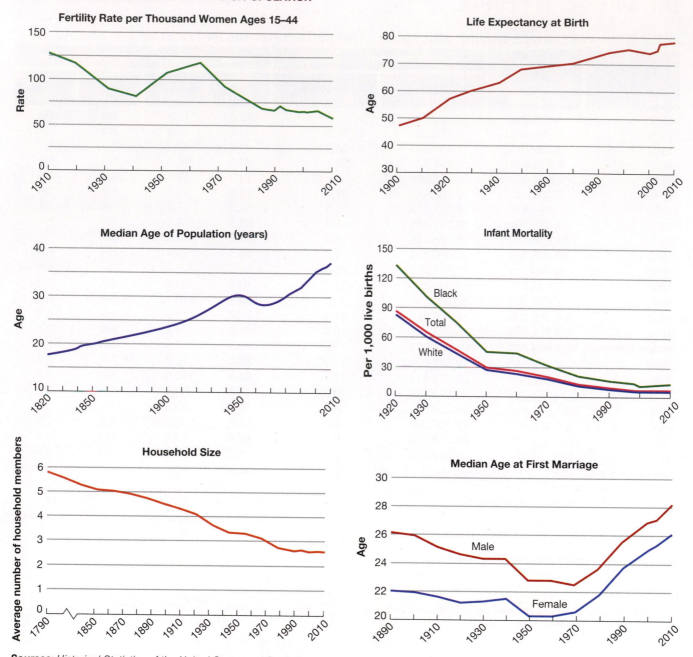

Sources: *Historical Statistics of the United States and Statistical Abstract of the United States,* relevant years.

ESTIMATED IMMIGRATION TOTALS BY DECADE

IMMIGRATION TOTALS BY DECADE			
YEARS	**NUMBER**	**YEARS**	**NUMBER**
1820–1830	151,824	1911–1920	5,735,811
1831–1840	599,125	1921–1930	4,107,209
1841–1850	1,713,251	1931–1940	528,431
1851–1860	2,598,214	1941–1950	1,035,039
1861–1870	2,314,824	1951–1960	2,515,479
1871–1880	2,812,191	1961–1970	3,321,677
1881–1890	5,246,613	1971–1980	4,493,314
1891–1900	3,687,546	1981–1990	7,338,062
1901–1910	8,795,386	1991–2000	9,095,417
		2001–2006	8,795,000
		2009	8,944,170

MAJOR SOURCES OF IMMIGRATION, 1820–2000

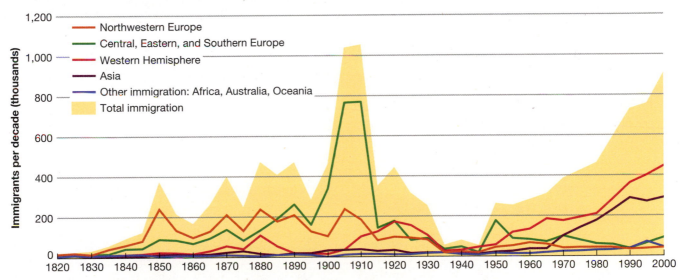

Sources: *Historical Statistics of the U.S., Colonial Times to 1970 (1975) and Statistical Abstract of the United States, 2001 (2002). Numbers do not include undocumented immigrants.*

THE AMERICAN WORKER

YEAR	TOTAL NUMBER OF WORKERS	MALES AS PERCENT OF TOTAL WORKERS	FEMALES AS PERCENT OF TOTAL WORKERS	MARRIED WOMEN AS PERCENT OF FEMALE WORKERS	FEMALE WORKERS AS PERCENT OF FEMALE POPULATION	PERCENT OF LABOR FORCE UNEMPLOYED
1870	12,506,000	85	15	NA	NA	NA
1880	17,392,000	85	15	NA	NA	NA
1890	23,318,000	83	17	14	19	4(1894=18)
1900	29,073,000	82	18	15	21	5
1910	38,167,000	79	21	25	25	6
1920	41,614,000	79	21	23	24	5(1921=12)
1930	48,830,000	78	22	29	25	9(1933=25)
1940	53,011,000	76	24	36	27	15(1944=1)
1950	62,208,000	72	28	52	31	5.3
1960	69,628,000	67	33	55	38	5.5
1970	82,771,000	62	38	59	43	4.9
1980	106,940,000	58	42	55	52	7.1
1990	125,840,000	55	45	54	58	5.6
2000	135,208,000	53	47	55	60	4.0
2009*	154,142,000	53.3	46.7	51.7	59**	9.9

NA=Not Available

*Data not strictly comparable with earlier years. See 2008 Statistical Abstract, Table 569, note 2.

** Females 16 years of age and older.

Sources: *U.S Census Bureau; Statistical Abstract of the United States (2006, 2008); U.S. Department of Labor,"Women in the Labor Force,"
Report 1026, December 2010.*

THE AMERICAN GOVERNMENT

PRESIDENTIAL ELECTIONS, 1789–2016

YEAR	STATES IN THE UNION	CANDIDATES	PARTIES	ELECTORAL VOTE	POPULAR VOTE	PERCENTAGE OF POPULAR VOTE
1789	11	GEORGE WASHINGTON John Adams Minor candidates	No party designations	69		
1792	15	GEORGE WASHINGTON John Adams George Clinton Minor candidates	No party designations	132 77 50 5		
1796	16	JOHN ADAMS Thomas Jefferson Thomas Pinckney Aaron Burr Minor candidates	Federalist Democratic-Republican Federalist Democratic-Republican	71 68 59 30 48		
1800	16	THOMAS JEFFERSON Aaron Burr John Adams Charles C. Pinckney John Jay	Democratic-Republican Democratic-Republican Federalist Federalist Federalist	73 73 65 64 1		
1804	17	THOMAS JEFFERSON Charles C. Pinckney	Democratic-Republican Federalist	162 14		
1808	17	JAMES MADISON Charles C. Pinckney George Clinton	Democratic-Republican Federalist Democratic-Republican	122 47 6		
1812	18	JAMES MADISON DeWitt Clinton	Democratic-Republican Federalist	128 89		
1816	19	JAMES MONROE Rufus King	Democratic-Republican Federalist	183 34		
1820	24	JAMES MONROE John Quincy Adams	Democratic-Republican Independent Republican	231 1		
1824	24	JOHN QUINCY ADAMS Andrew Jackson William H. Crawford Henry Clay	Democratic-Republican Democratic-Republican Democratic-Republican Democratic-Republican	84 99 41 37	108,740 153,544 46,618 47,136	30.5 43.1 13.1 13.2
1828	24	ANDREW JACKSON John Quincy Adams	Democratic National Republican	178 83	642,553 500,897	56.0 44.0
1832	24	ANDREW JACKSON Henry Clay William Wirt John Floyd	Democratic National Republican Anti-Masonic National Republican	219 49 7 11	687,502 530,189 33,108	55.0 42.4 2.6
1836	26	MARTIN VAN BUREN William H. Harrison Hugh L. White Daniel Webster W. P. Mangum	Democratic Whig Whig Whig Whig	170 73 26 14 11	765,483	50.9
1840	26	WILLIAM H. HARRISON Martin Van Buren	Whig Democratic	234 60	1,274,624 1,127,781	53.1 46.9
1844	26	JAMES K. POLK Henry Clay James G. Birney	Democratic Whig Liberty	170 105 0	1,338,464 1,300,097 62,300	49.6 48.1 2.3
1848	30	ZACHARY TAYLOR Lewis Cass Martin Van Buren	Whig Democratic Free Soil	163 127 0	1,360,967 1,222,342 291,263	47.4 42.5 10.1

Because candidates receiving less than 1 percent of the popular vote are omitted, the percentage of popular vote may not total 100 percent. Before the Twelfth Amendment was passed in 1804, the Electoral College voted for two presidential candidates; the runner-up became vice president.

YEAR	STATES IN THE UNION	CANDIDATES	PARTIES	ELECTORAL VOTE	POPULAR VOTE	PERCENTAGE OF POPULAR VOTE
1852	31	FRANKLIN PIERCE	Democratic	254	1,601,117	50.9
		Winfield Scott	Whig	42	1,385,453	44.1
		John P. Hale	Free Soil	0	155,825	5.0
1856	31	JAMES BUCHANAN	Democratic	174	1,832,955	45.3
		John C. Fremont	Republican	114	1,339,932	33.1
		Millard Fillmore	American	8	871,731	21.6
1860	33	ABRAHAM LINCOLN	Republican	114	1,339,932	33.1
		Stephen A. Douglas	Democratic	12	1,382,713	29.5
		John C. Breckinridge	Democratic	72	848,356	18.1
		John Bell	Constitutional Union	39	592,906	12.6
1864	36	ABRAHAM LINCOLN	Republican	212	2,206,938	55.0
		George B. McClellan	Democratic	21	1,803,787	45.0
1868	37	ULYSSES S. GRANT	Republican	214	3,013,421	52.7
		Horatio Seymour	Democratic	80	2,706,829	47.3
1872	37	ULYSSES S. GRANT	Republican	268	3,596,745	55.6
		Horace Greeley	Democratic	*	2,843,446	43.9
1876	38	RUTHERFORD B. HAYES	Republican	185	4,034,311	48.0
		Samuel J. Tilden	Democratic	184	4,288,546	51.0
		Peter Cooper	Greenback	0	75,973	1.0
1880	38	JAMES A. GARFIELD	Republican	214	4,453,295	48.5
		Winfield S. Hancock	Democratic	155	4,414,082	48.1
		James B. Weaver	Greenback-Labor	0	308,578	3.4
1884	38	GROVER CLEVELAND	Democratic	219	4,879,507	48.5
		James G. Blaine	Republican	182	4,850,293	48.2
		Benjamin F. Butler	Greenback-Labor	0	175,370	1.8
		John P. St. John	Prohibition	0	150,369	1.5
1888	38	BENJAMIN HARRISON	Republican	233	5,477,129	47.9
		Grover Cleveland	Democratic	168	5,537,857	48.6
		Clinton B. Fisk	Prohibition	0	249,506	2.2
		Anson J. Streeter	Union Labor	0	146,935	1.3
1892	44	GROVER CLEVELAND	Democratic	277	5,555,426	46.1
		Benjamin Harrison	Republican	145	5,182,690	43.0
		James B. Weaver	People's	22	1,029,846	8.5
		John Bidwell	Prohibition	0	264,133	2.2
1896	45	WILLIAM McKINLEY	Republican	271	7,102,246	51.1
		William J. Bryan	Democratic	176	6,492,559	47.7
1900	45	WILLIAM McKINLEY	Republican	292	7,218,491	51.7
		William J. Bryan	Democratic	155	6,356,734	45.5
		John C. Wooley	Populist Prohibition	0	208,914	1.5
1904	45	THEODORE ROOSEVELT	Republican	336	7,628,461	57.4
		Alton B. Parker	Democratic	140	5,084,223	37.6
		Eugene V. Debs	Socialist	0	402,283	3.0
		Silas C. Swallow	Prohibition	0	258,536	1.9
1908	46	WILLIAM H. TAFT	Republican	321	7,675,320	51.6
		William J. Bryan	Democratic	162	6,412,294	43.1
		Eugene V. Debs	Socialist	0	420,793	2.8
		Eugene W. Chafin	Prohibition	0	253,840	1.7
1912	48	WOODROW WILSON	Democratic	435	6,296,547	41.9
		Theodore Roosevelt	Progressive	88	4,118,571	27.4
		William H. Taft	Republican	8	3,486,720	23.2
		Eugene V. Debs	Socialist	0	900,672	6.0
		Eugene W. Chafin	Prohibition	0	206,275	1.4

*When Greeley died shortly after the election, his supporters divided their votes among the minor candidates.

Because candidates receiving less than 1 percent of the popular vote are omitted, the percentage of popular vote may not total 100 percent.

PRESIDENTIAL ELECTIONS, 1789–2016 (continued)

YEAR	STATES IN THE UNION	CANDIDATES	PARTIES	ELECTORAL VOTE	POPULAR VOTE	PERCENTAGE OF POPULAR VOTE
1916	48	WOODROW WILSON	Democratic	277	9,127,695	49.4
		Charles E. Hughes	Republican	254	8,533,507	46.2
		A. L. Benson	Socialist	0	585,113	3.2
		J. Frank Hanly	Prohibition	0	220,506	1.2
1920	48	WARREN G. HARDING	Republican	404	16,143,407	60.4
		James N. Cox	Democratic	127	9,130,328	34.2
		Eugene V. Debs	Socialist	0	919,799	3.4
		P. P. Christensen	Farmer-Labor	0	265,411	1.0
1924	48	CALVIN COOLIDGE	Republican	382	15,718,211	54.0
		John W. Davis	Democratic	136	8,385,283	28.8
		Robert M. La Follette	Progressive	13	4,831,289	16.6
1924	48	CALVIN COOLIDGE	Republican	382	15,718,211	54.0
		John W. Davis	Democratic	136	8,385,283	28.8
		Robert M. La Follette	Progressive	13	4,831,289	16.6
1928	48	HERBERT C. HOOVER	Republican	444	21,391,993	58.2
		Alfred E. Smith	Democratic	87	15,016,169	40.9
1932	48	FRANKLIN D. ROOSEVELT	Democratic	472	22,809,638	57.4
		Herbert C. Hoover	Republican	59	15,758,901	39.7
		Norman Thomas	Socialist	0	881,951	2.2
1936	48	FRANKLIN D. ROOSEVELT	Democratic	523	27,752,869	60.8
		Alfred M. Landon	Republican	8	16,674,665	36.5
		William Lemke	Union	0	882,479	1.9
1940	48	FRANKLIN D. ROOSEVELT	Democratic	449	27,307,819	54.8
		Wendell L. Willkie	Republican	82	22,321,018	44.8
1944	48	FRANKLIN D. ROOSEVELT	Democratic	432	25,606,585	53.5
		Thomas E. Dewey	Republican	99	22,014,745	46.0
1948	48	HARRY S TRUMAN	Democratic	303	24,105,812	49.5
		Thomas E. Dewey	Republican	189	21,970,065	45.1
		Strom Thurmond	States' Rights	39	1,169,063	2.4
		Henry A. Wallace	Progressive	0	1,157,172	2.4
1952	48	DWIGHT D. EISENHOWER	Republican	442	33,936,234	55.1
		Adlai E. Stevenson	Democratic	89	27,314,992	44.4
1956	48	DWIGHT D. EISENHOWER	Republican	457	35,590,472	57.6
		Adlai E. Stevenson	Democratic	73	26,022,752	42.1
1960	50	JOHN F. KENNEDY	Democratic	303	34,227,096	49.7
		Richard M. Nixon	Republican	219	34,108,546	49.5
		Harry F. Byrd	Independent	15	502,363	0.7
1964	50	LYNDON B. JOHNSON	Democratic	486	43,126,506	61.1
		Barry M. Goldwater	Republican	52	27,176,799	38.5
1968	50	RICHARD M. NIXON	Republican	301	31,770,237	43.4
		Hubert H. Humphrey	Democratic	191	31,270,533	42.7
		George C. Wallace	American Independent	46	9,906,141	13.5
1972	50	RICHARD M. NIXON	Republican	520	47,169,911	60.7
		George S. McGovern	Democratic	17	29,170,383	37.5
1976	50	JIMMY CARTER	Democratic	297	40,827,394	49.9
		Gerald R. Ford	Republican	240	39,145,977	47.9
1980	50	RONALD W. REAGAN	Republican	489	43,899,248	50.8
		Jimmy Carter	Democratic	49	35,481,435	6.6
		John B. Anderson	Independent	0	5,719,437	1.0
		Ed Clark	Libertarian	0	920,859	
1984	50	RONALD W. REAGAN	Republican	525	54,451,521	58.8
		Walter F. Mondale	Democratic	13	37,565,334	40.5
1988	50	GEORGE H. W. BUSH	Republican	426	47,946,422	54.0
		Michael S. Dukakis	Democratic	112	41,016,429	46.0

Because candidates receiving less than 1 percent of the popular vote are omitted, the percentage of popular vote may not total 100 percent.

PRESENTIAL ELECTIONS, 1789–2016 (continued)

YEAR	STATES IN THE UNION	CANDIDATES	PARTIES	ELECTORAL VOTE	POPULAR VOTE	PERCENTAGE OF POPULAR VOTE
1992	50	WILLIAM J. CLINTON	Democratic	370	43,728,275	43.2
		George H. W. Bush	Republican	168	38,167,416	37.7
		H. Ross Perot	Independent	0	19,237,247	19.0
1996	50	WILLIAM J. CLINTON	Democratic	379	47,401,185	49.0
		Robert Dole	Republican	159	39,197,469	41.0
		H. Ross Perot	Independent	0	8,085,295	8.0
2000	50	GEORGE W. BUSH	Republican	271	50,456,169	47.9
		Albert Gore, Jr.	Democratic	267	50,996,116	48.4
		Ralph Nader	Green	0	2,783,728	2.7
2004	50	GEORGE W. BUSH	Republican	286	60,693,281	50.7
		John Kerry	Democratic	252	57,355,978	48.3
		Ralph Nader	Independent	0	405,623	0.3
2008	50	BARACK OBAMA	Democratic	365	66,882,230	53.0
		John McCain	Republican	173	58,343,671	46.0
		Ralph Nader	Independent	0	726,462	0.6
2012	50	BARACK OBAMA	Democratic	332	65,544,032	50.9
		Mitt Romney	Republican	206	60,589,084	47.1
2016	50	DONALD TRUMP	Republican	290*	59,533,911*	47.8*
		Hillary Clinton	Democratic	228	59,742,182	47.9
		Gary Johnson	Libertarian	0	4,055,228	3.2

*The vote count is taken from New York Times on Nov. 9, 2016 and may differ from the actual final count as tallied by the U.S. government.

Because candidates receiving less than one percent of the popular vote are omitted, the percentage of popular vote may not total 100 percent.

THE AMERICAN ECONOMY

KEY ECONOMIC INDICATORS

YEAR	GROSS NATIONAL PRODUCT (GNP) AND GROSS DOMESTIC PRODUCT (GDP)A (IN $ BILLIONS)	STEEL PRODUCTION (IN TONS)	CORN PRODUCTION (MILLIONS OF BUSHELS)	AUTOMOBILES REGISTERED	NEW HOUSING STARTS	FOREIGN TRADE (IN $ MILLIONS)	EXPORTS IMPORTS
1790	NA	NA	NA	NA	NA	20	23
1800	NA	NA	NA	NA	NA	71	91
1810	NA	NA	NA	NA	NA	67	85
1820	NA	NA	NA	NA	NA	70	74
1830	NA	NA	NA	NA	NA	74	71
1840	NA	NA	NA	NA	NA	132	107
1850	NA	NA	592[d]	NA	NA	152	178
1860	NA	13,000	839[e]	NA	NA	400	362
1870	7.4[b]	77,000	1,125	NA	NA	451	462
1880	11.2[c]	1,397,000	1,707	NA	NA	853	761
1890	13.1	4,779,000	1,650	NA	328,000	910	823
1900	18.7	11,227,000	2,662	89,000	189,000	1,499	930
1910	35.3	28,330,000	2,853	458,300	387,000(1918=118,000)	1,919	1,646
1920	91.5	46,183,000	3,071	8,131,500	247,000(1925=937,000)	8,664	5,784
1930	90.7	44,591,000	2,080	23,034,700	330,000(1933=93,000)	4,013	3,500
1940	100.0	66,983,000	2,457	27,465,800	603,000(1944=142,000)	4,030	7,433
1950	286.5	96,836,000	3,075	40,339,000	1,952,000	9,997	8,954
1960	506.5	99,282,000	4,314	61,682,300	1,365,000	19,659	15,093
1970	1,016.0	131,514,000	4,200	89,279,800	1,434,000	42,681	40,356
1980	2,819.5	111,835,000	6,600	121,601,00	1,292,000	220,626	244,871
1990	5,764.9	98,906,000	7,933	133,700,000	1,193,000	394,030	485,453
2000	9,963.1	112,242,000	9,968	133,600,000[f]	1,569,000	781,918	1,218,022
2009	14,265	56,000,000	13,200	134,080,000	554,000	1,578,945	1,958,009

NA = Not available
a In December 1991 the Bureau of Economic Analysis of the U.S. government began using gross domestic product rather than gross national product as the primary measure of U.S. production.
b Figure for 1849.
c Figure for 1859.
d Figure is average for 1869–1878.
e Figure is average for 1879–1888.
f Does not include sports utility vehicles (SUVs) and light trucks.

FEDERAL BUDGET OUTLAYS AND DEBT

YEAR	DEFENSE[c]	VETERANS BENEFITS[a]	INCOME SECURITY[a]	SOCIAL SECURITY[a]	HEALTH AND MEDICARE[a]	EDUCATION[a], [d]	NET INTEREST PAYMENTS[a]	FEDERAL DEBT (DOLLARS)
1790	14.9	4.1[b]	NA	NA	NA	NA	55.0	75,463,000[c]
1800	55.7	0.6	NA	NA	NA	NA	31.3	82,976,000
1810	48.4(1814:79.7)	1.0	NA	NA	NA	NA	34.9	53,173,000
1820	38.4	17.6	NA	NA	NA	NA	28.1	91,016,000
1830	52.9	9.0	NA	NA	NA	NA	12.6	48,565,000
1840	54.3(1847:80.7)	10.7	NA	NA	NA	NA	0.7	3,573,000
1850	43.8	4.7	NA	NA	NA	NA	1.0	63,453,000
1860	44.2(1865:88.9)	1.7	NA	NA	NA	NA	5.0	64,844,000
1870	25.7	9.2	NA	NA	NA	NA	41.7	2,436,453,000
1880	19.3	21.2	NA	NA	NA	NA	35.8	2,090,909,000
1890	20.9(1899:48.6)	33.6	NA	NA	NA	NA	11.4	1,222,397,000
1900	36.6	27.0	NA	NA	NA	NA	7.7	1,263,417,000
1910	45.1 (1919:59.5)	23.2	NA	NA	NA	NA	3.1	1,146,940,000
1920	37.1	3.4	NA	NA	NA	NA	16.0	24,299,321,000
1930	25.3	6.6	NA	NA	NA	NA	19.9	16,185,310,000
1940	17.5(1945:89.4)	6.0	6.0	0.3	0.5	20.8	9.4	42,967,531,000
1950	32.2	20.3	9.6	1.8	0.6	0.6	11.3	256,853,000,000
1960	52.2	5.9	8.0	12.6	0.9	8.0	7.5	290,525,000,000
1970	41.8	4.4	8.0	15.5	6.2	4.4	7.3	308,921,000,000
1980	22.7	3.6	14.6	20.1	9.4	5.4	8.9	909,050,000,000
1990	23.9	2.3	11.7	19.8	12.4	3.1	14.7	3,266,073,000,000
2000	16.2	2.6	14.1	22.7	19.9	3.5	12.3	5,629,000,000,000
2010	19.1	3.0	18.9	24.0	2.8	13.5	197.0[e]	13,500,000,000,000

NA = Not available

[a]1791 figure.

[b]Figures represent percentage of total federal spending for each category. Not included are transportation, commerce, housing, and various other categories.

[c]Include straining, employment, and social services.

[d]1789–1791 figure.

[e]Congressional Budget Office, "Federal Debt and Interest Costs," December 2010.

Index

(map); seat of government, 108 (illus); Tea Act, 136–137, 137 (illus); urban paradox, 96–97

Boston Manufacturing Company, 250

Boston Massacre, 133–134

Boycotts: Abigail Adams and, 160; colonial, 130; commercial, 117; Daughters of Liberty and, 131

Bragg, Braxton, 420, 422

Brant, Joseph, 149, 154 (illus), 155, 158, 169

Brazil: Civil War and, 438; Netherlands and, 46; slavery in, 94, 338; Treaty of Tordesillas and, 33

Breed's Hill, Battle of, 141

Britain/British: *Alabama* claims, 459; art and artisans, 122; authors, 308; depressions in, economic, 223–224; Oregon boundary dispute, 363–364, 364 (map); property requirements, for voting, 163; Royal Navy, 157, 200; taxation, 132; textile industry, 190, 242, 322

British-American Convention of 1818, 232

British Empire, 1750–1763, 118–124. *See also* British Empire, colonial opposition to; Anglo-American friction, 121–122; end of French North America, 1760–1763, 120–121, 121 (map); fragile peace, 1750–1754, 118–119; frontier tensions, 122–124; Seven Years' War in North America, 1754–1760, 119–120, 119 (map), 120 (illus)

British Empire, colonial opposition to: 1760–1766, 124–129; 1766–1770, 129–133; 1770–1774, 133–137; 1774–1776, 137–143; African Americans, liberty for, 137–139, 138 (illus); Boston Massacre, 133–134; committees of correspondence, 1772–1773,

134–135; *Common Sense,* 141–142; Continental Congress, 139–140; customs racketeering, 1767–1770, 131–132; Declaration of Independence, 142–143, 143 (illus); ideology, 128–129; Intolerable Acts, 139; Olive Branch Petition, 140–141; Quartering Act, 1766–1767, 129; rebellion, 140–141; religion, 128–129; resistance, 128–133; Stamp Act Crisis, 1765–1766, 125–128, 128 (illus); Sugar Act, 1764, 125; Tea Act, 1773, 136–137, 137 (illus); Townshend Acts, 1767–1770, 129–130; western disputes, 135–136; "Wilkes and Liberty," 1768–1770, 132–133; women and colonial resistance, 130–131; Writs of Assistance, 1760–1761, 124–125

British expansion, 42–46. *See also* New England; colonial elites, 100–101, 100 (illus); colonial politics, 107–109; disputed territorial claims in West, 1783–1796, 199 (map); Enlightenment, 109–111; farmers and the environment, 95–96, 99; Georgia, 104; Great Awakening, 111–113; Jamestown, 43–44; mercantilist empires in America, 89–90; Native Americans, 103; New England, 45–46; new immigrants, 91–94, 92 (illus), 93 (map); New Jersey, 73–75; New York, 73–75, 75 (map); occupation of North America to 1750, 102 (map); Plymouth, 45–46; population growth and diversity, 91; Quaker Pennsylvania, 75–76; rural white men and women, 94–95; Sagadahoc, 43, 44; slavery, 94 (map), 95 (illus), 97–98, 100; Spain's borderlands, 104–106;

urban paradox, 96–97, 97 (illus); Virginia, 43–45

British tea, 130

Broken voyage, 220

Brook Farm, 290

Brown, Henry, 340

Brown, John: Harpers Ferry, 376, 387, 392; Pottawatomie massacre, 385–386

Buchanan, James: *Dred Scott v. Sandford,* 387–388, 390, 393; Lecompton constitution, 388–389; presidential election, 1856, 386–387

Bull Run, First Battle of (First Manassas), 409–410

Bull Run, Second Battle of (Second Manassas), 410

Bunker Hill, Battle of, 141

Burned-Over District, 278–279

Burns, Anthony, 379

Burnside, Ambrose, 411, 420

Burr, Aaron, 207, 215–216, 217–218, 220

Butler, Benjamin, 411

C

Cabeza de Vaca, Alvar Nuñez, 38–39

Cahokia, 12, 12 (illus), 13

Calhoun, John C.: Compromise of 1850, 376–377; as Jackson's running mate, 1828, 267, 269; nullification crisis, 269–271; presidential election, 1824, 267–268; relation with Jackson, 270; *South Carolina Exposition and Protest,* 270, 271

California: annexation of, 350, 359; Bear Flag Republic, 366; Compromise of 1850, 376–377, 377–380, 378 (map); gold rush, 370; overland trail to, 359–360; statehood, 377

California gold rush, 352, 370–371

Californios, 355

Calvinism/Calvinists: indentured servants and, 59; in Netherlands, 28, 42, 46

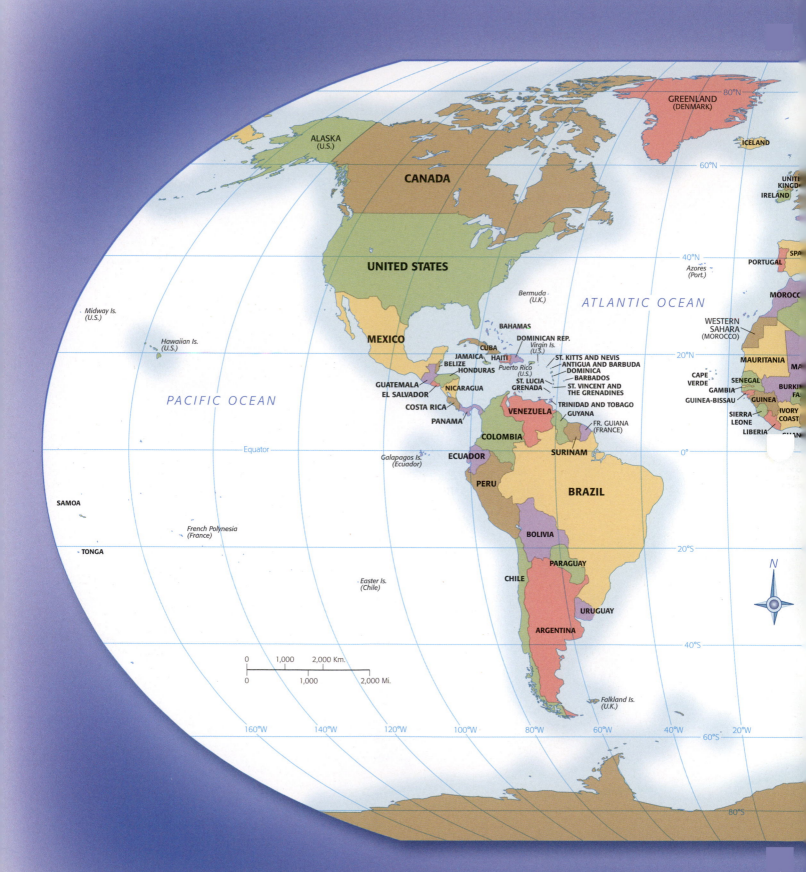